Standard C Object-Oriented Programming

SECOND EDITION

Standard C++ with Object-Oriented Programming

SECOND EDITION

Paul S. Wang

Kent State University

Brooks/Cole
Thomson Learning™

Australia • Canada • Mexico • Singapore • Spain • United Kingdom • United States

Sponsoring Editor: *Kallie Swanson*
Marketing Team:
 Chris Kelly, Samantha Cabaluna
Editorial Associate: *Grace Fujimoto*
Production Coordinator: *Kelsey McGee*
Production Service:
 Matrix Productions/Merrill Peterson
Manuscript Editor: *Frank Hubert*
Permissions Editor: *Sue Ewing*

Interior Design: *Cynthia Bassett*
Cover Design: *Lisa Henry*
Cover Illustration: *Judith L. Harkness*
Print Buyer: *Tracy Brown*
Typesetting and interior illustration:
 $T_{\!E\!}X$ *Consultants/Arthur Ogawa*
Cover Printing, Printing and Binding:
 Webcom, Ltd.

Copyright © 2001 by Brooks/Cole
A division of Thomson Learning
The Thomson Learning logo is a trademark used herein under license.

For more information about this or any other Brooks/Cole product, contact:
BROOKS/COLE
511 Forest Lodge Road
Pacific Grove, CA 93950 USA
www.brookscole.com
1-800-423-0563 (Thomson Learning Academic Resource Center)

All rights reserved. No part of this book may be reproduced, transcribed, or used in any form or by any means — graphic, electronic, or mechanical, including photocopying, recording, taping, Web distribution, or information storage and/or retrieval systems — without the prior written permission of the publisher.

For permission to use material from this work, contact us by
Web: www.thomsonrights.com
fax: 1-800-730-2215
phone: 1-800-730-2214

Printed in Canada

10 9 8 7 6 5 4 3 2

Library of Congress Cataloging-in-Publication Data
Wang, Paul S.
 C++ with object-oriented programming / Paul S. Wang — 2nd ed.
  p. cm.
 Rev. ed. of C++ with object-oriented programming. c1994.
 ISBN 0-534-37131-0
 1. Object-oriented programming (Computer science) 2. C++ (Computer program language) I. Wang, Paul S. C++ with object-oriented programming. II. Title.

QA76.64. W365   2000
005.13′3 — dc21   00-036771

To my mother, Chang Pei Wang,
on her 80th birthday:

Happy Birthday, Mom. . .

Contents

Introduction 1

ONE   C++ Primer Part I: Basics 8

- 1.1 Object-Oriented Program Structure 8
- 1.2 Functions 9
- 1.3 Running the First Example 12
- 1.4 Statements 12
- 1.5 The `while` Statement 13
- 1.6 Simple Conditional Statements 16
- 1.7 Characters and Character Input and Output 17
- 1.8 More Basic Constructs 20
- 1.9 Data Types and Declarations 26
- 1.10 Operators and Expressions 29
- 1.11 Enumerations 35
- 1.12 Arrays 37
- 1.13 Pointers 40
- 1.14 An Example 41
- 1.15 Iteration Control 42
- 1.16 Choices by `switch` 46
- 1.17 Summary 48
-       Exercises 48

TWO   C++ Primer Part II: Object-Based Programming 51

- 2.1 Data Abstraction and Encapsulation 51
- 2.2 Function Calls and Argument Passing 58
- 2.3 Command-Line Arguments 61
- 2.4 Environment Variables 62

2.5	The `string` Class	63	
2.6	Problem Solving with Objects	65	
2.7	C++ I/O Streams	70	
2.8	Error Handling	70	
2.9	Object-Based Thinking	73	
2.10	C++ Programming Tips	74	
2.11	Summary	77	
	Exercises	78	

THREE Key Constructs 80

3.1	Identifier Scoping	81
3.2	Namespaces	84
3.3	More on Declarations	86
3.4	Recursion	89
3.5	A Class of Fractions	93
3.6	Optional and Variable-Length Arguments	97
3.7	Overloading Functions	99
3.8	References	102
3.9	Read-Only Variables and Parameters	103
3.10	The `typedef` Declaration	105
3.11	Storage Allocation and Management	106
3.12	A Circular Buffer	109
3.13	Implicit Type Conversions	114
3.14	Explicit Type Cast	116
3.15	How to Use Header Files	117
3.16	Summary	119
	Exercises	120

FOUR Arrays, Pointers, and Generic Code 123

4.1	Array Concepts and Declarations	123
4.2	Pointers and Address Arithmetic	125
4.3	Two-Dimensional Arrays	133
4.4	A Matrix Class	135
4.5	A Class of Polynomials	138

4.6	Array Objects: vector	141
4.7	Sorting Text Lines with Objects	143
4.8	Pointers and Function Calls	151
4.9	Arrays, Pointers, and References	154
4.10	Multiple Indirection	154
4.11	Generic Programs	156
4.12	A Generic Sorting Program	162
4.13	Pointers and Dynamically Allocated Storage	165
4.14	Summary	168
	Exercises	169

FIVE Classes and Objects 172

5.1	Defining Classes	172
5.2	Creating and Initializing Objects	175
5.3	The Host Object	181
5.4	Internal-External Decoupling	182
5.5	Pocket Calculator Simulation	183
5.6	Built-in Operations for Objects	192
5.7	Object Destruction	193
5.8	Friends of a Class	195
5.9	Recursive Structures	197
5.10	Instance and Static Members	204
5.11	The Size of Objects	210
5.12	Generic Lists	211
5.13	Unions and Bit Fields	216
5.14	Summary	216
	Exercises	217

SIX I/O Streams and the Standard Library 219

6.1	Different Header Files	219
6.2	C-Style String Input and Output	220
6.3	String Objects	222
6.4	A String Tokenizer	225
6.5	Operations on Characters	228

- 6.6 Numeric Computations 229
- 6.7 The I/O Stream Library 230
- 6.8 Stream I/O for Objects 240
- 6.9 I/O Manipulators 242
- 6.10 Summary 244
  - Exercises 245

SEVEN Inheritance and Class Derivation 248

- 7.1 Class Derivation 249
- 7.2 Derived Classes and Objects 252
- 7.3 Public Derivation 255
- 7.4 Derivation Principles 258
- 7.5 Access Control Under Class Derivation 259
- 7.6 Private Derivation 261
- 7.7 Specialization of Generic Classes 263
- 7.8 Type Relations Under Inheritance 265
- 7.9 Assignment of Objects 267
- 7.10 Copying of Objects 271
- 7.11 Derived-Object Assignment and Copying 274
- 7.12 Object Assignment and Copying via Derivation 276
- 7.13 Multiple Inheritance 278
- 7.14 The I/O Stream Class Hierarchy 282
- 7.15 Summary 283
  - Exercises 284

EIGHT Operator Overloading, Iterators, and Exceptions 287

- 8.1 Operator Overloading 287
- 8.2 A Reference-Count String Class 290
- 8.3 Overloading [ ] 293
- 8.4 Overloading ++ and -- 294
- 8.5 Smart Pointers 295
- 8.6 Iterators 296
- 8.7 Nested and Local Classes 299

8.8	Robust Classes	302
8.9	User-Defined Type Conversions	303
8.10	Error and Exception Handling	306
8.11	Matrix with Exceptions	314
8.12	Managing Free Storage	316
8.13	Summary	319
	Exercises	320

NINE OOP Techniques 322

9.1	Programming with Plug-Compatible Objects	322
9.2	Run-Time Type Identification	330
9.3	A Generic Tree	335
9.4	Planning Uniform Public Interfaces	343
9.5	Destruction of Plug-Compatible Objects	352
9.6	Ordering Text Lines	354
9.7	Interfaces	357
9.8	Understanding Virtual Functions	359
9.9	Inheritance Planning	361
9.10	Object-Family Classes	363
9.11	Summary	371
	Exercises	372

TEN Templates 375

10.1	Basic Concepts	375
10.2	Function Templates	377
10.3	Class Templates	383
10.4	Template Compilation	388
10.5	A List Template	390
10.6	Class Template Specialization	397
10.7	Derived-Class Template	397
10.8	A Generic Hash Table	400
10.9	Generic Programming Approaches	407
10.10	Summary	409
	Exercises	409

ELEVEN Standard Containers 413

11.1 The STL 413
11.2 Standard Container Headers 414
11.3 Efficiency of Sequence Containers 416
11.4 Using `stack` 417
11.5 Associative Containers 418
11.6 Standard Container Iterators and `typedefs` 421
11.7 Generic Algorithms for Containers 426
11.8 Ordered Sets 429
11.9 Standard Functors 431
11.10 For More STL Information 434
11.11 Pointers to Members 434
11.12 Instance Functions as Functors 439
11.13 Summary 439
      Exercises 440

TWELVE Web CGI Programming 442

12.1 About Networking 442
12.2 Internet Basics 444
12.3 The World-Wide Web 446
12.4 What Is HTML? 448
12.5 Dynamic Generation of Web Pages 450
12.6 HTML Produced from C++ 452
12.7 Forms in HTML 455
12.8 HTTP Message Formats 456
12.9 Writing CGI Programs 458
12.10 Receiving Form Data 459
12.11 User Feedback Handling 461
12.12 More Information 464
12.13 Summary 465
      Exercises 465

THIRTEEN Object-Oriented Design 467

13.1 Decomposition Approaches 468

13.2	Object-Oriented Design Principles	469
13.3	Design Patterns	472
13.4	The CRC Method	474
13.5	Interfacing to Existing Systems	475
13.6	Pocket Calculator Simulation	479
13.7	Summary	488
	Exercises	488

FOURTEEN Compiling and Preprocessing 490

14.1	Compiling and Running C++ Programs	490
14.2	Preprocessing	492
14.3	Header Files	493
14.4	Symbolic Constants and Macros	494
14.5	Inline Functions Versus Macros	496
14.6	Conditional Text Inclusion	497
14.7	Once-Only Header Files	500
14.8	Standard Macros	500
14.9	Compilation and Execution	502
14.10	Summary	506
	Exercises	507

APPENDICES

A	Summary of C++ Constructs	509
B	Summary of Special Member Functions	515
C	C-Style Strings	516
D	Unions and Bit Fields	519
E	Interactive Debugging with dbx	525
F	Functions with a Variable Number of Arguments	528
G	Operator Precedence	531
H	Implicit Type Conversions	532
I	C++ Library Functions Common with C	534
J	C-Style Input/Output	542
K	Interfacing C++ and C Programs	547
L	Header Files	551

Index 552

Preface

C++ is one of the most popular languages for object-oriented programming (OOP), the centerpiece of object technology (OT) that is revolutionizing the software industry. OOP creates programs that are well organized, easy to understand and modify, flexible, and reusable in many different situations. It reduces complexity and makes software production and maintenance more economical. C++ has been standardized jointly by the International Standards Organization (ISO) and the American National Standards Institute (ANSI). The ISO/ANSI C++ standard (ISO/IEC FDIS 14882) was approved in November 1997.

New features introduced in Standard C++ include the Boolean type `bool`, exceptions, namespaces, run-time type identification, type cast notations, and template libraries with generic algorithms. Standard C++ also revised and extended a number of existing features including the wide character type, templates, and function call resolution. A new `string` class makes character strings easier to use.

This book is a revision of *C++ with Object-Oriented Programming*, covering Standard C++ comprehensively while preserving the proven approach. The C++ constructs are matched with clear and precise OOP concepts. Language mechanisms are explained individually and in combination to achieve OOP objectives. Object-based, object-oriented, and generic programming techniques are demonstrated in realistic programs to show their applications in practice. Chapter 12 shows how C++ can be applied for Web CGI programming.

OBJECT ORIENTATION

C++ is important because it is efficient and supports OOP well. Thus, OOP concepts and techniques are taught as an integral part of C++ programming. The approach brings OOP concepts down to earth so that they are easily grasped. Object orientation is introduced early and demonstrated with many complete examples. How these techniques are applied to solve problems and how they make programs more flexible and reusable are clearly shown.

Key OOP concepts such as data abstraction, encapsulation, information hiding, problem solving with objects, genericness, inheritance, and polymorphism are presented clearly and comprehensively. Basics on object-oriented design are also included. Again, these are illustrated by many C++ examples, including a bank account example that is carried through many chapters.

HANDS-ON APPROACH

The best way to learn programming is to write programs. With clear concepts and good examples, the text encourages the writing of interesting programs early. Chapters 1 and 2 form a primer introducing essential components of C++ and object-based programming to get started quickly. Materials on thinking with objects, C++ programming tips, and style guides help beginning programmers.

A pocket calculator simulation program is introduced in Chapter 5. This program evolves with each new chapter through programming exercises. Finally, in Chapter 13, a substantial pocket calculator program emerges that connects many key OOP concepts and C++ constructs.

COMPREHENSIVE COVERAGE

Standard C++ is presented comprehensively and in depth. The coverage anticipates the needs of students and describes Standard C++ as an integral, self-contained language. The examples evolve as new material is covered, providing many chances to revisit familiar code and to focus on the new concepts and features being introduced.

It is possible to use this book as the sole text for a course. Besides the basic topics, it covers the Standard Library, the I/O stream classes, templates, the Standard Template Library (STL), generic algorithms, program organization, use of header files, error and exception handling, preprocessing, and compilation (on UNIX® and on PC).

Object orientation is emphasized with topics on building software objects, comparing external behavior versus internal workings, reducing complexity with encapsulation, deriving new classes based on existing ones, writing generic codes that are reusable in many situations, creating software black boxes that are plug-compatible in usage, and establishing polymorphic procedures and objects that work with multiple types of objects. Also included are object-oriented design techniques, methods, and applications.

OOP MADE EASY

Standard C++ is a large and complex language. It is easy to get lost in the maze of new OOP concepts and the supporting C++ constructs. No effort is spared to make this complicated subject easy to grasp and understand. The approach begins with simple topics and key concepts as a foundation. Then, advanced topics are added in a logical sequence that is easy to follow. The materials are organized to anticipate questions and provide answers. Clear, interesting, and realistic examples show how to write object-oriented programs and how to apply the concepts and techniques introduced.

Inheritance, a key OOP feature, tends to be difficult for beginning programmers. A clear mental picture is painted of a derived class and its relation with a base class upon which it is built. Furthermore, specific principles on class derivation and its proper usage are supplied. Multiple inheritance is also covered with clarity and good examples.

Polymorphism and plug compatibility are central OOP techniques that require sophistication to use well. An entire chapter is devoted to this subject that provides enough material to challenge even the most advanced students.

WEB APPLICATION

CGI programs written in C++ can be fast and efficient. HTML forms and CGI programs for form processing are presented in a concise chapter that puts the OOP concepts and C++ techniques to good use. A C++ class library for CGI programming is given and explained. CGI programs using this library for form processing are presented.

FLEXIBLE USAGE

The book contains more than enough material for a three-credit programming course at the junior, senior, or beginning graduate level. No C background is assumed, but appropriate programming experience, to appreciate software complexity, is highly recommended. Knowledge of C or ANSI C will reduce the amount of work involved. At a lower level, the material in the beginning chapters should be covered carefully. Advanced topics such as user-defined free storage management (Section 8.12), CGI programming (Chapter 12), and object-oriented design (Chapter 13) can be omitted. At a higher level, Chapter 1 and Chapter 14 can be assigned to students as background reading to allow more class time for other topics.

For a class with substantial programming experience, generic programming, template writing, and object-oriented programming projects, as suggested by the end-of-chapter exercises, can be emphasized. In this case, the design considerations covered in Chapter 13 may be discussed much earlier.

The preprocessing and compilation material in Chapter 14 can be introduced (or assigned for reading by students) whenever the instructor feels it is appropriate in a course. Chapters 2 through 11 are central to this text and should prove challenging and rewarding to any reader.

The book can also be used as a valuable supplement to a general course on OOP, data structures, or object-oriented design with C++ implementation.

RIGHT FOR YOUR SYSTEM

C++ is presented in a system-independent manner. The examples will run on any reasonable C++ implementation including workstations, PCs, and multi-user servers. Chapter 14 gives general information on preprocessing, compiling, and executing programs. The Free Software Foundation offers g++, a good implementation of C++ for free downloading:

```
http://www.gnu.ai.mit.edu/software/gcc   (for UNIX)
http://www.delorie.com/djgpp/   (for PC)
```

EASY REFERENCE

As an instructional guide, this text follows an incremental approach, whereby new concepts are built on old ones to make understanding easy. However, the book is also a valuable reference tool. Information has been organized for easy reference with tables, figures, displayed syntax explanations, examples, and summaries. All key C++ constructs are collected in Appendix A for quick review. Appendix B summarizes usage of special member functions. Other appendices cover debugging, library functions, and the mixed use of C++ and C. Accurate cross-referencing and a comprehensive index help locate information contained in the book.

EXAMPLE PACKAGE

Throughout the text, concepts and programming constructs are amply illustrated with examples of practical importance. The example package is organized by chapter. There are about 400 files containing complete source codes that are ready to compile. The complete example package for UNIX and for PC is available from the Brooks/Cole Web site

www.brookscole.com

ACKNOWLEDGMENTS

The book has benefited from the previous edition, extensive classroom use, and feedback from industry. In particular, I wish to thank W. B. Adams of Goodyear Tire and Rubber Company, Technical Computer Operations (Akron, Ohio). The book has gone through several rounds of reviews, and I would like to thank the following reviewers for their suggestions and corrections:

William G. Albrecht	Florida Southern College
Richard Chang	University of Maryland
Julius Dichter	University of Bridgeport
Craig A. Adams	Houston Community College System
Hristina Galabova	Home Box Office, Inc.

Especially, I'd like to thank Hristina Galabova, a Kent State alumna, for her thorough review and thoughtful suggestions, resulting in many improvements.

The final draft of the book went through classroom trial at Kent State University in the spring of 2000. This resulted in many improvements. My appreciation goes to all the students who took the Object-Oriented Programming class. Thanks also go to Joyce Fuell, my assistant at the Institute for Computational Mathematics of the Department of Mathematics and Computer Science at Kent State University, for helping with the production of the manuscript. I would like to thank Kallie Swanson, the editor at Brooks/Cole for her expert handling of this publication, to Merrill Peterson at Matrix Productions for managing the production process, and to Arthur Ogawa at TEX Consultants for the LATEX style file, graphical art, index generation, and great composition.

My daughter Laura suggested the term *appendant*, and it proved to be very helpful in describing class derivation. She deserves all the credit. Finally, I'd like to thank my wife, Jennifer, and younger children, Deborah and David, for their understanding, support, and encouragement.

Paul S. Wang
Kent State University

Introduction

Object-oriented programming (OOP) has become the paradigm of choice for software development in industry as well as academia. OOP offers certain advantages over traditional programming approaches that make software easier to build, maintain, modify, and reuse. Knowledge of object-oriented (OO) techniques will make you a better programmer.

There are many programming languages that support OOP. Some, such as SMALLTALK, are pure and thorough in their object orientation. Others, such as C++, Java™, and CLOS (Common Lisp Object System), support a combination of object-oriented and traditional procedure-oriented programming. Among these, C++ remains a popular OOP language. The widespread acceptance of C++ can be attributed to two major factors. First, C++ provides a well-designed set of mechanisms to fully support OOP needs. Second, C++ is standardized internationally and an extension of ANSI C. Therefore, C++ is among the top choices for introducing OOP concepts and techniques to new and experienced programmers.

What Is OOP?

The central idea of OOP is to build programs using software *objects*. An object can be considered as a self-contained computing entity with its own data and programming. On modern workstations, for example, windows, menus, and file folders are usually represented by software objects. But objects can be applied to many kinds of programs. An object can be an airline reservation record, a bank account, or even an automobile engine. An engine object would include data that describe its physical attributes and programming that governs how it works internally and how it interacts with other related parts (also software objects) in an automobile.

A personnel management system would have engineers, secretaries, and managers as software objects. An air traffic control system would have runways, airliners, and passenger gates as software objects. Thus, in OOP, the software objects correspond closely to real objects involved in the application area. This correspondence makes the computer program easy to understand and manipulate. In contrast, traditional programming deals with bytes, variables, arrays, indices, and other programming artifacts that are difficult to relate to the problem at hand. Traditional programming also focuses mainly on the step-by-step procedures, called *algorithms*, to perform the desired tasks. For this reason, it is also known as *procedure-oriented* programming.

OOP Advantages

A large computer program is among the most complex mechanisms ever built. The cost of design, implementation, testing, maintenance, and revision of large software systems is very high. Thus, it is important to find ways to make these tasks easier and less frequent. In this direction, OOP has enormous potential.

For reasons that will become clear, OOP offers these main advantages:

- *Simplicity:* Because software objects model real objects in the application domain, the complexity of the program is reduced and the program structure becomes clear and simple.
- *Modularity:* Each object forms a separate entity with internal workings that are decoupled from other parts of the system.
- *Modifiability:* It is easy to make minor changes in the data representation or the procedures used in an OO program. Changes within an object do not affect any other part of the program provided that the *external behavior* of the object is preserved.
- *Extensibility:* Adding new features or responding to changing operating environments can be a matter of defining a few new objects by extending existing ones.
- *Flexibility:* An OO program can be very flexible in accommodating different situations because the interaction patterns among the objects can be changed without modifying the objects.
- *Maintainability:* Objects can be maintained separately, making locating and fixing problems and adding "bells and whistles" easy.
- *Reusability:* Objects can be reused in different programs. A table object, for instance, can be used in any program that needs to perform table lookups. Thus, programs can be built from prefabricated and pretested components in a fraction of the time required to build new programs from scratch.

OOP Concepts

The key concept of object orientation is the attachment of procedures to data. This concept changes the traditional segregation between data and programs. The wrapping together of procedures and data is called *encapsulation*, and the result is a software object. For example, a window object (Figure 1) in a graphical user interface system contains the window's physical dimensions,

INTRODUCTION

Figure 1 A WINDOW OBJECT

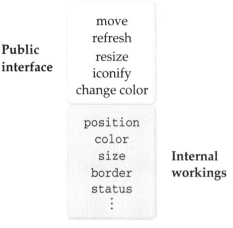

location on the screen, foreground and background colors, border styles, and other relevant data. Encapsulated with these data are routines (procedures) to move and resize the window itself, to change its colors, to display text, to shrink into an icon, and so on. Other parts of the user interface program simply call upon a window object to perform these tasks by sending well-defined *messages* to the object. It is the job of a window object to perform appropriate actions and to keep its internal data updated. The exact manner in which these tasks are achieved and the structures of the internal data are of no concern to programs outside the object. The *public interface* formed by the collection of messages understood by an object completely defines how to use that object. The hiding of internal details makes an object *abstract,* and the technique is sometimes referred to as *data abstraction.*

The separation of *public interface* from *internal workings* is not difficult to understand. In fact, it is common practice in our daily lives. Consider a bank teller, for example. Customers go to any bank and talk to any teller using the same set of messages: account number, deposit, withdrawal, balance, and so on. The way each bank or teller actually keeps records or performs tasks internally is of no concern to a customer. These tried-and-true principles simplify business at all levels and can bring the same benefit to organizing programs. As an OO program executes, objects are created, sent messages, and destroyed. These are the only allowable operations on objects. The internal (*private*) data or procedures in an object are off limits to the *public*. The decoupling of the private mechanisms in objects from routines outside the objects significantly reduces the complexity of a program.

It is often the case that more than one object of the same type is needed. For example, multiple windows often appear on workstation screens. Normally, objects of a given type are *instances* of a *class* whose definition specifies the private (internal) workings of these objects as well as their public interface. Thus, in OOP, a class would be defined for each different type of object required. A class becomes a blueprint for making a particular kind of object. A class definition and appropriate *initial values* are used to create an instance (object) of the class. This operation is known as *instantiation*. The term *object* can sometimes refer to either a class or to an instance of a class.

OOP provides easy ways to construct objects on top of other objects. There are two principal methods: *composition* and *inheritance*. Composition allows existing objects to be used as components to build other objects. For instance, a calculator object may be composed of an arithmetic unit object and a user interface object. Inheritance is a major OOP feature that allows the derivation of a similar or related object (the *derived object*) from another object (the *base object*). In C++, this is done through class derivation. A *derived class* can *inherit* the properties of its *base class* and also add its own data and routines. For example, a graphics window, a text window, and a terminal emulator window can all be derived from a basic window class. In addition, a check, an invoice, and an application form can all be derived from a basic business form class. Inheritance allows the extraction of commonalities among similar or related objects. It also allows classes in OO software libraries to be used for many different or unforeseen purposes. In these examples, derivation is from one base class, so it is called *single inheritance*. It is also possible to derive a class from several base classes (like inheriting characteristics from both parents) to achieve *multiple inheritance*.

Another hallmark of OOP is *overloading*, the assignment of multiple meanings to operators and function names. Such operators and functions are *overloaded* with different duties. For example, the operator +, primarily associated with the addition of numbers, can be overloaded to join one character string to another. Overloading can simplify programs and make the same operation work for many different types of operands.

Besides writing programs based on objects (*object-based programming*), OOP further encourages deriving new objects from existing ones, building object hierarchies, and making objects interchangeable in *polymorphic* programs. *Polymorphism* is the ability for the same procedure to work with different objects as interchangeable *black boxes*. It allows the creation of different (but related) objects that are compatible under a set of operations. If a problem-solving procedure is set forth using only these operations, then it works for all such objects.

For example, a procedure for driving a car can then be made under polymorphism to work for all types of vehicles that can be driven. Such procedures are polymorphic.

Obviously, OOP has many powerful concepts. C++ provides a set of well-designed language mechanisms to help achieve these goals. Only through actual programming can the many implications of these concepts be fully understood.

Evolution of C++

C++ is a general programming language that is compatible with ANSI C. In 1980, Bjarne Stroustrup of AT&T added classes and a few other features to C resulting in a language known as C with Classes. Later, in 1983 and 1984, several extensions were made, notably operator overloading and virtual functions, resulting in a language called C++. With a few further revisions and refinements, C++ became generally available in 1985. As C++ became widely used, new features and extensions were added to the language. These include multiple inheritance, templates, exception handling, namespaces, and run-time type identification. Standardization efforts for C++ began in 1987, and a draft standard was published in 1995. The final ISO/ANSI C++ standard (ISO/IEC FDIS 14882) was approved in November 1997. *The C++ Programming Language* (3rd ed.) by Bjarne Stroustrup is a good reference for details of the C++ standard.

As object orientation grew into a major trend, so did the use of C++ as a language. C++ supports both traditional procedural programming and OOP well. This is important because most real programs need a mixture of object and procedure orientations. Today, C++ is a very popular OOP language. All major computer vendors offer C++ on their machines. Implementations of C++ include Hewlett-Packard aC++, Sun Microsystems Visual Workshop C++, GNU g++ (C++ from The Free Software Foundation), and Microsoft Visual C++.

Features of C++

C++ provides all the usual facilities necessary for writing procedures. Major OOP features of C++ include classes, operator and function overloading, references, inline functions, single and multiple inheritance, virtual functions, and templates. There are also namespaces, template libraries, run-time type identification, and free storage management operators.

The C++ class defines software objects by enclosing data members as well as function members. Members can be designated *private*, *protected*, or *public*, providing a convenient way to define the public interface and the private domain of an object.

Class derivation is the C++ mechanism for inheritance supporting type relations and code reuse. Both single and multiple inheritance are possible. The virtual function mechanism supports polymorphism and allows the definition of interchangeable objects under a uniform external interface. The C++ abstract base class mechanism allows for extraction of commonalities among related classes as well as planning their interfaces.

The *template* facility supports *type parameterization*, allowing a function or a class to be defined with yet-unspecified types. The types only become known and fixed when a template is put to actual use in a program. Templates support writing generic programs that work for any data/object types.

As part of the C++ *Standard Library*, the STL (*Standard Template Library*) supports templates for container classes and generic algorithms. C++ also provides an object-based I/O library. I/O operators (>> and <<) make receiving and displaying data simple and straightforward. These operators can also be overloaded to input and output user-defined objects.

You will learn all about these and other features of C++ and how to use them effectively to write object-oriented programs.

Organization of Materials

This book introduces Standard C++ and its effective use for OOP. C++ is covered completely — from the basics to advanced topics. Knowledge of another programming language and enough programming experience are required. Prior knowledge of C will reduce the amount of work involved. Access to a C++ compiler is necessary. The material is suitable for a three-credit programming course or a course on C++/OOP at the undergraduate or beginning graduate level.

The material is organized and presented so that it is simple, concise, and easy to follow. The best way to learn programming is to write programs. Thus, you will begin writing whole programs early. Interesting examples and challenging exercises encourage this hands-on approach. The early chapters are quite basic and form a primer of information on many elementary aspects of C++, including objects, to get you started quickly. There are many simple examples, an object-based problem-solving guide, programming tips, and style suggestions. The pace, however, does pick up. When you are through, you will have gained a level of unusual proficiency in C++ and its use for OOP. A chapter on Web CGI programming puts C++ to use in an interesting and important application. The book contains enough advanced material to satisfy even experienced programmers.

INTRODUCTION

As a language that supports OOP, C++ contains many more features than a regular procedure-oriented language such as C or Pascal. It is important that each construct is covered well. This requires not only explaining the syntax and semantics of each construct but also illustrating how the construct can be applied to advantage. Furthermore, effective ways to combine different constructs in solving real problems are emphasized. OOP is introduced and integrated into the presentation so you learn OOP as a natural way of writing programs. Throughout the book, examples show how a problem is broken into logical chunks that are easy to tackle and how programs are modular, object-oriented, separately tested, and reusable. Many classes and programs are given in reusable form so they can be applied in many situations.

CHAPTER ONE

C++ Primer
Part I: Basics

Chapter 1 presents essential information for beginning C++ programmers and Chapter 2 introduces object-based programming. The two-part primer is carefully organized to get you off to a good start.

We begin with the overall program structure and basic information: program structure, constants, variables, expressions, arrays, functions, and simple input/output. The control-flow constructs `if`, `while`, `for`, and `do-while` are introduced. Testing the examples and their variations on your system is recommended.

Fundamental details are described completely but concisely in preparation for more interesting and central topics to follow. If you have some background in C, you may read through this chapter very quickly. However, since there are many differences between C and C++ programming even at the basic level, it is a good idea to look carefully at the examples. If a detail is required later, you can always find it here easily.

1.1 OBJECT-ORIENTED PROGRAM STRUCTURE

A program is a set of instructions, written in a programming language, to solve a given type of problem or to perform specific kinds of tasks. The source code of a C++ program consists of *functions* and *classes*. Functions codify the solution procedures required. Classes describe *objects* representing entities that interact at run time to perform desired tasks. Objects are used to closely model actual or logical entities in the problem domain. One important aspect of OOP is identifying these entities and their interactions in the solution process.

A function receives *arguments*, performs predefined computations on the arguments, and returns results. A *function call* activates (or *invokes*) a function, passes arguments to the function, and produces the values it returns.

A class is a blueprint for objects. It describes an object's data structures and operations. Once a class is defined, objects belonging to the class can be created and used in a program. A class provides a name under which data and function *members* are collected into one unit. This computing unit can be made to operate independently of other parts of the program. By using objects, a large program can be built with many small, independent, mutually interacting units. Object orientation can significantly reduce program complexity, increase flexibility, and enhance reusability.

For any program, one function must be named `main`. The function `main` is the *entry point*, the place where execution of the program begins. Aside from this basic structure, C++ is flexible. Functions and classes can be placed in one or several source code files.

Thus, in C++, procedures are coded by functions, which are explained here, and objects are defined by classes, which are introduced in Chapter 2.

1.2 FUNCTIONS

A function contains *statements* that specify a sequence of computing actions to be carried out and *variables* that store values needed and produced during the computations. Some of the variables may be objects, and the problem solution usually involves interactions among objects.

A function can be viewed as a self-contained computation procedure. The arguments are its input, and the computation result, or *return value*, is its output (Figure 1.1).

A well-organized procedure contains many small functions that perform well-defined duties. A function can call other functions and make use of objects in the course of its computations. In this way, a complex procedure is broken down into a series of steps that are individually straightforward but combine to achieve the given goal.

A function definition consists of a *header* and a *body*. The function header states the function name and the type of return value. The header also specifies

Figure 1.1   A FUNCTION AS A COMPUTATION UNIT

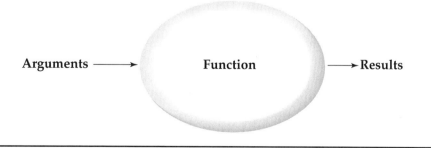

variables, known as *formal parameters*, which receive the incoming arguments. These formal parameters are used in the function body to perform computations.

The function body consists of a sequence of *declarations* and *statements* enclosed in braces, {}. A declaration supplies information to the C++ compiler, and a statement specifies actions for execution. The many different declarations and statements and their meanings are described as we proceed.

The general form of a function is

```
valuetype name ( type arg1, type arg 2, ... )    (function header)
{                                                (body begin)
        declarations and statements
}                                                (body end)
```

The `valuetype` specifies the type of the value returned by the function. If it is omitted, the function is presumed to return a value of type integer (`int`). If the function does not return a value, its `valuetype` is given as void.

Depending on the number of arguments needed, the function header may specify zero or more formal parameters. If there are no formal parameters, the parameter list is given as an empty list, (). Furthermore, the function body may contain zero or more declarations and statements. (Section 1.4 gives more basic information on statements.)

To begin, let's consider a very simple program that consists of just one function, main.

```cpp
#include <iostream>

int main()
{   int i = 10, j = 20;
    int k = (i + j)/2;
    std::cout << "i is " << i
              << " and j is " << j << std::endl;
    std::cout << "average is " << k
              << std::endl;
    return 0;
}
```

The header is simply the `int` return type, the function name `main`, and an empty list of formal parameters. An empty argument list cannot be omitted and indicates that the function takes no arguments.

The `main` function body begins with the declarations

```cpp
int i = 10, j = 20;
int k = (i + j)/2;
```

1.2 FUNCTIONS

establishing the three variables i, j, and k, each of type int (single-precision integer). A variable must be declared before it is used. A simple declaration consists of a *type name* followed by a list of variable names separated by commas and terminated by a semicolon. Each variable may also be given an optional *initializer* after an equal sign (=). The expression

```
(i + j)/2;
```

is evaluated, and the resultant value is used to initialize the variable k. There are different kinds of expressions. An *arithmetic expression* involves arithmetic operators such as +, -, *, and /. Generally, an *expression* is a constant, a variable, a function call, or an expression connected by operators.

Here are a few more variable declarations:

```
int age = 8;
float rate, speed;
char c, d;
```

These declare the variable age of type int, rate and speed of type float (single-precision floating-point), and c and d of type char (a single character).

Variables, such as i, j, and k, declared in a function body are used within the function and do not conflict with any variable with the same name used elsewhere. Therefore, such variables are said to be *local* to the function.

After the declarations in main, there are two output statements using the built-in output object std::cout. Standard C++ provides *I/O stream classes* that are used to establish objects to perform input and output. Further, C++ automatically provides each program with several built-in I/O stream objects for I/O to the terminal. The built-in I/O stream object std::cout sends output to the terminal screen. The std:: prefix here means cout is an identifier within the std *namespace*, the namespace of the C++ Standard Library. Data for output are passed to cout with the *output operator* <<, as in

```
std::cout << "average is " << k << std::endl;
```

A sequence of characters enclosed in double quotes is a *character string constant*. The integer k is displayed next followed by std::endl (Section 6.7), a platform-dependent *end-of-line* symbol, which is a NEWLINE character on UNIX® systems but the RETURN NEWLINE pair on MS/Windows™ systems. As you can see in the example, the operator << can be used consecutively to output a sequence of different quantities.

To use the Standard C++ I/O stream facility, a program must specify the line

```
#include <iostream>
```

near the beginning. It includes the *header file* iostream.[1] A header file supplies the necessary codes for using programs written in another file. This line must precede any code using the I/O stream. You should get in the habit of always putting this line at the beginning of any source code file that uses I/O.

The last statement

```
return 0;
```

terminates the program and returns a value known as the *exit status* to the invoking environment of this program to signal whether the program met with success or failure. A zero exit status is normal.

1.3 RUNNING THE FIRST EXAMPLE

By following a popular naming convention for C++ source code files, this example program can be put into the file average.C (or average.CPP) and then compiled. For example, on a UNIX system, a command such as

g++ average.C

compiles with the GNU C++ compiler **g++**. Your computer may have the C++ compiler under another name (e.g., **CC**) or may even provide a convenient program development environment. (Chapter 14 provides more general information on compilation and shows how to compile and run C++ programs on several widely used computer systems.)

After compilation, the executable program should be in a file under a standard name — for instance, a.out on UNIX systems. Your system may use another standard name. Now run the compiled program. These lines should appear:

```
i is 10
and j is 20
average is 15
```

As mentioned, the active parts of a function are its statements, the subject of Section 1.4.

1.4 STATEMENTS

A statement specifies program actions at run time. The computational steps in a function are expressed by a sequence of statements that performs in ways

---

[1]Note, there are headers with and without the .h suffix.

predefined by the language. The statements are *executed* one by one in the given order when the program runs.

C++ provides a full complement of statements that are described shortly. Generally, statements fall into two categories:

1. *Simple statement:* One single statement terminated by a semicolon (;).
2. *Compound statement:* Zero or more statements grouped together by { and }. A compound statement has the same structure as a function body. In fact, the function body is itself a compound statement. A compound statement can be used anywhere a simple statement can.

For example, each statement in the main function of average.C is a simple statement. Together they form the compound body of main. A compound statement is sometimes also referred to as a *block*.

A common programming mistake is to forget the semicolon terminator. When this happens in a program, because the C++ compiler cannot easily determine that a semicolon is missing, it almost always complains about some other alleged syntax problem. These erroneous complaints can be very confusing. So be sure to use the semicolon where it is needed:

1. A declaration always ends with a ;.
2. A simple statement is terminated by a ;.
3. There is no ; after a compound statement—in other words, after the closing } of a block.

For an example of item 3, see the while statement used by the factorial function in Section 1.5.

1.5 THE while STATEMENT

Let's consider another simple function—in this case, one that computes n factorial for a nonnegative integer n. Recall that n factorial is $n! = n * (n-1) * \cdots * 3 * 2 * 1$. Hence, $1! = 1, 2! = 2, 3! = 6$, and so on.

```
// factorial function computes n! for nonnegative n
/* version 1 */

int factorial(int n)
{       int ans = 1;
        while (n > 1)
        {     ans = ans * n;
              n = n - 1;
        }
```

```
        return ans;
}
```

Note that the first two lines in this example do nothing but are nonetheless very important. The C++ compiler ignores all characters starting from the two-character sequence // to the end of the line. Also ignored are all characters or lines enclosed in /* and */. These markers allow comments, auxiliary information, or *documentation* to be supplied to make a program easy to understand.

The function factorial is defined with one formal parameter n of type int. The return value is of type int also. If control flows off the end of a function or returns through a return with no argument, the return value is undefined and the function *valuetype* must be void.

In this factorial function, the while statement

```
while (n > 1)
{    ans = ans * n;
     n = n - 1;
}
```

specifies repeated execution of two statements forming a *loop*. The *condition* n > 1 (enclosed in parentheses) controls how many times the body of the while loop (enclosed in braces) is executed.

Figure 1.2   THE while LOOP

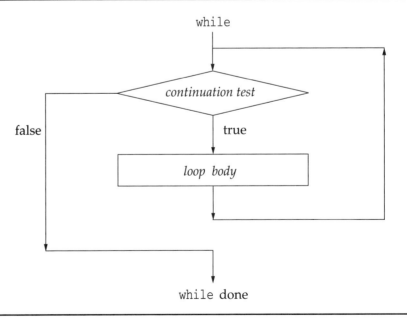

1.5 THE while STATEMENT

Here is the way while works (Figure 1.2):

1. Test the condition. If n is greater than 1 (the condition is true), then the body of while is executed once. If the condition is false, then the body is not executed, the while statement is finished, and control goes to the next statement.
2. Go back and execute the previous step.

Because the continuation of the loop depends on the condition being true, such a condition is known as a *continuation condition*. The variable n in this example is called a *loop-control variable* because its value changes for each repetition of the loop and it determines when the loop stops.

Take a particular value for n (say, 4) and follow the actions of this while loop to see how the variable ans actually becomes *n!* (24 in this case).

A Main Program for factorial

To test factorial, we can write a main program to call the function:

```cpp
#include <iostream>

int main()
{   std::cout << "Please enter n :";
    int n;                                     // declaration of n
    std::cin >> n;                             // input from keyboard
    if ( n >= 0 )
        std::cout << "factorial(" << n << ")=" // display answer
                  << factorial(n) << std::endl;
    else
    {   std::cerr << "factorial(" << n         // display error message
                  << ") undefined" << std::endl;
        return 1;
    }
    return 0;
}
```

The first statement in the main function displays a request for the user to enter the value of n. The second statement is a *declaration statement*, one that introduces a new variable into the program. After n is declared, an integer value is read into n using the built-in input object cin and the *input operator* >>. If n is nonnegative, then the return value of the call factorial(n) is displayed through cout. Otherwise (n is negative), a message is displayed through the built-in error-output object cerr, and the exit status 1 is returned to indicate failure.

Put the functions `factorial` and `main` (in that order) into a file; then compile and run the program. It should produce the message

```
Please enter n :
```

Now type in a small integer (say, 5) and then press RETURN. If it works correctly, the display

```
factorial(5)=120
```

should appear on your screen.

1.6 SIMPLE CONDITIONAL STATEMENTS

Let's now look at the `if` statement in the factorial example. The `if-else` statement provides *conditional branching* and can be used in the simple form

```
if ( condition )
     statement one
else
     statement two
```

The parentheses around the `condition` are mandatory. The condition is first tested to decide which one of the two given statements is executed. If the condition is true, then only `statement one` is executed; otherwise, only `statement two` is executed. Because a statement, by definition, can be either simple or compound, statement one or two here can be compound in the form { st_1; ... st_n; }.

The `else` part can also be omitted, resulting in the form

```
if ( condition )
     statement
```

The effect is to execute the given `statement` only if the `condition` is true. Failing this, the statement is skipped over, and control flows to the next statement after the `if` statement.

The following statement

```
if ( n > 0 )
      m = m + n;
else
      m = m - n;
```

assigns to `m` the absolute value of `n` plus `m`. The condition

```
n > 0
```

is a *relational expression*. It produces the logical value true only if the current value of n is greater than zero; otherwise, it produces false. The > is a relational operator. Table 1.1 lists the relational operators for numeric comparisons.

Do not confuse the relational operator == with the assignment operator =. If you use one less equal sign, the test condition becomes an assignment, which is perfectly legal in C++. The value of the assignment now, mistakenly, becomes the test result. This mistake will not cause compilation or execution errors; however, the answer produced will be wrong.

Logical constants, also known as *Boolean values*, are represented by constants of type bool: true and false. A test condition may produce a non-bool value: A zero value or null pointer (a zero-valued pointer) is treated as false, and all other values are treated as true. Because of this, the condition

```
if ( n != 0 )        // n not equal to 0
```

is the same as the simplified condition

```
if ( n )
```

1.7 CHARACTERS AND CHARACTER INPUT AND OUTPUT

For every C++ program, there are three standard I/O channels:

1. *Standard input:* The standard input channel reads from the keyboard and is represented by the built-in I/O stream object std::cin.
2. *Standard output:* The standard output channel outputs to the terminal screen and is represented by the built-in I/O stream object std::cout. Standard output is used for normal display to the terminal screen.

Table 1.1 RELATIONAL OPERATORS

Operator	Meaning
>	Greater than
<	Less than
==	Equal to
!=	Not equal to
>=	Greater than or equal to
<=	Less than or equal to

3. *Standard error:* The error output channel outputs to the terminal screen immediately without any intermediate character buffering or delay. It is represented by the I/O stream object std::cerr. Standard error is used for displaying error or diagnostic messages.

To illustrate character input and output, which are two of the most basic operations, we can write a program that does the following:

1. Reads characters from standard input.
2. Converts any uppercase characters into lowercase characters.
3. Writes all characters out to standard output.

We first write a function that converts uppercase characters to lowercase characters. The lower function is called with a character and returns the lowercase of this character:

```
#include <ctype.h>

char lower(char c)
{   if ( isupper(c) )              // if c is uppercase
        return tolower(c);         // turn c into lowercase
    else return c;                 // else c is unchanged
}
```

The library functions isupper and tolower (supplied by the header file <ctype.h>) make writing this function simple. The test isupper(c) returns nonzero (logical true) if c is an uppercase character. Otherwise, it returns zero (logical false).

So again, we use the if construct:

```
if (character is uppercase)
    compute and return lowercase value
else
    return character unchanged
```

Now all the main program has to do is call the function lower on each input character and output what lower returns:

```
#include <iostream>

int main()
{   char c;
    char lower(char c);                    // function prototype (1)
    while ( std::cin.get(c) != 0 )         // input character
        std::cout.put( lower(c) );
    std::cout.flush();
    return 0;
}
```

1.7 CHARACTERS AND CHARACTER INPUT AND OUTPUT

Note that the function `lower` is declared before it is used in the body of `main`. A function must be declared before it is used. The declaration

```
char lower(char c);
```

tells the C++ compiler that `lower` is a function that takes one argument of type `char` and returns a value of type `char`. In general, such a declaration takes the form of a function header terminated by a semicolon and is called a *function prototype*. Parameter names in a function prototype are optional but can provide valuable indications of the nature of the parameters. Thus, the preceding function prototype can also be given as

```
char lower(char);
```

The declaration on line 1 can be omitted if the function `lower` actually precedes `main` in the source code file.

The I/O stream objects `std::cin` and `std::cout` have internal routines or *member functions* that can be invoked to perform well-defined duties. For instance, the **get** member function of the object `cin`, when given a character variable c, reads from standard input a single character and assigns that character to c. A member function is accessed through an object by the notation

object.member

where the dot (.) is the *member-of* operator. The function call `std::cin.`**get**`(c)` returns zero only when end of file is reached. The *not equal to* sign `!=` is a relational operator. (See Table 1.1 for all available relational operators.) Thus, the `while` loop in our example will repeat until end of file is reached. When input is from the keyboard, a system-dependent convention is used to signify the end of input. For example, under UNIX you type ^D (control-D), under Windows you type ^Z (control-Z), at the beginning of a line.

After the character c is read, the character `lower(c)` is written to standard output by

```
std::cout.put( lower(c) )
```

where **put** is a member function of `cout`.

After the `while` loop is finished, `std::cout.`**flush**`()` is called to make sure that any buffered output is sent before the program terminates. Other useful facilities provided by the built-in I/O stream of C++ are covered as needed.

Put this program into a file (say, `lowercase.C`) and then compile and run it. Now type a mixture of uppercase and lowercase characters on the keyboard and press RETURN. You should see the same line displayed with all uppercase characters turned into lowercase characters. Type as many input lines as you like; then terminate the input properly.

1.8 MORE BASIC CONSTRUCTS

Having considered a few selected examples and having an idea of the overall structure of a C++ program, we are ready to examine some more frequently used expressions and statements.

The `for` Statement

C++ has the usual arithmetic operators +, -, *, and /. In addition, there is also the integer remainder operator % (e.g., 15 % 6 is 3). But there is no power, or exponentiation, operator. The `for` statement can be used in a power function to raise integers to integer powers:

```
int power(int a, int n)
{    int i, ans = 1;
     for (i = 1 ; i <= n ; i = i+1)
          ans = ans * a;
     return ans;
}
```

In this function, the `for` specifies a loop and takes the following general form:

```
for ( init statement
      cont condition ; incr expr )    (loop control)
      statement                        (loop body)
```

The loop body can be a simple or a compound statement. The loop control consists of an initialization statement (with its own terminating semicolon) and is followed by two expressions (a continuation condition and an increment expression) separated by another semicolon.

In the function power, the *init statement*

```
i = 1;
```

is executed before the `for` loop starts. The *cont condition*

```
i <= n
```

is then tested. If true, the *statement*, or body, of the `for` loop is executed once. The *incr expr*

```
i = i + 1;
```

is then executed, followed by a reexamination of the test condition. If it is true, the body is executed once again. If it is false, the `for` statement is finished. Figure 1.3 further illustrates the control flow of `for`.

The `for` is a specialized `while`, and the iteration keeps going only while the test condition remains true. Thus, it is possible for the body of the `for` to

1.8 MORE BASIC CONSTRUCTS

Figure 1.3 THE for LOOP

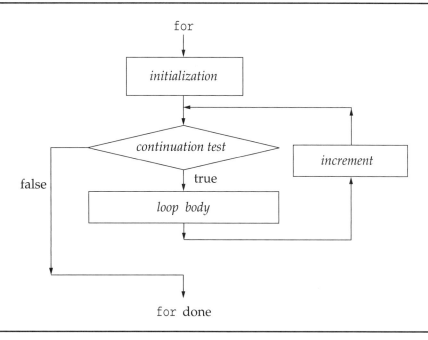

be *skipped without ever being executed* if the test condition is false to start with. It is also worth noting that only two semicolons are used in the loop control part of the for. (Details on the forms of expressions themselves are discussed in Section 1.10.)

The initialization statement can be a *null statement*, one that consists of just the ending semicolon and specifies a no-op, an operation that does nothing. It is possible to omit one or more parts in the for loop control. The absence of a part indicates a no-op. Thus, an infinite loop can be written as

```
for(;;) { /* loop body */ }          // infinite loop
```

It is also possible to write a for with a body that is empty or a null statement:

```
for ( /* control */ ) { }            // empty loop body
for ( /* control */ ) ;              // null loop body
```

In this case, the loop body is a no-op, and the effective computations would be contained in the loop control.

Instead of declaring the loop control variable i outside, it can be declared inside the for:

```
for (int i = 1 ; i <= n ; i = i+1)
    ans = ans * a;
```

Thus declared, the variable i is local to the for and its value is not accessible outside the for loop.

The function power assumes that the exponent n is nonnegative. It does not work for a negative n. Strictly speaking, there should be a check for the sign of n before the for loop is entered. Another concern is the size of the answer. If the answer exceeds the maximum size for the type int, power will fail. The handling of arithmetic overflow and underflow in C++ is implementation dependent. It could happen that the variable ans suddenly becomes zero when overflow occurs. These problems can be solved as you become more familiar with the language (Section 8.10).

Increment and Decrement Operators

The unary operators ++ (increment) and -- (decrement) are used to increase or decrease the value of an integer variable by 1 (which is especially useful in loops). Applied to a variable i, these special operators perform four separate functions in a single step:

1. Access the current value of i.
2. Add or subtract 1 from this value.
3. Assign the new value to i.
4. Produce the old or new i as the value of the expression.

Specifically, we can use

i++   (increment after — gives value of i and then adds 1 to i)
++i   (increment before — adds 1 to i and then gives value of i)
i--   (decrement after — gives value of i and then subtracts 1 from i)
--i   (decrement before — subtracts 1 from i and then gives value of i)

The idea is to combine referencing the value of a variable with assigning a new value to the variable to get shorter, more efficient code. For example,

```
j = 2 * i++;
```

means use the current value of i in the multiplication with 2 and then change the value of i by adding 1 to it. Thus, it is shorthand for

```
j = 2 * i;
i = i + 1;
```

1.8 MORE BASIC CONSTRUCTS

but more efficient. Similarly, the increment-before usage in

```
j = 2 * ++i;
```

is short for

```
i = i + 1;
j = 2 * i;
```

which is very different from the increment-after operation.

Here is the power function with the increment operator:

```
int power(int a, int n)
{      int ans = 1;
       for (int i = 1 ; i <= n ; i++)
            ans = ans * a;
       return ans;
}
```

Note that we could have written ++i instead of i++ in the loop control of the for because the value of this increment expression is not used.

A yet more efficient implementation of power combines n-- with while, a construct explained in Section 1.5:

```
int power(int a, int n)
{      int ans = 1;
       while (n-- > 0)
            ans = ans * a;
       return ans;
}
```

Note that n-- in the while condition here cannot be replaced by --n. However, assuming n is nonnegative, the relational expression n-- > 0 can be replaced by the simple n-- without changing the meaning of the while loop.

Use of the increment and decrement operators sometimes can make code more difficult to read and can contribute to program errors. You should strive for readability over terseness in your programming.

The do-while Statement

The while and the for loops test the continuation condition at the beginning of the loop. If the condition is false to begin with, the while or for loop body can be skipped without being executed. The do-while loop is the same as while, except it tests the continuation condition at the end of the loop (Figure 1.4). Therefore, a do-while loop body is executed *at least once*.

The general form of the do statement is

```
do statement while ( condition ) ;
```

Figure 1.4 THE do-while LOOP

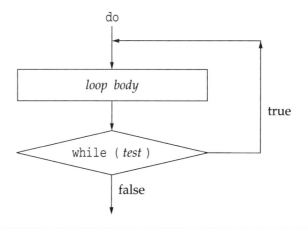

where the loop body is again a simple or compound statement.

The Multiway if Statement

We have seen the simple if-else statement and how to use it. Here is the general form of the if statement:

```
if ( expr1 )
      statement-1
else if ( expr2 )
      statement-2
...
      ...
else
      statement-i
```

There can be zero or more else-if parts. As stated before, the final else part is optional.

This pattern specifies a multiway branching: If expr1 is true, statement-1 is executed; otherwise, if expr2 is true, statement-2 is executed; ...; otherwise, if nothing is true, statement-i is executed. In other words, the logical expressions are examined in order, and the first true expression triggers the execution of the corresponding statement. At most, one of the statements is executed. Control then goes to the next statement beyond the entire if statement.

1.8 MORE BASIC CONSTRUCTS

To apply the if statement, we can write a function, compare, that takes two int quantities, a and b, and returns 1, 0, or −1, depending on whether a is greater than, equal to, or less than b, respectively:

```
int compare(int a, int b)
{    if ( a > b )
         return 1;
     else if (a < b )
         return -1;
     else
         return 0;
}
```

Actually, it is not necessary to insist on getting 1, 0, and −1 from compare. Following the convention established by the C++ library function strcmp (string compare, see Section 4.2), the return value should be positive, zero, or negative, depending on the relative size of the two quantities being compared. Hence, the function compare becomes simply

```
int compare(int a, int b)
{      return a-b;
}
```

A statement within an if can be another if to form a *nested* if statement. The function even_or_odd returns 2, 1, or 0 for a positive even, positive odd, or neither, respectively:

```
int even_or_odd(int a)
{   if ( a > 0 )                   // outer if begin
        if ( a % 2 == 0 )          // inner if begin
            return 2;
        else
            return 1;              // inner if end
                                   // outer if end
    return 0;
}
```

The arithmetic operator % computes the remainder (Section 1.10). With nested if statements, a good question to ask is: To which if does the else belong? There are two logical possibilities: (1) Associate the else with the inner if, making the statement part of the outer if another if-else statement; (2) associate the else with the outer if. This potential ambiguity is known as the *dangling else* problem. In C++, an else clause automatically goes with the immediately preceding open if. An if without an else can be closed by enclosing the if statement in {}, making it a compound statement.

1.9 DATA TYPES AND DECLARATIONS

There are only five *basic data types* in Standard C++: bool, char, int, float, and double. We have seen the type bool in Section 1.6 already. The effects of all C++ operators on the basic types are defined by the language.

Data Type char

We have used characters in a limited way without details of the character type. A char type is a single byte (typically, 8 bits), enough to hold one character in the character set. A common standard is ASCII (American Standard Code for Information Interchange). A char byte represents a character with an integer encoding defined in the character set. In ASCII, each character has a nonnegative integer code. For instance, the characters Z and z are represented by 90 and 122, respectively.

Like 'A' and 'Z'?, a character constant is specified within single quotes. The value of a character constant is merely its integer code. For example, in ASCII, '9' has numeric value 57. A character constant and its equivalent integer value are interchangeable in usage. However, by using the character constant notation, you can make your program *character-set-independent* and easier to read.

A few special characters are specified by two-character *escape sequences* such as '\n', the NEWLINE character discussed earlier. Table 1.2 contains a list of all such escape sequences.

Any constant, byte-size, bit pattern can also be specified using a notation with one to three octal (base 8) digits (0–7) or with one to two hexadecimal (base 16) digits (0...9, a...f, A...F). Some byte-size patterns (anything over 127) do not correspond to any character code in ASCII. Table 1.3 shows a sample of characters in various notations.

Table 1.2 CHARACTER ESCAPE SEQUENCES

\n	NEWLINE	\r	RETURN
\t	TAB	\v	VERTICAL TAB
\'	SINGLE QUOTE	\"	DOUBLE QUOTE
\\	BACKSLASH	\b	BACKSPACE
\f	FORMFEED	\a	BELL
\?	QUESTION MARK	\0	Null character
\0*ooo*	Octal byte	\x*hh*	Hexadecimal byte

1.9 DATA TYPES AND DECLARATIONS

To support larger character sets such as the 16-bit Unicode, C++ provides the wchar_t *wide character* type. The precise size of a wchar_t character is implementation dependent. A wide character constant is given in the form L'xy', where the number of characters between the single quotes and their meaning are implementation defined. For example,

```
wchar_t pi = L'\x03\xC0';    (Greek character π)
wchar_t wang = L'\x73\x8B';  (Chinese character for wang)
```

are Unicode characters.

Data Type int

The type int holds an integer quantity. The size (number of bits) of the int type is machine dependent and normally reflects the machine word size. In addition to int, there are short int and long int types. Again, their sizes are machine dependent. Typically, on a 32-bit computer, C++ offers a 16-bit short int, a 32-bit int, and a 32-bit or 64-bit long int. By omitting the int, these types may be specified simply as short or long.

The signed and unsigned Integers

Integer types such as int and char normally are interpreted with a leading *sign bit*. This means that if the leading bit is 0, the quantity is positive; otherwise, it is negative. Thus, if a char uses 8 bits, then the value ranges from −128 to 127. Hence, about half of the available representations are taken up by negative values.

In cases where the negative values are not needed, a representation with a leading sign bit wastes 50% of the possible values. However, this can be

Table 1.3   CHARACTER REPRESENTATIONS

Character	Constant	Integer Value	Bit Pattern	Octal Value	Hex Value
Zero	'0'	48	00110000	060	0x30
NEWLINE	'\n'	10	00001010	012	0xa
Plus sign	'+'	43	00101011	053	0x2b
A	'A'	65	01000001	0101	0x41
a	'a'	97	01100001	0141	0x61
^D	'\04'	4	00000100	04	0x4

avoided. The qualifiers signed and unsigned can be used on int, char, and other integer types to enable (the default) and disable the use of the sign bit. An unsigned number obeys integer arithmetic modulo 2^n, where n is the number of bits in the type. Therefore, for $n = 32$, unsigned int values range between 0 and $2^{32} - 1$. The signed and unsigned representations of a small positive integer are the same.

The maximum and minimum values of various data types are implementation dependent and are kept in the standard header files limits.h and float.h. Symbolic constants such as INT_MAX and INT_MIN (typically, $2^{31} - 1$ and -2^{31} on a 32-bit computer) are defined in limits.h.

The short test program

```
#include <iostream>
#include <limits.h>

int main()
{   unsigned int a = INT_MAX + 1;
    std::cout << a << std::endl;
    int b = INT_MAX + 1;
    std::cout << b << std::endl;
    return 0;
}
```

will show you the value of INT_MAX and the meaning of unsigned versus signed quantities.

Forms of Constants

An integer constant is composed of an optional sign (+ or -) followed by a sequence of digits. An integer given in octal or hex begins with a 0 (zero) or a 0x prefix, respectively. If an integer constant given in your program is large and does not fit into an int, the compiler will take it as a long. You can also use trailing characters to explicitly indicate long, unsigned, and so on, as shown in Table 1.4.

A single-precision floating-point type, float, has a size suggested by the machine architecture. A double-precision floating-point type, double, typically uses twice as many bits as float. There is also long double, which usually supplies yet more precision.

A floating-point constant contains a decimal point (3.1416), an exponent (31416e-4), or both. The type is assumed to be double unless the constant has a trailing f or F (float) or l or L (long double) (see Table 1.4).

Table 1.4 INTEGER AND FLOATING-POINT CONSTANTS

-9876	int	-9876L or -9876l	long
1234U or 1234u	unsigned	1234UL or 1234ul	unsigned long
025	Octal number	0xFFF	Hex number
025L	long octal	0xFFFul	unsigned long hex
3.14159	double	314e-2 or 314E-2	(3.14) double
3.1416f or 3.1416F	float	314e-2l or 314e-2L	long double

Variables and Identifiers

A variable is an *identifier* referring to a memory location holding a value. There is more to an identifier than just variable names. It can be a function name, a class name, a symbolic constant, and so on. An identifier consists of a sequence of letters, digits, and underscores (_) whose first character must not be a digit. Note that uppercase and lowercase letters are different. An identifier can be of any length. Identifiers containing a double underscore (__) or a leading underscore may conflict with implementation-generated identifiers or those used in libraries and should be avoided by application programs.

As mentioned before, the data type of a variable must be declared before it is used in a program. When a variable is declared, it can also be initialized. For example,

```
char shift = 'a' - 'A';
int i = 7;
float x = 1.2f;
long double pi = 3.141592653589793L;
```

In general, a variable can be initialized with arbitrary expressions involving constants, other variables, and function calls. The different types of expressions are described next.

1.10 OPERATORS AND EXPRESSIONS

Constants, variables, and function calls are the simplest sorts of expressions. When combined with operators, they form more involved expressions. Whether an expression is simple or complicated, it always gives a value.

An operator acts on operands. A *binary* operator takes two operands, and a *unary* operator takes only one operand. In an expression involving multiple operators, the order in which the operations are carried out is very important. In the expression

```
a + b / c
```

the division is carried out before the addition. Thus, the operator / takes *precedence* over +. Generally, arithmetic operators take precedence over logical operators, which take precedence over assignment operators. Consider an expression involving operators with the same precedence:

```
a / b * c         // equivalent to (a / b) * c
```

Its value can depend on the *associativity* of these operators. Most operators associate left to right, causing the expression to be evaluated from left to right. A few groups of operators associate right to left. (The relative precedence and associativity of all operators are shown in Appendix F.) Parentheses can be used to override the precedence and associativity rules, as in

```
(a + b) / c
a / (b * c)
```

The available operators and expressions are presented in the following subsections. For easy reference, the operators and expressions are summarized in Tables 1.5, 1.7, 1.8, and 1.9.

Arithmetic Expressions

Table 1.5 shows the variety of arithmetic expressions. When the divide operator / is used on two integers, an integer quotient is produced. Any fractional part is discarded. The increment and decrement operators can be used only on actual variables. Therefore, an expression such as (a+b)++ is incorrect.

Table 1.5 ARITHMETIC EXPRESSIONS

Expression	Description
a/(3.4+b)-3*c	Usual precedence and type conversions
i/4	Integer division truncates any fractional part
i % j	Integer remainder; denominator j should be positive
x*x*x	No built-in power operator
++i, j++	Pre/postincrement (integer only)
--i, j--	Pre/postdecrement (integer only)

1.10 OPERATORS AND EXPRESSIONS

The arithmetic operator `%` provides the remainder, or modulo operation, for integer operands. To compute `i` modulo `j` means to divide `i` by `j` and take the remainder. If both `i` and `j` are nonnegative, the result is nonnegative and smaller than `j`. Otherwise, the only guarantee is that the absolute value of the result will be smaller than the absolute value of `j`. Furthermore, `%` does not work for floating-point numbers. The modulo operation (mod for short) is useful in many situations.

Consider computing the next tab position, given any current column position. On a typical CRT terminal, tab stops are set eight columns apart. So the next tab stop is given by

```
c - (c % 8) + 8
```

for any current column position `c`.

Relational and Logical Expressions

We have already used some relational and logical expressions. The set of all *relational* operators is listed in Table 1.1. The *logical* operators are given in Table 1.6. All forms of relational and logical expressions are shown in Table 1.7.

The relational operators have higher precedence than the operator `&&` (logical and), which takes precedence over `||` (logical or). *Evaluation of a logical expression stops as soon as the logical value of the whole expression is determined.* This may leave some operands unevaluated. For example, the expression

expr1 `&&` *expr2*

is true only if both *expr1* and *expr2* are true. If *expr1* turns out to be false, the value of the whole expression must be false; therefore, *expr2* is not evaluated. Similarly, in evaluating

expr1 `||` *expr2*

if *expr1* is true, the value of the whole expression is true, and *expr2* will not be evaluated.

Table 1.6 LOGICAL OPERATORS

Operator	Meaning
`&&`	Logical operator *and*
`||`	Logical operator *or*
`!`	Logical operator *not* (unary)

Table 1.7 RELATIONAL AND LOGICAL EXPRESSIONS

Expression	Comment
false or 0	Logical false
true or nonzero	Logical true
a > b, a < b, a >= b, a <= b	Relational expressions have logical values
a == b, a != b	Equal, not equal
a > 0 && a < 1	True if first *and* second relations are true
a > 1 || a < -1	True if first *or* second relation is true
a || ! b && c	Logical expression: a *or* [(*not* b) *and* c]
a > b ? a : b	Conditional expression: if (a > b), then value is a; else b

The unary operator ! (logical not) *negates* the logical value of its operand. The negation turns true into false, and vice versa. The operator ! has precedence over all relational and other logical operators. For an example of a rather complicated logical expression, see the readLine function in Section 1.14.

C++ also features the *conditional expression* formed with the *ternary* operator ?:, which takes three operands:

expr0 ? *expr1* : *expr2*

The expression has value *expr1* if *expr0* is true and *expr2* otherwise. Thus, the expression

c = a > b ? a : b

sets c to max(a,b).

Assignment Expressions

An *assignment* is a statement as well as an expression because it produces a value—that of the left-hand side after the assignment is made. Hence, an assignment can be used anywhere an expression can. Furthermore, in the same spirit of the increment and decrement operators, the assignment operator = can combine with other operators to form efficient shorthand expressions. The allowable combinations are shown in Table 1.8.

1.10 OPERATORS AND EXPRESSIONS

Table 1.8 ASSIGNMENT EXPRESSIONS

Expression	Comment
a = b = 1	a = (b = 1)
(c = std::cin.get()) != EOF	Assignment expression used in a relational expression
a += b	Shorthand for a = a + b
a op = b	Shorthand for a = a op b Allowable op s: +, -, *, /, %, <<, >>, &, ^, |

To see assignment expressions in action, let's consider a function that computes the sum of the squares of the first n odd integers:

```
int sumSquares(int n)              // n is assumed positive
{   int sum = 1, i = 1;
    n *= 2;                        // n = n * 2
    while ( (i += 2) < n )
        sum += (i * i);
    return sum;
}
```

In sumSquares, the assumption is made that the argument n is positive. The while loop is completely bypassed for the case $n = 1$. The parentheses around i += 2 in the while condition are necessary because assignment operators have lower precedence than almost all other operators. For the same reason, the parentheses around i * i are unnecessary but included for readability.

Bitwise Operations

There is also a group of operators for dealing with data at the bit level. These include << (left-shift) and >> (right-shift) as well as the bitwise logical operators & (and), | (or), ~ (not), and ^ (exclusive or). The bitwise operators take only operands of integer types. Table 1.9 shows the available bitwise operations where the *ones complement* is obtained by flipping each and every bit of an integer. Unlike increment and decrement operators, bitwise operations do not alter their operands. Thus, j = i << 4 produces an integer value equal to left-shifting i by 4 bits without damaging the contents of i. If modifying i is what you actually desire, use

```
i <<= 4;
```

Table 1.9 INTEGER BITWISE EXPRESSIONS

Expression	Comment
n & 017	Bitwise *and*; value is n with all but lower 4 bits masked away
i | j	Bitwise i *or* j
i ^ j	Bitwise i *exclusive or* j
i << 4	Value is left-shift i by 4 bits
j >> 5	Value is right-shift j by 5 bits
~n	Ones complement of n

A 1-bit left-shift on an integer is normally equivalent to multiplying by 2. Thus, the preceding operation results in a value 16 times that of i.

Bitwise operations provide an alternative way to compute the next tab stop. By zeroing out the last three bits of the current column position c, you can use the expression

(c & ~07) + 8

to produce the position of the next tab stop. The bit pattern ~07 (bitwise not applied to octal 7) is all ones except the lowest three bits. It is used as a *mask* by the bitwise & operation to produce the same value as c but with the last three bits zeroed out.

Bitwise operations not only allow manipulations at the bit level, but they also provide an efficient way to perform certain arithmetic operations involving positive or unsigned integers. For example, left-shifting the number 3 by 1 bit gives 6. Conversely, right-shifting 6 by 1 bit gives 3.

Functions and Operators in C++

Note that the operators >> and << perform bitwise shifting as well as input/output. C++ supports *function overloading* and *operator overloading*, assigning multiple duties to functions and operators. Thus, a function/operator under the same name can perform different duties, depending on what arguments it receives. For example, take the left-shift operator <<. It can perform the added duty of sending data to an output stream object such as cout. The C++ compiler knows which one of the multiple duties an overloaded operator should perform by examining the declared types of the operator's operands.

For an operator to be overloaded, at least one of its operands must be an object (of user-defined type). Hence, the meaning of an operator in relation to

C++ built-in types cannot be changed by overloading, which is a reasonable policy. How to define classes and how to create objects are topics yet to be covered — not to mention overloading operators. But all of this is explained as we proceed.

Just as an operator is overloaded, so also can the same function name be overloaded to perform different duties (Section 3.7). The ability to overload can significantly reduce the number of functions, with different and often difficult-to-remember names, in a software system. Overloading also makes it easier to write *generic code*, routines that work for many different data types. These points will become clearer as your experience with OOP increases.

1.11 ENUMERATIONS

The *enumeration type* is a user-defined integer type consisting of a number of symbolic names, known as *enumerators*, representing constant integer values. Enumeration provides a convenient way to associate symbolic names to integer constants.

The declaration enum is used to establish a new enumeration type:

```
enum name { symbol₁[ = val₁],
            symbol₂[ = val₂],
            ...
          };
```

The declaration establishes *name* as a new enum *tag*. The constant integer values val_1, val_2, and so on are optional. For example,

```
enum Days { MON=1, TUE=2, WED=3, THU=4, FRI=5, SAT=6, SUN=7};
```

declares the enum tag Days and defines the constant enumerators MON, TUE, and so on. The integer values of the enumerators are explicitly specified here. If unspecified, the enumerators are given consecutive integer values following the last specified entry or from zero. Thus,

```
enum Days { MON=1, TUE, WED, THU, FRI, SAT, SUN };
```

is an equivalent declaration of Days. The values of the enumerators do not have to be distinct, allowing declarations such as

```
enum Days { MON=1, TUE, WED, THU, FRI, SAT, SUN,
            mon=1, tue, wed, thu, fri, sat, sun};
```

Enumerators must be declared before they are used. The names of the enumerators must also be distinct from other identifiers in the same scope (Section 3.1). This means that having used MON in Days, you cannot, in the same scope, use MON again in another enumeration type (say, WeekDays) or use MON as a variable.

Once an enumeration tag is established, *enumeration variables* of that type can be declared and used. An enumeration variable should take on only the values defined in the enumeration type:

```
Days j = MON;
```

Thus, the enumeration variable j is an integer variable intended to take on only the values MON through SUN inclusive.

Here is another example of enumeration type.

```
enum white_space
{    SPACE = ' ',
     NEWLINE = '\n',
     TAB = '\t',
     RETURN = '\r'};
```

Anonymous enumerations are declared by leaving out the name part. An anonymous enumeration is sometimes an alternative to #define constants (Section 14.4):

```
enum { TABLE_SIZE = 256,   TERMINATOR = -1 };
```

There are, however, significant differences between an enumeration constant and a symbolic constant established by #define. The latter is not restricted to representing integers and is effective in one file only, whereas the former must be an integer and obey scope rules.

Without explicit type-casting (Section 3.13), an enumeration variable can be assigned only an enumerator. Thus,

```
Days j = 2;          // error; cannot convert int to Days
```

does not work. C++ does not automatically convert an integer to an enumerator, but converting an enumerator to an integer is automatic. In particular, arithmetic operations involving enumeration variables and/or constants are performed by first converting to integers. Thus,

```
int k = MON + WED;          // o.k.
```

works just fine.

1.12 ARRAYS

Basic Concepts

An array is composed of consecutive memory locations, *array cells*, each of which holds data of the same type. For example,

```
int b[10];
```

declares b an array and defines for it ten cells, b[0] through b[9], each just large enough to hold a quantity of type int. Unlike some other languages, in C++, *array indexing goes from 0 to the dimension* − 1. This is important to keep in mind. Here are some typical usages:

```
b[0] = 17;
n = b[i+1] - 13;
for (i = 0 ; i < 10 ; i++) b[i] = 0;
```

The array b can be declared and initialized to hold the first ten prime numbers as follows:

```
int b[]={2,3,5,7,11,13,17,19,23,29};
```

When the array size is left unspecified, the C++ compiler figures out the dimension of b from the number of data items supplied. Figure 1.5 provides a graphical representation of the array b.

Once an array is created, its cells can be used to store and retrieve data of a given type. Cells are accessed using the index notation b[i], where each array cell can be thought of and treated as a separate variable. Thus, an array can be viewed as a set of subscripted variables.

Character Arrays

An array of characters is used to represent a *C-style string*. The notation

```
"Happy Birthday"           // string constant
```

specifies a string constant. Figure 1.6 shows the structure of an array containing

Figure 1.5 THE INTEGER ARRAY b

b[0]	b[1]	b[2]	b[3]	b[4]	b[5]	b[6]	b[7]	b[8]	b[9]
2	3	5	7	11	13	17	19	23	29

Figure 1.6 A STRING AS A CHARACTER ARRAY

this string. The special *null character* '\0' (BACKSLASH zero) is used to mark the end of a string. The null character has an integer value of zero.

A string may extend across multiple lines. A BACKSLASH at the end of a line continues a string to the next line:

```
"A long string across \
two lines"
```

The C++ Standard Library provides a string type (a class) that makes string operations easier and less error prone. See Section 2.5 for details.

The array can be created using a sequence of assignments:

```
char str[15];      // declare str character array length 15
str[0] = 'H';
str[1] = 'a';
     .             // and so on
     .
     .
str[12] = 'a';
str[13] = 'y';
str[14] = '\0';    // string terminator
```

An easier way to perform such initialization uses the notation

```
char str[15] = {'H', 'a', ... , 'a', 'y', '\0'};
```

A still easier, but entirely equivalent, way is to initialize using the following shorthand notation:

```
// convenient char array initialization
char str[] = "Happy Birthday";
```

As before, the compiler figures out how large to make str to accommodate the character string and the extra terminator at the end.

To illustrate the usage of strings, let's consider the function strEqual(x,y), which returns a bool to indicate whether the strings x and y are equal or not:

```
bool strEqual(char x[], char y[])     // array formal parameters
{   int i = 0;
    if ( x == y ) return true;        // same memory locations
    while (x[i] == y[i])
    {   if (x[i] == '\0') return true; // strings equal
```

```
        i++;
    }
    return false;                          // strings unequal
}
```

The strEqual function header declares two formal array parameters, x and y. In general, the notation

type var[]

as part of the formal parameter list declares *var* an array of the given *type*.

Follow the code to see how strEqual works. If the condition (x == y) is true, then x and y refer to the same memory location. This means that a string is being compared to itself, and 1 can be returned immediately. If x and y point to different memory locations, they can still contain the same characters and be equal. So we use a while loop to compare the individual characters to determine whether they are equal or not.

Now test strEqual with the main program:

```
///////    strEqual.C    ///////
#include <iostream>

// put function strEqual here

int main()
{   char a[]= "abcde";                  // array a
    char b[]= "abcde";                  // array b
    char c[]= "abcd";                   // array c
    if ( strEqual(a,b) )
       std::cout << "a is equal to b"
                 << std::endl;
    if ( ! strEqual(b,c) )              // ! is logical not
       std::cout << "b is not equal to c" << std::endl;
    return 0;
}
```

The Standard Library provides many common operations on C-style strings, including comparing two strings for equality. C++ also supports *string objects* that can be easier to use and less error prone than C-style strings. Refer to Section 2.5 for more on string objects.

1.13 POINTERS

Basic Concepts

A *pointer* is the address of the memory location where an object or a piece of data is stored. A pointer variable can be declared by preceding the variable name with *. Here are some examples:

```
int *i, *j;      // values of i and j are pointers to int
char *c;         // value of c is a pointer to char
long *k;         // value of k is a pointer to long int
float *x;        // value of x is a pointer to float
double *y;       // value of y is a pointer to double
```

The memory location where a variable stores its value is obtained by the *unary address-of operator* &. Thus,

```
int i = 512;
int *j;          // declare j to be an int pointer variable
j = &i;          // j is assigned the address of i
```

results in j being a pointer to where 512 is stored. To be specific, let's assume the value of i is stored at memory location 49132. The variable j then has the value 49132. To obtain the value 512 through j, we use the *unary value-of operator* *. For instance, *j + 2 gives 514. The notation *j is equivalent to a variable of type int. To illustrate this, consider

```
*j = 0;
```

This puts 0 where the value 512 was formerly, so i is now 0 also. The pointer concept is illustrated graphically in Figure 1.7.

Memory locations in a program are referenced relative to a starting location, and an address is usually, but not guaranteed to be, a value that can be stored in a single machine word.

Array Assignments

For an assignment u = v, the variable u normally gets a copy of the value of v. In C++, this is correct except for arrays. In fact, an array name (e.g., take b) is actually a *constant pointer* to the first cell of the array. Therefore, the array name cannot be used as a variable on the left-hand side of an assignment. Hence, the following is incorrect:

```
int foo[10], b[10];
foo = b;              // incorrect; array name foo is not a variable
```

Figure 1.7 THE MEANING OF A POINTER

To make an array assignment, we need a pointer variable of the correct type on the left-hand side of the assignment. To assign b to a variable x, we use the code

```
int *x;
x = b;      // array assignment is by pointer
```

Now the elements of b can also be accessed via x. Keep in mind that the cells of the array b are still where they were, only now x can also access them. Thus,

```
x[3] = 96;
```

results in b[3] containing 96 as well.

Similarly, when an array name is used in a function call, a pointer to the first cell is passed to the called function.

1.14 AN EXAMPLE

The readLine function reads a line from standard input, stores the line in a character array, and returns the length of the line. This function is useful in other programs to obtain user input.

```
int readLine(char s[], int len)   // len length of s
{   char c = '\0';
    int i = 0;
    len --;                        // leaving room at the end
    while ( i < len && std::cin.get(c) && c != '\n')
        s[i++] = c;
    if (c == '\n') s[i++] = c;
    s[i] = '\0';                   // string terminator
    return i;
}
```

The while condition in readLine is the most complicated expression we have encountered so far. It consists of three conditions connected by two logical operators. The effect is to read characters into the array s until either the array is full, the end of file is reached, or a '\n' is read. After the while, the '\n', if any, is deposited into the array, and then the string terminator '\0' is added at the end. The number i of actual characters read is then returned.

Normally, a text file, including that supplied through the keyboard, consists of complete lines, each terminated by a '\n' character. The last line in the file is no exception. The readLine function makes this assumption. Therefore, the returned value is always the number of characters read even when end of file is reached.

The file readLine.C can be established as follows:

```
#include <iostream>
// put definition of readLine here

int main()
{   const int SIZE = 100;
    char line[SIZE];
    int n;
    while ((n = readLine(line, SIZE)) > 0)
            std::cout << "n = " << n << "\t line= "
                      << line << std::endl;
    return 0;
}
```

Here the C++ const declaration (Section 3.9) makes a variable or function parameter *read-only*. A constant identifier SIZE is established for the quantity 100. A const identifier is used in place of the actual constant in the source code. Assignment to a const variable or function parameter is not allowed. Do not use numeric constants in programs; use constant identifiers with meaningful names instead. This approach not only makes programs easier to understand but also allows you to modify every occurrence of a constant by simply changing the const definition.

Compile and run the program to get an output that looks something like this:

```
n=8     line=ABC DEF
n=12    line=123 456 789
```

1.15 ITERATION CONTROL

Iteration is the repeated execution of a set of statements in a program. Such repetitions make it possible for a short program to perform a very large number of operations. The constructs while, for, and do-while are used to perform iterations.

An iteration is normally specified by the following components:

1.15 ITERATION CONTROL

1. *Control variables:* One or more variables that take on new values for each successive repetition.
2. *Successor statements:* One or more statements that assign new values to the control variables in preparation for the next repetition.
3. *Loop body:* A sequence of zero or more statements that is executed once for each repetition.
4. *Continuation condition:* A logical or relational expression tested before or after each repetition. If the condition is true, then the next repetition is performed; otherwise, control flows to the program statement just after the iteration construct.

In addition to normal termination via item 4, the loop body may contain statements that cause *early termination* of the iteration. An example is the function inString, which determines whether a string contains a particular character:

```
bool inString(char c, char *str)
{       int i = 0;
        while (str[i] != '\0')
        {   if (str[i] == c) return true;
            i++;
        }
        return false;
}
```

The control variable i, initially 0, is incremented by 1 for each repetition. Normal termination comes when the string str has been completely examined and no match for c has been found. Early termination via the return statement occurs as soon as a match for c is found in str. Here are a couple of calls to this function:

```
inString('g', "abcdefgh");
inString('/', filename);
```

A shorter implementation of inString uses the for construct:

```
bool inString(char c, char *str)
{       for (int i = 0 ; str[i] != '\0' ; i++)
            if (str[i] == c) return true;
        return false;
}
```

The break and continue Statements

In the inString example, we used the return to terminate an iteration early. This technique is restrictive and cannot be used to break out of an iteration without causing the entire function to return. The break statement is used in such situations. When break is executed, control transfers immediately to the first statement after the current iteration. An application of break is found in the function monotonic, which examines an integer array and returns 1 or 0, depending on whether the sequence of integers is *monotonic* or not. A sequence of values is monotonically increasing if each value is no smaller than the previous one. Similarly, a sequence is monotonically decreasing if each value is no larger than the preceding one.

```
bool monotonic(int a[], int n)              // n is dimension of a
{     int i;
      for (i = 0 ; i < n - 1 ; i++)
            if (a[i+1] < a[i]) break;
      if (i == n - 1) return true;          // increasing
      for (i = 0 ; i < n - 1 ; i++)
            if (a[i+1] > a[i]) return false;
      return true;                          // decreasing
}
```

Try this program with various increasing, decreasing, repeating, length-one, and other sequences of integers.

The continue statement is similar to break. But instead of breaking out of a loop, continue *goes to the end of the loop body*. Within while or do-while, this means that control transfers immediately to the test-condition part. Inside for, it transfers to the increment step. In other words, continue skips the rest of the loop body to reach the loop control of the next repetition. To demonstrate how this can be convenient, let's consider stringMatch, a function that determines whether a given character string, str, is contained in another character string, line. The function returns the starting index in line if a match is found and -1 otherwise.

```
int stringMatch(char str[], char line[])
{    if ( str == NULL || str[0] == '\0')   // str is empty
          return -1;
     int j, k;
     for (int i = 0 ; line[i] != '\0' ; i++)
     {    if ( line[i] != str[0] )         // first chars different
               continue;                   // skip rest of loop body
       // compare remaining characters
       // until first mismatch or end of string
          for ( j = i + 1, k = 1;
```

1.15 ITERATION CONTROL

```
                line[j]==str[k] && str[k] != '\0';
                j++, k++
            ) { }
        if ( str[k] == '\0')            // end of str is reached
            return i;                   // successful match
        else if (line[j] == '\0')       // end of line is reached
            return -1;                  // no match possible anymore
    }
    return -1;                          // failed to match
}
```

The function `stringMatch` uses a straightforward strategy. The string `str` in turn is matched with a series of substrings starting at `line[0]`, `line[1]`, and so on. A successful match returns the value 1. Otherwise, the next substring is used. The value -1 is returned when there are no more substrings to match with `str`.

In `stringMatch`, a nested `for` loop is employed. The outer `for` iterates over the substrings `line[0]`, `line[1]`, and so on. If the first character of the substring does not match `str[0]`, the program skips the rest of the loop body and continues with the next substring.

The inner `for` is interesting because it has an empty body and two loop-control variables, `j` and `k`. In addition, the *comma operator* (`,`) is used in the increment expression. Two expressions connected by a comma become one expression whose value and type are those of the second expression. Expressions connected by commas are evaluated sequentially from left to right. Such a sequence of expressions can be used anywhere a single expression can.

The algorithm used in `stringMatch` is unsophisticated and inefficient. One immediate improvement is to stop matching and return 0 as soon as the substring becomes shorter than `str` because no further match is possible. Try to implement this modification.

The `goto` Statement and Labels

Structured programming advocates avoiding the arbitrary transfer of control provided by the `goto` statement. In fact, it is possible to write code without ever using `goto`. Experts generally agree that `goto` should be used rarely if at all. However, sometimes `goto` can be used to advantage. Mainly, it is useful in breaking out of a deeply nested loop because `break` gets you out of only the immediately enclosing loop.

```
while ( ... )
    while ( ... )
    {
        . . .
```

```
        for ( ... )
        {
            ...
            if ( /* something wrong */ ) goto error;
            ...
        }
    }

    . . .

return ...;
error:    // take care of errors here
```

The general form of the command is as follows:

`goto label;`   (label must be in the same function)

A *label*, such as `error` followed by a colon (`:`), is placed in front of the target statement for control transfer. A `goto` label has the same form as a variable and can be attached to any statement in the same function as the `goto`. A label must be unique, appearing in only one place, although it can have several jumps to it.

1.16 CHOICES BY `switch`

While the `if-else if-else` construct remains the general-purpose decision-making mechanism, the `switch` statement provides a very handy way to select among a set of predefined choices. The syntax is as follows:

```
switch ( expression )
{
        case constant-expr1 :
            statements
        case constant-expr2 :
            statements
         ...
        default:
            statements
}
```

The `switch` construct is like a structured multiple `goto`. The switching *expression* is evaluated first. The resulting value is matched against each integer-valued constant `case` label. In a `switch`, all `case` labels must be distinct. Control is transferred to the matching `case` or to the `default` if nothing matches. There is no sequential case-by-case matching at run time; control is transferred directly.

1.16 CHOICES BY switch

If the optional `default` case label is not given and if nothing matches, the execution of `switch` is successfully completed.

Following control transfer to a `case` label, the statements at the selected label *and all statements under other case labels after it* will be executed in sequence. This behavior is called *fall through*, and it makes `switch` very different from a multiple `if`. The `break` statement can also be used to break out of the `switch` statement. It is often the last statement for each `case` in order to prevent fall through. With fall through completely prevented, the order in which the `case` labels are given becomes unimportant. At each `case` label, there can be zero, one, or more statements. This allows several case labels to precede one group of statements, making it convenient for certain situations.

Experiment with the following test program to familiarize yourself with these concepts about `switch`:

```
int main()
{   int j = 4;
    std::cout << "1: switch(" << j << ")" << std::endl;
    switch(j)
    {   case 1:
        case 3:    std::cout << "A: case 1 or 3";
        case 5:    std::cout << "B: case 5";
        default:   std::cout << "C: case default ";   // deliberate
        case 2:    std::cout << "D: case 2";
    }
    std::cout << std::endl;
    j = 2;
    std::cout << "2: switch(" << j << ")" << std::endl;
    switch(j)
    {   case 5:    std::cout << "E: case 5";
        default:   std::cout << "F: case default";
        case 2:    std::cout << "G: case 2";
    }
    std::cout << std::endl;
    return 0;
}
```

The output produced is as follows:

```
1: switch(4)
C: case default D: case 2
2: switch(2)
G: case 2
```

1.17 SUMMARY

Functions and objects are the basic building blocks of a C++ program. Functions codify procedures, and classes define independent computing agents called *objects* (introduced in Chapter 2). The source code of a program may involve many functions and classes contained in one or more files. Every program contains the special function main, which is the entry point of the program. Any program that uses the standard I/O objects std::cin, std::cout, and std::cerr should include the header <iostream>. The std:: prefix puts these identifiers in the std namespace, the namespace of the C++ Standard Library.

All items such as functions and variables must be declared before use. C++ is a language with strong typing: Every quantity has a type, and the compiler checks for type correctness in a program. There are only five basic data types: bool, int, char, float, and double. Type qualifiers such as short, long, and unsigned obtain size and sign variations of integer types (char and int).

An array is a sequence of memory locations to store data of a given type. A character string is an array of characters terminated by '\0'. Array elements are indexed starting from zero. Memory locations where data of a particular type are stored are represented by pointers. There is a close relationship between pointers and arrays.

Constants (regular or enum) and variables are combined by operators to form expressions. Type bool constants are true and false. Wide character type wchar_t can represent Unicode characters. There are arithmetic, relational, logical, increment and decrement, assignment, and bitwise operators. There is no power operator for exponentiation. Additionally, there is the ternary conditional operator (?:). Frequently used control-flow statements include if, while, for and do-while, break, continue, and switch. Control variables local to a for loop can be introduced inside the control part of the for statement, in which case the variable is local to the for statement.

C++ supports function and operator overloading, assigning multiple meanings to the same function or operator. Built-in operators can be overloaded to work with objects in ways specified by the programmer. Use of the operators >> and << for I/O is an example of operator overloading.

EXERCISES

1. Write a simple main program to display some single characters, strings, integers, and floating-point numbers using the cout object.

CHAPTER 1 EXERCISES

2. Certain identifiers are reserved by C++ and cannot be used for other purposes. Name ten reserved words in C++.

3. Take the factorial function and add a check to detect any negative input. If the argument is negative, an error message is displayed using std::cerr and the value zero is returned.

4. Explain why calling factorial(j) repeatedly with j being 0, 1, 2, ... is very inefficient. Write a more efficient function to produce a list of factorial values.

5. Write a program expand.C that replaces all TAB characters in its standard input (cin) by an equivalent number of spaces and sends the result to standard output (cout). (*Hint:* Follow the example lowercase.C.) You may assume that TAB stops are eight characters apart.

6. Consider the function readLine. What would happen if the line read is longer than the size of the array s? Add a check for this condition and insert the appropriate error-handling code for readLine.

7. Consider the bitwise shift operations of integer quantities. In what exact situations do the left- and right-shift operations actually correspond to multiplication and division by 2?

8. Write a function octalDisplay(int n) that displays the integer n in octal notation.

9. Consider the octalDisplay function in Exercise 8. Rewrite the function to use bitwise operations to achieve the modulo-8 and the divide-by-8 operations.

10. Examine the following function definition and spot any syntax problems. Try to compile it and see what your compiler says. Explain in detail the source of any error.

    ```
    int myabs(int a)
    {    if (a >= 0)
            {    return a; };
         else
            {    return -a; };
    }
    ```

11. Write a function stringCompare that compares two strings x and y. The returned value is 1, 0, or −1, depending on whether x is greater than, equal to, or less than y, respectively, using lexicographic (dictionary) ordering.

12. Write a function `isLeapyear` that takes an integer year and returns zero if false and nonzero if true. (*Hint:* Use the % operator.)

13. Write a program to count the number of decimal digits in any integer given to the program through `cin`.

14. When reading from `std::cin`, end of file is normally reached when the user types a control-D (or a control-Z or some other system-dependent character) at the beginning of a line. Find out what the convention is on your system.

15. A *bitonic* sequence of integers consists of one monotonic sequence of zero or more elements followed by another. For example, both 2,2,3,4,3,2 and 4,3,1,2,7 are bitonic. Using the `monotonic` function in Section 1.15 as a model, write a `bitonic` function.

16. Using `switch`, write a program to count the number of SPACE, TAB, NEWLINE, and FORMFEED characters in a file.

CHAPTER TWO

C++ Primer
Part II: Object-Based Programming

Building on the basics in Chapter 1, an overview of C++ is now presented with emphasis on introducing classes and objects. Enough is covered so that you can write interesting and complete programs.

Objects help achieve data abstraction and encapsulation, two important software qualities. Classes, specifying both data and functions, serve as blueprints to build objects. These concepts are introduced and illustrated by a bank account example. Descriptions of the Standard C++ `string` objects further reinforce these ideas.

An *object-based program* uses classes and objects for problem solving. Tasks are achieved by employing interacting objects in a solution process. The methodology is demonstrated by a simple exercise in plane geometry and a complete program.

Argument passing in function calls is described, covering passing by value and passing by reference in detail. The inline function feature used to avoid function call overhead is also shown. The way a C++ program receives arguments from its invoking environment is described. This information helps you in writing programs that receive arguments and options given to the program when it is first invoked.

Input and output (I/O) operations are critical for programming. Enough terminal and file I/O, with built-in C++ I/O objects, are introduced to give you a good start. Also included are error-handling techniques, source code formatting suggestions, and effective object-based thinking in C++.

2.1 DATA ABSTRACTION AND ENCAPSULATION

One of the most central features of OOP is the division of the whole program into smaller autonomous entities, called *objects*, with well-defined interactions. This feature significantly reduces overall complexity and enhances the quality of the program in many different ways. An object organizes data and related operations into a *black box*, which hides the internal data structures, representations, and procedures from outside view. A data structure is *concrete* when its exact details are fixed and exposed. Traditional programming approaches depend heavily on concrete data. OOP, on the other hand, emphasizes *data abstraction* and encourages hiding the details of data by presenting only the data's *behavior*. For example, if you do not know the details of car construction, you can still drive one effectively if you know behavior such as "steering clockwise makes the car turn right." This leaves the implementation of steering to the black box, which can use one of several alternatives: regular, power-assisted, rack-and-pinion, and so on. In addition to structures, the object also contains mechanisms, or procedures, that are necessary to operate the structures. These procedures are *attached* to the structures to form one inseparable unit. This technique is called *encapsulation*.

Classes and Objects

The C++ *class* construct supports data abstraction and encapsulation. A class describes the construction of an object and serves as a blueprint to build objects. It specifies the internal workings as well as the external interface of an object. A class has a name, or *tag*, and specifies *members* belonging to the class that may be data, functions, or objects. Once a class is defined, the class name becomes a new data type and is used to declare variables of that type. A class-type variable is an *instance* of a class and is called an *object* of that class.

To begin, let's consider a simplified class representing bank accounts:

```
///////    Account.h     ///////

class Account                              // class name
{ public:
      Account();                           // constructor   (1)
      Account(unsigned n, double b);  // constructor   (2)
      void deposit(double amt);      // deposit amt into this account
      bool withdraw(double amt);     // withdraw amt from this account
      double balance();                    // balance inquiry
      unsigned id();                       // get account number
      /* other public members */
   private:
      unsigned   acct_no;                  // account number
      double     acct_bal;                 // current balance
      /* other private members */
};
```

2.1 DATA ABSTRACTION AND ENCAPSULATION

Class names should appear as *capitalized nouns*, which is the style recommended and followed in this book. Here the class Account is declared following the general form:

```
class Name
{
      class body
};
```

If you are new to C++, you may sometimes forget the final semicolon in a class declaration. This can cause many unpleasant errors. One way to remember the semicolon is to type in the form class *Name* {   }; before entering the *class body*, which in itself can be very involved.

The class body consists of declarations for data members, function members, or both. Member declarations are supplied in the usual way—namely, with declarations and function prototypes. However, *no initializers are allowed for data member declarations*. Except for overloading, all members must have distinct names. The class Account contains the data members

```
unsigned   acct_no;        // account number
double     acct_bal;       // current balance
```

which are the identification number and current balance of a bank account. Function prototypes in a class definition specify member functions of the class. For example,

```
void deposit(double amt);
```

declares deposit to be a member function. The actual code for member functions usually resides in a separate implementation file.

Creating Objects

Once a class is declared, *objects* of the class can be created. A class is a blueprint to build objects of a particular type (Figure 2.1), and the objects are known as *instances of the class*. The class name becomes a type name and can be used to declare variables. *A class-type variable is an object of that class*.

For example, objects of type Account can be defined as follows:

```
Account susan(5551234, 600.0);    // object susan  (3)
Account jack;                      // object jack   (4)
```

The variable susan is an Account object with the given account number and a beginning balance of 600. The initialization of this object is through the Account constructor.

In class Account, the Account member (line 1) is special. In general, a member function with the same name as the class itself is called a *constructor*

Figure 2.1 CREATING OBJECTS

and is treated differently from other member functions. The purpose of a constructor is to perform initializations when an object is created. For example, the statement on line 3 allocates space for an Account object and passes the values in parentheses to the constructor:

```
Account(unsigned, double)
```

The result is an object represented by the variable susan. The constructor is defined as

```
public Account::Account(unsigned id, double amt) // constructor
{   acct_no = id;
    if ( amt > 0 ) acct_bal = amt;
    else acct_bal = 0.0;
}
```

which provides the desired initialization of the data members acct_no and acct_bal. No return type of any kind is allowed in declaring a constructor, which should never return a value. Note that the constructor function name Account is *qualified* by Account:: to attach the name to the Account class as a member. More will be said on this presently.

The variable jack is an object initialized by the constructor that takes no arguments.

```
public Account::Account() { }
```

A *no-args constructor* is also referred to as the *default constructor*.

Information Hiding and Member Access Control

An object can be thought of as an independent computing agent (a tiny computer) with its own storage and instruction set. The data members define the storage, and the function members provide the instruction set.

The C++ class construct also specifies access control to its members. In the class definition, members are sectioned into groups to achieve information hiding:

- *Public members* in a class can be accessed from anywhere in a program.
- *Private members* in a class can be accessed only by member functions of the same class.

All a user, or *client*, of a class needs to know is the public interface (Figure 2.2). As long as the public members are well documented, there is no need to know any implementation details. In the case of deposit, all that matters is putting a given amount, amt, into the account. Thus, knowledge of internal details is confined to member functions. The class Account is thus an *abstract data type*.

An object embodies the abstract data item. Values stored in an object constitute its internal *state*, and public members of an object form its interface to the outside (other functions and objects). Thereby, an object *encapsulates* (envelops) a set of data and function members. The encapsulating object is called the *host object* of its members. Many objects can be created from a class.

Although all members—function or data—are thought of as contained within each individual object, C++ achieves this effect without having to replicate the member functions. The memory required for each object is essentially for storing the data members.

The Account data members acct_no and acct_bal are private, so their access is limited to member functions such as id() and balance(). No operations

Figure 2.2   AN OBJECT

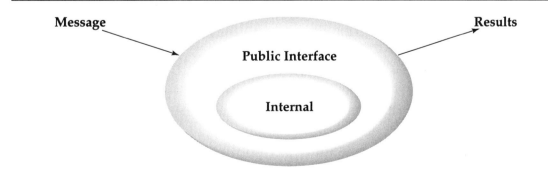

other than those specifically provided by the Account class can be performed on these private quantities. In designing a class, you, the OO programmer, must design the public/private grouping to support effective use and to maximize information hiding.

Member Access Notations

We already know that not every member of an object is accessible from the outside. When permitted, the members of an object are accessed with the *dot* (.), or *member-of*, operator. For example,

```
susan.deposit(25.60);      // deposit into Account object susan
double bal = susan.balance();
                           // retrieve balance of Account object susan
susan.withdraw(25.0);      // take 25 out of Account object susan
from.acct_bal -= 30.50;    // decrease balance of from account   (A)
to.acct_bal += 30.50;      // increase balance of to account     (B)
```

Because acct_bal is a private member, the assignments on lines A and B can be used only by member functions of Account.

Clearly, the general syntax to access a member in a host object is

object.member   (member access syntax)

Pointers to Class Objects

Pointers to class objects are also very useful. For example, the pointer variable acnt_ptr

```
Account* acnt_ptr = &jack;        // pointer to object jack
```

is initialized to point to the Account object jack. But it can also be assigned another value:

```
acnt_ptr = &susan;                // now *acnt_ptr is susan
```

When you are dealing with a pointer to an object, the members can be accessed directly through the pointer with the -> operator:

objptr -> member   (member access via pointer)

This notation is equivalent to (*objptr).*member*. An example is

```
acnt_ptr->deposit(11.79);         // deposit into Account susan
```

Member Functions

Generally, a class declaration is kept in a header file, which can be included by any file that wishes to use objects of the class. For example, the declaration for Account can be put in the header file Account.h. Member functions of a given class are usually defined in a separate *implementation file*, with a file name ending in .C (or .CPP). For instance, the Account.C file begins with

```
///////    Account.C    ///////
#include  "Account.h"

void Account::deposit(double amt)
{   if ( amt > 0 )
        acct_bal += amt;
}
```

While the file-inclusion notation

```
#include <iostream>
```

specifies a system-supplied header file, the notation

```
#include  "Account.h"
```

is used for a header file written by a user (Section 14.3).

The notation Account::deposit puts the name deposit within the *scope* (Section 3.1) of the class Account, making it a member function. The double colon (::) is the *scope operator*. If Account:: is not placed in front of the function name, then it is just a regular (unattached) function, not a member of class Account.

Note that deposit() takes only one argument, the amt to be deposited. There is no mention of the target account to make the deposit. As a member function, deposit is always attached to a specific account when it is called. In OOP, member functions are not pure procedures, but procedures attached to an object, such as an accelerator to a car. There is never a need to worry about which car you are driving when you depress the accelerator. Because objects are known as instances of a class, members in an object are known as *instance members*. Thus, deposit() is an *instance function*. Input to an instance function consists of its arguments and the *state of its host object* (Figure 2.3). To emphasize the point, some OOP literature refers to instance functions as *methods* and to invoking such functions as *passing a message* to an object. You should be aware of such widely understood OOP terms, even though these particular phrases are used only occasionally in the C++ context.

Because deposit is an instance function, it can access other members in the host object (e.g., acct_bal) directly, without using the *object.member* notation. All members in a class are accessible by member functions.

Figure 2.3 INSTANCE FUNCTION

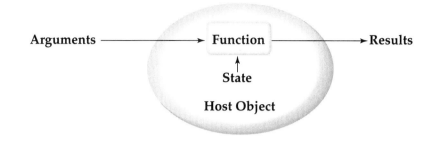

2.2 FUNCTION CALLS AND ARGUMENT PASSING

A function is either unattached or encapsulated in a class. The function header specifies the number and type of *formal parameters* required. In C++, a function is identified not only by its name but also by its formal parameter list. Thus, the same function name may be *defined more than once* with different formal parameters. This is known as *function overloading* (Section 3.7).

When a function is called, the correct number and type of arguments must be supplied. The arguments in the function call are known as the *actual arguments,* or simply *arguments*. The definition of factorial has a formal parameter n. In the function call factorial(j), the variable j becomes the actual argument. When a function call is executed, the data or objects referenced by the actual arguments are bound to the formal parameters and can be used in the body of the function. This binding is called *argument passing*.

When a function with more than one argument is called, *there is no guarantee of the order in which arguments are evaluated*. Therefore, no code should depend on any specific order of argument evaluation. Thus, the function call

```
power(i++, i);           // incorrect usage
```

is wrong because the result depends on which of the two arguments is evaluated first. You should use instead something like this:

```
i++;
power(i-1, i);
```

Parameters in a function header are formal in the sense that any name can be used for them without changing the meaning of the function. The same situation is found in mathematics where the notations $f(x) = x^2$ and $f(y) = y^2$ define the same function.

2.2 FUNCTION CALLS AND ARGUMENT PASSING

Formal parameters are local to a function. When a function call is made, a copy of the value of the actual argument is passed to the corresponding formal parameter. In other words, arguments are *passed by value*. With pass by value, a function can work only on copies of arguments, not on the actual arguments themselves. Therefore, the actual arguments have the same values before and after the function call.

When necessary, it is possible to modify data in the calling function. One way is by passing *pointers* as actual arguments. Recall that a pointer is the memory location, or address, of an object or a piece of data. Once the called function gets the address, it can proceed to modify information stored at that address. As a result, data in the calling function are altered indirectly.

Unlike basic data types and objects, there is no automatic copying of the elements in an array when it is passed as an argument. Instead, the address of its first element is passed. (This is the value of the array name.) Therefore, the formal array parameter becomes another name by which the same array elements can be accessed.

Reference Parameters

Pass by value can be expensive if the arguments represent large data objects. *Pass by reference* is a way to pass arguments without copying. C++ supports *reference* formal parameters for functions. A reference parameter is an alias for the actual argument passed (without copying) in a function call. An assignment to a reference parameter assigns a value to the corresponding actual argument. A reference parameter is used most often for the following purposes:

1. To pass an argument without making a copy of it (which is more efficient than pass by value).
2. To allow the called function to modify the actual argument.
3. To collect data produced by the called function.

You declare a reference parameter in a function header by putting the & character after the type name and in front of the parameter name. For example, the function

```
void swap(int& a, int& b)
{   int tmp = b;
    b = a;
    a = tmp;
}
```

uses two `int` reference parameters, a and b, to interchange the values of its actual arguments. In general, the `&` before a parameter declares a reference and is not to be confused with the address-of operator used in expressions. The line

```
int tmp = b;
```

may look a little suspicious at first because `tmp` is of type `int` but b is of type `int&`. It simply means that `tmp` gets the value of the actual argument represented by the `int` reference b. Thus, the following code works:

```
int r = 7, s = 11;
swap(r, s);        // now r is 11 and s is 7
```

The values are switched because a and b are reference parameters that become aliases for r and s, respectively, when swap is called. In other words, the effect of the call `swap(r,s)` is

```
int tmp = s;
s = r;
r = tmp;
```

Also recall the `std::cin.get(c)` usage. It works because `std::cin.get` takes a reference parameter (`char& c`). A reference parameter is one form of the C++ *reference*, a feature explained in Section 3.8.

Inline Functions

The C++ coding style sometimes calls for defining many small functions that are very simple. For such small functions, function call *overhead* (i.e., the argument-passing and the value-returning activities associated with a function call) becomes significant compared to the amount of time spent in the called function. To reduce this overhead and to increase code efficiency, C++ allows you to declare functions `inline`. For example,

```
inline int MAX(int a, int b)
     { return (a > b ? a : b); }

inline double ABS(double a)
     { return (a > 0 ? a : -a); }
```

A call to an `inline` function is *expanded* by the compiler so that the effective code is substituted at the place of call, and run-time function call overhead is avoided. An `inline` specifier advises the compiler to make an `inline` expansion if possible. An implementation may expand only `inline` functions containing straight-line code with only a few statements. Usually, no conditionals (`if`), loops (`while`, `for`), or other branching statements are allowed. In most situations, these limitations coincide with good programming practices.

Furthermore, a class member function completely defined inside the class declaration (Section 2.6) is automatically declared `inline`.

To expand a function `inline`, the compiler must have seen the function definition when compiling a file. This is usually done by including a header file where the definition of the `inline` function has been placed.

2.3 COMMAND-LINE ARGUMENTS

The `main` function is special in C++ because it marks the starting point for program execution and is not called by other functions in the program. However, it is possible to supply arguments to a C++ program when it is invoked. The *command-line arguments* are passed as character strings to the function `main`.

A `main` function expecting arguments is normally declared as follows:

```
int main(int argc, char *argv[])
```

The parameter `argc` is an integer. The notation

```
char *argv[]
```

declares the formal array parameter `argv` as having elements of type `char *` (character pointer). In other words, each of the arguments `argv[0]`, `argv[1]`,..., `argv[argc-1]` is a character pointer. The meanings of the formal arguments `argc` and `argv` are as follows:

argc   The number of command-line arguments, including command name
argv[n] A pointer to the *n*th command-line argument as a character string

If the command name is **cmd** and it is invoked as

cmd   *arg1 arg2*

then

argc   Is 3
argv[0]   Points to the command name **cmd**
argv[1]   Points to the string *arg1*
argv[2]   Points to the string *arg2*
argv[3]   Is 0 (NULL)

The parameters for the function `main` can be omitted if they are not needed.

Now let's consider a program that receives command-line arguments. To keep it simple, all the program does is echo the command-line arguments to standard output:

```
/////// the echo command ///////
#include <iostream>
```

```cpp
int main(int argc, char *argv[])
{   int i = 1;                  // begin with 1
    while (i < argc)
        std::cout << argv[i++]  // output string
                << " "          // output SPACE
                << std::endl;   // terminate output line
    return 0;
}
```

The program displays each entry of argv except argv[0]. To separate the strings, the program displays a SPACE after each argv[i], and the last argument is followed by the proper end of line.

Note that main is declared to return an int, and the last statement of main is

```
return 0;
```

The return value of main indicates, to the invoker of the program, whether the program executed successfully and terminated normally. This value is referred to as the *exit status*. For example, on UNIX systems, a zero exit status indicates successful or normal execution of the program, whereas a nonzero (usually positive) exit status indicates abnormal termination. Thus, it is advisable always to use a return statement in the main program, even though it works without one.

2.4 ENVIRONMENT VARIABLES

The parameters argc and argv of a main program reference the explicit arguments given on the command line (Section 2.3). Every time a program runs, another array of strings representing the *user environment*, called the *environment list*, is also passed to the program. This provides a way, in addition to the command-line arguments, to pass information to a program.

The environment list is always available in the system-defined global variable

```
extern char **environ;      /* environment strings */
```

Each environ[i] is an environment string in the form *name=value*. For example,

```
HOME=/users/fac/pwang      (UNIX)
PATH=/usr/local/bin:/usr/local:/usr/ucb:/bin:/usr/bin:.     (UNIX)
TERM=vt200     (UNIX)
PATH=C:\;C:\NETMANAG;C:\JDK1.2\BIN;C:\TOOLS\VIM46W32\VIM-4.6     (Windows)
```

The first three examples are from UNIX and the fourth is from Windows. The final element of the environ array is a zero pointer (NULL) to mark the end.

2.5 THE string CLASS

To access environ, include the header <stdlib.c>. Although direct search of environ is possible, it is simpler to access environment values with the Standard Library function **getenv**:

char * **getenv**(char * varName)

This function searches the environment list for a string whose *name* part matches the varName given and returns a pointer to the *value* part. If no match is found, then *varName* is not an environment variable and NULL is returned.

The function **getenv** makes it easy to retrieve environmental values. For example

```
#include <stdlib.h>

char* uname = getenv("PATH");     // obtain command path
char* tname = getenv("TERM");     // obtain terminal name
```

2.5 THE string CLASS

Account showed how a class is defined and used. Standard C++ provides many useful classes as part of the language. You'll get to know many of them as you make progress. One such class is string, in the std namespace, which makes operations on character strings easier and less error prone. Before string was introduced, the only way to represent a character string in C++ was the C-style string—an array of characters terminated by the '\0' character. Now you may find the string class a better choice in many situations.

To use the string class, you need to include the C++ header

```
#include <string>
```

To create a string object, simply use

std::string *str_obj*(*c_str*);

where *c_str* is a C-style string. For example,

std::string str1("Happy Birthday\n");

As an application, let's rewrite the stringMatch function (Section 1.15) using string objects.

```
int stringMatch(std::string& str, std::string& line)        // (1)
{   if ( str.empty() ) return -1;                            // (2)
    int j, k;
    int sl= str.size(), ll = line.size();    // string length (3)
    for (int i = 0 ; i < ll ; i++)
    {   if ( line[i] != str[0] )    // first chars different (4)
```

```
                continue;              // skip rest of loop body
    // compare remaining characters
    // until first mismatch or end of string
    for ( j = i + 1, k = 1;
          line[j]==str[k] && k < sl ;  // (5)
          j++, k++
        ) { }
    if ( k == sl ) return i;     // successful match
    else
        if (j == ll) return -1;  // no match possible anymore
    }
    return -1;                   // failed to match
}
```

The stringMatch function looks for str in line and returns the starting position in line if a match is found. Otherwise, -1 is returned. It receives string objects as references (line 1), checks if str is empty (line 2), obtains the length of the given strings (line 3), and compares characters (lines 4 and 5) to do the job.

You can use subscripts to access individual characters in a string object. For example, the function

```
void downcase(std::string& st)
{   int len = st.size();
    for (int i=0; i < size; i++)
        st[i] = tolower(st[i]);
}
```

changes all uppercase characters in the argument string to lowercase.

You can also concatenate strings using the + operator:

string s3 = s1 + s2;   (appends s1 and s2)

where s1 is a string object and s2 is a string object or C-style string. The string s3 is s2 appended to s1 while s1 and s2 remain unmodified. To modify s1, use

s1 += s2;

The string member function **compare** can be used

str.**compare**(*any_str*)   (compares strings)
str.**compare**(*i0*, *n*, *any_str*)   (compares substrings)

to compare the host *str* to *any_str* (C-style or string object), starting from index *i0* for *n* characters, if the first two args are given, or the entire string. The result is positive, negative, or zero indicating *str* is bigger than, less than, or equal to *any_str* in alphabetical order. See Section 6.3 for other useful member functions of the string class.

The Standard Library function call

getline(istream& *in*, string& *str_obj*, char *eol*)   (reads line into string)

reads from the istream object *in* into the string object *str_obj* until either the given end-of-line character *eol* (usually '\n') or the end of file is encountered. If the third argument *eol* is not given, then it is assumed to be '\n'. If the input length exceeds str.max_size(), the read operation fails (Section 2.7).

Section 2.8 contains a complete example that uses stringMatch().

2.6 PROBLEM SOLVING WITH OBJECTS

One important purpose of OOP is to solve problems better by using objects. To illustrate what this means in a simple way, let's consider a problem from plane geometry: Given four vertices A, B, C, and D in the x–y plane, determine whether $ABCD$ is a rectangle.

Clearly, one direct way to make the determination is to decide whether the neighboring sides of $ABCD$ are all mutually perpendicular. An ad hoc procedure could be written for this purpose, and the problem would be solved. But this is the traditional procedure-oriented approach.

The OO approach first identifies the interacting objects in the problem domain. Here the objects are the vertices and the sides. The sides are determined by the vertices, and the orthogonal properties of neighboring sides lead to the solution. Further analysis leads us to the identification of a two-dimensional vector as the object needed because it can represent a vertex or a side. Thus, for the OO solution of the given problem, a Vector2D class is first established.

A Simple Vector2D Class

Vectors in two-dimensional space are familiar geometric objects. A vector **v** has an x component and a y component:

$$\mathbf{v} = (x, y)$$

Vectors also have well-defined arithmetic and other kinds of operations. A class Vector2D is defined to model two-dimensional vectors:

```
///////    Vector2D.h    ///////

class Vector2D
{ public:
    Vector2D() {}                   // no-args constructor
    Vector2D(float a, float b)      // inline (1)
    {   x = a; y = b;      }
```

```
    Vector2D difference(Vector2D& a);
    float inner(Vector2D& a);
    bool isPerpendicular(Vector2D& a);
    bool nonzero()              // inline (2)
    {   return( x != 0.0 || y != 0.0 ); }
    void display();
    /* other members not shown */
private:
    float x, y;
};
```

For the class Vector2D, there are two private data members:

```
float   x, y;
```

They represent the *x*- and *y*-direction components of a vector. There is a no-args constructor and a constructor that initializes both vector components (line 1). The overloaded constructors and the member function nonzero (line 2) are defined completely in the Vector2D class declaration rather than merely being declared with a function prototype. Functions included in this way are automatically inline (Section 2.2).

The Default Constructor

The Vector2D constructor is overloaded as constructors usually are. One version takes two arguments and initializes the data members x and y. The other takes no arguments and does nothing. A constructor that takes no arguments must be present to allow the usage

```
Vector2D u;
```

where no initialization is intended. The no-args constructor is referred to as the *default constructor*. Two points can be made about supplying default constructors:

1. If a class defines no constructor at all, a default constructor that does nothing is supplied automatically.
2. If a class defines any constructor, no default constructor is automatically supplied. This is fine if the default constructor is not needed. However, if it is needed, an appropriate one must be given explicitly.

One trap that a C++ beginner may fall into is the use of

```
Vector2D u();     // warning
```

2.6 PROBLEM SOLVING WITH OBJECTS

to declare u as an object. This code instead declares u as a function returning a Vector2D value.

Implementing Vector2D

Let's turn our attention to the other member functions of Vector2D. The member function inner

```
float inner(Vector2D a);
```

receives a Vector2D object argument and returns a float value. The actual code for inner is defined in the file Vector2D.C:

```
///////// Vector2D.C ///////////
#include <iostream>
#include "Vector2D.h"

float Vector2D::inner(Vector2D& a)    // reference argument
{   return(x * a.x + y * a.y);   }
```

Again, because inner is a member function, it is allowed to access the private members x, y (in the host object) and a.x, a.y (in object a). Usually, data and function members can be accessed only through an established object of the class. For example,

```
Vector2D u(2.0, 3.0), v(4.0, 5.0);
u.inner(v);
```

computes the inner product of the vectors u (host object of inner) and v (argument to inner). Here the Vector2D v is passed to the member function inner of the object u. Because the data in the host object (u in this case) are already available, inner requires only one argument.

An object ought to know how to display itself. This can usually be done by defining a member function display. For Vector2D, it can be

```
void Vector2D::display()
{   std::cout << "(" << x << ", "
            << y << ")";
}
```

so the code v.display() produces the display

```
(4.0, 5.0)
```

The Vector2D member function difference subtracts the given Vector2D object v from the host object and returns their difference as a Vector2D object.

```
Vector2D Vector2D::difference(Vector2D& v)
{    Vector2D tmp;
```

```
        tmp.x = x - v.x;
        tmp.y = y - v.y;
        return tmp;
}
```

Another member function determines if a given vector v is perpendicular to the host object:

```
inline float ABS(float x)
        {  return (x > 0 ? x : -x); }

bool Vector2D::isPerpendicular(Vector2D& v)
{    return ( nonzero() && v.nonzero()
              && ABS(inner(v)) < 0.00000001 );
}
```

It makes sure both vectors are nonzero and their inner product is zero, up to a tolerance. Note that both `difference` and `isPerpendicular` take an argument passed by reference.

The OO Solution

Now that we have the `Vector2D.h` and `Vector2D.C` files in place, we can construct a solution for the rectangle problem that makes use of `Vector2D` objects. The approach is simple:

1. Represent the given vertices *A*, *B*, *C*, and *D* as four `Vector2D` objects.
2. Subtract neighboring vertices (2D vectors) to get the sides that are again 2D vectors.
3. Determine perpendicularity of neighboring sides.

Using `Vector2D` objects, our task is reduced to reading the four vertices from the user and testing whether the neighboring sides (as 2D vectors) are all perpendicular. Each point is read from user input into a vector by `getVec`:

```
///////    rectangle.C    ///////
#include <iostream>
#include "Vector2D.h"

Vector2D getVec(int i)   // input a point as vector
{    float x,y;
     std::cout << "x" << i << "= ";
     std::cin >> x;
     std::cout << "y" << i << "= ";
     std::cin >> y;
```

2.6 PROBLEM SOLVING WITH OBJECTS

```
      return Vector2D(x,y);    // explicit constructor call
}
```

The getVec function actually creates a new Vector2D object by making an explicit constructor call. The main program looks like this:

```
int main()
{  std::cout << "Enter vertices 0,1,2,3 "
             << std::endl;
   Vector2D p[4];                           // vector array       (A)
   for ( int i = 0; i < 4; i++)             // input all four points
      p[i] = getVec(i);
   Vector2D u = p[0].difference(p[3]);      // vector difference  (B)
   Vector2D v;
   for (int i = 0; i < 3; i++)              // process all sides
   {  v = p[i+1].difference(p[i]);          // vector difference  (C)
      if ( ! u.isPerpendicular(v) )         // check perpendicularity
      {   std::cout << "No, not a rectangle." << std::endl;
          return 1;
      }
      u = v;
   }
   std::cout << "Yes, a rectangle." << std::endl;
   return 0;
}
```

After the coordinates for the four vertices are read (in sequence), four vectors are in the array p[4] whose declaration (line A) invokes the Vector2D default constructor four times. A 2D vector u representing one side of the quadrilateral is then calculated by vector subtraction (line B). A second Vector2D object v is made for an adjacent side (line C). The perpendicularity of u and v is checked. After all sides are checked, the right conclusion can be made.

Assuming the file Vector2D.o has already been produced, compile rectangle.C with Vector2D.o and run the program.

The ability to work with vectors that correspond to real geometric objects allows the solution to be stated simply and elegantly with geometric concepts and also makes it much easier to explain and understand. More important, the Vector2D class can help in many other situations in plane geometry. Hence, the class has potential for reuse.

Furthermore, the object-based solution is easily adaptable to changes in the problem specification. For instance, determining whether $ABCD$ is a parallelogram involves almost no change to the program. You just add a member isParallel(Vector2D& b) to the Vector2D class if it is not already there.

2.7 C++ I/O STREAMS

Section 1.7 mentioned cin, cout, and cerr—three ready-made objects for I/O in each program. These objects are *instances* of the I/O stream classes that are part of the C++ Standard Library. To avoid global name conflicts, the Standard Library classes and objects are placed in a separate namespace std, which is the reason we use the prefix in std::cout. We have also seen the use of cin.get and cout.put for character I/O.

While these standard objects take care of terminal I/O, there are occasions when you want direct I/O from or to a specific file. This can be done by setting up new I/O objects connected to the desired files. The declarations

```
#include <iostream>
#include <fstream>              // needed for file I/O

std::ifstream in(infile);       // input from file
std::ofstream out(outfile);     // output to file
```

are used to establish objects for file I/O. The file names are C-style strings.

From your knowledge of C++ classes, you can deduce that the ifstream and ofstream classes have constructors supporting the declarations of in and out. If *outfile* is a new file, it will be created. Otherwise, its contents will be replaced. Once established, these file I/O objects are used in much the same way as cin and cout. Open files are automatically closed when your program terminates. An open file can also be specifically closed by calling the member function **close**:

```
in.close();
out.close();
```

For any istream object *in*, you can use

```
in.eof()      // true or false
in.fail()     // true or false
```

to test if the stream has reached the end of file or has failed.

For an example involving file I/O, see Section 2.8. Other input/output functions provided by the Standard Library are discussed in Section 6.7.

2.8 ERROR HANDLING

A very important aspect of programming concerns the handling of possible errors during the execution of a program. Many kinds of errors can occur at run time. The main program may be invoked with incorrect arguments. A function expecting a positive argument may be passed a negative value. Arithmetic

2.8 ERROR HANDLING

operations can overflow or underflow. A well-written program should detect errors and take appropriate actions.

Displaying Error Messages

The main program should first check the arguments supplied on the command line for correctness. If the arguments are unacceptable, a clear message should be displayed stating the nature of the error and its cause (if known). Use the object cerr for sending error messages to ensure that they appear on the terminal immediately without buffering. A conditional statement such as

```
if (argc != 3)
{   std::cerr << argv[0] << ": expects 2 arguments but was given "
            << argc-1 << std::endl;
    std::cerr << "Usage " << argv[0] << " input-file output-file";
            <<   std::endl;
    exit(1);
}
```

checks the number of command-line arguments supplied. Note that the value of argc is, by definition, the number of command-line arguments *plus 1*. Always identify the program unit or subunit displaying the error message. The command name identifies which program is announcing the error. When appropriate, a function name further narrows down the error location. In this example, the program refers to its own name as argv[0], which is better than assuming a specific file name.

After displaying an error message, a program may continue to execute, return a particular value not produced normally, or elect to abort. The Standard Library function **exit** is called to terminate the execution of a program:

```
#include <stdlib.h>

void exit(int status);
```

When **exit** is called anywhere in a program, program execution is terminated. For normal termination, *status* should be 0 (or EXIT_SUCCESS). For abnormal termination such as an error, a positive *status*, usually 1 (or EXIT_FAILURE), is used. To use **exit**, you should include the header file <stdlib.h>. The library function **abort**() can be called, and it produces a *core dump* file for postmortem analysis before exiting.

File I/O objects maintain internal error states that can be checked for any failure. For example, after the code

```
std::ifstream in(file);
```

you should use a test such as:

```
if ( in.fail() )
{   std::cerr << "Can't open " << file
              << std::endl;
    exit(1);
}
```

The ifstream class (Section 6.7) member function **fail**() returns true if the file failed to open. The same usage applies for an ofstream object.

An Error-Handling Example

Let's put the stringMatch function (Section 1.15) to use together with appropriate I/O and error handling. The intention is to define a **stringSearch** command that works with standard I/O when given no arguments or with specific I/O files.

```
///////    stringSearch.C    ///////
#include <iostream>
#include <string>
#include <fstream>
#include <stdlib.h>

/* put function stringMatch here */

void match(std::string& str, std::istream& in, std::ostream& out)
{   if ( str.empty() )          // str is empty
    {   std::cerr << "match: empty match string"
                  << std::endl;
        exit(1);
    }
    string line;
    while ( std::getline(in, line, '\n') ) // (a)
    {   if ( stringMatch(str, line) > 0 )  // (b)
            out << line << std::endl;      // (c)
    }
    out.flush();
}
```

The function match searches (line b) for str in each line from the given input stream in (line a) and outputs any matching lines to the output stream out (line c). Note that reference parameters are used. Failure to use reference parameters for I/O objects can prove unwise in most situations.

```
int main (int argc,  char* argv[])
{   if ( argc < 2 || argc > 4 )              // (1)
```

```
    {   std::cerr << "Usage:" << argv[0]
                << " str [infile [outfile]]" << std::endl;
        return 1;
    }
    std::string str(argv[1]);
    if ( argc == 2 )                            // use standard I/O
        match(str, std::cin, std::cout);
    else                                        // use file
    {   ifstream infile(argv[2]);
        if ( infile.fail() )                    // (2)
        {   std::cerr << argv[0] << ":can't open input file "
                << argv[2] << std::endl;
            return 1;
        }
        if ( argc == 3 )
            match(str, infile, std::cout);
        else // argc == 4
        {   ofstream ofile(argv[3]);
            if ( ofile.fail() )                 // (3)
            {   std::cerr << argv[0] << ":can't open output file "
                    << argv[3] << std::endl;
                exit(1);
            }
            match(str, infile, ofile);
        }
    }
    return 0;
}
```

The main program of stringSearch.C anticipates common errors: wrong number of arguments (line 1), failure to open the input file (line 2), and inability to open the output file (line 3). In the first case, a brief guide to command usage is displayed. Run this program on files and check your results against the UNIX **grep** command if available.

2.9 OBJECT-BASED THINKING

The traditional approach to program design involves breaking down a given problem into a number of steps. Each step is either simple and straightforward or may have to be broken down further. The sequence of steps forms a procedure that solves the given problem. This approach is known as *procedure-based decomposition*.

An OO program establishes objects, and these objects cooperate and interact to solve a problem. Thus, object orientation involves a whole new way of thinking. Program design begins with identifying the interacting entities, or objects, in a given problem. In a banking application, for example, objects can be accounts, customers, credit records, monthly statements, and so on. The key is thinking in terms of quantities present in the problem domain rather than programming artifacts in the computer language domain. An object may represent a physical item such as a monthly statement or a logical item such as a transaction. The objects must be self-contained and must correspond to well-understood concepts in the problem domain. Thinking with the *language of the problem*, not the language of the computer, is essential. Some objects may have to be further broken down into smaller constituent objects. This approach is known as *object-based decomposition*. Objects thus identified lead to software objects, defined by classes, that simulate real ones in the problem domain.

The interactions among the problem-domain objects must then be considered carefully to define the external behavior of the objects and their interdependence. Class definitions of the different objects can then be coded. The set of all public data and function members forms the *public interface* of objects in a class. The public interface must support the intended external behavior precisely. The public interface determines how objects are used by other parts of the program. Hiding behind the public interface are internal implementation details kept from outside access. Thus, object orientation decouples the internal workings of objects from the rest of the program and significantly reduces program complexity. Internal data and procedures can be modified without affecting other parts of the program as long as the public interface is preserved.

A good OO design takes into account features such as generalizations of the given problem, possible future extensions, reuse of existing code, ease of modification, and so on. These ideas will become more concrete as you become more familiar with C++ and OOP.

2.10 C++ PROGRAMMING TIPS

Here are some basic programming tips and things to remember to improve your C++ programs:

- Include `<iostream>` to use I/O streams in the C++ Standard Library, which is in its own namespace `std`. Add `<fstream>` for file I/O.
- Include `<stdlib.h>` to use Standard Library functions such as **exit**.
- Declare functions, variables, and classes before using them.
- Always terminate a declaration or a class definition with a semicolon.

2.10 C++ PROGRAMMING TIPS

- Terminate a simple statement, but not a compound statement, with a semicolon.
- A C-style character string is an array of characters terminated by `'\0'`. Consider using the C++ `string` class instead of the C-style string when you can.
- Use zero-based indexing for arrays. Hence, `int arr[100]` has its index running from 0 to 99.
- A character is represented by an integer and can be used as such. Logical values are of type `bool`.
- There is no exponentiation operator.
- The address-of operator `&` produces a pointer.
- The value-of operator `*` produces a value through a pointer.
- Except for reference parameters, arguments of functions are always passed by value.
- Loops in C++ use continuation conditions. The iteration ends when the condition becomes false.
- Logical false is zero, and logical true is anything else.
- Learn useful idioms such as `for(;;)` (infinite loop), `for(int i=0 ; i < j ; i++)`, `while(i--)`, and `while( std::cin.get(c) )`. (Idioms are pointed out throughout the book.)
- Apply the ternary operator `?:` to form conditional expressions; use the `%` operator to compute the remainder.
- Avoid hard-coded constants; use `const` identifiers instead.
- Avoid passing objects by value in function calls; use pass by reference whenever possible.

Function Style

If you develop a consistent formatting style in which to render your programs, you avoid syntax errors and make the programs readable. The function style used in this book is explained here with an example:

```
// logical function equal compares strings x and y
// returns true if x is equal to y, false otherwise

bool equal(char x[], char y[])              // (1)
{   if ( x == y ) return 1;                 // (2)
    int i=0;                                // (3)
```

```
    while (x[i] == y[i])                        // (4)
    {   if (x[i] == '\0') return true;          // (5)
        i++;                                    // (6)
    }   /* end of while */                      // (7)
    return false;                               // (8)
} // end of function equal                      // (9)
```

Use comments to document the purpose and the effects of the function, the meaning of the arguments, and the value returned. Format the function body as follows:

1. Start the function header flush with the left margin.
2. Format the function body as a compound statement. Line up the opening brace with the function name. Indent all statements one level.
3. Keep statements on separate lines for readability.
4. For the body of a statement, such as if, while, for, and so on, some programmers always prefer to use a block, even if it contains only one statement.
5. Keep a simple statement on one line. Some programmers may prefer using another line for the body of the if statement. That is all right as well.
6. Indent statements inside a block another level.
7. Line up the closing brace for while vertically with the opening brace. A comment can be added to clearly indicate the end of a multiline construct.
8. Always put a return at the end of a function if it returns a value.
9. Line up the closing brace of a function vertically with the opening brace. If the function is lengthy, a comment at the end will help as well.

Use names in all caps for symbolic constants, preferring const over #define (Sections 14.4 and 3.9). Give functions and variables meaningful names (in all lowercase), using the underscore (_) or capitalization to connect multiple words when appropriate.

Class Style

A consistent set of conventions for defining classes is also recommended:

1. Use capitalized nouns for class names. Join multiple words, and abbreviate if necessary, while capitalizing each word, as in Vector2D and GroupLeader.

2. Put each class definition in a separate header file, and be sure to use the once-only header feature (Section 3.15). Put member function definitions in a corresponding .C (or .CPP) file, which uses #include to include its own header file.
3. In a class definition, put public members first and carefully document public member functions with comments. Specify the meaning of arguments.
4. Give only extremely simple member functions inside the class definition.
5. If a class has any constructor, provide a default constructor.

Program examples in this book follow the formatting conventions closely. However, because explanations are usually included in the text, the examples tend not to be extensively commented.

2.11 SUMMARY

Objects encapsulate functions and data to form an independent computing unit. An object hides internal workings and is used only through its public interface, achieving data abstraction. The isolation of object internals from the rest of the program greatly simplifies the program. A class describes the structure of an object and specifies access control to class members, which can be data, functions, or other objects. Once defined, a class name becomes a user-defined type and is used to establish objects or instances of the class. A constructor is a special member function that initializes an object. A default constructor, which takes no arguments, is needed for establishing simple variables or arrays of class type. An object is the host of its members, and the members are accessed via the host object with the operators . and ->.

C++ provides the class string as a better alternative to C-style strings in many situations. The string class supplies useful operations such as **size**() (string length), **empty**() (test), **compare**() (comparing substrings), and access to individual characters by indexing. The + operator can be used to concatenate a string object with another or a C-style string. The **getline** library function can read a line from a given input stream into a string object.

Using objects to solve problems is natural and effective. An object-based solution involves identifying the interacting objects in the problem domain and building classes to model their behavior. A sequence of interactions among the objects can represent the solution to the given problem. Changes in the problem specification can be handled with modifications in the interactions. The Vector example makes these points clear.

Both unattached and member functions in C++ can be overloaded. When a function call is made, the actual arguments are evaluated in an unspecified order. Normally, arguments are passed by value; that is, the called function receives a copy of the arguments being passed. Pass by reference is accomplished using reference parameters. Inline functions can avoid run-time function call overhead. The function main can receive arguments supplied on the command line. The library function **getenv** can retrieve environmental values.

Important topics to consider in order to write interesting programs include establishing I/O stream objects for reading and writing files, handling of errors, object-based thinking, programming tips, and code formatting recommendations. This overview gives you a cross-sectional view of Standard C++ and sets the stage for learning the elaborate constructs of later chapters.

EXERCISES

1. Consider the Account class in Section 2.1. Add a member function void display() to this class.

2. Add a member function transfer() for the Account class that transfers a given amount from another account to the host account. Also implement the same function as a nonmember.

3. Consider class member function definition and invocation. If the function deposit can be defined as

   ```
   void Account::deposit(double amt)
   {    acct_bal += amt;    }
   ```

   why can it not be used with the notation Account::deposit(400.0); to deposit 400.0?

4. Consider the Account class in Section 2.1. Are the following declarations correct? Possible? Explain why.

   ```
   Account paul;
   Account mary;
   ```

5. Consider the default constructor definition inside the class Vector2D definition.

   ```
   Vector2D() { }
   ```

   Is a semicolon missing at the end? Explain.

6. Suppose `sally` is already declared as an `Account` object with an account identification and initial balance. Is the call `sally.Account(new_id, new_balance)` possible? Why?

7. How do you convert a C-style string to a `string` object? And vice versa? Is it possible to pass a C-style string to a function parameter declared as a `string`? Assign a C-style string to a `string` variable? Why?

8. Apply the library function **getline** in a program that counts the number of lines in any text file specified on the command line.

9. Write a reverse-echo program that takes all words on the command line and displays them backward, character by character.

10. Let words in a file be character strings separated by one or more white-space characters (SPACE, TAB, NEWLINE). Write a program to count the number of words in the input file (`cin`).

11. Modify the word-count program in Exercise 10 to take an optional argument, which is the name of the input file.

12. Add the '==' operator to the `Vector2D` class. Add the member function `is_parallel(Vector2D&)` to test whether a vector is parallel to the host vector object. Given any four points A, B, C, and D, use `Vector2D` objects to determine if ABCD is a parallelogram.

13. Define `Vector3D` to be a three-dimensional vector class.

14. NIM is a game in which two players alternate in drawing counters, pennies, or the like from a set of 12 arranged in three rows of three, four, and five counters, respectively. With each move, a player is allowed to draw either one, two, or three counters. The player who draws the last counter loses. Write a program to play NIM with one person or with two. (*Hint:* Consider a NIM board object.)

CHAPTER THREE

Key Constructs

Building on the basics of C++ and object-based programming, we now begin to present many subjects in depth. Key language features are discussed in combination with OOP techniques.

To avoid name conflict, identifiers in C++ can belong to different *namespaces*. Within a namespace, each identifier is uniquely distinguished by the spelling of its name. Identifiers also obey scope rules that limit the extent to which each identifier is known in a program. There are different scopes for identifiers, and familiarity with identifier naming and scoping is important for program writing.

Functions that call themselves directly or indirectly are *recursive*. Recursion is an important problem-solving technique. Two examples of recursion are given that are reused later in the book.

To further demonstrate object-based programming, a `Fraction` class is defined whose objects represent rational numbers. `Fraction` represents a typical abstract data type. It also motivates many other topics: canonical data representation, arithmetic operator overloading, object assignment, and the host-object pointer.

Effective use of function overloading is an important aspect of OOP, and the C++ overloading mechanism is described in detail. Usage, limitations, and invocation rules for overloaded functions are explained. How a function can take optional, variable-length, and read-only arguments is also shown.

Proper use of declarations is critical to programming. Rules for declaring and using local and global variables are given. Protecting per-file variables and sharing global variables across multiple files are explained. Additional declarations establish reference variables as well as alternative names for existing types.

Because not all data sizes are known at compile time, there is a need to allocate storage at run time. The free storage operators `new` and `delete` are described. A circular buffer object brings dynamic storage allocation and many other constructs together in an interesting application.

Reference parameters in function calls are important to avoid unnecessary copying of objects. Operands of operators and arguments of functions sometimes are converted from one data type to another to perform the operation. Rules for implicit and explicit type-casting are explained. Suggestions are given on how to use header files and organize programs into independently compilable modules.

Many subjects are introduced here, and a foundation is laid for later topics.

3.1 IDENTIFIER SCOPING

Identifiers are used in a program as names for functions, parameters, variables, constants, classes, types, and so forth. In Standard C++, identifiers can be defined in different *namespaces* (Section 3.2). Identifiers in one namespace cannot be confused with any in another namespace.

Within the same namespace, identifiers belong to different *scopes* (restrictive regions) and are regulated by *scoping rules*. A scope is a contiguous extent within the program source code. A larger scope encloses smaller scopes, and a smaller scope *nests* within an enclosing scope. Scopes in C++ are:

1. *Global or file scope:* The file scope is the largest scope. In a source code file, an identifier declared/defined outside of all local and class scopes is *global* and known from the point of declaration to the end of the file.
2. *Class scope:* A class creates a smaller scope nested within another scope (usually the file scope). Identifiers declared/defined in a class (e.g., member names) are known from where they are declared to the end of the class declaration.
3. *Local scope:* A function or block creates a local scope. Within a function or a block, an identifier is known from where it is declared to the end of the block. A local scope can be nested within the file scope, a class scope, or an enclosing local scope.

Exceptions to the rules are:

- A goto label is the only local scope identifier that is known to all parts of a function within which it is declared.
- Inline function bodies in a class declaration may use identifiers yet unseen in the same class scope.
- Default parameter values of a member function may use identifiers yet unseen in the same class scope.

In any scope, you may use an identifier from an enclosing scope. If a nested scope declares/defines an identifier with the same name as one from the enclosing scope, then the identifier from the enclosing scope is *hidden* and cannot be used directly.

Local Variables

A variable must first be introduced into a program before it can be used. The scope of a local variable extends from where it is defined to the end of its own block (compound statement). Formal parameters are local to the function. A variable declared inside a function/block is said to be *local* to the function/block. Local variables are private to the block in which they are declared and cannot be accessed from the outside. A local variable normally only comes into existence every time its declaration statement is executed and is destroyed automatically after its enclosing function/block is exited. Such variables are known as *automatic variables*.

Local variables are normally automatic. However, if a local variable is declared `static`, then it is not an automatic variable. Instead, it is created and initialized at compile time and retains its most recent value even after the function/block is exited. This same value is available when the function/block is entered again. Consider a function that keeps track of how many times it is called. The two lines

```
static int my_count = 0;
my_count++;
```

can be put in the function to do the job.

File Scope

A file scope, or global, identifier must be *defined* by a declaration outside of all functions and classes. A global identifier is known from its point of declaration to the end of the source code file. Class names are usually global. Unattached functions, such as `stringMatch` or **getline**, are also global. OOP discourages the use of unattached functions. Global enumeration symbols and `typedef` names (Section 3.10) are sometimes useful.

Because its value can be set and used by any function, a global variable provides a way, in addition to argument passing, for functions to communicate data. Unlike automatic variables, global variables always exist and retain their values until the entire program is terminated. You should avoid creating global symbols in your program and consider enclosing identifiers inside classes as much as possible.

When placed in file scope, the declarations

```
int overall_maximum;
int global_count = 0;
char name[]= "John Smith";
Vector2D v_i(1.0, 0.0);
Vector2D v_j(0.0, 1.0);
```

define the global variables `overall_maximum`, `global_count`, the character array `name`, and the `Vector2D` objects `v_i` and `v_j`. When a global variable is defined, it is allocated storage and is initialized with either zero or a supplied value. A variable can be defined only once. If the compiler detects an attempt to define a variable more than once, it complains and fails.

To use a global variable in a function, at least one of the following conditions must be met:

1. The variable has been defined earlier in the file.
2. The variable has been declared `extern` earlier in the file.
3. The variable has been declared `extern` in the function.

To use `v_i`, you can put the declaration

```
extern Vector2D v_i;
```

in the function. When many functions share an external variable, this coding can be tedious. It is easier simply to put the necessary `extern` declarations outside the functions at the beginning of a file — once and for all. In OOP, use of global variables is discouraged.

Scope Nesting

Identifier scoping can be illustrated further with an example:

```
long x;
float y;
int z;

void fn(char c, int x)     // parameter x hides global x
{    extern int z;         // refer to global z
     double y = 3.14159;   // local y hides global y
     { char y;             // hides first local y
         y = c;            // assign to second local y
         ::y = 0.3;        // assign to global y
     }
     y = y / 3.0;          // assign to first local y
     z++;                  // increment global z
}
```

Here we have a function nested in file scope and a local block nested within the function fn. The global variable `float y;` is hidden by the local `double y;` in the function fn. This local y is in turn hidden by the local variable `char y;` inside the block. As control exits the block, the variable y of type `double` resurfaces. This further illustrates the scope rules. (More is said about variables and their declarations in Section 3.3.)

Note how the *file scope operator* (::) is used to refer to the global variable y from within a local scope.

Class Scope

In C++, each class has its own scope. Enclosed in class scope are names for data, functions, `typedef`s, and `enum` constants. Even another class can be put inside a class scope. With the exceptions stated earlier, identifiers declared within a class are known from the point of declaration to the end of the class. Function and static member definitions in an implementation file can be regarded as being at the end of the class. A class scope identifier hides an identifier with the same name in the enclosing scope.

Unless qualified, a class member name is generally not recognized outside its class. A *class scope operator* (`ClassName::`) in front of an identifier explicitly specifies the class scope within which the identifier is interpreted.

Consider the `Vector2D` constructor:

```
Vector2D::Vector2D(float x, float y)
{   Vector2D::x = x;
    Vector2D::y = y;
}
```

Because the formal parameters hide the class scope data members x and y, the `Vector2D::` notation is required. The class scope operator is also used to access `static` members (Section 5.10) in classes.

Another way to qualify a name and put it in a specific class scope is to use the object member-of notation, as in the following examples:

```
sally.balance()           // refers to Account::balance
u.inner(v)                // refers to Account::inner
bob_ptr->deposit(11.79)   // refers to Account::deposit
```

Similarly, a class scope identifier hides a file scope identifier with the same name. Suppose there is also a file scope function `inner()`. In this case, a member function of `Vector2D` must use `::inner` to access the file scope function.

3.2 NAMESPACES

In C++, it is possible to establish multiple *namespaces*. An identifier in one namespace does not conflict with another having the same name in a different namespace. C++ software libraries are often defined in *user-defined namespaces* to avoid *polluting the global namespace* (the file scope) or conflicting with names

3.2 NAMESPACES

in application programs that use the libraries. Identifiers from the C++ Standard Library, supplied by header files without the .h suffix, are in the namespace std, whereas identifiers from libraries supported by C header files (with the .h suffix) are in the global namespace.

The *namespace definition*

```
namespace ns_name
{
    . . .         // any constructs
}
```

puts enclosed entities in namespace *ns_name*, which should be a unique symbol in global scope not used for other purposes. To put a large program in a separate namespace, all you do is enclose each file within a namespace declaration. A *nested namespace* is a namespace defined inside another namespace.

To use identifiers from another namespace, add the scope operator *ns_name*:: to qualify the identifier name. Usages std::cout and std::endl are examples you have seen. Always having to use the qualifying prefix can become bothersome. *Namespace declarations* with the using keyword tell the compiler that certain identifiers are from another namespace, so their simple names can be used directly. For example,

```
using std::cout;     // use cout
using std::cin;
using std::cerr;
using std::endl;
```

make each of the four identifiers usable directly as cout, cin, and so forth. If a namespace name is very long, a namespace alias can help:

```
namespace abc = someLongName;    // namespace alias
```

The alias *abc* now stands for the namespace *someLongName*.

Sometimes there can be too many namespace declarations. Then, you can place a *namespace directive* near the beginning of a file:

```
using namespace std;    // import all names from std
```

This namespace directive essentially unwraps the indicated namespace std into your namespace, allowing all names from std to be accessed as if they were in your namespace. This is convenient but makes name conflict more likely. In any case, you can always use the scope operator to distinguish conflicting names.

3.3 MORE ON DECLARATIONS

Knowing how declarations work and how to use them properly and effectively is just as crucial to programming as familiarity with classes, functions, statements, and expressions.

The C++ compiler takes expressions and statements in a source code file and produces corresponding machine codes to run on a particular computer. Unlike an expression or an executable statement, a declaration does not specify run-time code. Instead, declarations provide necessary or supplementary information so that the compiler can generate the required codes. In other words, declarations instruct the compiler, whereas executable statements specify program actions.

Some declarations, such as int and float, provide necessary information without which compilation of a C++ program cannot succeed. For example, to produce code for x + y, the compiler must know the types and sizes of x and y. This information is given by declarations such as int x; and double y;. Other declarations, such as the register and inline modifiers, give auxiliary information to help the compiler produce more efficient code.

Declarations and Definitions

When a declaration also causes storage allocation for a variable or constant or specifies a function/class body, it is called a *definition*. In a program, one definition at most is allowed for each variable, constant, function, and class. No repeated definition is allowed even if it is entirely the same. This is sometimes known as the *one definition rule* (ODR) in C++.

In addition to function and class definitions, declarations of automatic variables and declarations with initialization are common examples of definitions. However, declarations such as

```
extern int x;                      // external variable declaration
float cube_root(float);            // function prototype declaration
class Vector2D;                    // forward class declaration
float Vector2D::inner(Vector2D a); // member function prototype
```

are not definitions because they do not allocate storage. The storage for x should be provided by a unique definition somewhere else in the program. In a C++ program, multiple declarations of the same quantity, usually in different files, are allowed provided that all declarations are consistent.

File Scope Declarations We already know that a declaration placed inside a function or block is local and that a member of a class has class scope. A local declaration defines an automatic variable, unless the declaration is preceded with the `extern` modifier and not followed by an initializer—in which case, the variable refers to the same variable in file scope.

If a declaration is not placed inside any function, block, or class, it is called a *file scope declaration*. Function and class definitions are usually given at file scope.

For variables, if a file scope declaration is a definition, then it creates a file scope (global) variable. Since C++ disallows duplicated definitions, it is important to know when a file scope variable declaration becomes a definition:

1. A file scope declaration with an initializer is a definition. For example,

    ```
    int counter = 0;
    extern int max = 0;
    int a[] = {1,2,3,4,5};
    char name[] = "Wang";
    ```

2. A file scope declaration with `extern` but without an initializer is not a definition.

3. A file scope declaration without `extern` or an initializer is taken as a definition. For basic types, an initial value of zero is assumed; for class objects, the default constructor will be called for initialization.

Internal and External Linkage The C++ compiler compiles each source code file as a separate *compilation unit* and generates a corresponding .o file. When multiple .o files are put together into an executable program, global names of variables, objects, functions, and classes used across multiple files must be *linked together*. A global identifier in a file to be linked with like identifiers in other files has *external linkage*. Otherwise, the global identifier has *internal linkage* and is not linked with identifiers in other files with the same name. For example, a global variable `int population` shared by two source code files has external linkage.

Let's examine how linkage is determined. First of all, a file scope identifier automatically has external linkage, unless specifically declared otherwise. To make external linkage explicit, you can add the `extern` specifier in front of any global identifier declaration:

```
extern int population;
extern class Account;
```

External linkage allows use of the same global variables across files but brings with it the danger of global-variable-name conflicts between those files, especially if the files are written at different times or by different programmers.

A per-file global variable can be protected by putting it in an *unnamed namespace*

```
namespace                               // no name given
{   const int TABLE_SIZE = 64;
    int max;
}
```

which implies that the variables are used only in their source code file. Names in unnamed namespaces are not accessible from other files. Alternatively, you may declare a file scope identifier `static` to limit it to a single file.

Using Local and Global Identifiers

The following practical rules summarize concepts regarding declarations covered so far:

1. Declare a local variable anywhere inside a function or a block before using the variable. Such variables can be initialized. A local variable is automatic unless specified `static`. Declare class members in class declarations.
2. Define a global variable with external linkage exactly once in a file using a file scope definition with initialization.
3. A file scope function name or variable declared `static` is local to a file, whereas any construct placed in an unnamed namespace is local to a file. The latter alternative is recommended.
4. Place file scope `extern` declarations at the beginning of a file for all global variables defined in or used by other files. This is usually done by including the appropriate header files (see Section 3.15).
5. A function must be declared with a prototype before it is called. For functions returning `int`, such declarations can, but should not, be omitted. To use a function defined in another file, place the function prototype, with or without `extern`, at the beginning of the file.
6. A class must be declared before objects of that class can be established. This is usually done by including the header file supplied by the class.

Knowing how to declare global variables does not mean you should use them. Object orientation encourages encapsulation and discourages global data sharing.

Later in this chapter, coverage of C++ declarations continues with *type&* (reference), `const`, and `typedef`.

3.4 RECURSION

While object orientation focuses on classes and objects, it is still important to define functions and procedures for them. Often, the value of objects is directly related to the efficiency or intricacy of the algorithms they encapsulate.

Many problems are solvable by a type of algorithm that reduces the original problem into one or several smaller problems of exactly the same nature. The solutions of the smaller problems then combine to form the solution of the original problem. These subproblems can be further reduced by applying the same algorithm *recursively* until they become simple enough to solve. A recursive algorithm can be implemented most naturally by a recursive function.

Greatest Common Divisor

Consider computing the *greatest common divisor* (gcd) of two integers. The gcd of integers a and b is defined as the largest integer that evenly divides both a and b. The gcd is not defined if both a and b are zero. A negative a or b can be replaced by its absolute value without affecting the gcd. Hence, we can assume that a and b are nonnegative and not both zero. The recursive algorithm to compute $gcd(a, b)$ can be described by the pseudocode:

1. If b is zero, the answer is a.
2. If b is not zero, the answer is $gcd(b, a \bmod b)$.

It is interesting to note that the idea for this simple but effective integer gcd algorithm is credited to Euclid, a Greek mathematician (ca. 300 B.C.).

The recursive function for Euclid's algorithm is straightforward:

```
int gcd(int a, int b)      // integer greatest common divisor
{   if ( b == 0 )
        return a;
    else
        return gcd(b, a % b);
}
```

Note that the function gcd calls itself and that the value of the arguments for each successive call to gcd gets smaller (see Table 3.1 for an example). Eventually, the second argument becomes zero and the recursion unwinds: The deepest recursive call returns, then the next level call returns, and so on until the first call to gcd returns.

When a function is called recursively, each new invocation gets its own set of formal parameters and automatic variables, independent of the previous set. This is consistent with how automatic variables and formal parameters are normally treated.

Table 3.1 RECURSION OF gcd(2970,1265) = 55

Call Level	a	b
1	2970	1265
2	1265	440
3	440	385
4	385	55
5	55	0

The Recursion Formula

For many people, recursion is a new way of thinking that brings a powerful tool for problem solving. Given a problem, two questions can be asked:

- Do I know a way to solve the problem if it is small?
- For a larger problem, can it be broken down into smaller problems of the same nature whose solutions combine into the solution of the original problem?

If you answered yes to both questions, then you already have a recursive solution.

Recursive programs are concise and easy to write once you recognize the overall structure of a recursive program. All recursive solutions use the following sequence of steps:

1. *Termination conditions*: Always begin a recursive function with tests to catch the simple or trivial cases at the end of the recursion. A terminal case (e.g., remainder zero for gcd) is treated directly and the function call returns.

2. *Subproblems*: Then, break the given problem into smaller problems of the same kind. Each is solved by a recursive call to the function itself passing arguments of reduced size or complexity.

3. *Recombination of answers*: Finally, take the answers from the subproblems and combine them into the solution of the original bigger problem. The task is finished and the function now returns. The combination may involve adding, multiplying, or other operations on the results from the recursive calls. For problems such as the gcd, no recombination is necessary, and this step becomes a trivial return statement.

Let's look at another well-known recursive algorithm, the *quicksort*.

Quicksort

Sorting means arranging data items into a specified order. Items are sorted to make retrieval easier. Imagine trying to look up (retrieve) a phone number from an unsorted phone book! Among many competing sorting algorithms, the quicksort algorithm remains one of the fastest.

Let's consider arranging an array of integers in increasing order with quicksort, which applies recursion:

1. *Termination conditions*: If the array contains zero or one element, quicksort is done and it returns.
2. *Subproblems*: Pick any element of the array as the *partition element*, pe. By exchanging elements, the array can be arranged so that all elements to the right of pe are greater than or equal to pe and all elements to the left of pe are less than or equal to pe. Now apply quicksort to each of the smaller arrays on either side of pe.
3. *Recombination of answers*: After the two smaller arrays are sorted, the task is done. No additional efforts are needed.

```
void quicksort(int a[], int i, int j)
{       // sort a[i] to a[j] inclusive
        int partition(int a[], int, int);
        if ( i >= j || i < 0)
             return;
        int k = partition (a, i, j);   // k is position of pe
        quicksort(a, i, k-1);          // sort left subarray
        quicksort(a, k+1, j);          // sort right subarray
}
```

The function quicksort is called with the lower index i and the higher index j of the array. If j is greater than i, the function partition is called to select a partition element and to split the array into two parts. The returned value of partition is the index of the partition point. The smaller arrays to either side of pe are then sorted by calling quicksort recursively.

The function partition is not recursive, and a simple implementation is easy. Let's consider an efficient partition and see how it works.

The arguments to partition are the array a and the two indices low and high. The range of the array from a[low] to a[high] inclusive is to be partitioned. Basically, the middle element is chosen to be the pe. By searching simultaneously from both ends of the range toward the middle, elements belonging to the other side are located. Out-of-place entries are interchanged in pairs. Finally, the searches in opposite directions end when they meet somewhere in the range, pinpointing the location for the partition element.

The `partition` function begins by exchanging the rightmost element with pe. Starting from both ends, the left-to-right search locates an element greater than pe, and the right-to-left search finds an element less than pe. The two elements located are exchanged (with the `inline` function). Thereafter, the searches in opposite directions continue. Eventually, no more exchanges are needed, and the searches meet somewhere between `low` and `high` inclusive. This is the partition spot that contains an element greater than or equal to pe. The pe at the rightmost position is now interchanged with the element at the partition position. Finally, the index of the partition element is returned:

```
inline void exchange(int b[], int i, int j)
{       //  array b is modified
        int t = b[j];
        b[j] = b[i]; b[i] = t;
}

int partition(int a[], int low, int high)
{   // partition a[low] through a[high]
        register int pe;
        int i = low;
        int j = high;
    // choose middle element as partition element
        exchange(a, (i+j)/2, j);        // move pe to right end
        pe = a[j];
        while (i < j)
        {       while (i < j && a[i] <= pe) i++;
                while (i < j && a[j] >= pe) j--;
                if (i < j) exchange(a, i++, j);
        }
        if (i != high) exchange(a, i, high);
                                        // move pe to partition location
        return i;                       // return index of pe
}
```

Another feature of `quicksort` is that the reordering is performed *in place*. No auxiliary array is used, as is required by some other sorting algorithms. The best way to understand how quicksort works is to try, by hand, an example with fewer than ten entries.

Recursion is a powerful tool for problem solving. But a recursive function can be inefficient for making too many function calls. Once a recursive solution is fashioned, a nonrecursive implementation can be made for better performance. Recursive calls can always be eliminated by using stacks to manage changing parameter values. Sometimes, as is the case for gcd, no stack is even necessary.

3.5 A CLASS OF FRACTIONS

Now let's consider dealing with ordinary fractions like $\frac{1}{2}$ and $-\frac{1}{3}$. A fraction is, of course, the ratio of two integers: a numerator and a denominator. A user-defined type can be built for fractions by creating a class Fraction. The class supplies a set of necessary operations on fractions and hides implementation details of data representation and internal manipulations.

The Fraction.h file contains the class declaration:

```
///////   Fraction.h   ///////
#include <iostream>

class Fraction
{ public:
    Fraction() { }                          // default constructor
    Fraction(int n, int d);                 // constructor, d != 0
    Fraction operator- ();                  // unary negation
    Fraction operator- (Fraction& y);       // binary difference
    void display();
    bool operator==(Fraction& y)
    {   return( num == y.num && denom == y.denom );
    }
    bool operator> (Fraction& y);
    bool isZero() { return(denom == 1 && num == 0); }
    bool isOne()  { return(denom == 1 && num == 1); }
    bool isInt()  { return denom==1; }
    int floor();
    int ceiling();

    /* other members not shown */
  private:
    Fraction makeFraction(int n, unsigned d)
    {    Fraction ans;
         ans.num = n; ans.denom = d;
         return ans;
    }
    int num;                                // numerator
    unsigned int denom;                     // denominator
};
```

There are quite a few members in the Fraction class: the private data members num and denom, constructors, arithmetic and relational operators, logical tests, and so on. Only a few typical members are shown here so that the class definition remains uncluttered and thus easy to read. In practice, a full complement of member functions is included to support the intended use of the objects.

A class usually encapsulates a data structure with its manipulation procedures. In designing a class, an important task is to decide on the internal data representation, which is isolated from outside view. In this way, member functions keep the data representation consistent in any way that is appropriate; outside routines are not affected. Here are some internal representation items to consider:

1. A fraction is kept internally as a pair of integers: num and denom.
2. The numerator num is an int that can be positive, negative, or zero.
3. The numerator carries the sign of the fraction, and the denominator can be kept positive — hence, the type unsigned int. The denominator can never be zero.
4. Another design decision is whether to allow equal but different-looking fractions (e.g., $\frac{1}{2}, \frac{2}{4}, \frac{3}{6}$) to exist. If not, and equal fractions must have the same numerator and denominator, then all fractions must be reduced to the lowest terms. A data representation in which all equal quantities are represented uniquely is known as a *canonical* representation. Keeping fractions canonical is desirable here.
5. A fraction can be zero, and it is represented by num = 0 and denom = 1.

It is possible to design the Fraction class to help enforce these representational decisions and not to have them just as principles that anyone can choose to follow or ignore. This is one major advantage of object-based programming over traditional programming.

The fraction representation is formed by the Fraction constructor as follows:

```
///////   Fraction.C   ///////
#include "Fraction.h"

Fraction::Fraction(int n, int d)
{   if ( d == 0 )
    {   std::cerr << "Fraction: denominator is 0" << std::endl;
        exit(1);
    }
    if (n == 0) { num = 0; denom = 1; return; }
    if (d < 0) { n = -n; d = -d; }
    int g;
    if ( (g = gcd(n,d)) != 1 )                    // remove gcd
    {   num = n/g; denom = d/g;
    }
```

3.5 A CLASS OF FRACTIONS

```
       else {  num = n; denom = d; }
}
```

This constructor takes the given arguments n and d and constructs a fraction $\frac{n}{d}$. The denominator d should not be zero. The fraction is reduced by removing the gcd (Section 3.4) between n and d.

Let's now examine a representative set of member functions in the class Fraction. First of all, the functions isZero, isOne, and isInt have their entire definition contained within the class declaration. Class member functions so specified are inline and may be compiled without run-time function call overhead.

Functions can also be explicitly designated inline following the class declaration in a header file. For example,

```
inline void Fraction::display()
        {  std::cout << num << "/" << denom;  }

inline int Fraction::operator ==(Fraction& y)
        {  return( num == y.num && denom == y.denom );  }
```

As always, the class scope operator (Fraction::) puts the function names in the intended class scope. Only very simple functions should be inline; other functions should be defined in an implementation file (Fraction.C in this case).

The operator - has been overloaded here to handle the unary negation:

```
Fraction Fraction::operator -()                    // unary negation
{   return makeFraction(-num, denom);  }
```

Given a fraction

```
Fraction r(3, 4);
```

the unary negation -r is shorthand for the function call

```
r.operator-()
```

The answer is computed by constructing a fraction with a negated numerator. The private makeFraction function creates a fraction efficiently without computing a gcd. Because makeFraction only works when no simplification is necessary, access to it is restricted to member functions.

Object Assignment

The object assignment

```
Fraction s;
s = -r;
```

copies the return value of operator-() into s.

Without user-supplied definitions, very few built-in operations work on class objects. However, the assignment operation is so basic that it does have a default meaning on objects. Unless otherwise defined by the user, *object assignment* involves assigning each corresponding data member on the right-hand side to that on the left-hand side.

Arithmetic Operations

An example of fraction subtraction, as a typical binary arithmetic operation on fractions, follows:

```
Fraction Fraction::operator -(Fraction& y)   // fraction subtraction
{   if ( num == 0 )                          // trivial cases   (1)
        return makeFraction(-y.num, y.denom);
    else if ( y.num == 0 ) return *this;     // host pointer    (2)
    else                                     // subtract fractions
        return( Fraction(num * y.denom - y.num * denom,
                         denom * y.denom ) );
}
```

With the binary `operator-` defined, the infix notation

```
r - s              // r and s are Fraction objects
```

becomes shorthand for the function call

```
r.operator-(s)
```

Namely, the object s is passed to the member function `operator-(Fraction&)` of the object r. The reference parameter causes the argument s to be passed without copying.

Here is a simple main program that puts fractions to use:

```
///////    testFraction.C    ///////
#include "Fraction.h"

int main()
{   Fraction x(1,30), u(-1,60), v(-1,60);
    Fraction y;
    x.display(); std::cout << std::endl;
    y = x + u + v;
    y.display(); std::cout << std::endl;
    return 0;
}
```

The Host-Object Pointer

The fraction subtraction function uses the pointer `this` (line 2), which deserves careful explanation. Recall that an object is built using its class as a blueprint. Hence, an object is an instance of its class and contains data and function members specified by the class. Thus, members within individual objects are known as *instance members*. The host object for an *instance function* is the object containing that function. In C++, an instance function is called with an extra pointer argument, `this`, supplied by the compiler, which is a pointer to the host object and is known as the *self-pointer* or *host pointer*. This host pointer is crucial to the operation of an instance function. For example, the code (line 1)

```
if ( num == 0 )
```

is simply shorthand for the actual code executed:

```
if ( this->num == 0 )
```

Thus, when referring directly to another member in the same host object, an instance function really relies on the self-pointer (`this`) to do the job.

The self-pointer can also be used explicitly by instance functions when there is such a need. In fraction subtraction, `*this`, the host object itself, is the answer if zero is to be subtracted (line 2). The pointer `this` is not a fixed quantity; it depends on the host object in question. For host object r, it points to r; for host s, it points to s.

`Fraction` is another example of using `class` to build new data types from existing ones. `Fraction` is now an abstract data type because it is characterized only by its external behavior. Specific implementation details are hidden and immaterial to users of fractions. By attaching all related routines to the data, encapsulation is achieved. A fraction object is therefore self-sufficient, and it even knows how to display itself. By operator overloading, `Fraction` objects can be treated almost as built-in types (e.g., r - s).

3.6 OPTIONAL AND VARIABLE-LENGTH ARGUMENTS

A function usually takes a fixed number of arguments. But there are situations when it is convenient or even necessary to relax this rule. In C++, it is possible to define functions with optional arguments or even an *arbitrary* number of arguments.

Functions with Optional Arguments

An argument of a function becomes *optional* (may or may not be supplied in a function call) if it has been given a *default value*. Optional arguments must be grouped at the end of the formal parameter list. The = value syntax is used to supply a default value. For example, the class

```
class Time
{ public:
    Time() {}
    Time(int hr, int min, int sec = 0, char ap = 'A');    // (1)

    /*  other member functions  */

  private:
    int second, minute, hour;
    char a_or_p;      // 'A' or 'P'
};
```

can be defined to supply Time objects. Here an overloaded constructor takes zero, two, three, or four arguments. The default value for the fourth argument is 'A' (for A.M.). Thus, Time objects can be established as follows:

```
Time t1(2, 30, 0, 'P');    // 2:30 PM
Time t2(9, 15);            // 9:15 AM
Time t3(6, 15, 30);        // 6:15:30 AM
Time t4;                   // uninitialized
```

The default value can be supplied in a prototype declaration or the definition of a function. And it can be supplied anywhere in the source code as long as it is specified only once. The C++ compiler complains if a default value is supplied more than once. A default value cannot be supplied to an argument unless all arguments to its right have been made optional already. Therefore, the additional declaration

```
Time::Time(int, int = 0, int, char);
```

anywhere (after line 1) makes the min argument also optional. This is possible but not advisable. Rather, always supply all the default values in one prototype declaration at a place where any potential caller can see how to supply arguments. The usual place for such a prototype is in a header file, where the meaning of the arguments as well as other possible values for the optional arguments are clearly documented with comments.

To further ensure code clarity and consistency, it is good practice to use the same header for a function in all its declarations and prototypes. The default values can be commented out in all places but one. Thus, the implementation of `Time::Time` should look like this:

```
Time::Time(int hr, int min, int sec /* = 0 */, char ap /* = 'A' */)
{   hour = hr;
    minute = min;
    second = sec;
    a_or_p = ap;
}
```

If all arguments are optional, the function can be called with no arguments. When such a function is a constructor, it is not necessary to supply another default constructor. In fact, it is an error to supply one because a call with no arguments becomes ambiguous.

The initial value for an optional argument can be a constant expression or any expression involving no local variables. Specifically, global variables, static members (Section 5.10), and `enum` constants (Section 1.11) can be used.

C++ also supports writing functions that take an indefinite number of arguments. For example, the notation

```
int sum(int argcnt, ...)              // variable args notation
```

declares `sum` as a function of one or more arguments. The first parameter is `argcnt`, and it is of type `int`. The ellipsis (...) is a syntax element to indicate that the number and type of the remaining (undeclared) arguments may vary. See Appendix F for complete details.

3.7 OVERLOADING FUNCTIONS

Traditionally, a function performs a specific duty that is programmed for it. C++ supports *function overloading*, adding extra duties to existing functions. This is done simply by defining multiple versions of a function with the same name, but the versions must have different *signatures*. The function name and the number, order, and types of its formal parameters constitute a function's signature. Note that the function return type is not part of its signature. We have already used some overloaded constructors. As another simple example, consider the power function (Section 1.8) with the prototype

```
int power(int a, int n);              // integer power
```

You can overload `power` to compute powers of `double` quantities:

```
double power(double a, int n)
{   double ans = 1.0;
    for (int i = 0 ; i < n ; i++)
```

```
            ans *= a;                       // no overflow check
      return ans;
}
```

Now the same power can compute powers of int and double—how convenient! Furthermore, you can add the duty of computing powers of fractions:

```
Fraction power(Fraction a, int n)
{     Fraction ans(1, 1, 0);          // ans is 1
      for (int i = 0 ; i < n ; i++)
          ans = ans * a;              // * of Fraction
      return ans;
}
```

Note that the preceding defines power, not Fraction::power. Thus, you are not dealing with a member function of the class Fraction. Had you used Fraction::power, you would be adding a function in the scope of Fraction and not overloading the file scope function power. Hence, overloading occurs only if additional meanings are assigned to a function name in the same scope. When a function definition involves default arguments, it results essentially in several versions of an overloaded function taking different numbers of arguments.

There is no practical limit on how many different duties can be piled on the same function name. The added definitions can also be in different places or files in a program.

Distinguishable Signatures

To overload a function, the new definition must carry a signature *distinct* from all existing ones (in the same scope). For example, all of the following function prototypes have distinct signatures:

```
int power(int a, int n);              double power(Fraction a, float n);
int power(int a, short n);            double power(float a, int n);
int power(int a, unsigned n);         double power(int a, float n);
double power(double a, int n);        Fraction power(Fraction a, int n);
double power(float a, float n);       Fraction power(Fraction a, int* n);
```

Remember that the return value type is not part of the function signature. The C++ compiler produces an error message and the compilation fails if the overloading signature conflicts with an existing signature. For example, the following signatures conflict with one another:

```
double power(double a, int n);        // mutually
double power(double a, const int n);  // conflicting
double power(double a, int& n);       // signatures
```

For any type *TP* that is not a pointer or reference, the types *TP*, *TP&*, and const *TP*[1] cannot be distinguished when function signatures are compared. However, the types const *TP&* and *TP&* can be distinguished because read-only and read-write reference parameters are very different. For similar reasons, const *TP** and *TP** have different signatures. For example, the signatures

```
double power(double a, int& n);
double power(double a, const int& n);
```

do not conflict.

Since arrays are always passed as pointers in function calls, the types *TP** and *TP[]* (with or without array dimension) are not distinguishable as far as the signature is concerned.

Overloaded functions only give the appearance of having different functions with the same name. But in fact, each overloaded version is internally encoded by the compiler with a name that reflects the function's signature. Thus, in a compiled program, there are no functions with the same name.

In C++, operators can also be given extra duties. Operator overloading is similar to function overloading but becomes more involved for certain operators (Section 8.1).

Function Call Resolution

When a function call is made to an overloaded function, the C++ compiler automatically deduces, from the actual arguments, the correct version of the function, in the indicated scope, to invoke. This activity is termed *call resolution* and is performed by matching the number and type of the actual arguments with the function signatures visible at the points of call:

1. Determine the *set of viable functions*: A viable function is one that can receive the number and type of arguments in the call under argument type conversions.
2. Select the function that *best matches* the call.

The best is an *exact match* where the arguments match the parameter types exactly or with only trivial differences that the two signatures would be in conflict as overloaded functions. Next best are, in order, promotions, standard conversions, and user-defined conversions. See Section 3.13 for details on these conversions.

---

[1] It makes little sense to declare a pass-by-value parameter const anyway (see Section 3.9).

3.8 REFERENCES

Reference parameters (described in Section 2.2) are just one form of *references* in C++. A variable declared `type&` is a *reference* of the given `type` and must be initialized when declared. For example,

```
int a;
Account sally(55123, 450.0);
int& ra = a;              // ra is reference to a
Account& rsally = sally;  // rsally is reference to sally
```

The reference variables `ra` and `rsally` become aliases of the actual variables `a` and `sally`. The initializer of a reference must be an *lvalue*, an expression that can be used on the left-hand side of an assignment. Common lvalues include variables (x), array cells (a[i]), and dereferenced pointers (*ptr). Constants or results of expressions such as (2 * a + 3) are not lvalues. Thus, for example, the codes

```
int& wrong = 256;            // reference initializer
Fraction& bad = Fraction(2,3);  // must be an lvalue
```

are not possible. The general syntax for declaring a reference variable is

type& *refname* = *lvalue*;   (declaring a reference)

where `&` signifies a reference declaration and is not to be confused with the address-of operator. It cannot be because it is used after a type name. The initializer must be of the same or a compatible type. Several reference variables can be declared on one line, as in

```
int& ra = a, & rb = b;
```

A reference variable always refers to the actual variable given at initialization time. The association cannot be changed. Thus, the code

```
int c = 9;
ra = c;    // assignment to a
```

assigns the value of c to a rather than switching `ra` to refer to `c`. Both `ra` and `a` refer to the same memory location where an integer value is stored (Figure 3.1).

Figure 3.1   THE MEANING OF A REFERENCE

```
                                        a
        int& ra = a;      ra      [   int   ]
```

When a function takes a reference parameter, the formal reference parameter is considered initialized by the argument being passed each time the function is called. And such an argument must be an lvalue.

A function's return value can also be declared a reference — in which case, an lvalue not local to the function must be returned. Consider the function

```
int& maxi(int& x, int& y)
{   return (x > y ? x : y);  }
```

It returns a reference to its maximum argument, allowing usages such as

```
int a = 9, b = 9;
maxi(a,b) = 16;      // assigns 16 to b
maxi(a,b) -= 10;     // decreases b by 10
maxi(a,b)++;         // increases a by 1
```

The major purpose of references in C++ is to pass parameters into functions without copying. Avoiding copying can be important when large objects are passed to functions. Depending on the application, the receiving function may or may not modify an incoming reference. Whether it does is an important piece of information for the caller who passes an actual argument. The read-only nature of variables and parameters can be expressed easily in C++.

3.9 READ-ONLY VARIABLES AND PARAMETERS

The type qualifier const expresses the read-only nature of variables and objects. If a type name is preceded by const, it becomes a constant or read-only type. If a variable or an array element is declared read-only, the value of the variable stays constant and cannot be changed after initialization:

```
const float pi =  3.14159f;
const int lower_limit = 32;
const char greeting[] = "Hello There"    // read-only char string
```

Similarly, the pointer declaration

```
const char *str = "Happy Birthday";      // string constant
```

prevents any assignments through the pointer variable str. In Standard C++, a string literal is strictly read-only and of type const char*. For instance, *str = 'A' is illegal. However, the pointer variable str itself can still be set. Thus, ++str is perfectly all right.

The old-style code

```
char *str = "Happy Birthday";            // should add const
```

is *deprecated* by Standard C++ and should be avoided.

To declare a pointer variable itself read-only, use

```
char const * ptr = "Happy New Year";      // read-only ptr to char
```

To declare a read-only pointer that points to read-only array cells, use

```
const char * const qtr = greeting;
```

The compiler also disallows assignment of a pointer (reference) to read-only data to a regular pointer (reference) to protect the read-only data. For example,

```
char *s = str;                // error; s not const char*
const Account& ac = susan;
Account& act = ac;            // error; act not const Account&
Account act1 = ac;            // OK; act1 is a copy
```

The const qualifier is often used in function declarations. For example, the function header

```
bool stringMatch(const char str[], const char line[])
```

means calling the function stringMatch does not result in any modifications to the elements in str and line. The compiler checks for any illegal attempts to modify read-only data.

Similarly, it is important to indicate the read-only nature of reference formal parameters with const not only to prevent accidental modification but also to assure any caller of a function that the reference argument will not be damaged. For example, the member function operator-(Fraction&) can be improved with the code

```
Fraction Fraction::operator-(const Fraction& x);
```

The added const modifier ensures that the reference being passed will not be modified in any way. This code states that the right operand of Fraction::operator-() is read-only. But what about the left operand? It is the host object itself and can also be designated read-only with the code

```
Fraction Fraction::operator-(const Fraction& x) const;
```

The const keyword at the end indicates to the compiler that the host object will not be modified by the function. In writing member functions for a class, be sure to declare the host const for any function that does not modify the host object,[2] directly or indirectly. For example,

```
void display() const;
bool isEmpty() const;
```

---

[2]If the function does not access the host at all, then it should be declared static.

```
int compare(const string&) const;
Fraction operator+(const Fraction& x) const;
```

Let *cobj* be a read-only object.

```
const ClassName cobj = ClassName(...);
```

The compiler checks the calls

```
cobj.func( . . . );
&cobj->func( . . . );
```

to make sure *func* indicates read-only host. If not, the call is wrong and a warning is issued.

Usually, no data member can be modified in a const object. But if a data member is declared mutable, then its modification does not violate the read-only status of its host. The mutable keyword is useful in situations where you wish to allow certain data members to change while keeping all other members read-only.

It is always important to know whether modification is intended on a reference parameter or host object. Passing read-only reference parameters gives you the power/efficiency of pass by reference and the safety of pass by value.

An individual data member in a class can also be declared read-only — in which case, its initial value is set at object instantiation time by the class constructor (Section 5.2).

3.10 THE typedef DECLARATION

The typedef declaration is used to create new names for basic as well as user-defined types, including classes. The new type name should be either more descriptive or more compact to use. Once a new type name has been established, it can be used just like any other type name. Type names should also be distinct from other identifiers in the same scope:

```
typedef int Enrollment;            // Enrollment is int
typedef unsigned short Age;        // Age is unsigned short
typedef char *String;              // String is char *
typedef Fraction *Fracptr;         // Fraction pointer
```

Note that capitalized identifiers are used for new type names. This convention makes it simpler to distinguish typedef names from other names. With these new type names, clearer codes, as in

```
Age x;
String a, b = "hello there", argv[5];
```

can be used—in this case, to declare x unsigned short; a, b, and argv[0] through argv[4] char *.

Having seen some examples, we are ready for the general syntax of typedef. To establish a new type name Abc, just declare Abc as though it were a variable of the desired type and then precede the entire variable declaration with the modifier typedef. Hence,

```
typedef char * StringArray[];
```

defines the type name StringArray and allows the main function header to be written as

```
main(int argc, StringArray argv)
```

It must be pointed out that typedef does not actually create a new data type; rather, it simply gives a new name to an existing type. The class declaration, on the other hand, is used to define new types.

Besides aesthetics, the use of typedef simplifies complicated declarations and provides readability and documentation for a program. Clearly, an Age variable is more specific than an arbitrary int variable, and StringArray is more to the point than what it replaces. Later, when we deal with complex declarations or types defined in classes, typedef will come in handy. You'll also see that typedefs defined inside a class can supply useful information to clients of the class.

3.11 STORAGE ALLOCATION AND MANAGEMENT

When a variable is defined, storage for it is allocated by the compiler. Thus, variables and arrays declared in a program have storage allocated at compile time. The management of the compile-time allocation depends on the *storage class* of the variable: *automatic* or *static*. We are already familiar with the storage treatment for automatic variables.

Local variables with the static specifier and all global variables, with internal or external linkage, belong to the static storage class. Static-storage variables are initialized to zero by default. They also retain their storage location and therefore value, regardless of entry or exit of functions and blocks.

Compile-time-allocated data storage is managed implicitly, according to the rules just mentioned. Storage allocation at compile time is efficient and convenient but sometimes too restrictive. To avoid such restrictions, certain data storage can also be allocated and managed explicitly at run time.

Run-time storage techniques are often overlooked by beginning programmers. However, they are very important in C++ programming and deserve

3.11 STORAGE ALLOCATION AND MANAGEMENT

careful study. Their importance is underscored by the fact that C++ offers the special operators new and delete for treating dynamic storage.

Dynamic Storage Allocation with new

In addition to compile-time storage allocation, it is sometimes necessary in a program to allocate storage dynamically, or at run time. Unlike storage associated with automatic variables, dynamically allocated storage persists until explicitly deallocated. C++ provides the operators new and delete for the allocation and deallocation of storage at run time.

One frequent reason for dynamic storage is that certain data sizes are unknown at compile time. Consider a function, arrayAdd, that takes two int arrays, adds them, and returns the sum array. The result, of course, is an array whose size depends on the size of the argument arrays. If the space to hold the answer is to be allocated in the arrayAdd function, it must happen at run time. Similarly, if the size of a table is not known beforehand, either a huge table is reserved at compile time (to guard against all eventual sizes) or just enough dynamic storage is allocated for the job at hand. Run-time storage is allocated from a *free pool* reserved for this very purpose.

The operator new allocates storage at run time and is used in the forms

```
new    typeName        (allocate variable)
new    typeName[n]     (allocate array)
```

and new returns a pointer to the newly allocated space appropriate to hold data of the indicated type. The pointer returned is of type *typeName**. For example,

```
int *i = new int;
float *x = new float;
int *m = new int[20];           // array, space for 20 integers
Fraction *f = new Fraction;     // class object
```

are valid usages.

If new fails, meaning you have run out of free store, it throws the bad_alloc exception. It means new does not return, and the program breaks out of its normal control flow to produce an object carrying the run-time error condition (Section 8.10).

Except for arrays, initializers can be supplied for data storage allocated by new, as in

```
int *j = new int(11);               // initial value 11
float *x = new float(3.1416);       // initial value 3.1416
Fraction *f = new Fraction(2,3);    // calls constructor
```

For basic types, the optional initializer takes the form of (*expr*). For class objects, the initializer is an object or an argument list to a constructor that is called to perform the initialization.

A programmer can also request that the space allocated by `new` be at a specified address with

`new ( ptr ) type`

This expression returns a `type*` pointer that points to the same address as `ptr`. It is helpful in reusing a pool of space allocated and managed by a program and in the explicit placement of data in memory. Be sure to include the header <new> for this usage.

Dynamic Storage Deallocation with `delete`

Dynamically allocated storage is freed with the operator `delete` when the space is no longer needed. The `delete` operation must be explicitly invoked in a program in the form

`delete  ptr`

where `ptr` must be a pointer returned earlier by `new`. Freed space goes back to the pool of available space for dynamic allocation. Be careful not to free space that has not been dynamically allocated. Otherwise, data and even functions in your program can be destroyed in unpredictable ways. However, C++ guarantees that deleting a pointer with the value zero is not a problem. This means that a pointer to dynamic storage that is initialized to NULL can always be deleted. After `delete`, the value of `ptr` is invalid (most likely NULL), and `ptr` should not be dereferenced again.

Dynamically allocated arrays are freed using

`delete [ ] arrayname`

Again, `arrayname` must be a pointer returned by a call to `new` that created the dynamic array. The size of the array is known and need not be supplied to the `delete` call. Use `delete []` only to free an array.

When a dynamically allocated object is freed, the `delete` call automatically calls any *destructor* supplied by the class before freeing up the space. The destructor performs *deinitialization* operations specified for objects of a given class (see Section 5.7).

Applications of `new` and `delete` can be found in the circular buffer example given next.

3.12 A CIRCULAR BUFFER

To demonstrate some of the key points covered so far, let's consider implementing a *circular buffer* and also apply it in a program to count the total number of words in any given file.

A first-in/first-out (FIFO) character buffer is often useful as a data structure to transfer characters from a producer to a consumer. The provider of characters for the buffer is called the *producer*, and the receiver of characters from the buffer is called the *consumer*. In sequential processing, the producer and consumer are different parts of the same program. In concurrent (or parallel) processing, they can be independently running programs. The buffer is usually represented as a character array of an appropriate size. In the beginning, the buffer contains nothing and is therefore empty.

Normally, head and tail indices are used to keep track of the start of characters yet to be consumed and the start of empty spaces available in the buffer, respectively. The head advances as characters are consumed, and the tail advances as new characters are put into the buffer. When an index reaches the end of the buffer, it wraps around to the beginning. This wraparound property makes the buffer *circular* (Figure 3.2). Obviously, it is an error to consume from an empty buffer or produce into a full buffer.

Let's now define a circular buffer class, Cirbuf, to hide the implementation details and to supply just the right interface for producing into and consuming from a circular buffer object. Our program establishes a Cirbuf object with a given buffer capacity whenever there is a need. The Cirbuf.h header file is included by any file that uses a circular buffer:

```
///////    Cirbuf.h    ///////

class Cirbuf    // circular buffer
{ public:
```

Figure 3.2 CIRCULAR BUFFER

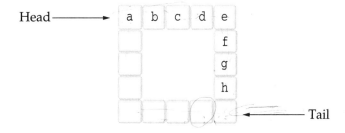

```cpp
    enum { D_SIZE = 16 };                    // default buffer size
    explicit Cirbuf(int size = D_SIZE);      // constructor (A)
    int produce(char c);                     // insert c into buffer
    int consume();                           // remove char from buffer
    bool isEmpty(){ return(length == 0); }   // buffer empty test
    bool isFull() { return(length == size); }// buffer full test
    ~Cirbuf();                               // destructor
  private:
    int head;              // first char in buffer
    int tail;              // first empty slot in buffer
    int length;            // number of characters in buffer
    int size;              // capacity of buffer
    char *cb;              // pointer to buffer
    void incr(int& x)      // index wraparound
    { if (++x == size ) x = 0; }
};
```

Note that the private data member cb points to the first cell of a character array dynamically allocated by the Cirbuf constructor. A default buffer size of 16 is used.

The explicit keyword in front of Cirbuf (line A) needs some explaining. Because any constructor taking exactly one argument also does double duty as an *implicit type conversion* operation (Section 8.9), we add the keyword explicit to remove the type conversion semantics so Cirbuf is only a constructor and not an integer-to-Cirbuf conversion operation. Be sure to declare any constructor taking one argument explicit if you don't want the associated implicit conversion semantics.

As discussed earlier, the index head points to the first character to be consumed in cb, and the index tail locates the slot for the next incoming character. The number of characters remaining in the buffer is length. The buffer is empty if length is zero. It is full if length becomes equal to size.

These details are important only to you, the designer of the Cirbuf class. Any program that uses a circular buffer object is isolated from these details and uses a Cirbuf object only through its public interface:

```cpp
int produce(char c);
int consume();
bool isEmpty();
bool isFull();
```

Note also that the isEmpty (isFull) test should be used before a consume (produce) operation. These operations together with the constructor and destructor are implemented in the file Cirbuf.C:

```cpp
///////    Cirbuf.C    ///////
#include <iostream>
```

3.12 A CIRCULAR BUFFER

```cpp
#include   "Cirbuf.h"
using std::cout; using std::cerr;       // namespace declarations
using std::endl;

Cirbuf::Cirbuf(int s /* = D_SIZE */)    // constructor
{    head = tail = length = 0;          // initial values
     size = s;
     cb = new char[s];                  // allocate buffer space
}

Cirbuf::~Cirbuf()
{    delete [] cb;                      // free up space
}
```

In the Cirbuf constructor, the operator new is used to dynamically allocate the character buffer of the desired capacity. Thus, the code

```cpp
Cirbuf a_buf(64);
Cirbuf *d_buf = new Cirbuf(128);
```

establishes a_buf and *d_buf as Cirbuf objects with the indicated capacities. When a Cirbuf object is destroyed, the buffer space should be freed. This is programmed into the destructor ~Cirbuf (Section 5.7), which is automatically invoked before a Cirbuf object is deallocated. During program execution, there are two occasions when a variable is destroyed:

1. When an automatic variable goes out of scope, as in

    ```cpp
    { Cirbuf a_buf(64); /* ... */ }
    ```

    The circular buffer object a_buf is established when the code block is entered and is destroyed when control leaves the block.

2. When dynamically allocated space (through new) is explicitly deleted, as in

    ```cpp
    delete(d_buf);
    ```

By allocating buffer space in the constructor and releasing it in the destructor, the handling of free storage is made transparent to the user of Cirbuf objects, reducing the likelihood of errors related to free storage management.

The implementations of produce and consume are straightforward. Note that each takes care of index increment with wraparound by a call to the private member function incr.

```cpp
int Cirbuf::produce(char c)             // insert c into buffer
{    if ( isFull() )                    // if buffer full
       { cerr << "produce: buffer full" << endl;
         return -1;                     // return error value
       }
```

```
      cb[tail] = c;
      length++;
      incr(tail);                        // increment with wraparound
      return 0;                          // normal return value
   }
   int Cirbuf::consume()                 // extract char from buffer
   {  char c;
      if ( isEmpty() )
      {  cerr << "consume: buffer empty" << endl;
         return -1;
      }
      c = cb[head];
      length--;
      incr(head);                        // increment with wraparound
      return c;                          // return character
   }
```

In testing the implementation, use a reasonably small size (say, 5) so that wraparound happens sooner. Take special notice of the way in which errors are handled. Instead of exiting, a value of −1 is returned. It is up to the calling function of consume or produce to detect the error and treat it appropriately.

When everything is working, establish the object file Cirbuf.o to combine with any file that uses a circular buffer object.

Circular Buffer Application

Let's put the circular buffer to use. Our example program counts the number of words, separated by SPACE, TAB, and/or NEWLINE characters, in the standard input. The WordCount class utilizes a Cirbuf object to store characters.

```
//////    WordCount.h    //////
#include "Cirbuf.h"        // use circular buffer

class WordCount
{ public:
   WordCount()
   { buf = new Cirbuf(128);
     wcnt = 0;
     word = false;
   }
   ~WordCount() { delete buf; }
   bool readin();                        // obtain input from cin
   void count();                         // count number of words
   int getCount() { return wcnt; }
```

3.12 A CIRCULAR BUFFER

```
    private:
      int wcnt;        // word count
      bool word;       // partial word indicator
      Cirbuf* buf;     // input buffer
};
```

The `WordCount` constructor dynamically allocates a `Cirbuf` of size 128, and the destructor frees this space. A producer member function `readin` obtains input characters and deposits them in the circular buffer until it is full. A consumer function `count` then takes characters out of the buffer and counts the number of words until the buffer is empty.

```
//////    WordCount.C    //////
#include <iostream>
#include "WordCount.h"
using std::cin;

bool WordCount::readin()          // obtain input from cin
{   char c;
    while ( ! buf->isFull() )     // while circular buffer not full
        if ( cin.get(c) )
            buf->produce(c);      // deposit into buffer
        else
            return false;         // input closed
    return true;                  // buffer full
}

void WordCount::count()           // count number of words
{   int c;
    while ( ! buf->isEmpty() )    // while buffer not empty
       switch( c = buf->consume() )
                                  // remove one character from buffer
       {  case ' ' :
          case '\t':
          case '\n':              // word delimiters
              if ( word ) wcnt++;
                                  // word complete
              word = false;       // partial-word indicator false
              break;
          default:
              word = true;        // partial-word indicator true
       }
}
```

Note how the partial-word indicator `word` is used to count one whole word across multiple invocations of `count` and to avoid counting words of length zero. Also note that WordCount is our first example in which a class creates and uses a member that is an instance of another class.

The main program testWordCount establishes a WordCount object counter and calls counter.readin() and counter.count() repeatedly until input is exhausted. It then makes one final call to counter.count() before reporting the final result:

```
//////   testWordCount.C   //////
#include <iostream>
#include "WordCount.h"
using std::cout; using std::endl;

int main()
{   WordCount counter;                          // WordCount object
    for (;;)
        if ( counter.readin() ) counter.count();
        else
        {   counter.count(); break;    }
    cout << "total " << counter.getCount()
         << " words" << endl;
}
```

Now the program is ready for some sample files. If your computer system has an independent word-count program (e.g., the UNIX **wc** command), it can be used to verify the output of the C++ program.

3.13 IMPLICIT TYPE CONVERSIONS

C++ is a strongly typed language that requires all quantities be declared a type before being used in a program. The compiler uses the type information to check for possible argument-passing errors and to generate efficiently running codes. Both primitive and user-defined types may need to be converted to a related type before an operation can be performed. The conversion is sometimes done *implicitly*, or automatically. At other times, it is done *explicitly*, or by program request.

Consider arithmetic operations. An arithmetic operator acting on operands of the same type produces a result of the same type. But if the operands are of different types, they must be converted to a common type before the operation is performed. For example, an integer must be converted to floating-point before an arithmetic operation with another floating-point number. Such conversions are made automatically according to a set of rules.

Since a char is just a small integer, characters can be used freely in arithmetic expressions involving integers or other characters (as in

Cirbuf::consume). If a char is converted to an int and then back to a char, no information is lost.

In general, implicit conversions are performed for integral and floating-point arithmetic operands, function arguments, function return values, and initializers. For example, a function expecting an int argument can be passed any arithmetic type that converts to an int, and the conversion is done by the compiler automatically. Implicit type conversion also takes place when the two sides of an assignment have different types; the right-hand-side value is converted to the type of the left-hand side. For instance, if a floating-point number (right-hand side) is assigned to an integer variable (left-hand side), the fractional part is truncated. Therefore, the function

```
int round(float f)
{    int g = f;                    // truncate fractional part
     float fracpart = f - g;
     return ( (fracpart < 0.5) ? g : g+1 );
}
```

performs the rounding of a float to the nearest integer.

When a double is converted to a float, whether the value is truncated or rounded depends on the C++ compiler for your specific machine.

Arithmetic Conversions

For binary arithmetic operations with operands of two different types, the operand of a *lower* type will be automatically converted to the operand of a *higher* type. (The precise rules can be found in Appendix H.) If there are no unsigned operands, the rules given in Table 3.2, applied sequentially, will suffice for most situations.

Note that when *integral promotion* is applied, a char, short, enum type, or an int bit field (Appendix D) is converted to an int if int can represent all

Table 3.2 ARITHMETIC CONVERSIONS

Rule	If One Operand Is	Convert Other Operand To
1	long double	long double
2	double	double
3	float	float
4	long int	long int
5	*integral promotions*	

possible values of the original type. Otherwise, it is converted to unsigned int. (Type conversion rules concerning pointers and references are discussed later when the need arises.)

Initialization and Argument Conversions

C++ uses the same semantics for function argument passing as variable initialization; certain argument conversions are performed automatically including standard conversions and user-defined conversions.

- *Standard Conversions:* numeric conversion (basically between any two numeric types), object pointer to void* conversion, Boolean conversions (nonzero to true, zero to false), and derived pointer (reference) to accessible base pointer (reference) conversion (Section 7.8)
- *User-Defined Conversions:* conversions defined by classes (Section 8.9)

However, argument conversions take place only if the function call has been matched with a function prototype supplying the necessary type information. The situation becomes more complicated when the function is overloaded (Section 3.7). It is best to avoid relying on implicit type conversion to pick a version out of a set of overloaded functions and to use explicit type-casting for an exact match (Section 3.7).

3.14 EXPLICIT TYPE CAST

A programmer can also request type conversion *explicitly* to force data of one type to become another. Standard C++ introduces the type-cast notation

type_cast_operator< *type* >(*expr*)

to request that the expression *expr* be converted to the given *type*. There are four type-cast operators for different kinds of conversions:

static_cast is used to make conversion between related types, between related pointer types, and from a pointer type to void*. It is also used to make compiler-supplied conversions explicit (to avoid warning messages). For example,

```
double d = 3.1415;
int i = static_cast< int >(d);                    // double to int
enum Days { MON=1, TUE, ... };
Days w = static_cast< Days >(i);                  // int to enum
float* ptr2 = static_cast< float* >(ptr1);        // double* to float*
```

Using static_cast, a short version of round can be written as:

```
int round(float f)
{   return static_cast< int >(f + 0.5);
}
```

reinterpret_cast is used to ask the compiler to interpret one type as another unrelated type, for example, casting void* to another pointer type, treating an integer as a pointer or vice versa, interpreting an unsigned int as several characters, or casting function pointers. Reinterpret casts are dangerous and less portable. Avoid them if you can.

const_cast is used exclusively to drop the read-only status of a type. For example,

```
const char* str = "Happy Birthday";
int i = strlen( const_cast< char* >(str) );
```

dynamic_cast is used for converting pointer or reference types in a class derivation hierarchy (Section 7.1) with run-time checks, usually from a base class pointer or reference to a derived class pointer or reference. Dynamic cast is performed at run time and checks the correctness of the cast (Section 7.8).

The old type-cast notation

type_name (*expression*)

converts the given *expression* to the named type. If no expression is given, the result is an undefined value of the named type. With this type-casting, the round function becomes:

```
int round(float f)
{   return int(f + 0.5);      // old-style casting
}
```

The old-style casting can be used in place of static_cast, const_cast, and reinterpret_cast.

The C-style casting that used to be allowed in C++ is now deprecated:

```
float x = 3.2;
(int) x;             // convert to int (deprecated)
(double) x;          // convert to double (deprecated)
```

3.15 HOW TO USE HEADER FILES

The primary purpose of a header file is to make functions, variables, arrays, objects, and other data objects that are defined in one separately compilable source code file accessible from another file. We already know about Standard C++ headers (Section 3.2). Let's think about establishing our own headers.

For a file source.C, the convention is to use a corresponding source.h as its header file (for certain cases, the .h suffix is not used). Any file, called a *client*, that wishes to use facilities provided by source.C will include the header source.h. Furthermore, the file source.C itself will #include its own header file as well. This ensures that declarations stay consistent for the source and clients. Figure 3.3 illustrates this source–client relation.

Often in practice, the client file uses facilities provided by a module consisting of many source code files. In this case, one header file should declare constructs made available by the module. The <iostream> is such a header file. This organization allows you to collect information affecting multiple files in one file (the header) so that any modifications can be made easily in one place only. Thus, the impossible question, If I modify this declaration, in what other places do I have to make a similar change? is completely avoided. Be sure to avoid possible duplicate inclusion of headers by using the *once-only* feature (Section 14.7).

So which declarations should go in a header file and which belong in the source code file itself? Use the following rules of thumb:

- Put class declarations to be used by clients in the header file.
- Do not put definitions, a declaration that allocates space, in a header file. For example, int arr[10]; and float x=3.14f; are definitions (Section 3.3).
- Use unattached functions sparingly. But declare in the header any unattached function to be accessible from another file with a function prototype (e.g., int gcd(int, int);).
- Avoid using global variables. Consider enclosing them in classes (Section 5.5). But declare in the header any global variables to be accessible from a client with the extern modifier. The same global variable should also be defined with an initializer in the source (.C) file.
- Include any #define constants to be used by clients in the header file. The constants NULL and EOF in iostream are examples.

Figure 3.3 SOURCE–CLIENT RELATION

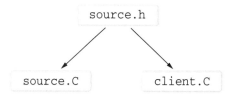

- Include inline function definitions, enumerations (enum), constants (extern const), and typedef (Section 3.10) declarations used by clients in the header file.
- Establish a pair of .C and .h files for each class or source code module. The .h file contains the class and other declarations to be used by a client of the class or module. The .C file implements the class or module with a member function and other definitions. The .C file should also #include its own header file.

In summary, a header file is often the *external interface* of a program module. All necessary declarations should be there so that a client just has to #include the header file to access all the facilities provided by the module. On the other hand, anything unnecessary for clients should be kept out of the header.

When there are multiple header files that may include other files, there is a distinct possibility that the same header file can be included more than once. Multiple inclusion of the same header file must be avoided (Section 14.7).

The examples given so far conform to these descriptions for header files. Many more examples can be found in later chapters.

3.16 SUMMARY

Identifiers can represent, among others, constants, variables, functions, classes, members, and types in a program. Identifiers can be in different namespaces and, within the same namespace, in different scopes. Identifiers are in the global namespace or a user-defined namespace. Standard C++ libraries are in the namespace std. Identifiers in one namespace cannot be confused with any in another. Within the same namespace, the same identifier is distinct in different scopes. There are file, class, function, and local scopes.

Depending on its scope, an identifier can be local to a function, block (internal variables), or class; known to all functions throughout one file but not to anything outside the file; or global and accessible by all parts of the same program in one or more files. Automatic variables are created and destroyed as their program blocks are entered and exited, whereas static variables retain their value independent of control flow.

Identifiers must be declared properly before use. Declarations are instructions to the compiler and do not result in executable code. File scope declarations are given outside of functions and classes and are used to declare or define global identifiers that may have *external* or *internal* linkage. A global variable is allocated at compile time and initialized to zero by default. The C++ one definition rule states that everything can be defined only once. The typedef feature can simplify declarations by giving meaningful names to complicated declarations inside or outside a class.

Identifiers are often used as variables. A C++ variable has three possible storage classes: automatic, static, and dynamic. C++ provides operators `new` and `delete` to dynamically allocate and release storage at run time. It is also possible for an identifier to serve as a reference to a variable or lvalue. A reference must be initialized when declared and thus becomes an alias for the given lvalue. Reference parameters are often used to avoid copying in argument passing and to collect return values from a function. Pass objects by reference whenever possible. When a reference or pointer argument does not collect a return value, it should be declared read-only with the `const` specifier to bar modifications to it. Whenever a member function does not alter its host, declare the host `const`.

Identifiers also serve as function names. Overloading assigns multiple meanings to the same function name. Different definitions for the same function name must have distinct signatures. The C++ compiler uses a systematic function call resolution procedure based on the number and types of the actual arguments to pick the correct version of an overloaded function. A function can have optional arguments with default values. Passing a variable number of arguments whose types are known only at run time is possible.

Identifiers and expressions have types. Built-in rules govern the conversion of types when an operator is given different data types. Type conversions also take place when passing arguments to a function and when explicitly requested in a program.

The two classes, `Fraction` and `Cirbuf`, show how a class encapsulates data and functions to define well-behaved objects. These examples illustrate topics presented in this chapter and demonstrate OOP techniques. Furthermore, they are revisited frequently in later chapters.

EXERCISES

1. Class member names have class scope and are generally not recognized outside the class without qualification. Can you think of any class members that are recognized without being qualified?

2. Write a `gcd` that is nonrecursive and that can take any `int` arguments, not just nonnegative ones.

3. Write a function `lcm` that takes two integer arguments and returns the *least common multiple* of all the arguments (e.g., `lcm(-15,12)` is 60). Modify `operator-` and `operator+` in `Fraction` to use `lcm`. (*Hint:* Use `gcd`.)

CHAPTER 3 EXERCISES

4. Write lcm (exercise 3) to take an arbitrary number of integer arguments.

5. Add to the class Fraction a member function floor, which returns the largest integer less than or equal to the fraction. (*Hint:* Consider both positive and negative fractions.) Also add const declarations in every appropriate place for Fraction.

6. Explain the meaning of each of the following declarations:

    ```
    const int* a;            const double& b;
    int * const a;           double & const b;
    const int * const a;     const double & const b;
    ```

    Does it make sense to have int & const a = i;?

7. A proper fraction lies between −1 and 1. Add to Fraction a member function isProper().

8. Add a member to CirBuf so that the capacity of a circular buffer object can be increased dynamically. The member prototype should be int grow(int n), which causes the capacity to increase by n characters. Any unconsumed characters in the buffer remain. A false is returned when grow() fails.

9. Examine closely the function partition used in our quicksort (Section 3.4). Can you show that, after the while loop, the element a[i] is not less than pe? Is it an improvement to the partition code to modify the exchange call to exchange(a, i++, j--)?

10. Given an array of distinct integers, write an efficient program to find the *median*, the element of the array whose value is in the middle. Namely, roughly half of the elements are over and half are under the median. (*Hint:* Modify partition.)

11. List the explicit conversion notations and explain their meaning using your own words.

12. Write a function sum that produces the total of an indefinite number of arguments uniformly of type int, float, or double. Make sum always return double for now.

13. Consider the following code for the function swap. Is there any syntax problem here? Does the function achieve its intended purpose? Why?

    ```
    void swap(int& a, int& b)
    {   int& tmp = b;
        b = a;
    ```

```
        a = tmp;
}
```

14. In a function header, does it make sense to declare as const any formal parameter other than a pointer or a reference? Why? Is it possible to use the same identifier both as a variable and as a function name? What about an enum tag? A typedef name?

15. Write a program that creates an array frac_arr with new, initializes each element frac_arr[i] with the Fraction object $\frac{1}{i+1}$, displays the array, and then deletes it.

16. A *stack* is a first-in/last-out buffer. If the numbers 1.0, 2.0, 3.0 are entered into the buffer in that order, then they are taken out of the stack in the sequence 3.0, 2.0, 1.0. The operation push enters an item on the top of a stack, and the operation pop removes an item from the top of the stack. These are the only two operations that are allowed to modify a stack. Following the circular buffer example in Section 3.12, implement a class Stack for type double.

17. Exercise RP-1: Use the Stack object in Exercise 16 to implement a program **rp** to evaluate a *reverse Polish* expression. For example,

    rp 3.1 -4.2 / 5.3 6.4 - 7.5 * +

    displays the value of 3.1 / -4.2 + (5.3 - 6.4) * 7.5. (*Hint:* Use the library function **strtod**.)

18. Compare and contrast a *file scope declaration* with an extern declaration.

19. (a) If you have a function sum at file scope and a function sum in a class, is the function sum considered to be overloaded? Why? (b) If the file scope sum has a different signature than the class scope sum, can you call the file scope sum from a class member function without using the scope operator ::?

20. A function compare is a natural candidate for overloading. Write versions that compare integers, floating-point numbers, strings, characters, and fractions.

21. In C++, the return type of a function is not considered part of the signature of a function. Does this prevent you from defining functions that, in effect, make the return value part of the signature? If not, explain the mechanism you would use.

CHAPTER FOUR

Arrays, Pointers, and Generic Code

The array is one of the most useful data structures in programming. Arrays are often encapsulated in classes as internal mechanisms. A single array can group many related data items of the same type for easy processing. *Random access* to stored elements is most efficient through *array indexing*. Arrays are usually one-dimensional (with one index). Multidimensional arrays are also possible. A matrix multiplication example illustrates the use of two-dimensional arrays.

The length of an array is static, or fixed at compile time. The vector class in the Standard Library is a versatile container class that works like an array with dynamically changing length. The vector class also supplies many useful member functions, including efficient random access to stored elements.

A pointer is a value that *points to* the memory location (address) of another value. Through such *indirection*, pointers provide flexibility in organizing and accessing data stored in a program. Arrays and pointers have a very intimate relationship, and pointers are made easier through array concepts. *Pointer arithmetic* is presented carefully and clearly. Pointer and reference parameters for functions, multiple indirection, and pointer arrays are also discussed.

A set of well-chosen applications demonstrates how arrays and pointers are used effectively in practice. Sorting text lines with objects provides a complete example that combines many of the constructs and techniques presented.

Pointers to functions, formal functional parameters, and the void * type are explained individually and then combined to write *generic programs*, which are programs that can be used on a multitude of data types.

4.1 ARRAY CONCEPTS AND DECLARATIONS

The array is the simplest data structure beyond the basic types such as char, int, and float. In earlier chapters, we have already seen some use of arrays. In general, an array is a section of consecutive *memory cells*, each large enough to hold a data element of the same predetermined type. Each cell in an array is also referred to as an *array entry* or *array element*. The declaration

```
char str[10];
```

establishes `str` as a *one-dimensional* array of ten entries, `str[0]`, `str[1]`, up to `str[9]`, each of type `char`. An array can be initialized when declared (Section 1.12). The initializers enclosed in braces (`{}`) must be constant expressions. Here is an array of two objects with initializers:

```
Fraction frac_arr[] = { Fraction(1,2),
                        Fraction(3,4) };
```

When an array of *objects* is declared, the no-args constructor is always used first to initialize each array element. Declaring an array involving objects whose class has no default constructor is an error. For example, the preceding `frac_arr` cannot be declared if `Fraction` has no default constructor.

The *index* notation `str[n]` refers to the $(n + 1)$th entry of `str`. In general, if there are k entries, the index goes from 0 to $k - 1$. The index notation is used to store and retrieve values in an array:

```
str[0]='A';
cout.put(str[0]);
str[1]='B';
cout.put(str[1]);
```

In other words, each array entry is used just like a variable of the declared type. The advantage is that array entries are indexed and can therefore be used effectively in loops. Although each array entry is like a variable, the array name is a constant representing the address (memory location) of the first entry of the array. Thus, `str` is a constant whose value is the location of `str[0]`. Because the array name is a constant, its value cannot be changed. Hence, an array name cannot be used on the left-hand side of an assignment or with a decrement or increment operator such as `str++`.

As an address, an array name can be assigned to a *pointer variable* of the appropriate type. Thus,

```
char *s;
s = str;
s[0] = 'Z';
```

is a roundabout way to assign the character `'Z'` to `str[0]`.

An array name can also be used in a function call as an argument. At the time of the call, the value of the array name (the address of the first entry of the array) is passed to the formal parameter in the called function. Array formal parameters are local variables and are usually used just like pointer variables. The function

```
bool strEqual(const char x[], const char y[]);
```

is an example.

Up to this point, we have used indexing with arrays and pointers. The index notation is easy to read and understand, but pointers can also be manipulated directly, as explained in Section 4.2.

4.2 POINTERS AND ADDRESS ARITHMETIC

Basic Pointer Concepts

A pointer variable is a variable whose value is the *address* of a memory location where a specific type of data is stored. When a pointer variable is declared, the data type it points to is specified. The notations

```
int *a, *b;
char *r, *s;
Account *u;
Fraction *f;
```

declare a and b as integer pointer variables and r and s as character pointer variables. The pointers u and f can hold addresses for an Account object and a Fraction object, respectively. Figure 4.1 shows a regular variable p at memory location 1200 and a pointer variable q at location 1204 without an initial value. A pointer declaration merely creates the pointer variable; it neither initializes the pointer variable nor allocates memory space for the variable to point to. *Therefore, before a pointer variable is used, it must be assigned the address of an array, a variable, an object, or some dynamically allocated space.* Figure 4.2 shows q getting the address of p. Therefore, the sequence

```
int *ptr_a;
int m[]={1,2,3,4};      // m is an integer array
ptr_a = m;              // pointer ptr_a assigned address of m
```

Figure 4.1 REGULAR AND POINTER VARIABLES

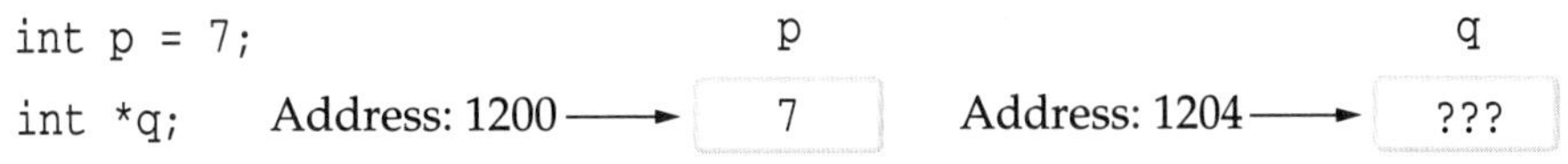

```
int p = 7;                          p                             q
int *q;     Address: 1200 ──▶    [ 7 ]     Address: 1204 ──▶    [ ??? ]
```

Figure 4.2 A POINTER VARIABLE WITH ADDRESS AS VALUE

```
                                    p              q
q = &p;         Address: 1200  →   [ 7 ]  ←      [ 1200 ]
```

```
// entries of m referenced through ptr_a
ptr_a[3]= ptr_a[0]+5*ptr_a[1];
```

results in m[3] being 11. Since ptr_a is a pointer variable of type int, it can be assigned the address of an integer array m. For a Vector2D pointer, the same guidelines apply:

```
Vector2D *v = new Vector2D[2];    // v points to allocated space
v[0] = Vector2D(0.0, 1.0);
v[1] = Vector2D(1.0, 0.0);
```

The Operators & and *

Two unary operators are important in dealing with pointers: &, the address-of operator, and *, the value-of operator. The address-of operator & produces a pointer to, or an address of, an lvalue: a variable or an array entry in memory. The statement

```
int *ap = &m[3];
```

assigns to ap the address of the int array entry m[3] and causes ap to *point to* m[3]. Similarly,

```
Vector2D *vp = &v[1];
```

assigns the address of the object v[1] to vp. The address-of operator & can be applied only to data stored in memory and does not work with constants, register variables, or expressions such as (a + b).

Taking the address of a reference gives the address of the variable referenced. For example,

```
Cirbuf b(256);            // circular buffer object
Cirbuf& cbuf = b;         // cbuf is reference to b
Cirbuf* b_ptr = &cbuf;    // b_ptr == address of b
```

Note that Cirbuf& is a reference type declaration and has *nothing* to do with the address-of operator &.

The value-of operator * is used to access a data item through a pointer. The * can be used on a pointer variable, a pointer constant, or any expression that produces a valid pointer value. After int *ptr_a = &a;, the notation

```
*ptr_a
```

stands for the variable a and behaves exactly the same. Thus, *ptr_a has the value of a, and

```
*ptr_a = 5;
```

is the same as saying a=5 because it stores 5 at the address where a stores its value. Note that the value of the pointer variable ptr_a itself is not changed by this assignment. In general, if ptr is a pointer of a certain type, then *ptr can be used as a variable of that type. The following code further illustrates this concept:

```
*ptr_a = i - 3          // ptr_a is a pointer variable, i integer
*m += 2                 // m is an int array
i = 5 * *ptr_a          // multiplication
( i >= *ptr_a )         // relational operation
++*ptr_a                // or (*ptr_a)++, increment *ptr_a
(*m)--                  // or --*m, decrement *m
```

The unary operators * and & have the same precedence as unary arithmetic operators and have higher precedence than binary arithmetic and relational operators. The parentheses are necessary in the last example because unary operators such as *, ++, and -- associate *right to left*. Hence,

```
*ptr_a--    and    *(ptr_a--)
```

are equivalent and would decrement the pointer variable ptr_a rather than the integer *ptr_a.

Another general observation that can be made of the * operator is that *ptr is always equivalent to ptr[0]. In fact, the compiler automatically converts the latter notation to the former. This is another reason why pointers are closely related to arrays.

Double Indirection

For an integer pointer variable ptr_a, it is clear what *ptr_a means. But what is &ptr_a? By definition, it is the address of ptr_a. In other words, &ptr_a is a pointer to an integer pointer. Thus, the artificial sequence

```
int k, *ptr_a, **ptr_b;    // ptr_b is a pointer to an int pointer
ptr_b = &ptr_a;            // ptr_b points to ptr_a
```

Figure 4.3 DOUBLE INDIRECTION

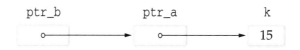

```
ptr_a = &k;          // ptr_a points to k (same as *ptr_b = &k)
**ptr_b = 15;        // k gets 15
```

results in the variable k being assigned the value 15, as illustrated in Figure 4.3. Here is how it works:

1. Since ptr_b points to ptr_a, *ptr_b is ptr_a.
2. Since ptr_a points to k, **ptr_b is k.
3. Thus, **ptr_b = 15 is the same as k = 15.

The same reasoning can be applied to unravel multiple indirections (Section 4.10).

Address Arithmetic

Address arithmetic calculates memory addresses using pointers. Thus, it is also known as *pointer arithmetic*. A pointer is an integer byte count identifying a memory location so many bytes away from a certain reference address, such as the beginning of a program. For instance, 15084 points to byte 15084 from the reference location. A pointer gives the beginning of a *data cell*, which may take 1 or more bytes, depending on the type of data stored there. The exact number of bytes for each data type is implementation dependent. On 32-bit computers, a char usually takes 1 byte and an int 4 bytes.

In practice, a pointer is often used to access a sequence of data cells stored in consecutive memory locations rather than just a single cell. To get from one such data cell to the next, you can use several convenient address arithmetic operations:

- Pointer + integer, resulting in a pointer.
- Pointer − integer, giving another pointer.
- Pointer − pointer, getting an integer.

A discussion of each of these operations follows.

Pointer + Integer Adding an integer quantity to a pointer is not as mysterious as it may seem. In fact, we have been doing it implicitly all along. The

4.2 POINTERS AND ADDRESS ARITHMETIC

familiar array notation b[3] retrieves the desired data by calculating its address based on the information that it is the third item after the cell at b, namely, b[0]. With *explicit address arithmetic*, the same address can be computed by

```
b + 3                    // &b[3] or address of b[3]
```

The result of this address addition is a pointer to b[3], as shown in Figure 4.4. Note that this is not adding 3; rather, it is adding three times the size of the data cell to the address represented by b.

Thus, if b is an int pointer and b is 15084, the pointer b+3 has value $15084 + 12 = 15096$, assuming that int takes 4 bytes. But if b is a char pointer, b+3 becomes $15084 + 3 = 15087$. When an address arithmetic expression such as b+3 is encountered by the compiler, it takes the size of the data cell into account and produces the appropriate code. This arrangement is convenient for programming and makes the program independent of the data type sizes on different computers.

As a result, the general rule holds: If ptr is a pointer and n an integer, then

```
ptr + n
```

is the pointer for the *n*th data cell from the one pointed to by ptr. And the expression

```
*(ptr + n)               // same as ptr[n]
```

is the same as ptr[n], where ptr can be a pointer variable or an array name.

To further illustrate pointer usage, let's consider a pointer version of the library function **strcmp**, which returns an integer value greater than, equal to, or less than zero if the C-style string r is greater than, equal to, or less than the string s, respectively:

```
int strcmp(const char *r, const char *s)
{   while (*r == *s)
    {   if (*r == '\0') return 0;       // strings are equal
        r++; s++;                        // advance pointers
    }
}
```

Figure 4.4   POINTER + INTEGER

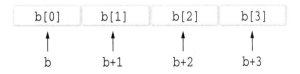

```
        return *r - *s ;                   // strings are not equal
}
```

The definition of strcmp depends on the fact that the string terminator is a zero-valued character.

As another example, consider a pointer implementation of the library function **strcpy**, which makes a copy of its second argument into the first argument:

```
char *strcpy(char *s, const char *cs)
{   char *tmp = s;
    while (*cs != '\0') *(tmp++) = *(cs++); // copy next character
    *tmp = '\0';
    return s;
}
```

The pointer variable tmp is first declared and initialized to s. Next, the while loop copies each character on the string cs until '\0' is encountered. Finally, the terminator '\0' is copied, and the pointer s is returned. The variable tmp is technically unnecessary because s can serve as a *return parameter* (Section 4.8).

A common source of error in copying by passing pointers is insufficient space to receive the data being copied. In this example, s is assumed to point to the beginning of a reserved space large enough to hold the entire string. The minimum number of bytes needed is

strlen(cs) + 1

where the '\0' terminator occupies the final byte. In this case, it is the responsibility of the calling function to ensure that enough space has been provided. If this is undesirable, the copying function may dynamically allocate space as in the function dstrcpy (dynamic string copy):

```
char *dstrcpy(const char *cs)
{    char *s, *tmp;
     unsigned size = strlen(cs)+1;           // or size_t size
     tmp = s = new(char[size]);              // allocate space
     while (*cs != '\0') *(tmp++)= *(cs++);  // copy next character
     *tmp = '\0';
     return s;
}
```

Note that the pointer returned by dstrcpy can later be freed with delete.

The Standard C++ string class (Section 6.3) provides many operations that are easier and safer to use than the preceding functions.

Pointer – Integer   Subtracting an integer from a pointer is the inverse of adding an integer. An example is contained in a pointer implementation of the

4.2 POINTERS AND ADDRESS ARITHMETIC

function match, which compares a string nm with the prefix of a name-value string nv:

```
//   Both nm and nv are strings:
//   nm is the target name to find, nv is in the form name=value
//   If the names match, value is returned, else NULL is returned.

char *match(const char *nm, const char *nv)
{   while ( *nm == *nv++ )
        if ( *nm++ == '=') return nv;     // field delimiter
    if (*nm == '\0' && *(nv-1) == '=')
        return nv;                         // match found
    return NULL;
}
```

Immediately after the while loop, the last step in determining a match is to pair the terminator of nm with the field delimiter =, one character before *nv. The pointer subtraction *(nv-1) gives the exact character needed.

For functions, such as match, that return pointers, it is conventional to return an invalid pointer NULL when the computation fails. The symbolic constant NULL is defined as zero in the header <stddef.h>. But if you include <iostream> or other frequent headers, you already have NULL defined. Although NULL can be assigned to any pointer variable, dereferencing it with * is a run-time error, which can crash the program.

With pointer subtraction, we have the alternative of going backward on a sequence of data cells. For instance, a loop may go from the end of an array to the beginning. This flexibility and power do not come without danger. Be careful not to *fall off the end* of the data cells by going beyond the proper range.

Pointer − Pointer   It is also valid to subtract one pointer from another. If p and q are pointers to entries of the same array, then

```
int n = q - p       // so p+n gives q
```

is an integer n that is the distance between cells p and q. In other words, p + n is q. Note that n can be positive, negative, or zero. Here is a pointer-based version of **strlen** that uses this feature:

```
int strlen(const char *s)    // computes length of string s
{   const char *t = s;
    while( *t++ != '\0' ) {} // go to end of string
    return t-s-1;            // length of string without terminator
}
```

In this version of **strlen**, the while loop, with an empty body, increments t until it reaches the end of the string. Then, the return statement computes the correct length of s via pointer subtraction.

Actually, the pointer variable t is incremented to one character beyond the terminating '\0'. So potentially, t now points to some address that may contain another type of data or may even be outside of the address space of the program. But this is only a problem if access is attempted—say, with *t.

Valid Pointer Operations

In this section, valid pointer operations are summarized for easy reference. The material here also contains some details not previously mentioned, as well as topics yet to come in this chapter.

- *Creation:* The initial value of a pointer has three possible sources: a constant pointer such as an array name, an address obtained with the & operator, or a value returned by a dynamic memory allocation operation.
- *Assignment:* Pointers of the same type can be assigned. Pointers of different types can be assigned only with an explicit cast (Section 3.14). However, a void * variable can be assigned a pointer of any type without explicit casting. An array name is a constant pointer and cannot be used on the left-hand side of an assignment. The NULL pointer (usually zero) can be assigned as a pointer value.
- *p ± integer:* Adding or subtracting an integer from a pointer also includes the operations p++, p--, p += 2, and so on. Such expressions are valid as long as the resulting pointer is within the range of the same array. A pointer is also allowed to go one step beyond the high end of an array. In other words, if p points to the last entry of an array, the pointer p+1 is valid as long as no attempt is made to access the nonexistent entry that it points to. Although most compilers do not check whether a pointer falls outside its range, it is good practice to make sure that it stays within the allowed bounds.
- *Pointer subtraction:* Pointers of the same type can be subtracted, yielding an integer that is positive, negative, or zero. In practice, only pointers to entries of the same array are subtracted.
- *Comparison:* Pointers to entries of the same array can be compared with ==, <, >, and so on. Any pointer can be checked for equality with the NULL pointer. A function returning a pointer usually returns NULL as an indication of error or failure. The calling function must compare the returned pointer with NULL to detect such an error.

- *Indirection:* For a pointer ptr of a certain type, *ptr becomes a variable of that type and therefore can be used in expressions and on the left-hand side of an assignment.
- *Indexing:* A pointer p, whether an array name or a pointer variable, can be used with an index subscript as in p[i], where i is a positive or negative integer. The notation is converted by the compiler to *(p+i). Again, it is the programmer's responsibility to make sure that the indexing stays within the bounds of the array.

4.3 TWO-DIMENSIONAL ARRAYS

Up to this point, all of the arrays we have seen use a single index or subscript. Such arrays are *one-dimensional*. It is possible to have arrays with more than one subscript. For example,

```
int a[2][4];
```

declares a to be a *two-dimensional* array with the first subscript going from 0 to 1 and the second ranging from 0 to 3. In other words, the array can be thought of as a rectangular grid of two rows and four columns (Figure 4.5). The actual memory organization of a two-dimensional array is still linear: A total of eight entries are allocated in consecutive memory cells (Figure 4.6). The array entries are stored by *rows*, with the first row followed by the second row and so on. Using pointer arithmetic, the organization by rows also means that the address &a[i][j] is given by

```
&a[0][0] + i*4 + j      // points to cell a[i][j]
```

where 4 is the number of columns of a. Thus, it is possible to access a[i][j] using the alternative notation

```
int *p = &a[0][0];
*(p + i*4 + j)          // value of a[i][j]
```

or equivalently

```
p[i*4 + j]
```

Figure 4.5 TWO-DIMENSIONAL ARRAY LOGICAL VIEW

a[0][0]	a[0][1]	a[0][2]	a[0][3]
a[1][0]	a[1][1]	a[1][2]	a[1][3]

Figure 4.6 TWO-DIMENSIONAL ARRAY MEMORY ALLOCATION

| a[0][0] | a[0][1] | a[0][2] | a[0][3] | a[1][0] | a[1][1] | a[1][2] | a[1][3] |

A two-dimensional array can be initialized as follows:

int a[][4]= { {0,1,2,3}, {4,5,6,7} };

Note that the range of the last subscript must be given explicitly. The initializer is a list of sublists for the rows. No sublist may contain more elements than the range specified in the declaration. On the other hand, it is always possible to initialize *less* than the full range for any row. Some sublists may even be empty ({}).

One natural question to ask at this point is, Why is the syntax

a[i][j]

used rather than the common notation for two-dimensional arrays

a[i,j]   // not used in C++

used in other programming languages? The answer is that a two-dimensional array is really just a one-dimensional array of elements that are themselves one-dimensional arrays. Thus, a[i][j] literally means (a[i])[j], and a[i] is a constant pointer, of type int *, pointing to the $i + first$ row of the two-dimensional array a. The following test program further illustrates many concepts related to pointers and the two-dimensional array:

```
int main()
{   const int RANGE=4;
    int a[][RANGE]= { {0,1,2,3}, {4,5}, {8,9,10,11} };
    int *p = &a[0][0];
    int *q = a[0];                          // p and q are the same
    int *r = a[1];                          // pointer to 2nd row
    int *s = a[2];                          // pointer to 3rd row
    std::cout << *(p+RANGE+1) << std::endl;    // a[1][1]
    std::cout << *(q+2*RANGE+2) << std::endl;  // a[2][2]
    std:std:::cout << *r << std::endl;         // a[1][0]
    std::cout << *(r-2) << std::endl;          // a[0][2]
    std::cout << s[3] << std::endl;            // a[2][3]
    return 0;
}
```

The variable a is created as a 3 × 4 two-dimensional array of consecutive integers. The second row is partially initialized. The pointers q, r, and s point

4.4 A MATRIX CLASS

to the first, second, and third row of a, respectively. A variety of notations have been used to access cells of a to reinforce your understanding of the two-dimensional array representation, as well as pointer arithmetic.

Having a basic understanding of arrays and pointers, we are now ready to apply them.

4.4 A MATRIX CLASS

Now let's consider writing a simplified Matrix class. The example illustrates the practical use of double arrays in numeric computing.

```
///////    Matrix.h    ///////
#include <iostream>

class Matrix
{ public:
    Matrix() { mat = NULL; }
    Matrix(int r, int c);                          // (1)
    Matrix(double* m, int r, int c);               // (2)
    ~Matrix() { delete mat; }
    double getElement(int i, int j) const;
    void setElement(int i, int j, double e);
    int rows() const { return nr; }
    int cols() const { return nc; }
    void times(const Matrix& b, Matrix& ans) const;
    void display() const;
  private:
    double rowTimesCol(int i, double* b, int j, int bc) const;
    void setUp(int r, int c);
    double* mat;              // the matrix
    int nr, nc;               // rows and cols
};
```

A Matrix object has nr rows and nc columns of double elements stored at mat in row-major format (one row after another). A Matrix object can be initialized with just dimensions (line 1) or a row-major array of double (line 2). These are implemented as follows:

```
///////    Matrix.C    ///////
#include <math.h>
#include "Matrix.h"

Matrix::Matrix(int r, int c) {    setUp(r,c);    }
```

```
void Matrix::setUp(int r, int c)
{   if ( r > 0 && c > 0 )
    {   nr = r; nc = c;
        mat = new double[r * c];
    }
    else
    {   mat = NULL; nr=nc=0;   }
}

Matrix::Matrix(double* m, int r, int c)
{   setUp(r,c);
    if ( mat != NULL )                                    // copy data
        for (int i=0; i < r*c; i++) mat[i] = m[i];
}
```

Functions for retrieving dimensions are simple and given in the header file. Functions to get/set entries check subscript ranges. The illegal double symbol HUGE_VAL (from <math.h>) is returned by getElement for illegal indices.

```
double Matrix::getElement(int i, int j) const
{   if ( 0<=i && i<nr && 0<=j && j<nc )
        return mat[i*nc+j];
    else return HUGE_VAL;                 // illegal value
}

void Matrix::setElement(int i, int j, double e)
{   if ( 0<=i && i<nr && 0<=j && j<nc )
        mat[i*nc+j] = e;
}
```

The member function times multiplies two matrices. The product of an $r \times s$ matrix A by an $s \times t$ matrix B is an $r \times t$ matrix C. (To appreciate this one, *say* the equation.) Each entry $C_{i,j}$ is given by the inner product of row i of A and column j of B. Here is a simple example.

$$\begin{pmatrix} 1 & 2 \\ 3 & 4 \\ 5 & 6 \end{pmatrix} \times \begin{pmatrix} a & b \\ c & d \end{pmatrix} = \begin{pmatrix} a+2c & b+2d \\ 3a+4c & 3b+4d \\ 5a+6c & 5b+6d \end{pmatrix}$$

The matrix multiplication function times is implemented as follows:

```
void Matrix::times(const Matrix& b, Matrix& ans) const
{   assert( nc == b.nr )   // compatible dimensions
    for (int i=0 ; i < nr ; i++)
    {   for (int j=0 ; j < b.nc; j++)
            ans.setElement(i, j, rowTimesCol(i, b.mat, j, b.nc));
```

4.4 A MATRIX CLASS

```
    }
}
```

The function times insists on compatible dimensions by using the assert macro, from <assert.h>, which calls abort() if the condition is not met. It then multiplies the host matrix with b and deposits the product in the reference parameter ans.

Nested for loops are used to compute elements of the result. The private function rowTimesCol computes the inner product of row i of the host matrix with column j of b. The result is stored as entry (i,j) in ans.

```
double Matrix::rowTimesCol(int i, double* b, int j, int bc) const
{   double sum=0.0;
    for (int k=0; k < nc; k++) sum += mat[i*nc+k] * b[k*bc+j];
    return sum;
}
```

The display function outputs the matrix in a two-dimensional format:

```
void Matrix::display() const
{   for (int i = 0; i < nr; i++)
    {   std::cout << std::endl << "( ";
        for (int j = 0; j < nc-1; j++)
            std::cout << mat[i*nc+j] << "  ";
        std::cout << mat[i*nc+nc-1] << " )" << std::endl;
    }
}
```

A fully developed Matrix class would have many other functions. The following program can be used to test matrix multiplication and display.

```
///////    testMatrix.C    ///////
#include "Matrix.h"

int main()
{   double a[2][3]= { {1.0,-2.0,5.0}, {1.0,2.0,3.0}};
    double b[3][2]= { {9.0,7.0},{-2.0,3.0},{-1.0,4.0}};
    Matrix x(*a, 2, 3);   // pass *a, not a
    Matrix y(*b, 3, 2);
    Matrix z(2,2);
    x.times(y,z);
    z.display();
    return 0;
}
```

And the output displayed is

```
( 8   21 )
( 2   25 )
```

At this juncture, let's study some typical applications of arrays and pointers to help sharpen the concepts presented. This example with exceptions added can be found in Section 8.11.

4.5 A CLASS OF POLYNOMIALS

Arrays and pointers are now applied in building a polynomial class. It is important that pointers are not studied in isolation but in conjunction with other constructs to solve problems. By doing so, the abstract rules of pointer usage become concrete and easy to grasp. The polynomial class again demonstrates techniques for data abstraction and program encapsulation.

With the exception of numbers, polynomials are the most basic mathematical structures. They are widely used in many fields of study. Consider establishing a class Poly for one-variable polynomials with integer coefficients. Such a polynomial has the familiar form

$$a_n x^n + a_{n-1} x^{n-1} + \cdots + a_1 x + a_0$$

where x is the variable and $a_n, a_{n-1}, \ldots, a_0$ are the coefficients. The polynomial has *degree n*, and the *leading coefficient* $a_n \neq 0$. For example,

$$3x^5 - 10x^2 + 21x - 8 \tag{4.1}$$

is a fifth-degree polynomial with four terms. Each term is a coefficient multiplied by a power of x. Such a polynomial can be represented by an int array recording the power-coefficient pairs of each term. For instance,

```
int pol[] = {5,3,2,-10,1,21,0,-8,-1};
```

gives the fifth-degree polynomial (4.1). The representation pol begins with the highest power, its coefficient, followed by the next highest power, its coefficient, and so on. A minus one (−1) is used as an end marker because no negative power is allowed for a polynomial. To conserve space, terms with a zero coefficient are not included. Table 4.1 shows how this representation works.

The polynomial representation and operations can be encapsulated in a Poly class declared with code similar to the following:

```
///////    Poly.h    ///////
#include <iostream>

class Poly
```

4.5 A CLASS OF POLYNOMIALS

Table 4.1 A POLYNOMIAL REPRESENTATION

Representation	Polynomial
int p1[] = {100,1,50,1,0,1,-1};	$x^{100} + x^{50} + 1$
int p2[] = {20,9,7,-29,-1};	$9x^{20} - 29x^7$
int p3[] = {0,8,-1};	8
int p4[] = {-1};	0

```
{ public:
    Poly() { pol = NULL; }                      // default constructor
    Poly(const int *p, int terms);              // constructor
    Poly operator+(const Poly& q) const;        // poly addition
    Poly operator-(const Poly& q) const;        // poly subtraction
    Poly operator*(const Poly& q) const;        // poly multiplication
    unsigned int deg() const                    // degree
      { return(pol[0] > 0 ? pol[0] : 0); }
    void display() const;                       // display host object
    /*   other members   */
  private:
    int length() const;    // length of pol
    int  *pol;
};
```

The constructor makes sure that the incoming terms are copied into free storage. The pointer p supplies n terms with 2*n integers but no end marker, which is strictly for internal use. A zero polynomial is instantiated if n is zero:

```
///////    Poly.C    ///////
#include "Poly.h"

inline MAX(int x, int y) {  return x > y ? x : y; }
inline MIN(int x, int y) {  return x < y ? x : y; }

Poly::Poly(const int *p, int n)                 // constructor
{   n = 2*n;
    pol = new int[n+1];                         // dynamic allocation
    for ( int i=0 ; i < n ; i++ ) pol[i] = *p++;
    pol[n] = -1;                                // terminator
}
```

The private member `length` counts how many `int`s are in the representation `pol`:

```
int Poly::length() const                        // private member
{  int i;
   for (i=0 ; pol[i] > -1 ; i += 2);
   return i+1;
}
```

The member function `operator+` is a little more complicated and can be defined as follows:

```
Poly Poly::operator+(const Poly& q) const
{   int *c, *a, *b, *tmp;
    unsigned len, d;
    len = length()+q.length()-1;
    d = 1+2*(1+ MAX(deg(), q.deg()));
    len = MIN(len, d);              // max length of answer
    tmp = c = new(int[len]);        // temporary space for result
    a = pol; b = q.pol;
    while (*a >= 0)                 // for each term of a
    {   while(*b > *a)              // terms in b of higher power
        {   *c++ = *b++; *c++ = *b++; }
        *c++ = *a;
        if (*a == *b)               // add terms of like power   (1)
        {   *c = *++a + *++b;
            if (*c++ == 0) c -= 2;  // terms cancel              (2)
            b++;
        }
        else *c++ = *++a;           // no terms to combine
        a++;
    }
    while (*b >= 0) *c++ = *b++;    // add leftover terms in b
    *c = -1;                        // terminator
    Poly ans(tmp, (c-tmp)/2);       // answer object             (3)
    delete tmp;                     // free temporary space
    return ans;
}
```

In `Poly::operator+`, the maximum size of the result polynomial is computed, and then that much space is allocated with `new` to hold the temporary result. The sum computation now continues depositing terms in `tmp` using `c` as a running pointer.

To compute the sum, each term of a is added to the unprocessed terms of b with a power greater than or equal to the current term. The resulting terms are stored in c. When two terms from a and b combine (line 1), a check is made

4.6 ARRAY OBJECTS: vector

to see whether the new term is zero due to cancellation. If so, the c pointer is decremented by 2 to lose the zero coefficient and its exponent (line 2). The iteration continues until all terms of a and b have been processed. Finally, the −1 terminator is inserted at the end of c.

Now all we have to do is establish a Poly object with the correct number of terms (line 3), free up the temporary space (which may be too large for the actual result), and return ans.

Note that ans is an automatic variable, so it is destroyed after operator+() returns. This is not a problem because a copy of the value of ans is returned and not ans itself. The situation is entirely the same as returning an int or a float local variable.

For testing purposes, various polynomials should be added and the results displayed. Having a member function display is handy:

```
using std::cout; using std::endl;

void Poly::display() const
{   int *p = pol;
    switch ( *p )
    {  case -1: cout << "0" << endl; break;    // zero poly      (A)
       case  0: cout << p[1] << endl; break;   // constant poly  (B)
       default:
          cout << '(';                          // display terms
          while ( *p >= 0 )
          {   cout << *p << " " << *(p+1);
              p += 2;
              if (*p != -1) cout << ", ";
          }
          cout << ")";
    }
}
```

A constant polynomial is displayed as an integer (lines A and B). Note the using declarations allow the direct use of cout and endl without the namespace (Section 3.2) scope operator std::.

It is clear that many other members must be defined before the Poly class is complete. But you can already write a main program to test the Poly class and to display some polynomials.

4.6 ARRAY OBJECTS: vector

Standard C++ supplies vector objects that can be used just like arrays but have certain advantages. The dimension of a vector grows dynamically. Random access to elements through indexing as well as inserting new elements at the end are very efficient.

You include the header file <vector> to use vectors. The code

```
#include <vector>
using std::vector;

std::vector<type> arr(size);
```

establishes arr as a vector object for *size* elements of the given *type*. For example,

```
vector<int> iv(16);         // vector of 16 ints
vector<Fraction> fv(32);    // vector of 32 fractions
```

establishes iv (fv) as a vector object for 16 ints (32 fractions). To declare a vector of objects, make sure the class has a default constructor.

A vector object can be indexed just like an array:

```
iv[0] = 10;
iv[1] = iv[0] - 4;
```

If the index is invalid, the value returned may be wrong. To keep indexing efficient, vector does not detect out-of-bounds indices.

Initial value can be supplied when instantiating a vector:

```
vector<double> dv(256, 0.0);    // vector of 256 entries, init to 0.0
vector<int> iv2(ia, ia+15);     // init by ia[0] to ia[14]
vector<string*> sv;             // empty vector of string*
```

A vector records its size. Thus, you can write code such as

```
for ( int i=0; i < dv.size(); i++ )
```

The vector has another important advantage over primitive arrays: You can insert elements at the end of a vector, and the size of the vector will grow as needed:

iv.**insert**(iv.**end**(), i);   Inserts i at back of iv (same as iv.**push_back**(i);)

It is possible to insert elements at the beginning or in the middle:

iv.**insert**(iv.**begin**(), j);   Inserts j at front of iv (linear time)
iv.**insert**(iv.**begin**()+i, j);   Inserts j just before iv[i] (linear time)

but these two operations are inefficient, incurring a cost proportional to the length of the vector. Choose another data structure if your application calls for frequent insertion/deletion at the beginning or in the middle of the elements.

The **begin**() member function of vector returns a pointer[1] to the first element while **end**() gets you one that points just beyond the last element.

Similarly, you can delete elements from the vector with

```
iv.pop_back();            Removes last element of iv
iv.erase(iv.begin()+i);   Removes element iv[i] (linear time)
```

The *capacity* of a vector is the maximum number of elements it can hold before having to *grow* into a larger vector. After instantiation, the vector capacity is the same as its size. The capacity grows, by ever-larger increments, as more elements are inserted. Growing a vector can involve copying all existing elements. You can reserve enough capacity for a vector initially to avoid unnecessary growing.

```
vector<Account> av;
```

```
av.reserve(512);          Capacity set to 512
av.push_back(susan);      Inserting account
```

A vector stores the value, a copy, of whatever is put on the vector. Thus, a copy of the account susan, not the object itself, is placed in av.

These operations and the fact that it grows in size automatically make a vector object easier to use than a primitive array in many situations. More information on vector as part of the Standard Template Library can be found in Section 11.2. Let's put vector to use in a practical application.

4.7 SORTING TEXT LINES WITH OBJECTS

Ordering or sorting lines of text is commonplace in data-processing applications. Let's now consider a simple sort program. The command **mysort** is used in the form

mysort [*key*]

It reads all lines with cin, sorts the lines by comparing the given *key* in the lines, and then writes out the sorted lines with cout. Each line is assumed to contain one or more fields separated by white spaces (SPACE or TAB). The *key* is an integer indicating which field to use for ordering the lines. If the *key* is unspecified, whole lines are compared.

---

[1] An *iterator* to be precise. See Section 8.6 for more information.

For example, suppose there are files containing course grades in the form

```
Laura Wang      A
Paula Kline     C
Richard Brown   B
```

The command **mysort** can be used on such files: Use key position 2 to sort by last name and key position 3 to sort by letter grade.

Taking an object-oriented view, we can identify two useful objects:

1. A TextLines object, which holds the input text lines, provides access to individual lines, knows how to interchange any two lines, and can output the ordered lines to any given output stream.
2. A SortKey object, which compares the designated keys within any two text lines.

With these objects, the implementation of the **mysort** command consists of the following major steps:

1. Establish a TextLines object, txtobj, to hold the input lines.
2. Establish a SortKey object based on the key position and delimiter characters.
3. Apply quicksort using these objects and then ask txtobj to display itself to cout.

All of this is tied together with a main program which first processes the command-line arguments and then performs the three steps just listed.

This example is more extensive than any we have seen so far. It puts pointers, strings, vector, and many other constructs to use in one example. Its description is organized according to the preceding outline. The example also shows how to break down a complicated program into independent objects that interact to perform the task at hand.

mysort: Building a Class of Text Lines

After a TextLines object is initialized, lines can be read and stored within the object. A vector of string*, with a default capacity of 512, is used to hold the text lines (lines 1 and 2). Because a vector can grow dynamically, there is no prior upper limit to the number of lines. Storing string pointers makes interchanging lines easy and efficient. The operations provided include reading text lines (input), interchanging lines (swap), inserting and removing

4.7 SORTING TEXT LINES WITH OBJECTS

a line, accessing individual text lines by indexing ([]), reporting the number of lines (length), and displaying the lines (display):

```
///////   TextLines.h    ///////
#include <iostream>
#include <vector>
#include <string>
using std::string; using std::istream; using std::vector;

class TextLines
{ public:
    TextLines(int cap=512) {  line.reserve(cap);  } //      (1)
    int length() { return line.size(); }
    void swap(int i, int j);                      // swaps lines
    void input(istream& in);                      // reads lines into host
    void remove(int i);                           // removes line i
    ~TextLines();                                 // destructor
    string* operator[](int i) const               // gets line i (2)
    {   return (i>=0 && i<line.size()) ? line[i] : NULL;
    }
    void display(ostream& out) const;
    bool insert(const string& l, int i);          // insert before line i
  private:
    int readLines(istream& in);                   // performs line reading
    vector<string*> line;                         // vector of string*
};
```

Overloading the [] operator (line 2) makes it possible to use indexing on a TextLines object. Thus, if txtobj is a TextLines object, then

```
txtobj[n];      // gives line n (a string*)
```

is a convenient way to obtain line n. The operator[] defined here checks the index and returns NULL for index out of range.

Also swap and remove are inline functions defined in the header file but outside of the class declaration.

```
inline void TextLines::swap(int i, int j)
{   string* tmp = line[i];
    line[i] = line[j];
    line[j] = tmp;
}

inline void TextLines::remove(int i)
{   delete line[i];
    line.erase(line.begin()+i);
}
```

Clearly, a TextLines object is useful whenever a program deals with lines of text from standard input or a file. This is another concrete example of building components that are reusable in many places—a significant advantage of OOP. A user of TextLines need not know how it is implemented. Access to the header file is enough. Implementation details are hidden in the TextLines.C file:

```
///////    TextLines.C     ///////
#include <iostream>
#include "TextLines.h"
using std::getline; using std::ios;
using std::cin;       using std::cout;
using std::cerr;      using std::endl;

void TextLines::input(istream& in)
{   int l = readLines(in);
    if (l > 0 ) return;
    if (l == -1)
        cerr << "TextLines: Failed to read input file" << endl;
    if ( l == 0 )
        cerr << "TextLines: Input file empty" << endl;
    in.setstate(ios::badbit);                        // input failed (A)
}
```

The member input calls the active routine readLines to read lines. The function readLines returns the number of lines read if successful. If the value returned is -1 or 0, appropriate error messages are displayed, and the badbit of the input stream is set (line A). Setting badbit causes in.bad() to return true.

The readLines function reads each line into a string using the **getline** function (line B) from the Standard Library (Section 2.5). The string is then inserted at the end of the vector to hold the lines (line D). Input failure is checked (line C), and an error code or the number of lines read is returned (line E).

```
int TextLines::readLines(istream& in)
{   int error = 0, count = 0;
    string* tl = new string();
    while( getline(in, *tl, '\n') )   //                       (B)
    {   if ( in.fail() )              // input failed          (C)
        {   error = -1; break; }
        line.push_back(tl);           //                       (D)
        count++;
        tl = new string();
    }
```

4.7 SORTING TEXT LINES WITH OBJECTS

```
        return(error ? error : count);      // lines read or err (E)
}
```

Inserting a line before line i is performed by calling vector::insert. The line is inserted at the end if i is just beyond the last line.

```
bool TextLines::insert(const string& l, int i)
{   if ( 0 <= i && i < line.size() )
        line.insert(line.begin()+i, new string(l));
    else if ( i == line.size() )
        line.push_back(new string(l));
    else return false;
    return true;
}
```

A simple loop displays all lines contained in a TextLines object. The destructor frees up dynamically allocated storage.

```
void TextLines::display(ostream& out) const
{   for ( int i = 0; i < line.size(); i++ )
        out << *line[i] << endl;
}

TextLines::~TextLines()
{   int len = line.size();
    while(len-- > 0) delete line[len];
}
```

mysort: Comparing Keys

Line sorting has two aspects: quicksort and key comparison. A SortKey object supplies the capability to identify and compare specific key positions.

When initialized, a SortKey object holds the key position and the delimiter string, quantities used by the private member function key to identify the sort key in a text line (string). An established SortKey object is used to compare two text lines.

Letting the user of **mysort** specify the key field and implementing a separate key-comparison object provide the kind of flexibility that characterizes good programs. On top of this, the field delimiters are also settable rather than hard-coded. Other useful delimiters include =, :, ., and ,.

```
///////    SortKey.h    ///////
#include <string>
using std::string;

class SortKey
```

```cpp
{ public:
    explicit SortKey(int pos = 0, const char* dlm = "\n\t \r")
    { delim = dlm;
      position = pos;
    }
    void setDelim(const char* s) { delim = s; }
// compare lines
    int lineCompare(const string& a, const string& b) const;
    int keyCompare(const string& k, const string& l) const
    { return k.compare(key(l)); }
  private:
    string delim;              // token delimiters
    int position;              // key token position
// extract key
    const string key(const string& s) const;
};
```

Care has been taken in using reference parameters and in declaring them const appropriately. You should do the same in your C++ programs.

The function key extracts the sort keys with member functions of string:

str1.**find_first_of**(*str2, i*);
str1.**find_first_not_of**(*str2, i*);

Examining *str1* from position *i*, the index of the first character that is (is not) contained in *str2* is returned. If no such character is found in *str1*, the constant string::npos is returned. The argument *str2* can be given either as a string object or a C-style string.

The functions are put to good use skipping field positions (line F) to extract the desired key (line G). An empty string object is returned if the line s does not contain the key field indicated by position.

```cpp
///////    SortKey.C    ///////
#include <iostream>
#include <string>
#include "SortKey.h"

const string SortKey::key
      (const string& s) const
{   int i = position;                         // key token position
    if ( i == 0 ) return s;                   // whole line as key
    int i0=0, i1=0;                           // start and end indices
    while ( i-- > 0 )                         // skipping        (F)
    {  if ( i1 == string::npos )
          return string();                    // key not found
       i0 = s.find_first_not_of(delim, i1);
       if ( i0 == string::npos )
```

4.7 SORTING TEXT LINES WITH OBJECTS

```
        return string();                        // key not found
        i1 = s.find_first_of(delim, i0);
    }
    if ( i1 == string::npos )
        i1 = s.length();                        // length of s
    return string(s, i0, i1-i0);                // key found         (G)
}
```

The `lineCompare` member function compares two text lines. Basically, `lineCompare` compares the two whole lines or, if a key position is given, compares the two key fields:

```
int SortKey::lineCompare
(const string& a, const string& b) const
{   if (position == 0) return a.compare(b);
    return key(a).compare(key(b));
}
```

The member function `compare` of `string` is handy here.

The function `lineCompare` returns positive, zero, or negative for line a greater than, equal to, or less than line b, respectively. This is consistent with the C/C++ convention and is what the `partition` routine of `quicksort` expects.

mysort: Ordering the Lines

The objective of this part of the program is to take the text lines in `txtobj` and sort them into order by comparing the appropriate keys.

The approach is to adapt the `quicksort` procedure used for integer arrays (Section 3.4) to the `TextLines` object `txtobj`. The recursive function `quicksort` itself is mostly the same as before. However, now `txtobj.swap` interchanges lines. Furthermore, the `partition` function uses `lineCompare` of the given `SortKey` to compare two lines using the user-specified keys:

```
///////     mysort.C     ///////
#include "TextLines.h"
#include "SortKey.h"

int partition(TextLines& txtobj, int l, int r,
              const SortKey& sk)
{   register int i=l, j=r;
    string piv;
// middle element as pivot
    txtobj.swap((i+j)/2,j);
    piv = *txtobj[j];                           // line j of txtobj
    while (i < j)
    {   while (sk.lineCompare(*txtobj[i], piv)  // compare sort keys
            <= 0 && i < j)   i++;
```

```
        while(j > i && sk.lineCompare(*txtobj[j], piv) >= 0)
              j--;
        if (i < j) txtobj.swap(i++,j);
     }
     if (i != r) txtobj.swap(i,r);
     return i;
}

void quicksort(TextLines& txtobj, int l, int r, const SortKey& sk)
{    int k;
     if ( l >= r || l < 0 || r < 0)  return;
     k = partition (txtobj, l, r, sk);
     quicksort(txtobj, l, k-1, sk);
     quicksort(txtobj, k+1, r, sk);
}
```

Making txtobj a reference formal parameter is critical to these sorting routines. The basic logic of quicksort and partition stays the same. The SortKey sk is instantiated by the main program:

```
#include <iostream>
using std::endl; using std::cout; using std::cerr;

int main(int argc, char* argv[])
{    if (argc > 2)
        { cerr << "Usage: " << argv[0] << " key_position" << endl;
          return 1;
        }
     SortKey sk;
     if (argc == 2) sk = SortKey(atoi(argv[1]));
     TextLines txtobj;
     txtobj.input(cin);
     if ( cin.bad() )                                              // (H)
        { cerr << "failed reading input." << endl;
          return 1;
        }
     quicksort(txtobj,0,txtobj.length()-1, sk);
     txtobj.display(cout);
     return 0;
}
```

The library function **atoi** converts a numeric string to an integer. The test on line H checks the condition set on line A in function TextLines::input.

All of the parts are now in place. The main program processes command-line arguments and sets up the SortKey object. The program then gets a TextLines object txtobj, reads input lines into it, applies quicksort passing to it sk to make comparisons, and then asks txtobj to display itself. The simple and clear structure of the main program testifies to the advantages of the OOP approach.

Compile the binary files `TextLines.o` and `SortKey.o` first and then simply combine `mysort.o` with them to get **mysort**. For example,

g++ mysort.o SortKey.o TextLines.o -o mysort

gets you the executable file `mysort`. Run it with

mysort 2 < somefile

to see `somefile` sorted by key field 2.

The examples in this section and Section 4.5 (found in `ex04/` of the code package) not only show array, pointer, `vector`, and `string` usage but also demonstrate how to identify interacting objects that can be programmed independently. Object orientation not only makes programs easier to write but, more important, also makes the components useful in many other situations.

4.8 POINTERS AND FUNCTION CALLS

Let's now turn our attention to the usage of pointers and arrays in function calls. All aspects of pointer usage related specifically to function calls are collected in this section for easy reference.

Passing Pointer Arguments

When a pointer is passed by value in a function call, a memory address is passed. In most cases, the address is the location of a variable, an array entry, or an object. If `x` is a variable, `ptr` a pointer variable, `arr` an array, `arr2` a two-dimensional array, and `obj` a class object, then the expressions in Table 4.2 are all valid forms of pointers.

To specify a simple pointer formal parameter `y` in a function header, the two forms

type *y   and   *type* y[]

are equivalent, and both are commonly used. The second notation implies that `y` is a pointer to the beginning of an array. Extending the equivalence, the forms

type **y   and   *type* *y[]

are again the same in function headers. Therefore, the command-line argument

char *argv[]

can, in a function header, also be written as

char **argv

Table 4.2 FORMS OF POINTERS

&x	Address of x
&obj	Address of class object
ptr	Value of pointer variable ptr
ptr++	Value of pointer variable ptr
arr or &arr[0]	Value of constant array name arr
arr + 2 or &arr[2]	Address of third entry of array arr
&arr2[0][0] or arr2[0]	Address of first entry of two-dimensional array arr2
&arr2[i][0] or arr2[i]	Address of first entry of row $i + 1$ in two-dimensional array arr2

When a pointer is passed to a function, the called function knows the type and the starting location of a piece of data but not necessarily where it ends. For example, the formal parameter int *y can be used to receive the address of a single integer or an array of integers. Clearly, some other arrangement must be made. Using a special terminator is a convenient way to define the extent of a data item. The conventional terminator '\0' for C-style character strings is a good example. Independent of whether there is a terminator, it is always possible to use another integer parameter to pass the size information into a called function, as in istream::**read** of the I/O stream library (Section 6.7).

There are two possible purposes for passing a pointer into a function:

1. To give the called function access to data without making a copy.
2. To have the called function initialize or modify the data.

The data in question may be global, local to the calling function, or allocated in the scope of some function in the chain of function calls. More details on these two modes of usage are discussed next.

Read-Only and Return Parameters

A data item passed by pointer or reference is *read-only* if it is not modified by the called function. The parameter of **strlen** is a typical example of a read-only pointer. Counting the number of characters does not modify a string. The const modifier (Section 3.9) should be used for such a formal parameter, allowing the compiler to detect any unintended attempt to modify the data. The treatment of such a violation is implementation dependent, but a warning is usually generated. Furthermore, in making a function call, it is critical to know whether an object passed by pointer will be modified or not. Used consistently, the presence or absence of `const` in a function prototype can convey this important information.

One reason for a function to modify an object passed by pointer or reference is to transmit results computed back to the calling function. Many library functions depend on this feature; **getline** is an obvious one. A parameter used to transmit computed results back to the calling function is known as a *return parameter*. The matrix multiplication routine `Matrix::times` (Section 4.4) uses just such a return parameter for the product matrix. When a function is called with a return parameter, it is the calling function's responsibility to allocate enough space of the correct type to accommodate the returned value.

Functions Returning Pointers

Just like the operator `new`, a function can also produce a pointer as a return value. However, be careful when you define a function that returns a pointer. The returned pointer must not point to a local variable in the scope of the returning function. An automatic variable in a function is destroyed after the function returns. Certainly, it does not make sense to return a pointer to something that disappears. For example, it is incorrect to use

```
int *bad(int x)
{   int y;
    y = x * x;
    return &y;      // wrong
}
```

This function produces no syntax error when compiled and will actually execute. Unfortunately, when the returned pointer is used, it may be pointing to a memory cell that has been destroyed (used for other purposes). A pointer that has lost its object in memory is referred to as a *dangling pointer* and should be avoided.

When a function returns a pointer, make sure that it points to one of the following:

- Memory cells supplied by the calling function.
- External data.
- Static data in the function.
- Dynamically allocated space.

The function `Poly::operator+()` (Section 4.5) is an example where a pointer to memory allocated by `new` is returned. When such a pointer is returned, there is the danger of the allocated space not being freed properly later.

A class destructor (Section 5.7) can often help in this regard. In other cases, clear documentation of the dynamic nature of the returned pointer must be provided to callers of the function.

4.9 ARRAYS, POINTERS, AND REFERENCES

A C++ reference is not a basic data type but an alias for a variable or a class object. In many situations where a pointer formal parameter is needed, a reference parameter can be used instead. Certainly, passing an argument by reference involves no copying, and changes made to a reference modify the original. When passing a reference argument, make sure it is an lvalue. A reference parameter is sometimes simpler to use than a pointer because there is no need for any indirection notations such as *ptr or ptr->member.

When passing arrays, it is advisable to pass pointers rather than references. An array name, not being an lvalue, actually cannot be passed to a reference parameter or used to initialize a reference variable. A pointer variable should be used instead. Thus,

```
void f(int* &ptr_ref);
int arr[] = {1,2,3,4};
f( arr );              // error; arr is a constant pointer
int* ap = arr;         // pointer variable ap
f( ap );               // o.k.
```

A function can also return a reference (Section 3.8). A local variable in the returning function is a bad choice as a reference return value. The variable is destroyed after the function returns. In addition, there can be neither pointers to references nor arrays of references.

4.10 MULTIPLE INDIRECTION

A variable x may be used to access a memory cell *directly* (Figure 4.7). The value of x is stored in its associated data cell. As stated before, however, the cell of a pointer variable ptr stores the address of another data cell whose content can be accessed *indirectly* through the value of ptr using the value-of operator *. The quantity *ptr can be treated just like a variable and can be used on the left-hand side of an assignment.

A pointer provides one level of indirection. It is possible to have *double indirection* if the value of *ptr is also a pointer. Referring again to Figure 4.7, the value of ptra is the pointer variable *ptra, and the value of *ptra is an int variable **ptra, which has the value 15.

4.10 MULTIPLE INDIRECTION

Figure 4.7 MULTIPLE INDIRECTION

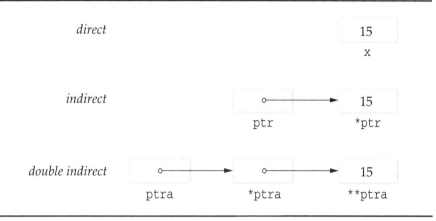

The declaration

```
int *ptr;
```

declares the variable ptr to be of type int *, not *prt of type int as some programmers may mistakenly suppose. Similarly, the declarations

```
char **c;
char ***d;
```

give c type char ** and d type char ***, respectively. A handy example of the type char ** is the array char *argv[] for command-line arguments. Thus,

```
c = argv;
```

is possible. In fact, we have already used a few variables of type char **, including the lines in the sorting example (Section 4.7).

To understand the meaning of d, think of it as the address of an array of different groups of text lines:

```
d[0]  is  line_group1
d[1]  is  line_group2
d[2]  is  line_group3
       ⋮
```

Multiple indirection tends to be confusing and error-prone. The situation can be helped by the appropriate application of typedef. Consider

```
typedef char *C_string;
typedef C_string *Lines;
typedef Lines *Groups_of_lines;
```

Now the variable d can be declared as

```
Groups_of_lines d;
```

making it much easier to deal with: The type of *d is Lines, the type of **d is C_string, and the type of ***d is char. (Section 4.13 contains an example that uses multiple indirection.)

By the way, typedef not only helps to decipher multiple indirections but also to simplify other complicated constructs, as we will see shortly. A class may have its own typedefs as part of the class declaration.

4.11 GENERIC PROGRAMS

Normally, functions are written to work on arguments of specific types. Thus, even if there is already a quicksort for an array of integers, there is still nothing to sort character strings, doubles, or fractions. However, with a combination of techniques, it is possible in C++ to write a type-independent, or *generic*, function that works for a multitude of different types of arguments.

Our discussions here ultimately lead to an implementation of quicksort that sorts arbitrary data in any caller-specified ordering. To achieve this goal, three distinct but related topics must be presented:

1. Pointers to functions.
2. Formal functional parameters.
3. The type void *.

These same mechanisms also help define generic classes (Section 5.12) where arbitrary types can be treated by objects of the class. Genericness makes programs widely applicable and reusable. C++ also offers a *template* mechanism (Chapter 10) that can be very useful when writing generic programs. For example, vectors of different types can be created with the simple template notation vector<*type*>.

Functional Variables and Arguments

Ordinarily, we think of the values of a variable or formal parameter as some kind of data or objects. A whole new dimension opens up when the values can be functions. Functions can be passed as arguments in a call, and the called function can apply the passed function in conjunction with its own preprogrammed procedures. An argument that is a function is known as a *functional argument*. Furthermore, an object can contain variables that are set to names of functions at (or after) initialization time.

4.11　GENERIC PROGRAMS

The flexibility provided by functional variables/arguments is tremendous. Imagine, now you can write a function that follows different procedures for different invocations. In other words, with functional arguments, a function not only works with different input data but also utilizes different incoming functions. Just consider how much more a sort program can do if it is supplied with the appropriate comparison function each time it is called.

Because the functional variable/argument is an extraordinary feature, not all languages support it. Fortunately, this feature is available in C++, and functional variables/arguments take the form of *pointers to functions*. Let's take a close look at how to use functional arguments, how they work, and what can be achieved with them.

Pointers to Functions

Once a function is defined, the function name preceded by the & operator is a pointer to the function—namely, the address where the function's definition begins in memory. A function pointer, just like any other pointer, can be assigned to pointer variables of the right type and also passed as an argument in a function call.

For example, given a function average defined as

```
int average(int x, int y)
{    return (x+y)/2;   }
```

we can write the following piece of code:

```
int (* fn)(int, int);       // declare function pointer variable fn
fn = &average;              // function variable assignment
int var = (* fn)(14,26);    // function call through pointer
var = fn(14,26);            // shorthand call through pointer
```

First, the functional variable fn is declared to be a pointer to any function that takes two int arguments and returns an int value. (The general syntax for functional variable declaration will be given presently.) Second, fn is assigned the address of the function average. Then, (* fn), or simply fn, can be used as a function name in making a call to average.

To produce a function pointer, the & in front of the function name can also be omitted. Thus,

```
fn = average;               // same as fn = &average
```

is fine, too. This notation is simpler and is used from now on. In case average is an overloaded function, a pointer to the correct version will be produced by deducing it from the signature used in declaring fn.

Declaring a functional variable may look complicated, but it is really simple. Just use the function prototype with the function name replaced by the notation (* var). Specifically, the general form

value_type (* *var*) (*args*);

declares the variable *var* to be a pointer to a function that takes the specified arguments and returns values of the given type.

A functional variable declaration looks strange because it deviates from the normal syntax of variable declarations. What confuses people is the position of the declared variable relative to the other parts in such a declaration. It may take a little getting used to, but the position is perfectly well defined: The variable is put *where the function name would be* in a function prototype. The examples in Figure 4.8 should help as well. More generally, complicated C++ declarations can be deciphered by realizing that *a declaration always spells out how the declared variable is used.* For example, the first declaration in Figure 4.8 shows that (*fn_a) (3.5, 6.7) is a function call that returns a float.

Since a functional variable declaration is somewhat long and complicated to look at, we can simplify things greatly by using typedef. For instance,

```
typedef int (* INT_FN)(int, int);
```

defines the type name INT_FN. Note that the type name is placed where the variable would be. INT_FN can then be used to declare any functional variable of that type. In particular, we can declare fn in the average example with

```
INT_FN fn;               // alternative declaration for fn
```

Figure 4.8 DECLARING FUNCTION POINTERS

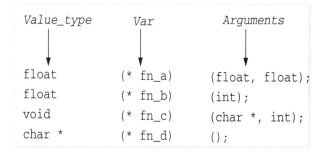

4.11 GENERIC PROGRAMS

Formal Functional Parameters   The purpose of a function variable, almost exclusively, is to pass a function name to another function or class object. To make things easy to understand, let's examine an artificial example:

```
int mystery(int a, int b, int (* fn)(int, int))
{    return fn(a,b);
}
```

Here the function mystery takes three arguments: two integers and a functional parameter fn. The declaration of the formal parameter fn is, as it should be, the same as declaring a variable of the intended type. By using the typedef INT_FN, we can code a simpler looking version of mystery:

```
int mystery(int a, int b, INT_FN fn)
{    return   fn(a,b);
}
```

The function mystery simply calls the function pointed to by fn and returns the value of the call. Here are some functions, in addition to average, that can be passed to mystery:

```
extern int gcd(int a, int b);
```
(The gcd function is defined in Section 3.4.)

```
int sqsum(int x, int y)
{    return (x * x + y * y);
}
```

Here is how to make calls to mystery. Note that the names average, gcd, and sqsum are pointers to the definitions of the functions:

```
int main()
{    cout << mystery(16, 30, average) << endl;    // is 23
     cout << mystery(3, 4, sqsum) << endl;        // is 25
     cout << mystery(312, 253, gcd) << endl;      // is  1
     return 0;
}
```

In fact, any function that takes two int arguments and returns an int can be passed to mystery.

The one topic that remains on our discussion list is the void * pointer, a mechanism to pass data or objects of arbitrary type and a necessary complement to the functional argument facility.

Genericness and void *

To write a function that applies the same algorithm in a variety of situations, we need the functional argument mechanism described earlier. But in most cases, we also need the ability to receive *data of arbitrary, or unspecified, types*. The ability of a function or class to work on different data types is known as *genericness*, and programs exhibiting such a capacity are *generic*.

Let's begin with a simple example of determining the length of an arbitrary array. The strategy is to write a function that takes the following two arguments:

1. An arbitrary array.
2. A test function for the end of the array.

The function arblen computes the length of the array any without knowing anything about its type. Thus, arblen is a generic array-length function. The functional parameter isEnd is the supplied function that detects the termination of the given array. What arblen does is simply call isEnd repeatedly and count the number of calls. The count is then returned when isEnd detects the end of the array:

```
typedef bool (* END_FN) (void *any, int index);

int arblen(void *any, END_FN isEnd)
{     int len=0;
      while ( ! isEnd(any, len) ) len++;
      return len;
}
```

A variable or formal parameter of type void * (pointer to unknown type) can receive a pointer of any type. This provides a way of passing data of arbitrary type into a function. Because the data type is unknown, there are very few allowable operations on a void * variable other than referencing (using the pointer value) and passing it to another function. In particular, indexing, value-of (*), increment, decrement, and other address arithmetic operations are illegal or unsafe on a void * variable. Even so, the void * type is critical to processing arbitrary data, as seen in the function arblen.

To test arblen, we define two terminator detecting functions, int_end and str_end, for nonnegative integer and character arrays, respectively:

```
bool int_end(int *a, int i)
{     return a[i] == -1;       // true or false
}

bool str_end(char *a, int i)
{     return a[i] == '\0';
}
```

4.11 GENERIC PROGRAMS

Now, for testing, we use the following `main` function:

```
int main()
{   char a[]="abcdefg";
    int b[]={0,1,2,3,4,-1};
    int i = arblen(a, reinterpret_cast< END_FN >(str_end) );
                                                          // length 7
    cout << "length of string = " << i << endl;
    i = arblen(b, reinterpret_cast< END_FN >(int_end) ); // length 5
    cout << "length of int array = " << i << endl;
    return 0;
}
```

Note that explicit type-casting, `reinterpret_cast< END_FN >(str_end)`, is used on the function pointers to make the argument match the declared formal parameter `isEnd` of `arblen`. This also allows passing the `void *` argument to `str_end`.

Since `void *` is so useful, a good question is, Can we also make use of `void &`, an arbitrary reference? Unfortunately, C++ does not permit `void &`.

The preliminaries are now finished. We are ready for some practical applications culminating in the implementation of a generic `quicksort`.

Sample Generic Functions

Let's consider how `void *` and functional arguments combine to define generic functions. Our first example is a function that checks to see whether all entries of an array satisfy some given condition. Questions such as

- Is every entry an even/odd number?
- Is every entry positive?
- Is every entry zero?
- Is every character lowercase?

are often asked. We can write one generic function, `and_test`, that takes care of them all. The *and* in the name expresses the concept of *logical-and*: All tests must be true before the answer is true:

```
typedef bool (* BOOLEAN_FN) (void *any, int index);

bool and_test(void *any, BOOLEAN_FN test, END_FN isEnd)
{     int len=0;
      while ( ! isEnd(any, len) )
      {    if ( test(any, len) == 0 ) return false;
           len++;
      }
```

```
            return true;
}
```

The type name BOOLEAN_FN also documents the fact that functions of this type must be *Boolean,* or one that returns a true or false value. The arbitrary Boolean test is applied to each array entry successively until the end is found by the supplied terminator detector isEnd. The first failed test causes and_test to return false. The value true is returned after the array is exhausted. Candidate functions to pass to the parameter test are

```
bool even(int *ip, int j) {   return (ip[j] & 01)==0;}
bool odd(int *ip, int j) {   return (ip[j] & 01)==1;}
bool clower(char *cp, int j) {   return islower(cp[j]); }
```

The function or_test is similar but is designed to answer questions such as:

- Is there an even/odd entry?
- Is there a negative entry?
- Is there a zero entry?
- Is there an uppercase character?

Again, the or indicates the *logical-or* concept: If at least one test is true, the answer is true:

```
bool or_test(void *any, BOOLEAN_FN test, END_FN isEnd)
{     int len=0;
      while ( ! isEnd(any,len) )
      {    if ( test(any, len) ) return true;
           len++;
      }
      return false;
}
```

4.12 A GENERIC SORTING PROGRAM

Our next example further illustrates the flexibility that functional arguments provide. Let's write a sorting program that can rearrange a sequence of items *of any type* into *any specified order,* thus making the sorting program generic and very reusable. The strategy is to modify the quicksort program to use the following three arguments:

1. An arbitrary array.
2. A caller-specified comparison function cmp.
3. A supplied element-interchange function swap.

4.12 A GENERIC SORTING PROGRAM

With the header file

```
///////    arbqsort.h    ///////

typedef int (* CMP_FN) (void *, int, int);
typedef void (* SWAP_FN) (void *, int, int);
extern void quicksort
        (void *any,     // arbitrary array to be sorted
         int l,         // start index
         int r,         // end index
         CMP_FN cmp,    // supplied comparison function
         SWAP_FN swap   // supplied interchange function
        );
```

the quicksort function is revised as follows:

```
///////    arbqsort.C    ///////
#include  "arbqsort.h"

void quicksort(void *any, int l, int r, CMP_FN cmp, SWAP_FN swap)
{   if ( l >= r || l < 0 ) return;
  // call with supplied functions
     int k = partition(any, l, r, cmp, swap);
  // recursive calls
     quicksort(any, l, k-1, cmp, swap);
     quicksort(any, k+1, r, cmp, swap);
}
```

The partition function, which is placed before quicksort in the actual file, now becomes

```
static
int partition(void *any, int l, int r, CMP_FN cmp, SWAP_FN swap)
{   register int i=l, j=r;
  // choose middle element as pe
     swap(any,(i+j)/2, r);                              // pe moved to r
     while (i < j)
     {   while (cmp(any, i, r) <= 0 && i < j) i++;  // use supplied cmp
         while(j > i && cmp(any, j, r) >= 0) j--;   // use supplied cmp
         if (i < j) swap(any,i++,j);                // use supplied swap
     }
     if (i != r) swap(any,i,r);                         // use supplied swap
     return i;
}
```

Note that indexing of any is not possible in partition because of its type
void *. But once its value is passed to the function cmp or swap, the formal
pointer parameter there can be used normally.

With these modifications, the generic quicksort can sort arbitrary arrays
when given appropriately supplied comparison and swap functions. To sort
integer arrays, the following set of functions can be defined:

```
int cmp_bigger(int x[], int i, int j) {  return x[i] - x[j]; }

int cmp_smaller(int x[], int i, int j) {  return x[j] - x[i]; }

void intswitch(int a[], int i, int j)
{   int s = a[i]; a[i] = a[j]; a[j] = s; }
```

The two different comparison functions cmp_bigger and cmp_smaller conform
to the type CMP_FN, and intswitch matches the type SWAP_FN. Now sorting can
be done with

```
int a[] = {5,3,-1, 9 , 22, 99};


// in increasing order
quicksort(a, 0, 5, reinterpret_cast< CMP_FN >(cmp_bigger),
                   reinterpret_cast< SWAP_FN >(intswitch));

// in decreasing order
quicksort(a, 0, 5, reinterpret_cast< CMP_FN >(cmp_smaller),
                   reinterpret_cast< SWAP_FN >(intswitch));
```

It is also a simple matter to convert the text-line sorting program in Section 4.7 to use the generic quicksort. For this purpose, the following functions
are needed:

```
int keycmp(TextLines *tl, int i, int j)
{    extern SortKey sortkey;
     TextLines& txtobj= *tl;
     return( sortkey.lineCompare(*txtobj[i], *txtobj[j]) );
}

void lineswap(TextLines *tl, int i, int j)
{    tl->swap(i,j);
}
```

Again, the two functions are written to match the types `CMP_FN` and `SWAP_FN`, information available from the `arbqsort.h` header file. With these functions, just use

```
quicksort(&txtobj, 0, txtobj.length()-1,
                reinterpret_cast< CMP_FN >(keycmp),
                reinterpret_cast< SWAP_FN >(lineswap));
```

to sort the `TextLines` object `txtobj`. Note that here we are sorting *text lines encapsulated in an object* with the same generic `quicksort` function, which drives home the point of handling data of arbitrary type.

The **qsort** library function (`<stdlib.h>`) implements quicksort for an arbitrary array with elements stored in consecutive memory locations. The `quicksort` defined in this section does not make assumptions on how the elements to be sorted are stored. Clearly, the basic sorting mechanism is in place and will remain unchanged. The header `arbqsort.h` provides the interface to client files of the generalized sorting facility. The application of this mechanism in a new area is simply a matter of providing the appropriate comparison and swap functions.

Standard C++ supplies a set of predefined generic functions (include `<algorithm>`) that can be used with generic container classes. The generic functions take functional arguments to perform tasks. The header `<functional>` supplies a variety of functions ready to use in such applications. These topics are covered in Chapter 11.

4.13 POINTERS AND DYNAMICALLY ALLOCATED STORAGE

We have already seen some uses of the operator `new` for dynamic storage allocation. In this section, let's consider how dynamic storage is applied in relation to arrays and pointers.

Allocating Two-Dimensional Arrays

Static allocation of two-dimensional arrays is very simple to code. But the syntax for dynamic allocation does not allow direct two-dimensional notations. Thus, codes such as

```
double** arr = new double[m][n];        // syntax error
```

are not possible. However, enough consecutive cells from free storage can accommodate all elements of a two-dimensional array and can be fabricated into the desired array structure.

The function `dyn_2d` returns a `double**` that can be used as a two-dimensional `double` array:

```
double** dyn_2d(int m, int n)
{   double* arr = new double[m*n];    // allocate data cells
    double** a = new double*[m];      // allocate pointer cells
    for ( int i=0 ; i < m ; i++ )     // initialize
    {   a[i] = arr + i*n;             // init m row pointers
        for (int j=0 ; j < n ; j++ )  // init array cells
            a[i][j] = 0.0;            // use as two-dimensional array
    }
    return a;
}
```

Enough storage for all consecutive data cells is allocated. In addition, storage for pointer cells for each row is allocated. The array and pointer cells are then initialized before the array name is returned. An overloaded version can also take care of freeing the storage properly:

```
void dyn_2d(double** a)
{   delete [] *a;      // free data cells
    delete [] a;       // free pointer cells
}
```

Dynamic Arrays of Pointers

Let's consider the representation of days in a month. One way to do this is to use short integers for the individual dates, an array of dates for each week, and an array of pointers to the individual weeks as a structure for the month. With a few `typedef`s, we can define a class `Month` to create any monthly calendar:

```
///////    Month.h    ///////
#include <iostream>
using std::ostream;

class Month
{ public:
    typedef short Date;
    typedef Date *Week;    // Week is short *
    enum Day {SUN=0, MON, TUE, WED, THU, FRI, SAT};
    Month(Date ndays, enum Day firstday);
    void display(ostream& out) const;
    ~Month();
  private:
    Week *month;           // internal representation
};
```

4.13 POINTERS AND DYNAMICALLY ALLOCATED STORAGE

The constructor initializes a month object when given the number of days in the month (ndays) and the day of the week for the first day of the month:

```
Month::Month(Date ndays, enum Day firstday)
{    Week w[7], wk;        // maximum 6 weeks
     short i=0;
     Day day;
     wk = w[i] = new Date[7];                                    // (1)
     for (day=SUN ; day < firstday ; day=static_cast< Day >(day+1))
                                                                 // (2)
     {    *wk++ = 0;    }
     for (Date d = 1 ; d <= ndays ; d++)                         // (3)
     {    *wk++ = d;
          if (day == SAT)
          {    wk = w[++i] = new(Date[7]); day=SUN; }            // (4)
          else day = Day(day+1);
     }
     while ( day != SUN )
     {    *wk++ = 0;day = Day( (day+1)%7 ); }                    // (5)
     month = new(Week[i+2]);                                     // (6)
     for (short j=0; j <= i; j++)
          month[j] = w[j];
     month[i+1] = NULL;        // NULL ptr terminator
}
```

For each week, seven Dates are allocated (lines 1 and 4) to record the days of the week where pointers returned by new are automatically cast to type Week (short *). Days unused in the first and last week are assigned zero (lines 2 and 5). The dates are filled in by the for loop (line 3). Note that arithmetic results involving enum variables are cast properly (lines 2 and 5).

The automatic array w records the weeks created. A dynamic array month is allocated (line 6), and the entries of w are copied into the data member month. Note that month is terminated by a NULL pointer. Figure 4.9 illustrates the organization of month.

To establish a Month object, use something like

```
Month m(31, Month::TUE);
```

Here the class scope notation is used to specify an enum constant defined in the Month class. (In Section 6.7, displaying a monthly calendar is again considered.)

Figure 4.9 THE ORGANIZATION OF Month WITH POINTERS

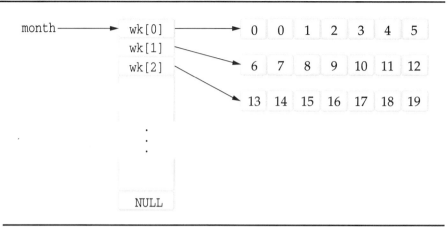

4.14 SUMMARY

The array and the pointer are closely related constructs that help store and manipulate data of any given type. Their mastery is essential for the low-level coding that is required of you. Such details should be encapsulated by objects when possible so that other parts of the program can ignore them.

An array stores elements of the same type in consecutive memory locations. The array name is a constant pointer to the first array cell. A two-dimensional array is actually a one-dimensional array whose elements are pointers to one-dimensional arrays of the same length. This scheme can be generalized into arrays of higher dimensions. Arrays allocated at compile time have fixed maximum dimensions. Arrays whose dimensions are known only at run time can be allocated dynamically.

The vector template supplies an attractive alternative to basic arrays. A vector is not limited to a fixed size and can be subscripted just like arrays. Besides, vector offers many useful operations such as **size**(), **insert**(), **erase**(), **push_back**(), and **pop_back**().

A pointer provides the ability to manipulate addresses and supplies a level of indirection to data or function access. The unary address-of operator & can be applied to any memory-based variable, class object, or array element to obtain a pointer. The unary value-of operator * is applied to a pointer, ptr, to access the value stored at that memory address. Furthermore, the notation *ptr can be used on the left-hand side of an assignment to store a new value at that location. Hence, the combination *ptr can be thought of and used as a variable of the appropriate type. Both pointer arithmetic and indexing are convenient to step through the cells of an array.

The TextLines class is a substantial OO programming example that uses a vector of pointers to represent a sequence of text lines internally. The class supplies access, interchange, input, and output functions for text lines, hiding the implementation details. The associated SortKey class helps locate and compare keys in text lines. The program **mysort** uses these objects and quicksort to sort text lines using user-specified keys.

A generic program is one that works for many different types of data items. The function pointer, functional arguments, the void * type, and implicit/explicit type-casting combine to provide one way to write generic programs. With these constructs, a generic quicksort is written to sort arbitrary data items or objects using any supplied comparison function. The generic quicksort is shown reused for integer and text-line sorting.

EXERCISES

1. Given the following declaration,

   int a[]={1,2,3,4,5};

   what are the values of the expressions (a) a - &a[3], (b) *(a+4), and (c) *(a+5)?

2. Explain the meaning of each of the following declarations:
   (a) char a[];
   (b) char *b;
   (c) char c[5]="";
   (d) int d[]={0,1,2};
   (e) int *e=d+1;
   (f) int f[20]={0,0,0,0};
   (g) char *g[];
   (h) char *g[]={a,b,c};
   (i) char **a;
   (j) char **a = &b;
   (k) typedef int (* C_FN)(char *, const char *);

3. Write a program to test the use of negative indices for arrays/pointers.

4. Rewrite the circular buffer class given in Section 3.12 with pointers and pointer arithmetic instead of indexing.

5. Consider the SortKey class. In practice, there is a need for a composite key, a key consisting of a primary key, a secondary key, and so on. When two items are compared under a composite key, the primary key is applied first. The secondary key is applied only if the two items are equal under the primary key and so on. Define a CompsitKey class, and use it in a sorting program that allows multiple sort keys. (*Hint*: A CompositeKey contains several SortKeys.)

6. Does the C++ compiler on your computer allow you to increment a void * pointer? If it does, give a good reason why you should not use it.

7. Is it possible to pass a void * actual argument to, say, an int * formal parameter in a function call? If this is not possible, can you specify *two* distinct ways to make such a call by explicit casting? Show your solution with actual working-code examples. (*Hint:* Cast the argument or the function.)

8. Consider references to pointers. Is there anything wrong with the following code? Why? If there is a problem, how do you fix it?

```
int a = 56;
int*& ptr_ref = &a;
```

9. Discuss the correctness and meaning of the following:

```
int i;
int & j = i;
int&* ptr1 = &j;
int* ptr2 = &j;
```

10. Modify the quicksort routine to remove duplicate entries in the input array. The routine should return the length of the final sorted array, which may be shorter than the given array before sorting. (*Hint*: partition should record positions of duplicate entries.)

11. Consider the address-of operator &. List the type of quantities to which it cannot be applied. Also consider the value-of operator *. List the type of quantities to which it cannot be applied.

12. Discuss the differences and equivalence of the following two notations. In what situations are these notations interchangeable?

   type x[];   and   *type* *x;

13. Discuss the differences and similarities of a two-dimensional array and an array of pointers.

CHAPTER 4 EXERCISES

14. In a class, is it possible to define two instance functions whose signatures differ only in the `const` declaration for the host object? If yes, can you give an example that has some practical use?

15. If a class `Xyz` has no default constructor, can you declare an array, a `vector`, with `Xyz` cells? Why?

16. Write a test program that inserts instances of class `Abc` into an empty `vector` making it grow. Detect how many `Abc` copy and destructor calls are made as the vector grows. What happens if you reserve a number of entries for the vector before running the same experiment?

17. Consider the destructor of `TextLines`. It deletes all strings kept on `line`. Is this correct? How can the class be certain that the strings have been allocated by `new`?

18. Write a simple class `Matrix` with `double` entries. Support the following public operations: (a) to create a matrix, given dimensions `m` and `n`, and a two-dimensional array of entries; (b) to delete any rows or columns; (c) to interchange any rows or columns; and (d) to display the matrix.

19. Write a quadruple-precision integer class with arithmetic operations +, -, *, and / and then `display` it. (*Hint*: Use an array.)

20. Write a function `toEach` that takes an array of arbitrary data items and applies a supplied unary function to each value stored in the array. For example, it can be used to increment each value by 1.

21. Add a multiplication operation to the `Poly` class.

CHAPTER FIVE

Classes and Objects

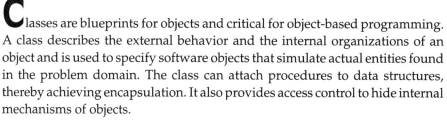

Classes are blueprints for objects and critical for object-based programming. A class describes the external behavior and the internal organizations of an object and is used to specify software objects that simulate actual entities found in the problem domain. The class can attach procedures to data structures, thereby achieving encapsulation. It also provides access control to hide internal mechanisms of objects.

Because the class is so important, we have been introduced to it informally early and have used it in many places already. It is now time for a thorough description of the C++ class so that we can see how it is used to implement software objects, learn to design an object's external interface, and acquire techniques for information hiding.

The important distinction between an *instance member* and a *class-wide member* is explained clearly. Examples show how class-wide members are useful.

Component objects can combine to form larger objects. A simulation program shows how to identify component objects and how to use them to model a pocket calculator. Study this example carefully because it forms the basis of a sequence of end-of-chapter programming exercises that eventually lead to a substantial OO program.

Furthermore, recursive classes that contain pointers to instances of the same class are described. A linked list example is given. The material leads ultimately to the definition of a generic linked list *container class* that can store arbitrary data types.

5.1 DEFINING CLASSES

The class provides a blueprint for constructing objects and is central to the OOP enterprise. In C++, a `class` is a user-defined type that has its own scope within which member data, functions, `typedef`s, `enum`s, and nested classes are encapsulated. A class must be declared or defined before it is used. The class definition has the general form

```
class Name
{
```

```
        class body
};
```

where the body contains zero or more *member declarations*:

- Data members are declared like variables, but initializers are not allowed.
- Function members are declared by function prototypes in the class body and usually defined elsewhere. Member functions completely defined in the class body are automatically declared `inline`. Normally, only very simple member functions are defined inside the class body.
- A function or data member is an *instance member* unless declared `static`, in which case it becomes a class-wide member.
- Member `typedef`s and `enum`s are declared as in other scopes.
- A member class, *nested class* (Section 8.7), is also possible.
- Except for overloaded functions, members in a class must have distinct names.

The class name is sometimes also referred to as the class *tag*. Class members have *class scope* (Section 3.1); they are generally known from the point of declaration to the end of the class, but not outside the class. Hence, members with the same name in different classes are distinct and do not conflict with one another or with names in file scope.

Once established, a class tag can be used to create *objects*, or *instances*, of the class. Thus, a class can be thought of as a blueprint to build objects. An object becomes an independent computing entity with its own memory (data members) and programming (function members). Objects belonging to the same class share the same set of function members but have their own separate data members.

Member Access Control

A class envelops its members and specifies permissions for outside access to them. Thus, *the class is the unit of information hiding and access control*. Accessibility to a class member depends on what code is making the access. If access to a member is allowed, then that member can be accessed within any instance of the class. Members may be private or public:

- *Private* members are accessible only by member functions in the same class. No other access is allowed. Private members hide data structures and internal procedures of an object.

- *Public* members are accessible from any part of the entire program. The collection of public members forms the external interface through which an object is used.

Unless otherwise designated, members in a class definition are private. We use the keywords public and private (followed by a colon) in the class body to designate the protection modes. A designation affects members following it up to the next designation or to the end of the class. The recommended class format is

```
class ClassName
{   public:
       /* public members    */

    private:
       /* private members   */
};
```

Because public members are the only ones important to a client of the class, they should be given first. The Account, Cirbuf, Fraction, Vector2D, and TextLines classes, among others, follow this format.

To further illustrate member access, let's add two more member functions to Fraction (Section 3.5):

```
Fraction Fraction::operator/ (const Fraction& y)
{   return Fraction(num * y.denom, denom * y.num); }

Fraction Fraction::operator* (const Fraction& y)
{   return Fraction(num * y.num, denom * y.denom); }
```

Obviously, these member functions can access not only the private data members num and denom in the host object but also those in another object, y, of the same class.

Class Declaration Styles

It is also possible either to declare class objects without first establishing a class name or to declare objects and the class name at the same time. For example, the two forms

```
class                              class Fraction
{                                  {
   /* class body */                   /* class body */
} obj1, obj2, obj3;                } obj1, obj2, obj3;
```

are equivalent insofar as the declaration of the objects obj1, obj2, and obj3 is concerned. The second form also defines the class name Fraction, which can be

5.2 CREATING AND INITIALIZING OBJECTS

used later to declare other Fraction objects. However, these forms, especially the first one, are not very useful in practice. The recommended style for class declaration is to

1. Define the class in a header file `ClassX.h`.
2. Put public members at the beginning of the class definition.
3. Include nonprivate inline member functions in or following the class definition in the header file.
4. Define other member functions in a separate file `ClassX.C`.

This scheme has already been applied in many examples, and it is followed throughout the book.

In C++, the keyword struct is also used to define a class. It is the same as class except for one difference: *Members in a class defined by struct are public unless designated otherwise*. We can achieve the same effect with the class keyword by beginning with public members. In practice, struct is seldom used in C++ code and is usually restricted to declaring pure data structures without function members. These two declarations are equivalent:

```
struct Name                      class Name
{    char*   last;               {   public:
     char    mid;                     char*   last;
     char*   first;                   char    mid;
};                                     char*   first;
                                 };
```

5.2 CREATING AND INITIALIZING OBJECTS

As mentioned earlier, a class definition is a blueprint for constructing objects. Thus, an object is referred to as an *instance* of a class. A class object is introduced into a program by declaring a variable whose type is the class name (e.g., Fraction r;). Such a declaration involves two separate actions to establish the desired object: *instantiation* (allocating memory) and *initialization* (assigning initial values to data members).

There is no complication with instantiation. The syntax to initialize an object, however, depends on whether the class has a *declared constructor*.

Data-Only Classes

Consider objects representing employees in a company. The simplest version is:

```
class Employee
{   public:
```

```
        enum  {SSN_LENGTH = 12, NAME_LENGTH = 32};
        char  name[NAME_LENGTH];   // full name
        char  ss[SSN_LENGTH]       // social security no.
        short age;
        float salary;
};
```

The class structures data but supplies no functions. In particular, no declared constructor is given. Another data-only class definition is:

```
class Date
{ public:
      unsigned month, day, year;
};
```

Again, there is no declared constructor. With these classes, objects and arrays of objects can be established as follows:

```
Date arrival, departure;              // Date objects
Date birthday = {11, 26, 1985};       // array-style init (1)
Date vacation = birthday;             // init by object
Date absence[12];                     // Date array
Employee representative;              // Employee object
Employee a_team[6];                   // Employees array
Employee newhire = {"John Doe",       // array-style init (2)
     "045-76-5555", 24, 38000.00};
```

Initializers given inside {} must be constants. An array of Employee objects is initialized in a similar way:

```
Employee pair[] = { { "Pat Brown",    // array-style init (3)
                      "000-11-6666"   // partial init
                    },
                    { "Diana Bell", "000-22-1234" }};
```

The *array-style initialization* (lines 1, 2, and 3) is restricted to objects without declared constructors. Furthermore, only public members can be so initialized. In practice, the array-style initializations are used only for classes without function and nonpublic members. The usual method for class initialization is through the appropriate constructors. It is also possible to initialize an object with an existing object of the same class. The initialization is performed by copying each data member. The same *memberwise copy* operation is performed when an object is assigned to another or passed by value in a function call.

The array-style initialization is tedious and rigid (requiring constant initializers). Furthermore, nonpublic members cannot be initialized because of lack of access. The class constructor mechanism replaces such initialization with a much easier approach.

Constructors

A special member function called a *constructor* facilitates object initialization. A constructor has the same name as the class and is automatically invoked after object allocation (Figure 5.1) to perform initializations. Objects of a class with a declared constructor are initialized following rules given in this section. The array-style object initialization (previous subsection) applies only to classes without declared constructors.

Adding a constructor to the class Date allows the data members to be private:

```
class Date
{ public:
      Date(unsigned m, unsigned d, unsigned y);  // constructor (1)
      Date();                                     // default constructor (2)
      void display()
      {  cout << month << '/' << day << '/' << year; }
  private:
      unsigned month, day, year;
};
```

Figure 5.1 LIFE CYCLE OF AN OBJECT

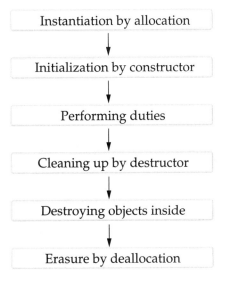

The constructor `Date::Date` is overloaded, as constructors usually are. With these constructors, `Date` objects can be established as follows:

```
Date birthday(mon, d, y);        // calls constructor with 3 args (i)
Date birthday = Date(mon, d, y); // longhand of (i)
Date appointment;                // calls default constructor (ii)
Date appointment = Date();       // longhand of (ii)
Date week[7]=
    { Date(mon1, d1, y1),        // (iii)
      Date(mon2, d2, y2)
    };                           // calls default constructor 5 times
```

The longhand forms are usually entirely the same but, depending on the compiler, may involve creating a temporary object and copying. Thus, they can be less efficient and should be avoided.

It is advisable always to define a no-args constructor, also known as the *default constructor*, for any class with declared constructors. Without the default constructor, declarations ii and iii would be impossible.

Be careful: The code

```
Date appointment();              // warning: a function prototype
```

is correct but does not establish an object. Instead, it declares `appointment` as a function returning a `Date` value.

For a class named *ClassX*, use the general form to define constructors:

```
ClassX::ClassX( args )   (constructor header)
: init-list              (optional initialization list)
{   constructor body     (assign initial values)
}
```

Unlike other functions, a constructor must be defined without a return type (not even `void`). A constructor never returns a value. Its exclusive mission is to perform initialization and to set up for a freshly allocated object. If a `return` statement is used within a constructor, it must be given no argument.

After the constructor header, an optional *init-list* preceded by a single colon (:) can be given. The init-list specifies desired initializations; the constructor body performs other setup chores if any. Code in the constructor should avoid calling member functions that may malfunction before the host is completely setup.

An init-list is a comma-separated list of member-initializers, with each *member-initializer* given in the form

member-id(*arglist*)   (a member-initializer)

5.2 CREATING AND INITIALIZING OBJECTS

For example, the `Date` constructor

```
Date::Date(unsigned m, unsigned d, unsigned y)
: month(m), day(d), year(y)              // init-list
{   /* empty body */  }
```

specifies the initialization of all three members of a `Date` object. Member initialization is performed in *declaration order* (in the class body) independent of the ordering of the member-initializers in the init-list. When initializing a member object, instance of another class, the *arglist* can supply either arguments to its constructor or an appropriate object.

The preceding `Date` constructor can also be written in the more familiar form

```
Date::Date(unsigned m, unsigned d, unsigned y)
{   month = m;  day = d;  year = y;  }     // three assignments
```

These two forms, however, are not equivalent in general. For initialization purposes, the init-list is the right choice. Strictly speaking, assignments in the constructor body are not initializations—a point made clear in the following discussion.

Initialization of `const` and Reference Members

An object may contain `const` and/or reference members. We already know unattached `const` or reference variables must be initialized when declared. In an object, however, `const` and reference members must be initialized by member-initializers in each constructor.

For example, suppose an `Account` object has a reference member `customer`:

```
class Account
{ public:

   /* public members */

  private:
    Name&    customer;          // reference member
    unsigned acct_no;           // account number
    double   acct_bal;          // current balance
    /* other private members */
};
```

The constructor must then supply an lvalue member-initializer for the reference member `customer`:

```
Account::Account(unsigned id, double amt, Name& n)
:  customer(n)                  // init reference member
{    acct_no = id;
```

```
        acct_bal = amt;
}
```

Note how the constructor also takes a reference n so that a Name object can be passed into an Account object. Be aware that using a const or reference member introduces complications for assignment of such objects (Section 7.9).

Initialization of Member Objects   The init-list is also useful when initializing a class member that is an object (class instance). Consider a class Appointment that contains a member what of type char* and a member when of type Date. The constructor

```
Appointment::Appointment(char *b, int month, int day, int year)
: what(b), when(month, day, year) { }
```

initializes when by a member-intializer

```
when(month, day, year)
```

which obtains the initial value by the call Date(month, day, year).
   As stated before, a member-initializer may supply arguments to a constructor or just give an object as initial value. Thus, another Appointment constructor is

```
Appointment::Appointment(char *b, Date dt)
: what(b), when(dt) { }
```

If the constructor does not specify the initialization of a member object, then that member object is initialized automatically by calling the object's default constructor.

Default Initializations   Data members of objects are generally initialized only through the constructor. A class member declaration must not contain an initializer.

```
class Date
{ public:
      /* ... */
   private:
      unsigned month = 1;      // illegal
      unsigned day = 1;        // illegal
      unsigned year = 2001;    // illegal
};
```

5.3 THE HOST OBJECT

Default values can be supplied to class members through the optional argument mechanism. To do this, the Date constructor can be modified as follows:

```
Date::Date(unsigned m = 1, unsigned d = 1, unsigned y = 2001)
: month(m), day(d), year(y)
{   /* empty body */  }
```

Because this definition can take from zero to three arguments, the old default constructor is no longer necessary and must now be removed. As a result, the simple object declaration Date tmp; is the same as Date tmp(1, 1, 2001);.

Default Constructors If a class declares no constructors, a default constructor, which takes no arguments and does nothing, is supplied by the compiler. Obviously, not every class can work with just this kind of default constructor. If any constructor is declared for a class, then no default constructor is automatically supplied. If the latter is needed, which is usual, it must be programmed in the class.

In summary, allocation and initialization are two distinct phases in object instantiation. Objects of classes with no constructors or nonpublic members are established in ways similar to built-in types. Constructors help automate object initialization and can perform other operations at initialization time. Objects of classes with declared constructors are initialized only through constructors. A default constructor should accompany other constructors to make declaring objects and object arrays possible.

5.3 THE HOST OBJECT

As independent computing entities, objects have data and function members. Data and operations in one object are distinguished from those in a different object, even if the two belong to the same class. An object is a *host* for data and function members in it. Such members are known as *instance members*. Instance members are always accessed through a host object:

```
host.member              for example, sally.acct_bal
host_ptr->member         for example, (&sally)->acct_bal
host.fn( args )          for example, sally.deposit(65.95)
host_ptr->fn( args )     for example, (&sally)->withdraw(19.95)
```

The same data member in different hosts has different values and memory locations. Function members are shared by all objects of the same class. When an instance function is invoked, the address of the host object is also passed to the function through an extra pointer parameter this (the host pointer). For an instance function, the host object provides an *operating context* consisting of the current values of all its data members. Therefore, the same member function can act differently depending on values in the host.

An instance function can refer to another member in the same object without indicating the host object explicitly. We have seen many such uses already. For example, in the circular buffer class (Section 3.12), the function Cirbuf::consume() uses the isEmpty() function in the same host object directly. Also, the operator-() in Fraction (Section 3.5) refers to denom directly. Such an unqualified member name does not refer to a fixed variable or function. Rather, it refers to a member *in the same host object as the function*. Specifically, the notations isEmpty() and denom are really shorthand for this->isEmpty() and this->denom, respectively.

Therefore, unqualified member names are interpreted relative to an implicit host object that invoked the instance function. An instance function can also explicitly refer to its host object through the built-in pointer this. For example, in the class Fraction, the member function operator- returns *this when subtracting zero. (More examples are given later.)

The Read-Only Host

The host object is an implicit argument to any instance function. Sometimes, it is desirable to specify the read-only nature of this argument. We have already seen how this is done (Section 3.9). The prototype

```
Fraction Fraction::operator-(const Fraction& f) const;
```

specifies that the member operator- of the class Fraction takes a read-only right-hand argument f, but the left-hand argument (the host object itself) is also read-only. Thus, if r and s are both fractions, the code r - s can be used with the assurance that neither r nor s will be modified.

Once a host is read-only, all its data members also become read-only.

5.4 INTERNAL-EXTERNAL DECOUPLING

An object encapsulates data and programming to form an independent computing entity. It also hides details of internal data structures and mechanisms by providing a public interface through which all outside access to the object is made. The *behavior* of an object is fully defined by its public interface, which you can rely on without knowledge or concern about the internal workings. The decoupling of the internal workings of objects from the rest of the

5.5 POCKET CALCULATOR SIMULATION

program greatly simplifies the interrelationships among program components and makes modifications much easier.

Public members form the interface, and other members are hidden from outside view. The Account, Vector2D, Fraction, Cirbuf, Matrix, and TextLines classes discussed earlier are good examples. Consider again the Poly class (first discussed in Section 4.5). Internally, Poly uses a *sparse representation* (Table 4.1), which excludes missing terms in a polynomial from the data structure. In situations where there are very few or no missing terms, a *dense representation*, listing every coefficient, becomes more compact and efficient. Thus, a polynomial

$$a_n x^n + a_{n-1} x^{n-1} + \cdots + a_1 x + a_0$$

can be encoded by the dense representation

$$(n a_n a_{n-1} \ldots a_1 a_0)$$

which uses an int array of length $n + 2$.

What modifications should we make if we want the program to use the dense instead of the sparse representation? If the external behavior of Poly is preserved, only member functions of Poly are affected; the rest of the program that uses Poly stays the same. The modified Poly class can be found in the code package (ex05/polynomial/).

As another example, consider the TextLines class (Section 4.7). Suppose we wish to use a linked list, instead of a vector, for storing the lines of text. We can simply do that internally within TextLines with a few changes. No clients of TextLines even need to know that anything has changed.

5.5 POCKET CALCULATOR SIMULATION

The power of the class as a data abstraction and encapsulation tool can be greatly magnified by building objects on top of other objects. In other words, larger classes can be specified to contain existing objects as components. This approach is illustrated here by a pocket calculator simulation program.

Suppose we wish to simulate the functions and behavior of a simple hand-held calculator by creating an executable program **calc**. The program **calc** supports the arithmetic operations +, -, *, /, and =, as well as the C (clear), A (all clear), and N (sign change) operations.

Here is a typical session with **calc**:

```
Calc:   0
32 +
Calc:   32
66 —
Calc:   98
```

```
5 =
Calc:  93
N
Calc:  -93
```

Each `Calc` display line has the `Calc:` prefix. User input is shown in italics. A session ends when user input ends with a ^D on UNIX or a ^Z on Windows.

Program Design

To simulate an actual calculator, it makes sense to implement it as a C++ object containing two component objects: a *compute engine* and a *user interface* (Figure 5.2):

- The user interface object deals with receiving keyboard input and displaying answers.
- The compute engine object executes operations on the given numeric data and stores the results.
- The calculator object controls these components to perform the overall job.

The `CalcEng` and `CalcFace` are *aggregate components* because they are integral parts of the whole, `Calculator`. A head is an aggregate part of a person, but a hat is not. Figure 5.2 also shows the graphical symbols for aggregation. The example follows the popular *model-control-view* design paradigm—the compute engine is the model, the interface is the view, and the calculator is the control.

Let's first examine the details of the calculator compute engine.

The `CalcEng` Class

The calculator engine object does the computing and provides four member functions in its *public interface*:

1. `operand` is used to enter numeric data into the compute engine.
2. `operation` is called to perform control and arithmetic operations.
3. `opcode` is called to obtain the internally kept operator code (+, *, etc.).
4. `output` is invoked to produce the argument currently stored.

Figure 5.2 CLASS WITH TWO AGGREGATE COMPONENTS

5.5 POCKET CALCULATOR SIMULATION

The calculator compute engine works with three fundamental quantities:

1. `ans` is the answer, or result of requested computations, initialized to `0.0`.
2. `op` is the operator code (or opcode), one of the characters "+-*/=", whose left operand is always `ans`.
3. `arg` is the right operand of `op`.

Here is the header file for the `CalcEng` class:

```
///////   CalcEng.h   ///////

class CalcEng
{ public:
      CalcEng();                            // constructor
      void operation(char c);               // perform operation
      void operand(double in) ;             // enter operand
      char opcode() const { return op; }    // returns current opcode
      double output() const                 // returns current argument
        { return(argcnt==2 ? (arg) : ans); }
  private:
      void compute();          // mostly performs ans = ans op arg
      void allclear();
      double ans, arg;
      char op;                 // operation code (operator)
      int argcnt;              // argument count
};
```

The private data member `argcnt` keeps track of how many operands have been given at any point in time. The public interface makes using a `CalcEng` object simple and logical while hiding implementation details, which will, however, be revealed at this time.

The member functions of `CalcEng` are contained in the file `CalcEng.C`, which begins with some include files and the class constructor:

```
///////   CalcEng.C   ///////
#include <math.h>       // for pow
#include "CalcEng.h"

CalcEng::CalcEng() { allclear(); }

void CalcEng::allclear()
{ ans = arg = 0.0; argcnt = 1; op = '='; }
```

Chapter 5 CLASSES AND OBJECTS

The initialization actions are performed by allclear, a function that also supports the 'A' operation discussed later. Numeric (double) data are entered into a CalcEng object using the member function

```
void CalcEng::operand(double in)
{   if ( op == '=' ) ans = in;      // as left operand
    else
    {   arg = in;                   // as right operand
        argcnt = 2;
    }
}
```

If the previous operation (still kept in op) is '=', then the data are assigned to ans (the left operand of the next operation). Otherwise, they are assigned to arg (the right operand) of the current op (one of "+-*/"). Once the operands are in place, an operation is triggered by calling operation with the next character code from the user:

```
void CalcEng::operation(char nc)     // nc is next opcode
{   switch( nc )
    {   case 'A': // All Clear
        case 'a':   allclear(); return;
        case 'N': // sign change
        case 'n':   if ( argcnt == 1 ) ans = -ans;
                    else arg = -arg;
                    return;
        case 'C': // Clear
        case 'c':   if ( argcnt == 1 ) ans = 0.0, op = '=';
                    else { arg = 0.0; argcnt = 1;}
                    return;
        default :  // +-*/=
                    compute();
                    op = nc;    // new opcode
    }
}
```

The operations A, N, and C are performed immediately. Others ("+-*/=") trigger computations implemented by compute before being recorded as the new value of op (the next calculation to perform). The compute function checks for the right number of operands and actually carries out arithmetic operations. Of course, its actions are guided by the currently stored value of op:

```
void CalcEng::compute()
{   if ( argcnt == 2 )
    {   switch( op )    // old value of op
        {   case '+':   ans += arg; break;
            case '-':   ans -= arg; break;
```

5.5 POCKET CALCULATOR SIMULATION

```
            case '*':   ans *= arg; break;
            case '/':   ans /= arg; break;
        }
        argcnt = 1;
    }
}
///////    End of CalcEng.C   ///////
```

Testing CalcEng   Since a class actually defines an independent computing entity, it always makes sense to test a class definition completely and separately. When combining classes into larger programs, all you have to do then is make sure the objects are interfaced correctly.

To test CalcEng.C, we use a main program such as:

```
///////    testCalcEng.C    ///////
#include <iostream>
#include "CalcEng.h"

int main()
{   CalcEng cal;
    cal.operand(9.8);
    cal.operation('+');
    cal.operand(1.2);
    cal.operation('/');
    cal.operand(2.0);
    cal.operation('=');
    std::cout << cal.output() << std::endl;
    return 0;
}
```

Of course, this simple program falls far short of a comprehensive test for the CalcEng class. Its purpose here is to show some typical test cases. In testing your own program, you should exercise all parts of the code and pay special attention to extreme and unusual cases. Compile CalcEng.C and testCalEng.C separately to produce the corresponding object files. Once tested, the CalcEng.o file is in place and ready to be combined with other programs.

The CalcEng class is finished. Now let's consider the user interface part of the calculator.

The CalcFace Class   I/O to the user is the responsibility of a CalcFace object. This object reads user input and displays calculator output. Its public interface has two functions:

1. Each call to input consumes a sequence of zero or more digits terminated by a character-coded operation entered by the user. The code and number are deposited in the return parameters c and *number*,

respectively. The return value of input indicates whether no number is supplied (OPONLY) or the input has been terminated (OFF).

2. The function showNumber displays a given number to the user.

Here is the header file for the CalcFace class:

```
///////    CalcFace.h    ///////
#include <iostream>
#include <string>
using std::string;  using std::cout;
using std::cin;     using std::endl;

class CalcFace
{ public:
    explicit CalcFace(char* k = "+-*/=NnAaCc" )
    {  keys = string(k); }
    int input(char& c, double& number);      // reads user input
    void showNumber(double number) const;    // displays number
    enum {OK=0, OPONLY=1, OFF=2, PREC=6};
  private:
    int inchar() const { return cin.get(); }
    void extractNumber(double&) const;
    void buildNumber(char c, int& i);
    int nump(char c);
    char   nbuf[PREC+2];    // buffer for input number
    string keys;            // keys recognized
};
```

The enum member PREC is the maximum number of digits allowed. Internally, the private member inchar produces the next input character or EOF upon end of file. The functions buildNumber() and extractNumber() are used by input() to treat numeric input.

The implementation file CalcFace.C begins with include files, an inline function, and the simple output member function showNumber:

```
///////    CalcFace.C    ///////
#include  <iostream>
#include  <strstream>
#include  "CalcFace.h"
using std::istrstream;

inline int CalcFace::nump(char c)
        { return( c == '.' || isdigit(c) ); }

void CalcFace::showNumber(double number) const
{ cout << "Calc:  " << number << endl; }
```

5.5 POCKET CALCULATOR SIMULATION

Although output is simple, simulating input from a calculator is more complicated. The strategy is to keep reading input characters and accumulating them in a character buffer nbuf (by calling buildNumber()) as long as they are part of a number. As soon as an operator character is encountered, the number is complete and both the number and the operator are obtained. If the number part is empty, then only an operator is entered. To simulate a calculator, the input number consists of digits with one possible decimal point. The istrstream in-memory input stream, from the C++ I/O stream library (Section 6.2), is used to convert a string representation of a decimal number into a double (in function extractNumber()):

```
void CalcFace::extractNumber(double& number) const
{   if ( nbuf[0] == '\0' ) number = 0.0;
    else
    {   istrstream tmp(nbuf, PREC + 1);
        tmp >> number;
    }
}
```

The function input returns three quantities: the operator (as a character in reference parameter op), a nonnegative input number (in reference parameter number), and OPONLY, OFF, or OK (as the function return value). Input is terminated when end of file is encountered (line 1).

The **find** function in the string class is handy here to determine if the character c is an operator (line 2). The call

str.**find**(*s*, *i0*)   (*i0* optional)

searches in the string object *str* for the character or string *s* and returns an index if found or string::npos if not. The optional index *i0* specifies a starting point to search.

The function input reads user input and returns the operator in op and the number, if any, in number. The return value OK means both op and number are obtained, OPONLY means only op is obtained, and OFF means end of all input (calculator turned off). The quantity PREC is the number of digits displayed.

```
int CalcFace::input(char& op, double& number)
{   char c;
    int current_position = 0, num=0;
    while ( (c=inchar()) != EOF )                    // (1)
    {   if ( keys.find(c) != string::npos )          // (2)
        {   op = c;
            if ( num )
            {   nbuf[current_position] = '\0';
                extractNumber(number);
                return OK;
```

```
            }
            else return OPONLY;
        }
        if ( nump(c) && current_position < PREC ) // (3)
        {   num = 1;
            buildNumber(c, current_position);
        }
    }  // end of while
    return OFF;    // end of input
}
```

Input characters not recognized or beyond the calculator's precision (PREC) are ignored (line 3). The private member buildNumber accumulates numeric input in the buffer nbuf:

```
void CalcFace::buildNumber(char c, int& i)
{ static int point_seen = 0;
  if ( i == 0 ) point_seen = 0;        // reset
  if ( i == 0 && c == '0') return;     // ignore leading zeros
  if ( c == '.' )                      // at most one decimal point
  {   if ( point_seen ) return;
      else point_seen = 1;
  }
  nbuf[i++] = c;                       // current_position++
}
```

Testing CalcFace

The user interface class CalcFace should be tested independently with a main program such as

```
///////    testCalcFace.C    ///////
#include <iostream>
#include "CalcFace.h"
using std::cout;  using std::endl;

int main()
{  CalcFace cf;
   char op;
   int ind;
   double number;
   while ( (ind = cf.input(op, number))
                      != CalcFace::OFF)
   {   cout << "operator is " ;          // display op
       cout.put(op) << endl;
       if ( ind == CalcFace::OK )        // got number
          cf.showNumber(number);
   }
```

5.5 POCKET CALCULATOR SIMULATION

```
        return 0;
}
```

Note how the `enum` quantities in `CalcFace` are referred to outside the class. Once tested, the `CalcFace.o` file is in place and ready to be combined with other programs.

Now let's see how relatively simple it is to use `CalcEng` and `CalcFace` objects in building a `Calculator` object.

The Calculator Class
Aside from the constructor, the `Calculator` class has just one publicly callable member, on. Like its real-life counterpart, it turns on a `Calculator` object:

```
///////    Calculator.h    ///////
#include    "CalcEng.h"
#include    "CalcFace.h"

class Calculator
{   public:
        Calculator() {}
        void on();
    private:
        CalcEng   eng;
        CalcFace  cf;
};
```

The private members `eng` and `cf` are objects of previously defined classes. To establish a `Calculator` object, its component objects are automatically built and their default constructors are called.

The on function implements the top-level loop of a pocket calculator. It uses the compute engine and the user interface to make the calculator work in the expected fashion:

```
///////    Calculator.C    ///////
#include "Calculator.h"

void Calculator::on()
{   int ind;
    char op;
    double number;
    cf.showNumber(eng.output());              // initial display
    while ( (ind = cf.input(op, number))      // calc loop   (1)
                    != CalcFace::OFF )
    {   if ( ind == CalcFace::OK )
            eng.operand( number );            // operand     (2)
        eng.operation( op );                  // perform op  (3)
```

```
        number = (op=='c' || op=='C')
                 ? 0 : eng.output();
        cf.showNumber(number);                      // display     (4)
    }
}
```

As long as there is more user input, the on function repeats these steps:

1. Obtains from the user interface object the next input number and/or operation.
2. Enters the number, if given, as the operand for the compute engine object.
3. Passes the indicated operation to the compute engine.
4. Displays the compute engine output via the user interface object.

Experimenting with a calculator object is now very simple indeed:

```
///////    mycalc.C    ///////
#include    "Calculator.h"

int main()
{   Calculator x;
    x.on();
    return 0;
}
```

Now create the executable program **calc** by combining the object files CalcEng.o, CalcFace.o, Calculator.o, and mycalc.o. Then, experiment with **calc** interactively to see how well it simulates a pocket calculator.

To end a session with this calculator, type the input-ending character ^D (UNIX) or ^Z (Windows).

5.6 BUILT-IN OPERATIONS FOR OBJECTS

A class gives rise to a user-defined type and objects with a well-defined public interface. A few operations for objects are so basic that C++ performs them without being explicitly programmed. These include

1. *Creating an object:* instantiation and initialization (Section 5.2).
2. *Assignment:* for example, frac_a = frac_b + frac_c for fractions.
3. *Argument passing:* for example, perpendicular(vec1, vec2) for vectors.
4. *Return value:* for example, return frac_a;.

5. *Address-of*: for example, `Poly* ptr = &poly_a`.
6. *Value-of*: for example, `*this`.
7. *Member-of*: for example, `frac_a.num` or `ptr->display()`.

Operations not built in must be defined by the class. Another built-in operation is object destruction as explained next.

5.7 OBJECT DESTRUCTION

C++ automatically destroys an object in exactly these three occasions:

1. When a local (automatic) object goes out of scope—for example,

   ```
   {  /* ... */
      Date d(1,14,1998);
      AddrEntry item(n1, a1);
      /* ... */
   }
   ```

   This often happens when a function call returns or when a compound statement ends.

2. When an object created by the operator `new` is specifically destroyed with the operator `delete`—for instance,

   ```
   Date *d = new Date(7,4,1776);
   /* ... */
   delete d;
   ```

3. Just before a program terminates, all global objects (those with static storage) are destroyed.

Thus, each object goes through a *life cycle* as shown in Figure 5.1. Before an object is deallocated, its destructor, if any, is called automatically. After the destructor call, any member objects in the object being destroyed are destroyed. When an object containing other objects is destroyed, the host destructor is executed first. The component objects are then destroyed in the reverse order of instantiation.

Destructors

While a constructor for a class automates initialization of objects just after instantiation, a destructor, another special member function, automates cleanup actions just before deallocation. Unlike the constructor, which you code in almost every class, you define the destructor only for classes with cleanup chores to perform before object deallocation. Such chores include resetting variable values, freeing dynamic storage, closing I/O streams, removing temporary files, refreshing windows, deleting menus, and so on. The destructor provides a way to supply appropriate actions that are automatically executed whenever an object is destroyed. The body of a destructor can contain calls to member functions that help with the cleanup chores.

The destructor is a member function with a name obtained by prefixing the class name with the character ~ (tilde). It is illegal for the destructor to specify a return type or to return a value. Furthermore, a destructor takes no arguments and therefore cannot be overloaded.

One example is the destructor for the `Cirbuf` class (Section 3.12):

```
Cirbuf::~Cirbuf() { delete [] cb; }   // free up space
```

which frees the character array cb created by the `Cirbuf` constructor with new. If an object contains a pointer to space allocated by new and if the object is destroyed without first freeing the dynamically allocated memory, then that storage is *lost* to the program. Explicit invocation of delete is tedious and error-prone. The destructor makes freeing of space reached through an object (Figure 5.3) automatic at object destruction time and brings some welcome relief to the programmer, who must otherwise free such spaces manually.

Another example is the class `Poly`, which can also use a destructor. The class `Poly` has a member pol, which points to allocated free storage. Thus, consider adding a destructor ~Poly:

```
Poly::~Poly()
{ delete [] pol; }
```

However, note that adding such a destructor causes other complications. It usually means also adding a class-defined assignment operator (Section 7.9) and a *copy constructor* (Section 7.10) to make the code robust. To avoid potential problems, remember to *pass objects in function calls by reference whenever possible*. You also make your code more efficient this way.

In addition to being invoked automatically before object deallocation, a destructor, like other member functions, can be called explicitly (with . or ->).

Figure 5.3 AN OBJECT WITH A POINTER TO FREE STORAGE

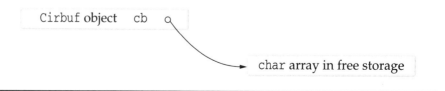

This is useful in situations where cleanup is needed without deallocating the object.

In C++, `delete` can be given either a pointer returned by `new` or a `NULL` pointer. Deleting a null pointer has no effect. For a destructor that frees up space, make sure that `delete` is applied only to these types of pointers.

If you find yourself coding a destructor for a class, you must also consider supplying a *copy constructor* and an *assignment operator*, as explained in Sections 7.9 and 7.10. We examine many more applications of the destructor later.

5.8 FRIENDS OF A CLASS

Normally, private members are not accessible by any function outside their class. This is how data hiding is enforced in C++. However, a few situations call for exceptions to this rule. The friend mechanism is used to specify such exceptions. In a class definition, the declaration

```
friend function-prototype
```

declares a specific function to be a *friend* of the class. A friend has the privilege to access the nonpublic members of the class. The `friend` declaration can occur anywhere in the class definition and is not subject to access-control designations. It is conventional to place all `friend` declarations at the beginning of a class definition.

A friend can be an unattached function or a member function of another class. Two friends are now introduced to the class `Fraction` (Section 3.5):

```
class Fraction
{    friend int compare(int, const Fraction&);
                                        // a friend function
     friend int compare(const Fraction&, int);
                                        // another friend function
   public:
     /* ... */
   private:
     int num;              // numerator
     unsigned int denom;   // denominator
};
```

The `friend` declarations can be added to `Fraction.h` even after `Fraction.C` has been compiled and there is no need to re-create `Fraction.o`. The added friend declarations simply inform the compiler that these two file scope comparison functions have access to nonpublic members of the `Fraction` class. The access privilege is necessary for compare to test the relative size of an integer and a fraction:

```
int compare(int i, const Fraction& r)      // usage: compare(i,r)  (A)
{   return(i * r.denom - r.num); }

int compare(const Fraction& r, int i)      // usage: compare(r,i)  (B)
{   return(r.num - i * r.denom); }
```

Of course, the result of the comparison is positive, negative, or zero, depending on whether the first argument is greater than, less than, or equal to the second one, a widely followed convention.

A good question at this point is, Why not implement compare as a member function of Fraction and avoid the friend mechanism? One reason is that it is not possible to implement both versions A and B as members. Specifically, the member definition

```
int Fraction::compare(int i) const      // usage: r.compare(i)
{   return(num - i * denom); }
```

can take the place of version B only. However, it is impossible to make i.compare(r) work because int is not a class.

When comparing two fractions, on the other hand, both the member and the friend options are open. The friend option gives symmetric treatment of the quantities being compared. The member option avoids making access exceptions to nonpublic members. Style dictates which option you choose.

Operators can also be friends. For example,

```
friend Fraction operator-(int, const Fraction&);
friend Fraction operator-(const Fraction&, int);
```

can be coded as

```
Fraction operator-(int i, const Fraction& r)
{    return Fraction(i*r.denom - r.num, r.denom);  }

Fraction operator-(const Fraction& r, int i)
{    return Fraction(r.num - i*r.denom, r.denom);  }
```

Again, it is not possible to implement both of these versions as member functions.

Sometimes, all member functions of a class X must be friends of another class Y. This can be done easily in C++ with

```
class Y
{    friend class X;      // all members of X are friends of Y
     /* ... */
};
```

Individual member functions of a class can also be made friends without making the whole class a friend. Just precede the selected function names with the class scope operator in the `friend` declaration.

The friend mechanism bypasses access control and allows nonmember functions access to the nonpublic members of a class. Use this mechanism sparingly and judiciously. While unnecessary use of the mechanism is inadvisable, some situations do require its use (Section 8.1).

Friends should be part of the design of a class. The information-hiding unit extends to include all friends of a class. If the internal workings of a class are modified without changing its public interface, all that may need modification are member and friend functions. Thus, the friend mechanism is used to facilitate information hiding and not to break it. Let's consider the linked list described next as an example.

5.9 RECURSIVE STRUCTURES

It has been mentioned that a class may have members that are also objects. But is it possible or desirable for a class to have a member that, in turn, is an instance of the *same class*? Very much so. Such classes define *recursive structures*. Among recursive data structures, the linked list is one of the most widely used.

The class implementation of a linked list is the topic here. But first, we need to know a little more about the linked list concept.

Linked List

Think of a grocery list as a structure with two members:

1. The name of a grocery item.
2. A grocery list of the remaining items.

In fact, this recursive structure is inherent to any list.

In C++, it is not possible for a class to declare a member of the same class type directly. The reason is that an object cannot be declared with a class tag not completely defined yet. Hence, the declaration

```
class List
{
    /* ... */
    List abc;      // List not defined yet
}
```

is incorrect. But a pointer to the class being defined can be used. Therefore, a recursive class is defined to contain member *pointers* to objects of the same class.

The List Cell   As a first example, consider a *linked list* of characters. Each cell of the list contains a character and a pointer to the rest of the list; that is, each list cell also points to the location of the next cell, like a "chain of elephants" (Figure 5.4). Unlike a rigid array, a linked list affords great flexibility at run time—it is simple to add, delete, and reorder items anywhere on the list. Each entry on the linked list is an object of the recursive class ListCell:

```
class ListCell                          // a recursive class
{    friend class List;
     private:                           // all members private
        char item;                      // item is a character
        ListCell* next;
        ListCell(char a = '\0',         // constructor
                 ListCell* ptr = NULL)
          : item(a), next(ptr) { }      // constructor init-list
};
```

The declaration

```
friend class List;
```

makes all member functions of class List friends of ListCell, granting them access to nonpublic members of ListCell (Section 5.8). Because all members, including the constructor, are private, the ListCell class is used exclusively by its friend class List, which encapsulates the recursive data structure and all list access and manipulation operations. Thus, ListCell is a *slave class* of List and placed in file List.C rather than in file List.h.

Each ListCell object stores a character in item and a pointer to the next cell in next. Here is how we construct a list:

```
ListCell* list_x = new ListCell('C');      //       (C)
list_x = new ListCell('B', list_x);        //     (B C)
list_x = new ListCell('A', list_x);        //   (A B C)
```

Figure 5.4   A LINKED LIST

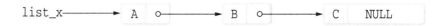

5.9 RECURSIVE STRUCTURES

A list cell containing the character C is first created with a call to new, and list_x points to this first cell. Another cell is created containing the character B and a pointer to the previous cell. Now list_x points to the second cell and is a list of two characters. This can be done a number of times to create a list of any length.

Linked List Design

Consider how the class List is designed. In designing any class, consideration should first be given to its public interface and external behavior. Internal mechanisms can then be designed and implemented to support the desired external behavior. For a linked list, what should the public interface do?

- *Build a list:* Establish a new list empty or with one item (constructors); add items to a list (putOn, append, insert).
- *Access list cells:* Access specific cells and search through a list (first, next, last, and find, each returning an item pointer ListCell* or NULL if no such cell exists).
- *Remove items:* Delete all cells with a certain item (remove); remove several cells from the front of the list (shorten).
- *Substitute items:* Replace an existing item with a new item (substitute).
- *Display the list:* Produce a display of the entire list or a sublist starting at any given list cell (overloaded display).

There can be many good interface designs for the same class. For a list class, there are so many other operations that it is impossible to cover all of them here.

Now let's examine how our design is implemented:

```
///////    List.h    ///////

class ListCell;  // defined in List.h

class List
{ public:
    List() : head(NULL) { }                 // empty list
    List(char c);                            // list with one cell
    ListCell* first() { return head; }       // first cell
    ListCell* last();                        // last cell
    ListCell* find(char c);                  // first item == c
    char content(ListCell* p);               // gets content
    bool substitute(char r, char s);         // substitutes r for first s
    int remove(char c);                      // removes c from entire list
```

```
    void remove(ListCell* cell);        // removes given cell
    int shorten(int n);                 // removes first n cells
    bool putOn(char c);                 // inserts c in front
    bool insert(char c, ListCell* c);   // inserts c after cell
    int append(char c)                  // inserts c at end
    { return insert(c, last()); }
    void display(ListCell* p) const;    // displays from p to end
    void display() const                // displays whole list
    { display(head); }
    bool isEmpty() const { return head == NULL; }
    ~List();                            // destructor
  private:
    ListCell* head;                     // first cell of list
    void free();                        // frees all cells
};
```

The single data member, head, is a pointer to the first list cell. All list cells used are allocated with new. Cells removed are freed immediately, and all cells are freed when a List object is destroyed (~List).

Linked List Implementation The implementation file List.C begins with the destructor. Because all cells are allocated by new, each list cell must be freed individually with delete at cleanup time. This is the duty of the private member function free:

```
///////   List.C   ///////
#include <iostream>
#include "List.h"

List::List(char c)                  // constructor
: head (new ListCell(c,NULL)) { }

List::~List() {   free();  }

void List::free()                   // private member
{   ListCell *n, *p = head;
    while (p)
    {   n = p->next;
        delete p;
        p=n;
    }
}
```

The member function shorten removes a number of cells from the beginning of the list. If the list can be shortened by the requested amount, n,

5.9 RECURSIVE STRUCTURES

zero is returned. Otherwise, a negative integer *listlength* − *n* is returned after removing all list cells:

```
int List::shorten(int n)
{   while (n-- && head)
       {   ListCell* tmp=head;
           head = head->next;
           delete(tmp);
       }
    return - ++n;
}
```

To remove all characters equal to c from the list, the member function remove(char) first processes all list cells starting with the second cell. Then, the first cell (head) is treated separately:

```
int List::remove(char c)
{   ListCell *tmp, *p = head;
    if ( p == NULL ) return count;
    int count = 0;
    while (p->next)              // treats all but head cell
    {   if ((p->next)->item == c)
        {   count++;
            tmp = p->next;
            p->next = tmp->next;
            delete(tmp);         // frees up storage
        }
        else  p = p->next;
    }
    if( head->item == c )        // treats head cell
    {   tmp = head;
        head = head->next;
        delete(tmp);
        count++;
    }
    return count;                // number of cells removed
}
```

Each cell removed is also freed. The total number of cells removed is returned by the function.

Inserting a new item at the beginning (putOn) or after a given entry e (insert) is relatively simple:

```
bool List::putOn(char c)
{    ListCell* tmp = new ListCell(c,head);
     if ( tmp )
     {   head = tmp;
```

```
            return true;
        }
        else return false;         // failed
}

// insert after entry e
int List::insert(char c, ListCell* e)
{   if ( e == NULL )               // inserts at head
            return putOn(c);
    ListCell* tmp = new ListCell(c,e->next);
    if ( tmp )
    {   e->next = tmp;
        return true;
    }
    else return false;             // failed
}
```

In each case, if the operator new fails (no more free storage), −1 is returned. The access functions last and find return a pointer to the list cell found (type ListCell*). Note how last treats an empty list:

```
ListCell* List::last()
{    ListCell* p = head;
     while( p && p->next ) p = p->next;
     return p;
}

ListCell* List::find(char c)
{   for( ListCell* p = head; p ; p = p->next )
        if( p->item == c ) return p;
    return NULL;                    // c not on list
}
```

The frequent idiom

```
for(ListCell* p=head; p!=NULL; p = p->next)   // idiom
```

follows pointers down a linked list efficiently. The member find locates the target character s to be substituted by r:

```
bool List::substitute(char r, char s)
{    ListCell* p = find(s);
     if( p == NULL ) return false;    // s not on list
     p->item = r;
     return true;
}
```

5.9 RECURSIVE STRUCTURES

The output of `display` is a list of characters separated by spaces enclosed in parentheses:

```
using std::cout;

void List::display(ListCell* p) const
{   cout << "(";
    while ( p )                 // displays from p to end
    {   cout << p->item;
        if ( p = p->next ) cout << " ";
    }
    std::cout << ")";
}
```

The overloaded `display` functions are

```
void List::display(ListCell* p);    // displays from p to end
void display() { display(head); }   // displays whole list
```

You may be tempted to use one display function with a default argument instead:

```
void display(ListCell* p = head);   // error
```

This cannot be done because a default argument initializer must be *an expression involving only data at fixed memory locations at compile time*. The location of head depends on its host object at run time. In general, instance members cannot be default argument initializers.

Try `List`, `ListCell`, and some of the member functions using the test file

```
///////    testList.C    ///////
#include "List.h"
using std::cout;  using std::endl;

void listTest()
{   List a('B');
    a.putOn('A');                       // (A B)
    a.append('D'); a.append('E');       // (A B D E)
    cout << endl;
    a.append('F'); a.display();         // (A B D E F)
    cout << endl;
    ListCell* lp = a.find('B');
    a.display(lp); cout << endl;
    a.insert('C', lp); a.display();     // (A B C D E F)
    cout << endl;
    a.remove('F'); a.shorten(2);        // (C D E)
    a.display(); cout << endl;
    // destructor called as function returns
```

}

```
int main()
{   listTest();
    return 0;
}
```

which, when compiled and executed, produces the following output:

(A B D E F)
(B D E F)
(A B C D E F)
(C D E)

A complete list class would have other member functions such as concatenating two lists, taking the union or intersection, copying a list, and assigning one list to another. The latter two operations require special member functions, as we will see in Sections 7.9 and 7.10.

The advantage of linked lists is the ability to insert and delete items anywhere in the list with ease. For instance, in a text editor program, each text line can be represented by a linked list of characters to make inserting and deleting characters easy.

The complete example can be found in the code package (ex05/list/). This example deals with characters, but the basic linked list structure and manipulations stay the same for integers, floats, strings, dates, or other data types. In fact, it is possible in C++ to define a list of arbitrary type. Such generality brings to programs much needed flexibility and reusability, as we will see in Section 5.12.

5.10 INSTANCE AND STATIC MEMBERS

A member in a class is either an *instance member* or a *class-wide member*. A member is an instance member unless declared `static`, which makes it class-wide. An instance member is attached to a *host object* and is accessed only through the host. For example, `susan.balance()` returns the balance for the `Account` object `susan`. Within an instance function, reference to the host object is made through the keyword `this`. In `balance`, the code `return acct_bal` is shorthand for `return this.acct_bal`. Thus, instance members *live within their host objects* and can access one another freely and directly within the host.

Instance members play an important role in object-based programming. But there are times when an attribute or operation must transcend the boundaries of individual objects. An error tolerance `delta` in the `Vector2D` class is an example. A monthly service fee can be part of the `Account` class but not

Figure 5.5 **STATIC MEMBER IN CLASS SCOPE**

```
Vector2D::              Account::
         delta                   fee
```

restricted to any individual `Account` object. A class-wide member is unique per class and exists independently of any instance (object) of a class. Thus, a class-wide data member can be used to share information among all objects of the class or to provide a value for other classes to use directly.

In C++, the following members are class-wide:

- Data or function members that are declared `static`
- `enum` members
- `typedef` members

Class-wide members are often simply referred to as static members. A static member is enclosed in the scope of its class but has no host object (Figure 5.5). A static member is accessible by all objects in the class and, if public, from the outside.

A static member can be accessed through any object of the class. Of course, the same static object is reached no mater what instance of the class you use. A static member can also be accessed directly, without using any instance of the class, by the notation

ClassName::*staticMemberName*

The `ios::badbit` is an example.

Static data members are often used for the following purposes:

- To provide values or structures for client programs.
- To store values or structures shared by all objects in a class.
- To pass data from any object to all other objects.
- To store results computed by collaboration among all objects.

Because a static member is not stored in each object, the storage savings can be significant if the static member is a large table or if many objects are used.

Static Member Functions

Declare a member function `static` when it is a procedure that works independently of any single object in the class. In other words, if a member function contains no references to instance members in the host, the function can be declared static.

The difference between a static and a instance member function is the existence of the host pointer this:

- A static function has no host object and therefore no access to this, explicitly or implicitly. Thus, a static function can refer to an instance member only through an explicit object.
- An instance member function can be called only through an object (the host) of its class and is instantiated with a pointer to the host (this).
- A static member function can be invoked either through an object or directly using the class scope operator *ClassName*::. It has no host pointer and cannot reference instance members without going through an explicit object.
- Constructors and destructors cannot be static.

The unattached gcd used in Fraction, for example, can be enclosed inside Fraction as a static function. The makeFraction function in Fraction is independent of any particular instance and should therefore be declared static as well. Also, s_to_d in Poly and nump in CalcFace can be made static.

When a class has only static members and no instance members, the class is not meant for establishing objects. It becomes a set of members enclosed in a class scope.

The next example, involving foreign exchange rates, illustrates the use of static members.

Foreign Exchange

Consider keeping a table of foreign exchange rates. Each table entry is an object of the class Rate:

```
///////    Rate.h    ///////
#include <iostream>
#include <string>
using std::cout;
using std::string;

class Rate
{ public:
    Rate(const char* name = "",            // currency name
         double r = 0.0)                   // exchange rate
      : cur(string(name)), amt(r) { }
    double getRate() { return amt; }       // retrieves rate
    void setRate(double r) { amt = r; }    // sets rate
    const string& id() { return cur; }     // retrieves currency name
```

5.10 INSTANCE AND STATIC MEMBERS

```
    void display()
    { cout << amt << "\t\t" << cur; }
  private:
    const string cur;                   // currency name
    double amt;                         // exchange rate
};
```

A `Rate` object records the name of a particular currency and its exchange rate. All necessary constructor, retrieval, and update members are provided as inline functions. The currency is stored in a `string` object.

The exchange rate table class `RateTable` stores a sorted array of `Rate` objects and has all static members.

```
///////    RateTable.h     ///////
#include "Rate.h"

class RateTable
{ public:
    RateTable() {}                              // default constructor
    static double rate(char *cur);              // gets rate
    static newRate(char *cur, double r);        // sets rate
    static void display(char *cur);             // displays one entry
    static void display();                      // displays rate table
  private:
    static int lookup(char *cur);               // table lookup
    static Rate table[];
    static unsigned len;
};

#define RATES    Rate("Britain (Pound)", 0.6967),   \
                 Rate("Canada (Dollar)", 1.4728),   \
                 Rate("Germany (Mark)", 2.0176),    \
                 Rate("European (Euro)", 1.0916),   \
                 Rate("Japan (Yen)", 106.10),       \
                 Rate("Mexico (New Peso)", 9.922),  \
                 Rate("Spain (Peseta)", 171.64),    \
                 /*       . . .               */   \
                 Rate("Taiwan (NT $)", 30.74)
```

The header file contains a symbolic constant (Section 14.4) `RATES`, which is later used to initialize an exchange rate table.

A static member is only declared in the class declaration. The memory space for a static member must be allocated by a definition contained in an implementation file (.C). The definition usually also supplies an initializer for the static member. This is the way static members are initialized, unlike instance members, which are initialized by a constructor.

For example, `table` and `len` are initialized in the `RateTable.C` file as follows:

```
///////    RateTable.C    ///////
#include <string.h>
#include "RateTable.h"
using std::endl;

Rate RateTable::table[] = { RATES };

unsigned RateTable::len = sizeof(RateTable::table)/sizeof(Rate);
```

Here the symbolic constant `RATES`, which can be modified in the `RateTable.h` file to add new currency entries and so on, is used to initialize the static member array `RateTable::table[]`.

In general, static member initialization notation is

type ClassName::static_member = initializer;

where *type* is the type of the *static_member*. The initialization is given at file scope in a .C file. Uninitialized static members are set to zero.

The compile-time operator `sizeof` (Section 5.11) helps compute the array length. Since the table could be fairly large, it makes sense to keep only one copy.

The member functions `rate` and `newRate` retrieve and set exchange rates, respectively:

```
double RateTable::rate(char *cur)
{   int index = lookup(cur);
    if ( index > -1 )
        return table[index].getRate();
    else
        return 0.0;    // no exchange rate
}

int RateTable::newRate(char *cur, double r)
{   int index = lookup(cur);
    if ( index > -1 )
    {   table[index].setRate(r);
        return 0;
    }
    else
        return -1;    // failed
}
```

Note that member functions are declared `static` in the class declaration only. It is an error to add the `static` modifier again outside the class declaration.

A single entry or the entire exchange rate table can be displayed with the overloaded `display` function:

```
void RateTable::display(char *cur)
{  int index = lookup(cur);
   if ( index > -1 )
   {   table[index].display();
       cout << endl;
   }
   else
       cout << "Entry " << cur << " not found." << endl;
}

void RateTable::display()
{  cout << "len =" << len << endl;
   for (int i = 0; i < len; i++)
   {  table[i].display();
      cout << endl;
   }
}
```

Table Lookup via Binary Search

A key operation is locating any given currency entry in the array `table`. Because the exchange rate table is assumed to be already in sorted order, we can use an efficient binary search routine, `lookup`, to find an entry quickly:

```
// table lookup with binary search

int RateTable::lookup(char *cur)
{    int low = 0, high = len-1, mid, test;
     while (low <= high)
     {   mid = (high + low)/2;   // mid point
         test = (table[mid].id()).compare(cur);
         if ( test == 0 ) return mid;
         else if ( test < 0 ) low = mid + 1;
         else high = mid - 1;
     }
     return -1;    // entry not on rate table
}
///////    End of file RateTable.C    ///////
```

The `string` function `compare` is used to identify the desired currency. The binary search proceeds by repeatedly going into the middle of the target search range to find the desired entry, which is a particularly efficient search method. The bsearch function available from <stdlib.h> performs binary search on an arbitrary sorted array where the elements are stored consecutively.

Test the exchange rate table using a simple main function

```
///////    testTable.C    ///////
#include <iostream>
#include "RateTable.h"
using std::cout; using std::endl;

int main()
{   RateTable::display();
    RateTable::newRate("Taiwan (NT $)", 34.5);
    cout << "revised entry" << endl;
    RateTable::display("Taiwan (NT $)");
    return 0;
}
```

In the test main program for RateTable, no class objects are used. Thus, the class RateTable is defined not to establish objects but to create a program package or module whose namespace is separated from the rest of the program. Although identifiers defined within the module are accessible to other parts of the program, the module name (RateTable in this case) must be explicitly mentioned.

enum and typedef Members

Enumerators and typedefs defined in the scope of a class are encapsulated in the class. Although such members are subject to normal access control, they are not instance members and are not stored in each class instance but in an area shared by all objects of the same class. Therefore, enum and typedef members are accessed, like static members, with the class scope operator.

Class-wide constants are usually declared as member enumerators to encapsulate information more completely. For example, the ios::in and ios::out are enumerators in the C++ I/O stream library class ios.

5.11 THE SIZE OF OBJECTS

We have already seen the use of the compile-time unary operator sizeof for computing RateTable::len in Section 5.10. This operator computes the size of built-in or user-defined data types. The expression

sizeof(*variable* or *type name*)   // parentheses optional

is replaced by the compiler with the number of bytes required to store a variable of the given type. Table 5.1 shows the typical values of some built-in types and

Table 5.1 `sizeof` EXPRESSIONS

Compile-time Expr	Typical Value
`sizeof(char)`	1
`sizeof(short int)`	2
`sizeof(int)`	4
`sizeof(long)`	4
`sizeof(float)`	4
`sizeof(double)`	8
`sizeof(`*any* `*)`	4
`sizeof(`*arrayname*`)`	*dim*∗`sizeof(`*entry*`)`
`sizeof(`*class-tag*`)`	*total sizes of data members and any padding*

the rules for computing the size of user-defined types. Using `sizeof` instead of hard-coded constant sizes makes a program independent of the local system and therefore more portable. Because some data must be aligned on certain word boundaries in memory, empty space, or *padding*, may be used in storing class members. The initialization of `len` in class `RateTable` is a good application of `sizeof`.

5.12 GENERIC LISTS

We are familiar with the class `List` (presented in Section 5.9). A `List` object represents a linked list of characters. But what about lists of integers, fractions, dates, vectors, addresses, and so on? What about lists of objects yet to be defined? Must we reinvent the wheel every time? No. Fortunately, there are ways to define such classes once and for all. Two approaches are available to achieve this goal:

1. We can use the *template* facility.
2. We can use the `void *` type and pointers to functions.

Templates are discussed in Chapter 10. The second approach creates lists storing items of type `void *` that can point to items of any desired type. Such a list is *generic*, or nontype-specific. A generic list class makes the code for list manipulation *reusable* whenever and wherever a linked list of some type is required. The generic approach presented here works not only for lists but also for any *container class* such as tables, sets, trees, graphs, stacks, and queues—just to name a few items.

Our generic list class `ArbList` can be defined by modifying the existing class `List`. You may be surprised at how few changes are needed. To begin with, the code for `ArbCell` is simply `ListCell` with `char` replaced by `void *`:

```
class ArbCell
{      friend class ArbList;
   private:
      Any item;                        // Any is void*
      ArbCell* next;
      ArbCell(Any c = NULL, ArbCell* ptr = NULL)
        : item(c), next(ptr) { }       // constructor
};
```

Storing pointers rather than the data items directly is the price for achieving genericness. For items of a basic type, the memory requirement doubles. For larger items such as strings and addresses, the storage increase is not significant at all.

To transform `List` into `ArbList`, we make two obvious changes: We replace all `ListCell` by `ArbCell` and all `char` by `Any`. Then, we must provide a way to check equality (for `find` and `remove`) of arbitrary items and to display them—tasks that are impossible for `void *` types. So an equality tester and a displayer function must be supplied when an `ArbList` object is initialized. These functions have knowledge of the item type and can therefore perform their tasks easily.

Here is the class `ArbList`:

```
///////   ArbList.h    ///////
#ifndef Arblist_SEEN__
#define Arblist_SEEN__
#include <iostream>
typedef void *Any;

class ArbCell;

class ArbList
{ public:
     typedef bool (* EQ_FN)(Any, Any);    // equality function type
     typedef void (* DISP_FN)(Any);       // display function type

     ArbList() : head(NULL) { }           // default constructor
     ArbList(Any c, EQ_FN eq, DISP_FN d); // constructor   (1)
     static ArbCell* next(ArbCell* p);    // next cell
     static Any content(ArbCell* p);      // content of list item
     static bool isEnd(ArbCell* p)        // end test
     { return p==NULL; }
```

5.12 GENERIC LISTS

```cpp
    ArbCell* first() const { return head;}  // first cell
    ArbCell* last();                         // last cell
    ArbCell* find(Any c);                    // first item equals c
    bool substitute(Any r, Any s);           // r for first s on list
    int remove(Any c);                       // c from entire list
    void remove(ArbCell* cell);              // removes given cell
    int shorten(int n);                      // removes first n cells
    bool putOn(Any c);                       // inserts in front
    bool insert(Any c, ArbCell* cell);       // inserts after cell
    bool append(Any c)                       // inserts at end
       { return insert(c, last()); }
    void display(ArbCell* p) const;          // displays from p to end
    void display() const                     // displays whole list
       { display(head); }
    bool isEmpty() const { return head==NULL; }
    ~ArbList();                              // destructor
  protected:                                 // (2)
    ArbCell* head;    // first cell of list
    void free();      // free all cells
    EQ_FN equal;      // supplied equality tester
    DISP_FN dispfn;   // supplied displayer
};
#endif /*arblist_SEEN__ */
```

Static members `content()` and `isEnd()` are added for a well-rounded public interface. The constructor (line 1) records the supplied equality tester and displayer in the members `equal` and `dispfn`. The access category `protected` (line 2) is like `private` but allows derived class access. Class derivation is the topic of Chapter 7.

```
///////    ArbList.C    ///////
```

```cpp
ArbList::ArbList(Any c, EQ_FN eq, DISP_FN d)
: head (new ArbCell(c,NULL)),
equal(eq), dispfn(d) { }
```

The `display` function now uses `dispfn`:

```cpp
// display from p to end
void ArbList::display(ArbCell* p) const
{   std::cout << "(";
    while ( p )
    {   dispfn(p->item);    // supplied displayer
        if ( p = p->next ) std::cout << " ";
    }
```

```
        std::cout << ")";
}
```

The functions remove and find use the supplied equality tester rather than the == operator:

```
int ArbList::remove(Any c)
{   ArbCell *tmp, *p = head;
    int count = 0;
    if ( p == NULL ) return count;
        while (p->next)                         // treats all but head cell
        {  if ( equal((p->next)->item, c) )    // uses equal tester
           {   count++;
               tmp = p->next;
               p->next = tmp->next;
               delete(tmp);                    // frees up storage
           }
           else  p = p->next;
        }
        if( equal(head->item, c) )              // treats head cell
        {   tmp = head;
            head = head->next;
            delete(tmp);
            count++;
        }
        return count;                           // number of items removed
}

ArbCell* ArbList::find(Any c)
{   for( ArbCell* p=head ; p ; p=p->next )
        if( equal(p->item, c) ) return p;      // equal tester
    return NULL;                                // c not on list
}
```

Other member functions not shown are simple translations from their List counterparts.

Now we can apply the generic ArbList. The example establishes lists of string objects from ArbList. The required displayer and equality tester functions are defined early in the file:

```
///////    testAList.C    ///////
#include <iostream>
#include <string>
#include "ArbList.h"
using std::cout; using std::endl;
using std::string;
```

5.12 GENERIC LISTS

```cpp
// linked list of strings via
//       generic ArbList class

void strDisplay(string* str)
{    cout << *str;    }

bool strEq(string* a, string* b)
{    return *a == *b; }
```

In the following main program, a list of strings slist is an instance of ArbList with the required functions supplied. Then, slist is used normally as a list of strings. Note that string* rather than string objects are always passed in the function calls:

```cpp
int main()
{    char* s[] = {"Zero", "Ten", "Twenty",
                  "Thirty", "Forty", "Fifty"};
     string a[] = {string(s[0]),string(s[1]), string(s[2]),
                   string(s[3]), string(s[4]), string(s[5])};

     ArbList
     slist( a + 1, reinterpret_cast< ArbList::EQ_FN >(strEq),
            reinterpret_cast< ArbList::DISP_FN >(strDisplay) );

     slist.putOn( a + 3 );
     slist.putOn( a + 5 );
     slist.display(); cout << endl;

     slist.putOn( a );
     slist.putOn( a + 2 );
     slist.append( a + 4 );
     slist.display(); cout << endl;

     slist.remove( a + 4 );
     slist.remove( a );
     slist.display(); cout << endl;

     slist.shorten(3);
     slist.display(); cout << endl;
     slist.shorten(1);
     slist.display(); cout << endl;
}
```

Run this program to produce the following output:

```
(Fifty Thirty Ten)
(Twenty Zero Fifty Thirty Ten Forty)
(Twenty Fifty Thirty Ten)
```

(Ten)
()

We have now successfully built a generic list class that can be applied in many applications.

5.13 UNIONS AND BIT FIELDS

A union is like a `class` except *all data members are stored at the same starting location*. Union is a construct for objects that can store a variety of different types at different times. The size of a `union` object is just as big as the largest data type it can hold. Otherwise, the `union` is just like a `class`.

A variable or class member can be declared to occupy a few bits in a single word. This ability allows you to pack information more tightly for certain applications. Such members are known as *bit fields* and are either signed or unsigned integer types with the number of bits specified after a colon (:).

See Appendix D for more information and examples on the `union` and the bit field.

5.14 SUMMARY

The class is a key construct for encapsulation and data abstraction. A class definition specifies members that are functions, data, `typedef`s, `enum` constants, and even classes. Instance members belong to a host object, whereas class-wide members are independent of class instances. Class members are designated `private` or `public` for access control. A class is a blueprint for making objects that are instances of the class. Each object can be viewed as an independent computing entity consisting of the instance members specified in the class. Data members are stored in the host object; instance functions have the special pointer `this` to access their host, implicitly or explicitly.

Public members of a class define its interface to the rest of the program and are accessible by any part of the program. Private members are accessible only by member functions in the same object or in an object of the same class. The `friend` declaration grants specific functions special access rights to the nonpublic members of objects of a class. Certain operations, such as `operator-(int, fraction)`, can be implemented only as friend functions.

A class definition cannot contain initializers for members. A constructor is a special member function for initializing data members and other setup chores. A constructor taking no arguments is called a *default constructor* and is needed for declaring objects without constructor arguments. An object of a class with no constructors whatsoever can be initialized with array-style initializers when declared. A constructor is called automatically when an object is created.

The destructor is another special member function for freeing dynamic storage and other cleanup chores just before an object is destroyed. Not all classes define destructors. Destructors are normally needed only when objects contain dynamic storage.

The design and implementation of a pocket calculator show how to break a problem into component objects and combine them to build larger objects. The interactions of these components closely simulate the behavior of actual objects, thus making the program elegant and easy to understand. Building upon existing objects to form larger objects is an important OOP technique. When an object contains other objects, the component objects are instantiated and initialized in declaration order before other members of the host object are initialized. When such an object is destroyed, the object destructor is first executed. Component objects are then destroyed in the reverse order of instantiation.

Except for a few built-in operations, all operations for user-defined types (class objects) must be supplied by a program. The built-in operations are initialization, pass as argument, return as function value, =, ., ->, &, and deinitialization by destructors.

A recursive structure can be defined with a class containing a pointer to an object in the same class. A linked list is a common recursive structure that affords great run-time flexibility. A generic list class is a typical container class that can be defined using pointers to function and the void * type. Such classes can be reused for applications requiring different or newly introduced types.

EXERCISES

1. Compare and contrast the two different class declarations class and struct.

2. Consider declaring an array of objects. Is a default constructor absolutely necessary? Illustrate your answer with examples.

3. In what aspects are constructors and destructors special members of a class?

4. Usually, a member is accessed only through a host object. Name all the cases you can think of where this rule does not apply.

5. What is the difference between initializing an object member using a member-initializer in a constructor init-list and assigning an initial value in the constructor body? Give examples to illustrate your point.

6. Consider static data members of a class. If the static member is private, how can it be initialized? Examine the `Poly` class (Section 5.4) and the member function `s_to_d()`. Should it be declared `static`? Why?

7. Consider a class `ClassX` and an object `obj` of this class. Assume that this class contains an enumerator member `Econst` and a `typedef` `Type`. Discuss the access notations `obj.Type`, `obj.Econst`, `ClassX::Type`, and `ClassX::Econst`.

8. A class has a number of members that are special in the sense that they have predefined meaning. Name the ones you know and explain their functions.

9. Exercise Cal-1: In OOP, one important design consideration is which part of the program contains what information. A good segregation of information helps the logic of the design. Consider the placement of information in the pocket calculator example. Which class should possess and provide the *precision* information? Which class should possess and provide the string of keys (+-*/...) allowed? Which other classes need to use this information but should not be the keepers of it? Modify the calculator classes accordingly.

10. Define a class `TicTacToeBoard` that records the game status, allows legal moves, and determines the game outcome. When designing this class, think about other simple board games, such as Othello, and what they have in common.

11. Consider the binary search algorithm used for looking up the foreign exchange table. Follow the generic sorting example in Section 4.12 and build a generic binary search function.

12. Consider objects that are read-only—namely, objects declared `const`. Does the read-only status of a host object prevent you from using certain member functions? Which ones? Why?

13. Take the `Poly` class and add all possible read-only declarations to it. (*Hint*: Do not forget the host object.)

14. Exercise Menu-1: Follow the `Calculator` example, design a program (class `Menu`) that can display a number of menu items as strings, and allow the user to make one selection. Design this program with generality and reuse in mind. (*Hint*: Write three classes and follow the model-control-view paradigm.)

15. A binary tree is a recursive structure with a root node that either contains just an item of a certain type (a leaf node) or contains an item, a left binary tree, and a right binary tree (an internal node). Define a `BTree` class together with appropriate functions.

CHAPTER SIX

I/O Streams and the Standard Library

Software libraries provide well-written and tested code for many useful purposes. A library is a very efficient way of making high-quality code available to programmers so that they do not have to "reinvent the wheel" every time a need for one of these routines arises.

To use a library-supplied construct (constant, variable, function, class, etc.), it must first be declared. Do this by including the correct header files. Once declared, the library-supplied entity can be used just as one of your own from a different file. Compiled codes from the Standard Library are usually automatically loaded, as needed, into your final executable program.

The C++ Standard Library contains many parts. Libraries for string manipulation, character operations, mathematical calculations, and I/O are described. A detailed description of the C++ I/O streams is given so you use them effectively. A systematic way of making the I/O operators >> and << work for user-defined objects is suggested.

Many library facilities are available. Some important ones are presented in this chapter. The Standard Template Library is presented in Chapter 11; others can be found in Appendices C, I, and J.

6.1 DIFFERENT HEADER FILES

To use different functions or classes provided by C++, you need to include different header files. Part of learning the Standard C++ libraries is to know which header file to include for what purposes. There are three sources of headers that come with C++:

1. Native C++ headers such as `<iostream>`, `<string>`, and `<vector>` that don't carry any .h suffix
2. Native C headers such as `<string.h>`, `<ctype.h>`, and `<stdlib.h>` that have the .h suffix

3. C headers turned into C++ headers such as <cstring> and <cstdlib> that drop the .h suffix and add the c prefix

When you #include a Standard C++ header (category 1 or 3), the symbols declared are in the std namespace. For example,

```
#include <iostream>
```

gets you std::cout, std::endl, and so on. Strictly speaking, you cannot use cout or cin directly unless you have added the

```
using std::cout;
using std::cin;
```

directives to your source code file.

When including a C header file such as <string.h>, the symbols you get are in the global namespace. So you can call **strcmp**(), for example, directly. If you prefer placing these symbols in the std namespace rather than in the global namespace, use the c-prefixed headers instead. For example, <cstring> gives you std::**strcmp**(). For simplicity, examples in this book do not use headers of type 3.

6.2 C-STYLE STRING INPUT AND OUTPUT

Character strings are among the most frequent structures in programming. C-style string input is easily handled through an I/O stream object. For example,

```
const int LEN = 64;
char buffer[LEN];
cin >> buffer;
```

The char* version of the overloaded input operator >> reads strings separated by white space (SPACE, TAB, RETURN, NEWLINE) into the given buffer. Here white space breaks up a string even inside double quotes. A string terminator '\0' (null character) is appended to the end of a string read into buffer.

If the input buffer does not have enough room, the trailing portion of the input string is lost. The *I/O manipulator* (Section 6.9) **setw**(*length*) prevents string input overflow. It limits input to no more than *length* characters at a time. Thus, to be safe, we can use a loop:

```
while ( in >> std::setw(SIZE) >> buffer )
```

String Composition and Extraction

At compile time, C-style string constants can be concatenated by juxtaposition (putting them next to each other). At run time, a string can also be composed from a mixture of strings, integers, floating-point numbers, and so on. The `ostrstream` class is designed for this purpose. An `ostrstream` object produces output similar to `cout` but in a preallocated character buffer instead.

Here is a simple example:

```
#include <iostream>
#include <strstream>
using std::ostrstream; using std::cout; using std::endl;

int main()
{   const int SIZE = 64;
    char buf[SIZE];
    ostrstream mystr(buf, SIZE);     // ostrstream obj
    float amt = 32.98;
    // compose string using mystr object
    mystr << "The price is $" << amt << '.' << '\0';     // (A)
    cout << buf << endl;             // displays C-style string
    return 0;
}
```

Note the correct header files to use. In `main`, a character buffer `buf` of capacity 64 is allocated. The buffer and its size are used in establishing `mystr`, an instance of the `ostrstream` class. The overloaded operator `<<` is used to compose a C-style string in `buf` through the `mystr` object (line A).

Compiling and running this program produces the following display:

```
The price is $32.98.
```

The buffer size should be large enough to receive a composed string. Otherwise, only the prefix that fits is contained in the buffer.

While an `ostrstream` object helps compose a string from all types of data, an `istrstream` object does just the opposite—it extracts different data from their C-style string representations. For example, the function `str_to_float` uses an `istrstream` object to convert the ASCII string representation of a floating-point number into `float`:

```
float str_to_float(const char* s)
{   istrstream tmp(s, strlen(s));
    float ans;
    tmp >> ans;
    return ans;
}
```

Of course, the extraction operator >> does not modify the string s in any way. The conversion fails if the leading part of s does not represent a valid floating-point number.

Similar to using cin, extraction of consecutive quantities separated by white spaces in a string is easy. For example, the main program

```
int main()
{   char *s = "3  -3.1 \t 3.1416";
    cout << s << endl;
    int a;
    float b, c;
    istrstream tmp(s, strlen(s));
    tmp >> a >> b >> c;
    cout << a+b+c << endl;
    return 0;
}
```

produces the following display:

```
3  -3.1      3.1416
3.0416
```

In applications where the extraction of a string is done only once, the creation of the named istrstream object tmp can be omitted in favor of an anonymous object:

```
istrstream (s, strlen(s)) >> a >> b >> c;
```

6.3 STRING OBJECTS

Standard C++ provides the string class to create objects and to supply many useful operations for ASCII character strings. Using string objects tends to be more robust and less error-prone than using C-style stings. Include the header <string> to use the string class. The <string.h> header is for traditional C-style strings whose operations are summarized in Appendix C.

Here common string operations are summarized. Standard C++ also provides a wstring class for wide character (wchar_t) strings. The string and wstring are char and wchar_t instantiations of the basic_string class template (Chapter 10), respectively.

Creating Strings

A string object contains a sequence of characters referred to as the *controlled sequence*. You may create string objects from C-style strings and other string objects. String constructors include:

```
string()                                    // empty string
string(char* s)                             // s
string(const string& str_obj)               // copy of str_obj
string(size_t n, char c)                    // n repeated chars
string(char* s, size_t n)                   // first n characters
string(const string& str_obj, size_t n)     // first n characters
string(char* s, size_t i, size_t n)         // up to n characters
string(const string& str_obj,               //    starting from char i
           size_t i, size_t n)
```

Generally, you may pass (assign) a C-style string to a string parameter (variable), making it easy to use string objects. The **c_str** member function returns a const C-style string stored in a string host object.

Performing string I/O

For string objects, free format input is supported:

```
in >> str_obj;      // extracts string object
```

reads the next space-delimited sequence of characters from the input stream in into the string object str_obj. The Standard Library function call

getline(istream& *in*, string& *str_obj*, char *eol*)

reads from the istream object *in* into the string object *str_obj* until either the given end-of-line character *eol* (usually '\n') or the end of file is encountered. If the third argument *eol* is not given, it is assumed to be '\n'. If the input length exceeds str.max_size(), the read operation fails and sets the failbit of *in*. In any case, the function returns a reference to *in*. The TextLines class (Section 4.7) example also illustrates **getline** usage.

The unattached **getline** function here is not to be confused with the **getline** member function of istream (Table 6.2), which reads a line into a char* buffer.

To output a string object *str_obj*, simply use

out_stream << *str_obj*;

where *out_stream* is cout or any other ostream or ofstream object.

Inspecting and Modifying Strings

Attributes of a given string object *str_obj* can be obtained:

str_obj.**length**()	(number of chars, same as *str_obj*.**size**())
str_obj.**empty**()	(true or false)
str_obj.**find**(*str2, i*)	(whole substring match)
str_obj.**find_first_of**(*str2, i*)	(1st char in *str2*)
str_obj.**find_first_not_of**(*str2, i*)	(1st char not in *str2*)

Each of the find functions returns an index of the first matching substring in *str_obj*, or string::npos if the match fails. In each case, the *str2* argument may be given as a single character, a C-style string, or a string object. The optional argument *i* is the starting position to search in *str_obj* and defaults to 0. The corresponding **find_last_of** and **find_last_not_of** searches from position *i* or the end toward the beginning of string *str_obj*.

The subscript notation *str_obj*[i] allows you to get/set individual characters in a string. For example, *str_obj*[0] = 'F' sets the first character of *str_obj* to 'F'. Make sure the index used is valid.

Comparing Strings

Comparing character strings under alphabetical order is also simple. Use the overloaded operators <, >, >=, <=, and == to compare two string objects.

The string member function **compare** can be used

str_obj.**compare**(*i0, n, any_str*)

to compare the host *str_obj* (starting from index *i0* for *n* characters if the first two args are given or the entire *str_obj* string) to *any_str* (C-style or string object). The result is positive, negative, or zero indicating *str_obj* is bigger than, less than, or equal to *any_str*.

Manipulating Strings

The + operator combines stings. The code

```
string s3 = s1 + s2
```

appends s1 and s2 and assigns the result to s3 while s1 and s2 remain unchanged. Also, s2 can be a C-style string. To actually change s1, use s1 += s2; or s1.**append**(s2). The **replace** function takes arguments in the same way as **compare**:

str_obj.**replace**(*i0, n, any_str*)

6.4 A STRING TOKENIZER

and replaces a portion of *str_obj* (starting from index *i0* for *n* characters if the first two args are given or the entire *str_obj* string) with *any_str*. The function returns *this.

To extract a read-only C-style string from a string object, use

```
const char* cs = str_obj.c_str();
```

6.4 A STRING TOKENIZER

One frequent operation on strings is to locate and process each token contained in the string. A *token* is a sequence of characters forming a meaningful unit such as a word, a number, an operator, or a variable. Tokens in a character string are separated from each other by one or more *delimiter* characters. Given any string and the delimiters, a program can extract consecutive tokens from the string for processing. As an example, let's write a Tokenizer class for exactly this purpose.

Here is the design of Tokenizer:

- To create a Tokenizer object, you supply a target string (str), a string of delimiters (delim), and a Boolean flag (want_delim) indicating if delimiters in str should also be returned as tokens. If want_delim is true, each delimiter in str is returned as a single-character token. Otherwise, only nondelimiter tokens are returned.
- After a Tokenizer (tk) has been instantiated, you can call tk.nextToken() to obtain the next token from the target string.
- To see if there are still more tokens to be returned, you test tk.moreToken().
- At any point, tk.tokenCount() gives the number of tokens remaining.
- The delimiters in tk can be changed at any time with tk.setDelimiter(*delim*).

In the header file, one Tokenizer constructor with two optional parameters is defined. Thus the simple code

```
Tokenizer tk1(str_obj);
```

gives you a tokenizer tk1 to extract tokens from *str_obj* separated by white space.

```
///////    Tokenizer.h    ///////
#include <string>
using std::string;

class Tokenizer
```

```
{ public:
    Tokenizer(const string& str,          // constructor
              const string& delim = WHITE,
              bool want_delim = false)
      : position(0), delimiter(delim),
        target(str), delimToken(want_delim) { }

    bool moreToken() const;                // true/false
    string nextToken();                    // returns string object
    int tokenCount() const;                // yet to be returned
    string setDelimiter(const string& delim)
    { delimiter = delim; }
  private:
    string next();
    string nextAll();
    static const string WHITE;    // init in Tokenizer.C
    int position;                 // to search for next token
    const string& target;         // the target string
    string delimiter;             // delimiters to use
    bool delimToken;              // delimiter as token flag
};
```

The implementation of `Tokenizer` depends heavily on operations supplied by `string`. Note how the white space constant `WHITE` is initialized.

```
///////    Tokenizer.C    ///////
#include "Tokenizer.h"

const string Tokenizer::WHITE=string("\r \n\t");     // white space

bool Tokenizer::moreToken() const
{ if ( position == target.length() ) return false;        // (1)
  if ( delimToken ) return true;
  int i0=target.find_first_not_of(delimiter, position);
  return i0 != string::npos;                              // (2)
}
```

If the current position reached beyond the last character index (line 1), `moreToken` returns `false` immediately. Otherwise, if delimiters are regarded as tokens, it returns `true`; if not, it looks for any nondelimiter character in the remainder of the target string (line 2).

The `nextToken` function calls `nextAll()` if delimiters are tokens or `next()` if not. It returns the next token as a `string` object. An empty string returned signifies the end.

```
string Tokenizer::nextToken()
{   if ( delimToken ) return nextAll();
```

6.4 A STRING TOKENIZER

```
      else return next();
}
```

The private function `next()` extracts a nondelimiter token and creates a string object. The indices `i0` and `i1` identify the start and the end of the next token to be returned.

```
string Tokenizer::next()
{  int i0=position, i1=position;           // start, end index
   if (i0 >= target.length()) return string();
   i0 = target.find_first_not_of(delimiter, i1);
   if (i0 == string::npos) return string();
                                           // no more nondelimiters
   i1 = target.find_first_of(delimiter, i0);
   if (i1 == string::npos) i1 = target.length();
                                           // no delimiter at the end
   position = i1;                          // for next search (3)
   return string(target, i0, i1-i0);       // token found (4)
}
```

Note how `next()` updates `position` and returns the token found (lines 3 and 4). The `nextAll()` function can be found in the example code package (ex06/token/).

The function `tokenCount` computes the number of tokens yet to be returned based on the flag `delimToken` and the current setting of `delimiter`.

```
int Tokenizer::tokenCount() const
{   if ( position == target.length() ) return 0;
    int count = 0;
    int i0=position, i1=position;
    while ( 1 )
    {  if ( i1 == string::npos ) return count;
       i0 = target.find_first_not_of(delimiter, i1);
       if ( i0 == string::npos )
          return (! delimToken ? count
                    : count + target.length() - i1);
       count++;
       if ( delimToken ) count += i0-i1;                  // (5)
       i1 = target.find_first_of(delimiter, i0);
    }
}
```

One way to implement `tokenCount` is to repeatedly call `nextToken` internally. But that is more expensive than the foregoing implementation, which increments a `count` rather than creates `string` objects. Note how the delimiters skipped are added to `count` (line 5).

To test `Tokenizer`, a function such as

```
void testToken()
{   string t("This is a test.");
    Tokenizer tk(t);
    while ( tk.moreToken() )
    {   cout << tk.tokenCount() << " = "
             << tk.nextToken() << endl;
    }
}
```

can be used. The `SortKey` class (Section 4.7) can be simplified using `Tokenizer`.

In-Memory String I/O Objects

String composition and extraction with C-style strings have been discussed in Section 6.2. Standard C++ makes in-memory I/O even more convenient with string I/O objects. A *string I/O object* is one that does I/O to a *dynamic string buffer* held in the object. String I/O objects are from the classes (see Figure 7.9):

```
istringstream           // string input objects
ostringstream           // string output objects
stringstream            // string I/O objects
```

Include the header `<sstream>` to use them. For example,

```
#include <sstream>

float amt = 32.98;
ostringstream o_str;
o_str << "The price is $" << amt;
```

Use `o_str.`**`str`**`()` to obtain the composed `string` object.

6.5 OPERATIONS ON CHARACTERS

Since a `char` is represented as a small integer, it can be used freely in arithmetic expressions involving other characters or integers. For example, the expression

```
'8' - '0'
```

yields the integer value 8 because the values of `'0'`, `'1'`, `'2'`, and so on are consecutive and form an increasing sequence. Also, an expression such as

```
c >= 'A' && c <= 'Z'
```

6.6 NUMERIC COMPUTATIONS

Table 6.1 CHARACTER FUNCTIONS

Function	Test For
int **isupper**(int c)	Uppercase letter (A–Z)
int **islower**(int c)	Lowercase letter (a–z)
int **isalpha**(int c)	Uppercase or lowercase letter
int **isdigit**(int c)	Decimal digit
int **isalnum**(int c)	**isalpha**(c) || **isdigit**(c)
int **iscntrl**(int c)	Control character
int **isxdigit**(int c)	Hexadecimal digit
int **isprint**(int c)	Printable character including SPACE
int **isgraph**(int c)	Printable character except SPACE
int **isspace**(int c)	SPACE, FORMFEED, NEWLINE, RETURN, TAB, vertical TAB
int **ispunct**(int c)	Printable character not SPACE, digit, or letter

Function	Meaning
int **toupper**(int c)	Convert to uppercase
int **tolower**(int c)	Convert to lowercase

used to test for c as uppercase works because the corresponding uppercase and lowercase characters are a fixed distance apart. Reliance on such features makes the expression dependent on the character set.

The header file <ctype.h> defines a group of useful character macros and functions (Table 6.1) that are implementation independent. Among these, **isupper** and **tolower** have already been used (Section 1.7). The various testing functions in Table 6.1 return zero for false and nonzero for true.

6.6 NUMERIC COMPUTATIONS

Also supported in the Standard Library are mathematical functions, such as *sin*, *sqrt*, and *log*, for floating-point computations. To use these functions, the header file <math.h> is needed. Appendix I contains a list of all mathematical functions.

The library functions work with type double (double-precision floating-point). This means that they take double arguments and return double values. For example, the *cos* function is double **cos**(double x).

Complex Numbers

Standard C++ also supports complex number computation with classes such as

```
complex<float>
complex<double>
complex<long double>
```

Just include the header <complex> to use complex objects and functions for them.

The normal arithmetic and equality operations are supported. Operations involving a complex<*type*> object and a *type* value (e.g., float, double) are also supported. For example,

```
double d = 3.14;
complex<double> c(2.0, 3.0);   // 2.0 + 3.0 i
c.real();                      // 2.0
c.imag();                      // 3.0
complex<double> r = d + c;     // 5.14 + 3.0 i
```

Complex numbers are in rectangular notation. These two member functions return the *radius* and *argument* in polar notation.

abs(c); (radius)
arg(c); ($-\pi <$ argument $\leq \pi$)

Complex functions include **pow, conj, cos, cosh, exp, log, log10, sin, sinh, sqrt, tan,** and **tanh**. In case of multivalued functions, the principal values are returned.

The I/O operators >> and << read and display complex numbers in the notation (*real, imag*).

6.7 THE I/O STREAM LIBRARY

Include the header <iostream> for basic I/O. We have already used the standard I/O objects cin, cout, and cerr in many examples. You need either the std:: prefix or the appropriate using declaration/directive to use these and other names supplied in the std namespace. Since I/O is an important topic, let's take a systematic look at the C++ iostream library.

The iostream library supports character I/O and consists of a number of related classes including

- *Basic I/O*: ios, istream, ostream, and iostream
- *File I/O*: ifstream, ofstream, and fstream
- *In-memory I/O with C-style strings*: istrstream, ostrstream, and strstream

- *In-memory I/O with string objects*: istringstream, ostringstream, and stringstream

These classes form a hierarchy (Figure 7.9), building more powerful classes from basic ones. Standard I/O is handled by the iostream class built on top of istream and ostream classes, which in turn depend on the fundamental ios class. Then, file and string I/O are built on top of the standard I/O facilities. These I/O streams are based on the char type. A complementary set of classes and objects (wcin, wcout, wofstream, wifstream, wios,[1] etc.) handles wide characters.

The object cin belongs to the istream class, whereas cout and cerr belong to the ostream class. The unbuffered error stream cerr is also complemented by a buffered stream, clog, used for logging of error and other messages produced by a program.

Opening and Closing Files

For each program, we always have the four ready-to-use objects for standard I/O as mentioned earlier. For file I/O, include the header <fstream>. I/O objects are connected with specific files with the following:

```
ifstream myin(filename, ios::in);           // for input   (1)
ofstream myout(filename, ios::out);         // for output  (2)
ofstream myout(filename, ios::app);         // to append at end
fstream myio(filename, ios::in | ios::out); // for input and output
```

The second argument for the first two calls (lines 1 and 2) is optional. We can also establish a file I/O object without its being attached to any file. The **open** member function is used later to attach such an object to a file. For example,

```
ifstream anyin;         // file input object
anyin.open(filename);   // attach to filename
if ( anyin.fail() )     // if open failed
{   ...
}
```

Table 6.5 provides more details on I/O stream error states.

Use the member function **is_open**() to test whether an I/O object is still open. To close a file, use **close**():

```
anyfile.close();
```

---

[1] Both ios and wios instantiate the basic_ios template; istream instantiates the basic_istream template; ostream instantiates the basic_ostream template, and so on.

To flush (force output) of the buffer of an output object, use **flush**(). Use the member function **sync**() to flush (discard unread characters in the input buffer) an input stream object.

I/O Operators << and >>

The bit-shift operators << and >> are overloaded to serve as output and input operators, respectively. A very simple way to perform output is with

```
cout << var;
anyout << var;
```

The type of the variable var determines the display produced. Besides a single variable, << can also handle any valid expression. In this case, you enclose the expression in parentheses to avoid precedence problems with <<. If var is of type char*, then a '\0'-terminated character string is displayed. The output manipulator **endl** outputs a system-dependent line terminator and flushes the output buffer:

```
anyout << var << endl;
```

If << is given a pointer, it displays the address of the pointer in hexadecimal notation. To display the address of a pointer to char, it must first be cast to void* to prevent it from being interpreted as a character string.

The input operator >> deposits input data into a variable of any basic type including char*. For example,

```
float a; int b;
cin >> a >> b;
```

reads correctly the input

3.1416   17

For >>, input tokens are always separated by white space, which is ignored. Thus,

```
char ch;
while( cin >> ch ) {  ...  }
```

reads, from standard input,

uv w
  xy   z

as six characters. (White space in the input can be read using other facilities, such as **get** and **getline**, explained later.)

6.7   THE I/O STREAM LIBRARY

We have already seen how the input operator >> is used to read character strings (Section 6.2). The >> operator is also very convenient in reading tabulated data. For instance, the loop

```
float x[3], y[3], z[3];
for ( int i = 0 ; cin >> x[i] ; i++ ) cin >> y[i] >> z[i];
```

reads correctly the data file

```
1.0    +2.0    3.0
0.1    -0.2    0.3
1.1    +2.2    3.3
```

The expression *obj* >> *arg* (or *obj* << *arg*) always produces a reference to the stream object *obj* as the value of the expression. This explains why << and >> can be concatenated. For example, the lines

```
cout << a << b ;
(cout << a) << b ;
```

are really the same. However, the logical test

```
while( cin >> x[i] )
```

works for a different reason. When cin (the value of cin >> x[i]) is tested, it must be converted from an istream object to a logical value. The istream class defines a special type-conversion rule that converts cin to zero or a positive integer depending on whether cin has been closed or not (Section 8.9).

The I/O operators >> and << can be further overloaded to perform I/O on class objects (Section 6.8), making their use even more general.

Reading and Writing

Several built-in member functions for I/O objects can be used to perform I/O on characters, whole lines, or a sequence of bytes. These are summarized in Table 6.2. Examples using **put** and **get** are shown in the table. There are three auxiliary member functions for input:

1. **peek**() returns the next input character (or EOF) to be examined without consuming it. The character remains to be read later.
2. **putback**(char c) puts at most one character back into the input stream.
3. **ignore**(int len = 1, int del = EOF) discards up to len characters until del is reached.

Table 6.2 I/O MEMBER FUNCTIONS

Function	Description
`obj.put(char c)`	Outputs c; returns ref to `obj`.
`obj.get(char& c)`	Reads character into c; returns ref to `obj`.
`int c = obj.get()`	Returns next character or `EOF`.
`obj.write(const char *s, int length)`	Outputs string of given `length`; returns ref to `obj`.
`obj.read(char *buf, int size)`	Inputs `size` number of bytes to `buf`; returns ref to `obj`.
`obj.getline(char *buf, int n, char delim = '\n')`	Puts at most n-1 bytes in `buf` up to `delim` or end of file; adds final `'\0'`; returns ref to `obj`.
`int obj.gcount()`	Returns number of bytes read by last `getline`.

Output Formatting

The C++ output stream defines a standard output format for its objects so that simple output can be performed easily. However, in some applications, the output must be programmed to appear in certain well-defined forms. Formatting is necessary, for example, when you want the entries in a table of numeric data to line up, the credits and charges on a bill to show as positive and negative amounts, or simply to render integers in octal or hexadecimal. How we achieve such effects through a formatting mechanism provided by output objects is our next topic of discussion, which uses the following formatting terminology:

- *Width*: This is the minimum number of character positions (*field*) for the next output item. The item is displayed in a field at least this wide. If necessary, *fill characters* (usually white space) are supplied to make up the width.
- *Justification*: Within a given field, the item is displayed *right* or *left* justified (flush with the right or left end of the field).
- *Base*: The radix base for displaying integers is decimal, octal, or hexadecimal.
- *Precision*: This specifies the number of significant digits displayed for a `float` or `double`.

Setting the width in an input stream limits the number of bytes read each time.

6.7 THE I/O STREAM LIBRARY

Tables 6.3 and 6.4 show functions and flags provided by output objects to control output format. Default settings are also indicated. The field width is normally zero. When the width is set with the **width**() function, only the next output item is affected. After that, the width resets to zero again automatically. Other format settings affect all subsequent output. All format functions return the old setting in case it must be restored later.

With **precision**(), we can improve, for example, the calculator display by modifying the showNumber() function of CalcFace (Section 5.5) to

```
void CalcFace::showNumber(double number)
{    cout.precision(PREC);
     cout << "Calc:   " << number << endl;
}
```

The function **setf**() sets and retrieves format flag settings, which are bit values that can be combined with logical or. For example, the code

```
cout.setf(ios::uppercase | ios::showpos );  // sets two flags
cout.setf(ios::hex, ios::basefield);
                         // resets basefield, then sets hex flag
cout << 54321 << endl;
cout << sqrt(2) << endl;
```

gives the following output:

```
D431                    // hex with uppercase D
+1.41421                // precision 6, leading +
```

Table 6.3 FORMAT FUNCTIONS

Format Request	Meaning
obj.**width**(int w)	Sets width to w; returns old width.
int w = obj.**width**()	Returns current width.
obj.**precision**(int n)	Sets precision to n; returns old value. Default precision is 6.
int n = obj.**precision**()	Returns current precision.
obj.**fill**(char c)	Sets fill character to c; returns old value.
char c = obj.**fill**()	Returns fill character (default SPACE).

Table 6.4   FORMAT FLAGS

Format Request	Meaning
long **flag** = obj.flags()	Returns current flag.
long **flag** = obj.flags(*nf*)	Sets flag to *nf*; returns old flag.
obj.**setf**(ios::oct, ios::basefield)	Sets base to octal.
obj.**setf**(ios::hex, ios::basefield)	Sets base to hexadecimal.
obj.**setf**(ios::dec, ios::basefield)	Sets base to decimal (default).
obj.**setf**(ios::right, ios::adjustfield)	Selects right justification (default).
obj.**setf**(ios::left, ios::adjustfield)	Selects left justification.
obj.**setf**(ios::scientific, ios::floatfield)	Uses scientific notation $[-]m.dde\pm xx$.
obj.**setf**(ios::fixed, ios::floatfield)	Prevents decimal-point motion (default).
obj.**setf**(ios::showpos)	Shows both leading + and −.
obj.**unsetf**(ios::showpos)	Shows leading − only (default).
obj.**setf**(ios::uppercase)	Uses uppercase in numbers.
obj.**unsetf**(ios::uppercase)	Uses lowercase in numbers (default).

For another example of output formatting, consider displaying a monthly calendar. Since we have already defined a class Month (Section 4.13), we simply add a display member function to Month:

```
#include "Month.h"
using std::cout;  using std::endl;

void Month::display(ostream& out) const
{       Week *mon = month;
        out << "SUN MON TUE WED THU FRI SAT" << endl;
        while ( *mon )
        {   Week wk = *mon++;
            for ( int d = SUN ; d <= SAT ; d++ )
            {   if ( wk[d] )
                {   out.width(3);                   // (1)
                    out << wk[d] << ' ';            // (2)
                }
                else out << "    ";
            }
            out << endl;
```

6.7 THE I/O STREAM LIBRARY

```
        }
}
```

In `Month::display`, the exact placements of the calendar dates are controlled with `out.`**`width`**`(3)` (line 1) as described. To line up the dates appropriately, we use a width of four characters for each column of the calendar (line 2). Here is a typical display:

```
SUN MON TUE WED THU FRI SAT
              1   2   3   4   5
  6   7   8   9  10  11  12
 13  14  15  16  17  18  19
 20  21  22  23  24  25  26
 27  28  29  30  31
```

File Updating

When the same file is opened for both reading and writing under the mode

`ios::in | ios::out`

the file is being updated *in place*; that is, you are modifying the contents of the file. In performing both reading and writing under the update mode, take care when switching from reading to writing, and vice versa. The C++ I/O stream library uses a *file-position* indicator (similar to a cursor in a text editor) to keep track of the location for the next I/O byte/character in a file. The file position is moved by each I/O operation. Before switching either way, a file-positioning operation (e.g., **seekp**) may be needed. These remarks will become clear as the update modes are explained.

The `ios::in | ios::out` mode is most efficient for making one-for-one character substitutions in a file. Under this mode, file contents stay the same if not explicitly modified. Modification is done by positioning and writing the revised characters over the existing characters. A **lowercase** command based on file updating can be implemented by following these steps:

1. Open the given file with the `ios::in | ios::out` mode.
2. Read characters until an uppercase letter is encountered.
3. Overwrite the uppercase letter with the lowercase letter.
4. Repeat steps 2 and 3 until end of file is reached.

Here is the implementation:

```
#include <iostream>
#include <fstream>
#include <ctype.h>
using std::cout; using std::cerr;
```

```cpp
using std::endl; using std::fstream;
using std::ios;

int main(int argc, char *argv[])
{   char c;
    if ( argc != 2 )
    {   cerr << "Usage: " << argv[0] << " file" << endl;
        return 1;
    }
    fstream fio(argv[1], ios::in | ios::out);
    if ( fio.fail() )
    {   cerr << argv[0] << ':' << " Cannot open"
                        << argv[1] << endl;
        return 1;
    }
    while ((c = fio.get()) != EOF)
        if ( isupper(c) )
        {   fio.seekg(-1, ios::cur);    // position for writing c
            fio.put(tolower(c));
        }
    fio.close();
    return 0;
}
```

After an uppercase character is detected, the file position is on the next character to read. Thus, the position indicator should be moved to the previous character to overwrite it. This is done here by

`fio.seekg(-1, ios::cur);    // back up one byte`

Then, the lowercase character is output. The rest of the file is processed in the same way.

The prototypes of the file-position-setting member functions are

```
istream& seekg(long offset, ios::seek_dir ori = ios::beg);
ostream& seekp(long offset, ios::seek_dir ori = ios::beg);
```

These two functions are essentially the same except that one belongs to the `istream` class and the other to the `ostream` class. For the `iostream` class, both are available. Note that these two functions set the same unique file I/O position.

After **seekg**/**seekp**, a subsequent I/O operation will access data beginning at the new position. The position is set to `offset` bytes from the indicated origin `ori`, which is one of the constants

`ios::beg`   (usually 0: the beginning of the file)
`ios::cur`   (usually 1: the current position)
`ios::end`   (usually 2: the end of the file)

Any time during I/O, the current file position can be determined by the member function **tellg**()/**tellp**(), which returns an offset from the beginning of the file.

When output is under the ios:app (append at end) mode, output will always be appended at the file's end and will not be affected by repositioning. However, the read position works normally; that is, it is moved by each I/O operation as well as by repositioning.

Binary Input and Output

It is usual to think of I/O as dealing with a sequence of characters. But performing *binary* I/O, where bytes rather than characters are being treated, is also possible. With binary I/O, a block of consecutive memory locations (e.g., an entire array or object) can be written out, byte for byte, into a file for later retrieval. If a binary file actually contains characters, it is no different from a text file. Otherwise, a binary file contains arbitrary bytes and usually cannot be examined or edited with a text editor. However, it is the most efficient way of reading and writing large amounts of data.

The member functions for binary I/O are

```
istream& read(const unsigned char *buf, int len);
ostream& write(const unsigned char *ptr, int len);
```

where buf (ptr) points to the data area in memory to receive (provide) len bytes.

To illustrate binary I/O, consider writing an array of Fraction objects to a file and later reading the data back in again. The sequence

```
Fraction uv[] = {Fraction(2,5), Fraction(3,6)};
ofstream out("Fraction.data", ios::out);
out.write((unsigned char*)(uv), sizeof(uv));
out.close();
```

puts two Fraction objects in the file Fraction.data. Clearly, the output of bytes is very simple and direct. The binary file can later be read back into a program by the code

```
Fraction ab[2];
ifstream in("Fraction.data", ios::in);
in.read((unsigned char*) ab, 2*sizeof(Fraction));
```

The objects read in should work normally. For example, they can be displayed to verify the data:

```
ab[0].display();
cout << endl;
ab[1].display();
```

Table 6.5 I/O CONDITIONS

Function	Description
obj.**eof**()	Returns true if obj has reached end of file.
obj.**bad**()	Returns true if an invalid operation has been requested.
obj.**fail**()	Returns true if an operation has failed or **bad**() is true (ios::badbit set).
obj.**good**()	Returns true if none of the above is true.
obj.**rdstate**()	Returns the internal error-state bit vector.
obj.**clear**(*bv*)	Sets error vector to *bv* or 0 if no argument.

Although efficient, binary I/O has its limitations. A binary file is very system dependent and usually cannot be moved to a different computer and be useful. Even on the same computer, a binary file can be used only by a program written in the same language that knows its data type or class definition. Furthermore, objects containing pointers (or references) cannot use direct binary I/O because the pointers (references) will be wrong when they are read back in again.

Error Conditions

In most cases, a call to an I/O member function returns a reference to its host stream object that can be used in a logical test to determine the success or failure of the operation. In addition, an iostream object maintains a set of condition flags recording the ongoing state of the object. Monitoring and setting these flags can be done through the four predicate member functions summarized in Table 6.5. Standard C++ also allows you to specify error states that will cause exceptions (Section 8.10).

6.8 STREAM I/O FOR OBJECTS

The stream operators >> and << are convenient for I/O operations. Each of the two operators takes an I/O stream object as the left operand. The operators already perform I/O for all built-in types because the stream library defines operator functions for all basic-type right operands. If these operators are also made to work for user-defined objects, then I/O operations can be made extremely easy—just apply these operators. A systematic approach is described here for overloading >> and <<.

To display fractions, for example, we can define a friend operator<< of the class Fraction:

```
ostream& operator <<(ostream& out, const Fraction& cf) // (1)
{   out << cf.num << '/' << cf.denom;
    return out;
}
```

With this operator function, output of fractions can be done using <<

```
fraction r(1,2), s(-3,4);
cout << r << ", " << s << endl;
```

just as easily as displaying strings or integers. The function header (line 1) is a frequent idiom:

- The left operand is an ostream object and should be the return value.
- Reference parameters are used to avoid copying objects.
- The object to be displayed is read-only.

If we write the public member function Fraction::display as

```
void Fraction::display(ostream& out = cout) const
{     out << num << '/' << denom;
}
```

then we can simplify operator<< to

```
inline ostream& operator <<(ostream& out, const Fraction& cf) //(2)
{    cf.display(out);
     return out;      // always return left operand
}
```

This version does not need to be a friend of Fraction and can be declared inline for more efficiency. The definition (line 2) is almost universal for all class types. Change one word and the operator function is adapted to another class. How much simpler can it get (Section 10.2)?

Now consider how >> is overloaded to input fractions:

```
istream& operator >>(istream& in, Fraction& f) // (3)
{    int num, denom;
     char c;
     in >> num >> c;
     if ( c == '/' ) in >> denom;
     else                        // sets error state (Section 6.7)
```

```
        {   in.clear( ios::badbit | in.rdstate() );
            return in;
        }
        f = Fraction(num, denom);                  // (4)
        return in;                  // always return left operand
    }
```

The function header (line 3) is another idiom. The reference object f is a return parameter receiving the input fraction through memberwise assignment (line 4). A file of fractions can now be read with >>:

```
3/4    18/19    -20/52
2/5    3/6       5/8
```

We can add an input function read to the Fraction class as a public member:

```
void Fraction::read(istream& in /* = cin */)
{   int num, denom;
    char c;
    in >> num >> c;
    if ( c == '/' )
        in >> denom;
    else                             // clear() sets error state
    {   in.clear( ios::badbit | in.rdstate()); return; }
    *this = Fraction(num, denom);   // calls constructor
}
```

We then simplify operator>> to

```
inline istream& operator >>(istream& in, Fraction& f)
{   f.read(in);
    return in;
}
```

Hence, if a class is built with the appropriate display and read functions, overloading >> and << becomes quite trivial. Follow these conventions consistently to make I/O of objects just as easy as built-in types.

6.9 I/O MANIPULATORS

We have discussed many flags and functions, such as **flush**(), **clear**(), **precision**(), and **width**(), that allow you to alter the state of an I/O object. I/O manipulators are function pointers or objects that work through the I/O operators >> and << to affect the state of an I/O object, making many operations easier.

6.9 I/O MANIPULATORS

The manipulator **setw** can limit the number of bytes read or written:

```
#include <iomanip>

char buffer[12];
while ( cin >> setw(12) >> buffer )
{   . . .
}
```

Lines 1 and 2 in the function `Month::display` can be rewritten as

```
out << setw(3) << wk[d] << ' ';
```

Standard C++ supplies a set of I/O manipulators that take no arguments in <iostream> (Table 6.6), enabling such usage as

```
cout << data << flush;
```

Additional manipulators that take one argument are declared in <iomanip> (Table 6.7).

Without arguments, an I/O manipulator can be implemented as a function that receives a reference I/O object argument and calls certain predefined member functions, such as flush(), in that argument. The manipulator is received, as a function pointer, by a member operator>> (operator<<) of an I/O

Table 6.6 I/O MANIPULATORS

Manipulator	Description
boolalpha, noboolalpha	Uses symbolic true and false.
showbase, noshowbase	Outputs octal/hex prefix.
showpoint, noshowpoint	Sets showpoint.
showpos, noshowpos	Outputs leading + sign.
skipws, noskipws	Skips certain leading white space on input.
ws	Discards all white space on input.
uppercase, nouppercase	Outputs X and E.
left, right, internal	Sets output adjustment.
dec, hex, oct	Sets integer base.
endl, ends	Terminates line, string, then flushes output.
flush	Flushes output.
fixed, scientific	Sets floating format.

Table 6.7 MANIPULATORS FROM `<iomanip>`

Manipulator	Description
`setioflags(f)`, `resetioflags(f)`	Sets, clears given bits for I/O flags.
`setbase(n)`	Sets output integer base.
`setw(n)`	Sets input or output width.
`setfill(c)`	Makes c the fill character.
`setprecision(n)`	Sets n digits after decimal point.

stream. The operator then invokes the manipulator with `*this`. For example, statement 1 triggers actions 2 through 4:

(1) `cout << endl;`
(2) `cout.operator<<( endl );`
(3) `endl( cout );`   (in `operator<<`)
(4) `cout.put( eol ); cout.flush();`   (in `endl`)

where `eol` stands for a platform-dependent end-of-line symbol.

With arguments, an I/O manipulator must be a constructor that creates a function object (Section 11.9) containing a predefined function and the argument values. Overloaded nonmember `operator>>` and/or `operator<<` are also defined to receive the manipulator objects and invoke their stored functions.

An I/O manipulator always returns a reference to the I/O stream.

6.10 SUMMARY

Standard C++ comes with an extensive Standard Library containing well-written and tested facilities for various useful purposes. Familiarity with the libraries allows you to apply them whenever there is a need.

To use a library facility, remember to include the required header files that provide the necessary declarations and the appropriate `using` declarations to use names supplied in other namespaces. Native C++ headers introduce entities in the `std` namespace while headers from ANSI C introduce entities in the global namespace. Through the header file `<string>`, you get `string` objects and a rich set of standard functions. The header `<sstream>` gives in-memory I/O objects. A `Tokenizer` uses `string` to break up tokens in a string and can be a handy class for applications.

The header file `<ctype.h>` gives access to a collection of character-set-independent operations on characters. Furthermore, through the header file math.h, C++ also has a set of mathematical functions for numeric computation. Complex numbers and their computations are supported; just include the header <complex>. The Standard Template Library is covered in Chapter 11. Other libraries not covered here are listed in several appendices.

The I/O stream is an object-oriented library for character I/O. The headers to include are <iostream> (for standard I/O), <fstream> (for file I/O), and <strstream> (for in-memory I/O). The I/O stream classes, their member functions, and the I/O operators >> and << are powerful and efficient tools for handling object-oriented I/O. There is a systematic way to overload these I/O operators for your own classes to make object I/O as easy as that for primitive types.

Output formatting is done with I/O stream formatting functions and flags. File I/O objects can be established in read (ios::in), write (ios::out), append (ios::app), or a logical combination of these modes. Member functions **get, put, write, read, getline, peek, putback,** and **ignore** are provided for I/O.

Random access I/O is also supported. The current read/write position in a file object can be set (examined) by **seekg/seekp** (**tellg/tellp**). The state of an I/O object is kept in flags accessed by member functions **eof, bad, fail,** and **good**.

A program can elect to cause failure exceptions upon designated I/O failures. I/O manipulators let you set I/O states and perform certain I/O operations through the convenience of the << and >> operators.

EXERCISES

1. Take the SortKey class (Section 4.7) and simplify its coding by using the Tokenizer in Section 6.4.

2. Apply the class Month in a program that formats and prints a calendar for a whole year.

3. Define operator>> and operator<< for Vector2D following the recommendations in Section 6.8.

4. Consider the pocket calculator program in Section 5.5. Modify the calculator display routine to show 16 significant digits.

5. Compare and contrast the Tokenizer class in Section 6.4 with the library function strtok for C-style strings (Appendix C).

6. Exercise Cal-1: Take the simple calculator example (Section 5.5) and extend it. (a) Add the square root function corresponding to the s(S) key. (b) Add the constant function with the k for "constant in" and K for "constant out." (c) Add one extra memory register and the add-to-memory (M), subtract-from-memory (m), and memory-recall (R) functions. (*Note:* The purpose is to simulate these facilities of a simple pocket calculator.)

7. Exercise Cal-2: Add to **calc** the ability to save a few intermediate results, in single-letter buffers, and to reuse them in subsequent computations.

8. How would you turn the **calc** program into one that uses octal numbers?

9. Consider the type double for floating-point computations. How many significant digits (precision) does it support on your computer? On a 32-bit computer?

10. Because the CalcEng class uses double, it can support more precision than the 6 used in the CalcFace class. Modify CalcFace so that an object is initialized with a precision up to the maximum allowed under double. This precision setting should control the number of digits allowed for input and display.

11. Using stream I/O, write a program that reads a text file and appends at the end of the file the length of each word in the file. (*Hint*: ios::in | ios::app.)

12. Add to **calc** the ability to save itself on disk so that later, when running **calc**, a user can retrieve the saved state and resume calculations. (*Hint*: Saving the compute engine part should be enough.)

13. Consider the **lowercase** implementation in Section 6.7. Instead of using **seekp**, can you use the **putback** feature to achieve the same effect?

14. Read in a file containing x, y, z coordinates on each line. The coordinates are in floating-point with five significant digits and separated by white space. Write a program to read this file and to produce a well-formatted output file (line up the decimal points in each column) showing y, x, z on each line.

15. Experiment with the error status functions of I/O objects. What happens if you use >> to read some random string into an int variable? What happens if you have too long a string of digits?

16. Examine the following program. Does it work? If not, can you fix it? If so, can you explain why? Any suggested improvements?

```
#include <iostream>
#include <string.h>
```

```
using std::cout; using std::endl;

int main()
{       char foo[]="abcd";
        char *bar="EFGHABCD";
        strcat(foo,bar);
        cout << foo << endl;
        return 0;
}
```

(*Hint*: C-style string operations are listed in Appendix C.)

CHAPTER SEVEN

Inheritance and Class Derivation

Object-based programmming is the foundation on which more advanced object-oriented programming techniques are built. One of the most critical OOP features is *inheritance*, a mechanism for building revised objects on top of existing ones. C++ supports inheritance with *class derivation*, defining new classes by extending existing classes without modifying them. Such a new class, called a *derived class*, *inherits* the members of one or more existing *base classes* and adds other members of its own. Inheriting from derived classes is also possible, giving rise to inheritance *hierarchies*.

The inheritance mechanism brings several major advantages to programming:

- *Reuse of existing code*: Avoid recoding what is already available. Simply use inheritance to import working and tested codes as a foundation.

- *Adaption of programs to work in similar but different situations*: Avoid writing largely similar programs all over again because the application, computer system, data format, or mode of operation is slightly different. Simply use inheritance to modify existing codes to suit.

- *Extraction of commonalities from different classes*: Avoid duplicating identical/similar codes or structures in different classes. Simply extract the common parts to form another class and allow it to be inherited by the other classes.

- *Organization of objects into hierarchies*: Form groups of objects that have an "is a kind of" relationship. For example, a savings account is a kind of bank account; a checking account is a kind of account; a sedan is a kind of automobile; a sports sedan is a kind of sedan; a manager is a kind of employee; and a square matrix is a kind of matrix. Such groupings give a program better organization and, more important, allow objects in the same hierarchy to be used as *compatible* types as opposed to completely unrelated types.

7.1 CLASS DERIVATION

C++ supports both single and multiple inheritance. In *single inheritance*, a class is derived from a *single* base class. For example, a class `JointAccount` can be derived from the class `Account`, or a `Manager` from `Employee`. In *multiple inheritance*, a class is derived from *several* base classes. The use of multiple inheritance and the *virtual base* (shared base) are described in this chapter. Skillful use of inheritance through class derivation contributes significantly to a well-designed OO program.

Both conceptual understanding and experience are important to achieving proficiency in this critical area of OOP. Material in this chapter is designed to present class derivation clearly and in practical terms. A vivid mental model of the derived class and objects will enhance understanding. Moreover, principles to guide your application of class derivation are also clearly stated. The important topic of information hiding and member access control under inheritance, often confusing to beginning programmers, is made simple and easy to grasp.

The first topic of discussion is the class derivation mechanism.

7.1 CLASS DERIVATION

The class `Account`, described in Section 2.1, is a simple class. Suppose we now wish to handle joint accounts. Each joint account has two owners instead of just one. Certainly, this is a small change from `Account`, and we can write a class `JointAccount` simply by copying the source code of `Account` and adding a joint owner and some related functions. But there is a better approach—deriving `JointAccount` from `Account` without changing it or duplicating the code.

The existing class `Account` written as a suitable base class for derivation is shown here:

```
///////    Account.h    ///////
#include <string>
using std::string;

class Account
{ public:
    Account(unsigned n, double b, const string& ss); // constructor
    Account() {}                    // default constructor
    void deposit(double amt);       // deposits amt into account
    bool withdraw(double amt);      // withdraws amt from account
    double balance() const;         // balance inquiry
    unsigned id() const;            // gets account number
    /* other public members */
  protected:
```

```
        unsigned  acct_no;              // account number
        string    ss;                   // owner ss no.
    private:
        /* other members */
        double    acct_bal;             // current balance
};
```

The `string` member `ss` records the social security number of the account owner. Members declared `protected` are just like `private` members except that they allow certain types of access from derived classes. Designating certain members `protected` in anticipation of future derivation is an important OOP design consideration. (More is said about this later.)

Joint Account

Now we can build the new class `JointAccount` on top of `Account` by class derivation:

```
///////    JointAccount.h    ///////
#include "Account.h"

class JointAccount : public Account       // derives from Account  (1)
{ public:
    JointAccount(unsigned n, double b,    // constructor
                 const string& owner,
                 const string& jowner);
    JointAccount() {}                     // default constructor
  private:
    string jss;                           // joint owner ss no.   (2)
};
```

The class header

```
class JointAccount : public Account
```

specifies `JointAccount` as a derived class of the base class `Account`. The general derived-class definition is

```
class Name : base-class list         (class derivation syntax)
{
     derived-class body
};
```

A list of comma-separated names of base classes, the *base-class list*, is given after a colon (:) following the name of the derived class. Each base-class name can be further qualified by one of the keywords `public`, `protected`, or `private`,

7.1 CLASS DERIVATION

depending on the type of derivation desired (Section 7.4). The keyword `private` may be omitted.

Whatever the type of derivation, a derived class *inherits* all[1] members of its base classes and adds new members of its own. Through inheritance (line 1), members of Account become *inherited members* of JointAccount. The derived class also adds a member jss (line 2) to record the social security number of the joint owner. The owner is recorded in the member ss inherited from the base class. Programming a joint account from scratch is avoided, and code from Account is reused.

A JointAccount object is initialized by the constructor:

```
///////    JointAccount.C    ///////
#include "JointAccount.h"

JointAccount::JointAccount (unsigned n, double b,
            const string& owner, const string& jowner)
  : Account(n, b, owner),      // calls base constructor   (3)
    jss(jowner)                // records joint owner
{ }
```

The inherited part of the object, or *base object*, is initialized by calling the base-class constructor (line 3) with appropriate arguments. Base-object initialization is specified at the beginning of the init-list (line 3).

Now we can establish and use a joint account object. For example,

```
JointAccount bill_mary(123456, 2500,
              "045-22-5555", "045-33-7777");
bill_mary.deposit(450.75);
cout << bill_mary.balance() << endl;
```

With class derivation, much recoding is avoided, and joint accounts are established with very little effort. Furthermore, the base Account class stays unchanged, ready to derive other types of accounts. And perhaps more important, any further refinement of Account is automatically reflected in JointAccount. This aspect of OOP is powerful, and its full implications will become clear only after we cover more related topics. Figure 7.1 shows the graphical representation of the base-derived relationship.

Although the subject of inheritance and class derivation is fascinating, it tends to be confusing because it is difficult to conceptualize. The presentation in Section 7.2 should remedy this situation.

---

[1] With the exception of constructors, destructors, and `operator=`.

Figure 7.1 CLASS DERIVATION

7.2 DERIVED CLASSES AND OBJECTS

Class Scope Nesting

A derived class is a composite class: It inherits members from the base (*inherited members*) and adds members of its own (*appendant members*). The derived-class scope is *nested* inside the base-class scope, like an inner code block nesting within an outer block. Figure 7.2 shows the scope nesting for JointAccount and Account. The call bill_mary.balance() refers to JointAccount::balance, and it is not defined in the scope JointAccount:: but in the enclosing scope Account::. This is how this particular call gets to the inherited member balance().

In general, consider any derived class Dd and the identifier Dd::xyz. If xyz is an appendant member of Dd, then it is what Dd::xyz refers to. Otherwise, the name xyz is searched for in the base class of Dd. If not found, the search continues up the derivation chain until file scope is reached. The search ends as soon as an identifier is found. Then, its accessibility is determined. The search will not continue even if access is denied.

Suppose some member function of JointAccount uses the identifier acct_bal. The identifier acct_bal is not found in the scope JointAccount::, so the search continues in the enclosing scope Account::, where the member acct_bal is found. Thus, this particular acct_bal refers to the inherited member acct_bal. The private status of acct_bal will deny such an access, and the

Figure 7.2 CLASS SCOPE NESTING

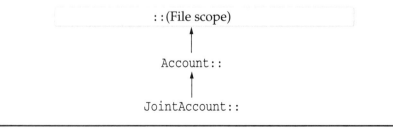

code is incorrect. This happens even if there is a file scope identifier `acct_bal` that can be accessed if reached.

The scope relation between the derived and the base class is basic to a good understanding of class derivation. Also important are the composition, initialization, and deinitialization of derived objects.

Derived-Object Composition

A *derived object*, such as `bill_mary`, is an instance of a derived class. For simplicity, consider single inheritance, where there is only one base class. A derived object, then, consists of two parts (Figure 7.3):

1. A *base object* composed of the data and function members as specified by the base class and properly initialized by a base-class constructor. In other words, the base-object part is built using the base class as a blueprint.
2. An *appendant part* consisting of additional data and function members defined in the derived class. The appendant part envelops the base object to form the derived object. Members in the appendant part are referred to as *appendant members*.

All inherited and appendant members are considered members of the derived object. A member function in the appendant part can refer to both types of members directly, using just the member name without mentioning the host object explicitly.

If the base object is itself a derived object, then it contains its immediate base object in exactly the same way. A derived class inherits all members, appendant and inherited, that can be inherited from its base class.

Figure 7.3 DERIVED-OBJECT COMPOSITION

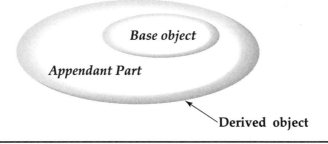

Derived-Object Construction and Destruction

As stated earlier, neither constructors nor destructors are inherited by derived classes. The initialization (deinitialization) of a derived object is done with a sequence of base and derived constructor (destructor) calls. The different constructors (destructors) collaborate to complete the task.

When a derived object is instantiated, enough memory space is allocated to accommodate all base objects and the appendant part. Then, a derived-class constructor initializes the object in two stages. First, the base-class constructors are invoked to initialize the base objects. For single inheritance, the immediate base constructor is called. For multiple inheritance, the base-class constructors are called in declaration order, the order in which they appear in the base-class list. After all base objects are initialized, the rest of the derived-class constructor is executed to initialize the appendant part.

A derived-class constructor specifies appropriate base-class constructor calls in its init-list. We have already seen how the `JointAccount` example used this feature:

```
JointAccount::JointAccount(unsigned n,  // derived-class constructor
        double b, const string& owner, const string& jowner)
: Account(n, b, owner), jss(jowner)     // init-list
{ }
```

If a base constructor call is not specified in the init-list, the base-class default constructor is called. The init-list may also initialize appendant members. However, it cannot specify the initialization of individual inherited members. Their initializations are done by the base-class constructor. If a base object is also derived, this procedure is applied recursively.

It is possible to initialize a base object by an existing object. For example, we can add a constructor to `JointAccount`:

```
JointAccount::JointAccount (Account acnt, const string& jowner)
: Account(acnt),          // init base object by object
  jss(jowner) { }
```

This is useful when turning an existing account (an instance of `Account`) into a joint account. An initialization object such as `acnt` can be any object that is convertible to the correct type implicitly or explicitly, including through user-defined conversions (Section 8.9).

When a derived object is destroyed, base- and component-object destructors are called automatically for deinitialization. The destructors are called in the reverse order of constructor calls.

7.3 PUBLIC DERIVATION

Free Checking Account

As another example of inheritance, let's now consider a free checking account that charges a monthly service fee only if the account balance drops below a preset minimum. A class FreeChecking can also be derived from the existing class Account (Figure 7.4):

```
///////    FreeChecking.h    ///////
#include "Account.h"

class FreeChecking : public Account
{ public:
      FreeChecking() {}                         // default constructor
      FreeChecking(unsigned n, double b,        // constructor
          const string& owner);
      void fee();                               // charges monthly fee
      bool withdraw(double amt);                // withdraws amt
      static void setMinbal(float m) { min_bal = m; }
      static void setFee(float f) { service_fee = f; }
      static float getMinbal() { return min_bal; }
      static float getFee() { return service_fee; }
  private:
      static float min_bal;
      static float service_fee;
      bool free;
};
```

Static functions (setMinbal, setFee, getMinbal, getFee) and data members (min_bal, service_fee) are used to set, get, and record class-wide quantities — minimum balance and service fee. A private flag free keeps the fee-free status of the account. The flag is maintained by the appendant member function withdraw() and used by fee(), the member function that charges a monthly fee, if any, to the account.

Figure 7.4 DERIVATION TREE

The constructor specifies how the base object and the appendant part are initialized:

```
///////    FreeChecking.C    ///////
#include <iostream>
#include "FreeChecking.h"
using std::cerr; using std::endl;

float FreeChecking::min_bal = 500.0;              // minimum balance
float FreeChecking::service_fee = 18.0;           // service fee

FreeChecking::FreeChecking                        // constructor
(unsigned n, double b, const string& owner)
:   Account(n, b, owner), free(b >= min_bal)      // init-list
{ }
```

Again, the constructor init-list contains a call to a base-class constructor. The flag `free` is also properly set. A bank normally requires an initial deposit more than the required minimum balance to open a new account. Nevertheless, the constructor checks the initial balance and sets the flag `free`.

A new `withdraw` function monitors the account balance and sets the flag `free` when necessary:

```
bool FreeChecking::withdraw(double amt)
{   bool ok = Account::withdraw(amt);                    // (1)
    if ( ok && balance() < min_bal ) free = false;       // (2)
    return ok;
}
```

The function calls the base `withdraw` function (line 1) and, after the withdrawal is made, checks the balance (line 2) and sets `free` accordingly. The status of the withdrawal is returned.

Two important points are worth noting:

1. The appendant member `withdraw()` has exactly the same prototype as its counterpart in the base `Account`. This is good because the same *message* (public function invocation) works for withdrawing from a simple basic account or a free checking account. Any other way would be unreasonable. Imagine asking bank customers to use different messages to withdraw funds from various types of accounts!

2. The free checking `withdraw()` completes its duty by asking the base `withdraw()` to perform basic processing and by supplying additional processing itself. Thus, processing common to all types of accounts should be implemented in the base `Account`; derived accounts add only their specialized processing.

7.3 PUBLIC DERIVATION

At the end of every month, the function `fee()` is called to charge a service fee to the account if required:

```
void FreeChecking::fee()
{  if ( ! free )
      if ( Account::withdraw(service_fee) )
         free = (balance() >= min_bal);    // reset free flag
      else
         cerr << "fee: Insufficient balance for account "
              << acct_no << endl;
}
```

The `free` flag is reset appropriately after a fee charge.

The `FreeChecking` class is quite simplified as it stands. Test it now with the following code:

```
///////    testFreeChecking.C    ///////
#include <iostream>
#include "FreeChecking.h"
using std::cout; using std::endl;

int main()
{  FreeChecking susan(555234, 750.0, "034-55-6789");
   cout << susan.balance() << endl;
   susan.deposit(25.50);                // inherited member (A)
   susan.withdraw(250);                 // appendant member (B)
   susan.fee();                         // appendant member (C)
   cout << susan.balance() << endl;
   susan.withdraw(30);                  // expensive move
   susan.deposit(100);                  // too late
   susan.fee();
   cout << susan.balance() << endl;
}
```

The account `susan` starts with a balance of 750.00. At the end of the first month, after a deposit of 25.50 and a withdrawal of 250, the account balance should be 525.50 because there is no service charge. But an unfortunate withdrawal of 30 results in a service fee of 18.00 for the following month. The deposit of 100 is too late to avoid the service charge, and the balance becomes 577.50. The program produces the expected output:

```
month 1: 525.5
month 2: 577.5
```

The class `FreeChecking`, somewhat more complicated than `JointAccount`, is a more realistic example of class derivation. `FreeChecking` defines an appendant member function `withdraw()`, which shields the base-class function with the same signature from view, as a result of class scope nesting. Thus, the call on line B invokes the appendant `withdraw()`, while the code on line A accesses the inherited `deposit()`.

To summarize, a derived class is usually a slight generalization, specialization, or modification of the base class. Often, this means you must add some preprocessing and/or postprocessing to existing functions in the base class. The derived `withdraw()` function is a typical example of adding some postprocessing after the base `withdraw()`. Thus, the design technique demonstrated here is that of collecting basic operations in the base class and allowing specialized preprocessing and postprocessing to be added by derived classes.

7.4 DERIVATION PRINCIPLES

A base class can be designated `public`, `protected`, or `private` giving rise to three types of class derivation. The base-class designation affects the accessibility of inherited members (Section 7.5) and the relation between the base type and the derived type (Section 7.8). A question often asked is, When do you use `public`, `protected`, or `private` derivation? The answer is not so simple because it depends on the situation. But here are a few rules of thumb:

1. *Use `public` derivation when a derived object is a kind of base object*. For example, a joint account is a kind of account, and a free checking account is another kind of account. The *is-a relationship* usually means that all or most of the public interface of the base object (an `Account`) also makes sense for the derived object (a `JointAccount`). Often, the is-a relationship also means that derived and base objects may be used together in applications as related/compatible data types. For instance, a list of accounts in a banking system may include many different types of accounts.

    A class `Manager` derived from the base `Employee` is another example of the is-a relationship. A manager is a kind of employee, so public derivation is appropriate.

    Thus, a public base class and a derived class have a type-subtype relationship. This is supported in C++ by implicit type-conversion rules that allow automatic conversion of a derived-type object, reference, or pointer to a corresponding quantity of a base type (Section 7.8).

2. *Use `private` derivation when a derived object is not considered a kind of base object and the base class simply supplies code to make the derived class easier*

to write. In other words, the appendant functions can use facilities provided by the base class. In this situation, the public interface of the base object makes little sense for the derived object and should be made inaccessible. For instance, a stack or a queue class can be derived from a linked-list class. But neither a stack nor a queue is considered a kind of linked list. Thus, private derivation is more suitable, as we see in Section 7.6.

In considering a derivation of class *Dd* from a base class *Bb*, make sure it is not because a *Dd* object contains a *Bb* object as a component. Consider the pocket calculator example. A calculator has two components: a compute engine and a user interface. Thus, the Calculator class has two components: a CalcEng object and a CalcFace object. Hence, the correct design for such a *has-a* or *uses-a* relationship is to employ component objects rather than class derivation.

On the other hand, a stack does not have a list component. It will be internally implemented as a list because it is convenient and the list class has already been defined. When *Bb* is a private base of *Dd*, often the relationship is that *Dd "is internally implemented as a" Bb*.

Therefore, a private base class and a derived class have no type-subtype relationship. In general, C++ does not automatically convert a derived object, reference, or pointer to a corresponding private base type (Section 7.8).

3. *Use* protected *derivation when you basically want a* private *base class but also want to make inherited members accessible from further derived classes.*

The accessibility of inherited members is discussed next.

7.5 ACCESS CONTROL UNDER CLASS DERIVATION

The discussion of class derivation introduced us to the protected member category of access control. In addition, there are the three derivation types arising from base-class designations: public, protected, and private. C++ has clear and specific rules governing what parts of the program, under what conditions, have access to appendant members (in the derived class) and to inherited members (in the base class). Access to the appendant members of a derived class is governed by normal member access rules. Access to inherited members, those in the base object, however, is a different matter altogether.

Access to Inherited Members

1. Access to inherited members by appendant members and friends of the derived class is independent of the base-class designation:

   - *Access is allowed to all nonprivate* (`public` *and* `protected`) *inherited members.*
   - *Access is not allowed to private members in the base class.* For example, an appendant member function of `JointAccount` has no access to `acct_bal` in the base object.

2. Access to inherited members from other functions depends on the base-class designation:

   - `public` *base*: All inherited `public` members are accessible as public members of the derived class; all inherited `protected` members are accessible as protected members of the derived class.
   - `protected` *base*: All inherited nonprivate members are accessible as protected members of the derived class. Thus, there is no access to these members except by appendant functions in a further derivation.
   - `private` *base*: No inherited members are accessible.

These access rules (accessibility) together with class scope nesting (visibility) give rise to some important implications. Private members from a base class are never accessible directly by appendant members. In a public derivation hierarchy, through each subsequent derived class, the combined set of public interfaces from its base classes is accessible. Furthermore, in a nonprivate derivation hierarchy, each subsequent derived class always has access to the combined set of public and protected members from its base classes. Table 7.1 summarizes access control under derivation.

Table 7.1 ACCESS CONTROL UNDER DERIVATION

Access from	Inherited Member		
	`public`	`protected`	`private`
Derived class and its friends	Yes	Yes	No
Subsequent derived class	If public/protected base	If public/protected base	No
Other outside functions	If public base	No	No

7.6 PRIVATE DERIVATION 261

To achieve finer control, accessibility and visibility of inherited members can be further modified by overriding and exempting individual inherited members:

- *Overriding*: By defining an appendant member of the same name, an inherited member, otherwise visible, is shielded from view. For example, `FreeChecking::withdraw()` overrides `Account::withdraw()`. Thus, the call `susan.withdraw(30)` invokes the appendant member. Outside access to the base member is possible with the class scope operator. So `susan.Account::withdraw(3)` is legal (ill-advised of course). Overriding is a result of identifier scoping under derivation (Section 7.2).

- *Exempting*: A nonpublic derivation makes *all* inherited members, accessible under public derivation, inaccessible. There is a way, however, to specifically exempt certain inherited members from this access limitation. Consider a `public` (`protected`) member *xyz* of the base class *BaseX* made invisible under nonpublic derivation. The accessibility of *xyz* can be restored by including the line

    BaseX::*xyz*;   // or
    using *BaseX*::*xyz*;

    in the `public` (`protected`) section of the derived-class definition. This exemption notation can be used only to restore accessibility to that allowed under public derivation. It cannot be used to promote or demote accessibility beyond that. Thus, a protected member does not become public, or vice versa, through exemption. These remarks will become clear after we see examples of nonpublic derivation.

7.6 PRIVATE DERIVATION

A stack is a common and useful data structure in programming. It is a last-in/first-out (LIFO) buffer resembling a stack of trays in a cafeteria (Figure 7.5).

Figure 7.5 A STACK

Chapter 7 INHERITANCE AND CLASS DERIVATION

A *push* operation puts an item on top of the stack, and a *pop* removes the top item from the stack. A *top* call accesses the value on top. You can also test if a stack is empty. Basically, these are the only allowable operations on a stack.

Suppose we wish to implement a class for the stack. An array can store the items being pushed and popped. However, an array is limited because it is fixed in dimension. Let's consider using a linked list to store the items. Because we already have a generic list class ArbList (Section 5.12), this approach should be easier. Besides, the list is dynamic and its dimension is not fixed. Furthermore, it does not cost anything to make the stack class generic:

```
///////    ArbStack.h    ///////
//   generic stack derived from generic list
#include <iostream>
#include "ArbList.h"

class ArbStack : private ArbList     // keyword private is optional
{  public:
       ArbStack() { }                // default constructor      (1)
       ArbStack(Any z);              // constructor
       bool push(Any z);             // pushes onto top
       Any top() const;              // value on top
       bool pop();                   // pops off top
       using ArbList::isEmpty;       // makes isEmpty accessible (2)
};
```

As noted, an unqualified base class is private. Also, if a derived constructor does not specify an explicit call to a base constructor, the default base constructor is called automatically. Thus, the code on line 1 is the same as

```
ArbStack() : ArbList() { }          // long version
```

The inherited public member isEmpty() is made accessible (line 2) so that it can be used to test whether a stack is empty. The inherited putOn() is used in two inline member functions:

```
inline bool ArbStack::push(Any z) { return putOn(z); }

inline ArbStack::ArbStack(Any z) { putOn(z); }
```

The only function remaining is pop(), which is defined in the implementation file:

```
///////    ArbStack.C    ///////
#include "ArbStack.h"

Any ArbStack::top() const
{   if ( isEmpty() ) return(NULL);    // top failed
```

7.7 SPECIALIZATION OF GENERIC CLASSES

```
        Any t = content(first());        // top item
        return t;
}

bool ArbStack::pop()
{   if ( isEmpty() ) return false;       // pop failed
    shorten(1);                          // stack popped
    return true;
}
```

Four `ArbList` functions are used in `pop()` and `top()`: `isEmpty()`, `first()`, `shorten()`, and `content()`. Reusing code in the base class `ArbList` makes `ArbStack` very simple indeed.

Test `ArbStack` using code similar to the following:

```
///////    testArbStack.C    ///////
#include <iostream>
#include "ArbStack.h"
// stack of integers via ArbStack

int main()
{   static int a[] = {0,10,20,30,40,50};
    ArbStack stack(a + 1);
    stack.push(a + 3);
    stack.push(a + 5);
    while ( ! stack.isEmpty() )
    {   std::cout <<  * (int *)stack.top() << " ";
        stack.pop();
    }
    std::cout << std::endl;
    return 0;
}
```

Note how `pop()` returns a `void *` pointer that must be cast before being dereferenced. The program produces the following output:

```
50 30 10
```

A queue can be derived using techniques similar to those used for `ArbList`.

7.7 SPECIALIZATION OF GENERIC CLASSES

Generic classes such as `ArbList` and `ArbStack` are general but awkward to use directly. It would be better, for example, to push and pop an `Employee` on a stack and not to constantly fuss with `void *` pointers, type-casting, and dereferencing.

With class derivation, we can easily *specialize* `ArbStack` to a type-specific stack—say, `EmpStack`. We can then use `EmpStack` to directly push and pop `Employee` items:

```
///////    EmpStack.h    ///////
// employee stack derived from ArbStack
#include "ArbStack.h"
#include "Employee.h"

class EmpStack : private ArbStack
{ public:
    EmpStack() { }                                 // default constructor
    EmpStack(Employee& x): ArbStack(&x) { }        // constructor
    bool push(Employee& x);                        // pushes Employee
    Employee& top();                               // Employee on top
    using ArbStack::pop;               // makes pop() accessible
    using ArbStack::isEmpty;           // makes isEmpty() accessible
};
```

Note how reference parameters are used to avoid copying objects. The fact that `EmpStack` is implemented as an `ArbStack` is hidden via private derivation. Therefore, the public interface of the base does not surface.

The appendant members `push()` and `pop()` are so simple that they are inline:

```
inline bool EmpStack::push(Employee& x)
      { return ArbStack::push(&x); }

inline Employee& EmpStack::top()
      { return *reinterpret_cast< Employee * >(ArbStack::top()); }
```

Because there is no automatic type-casting from `Any` (`void*`) to `Employee*`, we must use explicit type-casting. With the `EmpStack` class defined, pushing and popping employees on a stack are much more intuitive and less error-prone. The class specialization technique shown here is completely general and can be applied whenever a generic class must be made type-specific.

The derivation chain `ArbList`, `ArbStack`, and `EmpStack` demonstrates a simple inheritance hierarchy. Having layers of derivation and function calls is the price you pay for better software organization, reliability, and reusability. Declaring functions inline will help, and a good compiler will significantly reduce the overhead involved.

7.8 TYPE RELATIONS UNDER INHERITANCE

Inheritance and class derivation offer a powerful way to organize programs and group related objects. Indeed, a derivation hierarchy creates a set of related types that are compatible in use. The different types of accounts illustrate this point very well. In general, when type `DerivedX` is a type `BaseX`, it is logical to use a `DerivedX` object in place of a `BaseX` object. The reasoning is similar to using a `short` or an `unsigned` where an `int` is expected. In this situation, the type `DerivedX` becomes a *subtype* of `BaseX`.

Actually, such compatible uses have already been applied without being explained explicitly. In Section 2.8, the function

```
void match(string& str, istream& in, ostream& out)
```

is called either with standard I/O objects `cin` and `cout` or with file I/O objects:

```
match(str, cin, cout);
match(str, infile, ofile);
```

The reference parameter `out` can take on `cout` or `ofile`. This works because `cout` and `ofile` are objects derived from the same base (Section 7.14); the same goes for `cin` and `infile`. Type compatibility under inheritance provides this convenience and flexibility.

C++ supports type compatibility through type conversions. In addition to the conversions already discussed in Section 3.13, C++ performs implicitly a set of reasonable type conversions for objects related by inheritance. Other conversions among such related objects require explicit casting and/or user-defined conversion codes (Section 8.9). The kinds of implicit conversions performed are described next.

Inheritance-Induced Implicit Conversions

In argument passing, initialization, and assignment, implicit type conversions for inheritance-related objects are performed in the following cases:

1. Converting a derived object, reference, or pointer to a corresponding *public base type*: This implicit conversion supports the is-a relationship. It is the reason `cout` and `ofile` can be passed to the `match()` parameter `out`.

    It is safe to convert a derived object to a base object because there is always an instance of the base class in the derived object and the public interface of the base object is accessible.

    This implicit conversion is important for OOP because it allows the same function parameter to receive different objects in an inheritance hierarchy. For example, a function `Account::transfer(acnt)` should be able to take any account object acnt in a hierarchy rooted at `Account`.

2. Converting a *public base opm* (offset pointer to member, Section 11.11) to a derived opm: Again, because the base member is present within a derived object, the implicit opm conversion is safe.

3. Inside the appendant part of a derived class, conversions listed in items 1 and 2 are performed implicitly even if the base class is nonpublic.

Another way of looking at this is that *implicit derived-to-base conversion is allowed only if a base class is accessible.*

Also keep in mind that an object pointer is implicitly converted to void* when necessary (independent of class derivation). A void* pointer can be converted to an object pointer only through explicit casting.

Inheritance-Related Explicit Conversions

The `static_cast` operator is used to explicitly convert a base pointer (reference) to a derived pointer (reference). For example,

```
Account* bp;                              // base pointer
FreeChecking fc(. . .);                   // object with public base
bp = &fc;                                 // implicit conversion
FreeChecking *fcp =
    static_cast< FreeChecking* >(bp);     // explicit conversion (A)
```

The explicit cast (line A) actually restores the true type of bp.

With explicit `static_cast`, it is possible to mistakenly take a pointer (reference) to an actual base object and cast it into a derived pointer (reference). Such invalid casts can lead to run-time disasters. For *virtualized objects* (Section 9.1), casting from base pointer (reference) to derived pointer (reference) should be performed with the `dynamic_cast` operator (Section 9.2), which checks for the validity of the cast at run time.

Inheritance and Overloading

An appendant member function funcAbc *hides all inherited functions* funcAbc. Once you define at least one funcAbc in a derived class, the notation

```
derived_object.funcAbc(...);
```

accesses only those funcAbc defined in the derived class, thus hiding any and all inherited funcAbc. The inherited functions are not visible but still accessible by explicit scoping:

```
derived_object.BaseName::funcAbc(...);
```

When an overloaded function takes arguments that are objects, object pointers, or object references, the same call-resolution rules as listed in Section 3.7 apply. However, those rules must now be interpreted with inheritance-induced visibility and type conversion rules in mind.

Let *arg_type* and *par_type* be the argument object type and the declared formal parameter type, respectively. The match-preference rules as they relate to object arguments are:

- *Exact match*: *par_type* is *arg_type*, *arg_type*&, or const *arg_type*&.
- *Standard promotion*: Not applicable to objects.
- *Standard conversion*: Any inheritance-induced implicit conversion.
- *User-supplied conversion*: Class-defined conversion as described in Section 8.9.
- *No match or ambiguous match (more than one)*: An error.

7.9 ASSIGNMENT OF OBJECTS

Built-in Object Assignment

C++ understands how to assign one class object to another. Built-in assignment works only if the right-hand-side object has, or can be converted to, the same type as the left-hand-side object. The actual assignment is done *memberwise*; that is, data members are assigned individually. Consider the assignment of fractions

```
Fraction a, b(3, 4);
a = b;
```

or of compatible accounts

```
Account a1( . . . );
FreeChecking a2( . . . );
a1 = a2;
```

For a = b, the individual assignments a.num = b.num and a.denom = b.denom are performed. And for a1 = a2, the base part of a2 is assigned to a1 in a similar memberwise fashion. Of course, the right-hand side can also be a computation or function call that results in an object:

```
a = a - b;    // class Fraction member operator-
```

Combination assignment operators such as += and *= have no built-in meaning when applied to class objects even if the arithmetic operators operator+ and operator* are defined in the class. The only operators with prescribed meanings for objects are

    &   (address-of)
    .   (member-of)
    =   (assignment)

Any other operator must be explicitly defined in a class before it can be used on objects in that class. The general topic of operator overloading is discussed in Section 8.1. The focus here is on assignment of objects.

Conceptually, object assignment is implemented by an assignment operator that is either defined by the class or generated by the compiler. Built-in assignment is supported by the compiler-generated assignment operator and works fine for many classes. But there are situations that require class-defined assignment operators.

Class-Defined Object Assignment

For assigning objects containing pointers, for example, built-in assignment is usually inadequate. Consider two objects obj1 and obj2 in some class. Suppose obj1.str points to a character string string_1 and obj2.str points to a second character string string_2 (Figure 7.6). If the assignment

```
obj1 = obj2;
```

is performed, what is the result? Because obj1.str gets the value of obj2.str, both pointers now point to the second string, and it may well be that the address to the first string is lost (Figure 7.6). Furthermore, modification to string_2 via obj1.str affects obj2, and vice versa. Such coupling of objects as a side effect of assignment is almost always unexpected and unwanted.

The situation becomes much worse if obj1.str and obj2.str each points to dynamically allocated space that is freed automatically by the object destructor. Suppose obj1 is destroyed first and it frees (deletes) string_2. When obj2 is destroyed later, it also attempts to free string_2, resulting in a serious error that destroys the consistency of the free pool from which dynamic storage is allocated.

The preceding discussion points out a grave problem with using built-in assignment semantics for objects containing pointers to free store. Problems

7.9 ASSIGNMENT OF OBJECTS

Figure 7.6 SIDE EFFECT OF `obj1 = obj2`

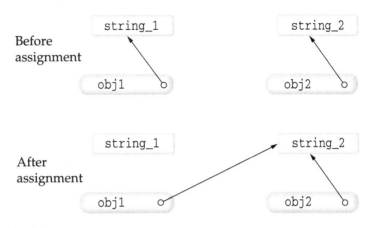

also exist for objects containing reference or `const` members, names of temporary files deleted by the destructor, or I/O streams closed by the destructor.

What is the solution to this problem? For a class where the default assignment semantics is inappropriate, the class must either *ban object assignment* or *define its own assignment operator* `operator=`. To make things clear, let's look at an example of class-defined `operator=`.

Class-Defined `operator=`

Recall the circular buffer class described in Section 3.12. A `Cirbuf` object contains, among other members, a `cb` pointer to a dynamically allocated character buffer. This buffer is freed by the destructor `~Cirbuf`. These characteristics make it necessary to define `operator=` if assignments of `Cirbuf` objects are required.

We can modify the `Cirbuf` class by adding a new member to the `Cirbuf` class definition:

```
Cirbuf& Cirbuf::operator=(const Cirbuf& b);    // Cirbuf assignment
```

This is a particular case of the general assignment prototype

ClassX& *ClassX*::operator=(const *ClassX*&);

for class-defined `operator=`. Here is the actual function definition:

```
///  add to Cirbuf.C  ///
Cirbuf& Cirbuf::operator =(const Cirbuf& b)
{   if (&b == this) return *this;    // check for a = a         (1)
    head = 0;                        // sets member values
    tail = length = b.length;
```

```
    if ( size != b.size )              // buffer size different   (2)
    {    delete [] cb;                  // frees old buffer
         size = b.size;
         cb = new char[size];           // new buffer
    }
    for (int i=0 ; i < length ; i++)    // copies all unconsumed chars
         cb[i] = b.cb[(b.head+i) % size];
    return *this;                       // returns host object    (3)
}
```

The purpose is, of course, to assign the given object b to the host object. First, a check is made (line 1) to determine whether the object is assigned to itself (e.g., a = a)—in which case, nothing needs to be done, except to return the host object. Then, head, tail, and length are assigned appropriate values. If the assignment involves two buffers of different sizes (line 2), the old buffer is freed and a new one with the correct size is allocated. All that is needed now is to copy the characters remaining in the buffer of the object b into the buffer of the host object. Finally, *this is returned.

The function header, trivial assignment check (line 1), and return statement (line 3) constitute a formula for defining operator=.

Test the user defined assignment of Cirbuf objects with the following code:

```
#include <iostream>
#include "Cirbuf.h"
using std::cout; using std::endl;

int main()
{   Cirbuf b1(64);                      // sets up b1
    b1.produce('A');
    b1.produce('B');
    b1.produce('C');
    char c = b1.consume();              // B C remain in b1
    {   Cirbuf b2, b3;                  // b2 and b2   capacity 16
        b2 = b1;                        // calls operator=
        cout << (c = b2.consume());
        cout << (c = b2.consume()) << endl;
        c = b2.consume();               // consumes empty buffer
        if (c > 0 ) cout << c;
        b3 = b2;                        // another = call
    }                                   // b2 and b3 destroyed
    cout << "from b1 ";                 // uses b1 some more
    cout << (c = b1.consume());
    cout << (c = b1.consume()) << endl;
    return 0;
}
```

The code tests not only the assignment operator but also its correct operation in conjunction with object destruction. The test should produce the following display:

```
BC
consume: buffer empty
from b1 BC
```

For classes where object assignment is not needed but becomes a problem if someone does it, you can bar such assignments by defining operator= as a private do-nothing function. If you want no Cirbuf assignments, you can define

```
private:       // prevents outside assignment
   Cirbuf& Cirbuf::operator=(const Cirbuf& b)
   { return *this; }
```

which causes any outside code that attempts to assign Cirbuf objects to get a compile-time access error.

7.10 COPYING OF OBJECTS

During the execution of a C++ program, there are many occasions when a copy of an object must be created. Such copies are often established automatically by the compiler without programmer intervention. Generally, a copy is needed under the following circumstances:

1. *When an object is passed by value in a function call.* For example, in the call

   ```
   vec1.inner(vec2)
   ```

   a copy of the Vector2D object vec2 is made and passed to the member function inner in vec1 (Section 2.6).

2. *When a function returns an object by value.* For instance, the function

   ```
   Vector2D Vector2D::operator-(Vector2D)
   ```

   returns a copy of a local Vector2D variable.

3. *When an object is initialized by another object.* For example,

   ```
   Vector2D vec3 = vec1;
   Vector2D vec4 = vec2 - vec1;
   ```

   where vec3 and vec4 are the copies made.

It is a good policy to avoid passing objects by value if pass by reference can be used. This way, you avoid the copying cost and complications associated with copying objects.

Built-in Object Copying

In each of the situations just listed, a copy is made of an existing object. Unless otherwise specified, C++ creates a copy of an object by copying each and every instance data member, of primitive or class type, in the object.

The memberwise copying actions are entirely similar to those for built-in object assignment. Object copying is performed by the *copy constructor*, a special class member that can be generated by the compiler or supplied by the class. Built-in copying is supported by the compiler-generated copy constructor. And for the same reasons as detailed in Section 7.9, the built-in copy semantics may not be adequate for certain objects, those with pointer members, for example.

Class-Defined Object Copying

When the built-in object copying semantics are not adequate, the correct actions can be specified by the class. This is done by *defining the copy constructor* explicitly.

Consider again the class `Poly` discussed in Section 4.5. The member `pol` points to a sequence of integers in free storage. To make the class work better, we should add a destructor:

```
Poly::~Poly() { delete [] pol; }
```

It is also clear that the class needs an `operator=` and a copy constructor. So we add the following lines to the class declaration:

```
~Poly();                             // destructor
Poly& operator =(const Poly& p);     // overload =
Poly(const Poly& p);                 // copy constructor
```

In general, a copy constructor is a constructor with the special prototype

`ClassX::ClassX(const ClassX&);`   (copy constructor)

or the equivalent but less restrictive alternative

`ClassX::ClassX(ClassX&);`

The `Poly` copy constructor must allocate free storage and copy the polynomial representation:

```
Poly::Poly(const Poly& p)                // copy constructor
    : pol(new int[p.deg() + 2])          // allocates free storage
```

7.10 COPYING OF OBJECTS

```
{   for (int i=p.deg()+1 ; i > -1 ; i--)
        pol[i] = p.pol[i];                      // copies representation
    cout << "copy constructor called" << endl;  // only for testing
}
```

Some display code is included just for testing purposes. In a copy constructor, data members in the host object have undefined values at the beginning. So make sure they are initialized before being used.

The assignment must also be specified in the class:

```
Poly& Poly::operator =(const Poly& p)
{   if (this == &p) return *this;
    unsigned pd = p.deg();
    if ( deg() < pd )                    // space not enough
    {   delete [] pol;
        pol = new int[pd + 2];
    }
    for (int i=0; i < pd+2; i++) pol[i] = p.pol[i];
    cout << "= called" << endl;          // testing only
    return *this;
}
```

With these improvements, we can test the Poly class again. Use the following main program, which is designed to show the effect of the copy constructor:

```
///////    testPoly.C   ///////
#include <iostream>
#include "Poly.h"

Poly testFn(Poly p, Poly q)              // value arguments (A)
{   p.display(); cout<<endl;
    q.display(); cout<<endl;
    Poly sum = p + q;                    // init by object
    sum.display(); cout<<endl;
    return sum;                          // return value
}

int main()
{   int p[]={7,-2,3,3,2,-15,1,-3,0,-9};
    int q[]={7,2,3,-3,2,15,1,3,0,9};
    Poly p1(p,5);
    Poly q1(q,5);
    p1.display(); cout<<endl;
    q1.display(); cout<<endl;
    p1 = testFn(p1, q1);                 // class-defined assignment (B)
```

```
        p1.display(); cout<<endl;
        return 0;
}
```

The value parameters in line A cause the function call in line B to trigger *implicit calls to the copy constructor* to make the copies required for passing to testFn. If such implicit copy constructor calls are undesirable for a class, you can use the explicit keyword to prevent implicit copy making. You may also place a do-nothing copy constructor in the private section to bar all copying, implicit or explicit.

Running the program should produce the following output:

```
(7  -2, 3   3, 2   -15, 1   -3, 0   -9)
(7   2, 3  -3, 2    15, 1    3, 0    9)
copy constructor called
copy constructor called
(7  -2, 3   3, 2   -15, 1   -3, 0   -9)
(7   2, 3  -3, 2    15, 1    3, 0    9)
copy constructor called
0
copy constructor called
= called
0
```

When you test this program, your output may show a different number of copy constructor calls because different C++ compilers have different levels of optimization to avoid making copies.

In summary, objects containing pointer, reference, or const data members, temporary files, or I/O streams usually cannot use the built-in object assignment or copying semantics. Classes with pointers to free storage should usually have all of the following defined:

- Destructor for freeing storage.
- Assignment operator=.
- Copy constructor.

You can bar assignment and copy construction for classes that don't need them by defining do-nothing versions as nonpublic members.

7.11 DERIVED-OBJECT ASSIGNMENT AND COPYING

As stated earlier, neither the assignment operator nor the copy constructor is inherited by a derived class. A derived class may supply code for either or both. If a derived class does not supply a class-defined copy constructor, one

7.11 DERIVED-OBJECT ASSIGNMENT AND COPYING

is generated for it that copies base and member objects by calling their copy constructors and copies other data members directly. A class-defined copy constructor must specify desired base- and member-object copy constructor calls on its init-list. (Again, default constructor calls can be omitted.)

The treatment of derived-object assignment is similar. If a derived class does not supply a class-defined assignment operator, one is generated for it that calls base- and component-object assignment operators and assigns other data members individually. A class-defined assignment operator takes care of calling (or not calling) base- and component-object assignment operators itself.

Let's consider a simplified example. The following base class has both a copy constructor and assignment operator:

```
class BaseX
{ public:
    BaseX() {}                                    // default constructor
    BaseX(int a, int b)                           // constructor
     : i(a), j(b) {}
    BaseX(const BaseX& obj){ i=obj.i; j=obj.j; } // copy constructor
    BaseX& operator=(const BaseX& obj);           // assignment
  private:
    int i, j;
};

BaseX& BaseX::operator=(const BaseX& obj)  // assignment
{  if (this == &obj) return *this;
   i = obj.i; j = obj.j;
   return *this;
}
```

The derived class also supplies a class-defined copy constructor and assignment operator:

```
class DerivedX : public BaseX
{ public:
    DerivedX() { }                            // default constructor
    DerivedX(int a, int b, int c)             // constructor
     : BaseX(a,b), k(c) { }
    DerivedX(const DerivedX& obj)             // copy constructor
     : BaseX(obj) { k=obj.k; }                // base copy constructor call
    DerivedX&
    operator=(const DerivedX& obj); // assignment
  private:
    int k;
};
```

```
DerivedX& DerivedX::
operator=(const DerivedX& obj)          // assignment
{  if (this == &obj) return *this;
   BaseX::operator=(obj);                // base assignment call
   k = obj.k;
   return *this;
}
```

Notice the base copy constructor call and the base assignment operator call. The integer data members really do not require copy or assignment operators, but they simplify the example.

If a base class does not have properly defined assignment and copying, these operations can be supplied in a derived class as explained next.

7.12 OBJECT ASSIGNMENT AND COPYING VIA DERIVATION

A class such as `ArbList` does not contain properly defined assignment and copy operations, which is all right as long as these operations are not required. To make the situation more robust, do-nothing assignment and copy constructors can be defined as private members to bar their use. When we want to make assignment and copy construction available for such a class, we can define a derived class that adds the desired operations.

For example, a generic list class `ArbList_ac` with proper assignment and copy operations is derived as follows:

```
///////    ArbList_ac.h     ///////
#include "ArbList.h"
// generic list with assignment and copy

class ArbList_ac : public ArbList
{ public:
    ArbList_ac() { }                              // default constructor
    ArbList_ac(Any c, EQ_FN eq, DISP_FN d)        // constructor
       : ArbList(c, eq, d) { }
    ~ArbList_ac() { }                             // destructor
    ArbList_ac& operator=(const ArbList_ac& x);   // assignment    (1)
    ArbList_ac& operator=(const ArbList& x);      // assignment    (2)
    ArbList_ac(const ArbList_ac& x)               // copy constructor (3)
       {   copy(x);  }
  private:
    void copy(const ArbList_ac& x);
};
```

7.12 OBJECT ASSIGNMENT AND COPYING VIA DERIVATION

`ArbList_ac` defines two assignment operators (lines 1 and 2) and a copy constructor (line 3). Line 2 makes assigning an `ArbList` object to an `ArbList_ac` object possible. The private function `copy()` is used for copying data members.

To allow `copy()` access to all data members, `ArbList_ac` can be made a friend of `ArbList`. Better yet, the nonpublic data members of `ArbList` can be declared `protected` to allow access from a derived class. Such planning ahead for derived classes is an important aspect of OOP.

The assignment operators `operator=()` are examined first:

```
///////     ArbList_ac.C      ///////
#include "ArbList_ac.h"

// assignment
ArbList_ac& ArbList_ac::operator =(const ArbList_ac& x)
{   operator=( static_cast< const ArbList& >(x) );  }     // (A)

// assignment of ArbList
ArbList_ac& ArbList_ac::operator =(const ArbList& x)      // (B)
{   if ( &x == this ) return *this;
    if ( ! isEmpty() ) free();
    copy( static_cast< const ArbList_ac& >(x) );
    return *this;
}
```

Note the use of static type casts. Without the cast, the call on line A won't go to the function on line B.

The actual copying is performed by the member function

```
void ArbList_ac::copy(const ArbList_ac& x)
{   equal = x.equal;               // copies data members
    dispfn = x.dispfn;
    ArbCell* lx = x.first();
    head = NULL;                   // empty list
    while ( ! isEnd(lx) )          // copies list
    {   append(ArbList::content(lx));
        lx = ArbList::next(lx);
    }

}
```

This `copy` member is also used in the copy constructor. It is good practice to share a piece of common copying code between the copy constructor and the assignment operator when possible.

Applications needing assignment or copying of lists can use `ArbList_ac` instead of `ArbList`. The complete program can be found in the code package (ex07/inhlist/).

7.13 MULTIPLE INHERITANCE

Deriving a class from one direct base class is single inheritance. Deriving from more than one direct base class is *multiple inheritance*. Multiple inheritance is a convenient way to define new objects that are combinations of existing types. For example, a TeachingAssistant can be derived from an Instructor and a Student class; MotorCycle from MotorVehicle and Bicycle; and IceCream from DairyProduct, Dessert, and FrozenFood. Although not as frequently used as its single-base counterpart, multiple inheritance provides a powerful dimension to OOP for both code reuse and program organization.

The easiest way to understand multiple inheritance is by studying an example. So let's apply multiple inheritance to derive a joint free checking account JtFrChecking from the existing JointAccount and FreeChecking, each of which happens to be already derived from the basic Account class:

```
///////    JtFrChecking.h     ///////
#include "FreeChecking.h"
#include "JointAccount.h"

class JtFrChecking                                  // multiple inheritance
: public JointAccount, public FreeChecking          // order insignificant
{ public:
    JtFrChecking() { }                              // default constructor
    JtFrChecking(unsigned n, double b,              // constructor
        char* owner, char* jowner);
};
```

Note that including the header files and defining the constructor do not take much work, and we easily obtain a new class. We now establish a joint free checking account:

```
JtFrChecking peter_lucy(23456, 750.0, "034-55-1111", "052-44-7777");
```

Multiple Base-Class Scopes

In single inheritance, the scope of a derived class is nested in its unique base class. When there are several direct base classes, a derived class is considered nested in each of the base scopes. To find an identifier under multiple inheritance, all the direct bases are searched at once. For example, if an identifier used in the scope JtFrChecking:: is not found there, both base scopes (scope FreeChecking:: and scope JointAccount::) will be searched at once. If there is only one match, then the identifier is found. Multiple matches result in

Figure 7.7 NONVIRTUAL MULTIPLE INHERITANCE

ambiguity and an error. If there is no match, then all bases of the base classes are searched at once and so on.

Hence, we have a slight complication: Both the JointAccount and the FreeChecking base objects contain an Account object (Figure 7.7). This means that peter_lucy contains two instances of Account. The duplication is legal but often unnecessary or even unworkable as is the case here. Certainly, an account with two different balances is not right.

Shared Bases

The C++ *virtual base* is the mechanism that is designed for the purpose of avoiding duplication of base objects. Simply declare virtual the base class whose instance should not be duplicated within a derived object. For JtFrChecking, we modify the declarations of JointAccount and FreeChecking as follows:

```
class JointAccount : public virtual Account    // (1)
{    /* class body as before */   };

class FreeChecking : public virtual Account    // (2)
{    /* class body as before */   };
```

The term *virtual base*, although less intuitive than *common base* or *shared base*, means exactly that. In the derived object JtFrChecking, there is just one Account object common to (shared by) the two base objects JointAccount and FreeChecking (Figure 7.8). If both virtual and nonvirtual instances of a base class exist (e.g., omitting the keyword virtual from line 2 but not from line 1), then there is a unique shared virtual instance plus other nonshared instances.

Since a virtual-base object (e.g., Account) is shared, should it be initialized by one of the derived classes (JointAccount or FreeChecking)? Or should each of the immediate derived classes perform its initialization as programmed by the following code?

```
FreeChecking::FreeChecking
(unsigned n, double b, char* owner)
```

Figure 7.8 VIRTUAL MULTIPLE INHERITANCE

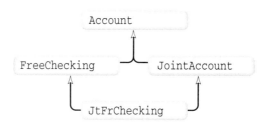

```
    : Account(n, b, owner),              // init virtual base (1)
      free(b >= min_bal)                 // init-list
    { }

JointAccount::JointAccount
(unsigned n, double b, char* owner, char* jowner)
    : Account(n, b, owner)               // init virtual base (2)
    { strncpy(jss, jowner, SS_LEN); }
```

The answer is none of the above. C++ actually shifts the duty of initializing a virtual-base object to the *most derived class*, the class at the end of the derivation chain in question. Thus, the JtFrChecking constructor

```
///////    JtFrChecking.C    ///////
#include "JtFrChecking.h"

JtFrChecking::JtFrChecking
(unsigned n, double b, char* owner, char* jowner)
    :  Account(n, b, owner),             // init virtual base (3)
       JointAccount(n, b, owner, jowner),   // (4)
       FreeChecking(n, b, owner)         // (5)
    { }
```

should contain a call to the Account constructor (line 3). If the explicit call is not given (line 3), the default Account constructor is called to initialize the virtual-base object. Other initializations (lines 1 and 2) are skipped entirely. Specifically, the calls on lines 4 and 5 skip their respective Account calls. Later, if a class is derived based on JtFrChecking, then it takes over the initialization of the virtual base Account.

To test the joint free checking account, use the following simple main program:

```
#include <iostream>
using std::cout; using std::endl;
```

7.13 MULTIPLE INHERITANCE

```
int main()
{   JtFrChecking peter_lucy(23456, 750.0,
                            "034-55-1111", "052-44-7777");
    cout << peter_lucy.balance() << endl;    // initial balance
    peter_lucy.withdraw(400);
    cout << peter_lucy.balance() << endl;    // after withdrawal
    peter_lucy.deposit(300);
    cout << peter_lucy.balance() << endl;    // after deposit
    peter_lucy.fee();
    cout << peter_lucy.balance() << endl;    // after service fee
    return 0;
}
```

Running this program produces the following output:

```
750
350
650
632
```

Multiple inheritance can also be used to add abilities quite unrelated to the original purpose of a class. Supplying logging operations to record information in files for later analysis is an example. To enable logging for class *Abc*, we can derive from both *Abc* and the Log class, *mixing in* logging operations with existing operations in class *Abc*. The resulting class offers objects that can be used as an *Abc* or a Log.

Base-Member Access Under Virtual Derivation

Access to members in a virtual-base object obeys the same public–private derivation rules given in Section 7.5. Making the base object unique actually reduces possibilities for access ambiguity. The call peter_lucy.balance() would be ambiguous if Account were not a virtual base because the compiler could not choose between JointAccount::balance() and FreeChecking::balance(). With Account as a virtual base, these versions of balance() become the same, thus eliminating the ambiguity. The same can be said about deposit() in the object peter_lucy.

The situation for peter_lucy.withdraw() is slightly different: It is redefined in the class FreeChecking but not in JointAccount. Thus, the call accesses the version defined in FreeChecking whether or not Account is made a virtual base.

Through multiple inheritance with a virtual base, we can access a unique base member via different routes: Getting to Account::balance() either through JointAccount or FreeChecking is one example. What if these routes involve different types of derivation that affect access permissions? For example, what if `Account` is a `private` base of `JointAccount`? In C++, if at least one of the multiple routes to arrive at the unique member is permissible, then access is granted.

Virtual-Base Object Initialization

A virtual-base object is not stored in a section of contiguous memory inside the derived object as are regular-base objects. It is stored independently, and its address is included in a derived object. This arrangement allows a virtual-base object to be easily shared by multiple subobjects within a derived object.

When a derived object is initialized, immediate virtual-base objects are initialized before other virtual-base objects. Other constructors are called in well-understood order after all virtual objects have been initialized. Destructor calls are always carried out in the reverse order of constructor calls.

7.14 THE I/O STREAM CLASS HIERARCHY

The C++ I/O stream library defines character-set-independent *class templates* (Section 10.3) such as

```
basic_ios
basic_istream
basic_ostream
```

from which character-set-specific I/O classes are *instantiated*. I/O classes for ASCII characters include `ios`, `istream`, `ostream`, `iostream`, and so forth. Corresponding classes for wide characters are also available. Here we'll focus on the I/O classes for `char`.

The C++ I/O stream class hierarchy is outlined in Figure 7.9 to give you a better idea of how the different I/O stream objects relate to one another and to show how class derivation can be used effectively in practice. At the base of Figure 7.9 is the `ios_base` class providing I/O error and exception handling. The `ios` class inherits the familiar `enum` members `ios::in`, `ios::out`, and so on from `ios_base` and supplies error testing functions such as **good**, **failed**, and so forth. Derived from `ios`, as a virtual base, are `istream` and `ostream`. Object assignment (class-defined `operator=()`) is added to `istream` and `ostream` by class derivation. These derived classes give rise to the standard `cin`, `cout`, `cerr`, and `clog`. Multiple inheritance is used to derive `iostream` from both `istream` and `ostream`. The derivations in Figure 7.9 are all public.

7.15 SUMMARY

Figure 7.9 I/O STREAM CLASS HIERARCHY

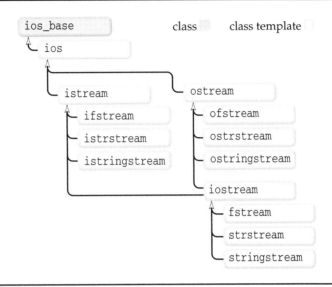

Class derivation is the C++ mechanism that supports inheritance by adding to or modifying existing classes without changing their code. A class can be derived from one or several base classes. A base class can be designated public, protected, or private, giving rise to three different types of derivation. Repeated derivation results in class hierarchies.

A derived class inherits all members of its base classes except constructors, destructors, and assignment operators. The derived-class scope is nested inside the scopes of its direct base classes. A derived-class identifier hides a base-class identifier of the same name. An identifier is located in the nested scope of a derivation hierarchy by following the derivation chain toward the root base class, searching base classes at the same level simultaneously, and ending at file scope. An identifier is first found; its accessibility is then determined. If more than one identifier is found, ambiguity results. Deriving a class from multiple base classes is multiple inheritance where avoiding duplicated indirect base classes is important.

A derived object is composed of base objects and an appendant part containing added members. The derived-class constructor and base-class constructors collaborate to initialize a derived object. Similarly, the derived-class destructor and base-class destructors cooperate to deinitialize a derived object.

Appendant members and friends of a derived class can always access the nonprivate inherited members. Access to inherited members from outside the derived class depends on the base-class designation. Section 7.5 contains a summary of access control rules under derivation.

Public derivation expresses the is-a relationship, whereas private or protected derivation facilitates code reuse and supports the is-implemented-as-a relationship. The has-a or uses-a relationship should be modeled with component objects within a class. The C++ implicit conversion rules between inheritance-related types are designed to support these relationships.

C++ defines only a few operations generally applicable to all objects: assignment, copying (initialization, argument passing by value, function return by value), address-of (&), and member-of (.). Most other operations on objects must be supplied by the class. Built-in assignment and copying work fine for objects without pointer/reference members or a nontrivial destructor. Other objects ought either to bar or to supply code for object assignment and copying:

ClassX& ClassX::operator=(const *ClassX&*);

and a copy constructor

ClassX::*ClassX*(const *ClassX&*);

When defining a copy constructor, implicit copying can be disallowed by declaring the copy constructor explicit.

When objects contain pointers to free storage, these operations are programmed to cooperate with the constructors and destructors for a well-rounded class. Assignment and copy constructors are not inherited, and a derived-class supplied definition must specify calls to appropriate base-class counterparts. Class derivation can be used to add the necessary assignment and/or copy constructor to an existing class.

EXERCISES

1. What is the fine and important distinction between an "inherited member" and a "member in the base class"? Consider the derived class JointAccount and the additional member

   ```
   int JointAccount::operator > (Account& a)
   {    return acct_no > a.acct_no;   }
   ```

   Is anything wrong with this member function other than the fact that it is a contrived example? Explain.

CHAPTER 7 EXERCISES

2. Does a `friend` of a base class have any special access privilege to members, inherited or not, of a derived class?

3. Which members of a base class are not inherited by a derived class? When a member is not inherited, what difference does it make? Explain and give an example. (*Hint*: Consider assignment.)

4. Is it possible to list the same base class more than once on the base-class list of a derived class? Is it possible to have a circular derived-base relationship: Class *RR* is derived from class *SS* and class *SS* is derived from class *RR*? If not, what prevents it from being done?

5. Enumerate the differences between a public and a private class derivation.

6. Consider the two member functions `DerivedX::xyz(char *)` and `BaseX::xyz(int)`. If `obj` is an object of `DerivedX`, which function does the call `obj.xyz(5)` invoke? Explain.

7. Derive an `OverDrawProtection` account from `FreeChecking`. For overdraw protection, a checking account would have a preset "credit line" of, say, 1000. If overdraw occurs, enough money (rounded up to the nearest 100) is transferred from the credit line into the account to cover the shortfall. Any account with a debit balance will incur the monthly fee no matter what the account balance is. The account charges interest on credit line balance with a settable rate on the *average daily balance*. Interest is charged to the account when the monthly fee is processed. Deposit into the account and repaying (part or all of) the credit line balance are two different account functions. The bank can increase/decrease the credit line for any account.

8. Under what situations can a derived object (reference, pointer) be passed to a base-type parameter? Under what situations can a base object (reference, pointer) be passed to a derived-type parameter?

9. Consider C++ built-in object assignment. If you assign objects that themselves contain member objects, how would the assignment proceed?

10. For class objects, list all the situations you can think of under which the built-in assignment may be inadequate and explain why. (*Hint*: `const`, reference.) Do the same for built-in copying.

11. Is it possible to pass an `ifstream` object to an `istream` formal parameter in a function call? What about an `istream&` parameter? Why?

12. Follow the `ArbStack` example (Section 7.6) and derive `ArbQueue` from `ArbList`.

13. Derive `EmpQueue`, a queue of employees, from the generic queue in Exercise 12.

14. Exercise Cal-1: Consider the improvements suggested for the pocket calculator program (Chapter 6, Exercise Cal-1). Instead of adding these new capabilities in the existing calculator classes directly, consider achieving the same with class derivation. Specifically, derive `NewEng` from `CalcEng` to add the new capabilities to the compute engine (change `private` to `protected` in `CalcEng`). The public interface of `NewEng` should be kept the same as `CalcEng`. Also, operations already implemented in `CalcEng` should not be duplicated in `NewEng`. It should simply add preprocessing and/or postprocessing to the base `CalcEng::operate()`. The `CalcFace` class should need no modification. The simple `Calculator` class can be modified to take a `NewEng` object.

15. Exercise Cal-2: Use the improved calculator program in Exercise 14 and further derivation to implement the calculator suggested in Chapter 6, Exercise Cal-2.

16. Extend the two-dimensional `Vector2D` class to *n* dimensions using dynamic storage allocation in the constructor. Also define the proper destructor, assignment, and copy constructor.

17. Explain the *is-a*, *has-a*, *uses-a*, *internally-implemented-as*, and *aggregation* relationship among objects.

18. Consider multiple inheritance and a virtual base that is a `public` base following one branch of the derivation chain and a `private` base following another. How does this affect the derived object's ability to access members in the virtual-base object?

CHAPTER EIGHT

Operator Overloading, Iterators, and Exceptions

Objects, classes, and inheritance provide enormous power for program organization, complexity reduction, and code reuse. However, as stated earlier, there are very few ready-made operations for objects. This is not an oversight on the part of C++; few operations make sense for all the varied kinds of user-defined types. Thus, to make a class of objects work well, your program has to define many of its operations, often through overloading operators. This is especially true for sophisticated classes.

Operator overloading is a C++ feature that can help make programs generic. Rules for operator overloading are presented in this chapter. The practical use of overloaded operators is demonstrated. Examples include =, +=, [], and smart pointers with ->.

Iterators make access to elements stored in encapsulating objects possible, and this concept is illustrated. Standard C++ iterator conventions are explained and demonstrated by a nested-class iterator for `Cirbuf`.

Knowing what errors may occur at run time and how to handle them is important for programming. Error values, error states, exceptions, error reporting, and error recovery are described. Exceptions are objects representing run-time errors. The definition, throwing, and catching of exceptions are discussed and applied in examples.

Also presented are class-defined type conversions and user-defined free store management with `new` and `delete`.

8.1 OPERATOR OVERLOADING

The three operators (&, ., =) have built-in meaning for class objects. Other operators do not work with objects unless definitions are supplied. Properly defining the meaning of appropriate operators can make class objects easier to use. We shall see that making the same operators work for different user-defined types can increase the genericness of programs.

You prescribe the meaning of an operator such as +, <<, and [ ] for class objects by defining *operator functions*. An operator function named "operator *op*" overloads the operator *op*. We have already seen some operator functions, including operator- for fractions and operator+ for polynomials. Note that there are two tokens in an operator function name, and it does not matter if they are separated by white space (operator +) or not (operator+). Either style can improve readability in a given situation.

Operator overloading helps OOP, for example, by making arithmetic operators such as + work for both basic types and objects such as fractions. We can thus write generic codes that work for all such arithmetic types. And by making I/O operators such as << work for basic and user-defined types, we can write I/O codes that work generically.

Table 8.1 shows all the operators that can be overloaded as well as the four that cannot be. However, there are certain restrictions to operator overloading:

1. At least one operand (argument) of the operator must be of user-defined type — that is, an object. Therefore, the meaning of an operator for built-in data types cannot be changed.
2. Operator functions cannot have default arguments.
3. The number of operands (or *arity*) for an operator cannot be changed.
4. Brand-new operators cannot be introduced. Thus, it is not possible to introduce a new operator such as **.
5. Operator precedence is built-in and fixed.
6. The four operators =, [ ], ( ), and -> can be overloaded only with member operator functions.

Table 8.1 OPERATOR OVERLOADING

Overloadable Operators							
/	%	^	|	~	!	<	>
+=	-=	*=	/=	%=	^=	&=	|=
<<	>>	<<=	>>=	==	!=	<=	>=
&&	||	++	--	,	->*	new	delete

Unary and Binary				Member Only				Not Overloaded			
+	-	*	&	=	[ ]	( )	->	.	? :	::	.*

Member or Nonmember

For all except four operators, the operator function can be defined as a class member or as an unattached function. For example, consider adding the operator += for the class Fraction. The intended meaning of f1 += f2 is f1 = f1 + f2. It is not illegal to use += for completely unrelated purposes, but it is usually ill-advised.

Taking the member route, we add the declaration

```
Fraction& operator +=(const Fraction&);
```

to the Fraction class declaration and the code

```
Fraction& Fraction::operator +=(const Fraction& fra)
{    *this = *this + fra;      // operator+ already exists
     return *this;
}
```

to the Fraction.C file.

Taking the nonmember route, we define the function

```
Fraction& operator +=(Fraction& f1, const Fraction& f2)
{    f1 = f1 + f2;
     return f1;
}
```

to perform the desired operations. Either style works fine in this case. The member function is declared with only one argument because the host object is always the implicit left operand; that is, the two expressions

```
f1 += f2                // member operator +=
f1.operator +=(f2)
```

are the same. The nonmember operator function takes two arguments. Thus,

```
f1 += f2                // nonmember operator +=
operator += (f1, f2)
```

are equivalent expressions.

In general, the expression x *op* y can access either the member or the nonmember implementation of *op*. When both forms are present, argument matching determines which one, if any, is called. Ambiguity results if there are several matches. Similar remarks can be made for unary operators.

Because direct invocations are possible, it is not an error to keep both the member and nonmember versions in a program even if they may cause ambiguity. One form is usually sufficient. When all operands are objects of the class, take the member route.

But there are situations when the nonmember route is your only choice. Consider overloading * for the `Fraction` class to take care of fraction-integer multiplication:

*Fraction * int* (case I: fraction × integer)
*int * Fraction* (case II: integer × fraction)

Case I can be treated by a member operator function, but case II cannot because a class object must be the left operand in order to invoke its member function with the operator notation. Everything else being equal, you should define both cases as nonmember functions. Here case II is coded as an unattached function:

```
inline Fraction operator *(int i, const Fraction& fra)
{   return   fra*Fraction(i, 1);
}
```

Case I can be similarly defined.

It is not necessary to discuss the overloading of each and every operator in Table 8.1 because most follow the rules already presented. Overloading of >> and << has been presented in Section 6.8. A number of other important cases are described in this chapter.

8.2 A REFERENCE-COUNT STRING CLASS

For objects with member pointers to free storage, one approach the user-defined copy constructor and the `operator=` can take is to make copies of data in free storage. Another approach involves *reference counting*.

In many applications, multiple objects with members pointing to the same free storage address present no problem. It is only the freeing of this storage by the destructor that causes difficulty. Consider an application in which many C-style strings in free storage will be used and the storage required should be minimized. Much space is saved by not making copies of the same string every time it is assigned, passed in a call, or returned from a function. This can be done by creating `Cell` objects that bind a reference count with a string in free storage. The count keeps track of how many pointers can access the `Cell` object. The string is freed only when the count drops to zero:

```
class Cell
{ friend class Refstr;
  private:
     Cell(const char *s);              // constructor
     char *str;                        // free storage string
     unsigned cnt;                     // reference count
```

8.2 A REFERENCE-COUNT STRING CLASS

```
      ~Cell() { delete [] str; }          // destructor
};

Cell::Cell(const char *s)
: str(new char[strlen(s)+ 1])
{    strcpy(str, s);                      // str in free storage
     cnt = 1;                             // reference count
}
```

The `Cell` class is used exclusively by its friend class `Refstr`, which manages strings with a reference count. The `Cell` code can be kept in the file `Refstr.C` for better information hiding. The `Refstr.h` file provides the reference string class:

```
///////   Refstr.h   ///////
#include<iostream>
#include<string.h>

class Cell;   // defined in Refstr.C file

class Refstr
{ public:
     explicit Refstr(const char *str= "");  // constructor
     Refstr(const Refstr& s);               // copy constructor
     Refstr& operator =(const Refstr& s);   // assignment
     int cmp(const Refstr& s) const;        // compares two strings
     unsigned getCount()                    // retrieves count
     {  return ptr->cnt;  }
     void display();
     ~Refstr();                             // destructor
  private:
     Cell *ptr;                             // ptr to ref count str
};
```

A new `Refstr` object is initialized by

```
///////  in Refstr.C
Refstr::Refstr(const char *s)
: ptr(new Cell(s)) { }
```

When a `Refstr` object is destroyed, the destructor is called:

```
Refstr::~Refstr()
{   if (--ptr->cnt == 0) delete ptr;       // calls ~Cell
}
```

Note that the storage is freed only when the reference count is zero. The `Refstr` copy constructor and assignment operator increase the reference count rather than make copies:

```
Refstr::Refstr(const Refstr& s)          // copy constructor
{   ptr = s.ptr;                         // assigns pointer
    ptr->cnt++;                          // increments count
}

Refstr& Refstr::operator = (const Refstr& s)
{   if (this == &s || ptr == s.ptr)
        return *this;                    // trivial assignment
    if ( --ptr->cnt == 0 ) delete ptr;   // last pointer gone
    ptr = s.ptr;
    ptr->cnt++;                          // increments count
    return *this;
}
```

These functions show you how to avoid copying to improve efficiency in your program. Other members for dealing with reference strings can be defined. For example,

```
int Refstr::cmp(const Refstr& s) const
{   if ( s.ptr == ptr ) return 0;        // same pointers
    else return strcmp(ptr->str, s.ptr->str);
}
```

compares two strings.

It is interesting to track `Refstr` objects and see how their reference counts change. Use the following test program:

```
///////     testRefstr.C    ///////
#include <iostream>
#include "Refstr.h"
using std::cout;
using std::endl;

int callcmp(Refstr a, Refstr b)
{   cout << "a ref count = " << a.getCount() << endl;
    return a.cmp(b);
}

int main()
{   Refstr s1("There"); Refstr s2("Here");
    Refstr s3("Hello"); Refstr s4 = s3;
    Refstr s5 = s2;
    cout << "s3 ref count = " << s3.getCount() << endl;
    s2 = s4;
```

```
            cout << "s3 ref count = " << s3.getCount() << endl;
            s1 = s3;
            cout << "s3 ref count = " << s3.getCount() << endl;
            callcmp(s1, s2);
            s4 = s5;
            cout << "s3 ref count = " << s3.getCount() << endl;
            return 0;
        }
```

Running this program produces the following output:

```
s3 ref count = 2
s3 ref count = 3
s3 ref count = 4
a  ref count = 6
s3 ref count = 3
```

The techniques presented here can also be used to build a reference-counting class from any given class — say, Abc. A pair of classes are needed:

1. A class AbcCell containing a reference count, a pointer to Abc, a constructor, and a destructor.
2. A class RefAbc with a pointer to AbcCell in free storage and an appropriately defined constructor, destructor, copy constructor, and assignment operator.

These two classes combine to give reference-count objects for Abc without modifying class Abc at all. In fact, class Abc may be a library facility whose source code is inaccessible.

8.3 OVERLOADING [ ]

The [] operator is often useful for an object that stores a sequence of values to be accessed by indexing just like an array. The way a class defines operator[] can control how the indexed element is used — as an rvalue or an lvalue.

The TextLines class (Section 4.7) provided an operator[] for read access to stored text lines:

```
class TextLines
{ public:
        TextLines()
        { line = vector<string*>(0);}
        string* operator[](int i) const          // for rvalue (A)
        {   return (i >= 0 && i < len ) ? line[i] : NULL; }
        int length() { return len; }
        /*  other members */
```

```
    private:
        int readLines(istream& in);
        vector<string*> line; // array of string pointers
        int len;              // number of lines
};
```

The operator[] on line A produces an rvalue allowing, for example, the code

```
string* ptr = txtobj[i];
key.lineCompare(*txtobj[i], *txtobj[j])
```

In practice, a pair of operator[] functions should be defined: one returning a read-only rvalue and the other an lvalue, which of course can also be used as an rvalue. For TextLines, this means replacing the function on line A with the pair of members:

```
string*& operator[](int i)           // for lvalue and rvalue  (B)
{   if (i >= 0 && i < len) return line[i]; abort(); }

const string* operator[](int i) const  // for read-only rvalue  (C)
{   if (i >= 0 && i < len) return line[i]; abort(); }
```

Version B returns a reference that can be used either as an lvalue or an rvalue. Version C returns a const string* rvalue and is needed when the host is a const object. With B defined, the following code for swapping two lines works:

```
string* tmp = txtobj[i];
txtobj[i] = txtobj[j];
txtobj[j] = tmp;
```

Overloading the unary * involves the same considerations as overloading [].

8.4 OVERLOADING ++ AND --

The increment and decrement operators ++ and -- are special because they can be used as prefix or postfix operators. Overloading ++ is discussed here. (Overloading -- is the same.)

To overload the prefix version of ++, use

```
type ClassX::operator ++();      (prefix ++ as class member)
type operator ++(type arg);      (prefix ++ as nonmember)
```

To overload the postfix version ++, a special signature must be used:

```
type ClassX::operator ++(int);        (postfix ++ as class member)
type operator ++(type arg, int);      (postfix ++ as nonmember)
```

The artificial second int argument does not even need a parameter name because it is just there to tell the C++ compiler that the postfix version of ++ is being overloaded.

Here is an example for the preincrement of a fraction:

```
Fraction Fraction::operator ++()
{   num += denom;
    return *this;
}
```

8.5 SMART POINTERS

Of the two member selection operators . and ->, only the latter can be overloaded and it is treated specially. Normally, -> is a binary operator taking a pointer as the left operand and a member name as the right operand. However, if its left operand is an object instead of a pointer to an object, the notation invokes the unary member function operator->. Specifically, the code

obj->mem

is interpreted as

(*obj*.operator->())->*mem*

where the function operator-> must return either a valid object pointer or an object with an overloaded ->.

As mentioned earlier, operator-> can be defined only as a member function. A typical application of the overloaded -> is in creating *smart pointer* objects — pointers that also perform additional work as programmed. To keep track of how often customers access their bank accounts, for example, we can define an AccountPtr class to access accounts:

```
#include "Account.h"

class AccountPtr
{   public:
        AccountPtr(unsigned n, double b)
         : ptr(new Account(n,b)), cnt(0) { }

        Account* operator ->()      // overloaded ->
        {  cnt++; return ptr; }
    private:
        unsigned cnt;
        Account* ptr;
};
```

Then, we can use codes such as

```
AccountPtr john(123456,640.75);
john->deposit(24.50);
cout << john->balance() << endl;
```

so that `john.cnt` keeps track of the number of times John's account has been accessed.

There are four operators (=, [], (), ->) that must be overloaded as member functions. Three of these have now been described. The function-call operator () can make objects behave like functions and is described in Section 11.9.

8.6 ITERATORS

In OOP, objects hide their internal workings and therefore reduce software complexity. But are there any downsides to this approach? Specifically, are any operations made harder or impossible to perform without knowledge of the internal structures? One is the operation of visiting every item contained in an object. Consider, for example, the circular buffer class (Section 3.12). Suppose there is a need to inspect each character still in a `Cirbuf` object without consuming any character. One way to achieve this is to provide another public member function for the iteration:

```
int Cirbuf::next(char& c)
{   static int ind = -1;
    if ( ind == -1 ) ind = head;
    if ( ind == tail ) return ind = -1;
    c = cb[ind++];
    ind = mod(ind);
    return ind;
}
```

A `static` variable `ind` is used to remember the index of the last character examined. The reference parameter c receives the next character. A nonnegative value is returned unless the end is reached. With the `next` function, a typical iteration can be written as follows:

```
Cirbuf mybuf(64);
char c;
/*   ...   */
while ( mybuf.next(c) > -1) cout << c;
```

The example is an attempt to iterate over items inside an object without knowledge of internal structures. The method is of limited use because *one iteration must be completely finished before another begins* and *calls to* next *from different host objects interfere with one another*.

8.6 ITERATORS

A more general solution involves defining an associated *iterator class* to provide systematic access to internal elements of objects in a target class. Consider a `CirbufIterator`:

```
class CirbufIterator                       // friend class of Cirbuf
{   public:
        CirbufIterator(Cirbuf& buf);       // constructor
        bool next(char& c);                // returns next char in c
    private:
        Cirbuf& b;                         // reference member
        int ind;                           // index
};
```

With this iterator class, iterations are performed as follows:

```
CirbufIterator it(mybuf);                  // iterator object
while ( it.next(c) ) cout << c;            // next char
```

Multiple iterations can also be ongoing without mutual interference. The constructor initializes the iterator

```
CirbufIterator::CirbufIterator(Cirbuf& buf)
: b(buf), ind(buf.head) { }
```

deposits the next item in its reference parameter, and returns nonzero unless the end is reached:

```
bool CirbufIterator::next(char& c)
{   if ( ind == b.tail ) return false;     // end reached
    c = b.cb[ind++];                       // next char
    ind = b.mod(ind);
    return true;                           // nonzero
}
```

The iterator is an important technique for hiding internal structures of objects while still providing necessary access from the outside. In some situations, the iterator can also be given other functions to perform as it scans through all the elements. Such chores include removing, adding, or substituting an element.

Here the iterator is a free-standing class. An often preferred alternative is to define the iterator as a *nested class* (Section 8.7).

Iterator Conventions

The Standard Template Library (STL) supplies a number of container classes such as `vector` and `list`. Each container supports *iterators*, used very much like pointers, to get and/or set elements in a container object. Let's describe the C++ iterator convention that can serve as a model for iterators of your own.

A container class *Xyz* holding type *T* elements defines encapsulated types (classes or `typedef`s) that *act as pointers to elements*:

- `iterator`: A type that behaves like *T**
- `const_iterator`: A type that behaves like const *T**

Thus, a `const_iterator` is for read-only iteration where we do not modify the values of the elements visited, whereas an `iterator` allows the setting of the visited elements.

A container *Xyz* must also provide member functions that return iterators:

- `obj.begin()`: Returns an iterator that points to the first element in the container `obj`. Normally two versions of `begin` are provided, one returning an `iterator` and the other a `const_iterator`.
- `obj.end()`: Returns an iterator that points to just beyond the last element in `obj`.

Under this convention, an iterator *itr* works just like a pointer or close to it. In particular:

- `*itr`: Gives a reference to the element to which the iterator object *itr* points, provided *itr* is not beyond the end. A class may also allow/disallow the use of *itr as an lvalue.
- `++itr`: Makes *itr* point to the next element or just beyond the end.
- `itr1!=itr2`: Returns true if the two iterators do not point to the same element.

Often, instead of defining iterator classes, we can simply add some `typedef`s to a container class. For example, the Standard C++ `vector` container (Sections 4.6 and 11.3) defines, for any given type *T*:

```
vector< T >::iterator        (as a typedef for T*)
vector< T >::const_iterator  (as a typedef for const T*)
```

A typical iteration loop looks like

```
for ( vector<int>::iterator itr = vec.begin();    // iterator
          itr != vec.end();  ++itr )
{   ...    }
```

Because `vector` iterators are actual pointers, all pointer operations are valid on them.

A simple program that computes the sum of all integers contained in a `vector` container further illustrates iterator usage.

```
#include <iostream>
#include <vector>
using std::vector; using std::cout; using std::endl;
```

```cpp
int main()
{   vector<int> v;
    v.reserve(16);                          // reserve capacity
    for (int i=0; i < 16; i++)
        v.push_back(i*i);
    int sum = 0;
    for (vector<int>::iterator itr=v.begin(); // iteration loop
         itr != v.end(); ++itr)
        sum += *itr;
    cout << "Sum is " << sum << endl;
    return 0;
}
```

Iterators that traverse the container backwards may also be provided. Other iterator operations, such as ==, --, and $itr \pm i$, may also be available as documented by the container class. Section 8.7 adds such an iterator to the class Cirbuf.

8.7 NESTED AND LOCAL CLASSES

A class defined within the scope of another class is a *nested class*. A class defined inside a function or a block is a *local class*.

A local class is known only to its local scope, and all its functions must be defined within the class itself. Normally, all members of a local class are public. Static members are not permitted; neither are references to automatic variables. The local class is seldom used or required.

A nested class, however, is sometimes useful as an encapsulation mechanism. Take the ArbList class (Section 5.12) for example. An alternative way to encapsulate the slave class ArbCell is to nest it within ArbList.

Simply revise as follows:

1. Move ArbCell, as is, into the class declaration for ArbList. Place it as a public member at the very end.
2. Move the forward declaration class ArbCell; from file scope to inside the ArbList class.
3. Any outside reference to ArbCell now becomes ArbList::ArbCell.
4. Any reference to Arbcell within ArbList remains the same.

```cpp
class ArbList
{ class ArbCell;                            // forward declaration
  public:
    typedef bool (* EQ_FN)(Any, Any);
```

```
        /* ... */
      public:
        class ArbCell
        { friend class ArbList;
          private:
            Any item;
            ArbCell* next;
            ArbCell(Any c = NULL, ArbCell* ptr = NULL)
            :  item(c), next(ptr) { }     // constructor
        };
    };
```

The complete example can be found in the code package (ex08/nest-class/).

In general, a nested class Inner is simply a member in the enclosing class Outer. The scope of Inner nests within that of Outer just like an inner block inside an outer block. Outer and Inner are otherwise just two different classes. In particular, neither has unusual access rights to members of the other.

Another application of nested class is to define iterators.

Adding Iterators to `Cirbuf`

Class nesting is useful for writing iterators. As an example, let's add a C++ container-style iterator to Cirbuf. Here is what we do:

- Add the nested class iterator to Cirbuf.
- Add the typedef for const_iterator.
- Hide iterator constructors as nonpublic members so only Cirbuf, a friend class, can instantiate Cirbuf::iterators.
- Add begin() and end() members to Cirbuf to return iterators.
- Make iterator a friend of Cirbuf so it can access hidden structures in the Cirbuf object under iteration.
- Define public operations in iterator to support ++, !=, and *.

Thus, we add the following code at the end of Cirbuf in file Cirbuf.h.

```
    public:                                               // in Cirbuf
      class iterator;
      typedef const iterator const_iterator;

      class iterator
      {  friend class Cirbuf;                             // (A)
         public:
           const_iterator& operator++() const             // (B)
           {   ++(const_cast< int& >(position));
```

8.7 NESTED AND LOCAL CLASSES

```
            return *this;
        }
        iterator& operator++()                  // (C)
        {   ++position;  return *this;  }

        bool operator !=(const iterator& b) const
        {   return position != b.position;  }

        char operator *() const                 // (D) rvalue
        {   return buf.cb[(buf.head + position)
                        % buf.size];
        }

        char& operator *()                      // (E) lvalue
        {   return buf.cb[(buf.head + position)
                        % buf.size];
        }
    private:
        iterator(Cirbuf& b, int i)              // (F)
            : buf(b), position(i)  { }
        Cirbuf& buf;    // buffer under iteration
        int position;   // current traversal position
    };
};
```

Remember that we need to model the type iterator after char* and the type const_iterator after const char *. If itr is of type iterator and c_itr of type const_iterator, this means

- *itr will return a char that can be used either as an lvalue or an rvalue.
- *c_itr will return a char that can be used only as an rvalue.
- ++ will increment both itr and c_itr.
- --, if implemented, will decrement both itr and c_itr.

Following these principles, operations ++c_itr (line B), ++itr (line C), *c_itr (line D), *itr (line E), and itr != cbuf.end() are supported in Cirbuf::iterator. Note how operator++ on line B has to artificially declare the host const and then casts away the const-ness of position to make things work.

Access to private members of Cirbuf (lines B and C) is possible because of the friend declaration on line D. Also add to Cirbuf the following member functions to return iterators.

```
    friend class Cirbuf::iterator;              // (G)
     iterator begin()                           // (H)
     { return iterator(*this, 0); }
```

```
const_iterator begin() const                    // (I)
{ return iterator(const_cast< Cirbuf& >(*this), 0); }

const_iterator end() const
{ return iterator(const_cast< Cirbuf& >(*this), length); }
```

The code on lines H and I return iterators for a read-write and a read-only host `Cirbuf`, respectively. Both call the private iterator constructor (line F) as a friend (line A). Obviously, line I is for read-only and line H is for read-write iteration.

With `Cirbuf::iterator` added, the following code for visiting elements in a circular buffer can be written:

```
#include <iostream>
#include "Cirbuf.h"

int main()
{   Cirbuf cbuf;
    cbuf.produce('A');
    cbuf.produce('B');
    cbuf.produce('C');
    for ( Cirbuf::const_iterator c_itr = cbuf.begin();
          c_itr != cbuf.end(); ++c_itr )
    {   std::cout << *c_itr;   }
    std::cout << std::endl;
}
```

8.8 ROBUST CLASSES

When writing C++ code, we may define a class so that it works only for a limited range of applications. Errors may occur when its objects are used for unintended purposes. For example, the `Cirbuf` class works well without a user-defined copy constructor as long as the copying of `Cirbuf` objects is avoided. Since there is no perceived need to initialize one `Cirbuf` object with another and since passing/returning circular buffers by reference is always easier and more efficient, copying is indeed easily avoided. `Calculator`, `CalcEng`, and `CalcFace` (Section 5.5) are typical examples of limited-application classes. Their objects are not intended for passing as arguments or for assignment to one another.

However, if another programmer comes along and uses objects from such a class in unforeseen ways that involve copying or assignment, errors will occur. One way to prevent assignment or copying is to include do-nothing `operator=` and copy constructor as nonpublic members in a class.

A user-supplied destructor, a copy constructor, overloaded operators such as =, +, -, *, and / as well as the I/O operators >> and << are features that help user-defined types behave increasingly like basic types (e.g., int). Adding these features makes a class more *robust*.

For a class without a nontrivial destructor, pointers to free store, temporary files, or I/O streams (e.g., Fraction), it is relatively easy to achieve robustness. In other situations, consider defining an appropriate destructor, an assignment operator, a copy constructor, as well as operators and iterators.

8.9 USER-DEFINED TYPE CONVERSIONS

Standard conversions for built-in types are applied implicitly and explicitly according to well-defined rules (Section 3.14). Automatic type conversions significantly reduce the number of overloaded operators and functions needed. Without conversions, x *op* y must be supported by many definitions covering all possible/desirable type combinations. For example, after defining the two friend functions

```
Fraction Fraction::operator+(const Fraction&, int);   // (1)
Fraction Fraction::operator+(int, const Fraction&);   // (2)
```

we can add a Fraction object not only to an int but also to a short, an unsigned, a char, and so on—all thanks to implicit conversions.

C++ knows about conversions among built-in types and among inheritance-related objects (Section 7.8). Other conversions for class objects are undefined unless appropriate type-conversion rules are specified. These user-defined type conversions can then be applied by the compiler when needed. Thus, *user-defined type conversions* help extend implicit and explicit type conversions to class objects. Conversions to and from a class type are discussed separately next.

Outward Conversion

A type-conversion class member

```
operator type ();       // convert host to type
```

is used to specify conversion of the host object to data of the given *type*. For example, to convert fractions to double, we add the following code to the class Fraction:

```
operator double()              // member of Fraction (3)
{  return   static_cast<double>(num)/static_cast<double>(denom);  }
```

With this member, a Fraction object fra can be explicitly converted to double using either of these two notations:

```
static_cast<double>(fra)
double(fra)                    // convert Fraction to double
```

Then, we can use codes such as

```
Fraction fra(22, 7);
if ( x > 3.1416 && x < static_cast<double>(fra) )
/* ... */
```

where x is a variable of type double. Type-conversion members can also be invoked using normal object syntax. Therefore,

```
fra.operator double()
```

works as expected.

The explicit conversion request in x < static_cast<double>(fra) is not always necessary. It can be omitted, and the code

```
x < fra                        // implicit conversion of fra
```

works fine because implicit conversion turns fra into type double.

Inward Conversion

The mechanism for converting data of another type into an object of a class is a constructor that takes exactly one argument of the foreign type. For example, to convert an int into a Fraction, we simply add the following constructor:

```
Fraction::Fraction(int j) : num(j), denom(1) { }    // (4)
```

The type-conversion notation is exactly that of a constructor call:

```
int i = 7;
fra = fra * Fraction(i);       // convert i to Fraction
/* ... */
```

Of course, an inward conversion, such as int to Fraction, is also applied implicitly. In fact, with the conversion specified on line 4, the mixed-arithmetic functions (lines 1 and 2) can be omitted without adversely affecting the codes

```
fra + i                        // works without (1), given (4)
i + fra                        // works without (2), given (4)
```

which call the member operator+(fraction) by implicitly converting i to Fraction using the constructor (line 4). However, if the Fraction-to-double conversion (line 3) is also defined, ambiguity results.

8.9 USER-DEFINED TYPE CONVERSIONS

Sometimes a constructor with only one argument is needed without the associated implicit type conversion. Then, simply add the keyword `explicit` in front of the constructor to suppress the implicit conversion semantics.

Conversion Ambiguity

The expression `fra + i` becomes ambiguous when `fra` can be converted to `double` and `i` can be converted to `Fraction`. Since both conversions are possible and there is no mechanism to indicate which to do first, the expression results in a compile-time error.

When multiple conversions are possible in a given situation but there is only one exact match, then there is no ambiguity. Thus, adding a `Fraction`-to-`float` conversion does not make the expression `double x = fra` ambiguous. Sometimes, there is more than one exact match. Consider classes `Xyz` and `Abc`. If `Xyz` defines an outward conversion to `Abc` and `Abc` defines an inward conversion from `Xyz`, then the code

```
Xyz var1;
Abc var2 = Abc(var1);     // ambiguous explicit conversion
Abc var2 = var1;          // ambiguous implicit conversion
```

is ambiguous because either `Abc(Xyz)` or `Xyz::operator Abc()` can be invoked. The explicit cast

```
static_cast<Abc>(var1)    // invokes Xyz::operator Abc()
```

is, however, not ambiguous because it is not confused with a constructor call.

Besides extending the applicability of operators and functions, user-defined conversions can also supply a convenient way for error handling as described next.

I/O Stream Conversions

User-defined conversion can be applied to report error or exception conditions. The common I/O stream conditions

```
while ( cin.get(c) )      // while input c successful  (A)

while ( cin >> x )        // while input x successful  (B)

ofstream ofile(/* ... */);
if ( ofstream )           // if open successful        (C)
```

involve logical tests on `istream` and `ostream` objects. When a class object is used in a logical expression, it must be converted either to some arithmetic type or to a pointer type. Thus, its class must define an unambiguous conversion to an arithmetic or a pointer type.

The I/O stream classes use a conversion generally defined as follows:

```
operator void*() const      // convert to void pointer
{   return fail() ? NULL : reinterpret_cast<void*>(-1); }
```

It is this kind of user-defined conversion that allows the convenient coding shown on lines A through C. The void* conversion is better than arithmetic conversions because it tends not to introduce ambiguity. Consider the conventions presented here in establishing your own error-reporting objects.

8.10 ERROR AND EXCEPTION HANDLING

For practical software projects, one important consideration is the handling of errors during program execution. Possible sources of run-time error include arithmetic overflow/underflow, division by zero, argument not within legal domain, results out of allowable range (too large or small), unexpected arguments, illegal pointers, array index out of range, free storage exhausted, no such file, disallowed file access, and I/O error.

Arithmetic and Mathematical Computation Errors

Overflow (underflow) occurs when a computation result is too large (small) and exceeds the limited precision of the data type used. For example, consider adding a positive integer to the largest positive int. What is the expected answer? Of course, the result will be incorrect because of overflow. Try it with your C++ program. You may very well find that the result is a negative int and that the program continues as if nothing wrong has happened. Generally, it is the programmer's responsibility to detect such errors when necessary.

The header files <limits.h> and <float.h> contain symbolic constants for the largest and smallest integral and floating-point values, respectively. For example, INT_MAX is the maximum int quantity, and INT_MIN is the minimum (most negative). Thus, for int a and b, the test

```
if ( a > 0 && (MAX_INT - a) < b )
```

predicts that a + b will overflow.

Error Indications from Mathematical Functions The standard mathematical functions (Appendix H) indicate domain and range errors. A *domain error* occurs when a function is passed an argument whose value is outside the valid interval for the particular function. For example, only positive arguments are valid for the **log** function. A *range error* occurs when the computed result is so large or small that it cannot be represented as a double.

The global variable errno defined in the header <errno.h> is used by system-supplied routines (library and system calls) to indicate error. When a domain error happens, errno is set to EDOM, a symbolic constant defined in <errno.h>, and the returned value is implementation dependent. For example, the call **sqrt**(-9.0) results in errno being set to EDOM. On the other hand, when a range error takes place, errno is set to ERANGE, and either zero (underflow) or HUGE_VAL (overflow) is returned. When an error occurs, an error message may also be generated by the library function.

Error Values

Standard Library functions return standard error values when they fail. The error indication returned must be consistent with the return value type declared for the function. At the same time, the error value must not be anything the function would ever return without failure. For library functions, the standard error values are

- EOF: Usually −1, used by functions normally returning a nonnegative integer.
- NULL: Usually 0, used by functions normally returning a valid pointer (nonzero).
- *Nonzero*: Used for a function that normally returns zero.

Again, it is up to your program to check for such a returned value and take appropriate actions. The following idiom is in common use:

```
if ( (value = call(...)) == errvalue )
{       // handle error here
        // output any error message to cerr
}
```

In your program, you can follow this error value technique. For example, the gcd(a,b) function normally returns a valid greatest common divisor that is a positive integer. Thus, zero or negative integer values can be used to report error conditions such as "both a and b are zero."

Error States

When a member function wishes to indicate error, an error flag or state variable in the host object can be set to a predefined value. This state variable is made accessible through the public interface of the object to determine whether an error or some exception condition has occurred. Error examination can be made even simpler by the class-defined conversion to void* (Section 8.9). The C++ I/O stream classes provide good examples (Table 6.5) for error states and error reporting.

The error state technique should be part of your class design when appropriate. For example, consider the CalcEng class. It should contain an error flag set internally to indicate overflow, underflow, square root of a negative quantity, and so on. Correct error reporting to the calculator user is thus made very easy.

Error Treatment and Recovery

After detecting an error or exception condition, a program has basically four alternatives:

1. *To ignore the error*: The program continues to execute as if nothing has happened. Normally, this is neither doable nor acceptable.
2. *To call* **exit**(*n*): If *n* is zero, this is a normal termination of the running program. If *n* is nonzero (usually positive), this is a normal exit with an abnormal *exit status*, a value transmitted to the invoking environment of your C++ program.
3. *To call* **abort**(): This call causes immediate program termination without cleanup actions associated with normal termination. On some systems, **abort**() may save information for a postmortem.
4. *The C-language* **setjmp** *and* **longjmp** *functions*: *Cannot be used under Standard C++ for error recovery. Instead, the C++ exception-handling mechanism should be used (next subsection).*

When a C++ program terminates normally (returning from main or calling **exit**()), destructors for static objects are called. The **atexit**() function (Appendix H) can be used to specify additional actions to be taken before program termination. This allows a program to release a lock, to remove a temporary file, or to perform some other critical action before termination. The **abort**() call causes immediate termination without any of these actions at exit.

Exception Handling

Standard C++ supports *exceptions*, a systematic way of representing, transmitting, and handling possible errors at run time. The C++ keywords try, catch, and throw are for exception-handling. With exceptions, you can write code to detect errors at run time and transfer control to central places where such

8.10 ERROR AND EXCEPTION HANDLING

errors are handled. Older C++ compilers may not fully support the exception mechanism described here.

The keyword `try` controls a code block (compound statement) whose execution errors can be caught and handled by codes supplied with the keyword `catch`. A *try block* has the general form:

```
try {     statements
    } catch(e-type₁ e)
      {   statements
      }
      catch(e-type₂ e)
      {   statements
      }
       . . . // any more catch clauses
      catch (...)  // optional catch-all clause
      {   statements
      }
```

At run time, if any statement within a `try` block leads, possibly through a sequence of function calls, to a `throw(exception_value)` call, control transfers from the point of `throw` up the function-call chain to the nearest enclosing `try` block (Figure 8.1). The `try` block captures the exception and matches it with

Figure 8.1 THROWING AND CATCHING AN EXCEPTION

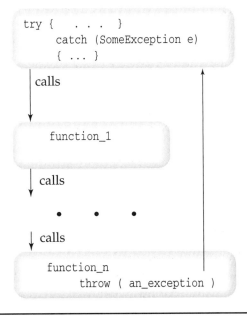

the parameter types of the *catch clauses* sequentially. Each catch clause is in the form of a function definition: with a parameter and a body of statements. The exception value is passed to the parameter e of the first matching clause and the statements executed. Only matching exceptions are caught. Uncaught exceptions are passed further up the call chain.

The catch-all clause

```
catch (...)      // if given, must be last catch clause
```

with a literal ellipsis (...) as the parameter, is optional but matches any exception thrown. If the try block executes without exception, control transfers to the first statement after the catch clauses.

Consider a simple example where we catch the "wrong argument" exception:

```
int main(int argc, char* argv[])
{   try                                      // try block
    {    long int a,b;
         get_ab(argc, argv, a, b);           // may throw exception
         long int d = gcd(a,b);              // may throw exception
         cout << "gcd(" << a << ","
              << b << ")=" << d << endl;
         /* other statements */
    } catch ( WrongArg& ex )                 // exception catch (1)
      { cerr << argv[0] << ": "
             << ex.errorMsg() << endl;       // handling         (2)
        return 1;                            //    codes         (3)
      }
      catch ( Overflow& ex )                 // exception catch (4)
      {
           /* handling overflow */
      }
      return 0;
}
```

The catch parameter can be any type but is usually an *exception class* type. For a particular kind of error, a distinct exception class can be defined to supply objects used in the throw and catch mechanism:

```
class WrongArg       // an exception class
{   public:
      explicit WrongArg(const char* msg)
      : err(msg) { }
      const char* errorMsg() const
      { return err; }
    private:
```

8.10 ERROR AND EXCEPTION HANDLING

```
        const char* err;
};
```

With the `WrongArg` class, a function (e.g., gcd) performs exception handling as follows:

```
long int gcd(long int a, long int b)
    throw(WrongArg)                        // exception specification (5)
{   if ( a==0 && b==0 )
        throw(WrongArg("gcd(0,0) undefined"));           // (6)
 // rest of nonrecursive gcd code
}
```

The `throw` (line 6) will be caught by the matching `catch` (line 1) for the `try` block in main, and the corresponding codes (lines 2 and 3) will be performed. If you delete line 3 from the catch body, control skips to the first statement after all the `catch` clauses. If an `Overflow` object were thrown, it would be caught by the `catch` on line 4.

Exception Specification

Possible exceptions that may result from calling a function can be *specified* as part of the function header declaration (line 5). The exception specification is simply

`throw( `*list of exception types*` )`   (as part of function header)

The function `get_ab` checks command-line arguments and obtains the two integers a and b whose gcd is to be computed. The function specifies `throw(WrongArg)` also.

```
#include <stdlib.h>     // for strtol

inline void THROW()
{ throw(WrongArg("needs 2 integer arguments")); }

void get_ab(int argc, char* argv[], long int& a, long int& b)
      throw(WrongArg)
{   if ( argc != 3 ) THROW();
    char* end[1];
    a = strtol(argv[1], end, 10);
    if ( end[0] != argv[1]+strlen(argv[1]) ) THROW();
    b = strtol(argv[2], end, 10);
    if ( end[0] != argv[2]+strlen(argv[2]) ) THROW();
}
```

The complete example, ex08/exception/gcdone.C, can be found in the code package.

In C++, it is not mandatory for a function to specify exceptions. But it is good programming practice to follow the *catch or specify* principle: *Each exception that may result from a function call must either be caught in the function or be specified by the function declaration.* If a function does specify exceptions, then these are the only exceptions that may emerge from the function at run time. If the function attempts to pass on an unspecified exception, the library function unexpected() is called automatically, which normally calls terminate() to abort program execution. The empty specification throw() guarantees that a function does not pass any exceptions up the call chain.

Standard Library Exceptions

The Standard Library defines a base exception class and derives two categories of exceptions:

- *Logic error*: an error due to the internal logic of a program. Logic error exception classes include invalid_argument, out_of_range, length_error, and domain_error.

- *Run-time error*: an error caused by the program execution that is not predictable beforehand. Run-time error exceptions include range_error, overflow_error, and underflow_error.

Each of these exception classes has an explicit constructor that takes a const string reference argument. This string is usually the error message associated with the exception object. The **what()** member function, inherited from exception, returns the string as a const char*. It is a good idea to derive your own exception classes from one of these classes. Be sure to include the <stdexcept> header file.

Normally, C++ I/O does not generate exceptions. Any error is recorded in the error state bits of an I/O object (Section 6.7). A program may specify a collection of error states to cause exceptions. The ios function **exceptions()** sets and gets the *exception states*. For example,

in_obj.**exceptions**(ios::badbit|ios::failbit);

sets the given exception state. Without an argument, **exceptions()** returns the exception state.

The exception thrown is ios::failure, a subclass of exception. Here is a simple demonstration program:

```
#include<iostream>
#include<fstream>
```

8.10 ERROR AND EXCEPTION HANDLING

```cpp
#include <stdexcept>
using std::cerr; using std::endl; using std::ifstream;

int main()
{   ifstream in;
    in.exceptions(ios::badbit|ios::failbit);
    try
    {   in.open("filexyz");      // open nonexistent file
        cerr << " should not reach this point! " << endl;
    } catch (ios::failure& e)
        {   cerr << "in catch:" << e.what() << endl; }
}
```

Defining Your Own Exceptions

In C++ code, a combination of error values, error states, and exceptions is used to handle run-time errors. A software module may want to catch/specify exceptions at entry points to the module so no unexpected exceptions get to application programs. A software module will define its own exception classes. Let's revisit the Fraction code. Recall the Fraction constructor (Section 3.5)

```cpp
Fraction::Fraction(int n, int d)    // d is not zero
{   int g;
    if ( d == 0 )
    {   std::cerr << " Fraction: Can't construct fraction"
                  << " with 0 denominator" << std::endl;
        abort();
    }
    . . .
}
```

Instead of aborting, the constructor may elect to throw an exception. To do this, you first define a new exception class:

```cpp
#include <stdexcept>

class ZeroDenominatorException : public invalid_argument
{   public:
        explicit ZeroDenominatorException (const string& s)
        : invalid_argument(s) {  }
};
```

and then modify the constructor code to throw the exception:

```cpp
#include <string>
```

```cpp
Fraction::Fraction(int n, int d) throw(ZeroDenominatorException)
{   if ( d == 0 )
    {   throw(ZeroDenominatorException(
            "Fraction constructor: 0 denominator"));
    }
    . . .
}
```

The fraction division can also be modified as follows:

```cpp
Fraction operator/ (const Fraction& y) const
                   throw(ZeroDenominatorException)
{   return Fraction( num * y.denom, denom * y.num );  }
```

See ex8/exception/fraction/ in the code package for the complete example.

8.11 MATRIX WITH EXCEPTIONS

Let's add exception handling to the simple Matrix class from Section 4.4 to further illustrate exception usage. All exceptions used by the matrix package are subclasses of MatrixException:

```cpp
///////    MatrixException.h     ///////
#include <stdexcept>

class MatrixException : public logic_error
{ public:
    explicit MatrixException(const string& s)
    : logic_error(s) { }
};

class Singular: public MatrixException
{ public:
    explicit Singular(const string& s)
    : MatrixException("Singular: "+s) { }
};

class InvalidIndex: public MatrixException
{ public:
    explicit InvalidIndex(const string& s)
    : MatrixException("Invalid index: "+s) { }
};

class IncompatibleDimension: public MatrixException
{ public:
```

8.11 MATRIX WITH EXCEPTIONS

```
        explicit IncompatibleDimension(const string& s)
         : MatrixException("Incompatible Dimensions: "+s) { }
};
```

Thus, `MatrixException` is a kind of `logic_error`, and there are `InvalidIndex`, `IncompatibleDimension`, and `Singular` matrix exceptions. The `setElement` method now throws `InvalidIndex` exceptions:

```
void Matrix::setElement(int i, int j, double e)
        throw(InvalidIndex)
{   if ( 0>i || i>=nr || 0>j || j>=nc )
        throw(InvalidIndex(string("setElement(")
                + int2String(i) + "," + int2String(j) + ")"
                + " of (" + int2String(nr) + " x "
                + int2String(nc) + ")" + " matrix." ) );
    mat[i*nc+j] = e;
}
```

The `getElement` method can be coded similarly. The auxiliary function `int2String` helps construct exception message strings:

```
string int2String(int i)
{   int SIZE = 64;
    char buf[SIZE];
    ostrstream mystr(buf, SIZE);
    mystr << i << '\0';      // terminated string
    return string(buf);
}
```

With exceptions, the `times` method can be revised as follows. Note the function now allocates space for the product matrix.

```
Matrix& Matrix::times(const Matrix& b) const
        throw(IncompatibleDimension)
{   if ( nc != b.nr )    // incompatible dimensions
        throw(IncompatibleDimension(int2String(nr)
                + " x " + int2String(nc) + " times "
                + int2String(b.nr) + " x " + int2String(b.nc)));
    Matrix *ans = new Matrix(nr, b.nc);
    for (int i=0 ; i < nr ; i++)
    {   for (int j=0 ; j < b.nc; j++)
            ans->setElement(i, j,
                rowTimesCol(i, b.mat, j, b.nc));
    }
    return *ans;
}
```

The test program `testMatrix.C` can use a single catch clause

```
catch(MatrixException& e)
{   cerr << e.what() << endl; abort(); }
```

to catch and treat all these matrix exceptions. See `ex8/exception/matrix/` in the code package for the complete example.

8.12 MANAGING FREE STORAGE

The special C++ operators `new`, `delete`, `new[]`, and `delete[]` make free storage convenient to use. Each calls a corresponding operator function to complete its duty:

```
void* operator new(size_t);         // for an object
void  operator delete(void*);

void* operator new[](size_t);       // for an array
void* operator delete[](void*);
```

For example, `new int` will eventually make the call

```
operator new( sizeof(int) )         // returns void*
```

which returns a `void*` pointer to the requested amount of space. More generally, the code

```
new(args) type     (general syntax for new)
```

results in the call `operator new( sizeof(type), args)`, activating the appropriate version of the overloaded `operator new`.

The global `operator delete` takes a `void*` argument and returns nothing. It cannot be overloaded. The expression `delete ptr` calls `operator delete( ptr )` to free space pointed to by `ptr`.

These special operator functions employ lower level routines, such as `malloc` and `free`, or some other operating-system-supplied procedures to manage free storage.

However, the built-in operations can be inadequate or inefficient for certain applications. In such situations, you, the programmer, can take over the management of free storage entirely or partially:

- By redefining the functions `operator new` and `operator delete` at file scope, you take over memory management completely.
- By overloading `operator new`, additional modes of free storage allocation can be supplied.

- By overloading operator new and operator delete as members, a class can assume its own memory management.

Global new and delete

Consider an application where two programs running concurrently must share memory to achieve a common task. To allocate and free storage in the shared memory area, library functions, such as shmalloc and shfree, are provided. The operators new and delete can work with shared memory by redefining operator new and operator delete globally:

```
#include <new>
#include <stdexcept>

void* operator new(size_t nb)          // global operator new()
     throw(bad_alloc)                  // must specify
{  void* p = shmalloc( nb );
   if ( p == NULL ) throw bad_alloc();
   return p;
}

void operator delete(void* p)          // global operator delete()
     throw()                           // no exceptions
{  if ( p ) shfree( p );               // delete NULL is safe
}
```

Note the exception-handling details for these operators. With these definitions, memory management through the operators new and delete deals with shared memory.

In general, operator new must have a first argument of type size_t, a typedef (usually unsigned) contained in stddef.h, and it must return a void* pointer to the space allocated. The signature and return type for operator delete are fixed.

Redefining the global new and delete is often too drastic a measure. In many applications, controlling the way certain objects are dynamically allocated is enough.

Member new and delete

When new (delete) is applied to allocate (deallocate) an object in free storage, the compiler will use an appropriate member operator new (operator delete) if defined in the class. (Otherwise, the global instance will be invoked.) These special member functions are automatically declared static because they are called either before an object is formed or after it has been destroyed.

Suppose dynamic allocations of fractions are to be done in shared memory. The goal is achieved simply by defining these operators for the class `Fraction`:

```
void* Fraction::operator new(size_t nb)  // member operator new()
{   void* p = shmalloc( nb );
    return p;
}

void Fraction::operator delete(void* p)  // member operator delete()
{   if ( p )  shfree( p );
}
```

Like the global operator, the member `operator new` can be overloaded. The member `operator delete` cannot be overloaded, but it may take either of two forms:

```
void ClassX::operator delete(void* p);              (case I)
void ClassX::operator delete(void* p, int size);    (case II)
```

For case II, the correct size of the space to be reclaimed will be passed as the second argument.

To change how arrays of objects are allocated and deleted, overload/redefine

```
operator new[]
operator delete[]
```

respectively.

Memory Exhaustion

A `bad_alloc` exception is thrown if `new` or `new[]` fails to allocate the required memory space. To make a program robust, this exception from `new` should be caught (be sure to include the headers `<new>` and `<stdexcept>`). But having to use a `try` block for each call to `new` and `new[]` is very tedious.

Upon memory exhaustion, `new` and `new[]` check to see if a *new-handler* function has been specified. The *new-handler* is called if given, otherwise `bad_alloc` is thrown. Thus, we can specify an appropriate new-handler to treat all memory exhaustion problems. Specify a handler with the call

```
#include <new>
```
set_new_handler(*handler_function*)

For example,

```
#include <new>
#include <stdexcept>
using std::cerr; using std::endl;
```

```
void noMemory() throw(bad_alloc)
{   cerr << "Memory Exhaustion!!" << endl;
    throw bad_alloc();
}

int main()
{   set_new_handler(noMemory);      // set new-handler
    ...
}
```

8.13 SUMMARY

Most operations on objects must be programmed explicitly. Operator overloading allows you to define what operators do for class objects. With the exception of four operators, all can be given user-supplied meanings by defining operator functions.

You have the choice of implementing an operator function as a member or a nonmember. When one (the left) or both operands are objects, the operator invokes the corresponding operator function (either the member or the nonmember implementation). When both exist within the same scope, argument matching is used to select the correct operator function.

Most operators follow the same overloading rules: =, [], (), and -> can only be overloaded by members. A set of useful conventions may also be followed to overload the I/O operators >> and <<. Reference counting is a novel approach to dynamic memory management that also involves the overloading of =. By adding appropriate operators and other special members, you can make a class more robust and its objects behave almost like basic types.

An iterator, in the form of a class-defined typedef or nested class, can provide access to elements encapsulated in objects. Standard iterators work like pointers to values. Standard C++ has a well-defined convention for defining and using iterators for container classes.

Implicit and explicit type conversions can be extended for objects by class-defined type-conversion rules. User-defined type conversion cuts down on the number of functions necessary to cover different argument type combinations. It can also be used for error reporting as demonstrated by the I/O stream class.

Execution errors can be treated in a number of ways: error return values, object error states, and exceptions. Exception objects representing predefined errors can be thrown and caught at run time. The keywords try, catch, and throw are used for exception handling. Basically, a function either catches or specifies each exception that may occur at run time. A function can guarantee no exceptions by explicitly specifying an empty throw list. Derive your own exception from the Standard C++ exception base classes by including <stdexcept>.

Overloading new and delete is different from overloading other operators. Only part of their operations can be modified through defining global or class scope operators (operator new and operator delete). By defining these special operator functions, you control free storage management.

EXERCISES

1. Consider the member versus nonmember implementation of overloaded operators. Both implementations are shown for Fraction += in Section 8.1. Suppose both are included in a program. Confirm that the program can be compiled without error. Would f1 += f2 still work? If not, how do you invoke each of the two operator functions?

2. Consider overloading [] in Section 8.3. Why do we need both versions?

    ```
    string*& operator[](int i)
    { if ( i >= 0 && i < len ) return line[i];  abort(); }

    const string* operator[](int i) const
    { if ( i >= 0 && i < len ) return line[i];  abort(); }
    ```

    Why can't just the first version suffice?

3. Define += and *= for fractions. Also make +, -, *, and / work as binary operators for mixed int and Fraction operands.

4. Consider the nested class iterator within Cirbuf (Section 8.7) and member functions of iterator. It is possible to supply the definition of the member functions in a separate cirbuf_iterator.C implementation file. Make this modification to the code and perform tests.

5. Define a class Amount that represents nonnegative amounts expressed in double. Make sure appropriate conversion is defined so that Amount objects can be used just like a double.

6. State and explain the *catch or specify* principle for exception handling recommended in this chapter.

7. Take the Cirbuf class and add exception handling. Consuming from an empty buffer and producing into a full buffer are now exceptions.

8. A member function always has the host object as an implicit argument. Do automatic type conversions apply to this argument? What implications can you think of as a result?

9. Consider user-defined free storage management (Section 8.12). If you define the two-argument

    ```
    void* Fraction::operator new(size_t nb, Fraction* p);
    ```

    without also defining the one-argument

    ```
    void* Fraction::operator new(size_t nb);
    ```

    what would happen? Why?

10. What happens on your system when int i = INT_MAX + 7; is done? What is the value of i now?

11. What happens on your system when the library function **sqrt**() is called with a negative number? Or when **log**() is given zero?

12. Verify that if a class defines operator void* correctly as suggested in Section 8.9, then conditions if (obj) and if (! obj) both work as expected.

13. Exercise Cal-1: Add error detection to the base CalcEng class through user-defined type conversion. Detect both overflow and underflow for the operations +, -, *, /, and ^. The implementation allows such tests as if (engine).

14. Exercise Cal-2: Modify the handling of the opcodes A (all clear) and C (clear) in relation to error handling in CalcEng. Note the behavior of C after an error on a real pocket calculator.

15. Do the **setjmp** and **longjmp** functions work under C++? Explain.

CHAPTER NINE

OOP Techniques

More advanced object-oriented programming (OOP) techniques build on classes, objects, and inheritance. OOP encourages programming at a higher level—manipulating objects as interchangeable "black boxes." This means making uniform interfaces for related objects and establishing generic programs for all *plug-compatible* objects. These topics are central to OOP and require a combination of C++ features.

By establishing common interfaces, related objects can be treated as black boxes that are manipulated the same way from the outside. Thus, these black boxes become interchangeable parts that are pluggable into another program. The ability to work with different black-box objects is generally known as *polymorphism*. The C++ *virtual function* mechanism allows type-dependent function calls at run time and is key to polymorphism. In this chapter, *run-time type identification* (RTTI) and virtual functions are described in detail. Practical use of plug compatibility is demonstrated by several examples.

A uniform public interface of plug-compatible objects takes careful planning. Designing base classes for inheritance is important. The C++ *abstract base class* facilitates the extraction of common operations and the preplanning of uniform interfaces. An ordered-sequence class is presented to serve as a schematic for building objects that can store, order, and retrieve arbitrary elements simply and efficiently. Then, the generic ordered-sequence object is applied to handle ordered lines in text files.

Finally, the concept of an *object-family class*, one whose objects represent different but related quantities, is introduced. Such classes encapsulate plug-compatible objects and aid in writing generic routines. A Number object-family class whose instances represent fractions, integers, and other types of numbers illustrates this technique.

9.1 PROGRAMMING WITH PLUG-COMPATIBLE OBJECTS

One enormous advantage of OOP is the ability to treat objects as black boxes and to deal with them only through their interfaces. If a set of similar or related black boxes supports a common interface, then we can write codes to use any such boxes without change. The fact that a computer motherboard can take different plug-compatible circuit boards from any vendor is an obvious example.

The concept of building and operating on *plug-compatible* objects is commonplace in daily life. Consider cars, for example. Having learned to drive one car, you can drive most other cars without changing your method of driving. Many different types of cars become interchangeable as far as you are concerned. The fact that one car's accelerator controls the fuel injection and another the carburetor does not affect the way you drive.

How C++ builds plug-compatible objects (cars) and defines *polymorphic operations* (driving) on them is our focus here. To illustrate this important technique, we will make bank accounts plug-compatible for certain well-defined operations such as transferring funds between accounts and printing a list of accounts.

Compatible Types and Polymorphism

By putting all different accounts in a public derivation hierarchy rooted at the base class Account, the different accounts become compatible types through class derivation. Because the derived types are considered a kind of Account, there is at least a chance of making them interchangeable. Since there already are a few types of account objects thus derived, the task at hand is simplified.

To make interchangeable use meaningful, these different account objects must support *either a uniform public interface or certain critical common operations*. To a degree, this has been done also: Account, FreeChecking, JointAccount, and JtFrChecking all support the same prototypes for balance(), deposit(), and withdraw(). Therefore, a piece of code that uses only the uniform interface has a chance to work for all these types of account objects.

Now we can write a transfer function to work on all different account types:

```
bool transfer(float amt, Account& from, Account& to)
{   bool flag = from.withdraw(amt);
    if ( flag ) to.deposit(amt);
    return flag;
}
```

The ability for the same program to work with more than one type of object is known as *polymorphism* (Figure 9.1). Consider transfer(), for example. Each of the parameters from and to can receive multiple types of account objects (Account, JointAccount, FreeChecking, etc.) instead of just one fixed type (*monomorphism*). The correct transfer procedure is performed by using the proper withdraw() and deposit() operations in different types of accounts.

Figure 9.1 POLYMORPHISM AND PLUG-COMPATIBLE OBJECTS

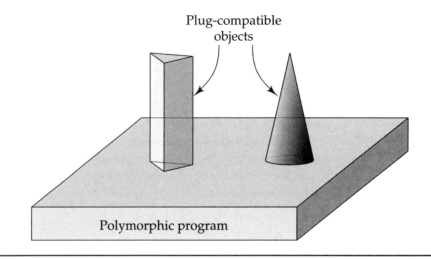

Two key techniques help the polymorphic transfer achieve plug compatibility:

1. *Using base-type pointer or reference parameters*: Here from and to are base references, so accounts of any type can be passed into transfer(). This is a result of type compatibility under inheritance (Section 7.8).
2. *Using only the uniform public interface*: Here withdraw() and deposit() are uniform, so the code makes sense for all different types of accounts.

But there is one difficulty: An actual argument (say, of type FreeChecking) referenced through the formal parameter from, which is of type Account&, causes the code from.withdraw(amt) to perform

from.Account::withdraw(amt)

rather than the desired

from.FreeChecking::withdraw(amt)

The reason is that the type of the parameter from is used at compile time to determine which class member to invoke. Because the type of from is Account&, from.withdraw() naturally invokes the member in Account, which is very disappointing indeed. The true type of the argument referenced by from would lead to the *correct* member function, but that true type is not known at compile time.

9.1 PROGRAMMING WITH PLUG-COMPATIBLE OBJECTS

This difficulty must be overcome before a *polymorphic* function, such as transfer(), can work correctly on plug-compatible objects. Any solution must somehow make the code

```
from.withdraw(amt)
```

1. Discover, at run time, the actual class of the object referenced by from.
2. Invoke the withdraw function defined by that class.

And the C++ *virtual function* is the answer.

Virtual Functions

C++ supports *virtual functions*. You can designate selected instance functions virtual to enable special run-time handling of their invocations.[1]

If a virtual function is invoked through a public base reference or pointer, then the actual type of the object, not that of the reference or pointer, is used to determine which one of a group of compatible virtual functions to call. Suppose a FreeChecking object fc is passed to the public base reference from of the transfer function. The call from.withdraw(amt) would indeed become fc.withdraw(amt) if withdraw() has been designated virtual. Similar effects take place if &fc is passed to an Account* pointer. However, the virtual function mechanism does not work if fc is passed by value to a parameter of type Account.

Thus, a virtual function really represents a group of functions, with identical prototypes, in a derivation hierarchy. A call to a virtual function is done through a base reference or pointer and treated specially at run time (Figure 9.2). Unlike regular functions, a virtual function call involves selecting one in a group of virtual functions to invoke, according to the actual host-object type at run time.

Now let's consider how virtual functions are declared and used. To make plug-compatible objects work, all uniform interface functions should be virtual. By declaring a base prototype virtual, any member function with the same prototype in a derived class (direct or indirect) is also automatically virtual and put in the same group of virtual functions. Thus, to make plug-compatible accounts, we revise the base class Account as follows:

```
///////    Account.h    ///////
#include <iostream>
using std::cout; using std::endl;
```

---

[1] Do not confuse virtual functions with virtual (shared) bases. Unfortunately, the same keyword is used for both purposes.

Figure 9.2 DYNAMIC VIRTUAL FUNCTION SELECTION

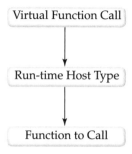

```
class Account
{ public:
    Account() {}
    Account(unsigned n, double b, char* ss);
    virtual void deposit(double amt);
    virtual bool withdraw(double amt);
    virtual double balance() const;
    virtual unsigned id() const;
    virtual void display(ostream& out = cout) const;      // (1)
    /* other public members */
  protected:
    enum {SS_LEN = 12};
    unsigned  acct_no;
    char      ss[SS_LEN];
  private:
    /* other members */
    double    acct_bal;
};
```

Declared virtual are the existing interface functions deposit(), withdraw(), balance(), and id() as well as a new function display(). As a result, there are five distinct virtual function groups here. These are the only changes to Account. Any corresponding interface functions in the derived account classes are now automatically virtual and included in their respective groups. While it is not necessary to add the virtual keyword to their declarations in a derived class, there is no harm in doing so.

For Account, we implement the virtual display() function as follows:

```
// in Account.C

void Account::display(ostream& out /* = cout */) const
```

```
{   out << "Account No: " << acct_no << endl
        << "Owner SS:   " << ss << endl
        << "Balance:    " << acct_bal << endl;
}
```

Once given (line 1), the `virtual` keyword need not be repeated when defining the function. Here are some counterparts of `Account::display()` in derived accounts:

```
void JointAccount::display(ostream& out /* = cout */) const
{   out << "Account No:     " << acct_no << endl
        << "Owner SS:       " << ss << endl
        << "Joint Owner SS: " << jss << endl
        << "Balance:        " << balance() << endl;
}

void FreeChecking::display(ostream& out /* = cout */) const
{   out << "Free Checking Account" << endl;
    Account::display();                       // inherited member (2)
}

void JtFrChecking::display(ostream& out /* = cout */) const
{   out << "Free Checking Account" << endl;
    JointAccount::display();                  // inherited member (3)
}
```

Each display function serves the need of its class. Clearly, they all have the same function prototype. Some enlist the help of inherited functions (lines 2 and 3).

To test the plug-compatible account objects, construct a simple test program as follows:

```
#include <iostream>
#include "acc.h"

// put the transfer function here

void show(Account* a[], int n)
{   for (int i=0; i < n; i++)
    {   a[i]->display();
        cout << endl;
    }
}

int main()
{   JtFrChecking jfc(23456, 750.0, "025-72-5555", "024-88-3333");
```

```
    JointAccount ja(55123, 1600.0, "043-12-4444", "034-21-2222");
    FreeChecking fc(66432,  600.0, "098-02-1111");
    transfer(300, fc, jfc);      // (4)
    fc.fee();
    transfer(200, ja, fc);       // (5)
    Account* acnt[3];
    acnt[0] = &jfc;
    acnt[1] = &ja;
    acnt[2] = &fc;
    show(acnt, 3);               // (6)
    return 0;
}
```

Here the header file acc.h includes all headers for the Account class hierarchy. Three different account objects jfc, ja, and fc are used to demonstrate plug compatibility. The function transfer is a polymorphic procedure that works for all types of accounts (lines 4 and 5). The function show is another polymorphic procedure that displays a sequence of accounts of various types (line 6). Such procedures work for all existing types of accounts and any additional types of accounts established in the future. As long as the public interface is preserved, the procedures work without modification.

Running this program produces the following output:

```
Free Checking Account
Account No:     23456
Owner SS:       025-72-5555
Joint Owner SS: 024-88-3333
Balance:        1050

Account No:     55123
Owner SS:       043-12-4444
Joint Owner SS: 034-21-2222
Balance:        1400

Free Checking Account
Account No: 66432
Owner SS:   098-02-1111
Balance:    482
```

Virtual functions are critical to polymorphism. A class or object is said to be *virtualized* if it has at least one virtual function. In some C++ literature, the definition *"a polymorphic object is an object with at least one virtual function"* is used. But we use the term *polymorphic* precisely as follows:

- A *polymorphic function* is one that can receive plug-compatible objects.
- A *polymorphic object* is one that contains plug-compatible components.

9.1   PROGRAMMING WITH PLUG-COMPATIBLE OBJECTS

We have seen the power of plug compatibility and how this OOP technique works. And it can be applied in many situations. We can make the `Calculator` class, for instance, polymorphic by using a `CalcEng` pointer instead of a `CalcEng` object directly. We can then use compatible derived compute engines in a `Calculator` object and create different calculator models by installing different engines inside.

Keys to Plug Compatibility

Programming with plug-compatible objects is achieved by a combination of OOP mechanisms and techniques. Its key ingredients, which represent the essence of OOP, are as follows:

1. *Interchangeable objects*: It must be possible to represent a collection of similar objects that are interchangeable under certain operations. Such objects usually have an is-a relationship and can be organized into a public derivation hierarchy under C++.
2. *Uniform public interfaces*: The interchangeable objects must have certain identical public interfaces to allow the same polymorphic procedure to work on all of them. This is achieved by maintaining a set of public interface functions with uniform prototypes throughout the class hierarchy.
3. *Polymorphic variables*: In a polymorphic function or object, interchangeable objects are represented by variables capable of referencing any plug-compatible type. In C++, polymorphic variables are public base pointer or reference types.
4. *Dynamic access of interchangeable operations*: By declaring the uniform interface functions `virtual`, the correct derived member function can be accessed through a polymorphic parameter. A class or object is *virtualized* if it has at least one virtual function.

As a further illustration, consider overloading the operator << for displaying any plug-compatible account:

```
ostream& operator <<(ostream& os, Account& a)
{    a.display(os);
     return os;
}
```

Notice how this short function works to allow output of any type of account object `acnt_obj` to any output stream by using the following deceptively simple code:

```
out << acnt_obj;
```

Figure 9.3 VIRTUAL TABLES

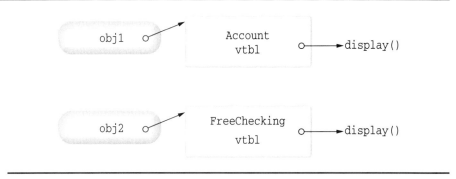

Virtual Function Tables

Virtualized objects, those with at least one virtual function, contain information leading to the correct virtual function at run time. A common implementation technique places in each virtualized object an extra pointer to a per-class *virtual function table* (*vtbl*) (Figure 9.3). A *vtbl* contains pointers to all virtual functions in its class. The table index of any particular virtual function is the same in *vtbl*s under the same derivation hierarchy. The compiler converts the name of a virtual function into a fixed *vtbl* index. And the run-time overhead for a virtual function call involves retrieving a function pointer from the object's *vtbl*.

9.2 RUN-TIME TYPE IDENTIFICATION

Recall that an object with at least one virtual function is called a *virtualized object*. The virtual function mechanism supplies an easy way to identify, at run time, the actual types of virtualized objects. Taking advantage of this, the Standard C++ *run-time type identification* (RTTI) system provides:

- *The* `dynamic_cast` *operator*: For casting pointers and references to virtualized objects
- *The* `typeid` *operator*: For identifying types and other type-related information for virtualized objects

The *type information* is typically attached as a `type_info` object through a pointer placed in the object's *vtbl* (Figure 9.3).

Figure 9.4 VALID DYNAMIC CAST

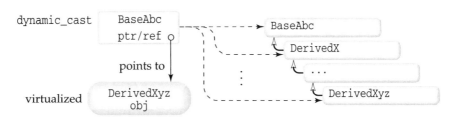

Operator dynamic_cast

Use `dynamic_cast` to cast pointers and references to virtualized objects. Consider the cast of a base pointer to a derived pointer:

```
BaseAbc* ptr = ...
dynamic_cast< DerivedXyz* >(ptr);
```

The `dynamic_cast` examines, at run time, the actual *True_Type* of the virtualized object to which `ptr` points and decides if the cast is valid. If cast is to *True_Type** or *Base_of_True_Type**, then the cast is valid (Figure 9.4). Otherwise, it is invalid. The same can be said about reference casting. If the cast is invalid, `dynamic_cast` returns a zero pointer (for pointer casting) or throws a `bad_cast` exception (for reference casting). Thus, for virtualized objects, always use `dynamic_cast` to explicitly convert a base pointer (reference) to a derived type. Here is a commonly used idiom:

```
fcp = dynamic_cast< FreeChecking* >(bp);
if ( fcp != NULL )
{       /* fcp is valid and can be used */
}
else
        /* handle invalid cast here      */
```

Operator typeid

In addition to the `dynamic_cast` operator, the *run-time type identification* (RTTI) mechanism of Standard C++ (Section 9.2) also supports the `typeid` operator. You use `typeid` to identify the types of variables and objects at run time. After including the header `<typeinfo>`, the code

```
typeid( type )
typeid( object )
typeid( expression )
```

returns a *read-only reference* to a `type_info` object associated with the *type*, *object*, or *expression*. The `type_info` object can be used to identify a type and to retrieve other information about that type. If *type* is unknown or *object* (*expression*) is invalid, a `bad_typeid` exception is thrown.

For example,

```
cout << typeid( obj ).name() << endl;
```

displays the encoded class name of `obj` as a C-style string.

Let `obj` be a *virtualized object* or a reference to it. Then `typeid(obj)` returns the actual run-time type of the object referenced. Thus,

```
Account* acnt_ptr = &freeChecking_obj;

typeid( *acnt_ptr ).name()                        // "FreeChecking"
typeid( *acnt_ptr )==typeid( FreeChecking )       // true
typeid( *acnt_ptr )!=typeid(freeChecking_obj)     // false
```

The `==` and `!=` operators are defined in the `type_info` class. If `obj` is not a virtualized object (or reference), `typeid(obj)` simply returns the `type_info` for the compile-time type of `obj`. Hence,

```
typeid( acnt_ptr ).name()                         // C-style string
typeid( acnt_ptr )==typeid( Account* )            // true
```

Use of `typeid`

Note that `typeid` is not a substitute for the virtual function mechanism. Testing `typeid` (or `dynamic_cast`) to determine which member function to call instead of using virtual functions is a mistake. This is because the `typeid` tests must be augmented each time a new subclass is added. No such modification is necessary with the virtual function approach.

So where is explicit type identification helpful? First of all, the name, a C-style string, in the `type_info` object is a piece of information not available through any other means. This string is implementation dependent but should have the class name in it. Hence, the name can be used for diagnostic purposes in debugging, tracing, or exception messages. A program can also store useful information related to classes in tables keyed by class-name strings. For example, if a program provides an *association list* `myBase` (a map, Section 11.5) storing the immediate base-class name of each class in a program, then the immediate base class of an object `obj` can be obtained by

```
type_info& baseName = myBase[ typeid( obj ).name ]
```

Consider an application that uses *object serialization*, writing certain objects to an output stream as a sequence of bytes. Serialized objects can later be read

9.2 RUN-TIME TYPE IDENTIFICATION

and reconstituted into objects of the right type. To do this, the serialization may begin with the C-style string name of the object type obtained through `typeid`.

As a concrete example of such object I/O, consider a program that writes out a fraction (line 2) and a complex (line 3) into a data file (line 1):

```
///////    objWrite.C    ///////
#include <iostream>
#include <fstream>
#include <complex>
#include <typeinfo>
#include "Fraction.h"
using std::endl; using std::ofstream; using std::complex;

int main()
{   Fraction f(2,7);
    complex< double > c(3.2, 9.8);
    ofstream out("obj.data");                         // (1)
    out << typeid(f).name() << endl << f << endl;     // (2)
    out << typeid(c).name() << endl << c << endl;     // (3)
    out.close();
    return 0;
}
```

The data file produced (under g++) is

```
8Fraction
2/7
t7complex1Zd
(3.2,9.8)
```

Here the name string for `Fraction` is preceded by a character count. The name for the template class `complex< double >` is coded in a similar way.

This data file can be read back into a C++ program to re-create the objects stored. The function `readNextObj` checks the type name string (lines A and C) to decide what type object to read and create (lines B and D):

```
///////    objRead.C    ///////
#include <iostream>
#include <fstream>
#include <string>
#include <complex>
#include <typeinfo>
#include "Fraction.h"
using std::cout; using std::endl;
using std::ifstream; using std::complex;

void* readNextObj(istream& in, string& type)
```

```
{   string end;
    if ( getline(in, type, '\n') )
    {   if ( type == typeid( Fraction ).name() )              // (A)
        {   Fraction* f = new Fraction();
            in >> *f;                                          // (B)
            getline(in, end, '\n'); // consumes rest of line
            return f;
        }
        if ( type == typeid( complex<double> ).name() )
        {   complex< double >* c = new complex<double>();      // (C)
            in >> *c;                                          // (D)
            getline(in, end, '\n'); // consumes rest of line
            return c;
        }
    }
    return NULL;
}
```

The main program calls readNextObj to obtain the type name string (in *t) and a void* pointer to the object read (line E).

```
int main()
{   ifstream in("obj.data");
    string* t = new string();
    void* obj_ptr;
    while ( (obj_ptr= readNextObj(in, *t)) != NULL )           // (E)
    {   if (*t == typeid( Fraction ).name())
            cout << *(reinterpret_cast < Fraction* >(obj_ptr)) // (F)
                 << endl;
        if (*t == typeid( complex<double> ).name())
            cout << *(reinterpret_cast< complex<double>* >(obj_ptr))
                                                               // (G)
                 << endl;
        delete obj_ptr;
    }
    in.close();
    return 0;
}
```

The void* pointer is converted to an object pointer based on the type name string (lines F and G).

The typeid operator is also useful in writing templates that check the incoming type (Section 11.6). Another potential use of typeid is in functions that can receive a wide variety of unrelated objects (through a void* pointer or an artificial catchall base type) and perform some computation, depending on the object types.

9.3 A GENERIC TREE

A tree is commonly used in programs to organize data items in a hierarchy. Each piece of data is placed in a *node*, and the nodes form a tree to express the hierarchical relations. Defined recursively, a tree is a single node, or a node with one or more subtrees (children). Each node is either a leaf node (with no child nodes) or an internal node (with one or more children). Each internal node is the parent of its children. Every node in a tree, except the root node, has a parent. Child nodes of the same parent are called siblings. A parse tree (Figure 9.5) is a typical application. Let's implement a generic tree to contain any type data. Our generic tree is a polymorphic object containing plug-compatible (virtualized) nodes. The example combines a number of C++ constructs and OOP techniques in a practical application.

Three main classes are involved:

- TreeNode: To instantiate leaf nodes, to serve as a base class for internal nodes, and to hold a data item of any type
- InNode: A kind of TreeNode, to instantiate internal (parent) nodes and to contain and manage child nodes
- ArbTree: A polymorphic structure to represent a tree using plug-compatible nodes and to provide common operations for a tree

ArbTree controls instantiation and destruction of parent and leaf nodes. Figure 9.6 shows the class design of the ArbTree.

Tree Nodes

The TreeNode records an arbitrary value and a pointer to the parent node. Methods set/get either attributes. The constructor initializes the value and parent fields. The virtual function isLeaf (line 1) returns true but will be

Figure 9.5 PARSE TREE OF x + y + 7 * z

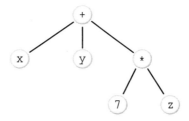

Figure 9.6 `ArbTree` DESIGN

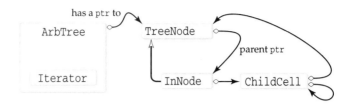

redefined in the derived class `InNode` to return `false`. The constructor is private (line 2) so only friend classes can instantiate `TreeNode` objects.

```
///////    TreeNode.h    ///////
typedef void* any;

class InNode;

class TreeNode
{   friend class ArbTree;
    friend class InNode;
  public:
    virtual bool isLeaf() const { return true; }            // (1)
    void setParent(InNode* p) { parent = p; }
    InNode* getParent() { return parent; }
    virtual void setValue(any it) { value = it; }
    virtual void* getValue() { return value; }
  protected:
    any value;
    InNode* parent;
  private:
    explicit TreeNode(any it=0, InNode* p=0)
                                            // private constructor (2)
      : value(it), parent(p) { }
};
```

While `TreeNode` gives leaf nodes, `InNode` provides internal nodes. The public derivation makes `InNode` a kind of `TreeNode`. A set of members helps access and manage child nodes. The virtual function `isLeaf` is redefined to return `false` (line 3). The private constructor means only friend classes can instantiate `InNode` objects.

```
class InNode : public TreeNode
{   friend class ArbTree;
  public:
```

9.3 A GENERIC TREE

```
      bool isLeaf() const { return false; }     // (3)
      TreeNode* getChild(int i);                  // 0-based indexing
      TreeNode* nextChild(TreeNode* ch);          // next sibling
      void addChild(TreeNode* n);
      bool deleteChild(int i);
      bool replaceChild(int i, TreeNode*);
      int getChildCount()
      { return childCount; }
   protected:
      ChildCell* children;          // list of children
      int childCount;
   private:
      explicit InNode(any v = NULL); // private constructor
      ChildCell* getCell(int i);
};
```

The slave class `ChildCell` provides a very simple linked list to store child nodes. Only `InNode` and `ArbTree` can create and manipulate `ChildCell`s.

```
class ChildCell
{   friend class ArbTree;
    friend class InNode;
   private:
      explicit ChildCell(TreeNode* c) { child = c; next=NULL;}
      TreeNode* child;
      ChildCell* next;
};
```

The `InNode` constructor calls its base-class constructor (line 4). Child nodes are added to an `InNode` object one at a time with `addChild` (line 5). The order of adding is significant.

```
///////    TreeNode.C    ///////
#include <iostream>
#include "TreeNode.h"

InNode::InNode(any it) : TreeNode(it)      // (4)
{ children = NULL; childCount = 0; }

void InNode::addChild(TreeNode* n)         // (5)
{   ChildCell* t;
    n->setParent(this);
    ChildCell* c = new ChildCell(n);
    if ( children == NULL ) children = c;
    else    // append child
    {   for( t=children; t != NULL && t->next != NULL;
```

```
                    t=t->next ) {}
        t->next = c;
    }
    childCount++;
}
```

Child nodes can be retrieved with the getChild(i) call, which returns a pointer to the desired child node. The internal function getCell is also used by the functions deleteChild and replaceChild.

```
TreeNode* InNode::getChild(int i)          // 0-based indexing
{   ChildCell* t = getCell(i);
    if ( t == NULL ) return NULL;
    return t->child;
}
```

The member function nextChild returns a pointer to the child node after the given node c within a host InNode. If c is NULL, the first child, if any, is returned.

```
TreeNode* InNode::nextChild(TreeNode* c)
{   if ( c == NULL && childCount > 0) return children->child;
    ChildCell *t1 = children, *t;
    for (t1 = children ; t1 != NULL ; t1=t1->next)
    {   if ( t1->child == c && t1->next != NULL )
            return t1->next->child;
    }
    return NULL;    // no child next to c
}
```

With tree nodes that can contain any value type, we can build a generic tree class.

Class ArbTree

ArbTree is the generic tree class that controls instantiation of tree nodes and supplies useful operations. The static functions leaf and parent instantiate TreeNode and InNode objects dynamically in free store, respectively. These are the only ways for an application to make a new tree node. To build a tree, we can first establish the nodes, link the nodes into larger and larger subtrees, and then finally use ArbTree(root) to get the tree object.

Member functions size and height compute the node count and tree height. Iterators for preorder, postorder, and inorder tree traversal are provided (lines 6 and 7). For example, nodes of the tree in Figure 9.5 in preorder are

```
+ x y * 7 z
```

9.3   A GENERIC TREE

The destructor frees all nodes and all `ChildCell`s.

```
///////    ArbTree.h    ///////
#include "TreeNode.h"

class ArbTree
{ public:
    class Iterator;
    enum TRAVERSAL {PREORDER, INORDER, POSTORDER};
    static TreeNode* leaf(any item=NULL, InNode* parent=NULL)
    { return new TreeNode(item, parent); }
    static InNode* parent(any item=NULL)
    { return new InNode(item); }
    static int size(TreeNode* n);        // node count from n
    static int height(TreeNode* n);      // height from n

    explicit ArbTree(TreeNode* r=NULL)
    : root(r) { }                                    // tree with root node
    int size() const { return size(root); }   // node count
    int height() const { return height(root); } // tree height
    /*   ...  */
    ~ArbTree() { free(root); }
    Iterator begin(TRAVERSAL ord=PREORDER)           // (6)
    { return Iterator(root, ord); }
    Iterator end(TRAVERSAL ord=PREORDER)             // (7)
    { return Iterator(NULL, ord); }
  protected:
    ArbTree(const ArbTree& t)                        // (8)
    { }   // prevents copy construction

    ArbTree& operator=(const ArbTree& t)             // (9)
    { return *this; }  // prevents assignment
  private:
    void free(TreeNode* n);
    TreeNode* root;    // root of tree
  public:
    /* nested Iterator class ... */
};
```

The copy constructor (line 8) and assignment operator (line 9) are protected from external use. The nested `Iterator` class keeps a pointer to the present node being visited in `current` and records the traversal mode in `mode`. Following the Standard Library iterator conventions (Section 8.6), the methods `begin` and `end` return iterator objects — for different traversals in this example.

The Iterator class for ArbTree, implemented as a nested class (Section 8.7), is given as follows:

```cpp
/* nested class in ArbTree */
  class Iterator
  { friend class ArbTree;
    public:
      Iterator& operator++();                          // increments
      TreeNode& operator*() { return *current; }       // returns node
      bool operator!=(const Iterator& b) const         // compares
      { return current!=b.current; }
    private:
      TreeNode* postNext();
      TreeNode* inNext();
      TreeNode* preNext();
      Iterator(TreeNode* n, TRAVERSAL ord)
        : current(n), mode(ord) { }
      TreeNode* current;    // node being visited
      TRAVERSAL mode;       // traversal mode
  };
```

The data field current records the present position of the iteration. Iterator functions include the obligatory preincrement (++), node access (*), and comparison (!=). Internal auxiliary functions help identify the next node in different traversal modes.

The ++ operator, from ArbTree.C, is

```cpp
ArbTree::Iterator& ArbTree::Iterator::operator++()   // next node
{ switch(mode)
    {   case POSTORDER: current=postNext(); break;
        case INORDER:   current=inNext();   break;
        default:        current=preNext();  break;
    }
    return *this;
}
```

The private function preNext finds the next node from current in preorder.

```cpp
TreeNode* ArbTree::Iterator::preNext()
{  if ( current == NULL ) return NULL;               // iteration ended
   if ( ! current->isLeaf() )                        // internal node
   {  InNode* n = dynamic_cast< InNode* >(current);
      if ( n->nextChild(NULL) != NULL )
          return n->nextChild(NULL);                 // first child node
   }
   TreeNode *d=current, *nd;
   InNode* p;
   while ( d != NULL )
```

```
    {   p = d->getParent();
        if ( p == NULL ) break;
        else nd = p->nextChild(d);
        if ( nd != NULL )  return nd;
        else d = d->getParent();
    }
    return NULL;            // no more next node
}
```

The `ArbTree` destructor calls `free` to release the entire tree structure, all nodes, and all `ChildCell`s in parent nodes.

```
void ArbTree::free(TreeNode* nd)
{   if ( nd == NULL ) return;
    if ( nd->isLeaf() ) delete nd;
    else
    {   ChildCell* t= (dynamic_cast<InNode*>(nd))->children;
        ChildCell* tmp;
        while ( t != NULL )
        {   tmp = t->next;
            free(t->child);
            delete t;
            t = tmp;
        }
        delete nd;
    }
}
```

Testing `ArbTree`

The following simple test program constructs a tree of ten nodes, with `char*` values, representing the mathematical expression

$$(a + b)(c - d)(e/f)$$

The main program constructs the tree (part A), displays nodes using prefix traversal iterators (part B), calls `displayPrefix` to display the expression in prefix notation (part C), and finally deletes the tree (line D).

```
///////    testArbTree.C    ///////
#include <iostream>
#include "ArbTree.h"
using std::cout; using std::endl;

int main(int argc, char* argv[]))
{   char* a[10] = {"*","+","-","/","a","b","c","d","e","f"};
    InNode* in[4];
    for (int i=0, j=4; i<4; i++)                            // (A)
```

```
        {   in[i] = ArbTree::parent(a+i);
            if ( i > 0 )
            {   in[0]->addChild(in[i]);
                in[i]->addChild(ArbTree::leaf(a+j++));
                in[i]->addChild(ArbTree::leaf(a+j++));
            }
        }
        ArbTree* t = new ArbTree(in[0]);
        cout << "Tree has " << t->size() << " nodes." << endl;
        ArbTree::Iterator s = t->begin(ArbTree::PREORDER);
        ArbTree::Iterator e = t->end(ArbTree::PREORDER);
        while ( s != e )                        // preorder traversal (B)
        {   valueDisplay(&(*s));
            ++s;
            if ( s != e )   cout << ", ";
            else cout << endl;
        }
        cout << endl;
        TreeNode& n = *(t->begin(ArbTree::PREORDER));
        prefixDisplay(&n);                                          // (C)
        cout << endl;
        delete t;                                                   // (D)
        return 0;
}
```

The output produced by this test program is

```
*, +, a, b, -, c, d, /, e, f    (prefix notation produced by B)
(* (+ a b) (- c d) (/ e f))     (prefix notation produced by C)
```

The `valueDisplay` function outputs the value field of a treenode.

```
void valueDisplay(TreeNode* n)
{   void* s = n->getValue();
    cout << *(reinterpret_cast< char** >(s));
}
```

The `prefixDisplay` produces output by this recursive procedure:

1. If n is a leaf node, display its value and terminate.
2. If n is an internal node, then
    a. display (.
    b. display value of the internal node.
    c. `prefixDisplay` each child node, with a leading space.
    d. display).
3. terminate.

```cpp
void prefixDisplay(TreeNode* n)
{   if ( n->isLeaf() )
    {   valueDisplay(n); return; }
    else
    {   InNode* op = dynamic_cast< InNode* >(n);
        cout << "(";
        valueDisplay(op);
        for ( int i=0; i < op->getChildCount(); i++ )
        {   cout<< " ";
            prefixDisplay(op->getChild(i));
        }
        cout << ")";
    }
}
```

The complete program for `ArbTree`, including code for `TreeNode` and `InNode`, can be found in the code package (ex09/arbtree/).

9.4 PLANNING UNIFORM PUBLIC INTERFACES

One key aspect of plug-compatible objects is maintaining a consistent set of public interfaces for classes in a derivation hierarchy, which is the main topic here.

A uniform public interface does not happen all by itself. It takes careful analysis, planning, and skillful coding. It often involves trial and error before a final design emerges. In C++, achieving uniform interfaces involves the following strategy:

- Begin with a desire to have a certain set of common operations defined for a collection of related objects.
- Design, in the base class, a set of virtual function prototypes to be followed by all derived classes. The set defines a uniform public interface and, often, also interactions between the base and derived classes. The goal is to make the desired common operations possible on the planned set of plug-compatible objects.
- Supply, in the base class, definitions for all or just some of the virtual functions. Supply missing definitions and redefine others in derived classes.

Thus, we can use the base class and its set of virtual functions to plan derived classes. A base class can define the uniform public interface and provide a code base for derivation (Figure 9.7).

Figure 9.7 ABSTRACT BASE CLASS

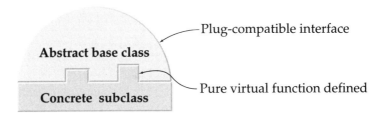

Abstract Base Class: Ordered Sequences

Consider items such as integers, names, dates, bank accounts, or any other objects that can be ordered into a linear sequence for easy manipulation and retrieval. Imagine creating objects representing such ordered sequences. An ordered-sequence object contains a number of elements and presents an external view of these elements organized in linear order. The external view is supported by the ability to refer to each element through an index $(0, 1, 2, \ldots)$.

Externally, an ordered sequence is characterized by the following public operations:

- Adding an element.
- Removing an element.
- Finding the index of an element by key.
- Retrieving an element by indexing.
- Detecting the length of the ordered sequence.

These operations form part of the public interface for any type of ordered sequence. Internally, an ordered sequence requires at least the following operations:

- Effectively sorting elements into order.
- Efficiently retrieving elements.

This analysis reveals that different ordered sequences have a great deal in common. The challenge is to extract the commonalities and form a single class from which each specific ordered sequence can inherit. If we let OrderedSeq be such a base class, then OrderedSeq must deal with elements and keys of unknown type. A derived class will specialize the element type and the key, if any.

More analysis and our experience with generic sorting (Section 4.12) soon lead us to the conclusion that sorting and searching can be done with common

9.4 PLANNING UNIFORM PUBLIC INTERFACES

routines contained in the base if a derived class supplies appropriate element interchange, element comparison, and key-to-element comparison operations with uniform call syntax. Adding and removing elements can also be done with a combination of base and derived operations.

Abstract Base Example

If our strategy is to have a set of common operations defined in the base class OrderedSeq and a complementary set of operations supplied by a derived class to form a fully operational class, we write OrderedSeq in the form of an *abstract base class*:

```
///////    OrderedSeq.h    ///////

class OrderedSeq  // abstract base class
{ public:
    OrderedSeq() : ordered(true), len(0) {} // default constructor
    unsigned length() const { return len; } // current length of seq
    virtual void remove(unsigned i)         // removes by index
        throw(out_of_range)   =0;
    virtual ~OrderedSeq() {}                // virtual destructor
  protected:
    virtual bool enter(void* any);          // false if failed
    virtual int  index(void* key);          // -1 if not found
    virtual bool append(void* any)   =0;    // at end, false if failed
    virtual void sort();                    // sorts into order
    virtual bool sorted() const             // false if seq not sorted
      { return ordered;}
    virtual void sorted(bool s)
      { ordered = s;}                       // sets sorted flag
    unsigned len;                           // sequence length
  private:
    virtual void swap(unsigned i, unsigned j) =0;
                                            // interchange items
    virtual int cmp(unsigned i, unsigned j) const =0;
                                            // compares items
    virtual int cmp(void* key, unsigned j) const =0;
                                            // compares key to item
    void quicksort(int l, int r);
    unsigned partition(unsigned l, unsigned r);
    bool ordered;                           // sorted flag
};
```

The abstractness of OrderedSeq comes from *pure virtual functions*, such as

```
virtual void remove(unsigned i) throw(out_of_range)  =0;
virtual void swap(unsigned i, unsigned j)=0;
```

that are marked undefined by the =0 notation. No objects can be established for a class with undefined pure virtual functions. Because pure virtual functions are inherited, a derived class is also abstract unless it supplies real definitions for all the pure virtual functions. Therefore, a pure virtual function forces a derived class to supply a real definition with the given prototype.

Thus, an abstract base class serves as a schematic for building derived classes rather than for establishing objects of its own. Without the proper operations supplied by a derived class, the base class OrderedSeq is useless. The abstract base prescribes interfaces and operations required of derived classes. Here the enter and index functions are protected because they take void* arguments. Their derived-class counterparts will be public to deal with specific types.

Note that the abstract OrderedSeq contains only two data fields: a length and an ordered flag indicating whether the sequence is sorted yet. Noticeably absent is a sequence of elements. No assumption is made on how the sequence of elements will eventually be stored. The base is designed to work together with all properly derived classes.

Extracting Common Operations

What common operations can we define in OrderedSeq when neither the elements of the sequence nor their type is known? Quite a few. In fact, you may be surprised at how many nontrivial operations can be supplied, given the right interface design between the base and the derived class.

To begin with, consider searching:

```
///////    OrderedSeq.C    ///////
#include "OrderedSeq.h"

// binary search gets index of entry matching key
int OrderedSeq::index(void* key)
{    if ( ! sorted() ) sort();              // sort when necessary
     int low = 0, mid, test;
     int high = length()-1;
     while (low <= high)                    // binary search
     {   mid = (high + low)/2;
         test = cmp(key, mid);              // call virtual cmp (1)
         if ( test == 0 ) return mid;
         else if ( test > 0 ) low = mid + 1;
         else high = mid - 1;
     }
     return -1;                             // entry not found
}
```

Note that if the sequence is not already in sorted order, it is sorted first. Then, an efficient binary search algorithm is employed to locate the desired element, calling upon the key-to-element comparison function (line 1). The pure virtual cmp(key, n), defined in a derived class, returns a positive, zero, or negative value, depending on whether the key is greater than, equal to, or less than the key contained in the element with index n. Either the index of the element is found or −1 is returned.

Now consider sorting using the quicksort algorithm:

```
void OrderedSeq::sort()          // basic sorting using quicksort
{   if ( sorted() ) return;
    quicksort(0, length()-1);
    sorted(true);
}

void OrderedSeq::quicksort(int l, int r)
{   if ( l >= r || l < 0 ) return;
    int k = partition(l, r);
    quicksort(l, k-1);
    quicksort(k+1, r);
}
```

The function partition(), where all the actual sorting work is done, relies on properly defined element comparison (cmp(i,j)) and interchange (swap(i,j)) virtual functions:

```
unsigned OrderedSeq::partition(unsigned l, unsigned r)
{   register unsigned i=l, j=r;
    swap((i+j)/2, r);                            // pe moved to r
    while (i < j)
    {   while (cmp(i, r) <= 0 && i < j) i++;     // virtual cmp
        while (j > i && cmp(j, r) >= 0) j--;     // virtual cmp
        if (i < j) swap(i,j);                    // virtual swap
    }
    if (i != r) swap(i,r);                       // virtual swap
    return i;
}
```

Having common searching and sorting defined in the abstract base class is already quite good, but more can be done:

```
// enter puts new element at end of array and
// invalidates ordered flag
bool OrderedSeq::enter(void* any)
{   bool ok = append(any);       // virtual append
    if ( ok )
```

```
        {   sorted(false);         // append succeeded
            len++;
        }
        return f;
}
```

The common `enter()` asks the virtual function `append()` to put a new element at the end of the sequence and invalidates the flag `ordered`. Multiple elements can be entered without resorting the sequence after each `enter()` call. Reordering is deferred until the next retrieval from the sequence.

Some pure virtual functions are not part of the public interface but part of the internal operations required by member functions. For example, the element interchange and comparison functions are required by `partition`, and `append` is needed by `enter`.

To fully appreciate the power and convenience of `OrderedSeq`, let's use it to form a specific sequence. The following example shows how to derive from an abstract base class and how to use it as a schematic for building uniform interfaces.

Derived Class: Ordered Dates

Consider applying the abstract base class `OrderedSeq` to form a sequence of dates. A simple date object is an instance of the class:

```
///////    Date.h    ///////
#include <iostream>
using std::cout;

class Date
{   public:
        Date();
        Date(unsigned m, unsigned d, unsigned y)
           : month(m), day(d), year(y)   { }
        int cmp(const Date& d) const;
        void display()
           {  cout << month << '/' << day << '/' << year; }
    private:
        unsigned month, day, year;
};
```

The class provides `Date` objects that can be compared for ordering. Objects of the `DateSeq` (date sequence) class represent ordered sequences of dates:

```
///////    DateSeq.h    ///////
#include <iostream>
```

9.4 PLANNING UNIFORM PUBLIC INTERFACES

```cpp
#include <vector>
#include <stdexcept>        // to use exceptions
#include "Date.h"
#include "OrderedSeq.h"
using std::out_of_range;    // exception

class DateSeq : public OrderedSeq
{ public:
     const Date& operator[](unsigned i)    // (A)
         throw(out_of_range);
     bool enter(Date& d)                   // (B)
     {  return OrderedSeq::enter(&d); }    // adds d, false if failed
     int index(Date& d)                    // (C)
     {  return OrderedSeq::index(&d); }    // -1 if not found
     void remove(unsigned i)               // removes by index
         throw(out_of_range);
  protected:
     bool  append(void* date);             // adds any at end,
  private:
     void swap(unsigned i, unsigned j);    // swaps elements
     int cmp(unsigned i, unsigned j) const; // compares elements
     int cmp(void* date, unsigned j) const;
                                           // compares key to element
     vector<Date*> dates;                  // vector of Date pointer
};
```

The class adds indexing with [] for read-only access to stored dates (line A). The function may need to sort the sequence before indexing. The index i is checked, and an out_of_range exception can be thrown.

The class also adds type-specific enter (line B) and search by key (line C). These functions deal with Date references and forward the call to their base-class counterparts that deal with void* pointers.

The virtual functions

```cpp
void remove(unsigned) throw(out_of_range)    // (I)
bool append(void*)
void swap(unsigned, unsigned)
int cmp(unsigned, unsigned) const
int cmp(void*, unsigned) const
```

follow the prototypes set forth by the abstract base class OrderedSeq. An exception specification (line I) is not part of the function signature. But, it is good practice to make derived and base virtual function exception specifications compatible.

A vector of Date pointers is kept internally. Interchange of elements on the pointer array is very easy. Comparisons are simply done by calls to Date::cmp(), as shown by the following inline functions:

```
inline void DateSeq::swap(unsigned i, unsigned j)
      { Date* tmp = dates[i];
        dates[i] = dates[j];
        dates[j] = tmp;
      }

inline int DateSeq::cmp(unsigned i, unsigned j) const
      { return dates[i]->cmp(*dates[j]); }

// key-to-element comparison
inline int DateSeq::cmp(void* date, unsigned j) const
      { Date* tmp = (Date*) date;
        return tmp->cmp(*dates[j]);
      }
```

The operator[], defined in DateSeq.C, makes sure the sequence is sorted before returning the indexed item. The function can throw an out_of_range exception.

```
///////   DateSeq.C    ///////
#include "DateSeq.h"

const Date& DateSeq::operator[](unsigned i)
    throw(out_of_range)
{   if ( i >= len )
       throw( out_of_range("DateSeq: Index too large") );
    if ( ! sorted() ) sort();
    return *dates[i];
}
```

It allows elements in an object ds of DateSeq to be retrieved by index:

```
Date* pta = ds[i];
```

This is, of course, important to applications requiring ordered dates. The append() function uses the vector::**push_back** function to add a Date pointer to the end of the sequence.

```
bool DateSeq::append(void* date)     // appends entry at end
{   dates.push_back(reinterpret_cast<Date*>(date));
    return true;
}
```

Removing an element from the ordered sequence is done by moving all entries below it up one notch:

```
void DateSeq::remove(unsigned i)     // deletes entry i
    throw(out_of_range)
{   if ( i < len )
    {   for ( int j=i ; j < len ; j++ )
            dates[j] = dates[j+1];
        len--;
        return;
    }
    throw( out_of_range("DateSeq: Index too large") );
}
```

Following the abstract base makes it relatively straightforward to get `DateSeq` implemented correctly. Now test it with some typical operations:

```
#include "DateSeq.h"
using std::cout; using std::endl;

int main()
{   Date d[10] = {Date(2,12,1949), Date(4,20,1949),
                  Date(3,15,1949), Date(11,6,1986),
                  Date(7, 4,1996), Date(2,12,1959),
                  Date(4,20,1959), Date(3,15,1959),
                  Date(11,7,1986), Date(7, 3,1996)};
    DateSeq mydates;
    int i;
    for (i=0; i < 10; i++)                    // enters 10 dates
            mydates.enter(d[i]);
    for (i=0; i<mydates.length(); i++)
    {   mydates[i].display(); cout << endl;  // displays date list
    }
    i = mydates.index(d[6]);
    mydates.remove(i);
    cout << endl << "Entry " << i << " removed" << endl;
    i = mydates.index(d[6]);                  // access should fail
    d[6].display();
    if ( i == -1 ) cout << " entry not found" << endl;
    return 0;
}
```

Running the program produces the following output:

```
2/12/1949
3/15/1949
4/20/1949
```

```
2/12/1959
3/15/1959
4/20/1959
11/6/1986
11/7/1986
7/3/1996
7/4/1996

Entry 5 removed
4/20/1959 entry not found
```

Through this example, we have seen how the abstract base class OrderedSeq is applied and how the base and derived functions cooperate.

Ordered Bank Accounts Now let's consider an example in which we establish a sequence of ordered bank accounts. The only difference here from our sequence of dates is that, while there is just one kind of date, there are many kinds of accounts. However, we should not encounter any major difficulty.

Here is all that we need to do:

1. Make sure the base class Account has a virtual function cmp() for comparing accounts. Ordering can be based on social security number, name of owner, and so on.
2. Derive AccountSeq from OrderedSeq with an internal Account* pointer array. Follow the DateSeq model.

That's it. Done! Consider what has been achieved. An instance of AccountSeq is an object in the OrderedSeq hierarchy, and it reuses all the common codes in the base. AccountSeq, in turn, contains a sequence of plug-compatible accounts all in the Account hierarchy. An AccountSeq object can be used to establish a sequence of accounts of any single type or mixed types. And common banking operations can be applied to all accounts in a sequence.

9.5 DESTRUCTION OF PLUG-COMPATIBLE OBJECTS

Recall that a destructor performs deinitialization just before an object is deallocated. When plug-compatible objects have no user-supplied destructors, no complications occur because of object destruction. The problem that user-defined destruction causes and its solution are described next.

9.5 DESTRUCTION OF PLUG-COMPATIBLE OBJECTS

Consider a revised FreeChecking that defines its own destructor, perhaps to free up dynamically allocated transaction records. Such a destructor would look like

```
FreeChecking::~FreeChecking()
{   delete transac;   }
```

where transac is a pointer to free storage of type Transactions*, for example.

This destructor is invoked every time a FreeChecking object is destroyed, except when the object is destroyed through a base pointer (Account*). To see the problem clearly here, consider show(), the account display routine, which deletes each object after it has been displayed:

```
void show(Account** a, int n)
{   for (int i=0; i < n; i++)
    {   a[i]->display();
        cout << endl;
        delete a[i];      // deletes object via base pointer
    }
}
```

Because delete is given an Account*, the destructor called is ~Account() and not ~FreeChecking() as desired. The C++ *virtual destructor* mechanism solves this problem. When a base destructor is designated virtual, as in

```
virtual ~Account() {}
```

for example, all derived destructors, explicitly supplied or not, are automatically virtual. The effect is familiar: If an object with a virtual destructor is destroyed through a base pointer, the destructor associated with the actual object is invoked. This happens despite the fact that a derived destructor has a name different from that of the base destructor. It is interesting to note that this fact alone distinguishes virtual destructors from other virtual functions. Destructors, virtual or not, are always invoked in the reverse order of constructor calls.

With an understanding of the virtual destructor, we can now see that the abstract base class OrderedSeq should also declare a virtual destructor

```
virtual ~OrderedSeq() {}
```

It is normally a good idea to declare a destructor for a virtualized class virtual.

9.6 ORDERING TEXT LINES

Arranging lines of text in sorted order for easy retrieval and update is important in many practical applications. Text lines are usually ordered by a user-supplied key field contained in each line. We have already seen one application of sorting text lines. Now let's create a class TextLineSeq by deriving from the abstract base class OrderedSeq. TextLineSeq is implemented as a wrapper for TextLines (Section 4.7) to conform to OrderedSeq (Figure 9.8).

```
///////    TextLineSeq.h    ///////
#include <iostream>
#include <stdexcept>
#include "../../ex4/sortline/TextLines.h"
#include "../../ex4/sortline/SortKey.h"
#include "OrderedSeq.h"
using std::out_of_range;      // exception

class TextLineSeq : public OrderedSeq
{ public:
     TextLineSeq(SortKey& k) : key(k) {}
     const string& operator[](unsigned i)
                              // returns line i >= 0, may sort first
         throw(out_of_range);
     bool enter(string& l)          // adds line, false if failed
     { return OrderedSeq::enter(&l); }     // (1)
     int index(string& key)      // finds line by key, -1 not found
     { return OrderedSeq::index(&key); }    // (2)
     void input(istream& in);             // reads into sequence
     void remove(unsigned i)              // deletes line i >= 0
     { txtobj.remove(i); len--; }         // (3)
     void output(ostream& out=cout);      // may sort first
  protected:
     bool append(void* line);             // appends line at end
  private:
     int cmp(unsigned i, unsigned j) const;
```

Figure 9.8 DESIGN OF TextLineSeq

9.6 ORDERING TEXT LINES

```
        int cmp(void* k, unsigned j) const;
        void swap(unsigned i, unsigned j)     // interchanges lines
        {  txtobj.swap(i,j);  }               // (4)
        SortKey& key;                         // sort key manager
        TextLines txtobj;                     // (5)
};
```

The text lines are ordered according to a key position managed by the prescribed SortKey object given to the constructor. The sort key within a line of text is determined by a numeric position and a set of delimiter characters kept in the SortKey object (Section 4.7). Lines are ordered differently given different sort keys. The private reference field key is initialized on the constructor init-list.

The enter and index functions call their counterparts in the base class (lines 1 and 2). Removing a line (line 3) is done by forwarding the operation to the internal TextLine object (line 5).

Line swapping is simply forwarded to txtobj (line 4). The virtual cmp functions are defined to use sortkey-controlled operations lineCompare and keyCompare.

```
inline int TextLineSeq::cmp
(unsigned i, unsigned j) const
{   return key.lineCompare(*txtobj[i], *txtobj[j]);
}

inline int TextLineSeq::cmp
(void* k, unsigned j) const
{   return key.keyCompare(
        *(reinterpret_cast<string*>(k)),
        *txtobj[j]);
}
```

To display, first make sure the sequence is in order. Then simply ask txtobj to display itself.

```
inline void TextLineSeq::output(ostream& out)
{   if ( ! sorted() ) sort();
    txtobj.display(out);
}
```

Read-only indexing (0-based) access to the lines is provided by operator[], which may throw an out_of_range exception.

```
//////    TextLineSeq.C    //////
#include "TextLineSeq.h"

const string& TextLineSeq::operator[](unsigned i)
```

```
        throw(out_of_range)
{   if ( i >= len )
        throw( out_of_range("TextLineSeq: Index too large") );
    if ( ! sorted() ) sort();
    return *txtobj[i];
}

void TextLineSeq::input(istream& in)
{   txtobj.input(in);
    sorted(false);
    len = txtobj.length();
}
```

Reading text lines from an input stream into the sequence is easily done by asking `txtobj` to perform the input, setting the `ordered` flag to `false`, and recording the sequence length.

The virtual `append` that supports the `enter` operation now simply inserts into `txtobj`.

```
bool TextLineSeq::append(void* l)      // append entry at end
{   bool ok =
    txtobj.insert(*reinterpret_cast<string*>(l),
                  txtobj.length());
    if ( ok ) { sorted(false); len++; }
    return ok;
}
```

The complete example is in ex09/order/ of the code package. `TextLineSeq` is a practical class for handling text lines. Here is a main program to test it.

```
///////    testTextLineSeq.C    ///////
#include <iostream>
#include <fstream>
#include "TextLineSeq.h"
using std::cout; using std::endl; using std::cerr;

int main(int argc, char* argv[])
{   if (argc > 3 || argc < 1)
    {   cerr << "Usage: " << argv[0] << " [ key ] file" << endl;
        abort();
    }
    int keypos=0;
    if (argc == 3)
    {   keypos=atoi(argv[1]);
        argv[1] = argv[2];
    }
```

```
        ifstream myin(argv[1]);
        if (! myin) cerr << "Cannot open file " << argv[1] << endl;
// instantiate sequence
        SortKey key(keypos);
        TextLineSeq seq(key);
        seq.input(myin);
        seq.output();
// interactive search
        cout << "Input search key:";
        string& str = *(new string());
        getline(cin, str, '\n');          // read into str
        int i = seq.index(str);
        cout << "index for " << str << " is " << i << endl;
        try {   cout << seq[i] << endl;    // try block
            }  catch (out_of_range& e)
              {   cerr << e.what() << endl; }
        return 0;
}
```

After checking command-line arguments and obtaining the key position, a SortKey and a TextLineSeq object seq are established. Lines of text are read into seq from the given file, and the sorted version is displayed. Then, the program asks the user to input the search key of some entry to retrieve. The index of the line found and the line itself are also displayed. The potential index out_of_range exception is caught. When run on a file of grades, the program produces such output as the following:

```
texttest 2 grades

Joe   Brown       C
Susan Gray        I
George Lee        S
John  Smith       A
Mary  Taylor      B

Input search key:Lee
index for Lee is 2
George Lee        S
```

9.7 INTERFACES

An abstract base class can enforce a planned public interface and can also provide partial (or default) implementations. It is a powerful tool for building plug-compatible objects. A completely abstract base class is also very useful as a device to define public interfaces for other objects to follow. Let the term *interface* mean *a totally abstract base class* with the following properties:

- All members are public.
- All functions are pure virtual.
- Other members may include `static const` data fields, `enum` constants, and `typedef`s.

Through multiple inheritance, we can mix several base classes and interfaces in one derived class. Objects of such classes can be plug-compatible in different ways. Thus, a *Solver* subclass, for example, can provide user help by implementing the *Help* interface, produce log files by implementing the *Logfile* interface, and supply documentation through the *Document* interface.

As an example, let's formalize the I/O conventions set forth in Section 6.8 with the IOable interface.

```
////////    IOable.h    ///////

class IOable                      // an interface
{ public:
    // displays host object
       virtual void display(ostream& out = cout) const =0;

    // reads into host object
       virtual void read(istream& in = cin) =0;
};

inline ostream& operator <<(ostream& out, IOable& any)
{    any.display(out);
     return out;
}

inline istream& operator >>(istream& in, IOable& any)
{    any.read(in);
     return in;
}
```

IOable defines two pure virtual functions as requirements for its subclasses. Any subclass of IOable will implement the two required functions for the intended purposes. Once a class implements the IOable interface, its objects can be used with the >> and << I/O operators as defined by the preceding inline functions.

Now we can make `Fraction` objects `IOable` by

```
class Fraction : public IOable
{ public:
    /* ... */
    void read(istream& in = cin);            // input fraction
    void display(ostream& out = cout) const; // display fraction
    /* ... */
};
```

without having to overload >> or << again specifically for `Fraction`.

Existing classes can be made `IOable` through multiple inheritance. As an example, let's mix in `IOable` with `TextLineSeq`.

```
///////    TextLineSeq_IO    ///////
#include "TextLineSeq.h"
#include "../interface/IOable.h"

class TextLineSeq_IO : public TextLineSeq, public IOable
{ public:
    TextLineSeq_IO(SortKey& k)
     : TextLineSeq(k) {}
    // displays host object
     void display(ostream& out = cout) const
     {   (const_cast< TextLineSeq_IO& >(*this)).output(out);
     }
    // reads into host object
     void read(istream& in = cin)
     {   input(in);    }
};
```

Note that `const_cast` is used to cast away the `const` before calling `output`, which may alter the host object by sorting it.

Now the following code is made possible:

```
TextLineSeq_IO txtobj(key);
myin >> txtobj;    // input operation
cout << txtobj;    // output operation
```

9.8 UNDERSTANDING VIRTUAL FUNCTIONS

We have seen how useful plug-compatible objects are. We know what a critical role virtual functions play in the overall scheme of a derivation hierarchy. However, the concept of a virtual function can still be somewhat difficult at first. The following points should help sharpen your mental picture of virtual functions:

1. Once a base prototype is designated `virtual`, all derived-class functions with the same prototype are automatically virtual, with or without explicit virtual declaration, and form a set of functions to be selected at run time. Designate a function virtual to allow derived classes to supply revised definitions for it.

2. When a virtual function is invoked through a base-type pointer or reference, the actual run-time type of the object determines which virtual function to call.

3. A pure virtual function is one that is left undefined with the =0 notation. The presence of pure virtual functions makes a class abstract.

4. A direct call of a member virtual function by another member function is considered to be an invocation through the host pointer `this`. (The calls to `swap` and `cmp` in the `partition()` function of the `OrderedSeq` class are examples.) This feature allows functions in the base class to call virtual functions to be supplied in derived classes.

5. Only instance functions can be virtual. Constructors, `new`, and `delete` are the only class members that cannot be virtual. However, destructors can be virtual despite having different names.

6. A pure virtual function can be left undefined but must be defined by a derived class before instances can be established.

7. The access protection designation (`public`, `protected`, or `private`) of a virtual function is determined by the base class (the pointer/reference type), not by the class of the actual object.

8. Virtual functions can be implemented as `inline` functions. Virtual functions cannot be static.

9. There are three situations when a virtual function invocation is fixed at compile time:

   - When a virtual function is invoked through an object instead of a pointer or reference. Here the call loses its virtualness and is just like any regular-member function call.
   - When a virtual function call explicitly specifies the class scope. (The call `JointAccount::display()` in the function `JtFrChecking::display()` is an example.)
   - When a virtual function is called within either a constructor or a destructor, the version defined by the class itself is always invoked

because the derived object is either not yet constructed or already destroyed.

- The run-time behaviors of `typeid` and `dynamic_cast` depend on virtualized objects, those with at least one virtual function.

9.9 INHERITANCE PLANNING

For a class, the `public` members represent an interface to outside functions. The combined `public` and `protected` members represent an interface to a derived class. When writing a class as a base for further derivation, this second interface, as well as certain other factors, must be considered carefully. Without proper planning, derivation from an existing class quickly runs into problems. Often, we can solve these problems by revising the base classes in question, assuming we have access to the base source code and are allowed to modify it. The situation is quite different when modifying the base is not possible.

The essential principle in planning for inheritance is a well-formed model of the overall behavior of the base object in relation to derived objects. This model facilitates decisions in the following critical areas:

1. *Protected or private*: Consider whether a `private` member should be designated `protected` instead to allow access by a derived class.
2. *Virtual or nonvirtual*: Decide whether a function should be designated `virtual`. If a function is expected to be redefined by a derived class, it should be designated `virtual`. Ideally, virtual functions should also be written so that preprocessing, postprocessing, or both can be easily added in a derived class. When in doubt, always make a base function `virtual`. Usually, the only price you pay is some performance degradation. The destructors in a class hierarchy are usually designated `virtual`.
3. *Shared base or not*: When the base class is itself derived, like `JointAccount`, whether its base is shared (`virtual`) affects future multiple inheritance. For a public derivation hierarchy, there is normally no need for duplicated base objects, and declaring base classes `virtual` usually makes good sense. The way a virtual base can be initialized should be clearly documented in a derived class because further derived constructors must call the correct virtual-base constructor.
4. *Subclass interface*: A base class has a public interface and a *subclass interface*. The latter is designed with derived classes and future extensions in mind and supported by `protected` members.

5. *Member function overloading*: When the base class contains an overloaded member and a derived class redefines one version of it, the remaining versions in the base class become hidden and no longer form part of the accessible interface for a derived object. Take this into account when naming base-class members.
6. *Pure virtual functions*: Use these to plan derived-class interfaces and virtual functions to be supplied by a derived class.
7. *Interfaces*: Completely abstract classes can specify the public interfaces required to conform to certain purposes. Such interfaces can be mixed in with other objects through multiple inheritance.

Virtual-Function Composition

A derived class often redefines a base virtual function to augment its capabilities. For example, the `FreeChecking` member

```
bool FreeChecking::withdraw(double amt)
{   bool ok = Account::withdraw(amt);        // call base withdraw
    if ( ok )                                // added processing
       if ( free && balance() < min_bal )
          free = 0;
    return ok;
}
```

first calls the base `withdraw()` and then performs some additional processing. In general, a derived class may add either *preprocessing, postprocessing,* or *both* to a base virtual function to achieve more complicated behavior. This method of composing functions via derivation is an important inheritance technique. However, we must do a certain amount of planning to use it effectively.

Consider the top-level loop of the pocket calculator:

```
void Calculator::on()
{     int ind;
      char op;
      double number;
      cf.showNumber(eng.output());
      // calculator top-level loop
      while ( (ind = cf.input(op, number))    // loop control
                 != CalcFace::off )
      {   if ( ind == CalcFace::ok )          // loop body
             eng.operand( number );
          eng.operate( op );
          number = (op == 'c' || op == 'C') ? 0 : eng.output();
          cf.showNumber(number);
```

            }
}

As it stands, it is impossible for a derived class to augment the loop body unless we rewrite the complete function `on()`. To allow for future composition, we extract the loop body from the loop control to form another virtual function `perform()`:

```
void Calculator::on()
{       int ind;
        char op;
        double number;
        cf.showNumber(eng.output());
        while ( (ind = cf.input(op, number))    // loop control
                    != CalcFace::off )
        {   perform(ind, op, number);
        }
}

// extracted loop body
void Calculator::perform(int ind, char op, double number) // virtual
{       if ( ind == CalcFace::ok )
            eng.operand( number );
        eng.operate( op );
        number = (op == 'c' || op == 'C') ? 0 : eng.output();
        cf.showNumber(number);
}
```

In this way, preprocessing and/or postprocessing can easily be added to the loop body in a derived class of `Calculator`. The loop control part can also be replaced or modified without affecting the loop body.

For maximum efficiency, we should plan even further ahead. The added preprocessing and/or postprocessing parts should also be defined as virtual functions so that future derived classes can augment or modify these parts, thus allowing full flexibility in composition in a derivation chain.

9.10 OBJECT-FAMILY CLASSES

With plug-compatible objects, programs are more generic and the same code can be applied to various objects through base pointers and references. Compatibility through pointers or references is very handy. However, in some situations, related quantities should be treated as instances of the same class so that they operate correctly and combine into new instances in the same class. In other words, we sometimes need *a class to encompass a family of objects*.

Consider different kinds of numbers, for example: integers, fractions, real, imaginary, and complex. In some applications, it is convenient to treat different numbers as objects of the same `Number` class. When two fractions are added, an integer may result. Representing this result as an integer is nicer than representing it as a fraction that is equal to an integer. When two complex numbers are multiplied, a real number may emerge. Again, representing such an answer by a real number is nicer than representing it as a complex number with a zero imaginary part. In other words, arithmetic operations should work on mixed kinds of numbers. The actual type of the result depends on its value.

Such a `Number` class allows us to build, for instance, a class of polynomials with `Number` coefficients or a class of matrices with `Number` entries. Such classes are of course much more generic.

A family class such as `Number` can be achieved in C++ with a combination of mechanisms. Here is the overall strategy:

- `Number` is defined as an *envelope* class whose objects represent many different subtypes of numbers and whose functions supply operations for all subtypes in the family. Mixing of subtypes is allowed.
- Distinct subtypes of numbers are defined as derived classes of `Number`.
- A `Number` object has an internal (`private`) pointer of type `Number*`, which can point to different derived objects of `Number`.
- Operations requested through the envelope class `Number` are *forwarded* to the actual objects to be carried out by virtual functions.
- The forwarding mechanism is also used by derived virtual functions to resubmit requests that need more type information.
- Results computed are again instances of `Number`, which supplies constructors to build numbers of various kinds.

To see exactly how this strategy works, let's consider a simplified example involving three classes:

1. `Number`, the envelope class for the family.
2. `Fraction`, derived from `Number`.
3. `Integer`, derived from `Number`.

The `Number` Envelope

The `Number` class serves both as an envelope containing the various subtypes of numbers and as a base class for the derived subtypes. Let's first examine the header.

9.10 OBJECT-FAMILY CLASSES

The Header File `Number.h` The public interface includes constructors, a destructor, a copy constructor, and assignment, display, arithmetic, and other usual operations involving numbers. Those functions declared virtual are redefined by various types of numbers as derived classes of Number. The actual number is represented by a base pointer. So a Number object is represented internally by a Number* pointer, which can point to any derived object of Number and thus allows Number objects to represent many different subtypes of numbers (Figure 9.9). (How subtypes of numbers are created, operated on, and destroyed is explained later.)

Here is the header:

```
///////    Number.h    ///////
#include <iostream>
using std::cout;

class Number
{public:
    Number(): ptr(0) {}                            // default constructor
    Number(int a);                                 // integer constructor
    Number(int a, int b);                          // fraction constructor
    Number(const Number&);                         // copy constructor
    Number& operator =(const Number&);             // assignment
    virtual void display(ostream& out=cout) const
    { ptr->display(out); }
    virtual Number operator+(const Number& n) const
    {   return ptr->operator+(n); }                // arithmetic    (1)
    virtual Number operator/(const Number& n) const // operations
    {   return ptr->operator/(n); }                //               (2)
/* other public members */
    virtual ~Number(){ delete ptr; }               // destructor
 private:
    virtual Number* copy() const                   // utility function
```

Figure 9.9 ENVELOPE AND SUBTYPE OBJECTS

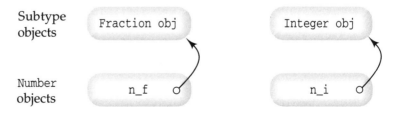

```
    { return ptr->copy() ;}
    Number* ptr;                              // ptr to actual number
};
```

To keep things simple, only addition and division operations are considered. Generalizations will become obvious.

Arithmetic involving two objects of the type Number is difficult unless the exact subtype of each object is known. In other words, an arithmetic operation must first deduce whether two fractions, two integers, or an integer and a fraction are being treated. The key is to use the virtual mechanism twice, once to deduce the subtype of each operand.

Consider two Number objects, n_i and n_f, where n_i is actually an integer and n_f is a fraction. This means that n_i.ptr points to a derived object of subtype Integer, and n_f.ptr points to a derived object of subtype Fraction. Let's trace how the division operation

```
n_i / n_f
```

is performed. The operation is directly interpreted as the call n_i.operator/(n_f) (line 2), which leads to another call

```
n_i.ptr->operator/(n_f)
```

This second call forwards n_f, through the virtual function mechanism, to the operator/ function in the object *n_i.ptr, which happens to be of type Integer. At this point, the subtype of the left-hand operand n_i has been deduced.

A set of protected virtual functions in the class Number is central to the determination of the actual type of the right-hand operand (e.g., n_f):

```
// more members for class Number
 protected:
   virtual Number AddFra(const Number& n) const  // host is Fraction
   {  return n.ptr->AddFra(*this); }             // *this + n
   virtual Number DivFra(const Number& n) const  // host is Fraction
   {  return n.ptr->DivFra(*this); }             // *this / n
   virtual Number AddInt(const Number& n) const  // host is Integer
   {  return n.ptr->AddInt(*this); }             // *this + n
   virtual Number DivInt(const Number& n) const
                                                 // host is Integer (3)
   {  return n.ptr->DivInt(*this); }             // *this / n      (4)
 /* other protected members */
```

Again, only functions for addition and division are shown. Each of these protected functions is called only by a specific derived class of Number. For example, Number::AddFra(n) knows its host object is a Fraction, and Number::DivInt(n)

knows its host is an Integer (line 3). In the latter case, for example, to find the subtype of n, the call (line 4)

```
n.ptr->DivInt(*this)     // arg is Integer (5)
```

is made through n.ptr leading to the virtual function DivInt() in the derived object *n.ptr. Thus, the call (line 5) knows the type of its host and its operand (an Integer) and can therefore simply carry out the desired operation and return a Number result. (This will be considered again after the codes for DivInt() in the derived classes are shown, and we will also return to n_i / n_f.)

The remainder of the Number.h file contains some inline functions:

```
//   Number.h (continued)
#include "Fraction.h"                          // (A)
#include "Integer.h"

inline Number::Number(int a)                   // make integer
     : ptr(new Integer(a)) { }

inline Number::Number(const Number& n)         // copy constructor
     : ptr(n.copy()) { }

///////     End of Number.h      ///////
```

Because of the mutual reference among Number, Fraction, and Integer, all headers must be *once-only* (Section 14.7). In Number.h, some #include lines (e.g., line A) must be put in an appropriate place in the middle of the file rather than at the beginning.

Implementation of Number

Most functions of Number are simple enough to be inline. Two functions — a class-defined assignment and a fraction-or-integer constructor — are placed in Number.C:

```
///////     Number.C     ///////
#include "Number.h"
#include <assert.h>

Number& Number::operator=(const Number& n)   // assignment
{   if (&n == this) return *this;
    if ( ptr != NULL ) delete(ptr);
    ptr = n.copy();
    return *this;
}

Number::Number(int n, int d)                  // constructor
{   assert(d != 0);
```

```
        if ( d < 0 )
        {   n = -n;  d = -d;   }                  // make d > 0
        int c = gcd(n,d);
        if ( c != 1 )                             // remove gcd
        {   n /= c;
            d /= c;
        }
        if ( d == 1 )
            ptr = new Integer(n);
        else
            ptr = new Fraction(n,d);
}
```

These functions are straightforward. Let's now examine the Fraction class.

The Fraction Subtype

The derived class Fraction takes care of the actual representation of a fraction number and supplies operations exclusively on fractions, as well as procedures involving a fraction and a number of another subtype. To ensure that all numbers are created and used uniformly through the envelope class Number, a derived subtype, such as Fraction, contains no public members. Each is used by Number and other derived classes in the family through friendship:

```
///////    Fraction.h    ///////
#include "Number.h"

class Fraction : public Number
{   friend class Number;
    friend class Integer;
 protected:
    Fraction(int n, int d)                        // constructor
      : num(n), denom(d) { }
    Number operator+(const Number& n) const;      // n subtype unknown
    Number operator/(const Number& n) const;      // n subtype unknown
    Number AddFra(const Number& f) const;         // f + *this (1)
    Number DivFra(const Number& f) const;         // f / *this (2)
    Number AddInt(const Number& i) const;         // i + *this (3)
    Number DivInt(const Number& i) const;         // i / *this (4)
    void display(iostream& out=cout) const;
 private:
    int num;                   // numerator
    unsigned int denom;        // denominator
    Number* copy() const
```

9.10 OBJECT-FAMILY CLASSES

```
    { return new Fraction(num, denom); }
};
```

Except for the constructor, all Fraction functions are virtual following the interface set down by the base class Number. Arithmetic operations are forwarded from Number to Fraction operator functions such as these:

```
inline Number Fraction::operator +(const Number& n) const
    { return Number::AddFra(n); }

inline Number Fraction::operator /(const Number& n) const
    { return Number::DivFra(n); }

////////    End of Fraction.h    ////////
```

Knowing the host object is of type Fraction, these operator functions can call type-encoded functions *OprFra()* in Number. These base-class functions will forward the operands to the corresponding type-encoded functions, such as those on lines 1–4, in a derived class.

The member Fraction::DivInt() divides an Integer by the host Fraction, as shown in its implementation in Fraction.C:

```
////////    Fraction.C    ////////
#include <iostream>
#include "Number.h"

Number Fraction::DivInt(const Number& i) const    // i / *this
{   const Integer& ii = dynamic_cast< const Integer& >(i);
    return Number(ii.val * denom, num);
}
```

The reference parameter i is first explicitly cast before computing the answer and returning a Number object.

Similarly, Fraction::AddInt() is coded as follows.

```
Number Fraction::AddInt(const Number& i) const    // i + *this
{   const Integer& ii = dynamic_cast< const Integer& >(i);
    return Number(ii.val * denom + num, denom);
}
```

The `Integer` Subtype

To complete the picture, let's examine the `Integer` class. It is similar to `Fraction`, so the rules for adding more subtypes to the `Number` family should become very clear:

```
///////    Integer.h     ///////
#include "Number.h"

class Integer : public Number
{  friend class Number;
   friend class Fraction;
 protected:
   Integer(int i) :val(i) {}                       // constructor
   Number operator+(const Number& n) const    // n subtype unknown
   {  return Number::AddInt(n); }
   Number operator/(const Number& n) const    // n subtype unknown
   {  return Number::DivInt(n); }
   Number AddFra(const Number& f) const;      // f + *this
   Number DivFra(const Number& f) const;      // f / *this
   Number AddInt(const Number& i) const;      // i + *this
   Number DivInt(const Number& i) const;      // i / *this
   void display(iostream& out=cout) const
   {  out << val ; }
 private:
   int val;
   Number* copy() const
   {  return new Integer(val); }
};
```

The integer division operation `Integer::DivInt`, which computes (i / *this), is coded as follows:

```
///////    Integer.C     ///////
#include "Number.h"

Number Integer::DivInt(const Number& i) const
{  const Integer& ii = dynamic_cast< const Integer& >(i);
   return Number(ii.val, val);
}
```

All three classes — `Number`, `Fraction`, and `Integer` — have been described. Now we can summarize the steps for the n_i / n_f computation:

```
1. n_i / n_f                  // invokes Number::operator/
2. n_i.operator/(n_f)         // forwards n_f to Integer::operator/
3. n_i.ptr->operator/(n_f)    // calls Number::DivInt(n_f)
```

```
4. n_i.ptr->Number::DivInt(n_f)   // calls Fraction::DivInt(*this)
5. n_f.ptr->DivInt(*n_i.ptr)
                    // divides Integer *n_i.ptr by Fraction *n_f.ptr
```

The technique is known as *double dispatching*: The first dispatching (steps 2 to 3) identifies the true type of n_i, and the second dispatching (steps 4 to 5) identifies the true type of n_f.

To see how things work together, we can run a test program:

```
#include "Number.h"
using std::endl;

int main()
{   Number f(4,6);
    Number i(3);
    Number g(-3,2);
    Number k = f + i;
    k.display(); cout << endl;
    k = f + g;
    k.display(); cout << endl;
    k = f / g;
    k.display(); cout << endl;
    k = k / f + f;
    k.display(); cout << endl;
    return 0;
}
```

Compiled and run, this program produces the following display:

```
11/3
-5/6
-4/9
0
```

The material in this section deserves careful study. Many subtleties exist that you may miss in a first reading. Experiment with the code to get a feel for its nuances and an appreciation of its sophistication.

9.11 SUMMARY

Polymorphism is a higher form of OOP activity that involves making generic operations apply to different types of objects that are plug-compatible. Several techniques are involved in polymorphism: uniform public interfaces, is-a relationships with class derivation, implicit conversion of derived reference/pointer to base reference/pointer, and run-time routing of function calls via the virtual function mechanism. A virtualized object is any that has a virtual function member. The RTTI also supports dynamic type-casting (`dynamic_cast`) and type identification (`typeid` operator) for virtualized objects.

A class presents one interface to the public and another to its derived classes. Careful planning is necessary to alleviate potential problems in future derivations. The abstract base class with pure virtual functions can be used to make planning for uniform interfaces easy. The technique is demonstrated by an `OrderedSeq` class, which results in a program reusable in all situations that involve searching and sorting. In planning classes for derivation, careful consideration should be given to how functions are written so that virtual-function composition can be easily and effectively achieved.

An interface is a totally abstract base class whose purpose is to regulate public interfaces for polymorphic use.

The compatible-object idea extends to the object-family class, which collects related plug-compatible objects within one single class. This organization also allows operations that construct new instances of such objects. The `Number` class illustrates this sophisticated concept.

A working class hierarchy does not happen by accident. Careful design and planning are required.

EXERCISES

1. Consider the declaration of a virtual-base class. Can the keyword `virtual` be put in front of `public`? `private`? `protected`?

2. Consider the nonvirtual version of `JtFrChecking`. Can a `JtFrChecking` constructor call the `Account` base constructor in this case? Why?

3. Consider the function

    `void show(Account* a[], int n)`

    in Section 9.1. If the function is declared as

    `void show(Account a[], int n)`

    would it still work as a polymorphic function? Why?

4. If a base class is declared `virtual` for some but not all derivations, what happens if you derive from these derived classes mixing virtual and nonvirtual versions of the same base class? Explain and give examples.

5. What is the overhead, in terms of speed and program size, incurred by declaring a member function `virtual`?

6. Consider binary I/O (Section 6.7) for polymorphic objects. What difficulties, if any, do you anticipate?

7. Consider `dynamic_cast`. In what situations should `dynamic_cast` be used? Does it work on all types or just certain types? Explain.

8. Exercise ObjIO-1: Expand the object I/O program in Section 9.2 and include several other object types.

9. Add a pure virtual function `display()` to `OrderedSeq` and supply its proper definition in `DateSeq`.

10. Consider the ordered dates example and the class `DateSeq`. Modify the class definition so that the pointer array `dates` is not fixed in length. It is initialized to zero length and becomes longer by a predetermined increment every time a new element comes into a full array. Make sure you free all dynamically allocated storage properly.

11. The `sort()` provided by `OrderedSeq` is the quicksort, one of the most efficient sorting algorithms known. Nevertheless, the fact that `sort` is `virtual` means it can be replaced by another sorting routine in a derived class if desired. Try to supply another sorting routine this way.

12. Consider class `Xyz` derived from class `Abc`. Both `Abc` and `Xyz` define the virtual function `int vfun()`. If a call to `vfun` is placed in an `Abc` constructor, which version of `vfun` will be called? If a call to `vfun` is placed in an instance function of `Abc`, then which version will be called? Explain.

13. Define a `sortable` interface. Show how any class conforming to the interface can be given to polymorphic sorting functions to perform the sorting.

14. Exercise Cal-1: Consider the improvements to the calculator program (Chapter 7, Exercises Cal-1 and Cal-2). Make the derived compute engine objects plug-compatible. Modify the `Calculator` class so that it uses a plug-compatible compute engine derived from `CalcEng`. Run `Calculator` objects initialized with different engines. Also break up the main computation loop of the calculator to allow derived classes to add preprocessing/postprocessing to each loop iteration. (*Hint*: Use a `CalcEng*` member.)

Chapter 9   OOP TECHNIQUES

15. Consider the generic tree program in Section 9.3. As it stands, the program supports only read-write iterators. But the principle *a const container can return only const iterators* should be followed. Add to ArbTree typedefs iterator and const_iterator following the conventions described in Section 8.6. Then, add member functions to return both types of iterators and make other necessary revisions to ArbTree::Iterator.

16. Consider the semantics for the preincrement and the postincrement operator ++. Add the member function operator++(int) to the class ArbTree::Iterator.

17. Consider virtual destructors (Section 9.5). When delete is applied to an Account*, which points to a FreeChecking object, what destructors are called and in what order?

18. What friend functions, if any, can be virtual?

19. Is it allowable to have the base version of a virtual function declared public and a derived version protected or private. If so, what effect, if any, is there when the virtual function is used?

20. Consider the object-family Number. What functions must be added to Number, Fraction, and Integer to support the additional binary arithmetic operations * and -?

21. Add the function prototypes in Exercise 20 to the appropriate class declarations.

22. Consider the forwarding operations in Number, Integer, Fraction, and so on. For example, consider the member function of Integer

    ```
    Number operator *(const Number& n) const
    {   return Number::TimInt(n); }
    ```

    Why can't this be written as

    ```
    Number operator *(const Number& n) const
    {   return n.TimInt(*this); }
    ```

    directly, since that is what Number::TimInt is going to do anyway?

23. Define the functions needed in Exercise 21 and test the revised object-family.

24. Take the polynomial class defined in Section 4.5 and make its coefficients Number objects. See how simple it is to work on polynomials with integer and fraction coefficients.

CHAPTER TEN

Templates

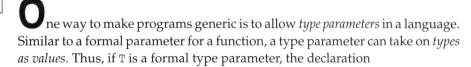

One way to make programs generic is to allow *type parameters* in a language. Similar to a formal parameter for a function, a type parameter can take on *types as values*. Thus, if T is a formal type parameter, the declaration

```
T x, y, z;
```

declares three variables whose type depends on the value of T. Allowing functions, classes, and other constructs to contain type parameters gives a programmer the ability to write *program templates*, which turn into fully completed codes when the type parameters take on values.

C++ supports type parameterization with the *template* construct. The template feature is an important technique for writing generic code. However, the level of support for templates among different C++ implementations may not be uniform. As vendors strive to make their C++ compilers Standard C++ compliant, this situation should improve rapidly.

This chapter introduces basic template concepts and then describes both function templates and class templates. Complete example templates are given and put to use. The template technique is applied, in combination with other C++ features, to define a widely applicable generic hash table class. The pros and cons of the template, void*, and polymorphism approaches to generic programming are also discussed.

10.1 BASIC CONCEPTS

A C++ *template* is a program skeleton specified by putting "placeholders" into ordinary program codes. Once the placeholders are filled, a template produces actual definitions or declarations. By filling the placeholders with different quantities, many different codes can be produced from a single template. Each specific version thus produced is known as an *instantiation* of a template. Thus, a template is a mechanism for generating programs.

The placeholders are *template formal parameters* that take on different values including type names such as int and Fraction. C++ supports templates for functions and classes.

With templates, we can write functions and classes that work for any appropriate primitive and user-defined types. Consider, for example, the power function discussed in Section 3.7. Such power functions can be defined once and for all by the template

```
template <typename T>              // T is type parameter
T power (T a, int exp)
{   T ans = a;
    while ( --exp > 0 ) ans *= a;  // *= of type T
    return ans;
}
```

Clearly, the power definition involves the type parameter T. T can be given the value int, double, Fraction, Complex, or any other type including those yet to be defined. Of course, the function will work only for those types where the operator *= is defined. Thus, appropriate operator overloading is one aspect of templates.

The general form of a template is

```
template < type1 T1, type2 T2,... >   (template header)
normal declaration or definition      (involving T1, T2,...)
```

The *template header* begins with the keyword template followed by one or more *template formal parameters* in angle brackets. A template header controls the immediately following declaration or definition, which must make use of the template formal parameters. A template parameter can be one of the following:

- *Type parameter*: The special notation "typename *T*" means *T* is a type parameter that can be given any type as a value. The keyword typename, introduced in Standard C++, is interchangeable with the keyword class in the template header.
- *Nontype parameter*: Normal function-style parameters, such as int i or CMP_FN cmp, specify nontype parameters.

For example, the function template

```
template <typename T, int N>
T max(T arr[N])
{   T ans=arr[0];
    for (int i=1; i<N; i++)
        ans = (ans > arr[i] ) ? ans : arr[i];   // > of type T
    return ans;
}
```

has a type parameter T and a nontype parameter N. The function generated would work for any type T where the > operator works.

A template tells the compiler how to make an actual declaration or definition once the template parameters are bound. For example, the code

```
Fraction x, y(1,2);
x = power(y, 3);       // triggers template instantiation
```

causes the compiler to instantiate the power template with T replaced by Fraction, resulting in the complete definition of a Fraction version of power.

The following simple main program causes three function template instantiations:

```
int main()
{   int i = 5, j = 2;
    double b = 12.345;
    cout << power(j,i) << endl;  // T is int
    cout << power(b,i) << endl;  // T is double
    int a[] = {1,2,3,4,5,6,7};
    cout << max(a) << endl;      // T is int, N is 7
    return 0;
}
```

With these basic concepts in mind, let's examine function and class templates in detail.

10.2 FUNCTION TEMPLATES

One technique we can use to make functions generic involves the void* pointers mentioned in Section 5.12. This technique has its strength and its weakness. The function template mechanism offers an alternative that can be very attractive because it defines a potentially unbounded set of overloaded functions with a single construct. Each function in this set is a *template function* and an *instance* of the function template. An appropriate template function is produced automatically by the compiler when needed.

Function Template Definition

To see the power of function templates, consider, for example, a generic binary search. The header file provides the function prototype and documentations:

```
#ifndef bsearch_SEEN__
#define bsearch_SEEN__
////////    bsearch.h    ////////
// Generic binary search template prototype
```

```
template<typename T1, typename T2>   // template header
int bsearch(T1 arr[],                // ordered array of any type T1
            T2 key,                  // search key of any type T2
            int low, int high,       // inclusive search range
            int (* cmp)(T1, T2)      // comparison function
           );

// cmp(arr[i], key) compares arr[i] with key and returns -1, 0, 1
// bsearch returns the index of the entry found or -1 if not found
#endif
```

Any client program that wishes to use the binary search simply includes this header and calls bsearch() with an appropriate cmp argument. The #ifndef once-only feature (Section 14.7) is shown here to underscore its importance when you are using the template mechanism.

In the bsearch template, both template parameters, T1 and T2, are type parameters. The actual implementation of the function template is in a different file:

```
///////    bsearch.C    ///////
// Generic binary search
#include "bsearch.h"

template<typename T1, typename T2>            // template header
int bsearch(T1 arr[], T2 key, int low,
            int high, int (* cmp)(T1, T2))
{   int mid, test;
    while (low <= high)
    {   mid = (low + high) / 2;
        test = cmp(arr[mid], key);            // -1, 0, +1
        if (test > 0) high = mid - 1;
        else if (test < 0) low = mid + 1;
        else return mid;                      // found
    }
    return -1;                                // not found
}
```

The binary search algorithm is implemented for an array of type T1 using search keys of type T2. Since these are known types for any instance, variables of type T1 or T2 are treated no differently in the function body than are any other quantities of known type.

To write function templates systematically, follow these steps:

1. Write a specific version of the function with all fixed types.
2. Compile and test the function.

10.2 FUNCTION TEMPLATES

3. Consider how the function would behave if selected types are replaced by other types and what properties a type must have for the function to work properly. Pay special attention to the type char*.
4. Replace selected types in the function with type parameters and add the template header.

Now let's apply the binary search function template:

```
///////    test_bsearch.C    ///////
#include <iostream>
#include <string.h>
#include "bsearch.h"                    // need template prototype
using std::cout; using std::endl;

char *getkey(char *s, unsigned int i)
{   for ( int j = 1; j < i; j++)        // skipping fields
        while ( *s++ != ' ' );          // single space delimiter
    return s;
}

int cmpLastname(char *ent, char *key)
{    char *k = getkey(ent, 3);
     return strcmp(k, key);
}

int main()
{   char *names[] = {"George M. Blum", "Ruth B. Boland",
            "Bill C. Johnson", "David P. Moses", "Debra S. Rice",
            "John A. Smith", "Paul S. Wang"};
    const int LEN = sizeof(names)/sizeof(char*);
    int j = bsearch(names, "Rice", 0, LEN-1, cmpLastname);       // (1)
    if (j >= 0 ) cout << names[j] << endl;

    j = bsearch(names, "Doe", 0, LEN-1, cmpLastname);            // (2)
    if (j < 0 ) cout << "Doe not found" << endl;
    return 0;
}
```

This simple application shows the use of bsearch to retrieve a name from an ordered array of names with the last name as a key. The first invocation (line 1) triggers the instantiation of the template with T1 = char* and T2 = char*. The second call (line 2) triggers no instantiation because it calls an existing function.

Function Template Instantiation

Template parameters are *formal* in the sense that there is no difference between the following declarations:

```
template <typename A, typename B>      template <class T1, class T2>
int funcXyz(A, B);                     int funcXyz(T1, T2);
```

Both type and nontype template parameters can be used. However, *each template parameter must appear, in some form, within the function signature at least once*. Remember that the return value type is not part of the signature. Given values to the template parameters T1 and T2, the bsearch function template can generate the full definition of a *template function* to perform binary search involving specific types (Figure 10.1). The template function is an *instance* of the function template and is sometimes also known as a *specialization* of the template.

The C++ compiler instantiates function templates automatically. When the compiler encounters a particular template function call for the first time, the function is still undefined. However, the function template together with the function call signature provides enough information to build the needed function from the function template right then and there.

Values for the template parameters are deduced by comparing the function template signature with the function call signature using the following *function template argument deduction* procedure:

1. The formal parameters in the function template signature are examined in turn.
2. Each formal parameter involving a template parameter is matched with the corresponding actual argument in the function call. A successful match binds the type parameter.
3. All matches of template parameters must be exact without nontrivial conversions (Section 3.7), but conversion from a derived template class type (Section 10.3) to an accessible base template class type (Section 10.7) is allowed.

Figure 10.1 FUNCTION TEMPLATE INSTANTIATION

10.2 FUNCTION TEMPLATES

4. Formal parameters not involving template parameters can receive arguments following the usual functional-call type conversions.

If all formal parameters match the incoming arguments and the match produces consistent template parameter values, template instantiation takes place.

Function template instantiation also occurs when the location of a template function is taken. For example, the declaration

```
float (* fn)(float, int) = &power;    // template function pointer
```

causes the instantiation of the power function template. It is also possible to explicitly specify the template parameters and bypass template argument deduction. For example,

```
void someFunction(double* arr, int n)
{
    ...
    // explicit template function call
    double m = max<double,n>(arr);
    ...
}
```

where the notation max<double,n> specifies the max function template (Section 10.1) and its template arguments explicitly and causes a direct instantiation. Arguments passed to such a function follow the normal argument conversion rules. The *explicit function template call* technique should be used only where automatic instantiation won't work, as in the preceding example.

Function Template Specialization

Consider the function template

```
template <typename T>
int compare(T a, T b)
{   if ( a > b ) return 1;              // using > for T
    if ( a == b ) return 0;             // using == for T
    return -1;
}
```

This template works for all user-defined types where > and == have been defined. It also works automatically for all primitive types, except char*. How do we plug this hole? We specify, together with the template definition, a special case for char* as follows:

```
template<>                              // compare template specialization
int compare<const char*>(const char* a, const char* b)
{   return strcmp(a, b);  }
```

The preceding is a *template specialization definition*. It prescribes the special case compare<const char*> for the compare template. The template<> prefix indicates a specialization that requires no formal template argument. And the

`<const char*>` after the function name means "use this specialization when the template argument to bsearch is `const char*`". This specialization can be written in the short form:

```
template<>                          // short-form specialization
int compare(const char* a, const char* b)
{   return strcmp(a, b);   }
```

because the `<const char*>` part can be deduced from the argument types. To completely handle `char*`, we also need

```
template<>
int compare(char* a, char* b)
{   return strcmp(a, b);   }
```

If one wishes, another specialization can be added to handle comparison of pointers in general:

```
template<typename T>
int compare(T* a, T* b)
{   if ( a == b || *a == *b ) return 0;
    else if ( *a > *b ) return 1;
    else return -1;
}
```

When resolving a call to compare, the more specialized version is used. Thus, comparing C-style strings is not handled by the general pointer version here.

Template Function Call Resolution   A function template generates a set of functions with the same name. The set can be further overloaded with individual nontemplate functions or even additional function templates. For example,

```
template <typename T>
T abs(T a)                                        // (1)
{   return (a > 0 ? a : -a);   }

#include <complex>
template <typename T>
double abs(complex<T> c)                          // (2)
{   return c.abs();   }
```

Here the template on line (2) is *more specialized* than that on line (1) because any call that matches (2) also matches (1) but *not conversely*.

When resolving a function call in the presence of template and ordinary functions with the same name, the compiler tries to find a best match. Among equally good matches, preference is given to the *nontemplate* versions. Specifically, these steps are used:

1. Add to the normal set of candidate functions any template functions (at most one from each different function template) that can be instantiated from the current call. Among the candidate template functions, if one is from a more specialized template than another, drop the less specialized one from consideration.
2. Find the best-match candidate functions as described in Section 3.7 with the condition that template arguments must be passed without promotions or conversions. If exactly one best-match is found, call that function.
3. If a template function and a regular function are equally good matches, call the regular function.
4. Otherwise (no match or multiple good matches), the function call is an error.

Thus, we can replace selected template functions with specialized individual versions that override their template function counterparts. We often do this when we want to handle special cases or increase code efficiency.

Note that optional arguments and variable-length arguments are generally not supported under function templates.

10.3 CLASS TEMPLATES

Templates can also make classes generic and useful in a wide variety of situations. One important application of a class template is establishing generic container classes such as vectors, lists, ordered sequences, and hash tables. A class template simply involves a template header followed by a normal class definition.

Class Template Definition

Consider a template for n-dimensional vectors in geometry:

```
#ifndef VectorND_SEEN__
#define VectorND_SEEN__
///////    VectorND.h    ///////
// n dimensional vector of type T elements

template <typename T, int n>              // template parameters
class VectorND
```

```
{   friend VectorND<T,n> operator*<T,n>    // friend syntax   (1)
           (int m, const VectorND<T,n>& v);
  public:
    VectorND() { }                          // default constructor
    explicit VectorND (T v0);               // init elements to v0
    explicit VectorND (T v[n]);             // init elements by array
    T& operator[](int i);                   // index notation, i >= 1
    const T& operator[](int i) const;       // read-only access
    T inner(const VectorND<T,n>& v) const;  // inner product
    VectorND<T,n> operator +(const VectorND<T,n> v) const;
    void display() const;
/* other members */
  private:
    T vec[n];                               // internal array of type T  (2)
};

//// function prototypes
template <typename T, int n>                                         // (3)
VectorND<T,n> operator*(int m, const VectorND<T,n>& v);

template <typename T, int n>                                         // (4)
VectorND<T,n> operator*(const VectorND<T,n>& v, int m);
```

The once-only header construct is explicitly shown here because it is indispensable for class templates. The practice has long been recommended, however, for *all header files*.

Friend declarations in templates use the function specialization notation (line 1). Template prototypes for nonmember functions are also given in the header file (lines 3 and 4).

The template parameter n allows us to use static allocation for the internal array vec (line 2). The class template defines a set of *template classes*, each of which is denoted by VectorND<*T, n*>. For example,

```
VectorND<int,2>     iv(0);      // 2-dimensional int vector
VectorND<double,3>  dv1(0.0);   // 3-dimensional double vector
VectorND<float,16>  dv2(0.0);   // 16-dimensional float vector
```

The value passed to the template parameter n must be a constant expression of a type that matches the declared type of n exactly (without nontrivial conversions).

Member functions are, as usual, defined in a separate file, which begins with the constructor:

```
///////    VectorND.C    ///////
#include <iostream>
#include <stdlib.h>
```

10.3 CLASS TEMPLATES

```
#include "VectorND.h"

template <typename T, int n>
VectorND<T,n>::VectorND(T a[n])    // constructor for VectorND<T,n>
{   for ( int i=0 ; i < n ; i++ )
        vec[i] = a[i];
}
```

The scope operator `VectorND<T,n>::` puts the constructor in the scope of the template class `VectorND<T,n>`. We can similarly define the `operator+()` member:

```
template <typename T, int n>
VectorND<T,n>          // return type
VectorND<T,n>::operator+(const VectorND<T,n>& a) const
{    VectorND<T,n> ans;
     for ( int i=0 ; i < n ; i++ )
         ans.vec[i] = a.vec[i] + vec[i];
     return ans;
}
```

Normal vector subscript notation is supported by

```
template <typename T, int n>
T& VectorND<T,n>::operator [](int i)    // base 1 indexing
{  if ( i > 0 && i <= n )
      return vec[i-1];                  // internal base 0 indexing
   else
   {  cerr << "VectorND index out of range" << endl;
      exit(1);
   }
}
```

which returns a reference `T&`. Component access for a read-only `VectorND` is also supported by the same `operator[]` code with the function header replaced by

```
const T& VectorND<T,n>::operator [](int i) const
```

As these examples show, the only differences between a template member function and an ordinary member function are the template header and the template class name (`VectorND<T,n>`).

Integer-vector multiplication functions serve as examples for unattached function tempates associated to a class:

```
template <typename T, int n>      // a friend of VectorND<T,n>
VectorND<T,n>  operator*(int m, const VectorND<T,n>& v)
{    VectorND<T,n> ans;
```

```
            for (int i=0; i<n; i++) ans.vec[i] = v.vec[i]*m;
            return ans;
    }

    template <typename T, int n>      // no friend status
    VectorND<T,n>  operator*(const VectorND<T,n>& v, int m)
    {     return m*v;   }
```

Now let's put the VectorND class template to use:

```
///////      testVectorND.C     ///////
#include <iostream>
#include "VectorND.h"
using std::cout; using std::endl;

int main()
{   VectorND<double,3> dv1, dv2;                // VectorND objects
    for ( int i=1 ; i <= 3 ; i++ )              // assign to components
    {     dv1[i] = i/2.0;
          dv2[i] = -i/4.0;
    }
    VectorND<double,3> dv = dv1 + dv2;          // operator+
    dv.display(); cout << endl;
    double in = dv1.inner(dv2);
    cout << "inner product = " << in << endl;
    dv = 10*dv;                                 // int*VectorND
    dv.display(); cout << endl;
    return 0;
}
```

The complete example can be found in the code package (ex10/VectorND/).

The pair Template

As another example of template definition, let's look at the Standard Library template pair in <utility>:

```
template<typename T1, typename T2>
class pair
{ public:
    typedef T1 first_type;                      // type names
    typedef T2 second_type;
    pair() : first(T1()), second(T2()) {}       // default constructor
    pair(const T1& a, const T2& b)              //                      (1)
      : first(a), second(b) {}
```

10.3 CLASS TEMPLATES

```
    template <typename U1, typename U2>   // member template (2)
        pair(const pair<U1, U2>& p)        // copy or convert
        : first(p.first), second(p.second)
        { }
    T1 first;
    T2 second;
};
```

A pair stores two elements, first and second.

```
pair<string, int> p1("age", 8);    // uses constructor on line 1
pair<string, double> p2;           // uses default constructor
```

The constructor notation $T()$ gives the default value for type T. When T is a primitive type, the value is 0 converted to that type. The *primitive-type constructor* notation is especially useful in template writing. Thus, first and second in p2 are initialized to the empty string and 0.0, the default values of the respective types.

The element types in pair are given as the in-template typedefs first_type and second_type, accessible using the notation:

```
pair<string, int>::first_type
```

The copy/conversion constructor (line 2) allows initialization of one type pair by another, as long as the element types can be converted.

```
pair<string, double> p3(p1);    // ("age", 8.0)
```

Pairs are useful for functions returning two values instead of just one. They are also used to store associations in the C++ associative array map (Section 11.5).

Class Template Instantiation

A *template class* is a class built from a template. When the compiler encounters a template type specifier such as

```
VectorND<double,3> dv1;
```

which requires the class definition for VectorND<double,3> for the first time, it takes the given template arguments and builds a proper class definition automatically (Figure 10.2). A template type specifier (e.g., VectorND<double,3>) can be used just like an ordinary type specifier, including inside other templates.

Declaring a pointer or reference

```
VectorND<float,2> *fv2;     // no immediate template instantiation
VectorND<int,7> &iv3;       // no immediate template instantiation
```

Figure 10.2 **CLASS TEMPLATE INSTANTIATION**

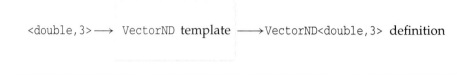

does not cause immediate class template instantiation. The instantiation is made only when the need for the class definition arises:

`iv3[2] = 0;`

Member functions of a class template are function templates with the same template header as the class. A template member function is instantiated when the compiler first sees a call to it.

10.4 TEMPLATE COMPILATION

When a file that uses a template is compiled, the compiler must have access to the template definition in order to perform any required instantiations. Standard C++ has two *template compilation models* providing two different ways to make the definition of a template available at compile time:

1. *Inclusion compilation model*: Put the template definitions in header files to be included by other files that use the template. This is the same method used for inline functions. The inclusion model is fine for short templates. But for large template files, it makes the header complicated and hard to manage.

2. *Separate compilation model*: Put template definitions in implementation files (.C) and establish header files for template declarations that are included by application files. The .C files for templates are compiled separately. This way, the file organization for templates is just like that for regular class or function files. The keyword `export` is placed in front of each template definition in the implementation file. Compilers supporting the separate compilation model make exported template definitions available, in an implementation-dependent way, for compiling application files later.

For separate compilation, in `bsearch.C`, we have

```
export template<typename T1, typename T2>      // exports template
int bsearch(T1 arr[], T2 key, int low, int high,
            int (* cmp)(T1, T2)  )
```

```
{ ...
}
```

And in `VectorND.C`, we have, for example,

```
export template <typename T, int n>     // exports template
T& VectorND<T,n>::operator [](int i)
{   ...
}
```

Now `VectorND.C` and `testVectorND.C` are separately compiled and linked. Run the program to produce the following vector display:

```
(0.5  1   1.5)(-0.25  -0.5  -0.75)
inner product = -1.75
(0.25  0.5  0.75)
```

Explicit Template Instantiation

Among C++ compilers, support for template compilation is not uniform, and some compilers still do not support the `export` keyword well or at all. If you don't want to fall back to the inclusion model, you may try the *explicit template instantiation* method. In each template implementation file (e.g., `VectorND.C`), add explicit template instantiation declarations at the end of the file. For example, the instantiation declaration

```
template
int bsearch<char*, char*>               // function explicit instantiation
   (char**, char*, int, int, int(*)(char*,char*));
```

may be placed at the end of the file `bsearch.C` to instantiate the indicated version of the `bsearch` function. And the instantiation declarations

```
template class Vector<double,3>;        // class explicit instantiation
template class Vector<int,16>;          // class explicit instantiation
```

can be placed at the end of the file `VectorND.C` to cause the instantiation of the indicated classes together with all their methods.

Compiling these `.C` files produces `.o` files that include the specified instantiations. Make sure you declare all instantiations required for your application program.

Explicit template instantiation can make compilation much faster by eliminating potential multiple instantiations of templates. Your compiler may require a command-line option and other source code file preparations to make this work. For GNU **g++**, follow these steps:

1. Include explicit template instantiations in all template implementation files.

2. Add the #pragma interface line at the beginning of each template header file.

3. Add #pragma implementation at the beginning of each template implementation (.C) file.

4. Use the *external template* compiler option for **g++**. For example,

   g++ -fexternal-templates VectorND.C testVectorND.C

Template examples in the code package contain explicit instantiation code for compilation by **g++**. See your GNU online documentation for more information.

10.5 A LIST TEMPLATE

We have already seen an implementation of a generic linked list using void* and function pointers (Section 5.12). A template provides us with a simpler alternative. The idea is straightforward: Make the value type of a list cell a type parameter. Most of the existing codes for the linked list will then stay unchanged. We only have to put them in a template setting.

Again, three classes are involved: List, a nested Iterator, and a nested slave class Cell.

```
///////   List.h   ///////
#pragma interface
#include <iostream>
using std::cout; using std::endl; using std::ostream;
// linked list template
// type T must define operator== and overload <<

template <typename T>
class List
{ class Cell;                                 // (A)
  class Iterator;
  public:
    List() : head(NULL) { }                   // empty list constructor
    List(T& c)                                // list with first cell
        : head (new Cell(c)) { }              // (B)
    Cell* last() const;                       // last cell
    Cell* find(T& c) const;                   // first value equals c
    bool substitute(T& r, T& s);              // r for first s on list
    int remove(T& c);                         // c from entire list
    void remove(Cell* cell);                  // remove given cell
```

10.5 A LIST TEMPLATE

```cpp
        int shorten(int n);                 // remove first n cells
        static T& content(Cell* p)          // (C)
            { return p->getValue(); }
        bool putOn(T& c);                   // insert in front
        bool insert(T& c, Cell* cell);      // insert after cell
        int append(T& c)                    // insert at end
            { return insert(c, last()); }
        int isEmpty() const { return head==NULL; }
        void display(Cell* p,               // display from p to end
            ostream& out=cout) const;
        void display(ostream& out=cout) const
            { display(head, out); }         // display whole list
        ~List();                            // destructor

// nested slave class
    class Cell
    {   friend class List<T>;               // (D)
        friend class List<T>::Iterator;
      public:
        T& getValue() { return val; }
        void setValue(T& v) { val = v; }
        T& val;                             // (E) ref type T
      private:
        Cell* next;
        Cell(T& c, Cell* ptr = NULL)        // (F)
            : val(c), next(ptr) {}          // constructor
    };
  private:
    static bool equal(const T&,
          const T&);                        // value equality test
    Cell* head;                             // first cell of list
    void free();                            // free all cells

// nested Iterator
  public:
    class Iterator
    {   friend class List<T>;
      public:
        Iterator& operator++();                             // (G)
        const Iterator& operator++() const;
        T& operator*() { return cur->getValue(); }
        const T& operator*() const                          // (H)
            { return cur->getValue(); }
        bool operator!=(const Iterator& b) const
```

```
                { return cur!=b.cur; }
        private:
            Iterator (Cell* c) : cur(c) {}
            Cell* cur;
    };

    typedef Iterator iterator;
    typedef const Iterator const_iterator;

    iterator begin() { return Iterator(head); }          // (I)
    const_iterator begin() const { return Iterator(head); }
    iterator end() { return Iterator(NULL); }            // (J)
    const_iterator end() const { return Iterator(NULL); }
};
```

The template version of the list class no longer involves function pointers. Instead, element comparison and display functions now depend on overloaded operators associated with the parameterized type T: *Type T must define operator== and overload <<.* The class definition is shortened here to show just a few members with various class template notations: forward nested class declaration (line A), nested class instantiation (line B), and static function (line C).

The nested Cell has List<T> and List<T>::Iterator as friend classes (line D). The Cell value val is of type T& (line E), so only a reference to type T is stored instead of a copy, which could be large since T can be any type. Note that making and storing copies should be avoided in template writing because the sizes of the parameterized types can be large. Using reference parameters in templates (line F) is thus common practice.

The nested Iterator class has List<T> as a friend. The conventional typedefs iterator and const_iterator are defined. Iterator instances can be created only by calling versions of begin() and end(). Note the implementation principle: *a const container can only return a const_iterator* (lines I and J). The * and ++ operators for List<T>::Iterator work for both types of iterators (lines G and H).

At the end of List.h, we also overload << for displaying lists.

```
template <typename T>
ostream& operator<< (ostream& out, const List<T>& list)
{   list.display(out);   return out;  }

template <typename T>
ostream& operator<< (ostream& out, const List<T>* l)
{   l->display(out);   return out;  }
```

10.5   A LIST TEMPLATE

The file `List.C` consists mostly of member functions with the added template header

`template <typename T>`

and the class scope operator `List<T>::`. A few typical definitions are shown here:

```
///////   List.C    ///////
#include "List.h"

template <typename T>
List<T>::Cell*  List<T>::last() const
{   List<T>::Cell* p = head;
    while( p && p->next ) p =  p->next;
    return p;
}

template <typename T>                                   // (i)
bool List<T>::equal(const T& r, const T& s)
{   return r==s;  }

template <typename T>
List<T>::~List() {   free();  }

template <typename T>
bool List<T>::putOn(T& c)
{   List<T>::Cell* tmp = new List<T>::Cell(c,head);
    if ( tmp ) { head = tmp;  return true; }
    else return false;      // failed
}

template <typename T>
bool List<T>::substitute(T& r, T& s)
{   for( List<T>::Cell* p = head; p ; p = p->next )
        if( equal(p->getValue(), s) )
        {   p->setValue(r);
            return true;
        }
    return false;   // s not on list
}

// display from p to end
template <typename T>
void List<T>::display(List<T>::Cell* p, ostream& out) const
```

```
{   out << "(";
    while ( p )
    {   out << p->getValue();                   // (ii)
        if ( p = p->next ) out << ", ";
    }
    out << ")";
}

template <typename T>                           // (iii-a)
List<T>::Iterator& List<T>::Iterator::operator++()
{   if ( cur != NULL ) cur = cur->next;
    return *this;
}

template <typename T>                           // (iii-b)
const List<T>::Iterator&
List<T>::Iterator::operator++() const
{   if ( cur != NULL )
         (const_cast< Iterator* >(this))->cur = cur->next;
    return *this;
}

///// explicit template instantiation
/////    --- for use by testList.C
#include "Employee.h"
template class List<Employee>;                  // (iv)

template ostream& operator<< < Employee >       // (v)
    (ostream& out, const List<Employee>& list);

template ostream& operator<< < Employee >       // (vi)
    (ostream& out, const List<Employee>* list);
```

The codes on lines i and ii show the use of overloaded operators associated with the type T. This is an advantage of the template implementation over the void* method, which requires function pointers. The ++ operators for the nested iterator are shown on lines iii-a and iii-b. Note how const_cast is used to allow incrementing a List<T>::const_iterator.

The template explicit instantiation (Section 10.4) technique is used to instantiate the List<Employee> class (line iv), the << operator for a List<Employee> object (line v), and a List<Employee>* pointer (line vi).

10.5 A LIST TEMPLATE

Applying the `List` Template

Consider manipulating lists of employees. The `List` class template makes this simple:

1. Make sure the `Employee` class has the `operator==` and overloaded `<<`.
2. Use `List<Employee>` to instantiate list objects.

We wish to experiment with a list of employees using the list template. Here is a simplified `Employee` class:

```
///////    Employee.h    ///////
#include   <iostream>
#include   <string.h>
using std::ostream; using std::cout;

class Employee
{  public:
       Employee() {}
       Employee(char* n, unsigned a, char* s)
       :   name(n), age(a), ss(s)   { }
       char* id() { return ss; }
       int operator ==(const Employee& a) const
       { return strcmp(ss, a.ss)==0; }
       void display(ostream& out = cout) const ;
   private:
       char*    name;          // full name
       unsigned age;
       char*    ss;            // social security number
       float    salary;
};

ostream& operator<< (ostream& out, const Employee& e);
ostream& operator<< (ostream& out, const Employee* e);
```

The `Employee` type has the required `operator==` and overloads the `<<` output operator. Actual overloading of `<<` is done in the implementation file:

```
///////    Employee.C    ///////
#include <iostream>
#include "Employee.h"
using std::ostream;

void Employee::display(ostream& out) const
{    out << name << "   age=" << age << "   ss=" << ss;
}
```

```
ostream& operator<< (ostream& out, const Employee& e)
{   e.display(out);
    return out;
}

ostream& operator<< (ostream& out, const Employee* e)
{   e->display(out);
    return out;
}
```

To see how employee lists are created and used and to test the `List` template, consider the following code:

```
////////    testList.C    ////////
#include <iostream>
#include "List.h"
#include "Employee.h"

int main()
{ Employee a[] = {
        Employee ("Big Mac", 39, "023441288"),
        Employee ("John Doe", 32, "083467890"),
        Employee ("Jen Sun", 24, "123451282"),
        Employee ("Joe Dregs", 27, "223451228"),
        Employee ("Yu Hong", 28, "323452128"),
        Employee ("Sam Smith", 29, "423415228") };

    List<Employee> weekly( a[1] );
    weekly.putOn( a[3] );    weekly.putOn( a[5] );
    cout<< weekly << endl;

    weekly.putOn( a[0] );    weekly.putOn( a[2] );
    weekly.append( a[4] );   cout<< weekly << endl;

    weekly.remove( a[4]);    weekly.remove( a[0] );
    cout<< weekly << endl;

    weekly.shorten(3);   cout<< weekly << endl;
    weekly.shorten(1);   cout<< weekly << endl;
    return 0;
}
```

Here `Employee` objects, through reference parameters, are put on the list. Just as easily, `Employee*` pointers can be put on the list:

```
List<Employee *> weekly( a+1 );
```

To put copies, not the objects themselves, on the list, copying can always be done first:

```
Employee copy = a[1];
weekly.putOn( copy );
```

Standard C++ supplies a built-in `list` class template for a doubly linked list (Section 11.2).

10.6 CLASS TEMPLATE SPECIALIZATION

The `List` template works for many built-in and all user-defined types with properly overloaded == and << operators. However, some cases require more than simply using List<*type*>. Consider List<char*>, for example. Since it is impossible to overload == for the type char*, certain list operations, such as substitute(), will work incorrectly because of how the member equal is defined (line i).

This difficulty can be overcome with the template specialization mechanism. If the following member template function

```
template<>               // specialize template member function
bool List<char*>::equal(char* const &r, char* const &s)
{   return (! strcmp(r,s));   }
```

is defined before List<char*> is used, then it overrides the template-supplied member function of the same exact signature. One or a few member functions — even the entire class — can be redefined for particular type values to make things work correctly or more efficiently.

The reason the `List` template had the equal() function in the first place was to allow the abovementioned specialization. It is not a bad idea to include the specialized List<char*>::equal() at the end of the file List.C.

10.7 DERIVED-CLASS TEMPLATE

For an example of class templates involving derivation, consider an implementation of Stack<T>, a template class derived from List<T>:

```
///////    Stack.h    ///////
#include "List.h"

template <typename T>
class Stack : private List<T>             // private is optional
{ public:
```

```
    Stack() { }                          // default constructor
    Stack(T& z) { putOn(z); }            // constructor
    bool push(T& z) { return putOn(z); } // push reference z
    bool top(T& z) const;                // returns false if failed
    bool pop();                          // returns false if failed
    using List<T>::isEmpty;              // make isEmpty visible
};
```

Obviously, transforming the Stack class in Section 7.6 into a template is almost a mechanical procedure. The pop() requires special attention for correct error handling. It returns false as a failure indication and puts the popped item in the reference parameter.

```
///////    Stack.C    ///////
#pragma implementation
#include "Stack.h"

template <typename T>
bool Stack<T>::top(T& z) const
{   if ( isEmpty() ) return false;   // pop failed
    z = *begin();
    return true;                     // pop succeeded
}

template <typename T>
bool Stack<T>::pop()
{   if ( isEmpty() ) return false;   // pop failed
    shorten(1);                      // stack popped
    return true;                     // pop succeeded
}

// explicit template instantiation for use in testStack.C
template class Stack<char*>;
```

When the Stack template is instantiated (e.g., with Stack<char*>), it also causes instantiation of the base template class List<char*> if it has not been instantiated already.

To see how the Stack template is used, consider the following simple test program:

```
///////    testStack.C    ///////
#include <iostream>
#include "Stack.h"
using std::cout; using std::endl;

int main()
{   char* a[] = {"aa","bb","cc","dd","ee","ff"};
```

10.7 DERIVED-CLASS TEMPLATE

```
        Stack<char*> mystack(a[1]);
        mystack.push(a[3]);
        mystack.push(a[5]);
        char* s;
        while ( mystack.top(s) )
        {    cout << s << " ";
             mystack.pop();
        }
        cout << endl;
        return 0;
}
```

Run the program to produce the following output:

`ff dd bb`

With `Stack<T>`, other types of stacks should be just as easy to handle.

C++ I/O Templates

As stated earlier, Standard C++ supports both ASCII and wide character I/O. The I/O stream library is actually organized as a hierarchy of class templates allowing the instantiation of I/O classes supporting any well-defined character sets. The template basic_xyz gives rise to the ASCII stream xyz. For example, the class istream is a typedef for

`basic_istream<char>`

Figure 10.3 shows the I/O stream class template hierarchy.

Figure 10.3 I/O STREAM TEMPLATE HIERARCHY

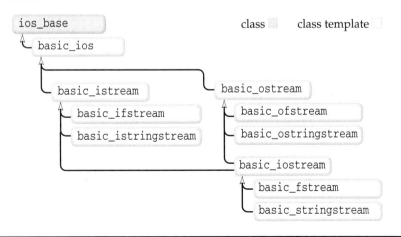

10.8 A GENERIC HASH TABLE

A *hash table* is an ingenious method to store and retrieve data that avoids sorting and searching and provides direct random access to the items stored. By applying a combination of OOP techniques, we will implement a hash table template for all types of records.

Basic Concepts

A hash table stores a data item, called a *record*, by taking a part of the record, known as a *key*, and computing an index from it. The index determines where in the hash table a particular record is stored or retrieved. For instance, the name part of an address record can be a key that is transformed into an integer index by, say, adding the integer representation of its characters together.

The action of turning a key into an integer index is called *hashing*. A *hash function* takes a key and computes an integer index called the *hash code* whose value lies in the proper range. The hash function is designed to give different hash codes for different keys, but this cannot be guaranteed. Normally, there is a chance of two different keys producing the same hash code. When this happens, we say that the two records have *collided*.

The linked list offers a good solution to the problem of collision: The hash table entries are linked lists, and records with the same hash code are stored in the same linked list, located at the hash address. If the hash table is large enough and if the hash function is well designed, collision should occur infrequently, and the linked lists are kept very short.

Thus, when properly used, the hash table offers a data organization in which most records are accessible directly at their hash code location. Only once in a while will a sequential search down a very short list be necessary to locate a record. With the hash table, the need to keep records in sorted order is avoided entirely. Adding new records and removing old ones are simple operations that do not involve reordering or other time-consuming operations.

A Hash Table Template

Since the hash table is so ingenious, we should apply it wherever appropriate. Thus, it would be very convenient if a template HashTable is defined to allow codes such as

```
HashTable<Rate> rateTable(size);
HashTable<Employee> thirdShift(size);
```

10.8 A GENERIC HASH TABLE

The `HashTable` supports several basic operations:

1. Adding a record.
2. Retrieving a record matching a given key.
3. Removing a record.
4. Inquiring whether a record is already on the hash table.
5. Finding the number of records contained on the table.

These are reflected by the public interface of `HashTable`:

```
///////    HashTable.h    ///////
#include "List.h"

template <typename T>
class HashTable
{ public:
    typedef char* (* KEY_FN)(T&);    // client-supplied key function
    enum {H_MULT=2640025017u};       // default multiplier
    HashTable(KEY_FN fn, unsigned k = 8,    // constructor
              unsigned m = H_MULT);
    void put(T& a);                       // enters record a
    bool get(const char *key, T& r);      // returns record in r
    bool rid(const char* key);            // removes record
    bool isOn(char* key) const;           // is record on table?
    unsigned length() const { return len; }
                                          // returns length of table
    ~HashTable();
  private:
    List<T>** ht;                         // table of linked lists
    KEY_FN getkey;                        // key function
    unsigned hash(const char*) const;     // built-in hash function
    bool onList(List<T>& l,               // is record on list l?
                char* key) const;
    unsigned len;                         // no. of entries on table
    unsigned mult;                        // hash multiplier
    unsigned bits;                        // hash table 2^bits
};
```

Internally, a pointer array ht is used whose entries point to linked lists that store the records (Figure 10.4). Unused entries of ht contain NULL pointers.

The size of the dynamically allocated pointer array ht should be set depending on how many records the hash table is expected to handle. If we expect up to 500 records, a size slightly larger (say, 600 to 700) can be used to reduce the chance of collisions.

Figure 10.4 A HASH TABLE

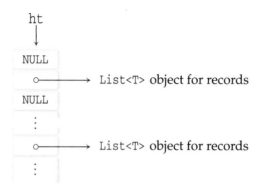

When a hash table object is established, two arguments are passed to the constructor:

1. k: The table size is set to 2^k or a default of 256. Keeping the size a power of 2 makes hashing much easier.
2. m: The *multiplier* m is used in the internal hash function to produce the hash code. The default multiplier is a good choice.

The key is assumed to be a character string, and a HashTable<T> object is instantiated with a key extraction function (of type KEY_FN), stored as getkey, that can be called to obtain a key from any record of type T. This function can always transform any nonstring key into a string by turning bytes into characters.

Hash Table Implementation

The constructor initializes bits, mult, and len:

```
///////    HashTable.C    ///////
#include <iostream>
#include <string.h>
#include <limits.h>
#include "HashTable.h"

template <typename T>
HashTable<T>::HashTable
(KEY_FN fn, unsigned k /* =8 */, unsigned m /* =H_MULT */)
 : getkey(fn), bits(k), mult(m), len(0)
{   int size = 1 << bits;
```

10.8 A GENERIC HASH TABLE

```
        ht = new List<T>*[size];
        for ( int i = 0; i < size; i++ ) ht[i] = NULL;
}
```

It also allocates the pointer array (`List<T>** ht`) and initializes all entries to NULL. The destructor frees each list pointer, triggering the list class destructor. Then, the `ht` pointer array is freed:

```
template <typename T>
HashTable<T>::~HashTable()
{   int size = 1 << bits;
    for ( int i = 0; i < size; i++ )
        if ( ht[i] ) delete(ht[i]);      // triggers List<T>::~List()
    delete(ht);
}
```

Now let's examine the design of the private member function `hash()`, which produces a hash code from any given character string key. The hashing is done in two stages:

1. Convert the character string into an `unsigned int`.
2. Randomize the `unsigned int` into a hash table index.

The file scope function `str_to_u` takes a string and converts it into an `unsigned int` value. This is done by treating the string as a sequence of `unsigned int` quantities and multiplying them together with a selected constant — 7u here:

```
static unsigned str_to_u(const char *str)
{       unsigned value = 7u;
        char c;
        while ( (c = *str) != '\0' )
        {       value *= c;
                str++;
        }
        return value;
}
```

The actual hash index is then produced by `unsigned` multiplication of the value produced by `str_to_u()` with the hash multiplier `mult` and right-shifting the result so that only `bits` of its leading bits remain. The hash code thus produced is random and falls within the proper range:

```
#include <limits.h>

template <typename T>
unsigned HashTable<T>::hash(const char* key) const
{       unsigned val = 0;
```

```
            val = str_to_int(key);
            return( (val*mult) >> (CHAR_BIT*sizeof(unsigned) - bits));
      }
```

The symbolic constant CHAR_BIT, usually 8, is defined in <limits.h>. There is much depth to the selection of the hash multiplier.[1] The one used here is based on *Fibonacci hashing* and should work well for all 32-bit computers.

Hash Table Operations
The private function hash() is used by the public members put(), get(), and rid(). The member put() enters a record into the hash table:

```
template <typename T>
void HashTable<T>::put(T& r)           // enter record r
{     char *key = getkey(r);            // obtain hash key
      unsigned hc = hash(key);          // compute hash code
      List<T>* l = ht[hc];
      if ( l == NULL )                  // location not used before  (1)
      {  ht[hc] = new List<T>(r);       // make a new list
         len++; return;
      }
      if ( ! onList(*l, key) )          // if not already on list    (2)
      { len++;  l->putOn(r); }          // put record on list
      return;
}
```

To enter a record r, its hash code hc is computed first. If the pointer ht[hc] is NULL, then r is put on a new list, and the address of the new list is assigned to ht[hc] (line 1). Otherwise, collision occurred, and r is put on the existing list if it is not already on that list (line 2). Note that since onList() is a static member function within a template, it is shared by all instances of HashTable<T> for any specific type T.

The member rid() removes a record from the hash table:

```
template <typename T>
bool HashTable<T>::rid(const char* key)
{     unsigned code = hash(key);
      List<T>* a = ht[code];
      if ( !a ) return false;
      T val;
      List<T>::Iterator it = a->begin();         // (3)
      for (; it != a->end(); ++it)
      {  val = *it;
```

---

[1] See D. E. Knuth, *The Art of Computer Programming* (Reading, MA: Addison-Wesley, 1973), vol. 3.

```
            if ( strcmp (key, getkey(val)) == 0 )
            {   a->remove(val);   len--;
                if ( a->isEmpty() )
                    ht[code] = NULL;                    // (4)
                return true;
            }
        }
        return false;
    }
```

A list iterator object is used to find the target entry (line 3). After a record is removed, the pointer is reset to NULL if the list of records becomes empty (line 4).

The retrieval function `get()` is similar:

```
template <typename T>
bool HashTable<T>::get(const char* key, T& rval)
{   List<T>* a = ht[hash(key)];
    if ( !a ) return false;
    T val;
    List<T>::Iterator it = a->begin();
    for (; it != a->end(); ++it)
    {   val = *it;
        if ( strcmp (key, getkey(val)) == 0 )
        {   rval = val;
            return true;       // entry found
        }
    }
    return false;              // not found
}
```

The function returns the entry matching the given `key` in the `rval` parameter. It returns `false` if the requested entry is not found. With these codes, other member functions are easy to write.

The explicit instantiation

```
#include "Employee.h"
template class HashTable<Employee>;
```

can be placed at the end of the file `HashTable.C` for experimenting with a hash table of employees described next.

Using the Hash Table Template

Now let's use the hash table template for a table of `Employee`. The source code files involved are

- `Employee.h` and `Employee.C` for employee objects (Section 10.5).
- `List.h` and `List.C` for the list template (Section 10.5).

- HashTable.h and HashTable.C for the hash table template.
- testHashTable.C for the application.

To test the hash table template, consider the following code:

```
///////    testHashTable.C    ///////
#include <iostream>
#include "HashTable.h"
#include "Employee.h"
using std::cout; using std::endl;

char* empId(Employee& e)       // getkey function
{   return e.id();      }

int main()
{    Employee a("Big Mac", 39, "023441288");
     Employee b("John Doe", 32, "083467890");
     Employee c("Jen Sun", 24, "123451282");
     Employee d("Joe Dregs", 27, "223451228");
     Employee e("Yu Hong", 28, "323452128");
     Employee f("Sam Smith", 29, "423415228");
     Employee z;
  // very small hash table for testing
     HashTable<Employee> ht(empId, 1);
     ht.put( b ); ht.put( a ); ht.put( c );
     ht.put( d ); ht.put( e ); ht.put( f );
     if ( ht.get("333415228", z) )
         cout << z << endl;
     else
         cout << "333415228 not found" << endl;
     ht.rid(empId(a));
     if ( ! ht.isOn(empId(a)) )
         cout << "023441288 not found" << endl;
     if ( ht.get("083467890", z) ) cout << z << endl;
     else
         cout << "083467890 not found" << endl;
     cout << ht.length() << "=len"<< endl;
     ht.rid(empId(d)); ht.rid(empId(e));
     cout << ht.length() << "=len"<< endl;
     return 0;
}
```

The complete example can be found in ex10/hash/ of the code package. Compile and run this program to produce the following output:

```
333415228 not found
023441288 not found
```

```
John Doe   age=32   ss=083467890
5=len
3=len
```

10.9 GENERIC PROGRAMMING APPROACHES

Genericness in programming can be achieved through void *, templates, and polymorphism. These approaches have their strengths and weaknesses.

Template Versus `void*`

The combining of void* and functional arguments can make programs generic. The technique depends on the conversion of void* pointers to pointers of known types, usually through function calls. Applying such a program for new types of data often means supplying the right functions with the desired type conversions. The scheme forces the use of pointers, even for primitive types. For example, a void*-based arbitrary list (Section 5.12) handles ints or doubles only through int* or double*, which is, of course, less efficient.

The template mechanism avoids many of the abovementioned problems by building a new function or class for each new application. Thus, a template function or class can be just as efficient as a regular function or class. The C++ built-in container classes such as list and set demonstrate the usefulness of templates. However, the template approach, as it currently stands, has these drawbacks:

1. Template definitions (source code) must be made available to compile application programs. Otherwise, explicit prior instantiations must be made for all template instances used in the applications. Such explicit instantiations become impractical for commercial template libraries.
2. A template duplicates many similar functions among multiple instantiations and can make a program much larger than necessary.
3. Support for templates, especially the export construct, is not uniform across C++ compilers yet. Thus, template codes may require special attention for compilation and can have portability problems.

These shortcomings are not present for the void* method. On the other hand, nontype parameters provide a degree of freedom for templates unavailable under any other technique. The two approaches can complement each other. For example, to avoid generating duplicated codes, a container class template can have a pointer specialization that uses a void* implementation to avoid duplication.

Polymorphism Versus Template and `void*`

Consider the ordered sequence example: `OrderedSeq` abstract class, and the derived `DateSeq`, `TextLineSeq` classes (Section 9.4). It demonstrates the combination of `void*` and polymorphism to achieve genericness. It is an interesting exercise to redesign and reimplement this facility using the template technique. The `Ordered` template is instantiated with a key type and a value type

Ordered< *key_type*, *value_type* >

enabling you to use Ordered< Date, Date > and Ordered< Name, Address> directly.

Polymorphism depends on type relations under class derivation and the virtual function mechanism to achieve genericness among a set of objects related by the is_a relationship. It goes beyond *writing type-independent code* to *organizing code common to an object category*. Rather than operating on completely unknown types, as in the `void*` and `template` approaches, polymorphic programs operate effectively knowing key behaviors common to an extensible hierarchy of objects.

Polymorphism does not instantiate from source code as templates, and it does not depend on separately defined functions for behavior as does the `void *` approach. We can say that polymorphism is much more object-oriented.

Polymorphism does not automatically cover all types as the other two approaches do. Some OO languages remedy this by defining a *catchall* class from which all other classes are automatically derived. The `object` class in Java is an example. Thus, an `object` reference (or pointer) acts much like a `void*`. Primitive types can have class wrappers, such as `string` as a wrapper for `char *`, so they can also be treated as `object`s.

Because templates can be derived, it is possible to have polymorphic templates, thus combining the powers of these two techniques.

Perhaps this is the most important difference. Polymorphism allows generic programs to use common behaviors of acceptable objects and automatically regulates which objects are plug-compatible types. On the other hand, the template and `void*` approaches generally only allow generic operations independent of the unknown types. Even if you attach conditions on the acceptable types, a compiler cannot guarantee that a parameterized type conforms to the conditions. Hence, the latter are usually restricted to building containers.

10.10 SUMMARY

The C++ template facility supports type parameterization for writing generic programs. There may still be variation in template support among C++ compilers.

Generally, both function and class templates can be written. The template header specifies a list of template formal parameters within angle brackets, and its scope extends to the end of the immediately following declaration or definition. A template may have type and nontype parameters. The keyword `typename` or `class` declares type parameters, and a type parameter can be used just like an ordinary type name within the template code.

For function templates, each template parameter must appear at least once in the function signature. A function template defines a potentially unbounded set of overloaded functions. The first call to a template-made function instantiates the template and defines the function. A function can be overloaded in the ordinary way and have one or more template definitions supplying additional instances. The C++ compiler follows specific rules in resolving calls to such functions.

A template class name takes a form such as `VectorND<double,16>` and can be used wherever a normal type name is used. Encountering a new template class type triggers the instantiation of the required class from the template. Member functions of a template class are instantiated when first called. Template functions and classes can be *specialized* by supplying explicit definitions for particular cases. Template specializations can fix difficult cases or increase the efficiency of a template.

Template, `void*`, and polymorphism have their strengths and weaknesses as generic programming techniques. They can also complement one another when used in combination.

EXERCISES

1. The template facility of C++ may not be supported uniformly by all versions of C++ compilers. Check your compiler to see whether this feature is implemented. In particular, check your compiler to see if/how it supports the *separate compilation model*.

2. Write a function template for `swap()` used in sorting.

3. Consider the following code:

```
#include <iostream>
using std::cout; using std::endl;

template <typename T1, typename T2>
T2 myFunc(T1 x, T2 y) { return x-y; }

int funCall(int a, int b)
{
   return myFunc(a, b);        // calls myFunc
}

int myFunc(int y, int x)       // redefines myFunc
{   return x+y; }

int main()
{   cout << funCall(9,6) << endl;
    cout << myFunc(7,11) << endl;
    return 0;
}
```

Would this code compile successfully? If it runs, what output would you expect? Explain.

4. Write a function template `toString` that takes an argument of any type and returns a `string` object that contains the string representation of the argument. For example, `toString(pi)` where `pi` is a `double` would produce a `string` object with `"3.1416159"` in it. (*Hint*: It works with any type that can be displayed with `<<`.)

5. Write a template function `fromString` that takes a reference argument `ans` of any type and a `string`. It would read the string and produce a value in `ans`. (*Hint*: It works with any type that can be read with `>>`.)

6. Consider the specialized template function `compare` in Section 10.2. If instead of a specialized template function, we define it as a regular function

```
int compare(const char* a, const char* b)
{   return strcmp(a, b);   }
```

What would be the difference?

CHAPTER 10 EXERCISES

7. Consider automatically allocating two-dimensional arrays of any type (see Section 4.13). Write a class template

   ```
   template <typename T>
   class Array2D;
   ```

   that dynamically allocates/deallocates a two-dimensional array to store elements of type T. Array2D can be used as follows:

   ```
   Array2d<double> d_arr(m, n);   // m x n array of doubles
   d_arr.at(i,j)                  // checks range and gets element at (i,j)
   d_arr.at(i,j) = 3.14;          // checks range and sets element at (i,j)
   ```

8. Is there an easy way to declare all instances of a certain function template to be friends of a class? Of all classes derived from a template?

9. Consider the list of employees in Section 10.5. Write a test program that displays every other employee on a list using an iterator.

10. Consider a generic Stack. Write a template class Stack by deriving from the C++ Library template class vector. Pay attention to the efficiency of the push and pop operations.

11. Suppose you want to establish a list of dimension-16 double vectors. How would you do this with the List and the VectorND templates?

12. Does your C++ compiler allow operators to be defined as templates? Can templates be written for inline and static functions? (*Hint*: Experiment.)

13. Take the VectorND class template and improve it by having its operator[] members throw an exception rather than exiting.

14. Does the sizeof operator work with template formal types?

15. Consider template class specialization. The list template in Section 10.5 depends on the overloaded << for display. Does this work for all types T? If not, what types would cause difficulty? How do you propose to fix it?

16. Take the test program for the hash table template (Section 10.8) and modify it for a hash table of text lines as character strings.

17. Write a more complicated test program for the hash table template that involves more than one type of hash table.

18. Follow the str_to_u() example and write a function template

    key_to_u(T key, int len)

    that takes a key of any type and of size len and computes an unsigned result. Also explain why str_to_u() is implemented as a file scope function instead of as a member function.

19. Add operator[] to the HashTable template using a key as the index. Define a version for rvalue use and another for lvalue use.

20. Add an iterator and associated typedefs to the HashTable template.

CHAPTER ELEVEN

Standard Containers

Containers are objects that store data elements and provide for their manipulation. Arrays, lists, stacks, vectors, trees, and hash tables are examples we have seen. A *generic container* can store data of any type and be useful in many applications.

Standard C++ offers a variety of generic containers together with related facilities to make them useful. The genericness is achieved through templates, and the library is known as the *Standard Template Library* (STL). The standard containers are convenient and can simplify many routine programming tasks. Generic algorithms work on any compatible containers through standardized *iterators* that behave like pointers to values in a container. Further, the STL provides functors (function objects) that work together with generic algorithms.

The *offset pointer to member* (opm) is a *variable member name* facility for additional program flexibility. The declaration, assignment, and dereference of opms (with .* and ->*) are clearly described in this chapter. Offset pointers to member functions can also be adapted as functors. Examples show their power and utility.

11.1 THE STL

The STL is part of the C++ Standard Library (Chapter 6). The centerpiece of the STL is a set of generic *sequence containers* (one-dimensional sequence of values) and *associative containers* (values stored and accessed by keys). The special-purpose containers `stack`, `queue`, and `priority_queue` are *container adaptors* that can use an internal implementation of any user-specified container as long as that container supports certain necessary operations.

Major parts of the STL are:

- *Containers*: Class templates and associated function templates that generate classes and functions to store and manipulate elements of any type, including
  - sequence containers: `vector`, `deque`, and `list`
  - container adopters: `stack`, `queue`, and `priority_queue`

Figure 11.1 ALGORITHM-CONTAINER INTERFACES

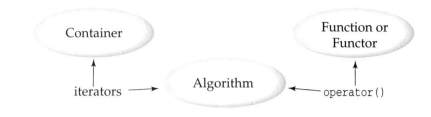

- sorted associative containers: set, multiset, map, and multimap
- hashed associative containers: hash_set, hash_multiset, hash_map, and hash_multimap

- *Iterators*: Container-supplied types that behave like pointers to values and allow systematic visits to the stored elements
- *Generic algorithms*: Function templates that apply familiar procedures such as searching and sorting to any container through its iterators, possibly using user-supplied functions or *functors*
- *Functors*: Function objects, taking one or two arguments, that can be given to generic algorithms that apply them to any given container

The iterators follow a well-designed convention (Section 8.6) to allow the generic algorithms to work on any container. Thus, iterators serve as glue to hold the containers and algorithms together. And the application operator operator() allows algorithms to use any user-supplied function or functor (Figure 11.1). Each of these topics is outlined and illustrated with practical examples. The material provides a starting point for exploring the many facilities in the STL.

11.2 STANDARD CONTAINER HEADERS

As part of the Standard Library, the STL is in the std namespace. You include an appropriate header file to use a container:

- <vector> header: vector< *T* > vec; Gives a one-dimensional, dynamically growing array of type *T*. We have seen a good number of vector operations in Section 4.6 and in the TextLines example (Section 4.7). Additional operations include:
  - vec[*i*]: Accesses element *i* as rvalue or lvalue without range check.

- vec.**at**(*i*): Accesses element with range check; throws out_of_range exception.
- vec.**back**() and vec.**front**(): Accesses first and last element (as lvalue or rvalue).
- vec1 == vec2: Returns true if the vectors have the same size and == elements.
- vec1 < vec2: Returns true if vec1 is less than vec2 in the lexicographical sense.

- <deque> header: deque< *T* > dq; Gives a *double-ended queue* with optimized operations at the front and the back. It basically offers the same operations as vector and adds **front**(), **push_front**(), and **pop_front**().

- <list> header: list< *T* > l; Gives a doubly linked list that is efficient for element insertions and deletions. A list provides most vector operations (no indexing) and adds the following:
  - **push_front**(const *T*& x), **pop_front**()
  - **splice**(iterator it, list& x, p1, p2): Inserts a list x, or part of it, into the host list at point it (and removing the elements from their source list x), where it. The optional p1, p2 are list iterators to indicate a sublist of x.
  - **sort**() and **sort**(fn): Sorts the host list into ascending order using < (or the given predicate fn) to compare the elements.
  - **merge**(x): Merges the list x, removing all its elements, into the host list. Both lists must already be in sorted order.

- <stack> header: stack< *T* > stk; Gives a stack, based on a deque by default, that offers **size**(), **pop**(), **top**(), **push**(const *T*& x), and the **empty**() check. Note that **pop**() does not return any value.

- <queue> header: queue< *T* > q; Gives a first-in/first-out structure, based on a deque by default, that offers **size**(), **push**(const *T*& x) at back, **pop**() off front, **back**() and **front**() (both as lvalue or rvalue), and the **empty**() check. Further, priority_queue< *T* > pq(*comp*); gives a queue where the priorities of the elements are sorted in decreasing ordered by the given less-than functor *comp* (or < by default). The largest element is at the head of the queue. For a priority queue, **front**() (**pop**()) returns (removes) the element with the highest priority.

- <map> header: map< *T* > ar; Gives a sorted associative array to store and retrieve elements using keys of any type. Elements are stored as key-value pairs in increasing key order (given by a predicate object). All keys are distinct. See Section 11.5 for more details and an example. The header also provides `multimap`, which allows multiple entries with the same key.

- `<set>` header: `set< T > s;` Is like a `map` with keys being the values. So a `set` stores values in sorted order and supports efficient set membership operations (Sectior 11.8).

Of these containers, `vector` and `map` are typical. Once you understand how these work, the other containers are similar. Examples of `vector` usage can be found in Sections 4.7 and 9.4. We discuss `map` in Section 11.5.

In addition to the containers already listed, there are also `<bitset>` for an array of bits (`bool`). The `<hash_map>` and `<hash_set>` headers supply hash table versions of map and set (`hash_map, hash_multimap, hash_set, hash_multiset`). Appendix L lists all header files available.

Containers such as `set` and `priority_queue` and generic algorithms such as **sort** use a function (or function object) for ordering, priority, or other purposes. Function objects are discussed in Section 11.9.

11.3 EFFICIENCY OF SEQUENCE CONTAINERS

A strength of STL containers is the near uniform interface of the container classes. As a result, a program using `vectors` can use `lists` with almost no modification. The freedom to change the underlying data structure for a program is very attractive.

The sequence containers `vector`, `deque`, and `list` are characterized by operations they support most efficiently. Understanding the characteristics will help you choose which one to use in your application.

Vectors support fast random access to sequences of varying length and fast insertion and deletions at the end. Use `vector` if speed of random access is most important and if few insert/delete operations, other than at the end, are needed. Insertion/deletion at the beginning cost $O(n)$ (proportional to the length of the sequence).

Deques provide constant time insertion/deletion at both ends and constant time random access (with a larger constant than `vector`).

Lists are more efficient for insertion/deletion in the middle of the sequence. But random access becomes $O(n)$. However, iterating up/down a list is supported well.

We have already seen examples using `vectors` (Section 4.7). Now let's look at an application of `stack`.

11.4 USING stack

Consider the problem of detecting if all the parentheses are properly balanced within a document or a sequence of characters. For our example, let's assume round, square, and angle brackets are present:

```
( [ ] ) < >     balanced
())             not balanced
(<)>            not balanced
><              not balanced
```

Intervening text between brackets are ignored.

We will write a predicate function balance that puts the standard stack to work.

```
///////    balance.C    ///////
#include <stack>           // use standard stack
using std::stack;

bool isOpen(char c)
{   return (c=='(' || c=='[' || c=='{' || c=='<'); }

char isClose(char c);

bool balance(istream& in)
{   stack<char> stk;                    // stack
    char c;
    while ( in >> c )
    {   if ( isOpen(c) ) stk.push(c);   // push open bracket
        else if ( c=isClose(c) )        // close bracket
        {   if ( stk.empty() )          // (1)
                return false;           // imbalance
            else if ( c==stk.top() )    // if matching
                stk.pop();              // pops matching open bracket
            else return false;          // bracket mismatch
        }
    }
    return stk.empty();                 // balanced if empty
}
```

The balance function is a predicate (returns true or false) that pushes open brackets onto a stack stk and pops off the matching open bracket when a closing bracket is read. It is important to make sure a stack is not empty before popping (line 1).

The auxiliary `isClose` function doubles as a predicate while returning the matching open bracket.

```
char isClose(char c)
{   switch(c)
    {   case '>': return '<';
        case '}': return '{';
        case ']': return '[';
        case ')': return '(';
    }
    return '\0';
}
```

In this program, we used a stack implemented by an internal `deque`. It is possible to elect either `vector` or `list` as the internal implementation:

```
stack< char, vector<char> > stk;
stack< char, list<char> > stk;
```

But the default `deque` implementation should prove best in most cases.

11.5 ASSOCIATIVE CONTAINERS

An associative container couples stored elements with symbolic names, or even objects, that serve as *keys* to retrieve the elements (*values*). Think of it as an array with *noninteger indices* called keys. For example, capital cities can be stored and retrieved by names of countries, bank accounts by customers, stock quotes by ticker symbols, and so forth.

The STL `map` is a *sorted associative container* for arbitrary keys and values. All keys are distinct and stored in sorted order. Random access to values is by binary search. The `OrderedSeq` we have seen in Section 9.4 is similar to such a container. A `multimap` is a map that allows duplicated keys. A `set` (`multi_set`) is a `map` (`multi_map`) where the key is the value.

Instead of sorting the keys, we can store values by hashing the keys. The `hash_map`, `hash_set`, `hash_multimap`, and `hash_multiset` are hashed versions of their sorted counterparts.

Let's focus on `map` here. The declaration

```
map< key_type, value_type > asc;
```

establishes `asc` as an associative container with the given key and value types. For example,

```
#include <map>
using std::map;
```

11.5 ASSOCIATIVE CONTAINERS

```
map<string, Quote> stock;
```

establishes `stock` as an associative container with `string` keys (for ticker symbols) and `Quote` objects as values. Now we enter some entries into `stock`

```
stock["IBM"]  = quote1;          // (A)
stock["SUNW"] = quote2;          // (B)
```

Later, the *subscript notation*

```
stock["IBM"]      // returns quote1 (C)
```

can be used to retrieve quotes in `stock`. One important point to note is the subscript notation (on line A, B, or C) *will insert a default value into the* `stock` *map if an entry with the given key does not already exist*. The default value is created by calling the default constructor of the value type or 0 for primitive types.

Thus, operations on line A actually store a default `Quote` before assigning the given `quote1` to it. The same can be said about line B. This is not the most efficient way.

A `map` container actually stores key-value pairs (type `pair< T1, T2 >`, Section 10.3). The `value_type` typedef of a `map` is a pair. You can use the **insert** function to enter a key-value pair into a map instead of the more expensive subscripting method on lines A and B.

```
typedef map<string, Quote>::value_type qpair;
stock.insert( qpair("IBM", q1) );  // more efficient than line A
```

It is very important to make sure a value is actually in the `map` before retrieving it with indexing:

```
if ( stock.find("IBM") != stock.end() )
    q2 = stock["IBM"];
```

Otherwise, a default quote is entered for any nonexistent entry. Let's look at an example of using map in a practical application.

URL Decoding

Forms on the Web are filled out by a remote user and sent to a CGI program (Section 12.5) at the Web server site for processing (Section 12.5). Data collected by a form is in *URL-encoded* format:

```
name=Paul+S%2E+Wang&address=Math%2fCS%2C+Kent+State+U%2E%2C+OH&
email=pwang%40icm.mcs.kent.edu
```

as one continuous sequence of characters. Form data contain *key=value* pairs separated by & characters. A space is encoded as a + sign. Other nonalphanumeric characters are represented by three-character codes

%XY

where *XY* is the ASCII code in hexadecimal for the character. For example

```
%2f  is  /
%2C  is  ,
%2E  is  .
```

A program receiving the encoded form data must first decode it. The FormData class (Section 12.10) has a member function unpack() to URL-decode the string kept in the member content and to store the resulting key-value pairs in the member associative container

```
map<string, string> data;
```

The Tokenizer (Section 6.4) makes it easy to split tokens delimited by & (line 1) or = (line 2):

```
void FormData::unpack()
{   Tokenizer tk(content, "&");                          // (1)
    string s1;
    while ( tk.moreToken() )
    {   Tokenizer nv(s1=tk.nextToken(), "=");            // (2)
        int count=nv.tokenCount();
        if (count == 2) // assume one or two tokens
        {   string key = nv.nextToken();
            string value = nv.nextToken();
            urlDecode(value);                            // (3)
            data[key]=value;                             // (4)
            name.push_back(key); // recording key names
        }
        else if (count == 1) data[nv.nextToken()]="";    // (5)
    }
}
```

Having obtained the key and value, we then decode the value part by calling urlDecode (line 3) and enter the result into data (line 4) for easy retrieval by code such as

```
const string& FormData::operator [](string key)
{   if (data.find(key) != data.end()) return data[key];
    else  return empty;                                  // empty string
}
```

Unspecified values are entered as empty strings (line 5).

The `urlDecode` function takes the string s to be decoded in reference form and modifies s by replacing any + character with a space (line A) and any three-character combination %*XY* with the correct ASCII character (lines B–D). The library function **strtol** (<stdlib.c>) is very helpful in converting the two-character C-style string x to an integer value hex (line C). The value hex is then cast into the desired character (line D).

```
void FormData::urlDecode(string& s)
{   int x1, x2, len = s.size(), pos=0;
    char c, space = ' ';
    for (int i=0; i < len; i++)
    {   c = s[i];
        if ( c == '+' )  s[pos++] = space;       // (A)
        else if ( c == '%' )                     // (B)
        {   char x[3] = {s[++i], s[++i], '\0'};
            char* t = x;
            int hex=strtol(x, &t, 16);           // (C)
            if (*t != '\0')  // hex seq invalid
            {   s[pos++]=c;
                s[pos++]=x[0];
                s[pos++]=x[1];
            }
            else s[pos++]=static_cast<char>(hex); // (D)
        }
        else if ( pos == i ) pos++;
        else s[pos++]=c;
    }
    s.erase(pos,len-pos);   // shorten string
}
```

11.6 STANDARD CONTAINER ITERATORS AND typedefs

The various standard containers already offer much convenience for programming. Still, C++ makes them more useful by supplying generic algorithms that can work with any standard container or any other container conforming to the conventions. The generic algorithms are function templates for common operations such as searching, sorting, and so on.

To make containers and algorithms work together in an interchangeable fashion, a common interface is needed. The STL interface convention involves container-supplied typedefs and iterators. Both of these are described here. The standard algorithms are discussed in Section 11.7.

Container `typedefs`

A standard container makes a number of `typedefs` available for application programs to use. The `typedefs` may include

- `value_type`: The type of values stored in the container. For example, `value_type` is `char*` for `vector<char*>` and `Account` for `list<Account>`.
- `reference`: A reference type to values stored in the container.
- `const_reference`: A `const` reference type to values stored in the container.
- `iterator`: A type that behaves like a pointer to the value stored and allows you to read and write each stored element in a forward direction from beginning to end.
- `const_iterator`: A read-only iterator.
- `reverse_iterator`: An iterator that goes backward from end to beginning.
- `const_reverse_iterator`: A read-only reverse iterator.
- `difference_type`: The result type of subtracting two iterators, usually `int`.

Container-supplied types also allow you to write programs on containers without hard-coding the types involved. For example, we can compute the average of values stored in any container by writing a function template `average`:

```
///////    average.h     ///////
#include <typeinfo>
#include <stdexcept>

class invalidValue;
inline bool numericType(const type_info& type);

template<typename CT>
double average(const CT& ctn)
     throw( invalidValue )
{    const type_info& t = typeid(typename CT::value_type);    // (1)
     if (! numericType( t ) )                                 // (2)
        throw( invalidValue(t.name()) );                      // (3)
     double ave =0.0;
     double d = ctn.size();
     for ( typename CT::const_iterator itr = ctn.begin();
           itr != ctn.end();
           ++itr )
     {   ave += *itr/d;   }                                   // (4)
```

```
        return ave;
}
```

The template average is instantiated with a container type CT. The typeid of the value_type from the CT is obtained (line 1) and checked to see if it is a numeric type (line 2). The notation

typename CT::value_type   (declaring a type name)

tells the compiler that CT::value_type is a type name. Otherwise, unless it has seen the class CT already, the compiler has no way of knowing that CT::value_type is a type name. If the value type is not numeric, an exception is thrown (line 3). The average is computed as a double (line 4).

```
inline bool numericType(const type_info& type)
{   if ( type==typeid(int) | type==typeid(int&) |
         type==typeid(unsigned int) |
            . . .
         type==typeid(double)
       )    return true;
    else    return false;
}

class invalidValue : public invalid_argument
{ public:
     explicit invalidValue (const string& s)
       : invalid_argument(s + " is not a numeric type.")
       { }
};
///////    end of average.h    ///////
```

Now average can be used to compute the average of numeric values in any container. Let's put the average function template to use:

```
///////     average.C    ///////
#include <iostream>
#include <vector>
#include "average.h"
using std::cout; using std::endl; using std::vector;

int main()
{   int a[] = {5, 3, 62, 99, 32, 98, 66};
    int d = sizeof(a)/sizeof(int);
    vector<int> v(a, a+d);          // vector of 7 ints
    cout << "average = " << average(v) << endl;
    return 0;
}
```

Run this program and see what output is produced. Use a different container (e.g., list) and verify that average also works.

Container Iterators

A basic iterator visits elements in a forward direction and may allow read and/or write operations on the elements. A *bidirectional iterator* can be incremented (++itor) as well as decremented (--itor). A *random-access iterator* allows itor±*integer*. Table 11.1 lists the iterators provided by standard containers. Section 8.6 discussed many fundamental concepts related to iterators. We won't repeat them here.

A container also provides member functions that return iterators. For example,

```
const vector<string> vec;
/* ... */
vector<string>::const_iterator it = vec.begin();
while ( it != vec.end() )
{   /* ... */
    cout << *it << endl;
    ++it;
}
```

In general, the container member functions **begin**() and **end**() return the front and back iterator, and the functions **rbegin**() and **rend**() give the first and last reverse_iterator, respectively. A const host container returns only const iterators.

The operator== and operator!= can be used to compare iterators. If you call certain container operations, such as deleting or inserting an element during an iteration, iterators obtained before the container modifying operation can become invalid. Each container documents such operations. Generally, it is a bad idea to perform unrelated container modifying operations during an iteration.

Table 11.1 STANDARD CONTAINER ITERATORS

Container	Iterator	Container	Iterator
vector	random-access	list	bidirectional
deque	random-access	map	bidirectional
multimap	bidirectional	set	bidirectional
multiset	bidirectional	valarray	random-access

I/O and Other Iterators

Include the header `<iterator>` to use a number of classes and templates that help declare and manipulate iterators. The functions

```
advance(itr, n)        // itr += n
distance(itr1, itr2)   // returns itr2-itr1
```

work on any appropriate type of iterators.

An `insert_iterator` object helps the assignment or copying of elements into a container of unknown size by turning assignments into insertions. For example,

```
#include<set>
#include<iterator>

int primes[] = {1, 2, 3, 5, 7, 11, ... };
set<int> smallPrimes;                    // ordered set of ints
insert_iterator< set<int> >              // type
   i_itr(smallPrimes,                    // the receiving container
         smallPrimes.begin()             // initial insertion point
        );
for (int i=0; i<6; i++) *i_itr = primes[i]; // insert into set
```

inserts into the `set` `smallPrimes` the first six integer primes by assigning each to an `insert_iterator`. The ++ operator of `insert_iterator` increments the insertion point.

An `ostream_iterator` helps send objects to an output stream:

```
ostream_iterator < int > o_itr(cout, " ");
o_itr = *smallPrimes.begin();        // output 1st prime
```

Here each `int` is sent to `cout` followed by a space.

Three more iterators are available in `<iterator>`:

```
istream_iterator     // reads from an input stream
istreambuf_iterator  // reads from an input stream buffer
reverse_iterator     // reverses the traversal order of an iterator
```

See Section 11.8 for an example that uses `istream_iterator` to fill a container from a file. The header `<iterator>` also supplies operators +, -, !=, ==, <, <=, >, and >= that work on the preceding three iterators.

11.7 GENERIC ALGORITHMS FOR CONTAINERS

By including the header <algorithm>, you can apply many useful generic algorithms on containers. For example, the function template **find** is a generic algorithm:

find(*first*, *last*, *value*)   (returns an iterator)

takes two read-only iterators (*first* and *last*) and checks from *first* to just before *last* for an element == to the given reference *value*. If an element is found, an iterator is returned; otherwise, *last* is returned. The fact that the argument iterators can come from almost any container makes **find** generic. A map defines its own **find** operation, and we should not use the generic **find** on a map.

To find a string in a vector<string> container vs, you use the code

```
#include <vector>
#include <string>
#include <algorithm>
using std::string; using std::vector; using std::find;

vector<string>::iterator it =
     find(vs.begin(), vs.end(), "treasure");
if ( it == vs.end() )
     /* not found      */
else
     /* *it == "treasure" */
```

Note that the == operation defined by the value type is used to determine equality. This simple example shows how iterators glue containers and generic algorithms together.

While finding an equal value in a container is useful, what's more interesting is finding an element that satisfies some arbitrary given condition. The **find_if** function is a generic algorithm that finds the first element satisfying any given predicate:

find_if(*first*, *last*, *pred*)   (finds element satisfying predicate)

where *pred* is a predicate, a function that, when applied to an element in the container, returns true or false. For example,

```
bool too_long(const string& str)
{   return str.size() > 256;   }

it = find_if(vs.begin(), vs.end(), too_long);
```

11.7 GENERIC ALGORITHMS FOR CONTAINERS

The argument *pred* can be either a function or a *functor*. A functor is simply an object using its `operator()` to behave like a function. The C++ header `<functional>` gives many useful unary and binary functors that are generic (Section 11.9). These functors can work on arbitrary types.

The **for_each** container algorithm applies a given unary function or functor to each element in the given range. For example, we can first define a generic functor sum.

```
template <typename T>
class Sum    // generic functor
{ public:
    Sum(T init=0) : ans(init) {}
    void operator() (T x) {  ans += x;  }
    T result() const {  return ans;  }
  private:
    T ans;
};
```

The sum of all elements in a vector<double> vd; can be computed by

```
Sum<double> s(0.0);
s = for_each(vd.begin(), vd.end(), s);    (applies s)
double ans = s.result();
```

Note that **for_each** returns its third argument which, being a functor, can carry the answer within. The **for_each** function template is defined as follows:

```
template<typename IT, typename FCT>
FCT for_each(IT first, IT last, FCT fn)
{   while ( first != last) fn(*first++)
    return fn;
}
```

Let's define a new container algorithm and_test which takes a predicate and tests to see if every element in range satisfies the given predicate.

```
template<typename IT, typename FN>
bool and_test(IT first, IT last, FN pred)
{   while ( first != last)
    {   if ( ! pred(*first) ) return false;
        ++first;
    }
    return true;
}
```

The and_test is applied to a container in the obvious way:

```
bool ok = and_test(ct.begin(), ct.end(), positive);
```

where `positive` is a boolean function, to test if each element in the container `ct` is positive.

More Container Algorithms

With a basic understanding, you now are able to tackle the over 60 function templates in `<algorithm>`. Most algorithms work on sequences specified by iterator parameters. The sequences can be from the same or different containers. You'd find template functions for:

- *Comparing two containers*: **find_first_of** (finds the first element in one sequence that is also in another sequence), **mismatch** (returns a `pair` of iterators representing the first positions where two sequences differ), **search** (searches for one sequence in another), **equal** (returns `true` if the first sequence is a prefix of the second sequence)

- *Producing a container with elements from another*: **copy** (copies the entire first sequence into the second sequence, by assignment, starting at a given position), **transform** (copies each element transformed by a given unary operation), **unique_copy** (copies without duplicates from a sorted sequence)

- *Filling a container with elements*: **fill** (fills a sequence with copies of a given value), **generate** (fills a sequence with successive values generated by a given functor)

- *Removing/replacing elements*: **remove** (removes from a sequence all elements equal to a given value), **replace** (replaces in a sequence all `value1` by `value2`), **unique** (removes duplicates in a sorted sequence)

- *Sorting*: **sort**, **binary_search** (finds a value in a sequence; returns true or false), **reverse** (reverses the order of elements in a sequence)

- *Merging sets*: **set_union** (merges two sorted sequences into a sorted result sequence without duplicates), **set_intersection** (builds a sorted result sequence of elements in both sorted sequences one and two), **set_difference** (builds a sorted sequence of elements in sorted sequence one but not in two)

For example,

```
#include <algorithm>
using std::remove; using std::copy;
int even[] = {0,2,4,6,8,10};

remove(even, even+sizeof(even), even[0]);  // returns end iterator
```

removes all elements equal to `even[0]` in the given range. It does this by copying each nonmatching element to the first available free position resulting in {2,4,6,8,10,10}. The new sequence is in the range 0 through 4. Hence, for this example, **remove** does the following copying:

```
copy(even+1, even+sizeof(even), even);
```

Let's apply the **sort** algorithm to sort integers in a container.

```
///////    vecSort.C    ///////
#include <iostream>
#include <vector>
#include <algorithm>
using std::cout;  using std::endl;

int main()
{  int a[] = {5,3,-1, 99, 32, 98, 66};
   int d = sizeof(a)/sizeof(int);
   std::vector<int> v(a, a+d);         // creates vector of 7 ints
   std::sort(v.begin(), v.end());      // ascending order (A)
   for (vector<int>::iterator itr=v.begin();
        itr != v.end(); ++itr) cout << *itr << " ";
   cout << endl;
   return 0;
}
```

The generic algorithm **sort** uses a built-in *less than* function to sort in ascending order. To sort in descending order instead, replace line A with the code

```
std::greater<int> fn;                    // instantiate functor fn
std::sort(v.begin(), v.end(), fn);       // use fn for ordering
```

where `greater` is a functor available by including the header `<functional>` (Section 11.9).

Each generic algorithm tends to involve a small loop. You can find the source code in a header file included by `<algorithm>`. See Section 11.10 for resources with more details.

11.8 ORDERED SETS

A `set` is a `map` where the keys are the values. In other words, a `set` stores a sequence of distinct read-only elements. The elements are kept in increasing or user-defined order.

```
#include <set>
set< string > strSet;          // alphabetical order
```

```
set< int > intSet;                  // increasing order
set< int, greater<int> >            // decreasing order
    intSet2( greater<int>() );      // functor from <functional>
```

Set member functions include **find**, **size**, **insert**, **erase**:

`intSet.`**`insert`**`( primes[i] );`	(inserts into sequence)
`intSet.`**`erase`**`( 7 );`	(removes 7 from sequence)
`int n = intSet.`**`size`**`();`	(returns length of sequence)
`if ( intSet.`**`find`**`( 7 ) != intSet.end() )`	(finds 7)

See the header file for more details and other members.

Let's look at an example that fills a set from a file `zipcode.txt` with eight zip codes separated by white space:

```
44312 44224 44242 44305 44312 44319
44407 43120
```

The strategy is to establish an `istream_iterator` for the input file and use the generic **copy** to fill a set<string> object.

```
#include<iostream>
#include<fstream>
#include<algorithm>
#include<string>
#include<set>
#include<iterator>
using std::cout;      using std::endl;
using std::string;    using std::set;    using std::copy;
using std::ifstream;  using std::insert_iterator;
using std::istream_iterator;

int main()
{   ifstream infile("zipcode.txt");
    if ( ! infile ) return 1;
    istream_iterator<string> in(infile);                       // (1)
    istream_iterator<string> eos;                              // (2)
    set<string> zip;
    insert_iterator< set<string> > i_itr(zip, zip.begin());    // (3)
    copy(in, eos, i_itr);                                      // (4)
    cout << zip.size() << " distinct zip codes read:" << endl;
    for ( set<string>::iterator it = zip.begin();
                                it != zip.end(); ++it )
        cout << *it << " ";
    cout << endl;
    return 0;
}
```

The istream iterators in (line 1) and eos (line 2) serve as the begin and end input iterators in the **copy** operation (line 4). The insert iterator i_itr makes each assignment into an insert operation into the container zip (lines 3 and 4). Note that ++i_itr does nothing other than return a reference to *this.

The output of this program is

```
7 distinct zip codes read:
43120   44224   44242   44305   44312   44319   44407
```

If we use a multiset instead of a set, the duplicated 44312 shows up twice. Because the program uses generic operations, it works if a vector or list is used instead of a set, provided that ordering is not important. If the intended application of zip is to check if certain zip codes are in the sequence, then set is a good choice because set insert and find operations are very efficient—the cost is $O(\log n)$ where n is the sequence length.

11.9 STANDARD FUNCTORS

What Is a Functor?

A functor is a function in the form of an object. If an object *fn_obj* has the *application operator*, operator(), defined, then the code

fn_obj(*args*);   (means *fn_pbj*.operator()(*args*))

looks, feels, and acts like a function call. Thus, if a class defines operator(), its objects can act as functions and are known as function objects or *functors*.

Functors have advantages over functions in several important ways:

- A function usually does not retain information across invocations. In other words, one function call has nothing to do with the next call. A functor can keep *state information* across invocations. The Sum functor in Section 11.7 is a clear example.

- A function can use static local variables to carry information from one call to the next. But one sequence of calls must be finished before another unrelated sequence of calls begins. Otherwise, the two call sequences interfere with each other through the static variables. On the other hand, distinct functors can take care of different call sequences at the same time without mutual interference. For example, one Sum functor can sum elements in one container while another Sum functor can do the same for another container.

- A functor can have auxiliary member functions, such as result() in Sum, to help achieve its purpose. A functor can be initialized differently and can be set to different operating modes (e.g., <iomanip>).

- Functors, as objects, can be organized in class hierarchies and can employ polymorphism.

A standard container algorithm (e.g., **for_each** or **find_if**) is a function template, and its function parameter can take a function or a functor as argument.

Standard Library Functors

By including the header file <functional>, you can use functors from the Standard Library. There are unary and binary functors derived from the base classes:

```
template<typename ARG, typename RESULT>
class unary_function
{ public:
    typedef ARG argument_type;
    typedef RESULT result_type;
};

template<typename ARG1, typename ARG2, typename RESULT>
class binary_function
{ public:
    typedef ARG1 first_argument_type;
    typedef ARG2 second_argument_type;
    typedef RESULT result_type;
};
```

The functors supplied basically cover the logical, relational, and arithmetic operators in C++ (Table 11.2). Each of these is defined very simply. For example, the **plus** functor is

```
template<typename T>
class plus : public binary_function<T, T, T>
{   T operator()(const T& x, const T& y) const
      { return x + y; }
};
```

and the predicate **greater** is

```
class greater : public binary_function<T, T, bool>
{   bool operator()(const T& x, const T& y) const
      { return x > y; }
};
```

11.9 STANDARD FUNCTORS

Table 11.2 STANDARD FUNCTORS

Functor	Meaning	Functor	Meaning
equal_to	==	plus	a+b
not_equal_to	!=	minus	a-b
greater	>	multiplies	a*b
less	<	divides	a/b
greater_equal	>=	modulus	a%b
less_equal	<=	negate	-a
logical_and	&&	logical_or	||
logical_not	!		

To create functors, follow normal object creation notations:

```
std::greater<int> fn;
std::greater<int> fn = std::greater<int>();   // longhand
```

Functors are useful with container algorithms. For example, to find the first element where two containers differ, you might use

```
typedef vector<double>::iterator vi;
pair<vi, vi> ans
          = mismatch(vd1.begin(), vd1.end(), // for 1st vector
                     vd2.begin(),            // for 2nd vector
                     equal_to<double>()      // functor
                    );
```

The pair of iterators returned gives the first place, in each of the two containers, where they differ.

Functor Manipulation

By including <functional>, you get not only a set of predefined functors, as listed in Table 11.2, but also some *functor generation* functions that can take a given functor and turn it into a related functor.

The **binder1st** and **binder2nd** template takes a binary functor and binds a given value to its first and second argument, respectively. The resulting functor takes only one argument. For example,

binder2nd(less<double>(), 3.5)   (unary functor for '< 3.5')
binder1st(less<double>(), 3.5)   (unary functor for '3.5 <')
binder1st(equal_to<int>(),99)   (unary functor for '== 99')

You can also use negators

not1(*unary_predicate*)
not2(*binary_predicate*)

These binders and negators work only with functors, not functions. The code

ptr_fun(*function_pointer*)   (adaptor takes any function pointer)

turns the given function pointer into a functor so it can be used in binders or negators.

11.10 FOR MORE STL INFORMATION

An overview and some insights have been provided here to get you started with the STL. For complete details, you may refer to *The Standard Template Library* (Upper Saddle River, NJ: Prentice Hall, 1998) by P. J. Plauger, Alexander Stepanov, Meng Lee, and David R. Musser.

The *Dinkum C++ Library* is a complete Web-based C++ API reference that can be obtained from www.dinkumware.com.

11.11 POINTERS TO MEMBERS

Ordinary pointers represent the address of a variable, an array cell, or even a function. Their use makes programs more general. However, the pointer concept has yet to be applied to members of objects or classes. Two cases can be distinguished:

1. An ordinary pointer is used for an individual data member within a specific object or a static member.
2. An *offset pointer* is used to point to *an instance member of a class* that can be associated with any object of the class.

These cases are discussed separately next.

Ordinary Pointers

Recall the Employee class

```
class Employee
{   public:
        enum      {SIZE=32, ss_SIZE=12};
        char      name[SIZE];     // full name
        char      ss[ss_SIZE];    // social security no.
        unsigned  age;
        float     salary;
};
```

and the object newhire of this class. Pointers to members of newhire can be established as follows:

```
float *f_ptr = &newhire.salary;    // declare f_ptr
unsigned *u_ptr = &newhire.age;
char *str_ptr;                     // declare str_ptr
str_ptr = &newhire.ss;
```

Here the code is no different from that of ordinary pointers. In general, the address of any data member in a specific object can be assigned to (or initialize) an ordinary pointer variable.

Offset Pointers

For any object (e.g., Fraction fr(3,5)), the member selection notations

```
fr.num
(&fr)->denom
```

always require explicitly stated member names (num and denom in this case). Is it possible or desirable to use something like

```
fr.var
```

where *var* is a *variable member name*? The expression produces either fr.num or fr.denum, depending on the value of *var*. The flexibility is desirable, and C++ supports this through the *offset pointer to member*, or *opm*, mechanism.

An opm is a special pointer that gives the offset, or distance, relative to the beginning address of an object. Given an object and an opm, a specific member in the object is located. C++ extends the syntax for ordinary pointers to opms. For example,

```
int Fraction::* nd_ptr;          // opm variable nd_ptr
nd_ptr = & Fraction::num;        // assigns opm value
nd_ptr = & Fraction::denom;      // assigns new opm value
```

Here an opm variable `nd_ptr` is established that can hold either of the two possible opm values. The offset pointer declaration is formed by simply prefixing the usual * with a class scope operator *ClassX*:: to indicate the class involved. Thus, an opm has both a type and a class name attribute. The opm `nd_ptr` can point to any `Fraction` member of type `int`. The value obtained by the notation

```
& Fraction::num                 // produces offset value
```

is not a regular memory address but an offset (or relative position) from the beginning location of any `Fraction` object where the `int` member `num` would be stored. The general offset value notation is

&*ClassX*::*member*

An offset is computed only if access to the member is allowed.

After being set to the offset of either `num` or `denom`, `nd_ptr` can be used to access that member within any given `Fraction` object with the C++ operators .* and ->*, respectively:

```
Fraction r(1,2), s(6,15);       // two Fraction objects
int a = r.*nd_ptr;              // same as r.num or r.denom
Fraction *fp = & s;
a = fp->*nd_ptr;                // same as fp->num or fp->denom
```

In general,

- *obj*.**opm* dereferences the given *opm* in the given object *obj*.
- *obj_ptr*->**opm* dereferences the given *opm* in the object pointed to by *obj_ptr*.

To appreciate the flexibility afforded by the opm, consider a function `prod` that takes an opm pointer parameter:

```
int prod(Fraction fa[], int dim, int Fraction::* opm)
{   int ans=1, i;
    for ( i=0 ; i < dim ; i++ )
        ans *= fa[i].*opm;
    return ans;
}
```

The function `prod` takes a fraction array `fa`, its dimension `dim`, and an opm as arguments. It computes the product of either the numerators or the denominators of the given fractions, depending on the value of opm.

A simple demo function illustrates how `prod` is called:

```
void opmdemo()
{   Fraction ar[] = {Fraction(1,2),       // array of fractions
                     Fraction(2,5),
                     Fraction(3,7)};
```

```
    int np = prod(ar, 3, & Fraction::num);    // friend access (1)
    int dp = prod(ar, 3, & Fraction::denom);  // friend access (2)
    std::cout << np << std::endl;             // prod of num = 6
    std::cout << dp << std::endl;             // prod of denom = 70
}
```

The function `opmdemo` must be made a friend of `Fraction` before the offsets (lines 1 and 2) of the private members can be taken. Note that the function `prod()` does not need friend status.

The discussion so far has focused on pointers to data members. Pointers to function members are also useful. Only opms, not ordinary function pointers, can point to instance member functions as described next.

Pointers to Member Functions

To appreciate the utility of pointers to member functions, consider the movement of a chess piece or a cursor on a game board displayed on a computer screen. A `Board` class keeps the board status and supplies member functions for making the basic moves. Let there be four basic moves: up, down, left, and right. There is also a general move function that combines a number of basic moves to achieve its goal.

To simplify things, a `typedef` is used:

```
class Board;
typedef void (Board::* B_MOVE)(unsigned);
B_MOVE opmf;   // offset pointer to member function
```

A `B_MOVE` variable `opmf` is an offset pointer to a member function. It can point to any member function of the class `Board` that takes one argument of type `unsigned` and returns nothing. Because an instance member function needs a host object for its invocation, it cannot be accessed through the ordinary function pointer mechanism.

The `Board` class looks something like this:

```
class Board
{  public:
      Board(unsigned x0, unsigned y0);
      void up    (unsigned n = 1);          // basic moves
      void down  (unsigned n = 1);
      void left  (unsigned n = 1);
      void right (unsigned n = 1);
      void move(int m, B_MOVE h, int n, B_MOVE v);
   /* other members */
   private:
      unsigned int x;       // current x position
```

Table 11.3 OFFSET POINTERS TO MEMBER NOTATIONS

Notation	Description
`Type ClassX::* opmd;`	Declares *opmd* data opm.
`Type (ClassX::* opmf)(...);`	Declares *opmf* function opm.
`& ClassX::xyz`	Gets offset value of member.
`obj.*opmd`	Dereferences *opmd* in *obj*.
`objptr->*opmd`	Dereferences *opmd* in **objptr*.
`(obj.*opmf)(...)`	Calls function in *obj* via *opmf*.
`(objptr->*opmf)(...)`	Calls function in **objptr* via *opmf*.

```
    unsigned int y;      // current y position
    /* other members */
};
```

The general move function applies the specified basic moves a given number of times:

```
void Board::move(int m, B_MOVE h, int n, B_MOVE v)
{   (this->*h)(m);   // use opm to member function
    (this->*v)(n);
}
```

The parentheses in the expression (this->*h) are necessary to use it as a function. Here is a piece of code that uses the general move:

```
B_MOVE u = & Board::up;          // & cannot be omitted
B_MOVE d = & Board::down;
B_MOVE l = & Board::left;
B_MOVE r = & Board::right;
Board ab(7,10);
ab.move(2, u, 3, r);             // moves up 2 and right 3
```

For better encapsulation, it is possible in this case to make B_MOVE a typedef member and to define u, d, l, and r as properly initialized static members of Board.

Because opms are not ordinary pointers, they do not obey type-conversion rules for pointers. In particular, an opm cannot be converted to a void*. The offset pointers to member notations are summarized in Table 11.3.

Pointers to Static Members

Pointers to static data or static function members are ordinary pointers, not opms. Therefore, the opm notations are not used for static members. The address-of (&) and value-of (*) operators work with normal pointer syntax for pointers to static members.

11.12 INSTANCE FUNCTIONS AS FUNCTORS

Now that we have been introduced to the opmf, the *member function adaptors* can be discussed. Basically, the function templates mem_fun and mem_fun_ref, provided in <functional>, can turn a given opmf into a functor suitable for use with algorithms for standard containers.

- The function template **mem_fun_ref** returns a functor for use with a container whose elements are objects.
- The function template **mem_fun** returns a functor for use with a container whose elements are object pointers.

For example, suppose accounts is a vector or list of FreeChecking accounts, and we wish to invoke the fee() member of each account in accounts. Can we use the for_each generic algorithm and give it the fee() function to invoke? Not directly because **for_each** takes a function or functor, but not an instance function or opmf.

What we can do is turn &FreeChecking::fee into a functor and then pass that functor to **for_each**:

```
for_each(accounts.begin(), accounts.end(),
    mem_fun_ref(&FreeChecking::fee));
```

The preceding assumes that accounts contains FreeChecking objects or references. If the accounts object contains pointers (FreeChecking*), then you would use the **mem_fun** adapter instead.

11.13 SUMMARY

The C++ Standard Library supplies, through the Standard Template Library (STL), generic sequence containers, sorted and hashed associative containers, and container adaptors. The sequence containers are mostly interchangeable in usage but support different operations more efficiently. Associative containers function as arrays whose elements are accessed with symbolic indices called keys. The keys, when stored in sorted order, achieve $O(\log n)$ retrieval time. When hashed, they achieve constant retrieval time.

The generic containers provide typedefs and iterators to work with generic procedures (<algorithm>). STL iterators work like pointers to values in the container. Through iterators, a generic algorithm, such as **find**, **find_if**, and

sort, can work with any acceptable type of containers. Algorithms can take user-supplied functions, in the form of a function pointer or functor, to perform computation on containers.

A variety of unary and binary functors, for relational, logical, and arithmetic operations, is supplied (`<functional>`). You can write you own functors as well as adapting existing functors, or function pointers, to suit your applications.

An ordinary pointer is used for a static member or a data member in a single object because there is a unique memory address where the member is stored. Offset pointers (opms), on the other hand, can point to class members within any instance of the class. An opm specifies the location of a member relative to the beginning address of an object. Opms provide the ability to use variables and formal parameters whose values are names of class members. Thus, a program is not limited to explicitly stated member names. The operator `&ClassX::` returns offset values, and the operators `.*` and `->*` dereference opm variables.

Offset pointers to instance functions can be adapted, via **mem_fun** and **mem_fun_ref**, as functors for use with containers storing object pointers and object references, respectively.

EXERCISES

1. Take the HashTable template (Section 10.8) and revise it so it stores a key-record pair rather than just the record. (*Hint*: Use pair from <map>.)

2. Consider the HashTable template (Section 10.8) and the hash_map in the C++ library. From an application viewpoint, what are the major differences? In what situations would you use HashTable? hash_map?

3. Exercise ObjIO-2: Consider the expanded object I/O program (Chapter 9, Exercise ObjIO-1). Use a map to eliminate the multiple if statements.

4. What does the notation std::greater< int >() mean? Explain in detail.

5. Write a functor MaxElement that can be used with **for_each** to return an iterator that points to the maximum element in the container. Of course, the maximum is defined by a greater functor given to MaxElement or it will use > as a default.

6. How would you apply the result of Exercise 5 to find the longest string in a container of strings, C-style? string object? As indicated in Section 11.11, modify the Board class to contain the type B_MOVE and the appropriately initialized static members u, d, l, and r. With these modifications, show what a call to move now looks like.

7. Take the zip code program in Section 11.8 and make the set store the elements in decreasing order. (*Hint*: Use the greater functor.)

8. The zip code program in Section 11.8 uses generic algorithms that work for many different containers. Revise the program to use a List, a string array of dimension 8.

9. Write a container map2 that is a two-way map. That is, you can store a key-value couple into a map2 and you can retrieve a value by a key and also a key by a value.

10. Consider the unary address-of operator & applied to class member functions. Can it be applied to a constructor? A destructor? An overloaded member function? Explain how it works.

11. Consider pointers to members. Can an opm point to a static member? Why?

12. Does an opm for a base class work with a derived object? Yes, no, or sometimes? Explain.

13. Consider the member function adaptors **mem_fun** and **mem_fun_ref**. Do they work for member functions taking one or more arguments? Explain.

14. The **mem_fun** is a template class. Figure out how it's written.

CHAPTER TWELVE

Web CGI Programming

The Internet and the World-Wide Web are dominant forces in computing. Let's apply our knowledge of C++ and OOP to programming for the Web. In particular, we will look at writing C++ programs to process forms that people fill out on the Web.

To handle forms, your program basically obtains the input provided on the form by the user, checks and processes it, and then provides a reply to the user. A form processing program cooperates with the local Web server program to complete its mission.

A program can cooperate with the Web server by following the *common gateway interface* (CGI) protocol. CGI governs exactly what information comes from the Web server, how to obtain the data, and how to prepare and send the reply.

Enough background information about the Web and CGI is included to enable you to write CGI programs in C++ with confidence. A class `Html` helps generating Web pages in HTML. A class `FormData` supplies all the usual CGI operations for handling user input. These classes are applied in a user feedback example.

12.1 ABOUT NETWORKING

A *computer network* is a high-speed communications medium connecting many, possibly dissimilar, computers or *hosts*. A network is a combination of computer and telecommunication hardware and software. The purpose is to provide fast and reliable information exchange among the hosts and between *processes*, or executing programs, on different hosts. The World-Wide Web is one of the most widely used Internet services. Others include electronic mail, file transfer, remote job entry, and remote login, to name just a few.

A network extends greatly the powers of the connected hosts. Modern computers and networks are so integrated it is hard to tell where the computer ends and where the network begins. The view that "the network is the computer" is more valid than ever before, and companies slow to adopt this view are scrambling to implement *network-centric* solutions to their data processing needs.

Networking Protocols

For computers from different vendors, running different operating systems, to communicate on a network, a detailed set of rules and conventions must be established for each host to follow. Such rules are known as *networking protocols*. Protocols govern such details as

- Address format of hosts and processes.
- Data format.
- Manner of data transmission.
- Sequencing and addressing of messages.
- Initiating and terminating logical connections.
- Establishing remote services.
- Accessing remote services.

Thus, for a process on one host to communicate with another process on a different host, both processes must follow the same protocol. A protocol is usually viewed as having logical layers that come between the process and the networking hardware (Figure 12.1). The corresponding layers on different hosts perform complementary tasks to make the connection between the communicating processes.

Among common networking protocols, the *Internet protocol* (IP) suite[1] is the most widely used. IP is the basic protocol for the *Internet* (Section 12.2), which is by far the most predominant worldwide network. The World-Wide Web is a service that uses HTTP (the Hyper Text Transfer Protocol), which is based on Internet protocols.

If your computer system is on a network, chances are that you are already connected to the Internet. This means you have the ability to, almost instantaneously, reach across great distances to obtain information, exchange messages, retrieve data, interact with others, do literature searches, and much more all without leaving the seat in front of your workstation. If your computer is not directly connected to a network but has a high-speed modem, you can reach the Internet through *Internet service providers* (ISP).

---

[1]Including TCP, UDP, and others.

12.2 INTERNET BASICS

Network Addresses

An address to a host computer is like a phone number to a telephone. Every host on the Internet has a unique network address that identifies the host for communication purposes. The addressing scheme is an important part of a network and its protocol. For the Internet, each host has a unique *IP address* represented by 4 bytes in a 32-bit quantity. For example, tiger, a host at Kent State, has the IP address 131.123.2.223. This *dot notation* (or *quad notation*) gives the decimal value (0 to 255) of each byte.[2] The IP address is similar to a telephone number in another way: The leading digits are like area codes and the trailing digits are like local numbers.

Because of their numeric nature, the dot notation is easy on machines but hard on users. Therefore, each host also has a unique *domain name* composed of words, rather like a postal address. For example, the domain name for tiger is tiger.mcs.kent.edu (at Department of Mathematics and Computer Science, Kent State University). With the domain names, the set of Internet host names is recursively divided into disjoint domains. The address for tiger puts it in the kent subdomain within edu, the top-level domain for educational institutions. Other top-level domains include gov (government offices), mil (military installations), com (commercial outfits), net (network service providers), uk (United Kingdom), cn (China), and so on. Within a local domain (e.g., mcs.kent.edu), you can refer to machines by their host name alone (e.g., tiger, dragon, horse), but the full address must be used for machines outside.

Agencies on the Internet register all IP addresses, so each IP address is unique. All network applications that require a host address should work whether a domain name or an IP address is given. In fact, a domain name is first translated to a numeric IP address before being used.

Data on the Internet are sent and received in *packets*. A packet envelops transmitted data with address information so the data can be *routed* through intermediate computers on the network. Because there are multiple routes from the source to the destination host, the Internet is very reliable and can operate even if parts of the network are down.

---

[2]To accommodate the explosive growth of the Internet, the next generation IP (IPv6) will support 128-bit addresses.

Figure 12.1 CLIENT AND SERVER

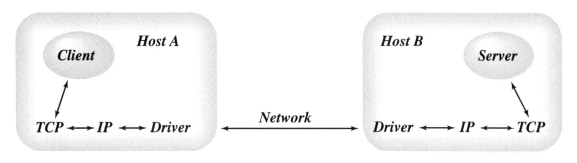

Client and Server

Most commonly, a network application involves a *server* and a *client* (Figure 12.1):

- A *server* process provides a specific service on a host machine that offers such a service. Example services are remote host access (telnet), file transfer (ftp), and the World-Wide Web (http). Each network-wide service has its own unique *port number* that is identical across all hosts. The port number together with the Internet address of a host identifies a particular server anywhere on the Internet. For example, the standard port for ftp is 21, and for http it is 80.

- A *client* process on a host connects with a server on another host to obtain its service. Thus, a client program is the agent through which a particular network service can be obtained. Different agents are usually required for different services.

A Web browser, such as Netscape Navigator® or Microsoft® Internet Explorer, is a Web client. It runs on your computer and helps you retrieve information from Web servers on other computers on the Internet.

One of the first requirements for retrieving remote information is to specify the address of that information. We describe network addresses next.

The Domain Name System

Every host on the Internet has a unique four-part numeric IP address and a domain name. The set of all host names changes dynamically with time due to addition/deletion of hosts, regrouping of local work groups, reconfiguration of subparts of the network, and so on. So new domain names, new IP addresses,

Figure 12.2 THE DOMAIN NAME HIERARCHY

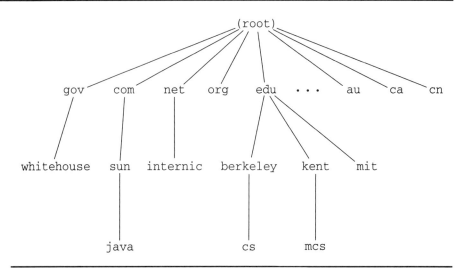

and new domain-to-IP associations can be introduced at any time by any site. The *domain name system* (DNS) provides a distributed database service that supports dynamic retrieval of information contained in the system. A network client program such as a Web browser normally uses the DNS to obtain address information for a target host before making contact with a server. The dynamic DNS supplies a general mechanism for retrieving network address information.

Each host has an official domain name. And it may choose to have several nicknames, called *aliases*. For example, the Web server computer www.mcs.kent.edu, also known as info.mcs.kent.edu, is actually the host aegis.mcs.kent.edu.

12.3 THE WORLD-WIDE WEB

The *World-Wide Web*, alternatively known as WWW, W3, or simply the Web, is a very successful distributed information dissemination and retrieval system. There is no central control or administration for the Web. Anyone can potentially put material on the Web and retrieve information from it. The Web consists of a vast collection of *documents* that are located on computers throughout the world. These documents are created by academic, professional, governmental, and commercial organizations as well as by individuals. The documents are prepared in special formats and retrieved through a *Web server* program on each computer that provides Web service. Web documents may be recorded in fixed files or generated on-the-fly by programs. Each Web document can contain (potentially many) links to other documents served by different servers in other locations and therefore become part of a "web" that spans the entire globe. New materials are being put on the Web continuously, and instant access to this collection of information can be enormously advantageous.

A *Web browser* is a program that helps a user obtain information from the Web. Given the location of a target document, a browser client connects to the correct Web server and allows you to select information for retrieval or to follow links to retrieve other documents. Using a browser, you can obtain information supplied by *Web servers* anywhere on the Internet. Today, widely used Web browsers include Netscape's Netscape Navigator and Microsoft's Internet Explorer.

Hypertext

A Web browser communicates with a Web server through an efficient *hypertext transfer protocol* (HTTP) designed to work with *hypertext* and *hypermedia* documents that may contain regular text, images, audio, and video. Parts of the document may also represent links to other documents. Each server handles its local documents. A Web browser can follow the links to contact different servers to retrieve information. On the Web, documents can take on many different formats for text, images, video, and sound. Native Web documents are prepared in the *Hypertext Markup Language* (HTML). The Web employs an open addressing scheme allowing links to many kinds of documents and services. Consequently, a Web browser provides the ability to access a wide variety of information on the Internet. After a piece of information is retrieved, the browser can also display the information for viewing.

URL

To retrieve information, you give your Web browser a *Uniform Resource Locator* (URL). A URL is basically an address for a document or service on the Internet. The URL enables a browser to obtain a service or to locate a particular document, contacting an appropriate network server if necessary.

A full URL usually has the form

`scheme://server[:port]/[pathname]`

The `scheme` part indicates the information service type and therefore the protocol to be used. Here are some common schemes.

- `http`: Service is Web. The file located is retrieved by the Web-defined hypertext transfer protocol (HTTP).

- `ftp`: Service is FTP. The URL locates a file, a directory, or an FTP server. For example, `ftp://ftp.mcs.kent.edu/pwang/`.
- `telnet`: Service is Telnet for remote login to another host. No *pathname* is needed. For example, `telnet://icm.mcs.knet/`.
- `mailto`: Service is Internet email. The user is allowed to send email to a specified address. The form is `mailto:userid@email-address`.
- `file`: Locates a file on the local system. The server part is omitted. For example, `file:///usr/local/file`.

The *server* identifies a host and a server program. The optional port number is needed only if the server does not use the default port (e.g., 80 for `http`). The remainder of the URL, when given, is a file pathname. If this pathname has a trailing / character, it represents a directory rather than a single file. The suffix (`.html`, `.txt`, `.gif`, etc.) of a data file indicates the type of file.

The pathname can also lead to an executable program that produces a valid document as its output. Such a program is often a *gateway*, conforming to the common gateway interface (CGI), and usually referred to as a CGI program. For security reasons, such executables are located only in controlled directories. URLs for executables can have *path info* and *query sting* attached at the end as explained in Section 12.8.

Within an HTML document, you can link to another document served by the same Web server by giving only the *pathname* part of the URL. Such URLs are *partially specified*. A partial URL with a / prefix (e.g., `/file_xyz.html`) refers to a file under the *server root*, the top-level directory controlled by the Web server. A partial URL without a leading / points to a file relative to the location of the document that contains the URL in question. Thus, a simple `file_abc.html` refers to that file in the same directory as the current document. It is also possible to include an in-document reference location at the end of the URL (Section 12.4).

12.4 WHAT IS HTML?

Documents for the Web are set in the Hypertext Markup Language (HTML). A hypertext document specifies the display format of its content and links, with URLs, to other documents and even programs.

A document written in HTML contains ordinary text interspersed with *markup tags* and uses the `.html` or `.htm` filename extension. The tags mark portions of the text as title, section header, paragraph, reference to other documents, and so on. Because the tags supply explicit structure and formatting information, line breaks and extra white space between words in the text are generally ignored. In addition to formatting, HTML tags are used to include

12.4 WHAT IS HTML?

graphic images, link to other documents, mark reference points, generate forms or questionnaires, and invoke certain programs. Various visual editors or *page makers* are available that provide a GUI environment for creating and designing HTML documents. The *Netscape Composer* is an example. If you don't have ready access to such tools, a regular text editor can be used to create HTML documents. An HTML tag takes the form <TAG>. A *begin tag* such as <H1> (level-one section header) is paired with an *end tag*, </H1> in this case, to mark text in between. Table 12.1 lists some frequently used tags.

Here is a sample HTML file:

```
<HTML><HEAD>
<TITLE>A Sample HTML File</TITLE>
</HEAD><BODY>
<H1>Introduction</H1>
<P>
    Here is the first paragraph
<P>
followed by the second paragraph and a list of things:
<OL>
<LI> Apples
<LI> Oranges
</OL>
</P></BODY></HTML>
```

Pictures can be included in-line with text by the tag <IMG SRC="*URL*"> where the *URL* points to an image file.

Table 12.1 SOME HTML TAGS

Document Feature	HTML Tags
Document Title	<TITLE>...</TITLE>
Level *n* Heading	<H*n*>...</H*n*>
Paragraphs	<P>...<P>...</P>
List Item	<LI> ...
Unnumbered List	<UL>...</UL>
Numbered List	<OL>...</OL>
Description List	<DL>...</DL>
Description Item	<DT>...
Description Body	<DD>...
Comment	<!-- ...... -->

12.5 DYNAMIC GENERATION OF WEB PAGES

Documents available on the Web are usually prepared and set in advance to supply some fixed content, either in HTML or in some other format such as plain text, GIF, or JPEG. These fixed documents are *static*. A Web server can also generate documents on-the-fly that bring these and other advantages:

- Customizing a document, depending on when, where, who, and what program is retrieving it.
- Collecting user input and providing responses to the incoming information.
- Enforcing certain policies for outgoing documents.

Dynamic Web pages are not magic. Instead of retrieving a fixed file, a Web server simply calls another program to compute the document to be returned. As you may have guessed, not every program can be used by a Web server in this manner. Such a program must conform to the CGI.

Recall that a URL can refer to an executable program. Thus, a link in a document can lead to the execution of an *external program* whose standard output is returned by the HTTP server as the information retrieved by following the link. For example, the link

```
<A HREF=http://monkey.mcs.kent.edu/cgi-bin/demo>a cgi demo</A>
```

leads to a request for the HTTP server on the host monkey to execute a program demo. Such external programs are known as *gateways*, and the interface between the HTTP server and a gateway follows the CGI protocol (Figure 12.3). For security reasons, CGI programs usually must be placed in specially designated locations known as *cgi-bin* directories. Basically, the Web server supplies parameters and input data to the gateway and obtains its standard output, which must be in valid HTTP format.

CGI specifies how an information server, mainly the HTTP server, interfaces with an external program, called a gateway. Instead of using built-in facilities, a server calls gateways to perform a variety of tasks such as form processing and database queries. CGI specifies four interface components:

1. *Command line*: Form of the command line by which the server invokes the gateway
2. *Environment variables*: Environment values transmitted from the server to the gateway
3. *Standard input*: Information sent to the gateway through its standard input

12.5 DYNAMIC GENERATION OF WEB PAGES

Figure 12.3 **WEB CGI INTERFACE**

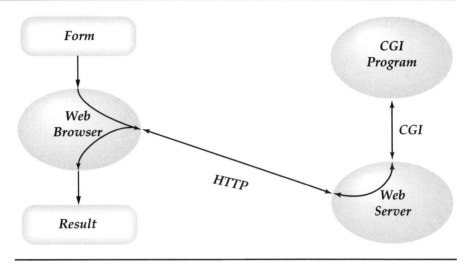

4. *Standard output*: Format of information sent back by the gateway to the server through the standard output

To send output, a CGI program uses standard output. It first sends the two lines

```
Content-Type:  MIME-type
empty line
```

to indicate the data type of the content and then sends the body of the data. MIME *standard content types* include:

1. text: Textual information in a number of character sets and formats
2. image: Still image (picture) data
3. audio: Audio or voice data
4. video: Video or moving image data, possibly containing audio as well
5. multipart: A message containing possibly differing types of data
6. application: Other types of application data or binary data, useful for mail transfer of files
7. message: An embedded mail message

Content-type names are not case sensitive. Types may also have *subtypes* and *attributes*. Table 12.2 shows a set of common content types.

Table 12.2 SOME MIME CONTENT TYPES

```
Content-Type: text/plain; charset=ISO-8859-1
Content-Type: text/plain; charset=us-ascii
Content-Type: multipart/mixed
Content-Type: text/richtext
Content-Type: audio/au
Content-Type: image/gif
Content-Type: video/mpeg
Content-Type: application/postscript
Content-Type: application/octet-stream
```

12.6 HTML PRODUCED FROM C++

Let's look at a simple CGI program that, when activated, produces an HTML page containing a greeting and the local time on the server machine.

We define the following Html class for sending hypertext back to the user:

```
///////    Html.h     ///////
#include <iostream>
using std::cout;

class Html
{ public:
    Html(char* f1=NULL, char* f2=NULL)
      : bodyOpen(f1), bodyClose(f2),              // (I)
        version("<!DOCTYPE HTML PUBLIC "          // (II)
          "\"-//W3C//DTD HTML 3.2 //EN>\"\n")
    { started = false; }
    void leader(char* title);
    void trailer();
    static void send(char *s);
    static void sendFile(char* file);
    char* version;                                // (III)
  private:
    char* bodyOpen;
    char* bodyClose;
    bool started;
};
```

The class makes sending an HTML page to standard output easy. You instantiate an Html object with optional front and back parts for the body as files

12.6 HTML PRODUCED FROM C++

(line I). The HTML version is set to 3.2 in English (line II) but can be changed by setting the member `version` (line III).

The `leader` function outputs to standard output

1. The content-type line, ending in the required \r\n.
2. The mandatory empty line \r\n that precedes the message body.
3. The version line, HTML header, and title.
4. If bodyOpen is given, then output that file. Otherwise, output the simple <BODY> tag.

```
///////    Html.C    ///////
#include <fstream>
#include "Html.h"
using std::ifstream;

void Html::leader(char* title)
{   if ( started ) return;
    cout << "Content-Type: text/HTML" << "\r\n\r\n"
         << version
         << "<HTML><HEAD><TITLE>"
         << title << "</TITLE>\n";
    if ( bodyOpen==NULL )
         cout << "</HEAD><BODY>\n";
    else sendFile(bodyOpen);
}
```

A `bodyOpen` file can contain custom background color, banner, logo, and navigation menu designed for a particular Web site.

After calling `leader()`, a CGI program can use `send()` repeatedly to output C-style strings for the message body. Finally, `trailer()` is called to output the tail end of the body and close the HTML page.

```
void Html::trailer()
{   if ( bodyClose==NULL ) cout << "</BODY>\n";
    else sendFile(bodyClose);
    cout << "</HTML>\n";
}
```

The static `sendFile` function can also be used to send out any text or binary file:

```
void Html::sendFile(char* file)
{     if (! started ) leader("No Title");
      ifstream in(file);
      unsigned char c[1];
      while ( in.read(c, 1) ) cout.write(c,1);
}
```

Figure 12.4   TIME TO WELCOME

With the Html class, our CGI program welcomeTime.C can be written as follows:

```
#include "Html.h"
#include <time.h>

int main()
{   static time_t tod;
    Html page;
    page.leader("Time to Welcome");
    page.send("<center><font size=+2><strong>");
    page.send("Welcome");
    page.send("</strong></font></center>");
    page.send("<p>");
    page.send("We appreciate your visit.<p>Our local time is<p>");
    page.send("<em>");
    time(&tod);                  // time as integer
    page.send(ctime(&tod));      // time string
    page.send("</em>");
    page.trailer();
    return 0;
}
```

Compile the program and put the executable welcomeTime in the cgi-bin/ for host www.super.com and make it executable by everyone. Then the URL

http://www.super.com/cgi-bin/welcomeTime

triggers the program resulting in output whose display is shown in Figure 12.4.

This simple CGI example shows only how to produce output. In most applications, a CGI program will process input collected from a Web user and then construct a resulting Web page depending on the input. The HTML FORM tag collects user input to be processed by the back-end CGI.

12.7 FORMS IN HTML

Usually, an HTML document supplies information to users on the Web. But it is also possible to collect information from a user. With the HTML *form* facility, you simply create a form to be filled out by the user and then process the collected information appropriately.

An HTML form, marked by <FORM> and </FORM>, usually consists of these four important parts:

1. Text indicating what information is being sought
2. Blanks, marked by the <INPUT> tag, to be completed by the user
3. A button, marked by the <submit> tag, for the user to send the completed form back
4. A CGI program, specified by the ACTION parameter of the <FORM> tag, to process the collected information and to produce appropriate output that is returned to the user

Figure 12.5 shows a simple form in HTML. When a Web browser gets a form, it displays the form and allows the user to complete it interactively. Figure 12.8 shows a simple user feedback form. Clicking the submit button causes the browser to send the completed form, in a well-defined format, back to the server. Then, the server invokes the gateway specified by ACTION and feeds it the information on the completed form. The ACTION program not only processes the information supplied by the server but also constructs, on-the-fly, correctly formatted output that is sent back to the server. The server

Figure 12.5 A FORM IN HTML

```
<FORM METHOD="POST" ACTION="/cgi-bin/newaddr">
<PRE>
Full name        <INPUT NAME="fname" MAXLENGTH="30" SIZE="35">
Email address    <INPUT NAME="email" MAXLENGTH="30" SIZE="35">
                 <INPUT TYPE="submit" VALUE="Submit">
</PRE>
</FORM>
```

interprets the output of the external program and returns it to the browser as a consequence of completing the form.

The ACTION program newaddr (Figure 12.5) can be an executable written in any language, including C++.

12.8 HTTP MESSAGE FORMATS

On the Web, browser-server communication follows the HTTP protocol. Before writing CGI programs for form processing, it is good to have a basic understanding of HTTP. Here is the framework of an HTTP transaction:

1. *Connection*: A browser (client) opens a connection to a server.
2. *Query*: The client requests a resource controlled by the server.
3. *Processing*: The server receives and processes the request.
4. *Response*: The server sends the requested resource back to the client.
5. *Termination*: The transaction is done and the connection may be closed.

HTTP governs the format of the query and response messages (Figure 12.6). The header part is textual, and each line in the header should end in RETURN and NEWLINE, but it may end in just NEWLINE. The initial line identifies the message as a query or a response:

- *A query line has three parts, separated by spaces*: A *query method* name, a local path of the requested resource, and an HTTP version number. For example,

    GET   /path/to/file/index.html   HTTP/1.1

    or

    POST   /path/script.cgi   HTTP/1.1

Figure 12.6 HTTP QUERY AND RESPONSE FORMATS

```
initial line                                (different for query and response)
HeaderKey1: value1                          (zero or more header fields)
HeaderKey2: value2
HeaderKey3: value3

                                            (an empty line with no characters)
Optional message body contains query or response data. The amount and type
of data in the body are specified in the headers.
```

Figure 12.7 CGI URL

http://*host:port*/cgi-bin/*progname* `path-info` `query-string`

- A UNIX-style file/dir name starting with a / character specifies *path-info* value.
- ? followed by url-encoded string specifies *query-string* value. Also treated as command-line args if string contains no explicit =.

The GET method simply requests the specified resource and does not allow a message body. A GET method can invoke a CGI program by specifying the CGI path, a question mark (?), and then a *query string*:

```
GET /cgi-bin/newaddr?name=value1&email=value2    HTTP/1.0
```

The full-blown structure of a GET URL is shown in Figure 12.7. Unlike GET, the POST method allows a message body and is designed to work with a CGI URL.

- *A response (or status) line also has three parts separated by spaces*: An HTTP version number, a status code, and a textual description of the status. Typical status lines are:

```
HTTP/1.0    200    OK
```

for a successful query, or

```
HTTP/1.0    404    Not Found
```

when the requested resource cannot be found.

The POST Query

A form is usually submitted as a POST query. But it is still possible to submit a form as a GET query. A Web server often handles form submission by calling a CGI program. A POST query includes:

- A URL which usually specifies a CGI program.
- `Content-Type` and `Content-Length` headers.
- A message body.

A CGI program reads the message body from standard input and processes it. The POST query content type is usually

```
application/x-www-form-urlencoded
```

which means the content body is *URL-encoded* (Section 11.5). Here is a sample HTTP POST query:

```
POST /cgi-bin/suggest HTTP/1.1
HOST: horse.mcs.kent.edu
From: jDoe@great.enterprise.com
User-Agent: Netscape 4.6
Content-Type: application/x-www-form-urlencoded
Content-Length: 132

name=John+Doe&email=jDoe@great.enterprise.com&...
```

In Section 11.5, we have presented a version of the urlDecode() function that URL-decodes a string for the FormData class.

12.9 WRITING CGI PROGRAMS

CGI programs can be written in high-level scripting languages such as UNIX Shell or Perl. But they can be in any language, including C++ for efficiency. Here are the interface considerations for a CGI program:

- A CGI script must usually be placed in a special directory, known as *cgi-bin*, where programs accessible through the Web server are placed.
- A CGI script obtains URL-encoded query data through standard input under the POST method and through the QUERY_STRING environment variable under the GET method.
- A CGI script can access command-line arguments.
- A CGI script can access environment variable settings transmitted to it by the Web server.
- A CGI script's standard output goes to the Web server, which relays the data back to the CGI client.

A CGI script follows the simple processing sequence:

1. Process command-line arguments as appropriate.
2. Obtain form input data.
3. Process the input data and accomplish intended tasks.
4. Send a response through standard output.
5. Terminate.

To send back a response, the Html class (Section 12.6) can be very helpful.

12.10 RECEIVING FORM DATA

A C++ class `FormData` is given here which automates receiving URL-encoded form data.

- Incoming form data are read, parsed, decoded, and stored by the `FormData` constructor call.
- Form data values can then be retrieved by name-value association (line 2).
- The query method (line 3) and the original undecoded content (line 4) are also made available.
- Whether a name has any value can also be determined (line 5).
- Errors are represented by internal error states (line 8), which can be tested (line 6). The associated error messages can be displayed (line 7).

```cpp
///////    FormData.h    ///////
#include <iostream>
#include <string>
#include "../ex06/token/Tokenizer.h"
#include <map>
using std::string; using std::map;
using std::ostream; using std::cerr;

class FormData
{ public:
    FormData();                                                 // (1)
    const string& operator [](string key);                      // (2)
    void enter(string key, string value)
    {   data[key]=value;   }
    const string& getMethod() const                             // (3)
    {   if ( error==NO_E ) return method;   }
    const string& getContent() const
    {   if ( error==NO_E ) return content;   }                  // (4)
    bool hasValue(string key) const                             // (5)
    {   return (data.find(key) != data.end());   }
    bool operator !() { return error != NO_E; }                 // (6)
    void displayError(ostream& out=cerr) const;                 // (7)
    enum ERROR {NO_E, METHOD_E, LENGTH_E, CONTENT_E};           // (8)
  private:
    ERROR inputContent();
    void unpack();
    static void urlDecode(string& v);   // v decoded
    map<string, string> data;           // decoded form data
    string content;                     // original form data
```

```
    string method;                       // query method
    string empty;                        // empty string
    ERROR error;                         // error state
};
```

The constructor initializes data fields, reads incoming form data (line a), and performs decoding (line b). The unpack() function has been discussed in Section 11.5.

```
///////    FormData.C    ///////
#include <stdlib.h>
#include "FormData.h"

FormData::FormData()
{   content = empty = method = "";
    error = inputContent();              // (a)
    if ( error == NO_E ) unpack();       // (b)
}
```

To obtain input form data, inputContent first determines the query method (line c). For the POST method, the content length is obtained from the environment variable CONTENT_LENGTH (line d), converted to an integer (line e), and used to read the form data from standard input (line f).

```
FormData::ERROR FormData::inputContent()
{   char *s = getenv("REQUEST_METHOD");              // (c)
    if (s == NULL) return METHOD_E;                  // no method
    method = s;
    if (method == "POST")
    {   s =getenv("CONTENT_LENGTH");                 // (d)
        if (s == NULL || *s=='\0') return LENGTH_E;  // no length
        char* t = s ;
        int len=strtol(s, &t, 10);                   // (e)
        if ( *t != '\0' ) return LENGTH_E;           // invalid length
        char c;
        while (len-- > 0  && cin.get(c))             // (f)
             content += c;
        if (len > 0) return CONTENT_E;               // missing content
    }
    else if (method == "GET")
    {   s = getenv("QUERY_STRING");                  // (g)
        if (s == NULL || *s=='\0') return CONTENT_E;
        content = s;
    }
    else    return METHOD_E;                         // unknown method
```

```
        return NO_E;
}
```

For the GET method, the environment variable QUERY_STING (line g) contains the form data. After creating a FormData object, a CGI program checks for error before proceeding:

```
FormData form;
if ( ! form )   displayError();
```

The error display function tells what kind of error took place:

```
void FormData::displayError(ostream& out) const
{   switch(error)
    {   case METHOD_E:
            out << "Invalid REQUEST_METHOD." << endl;
            break;
        case LENGTH_E:
            out << "Invalid CONTENT_LENGTH." << endl;
            break;
        case CONTENT_E:
            out << "Missing content." << endl;
            break;
    }
}
```

The complete FormData class can be found in the example package.

12.11 USER FEEDBACK HANDLING

The Html and the FormData classes are handy tools for writing CGI programs in C++. Let's put them to use in handling user questions, suggestions, and comments for a Web site. A form can gather the feedback from Web users, and a CGI program can log the information and send back acknowledgments.

The Form

Here is a simple feedback form in HTML:

```
<html><title>Feedback</title>
<body bgcolor="cyan">

<form action="/cgi-bin/suggest" method="post">
We welcome your feedback!
<p>
<table border=0>
```

Figure 12.8 USER FEEDBACK FORM

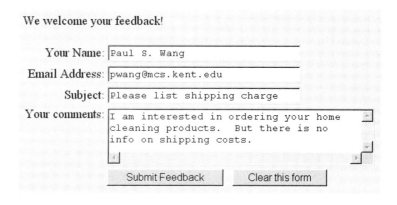

```
<tr>
   <td align=right>Your Name:</td>
   <td align=left><input name="name" size=40></td>      <!-- 1 -->
<tr>
   <td align=right>Email Address:</td>
   <td align=left><input name="email" size=40></td>     <!-- 2 -->
<tr>
   <td align=right>Subject:</td>
   <td align=left><input name="subject" size=40></td>   <!-- 3 -->
<tr>
  <td align=right valign=top>Your comments:</td>
  <td align=left><textarea name="comment"               <!-- 4 -->
      rows=4 cols=50> </textarea></td>
<tr>
  <td align=right> </td>
  <td align=left><input type="submit" name="submit"
                        value="Submit Feedback">
     <spacer type="horizontal" size="10">
     <input type="reset" value="Clear this form"></td>
</table> </body> </html>
```

The form uses a table construct to align the form entries (Figure 12.8). Entries in the form are name (line 1), email (line 2), subject (line 3), and comment (line 4).

Feedback Handling CGI Program

The main function for our CGI program first constructs a logfile name using the time of day (tod) so concurrent feedback submissions do not present a

12.11 USER FEEDBACK HANDLING

problem (lines 1 and 2). The Html object (Section 12.6) page is used for sending a reply (line 3). A FormData object (Section 12.10) form obtains the user input from the form (line 4). If something is wrong with the form input, an error reply is sent (line 5). The user input is then logged (line 6), and the user is acknowledged (line 7).

```
int main()
{   const char *LOGDIR = "feedback_log/";     // log directory
    const int SIZE = 256;
    char logfile[SIZE];
    ostrstream mystr(logfile, SIZE);           // (1)
    time_t tod;
    time(&tod);
    mystr << LOGDIR << tod << ".txt" << '\0';  // (2) file name
    Html page;                                 // (3) output object
    FormData form;                             // (4) input object
    if ( ! form || ! form.hasValue("subject")
                || ! form.hasValue("email")
                || ! form.hasValue("comment")
       )
    {   errorReply(page);   return 1; }        // (5)
    ofstream out(logfile);
    if ( ! out ) { sorryReply(page); return 1; }
    enterLog(out, form, tod);                  // (6) log feedback
    okReply(page, logfile);                    // (7) thank user
    return 0;
}
```

The acknowledgment is sent by okReply:

```
void okReply(Html& page, char* file)
{   page.begin("Thank You");
    page.send("<h3>Thank You</h3><p>"
        "Your message has been logged.<p>"
        "We confirm receipt of the following:"
        "<p><pre>\n\n");
    page.sendFile(file);                       // (8)
    page.send("\n</pre>");
    page.end();
}
```

which includes the exact file logged (line 8).

Submitting the form in Figure 12.8 to the preceding CGI program produces the acknowledgment shown in Figure 12.9.

Figure 12.9 FEEDBACK ACKNOWLEDGMENT

You'll find the complete CGI programs in the code package (ex12/) where you can also find a Makefile and a testCGI script that help you test a stand-alone CGI program before testing it on the Web.

12.12 MORE INFORMATION

The material here gets you started on CGI programming in C++. Obviously, much more information is needed for a complete picture of CGI specification, HTML forms, HTTP, and other Web-related issues for e-business and e-commerce.

Good starting points on the Web for such information are the World-Wide Web Consortium (W3C) and the National Center for Supercomputing Applications (NCSA):

- W3C: www.w3c.org
- NCSA: hoohoo.ncsa.uiuc.edu/cgi/interface.html

12.13 SUMMARY

The World-Wide Web is the premier information dissemination and retrieval facility on the Internet. Web servers and clients (Web browsers) use the HTTP protocol. Web pages are written in HTML and can link to other documents of many types. Resources on the Web are located by URLs. A URL indicates service scheme, host address, and file location of a resource.

A URL can also identify an executable program, known as a CGI program. A CGI program can receive input from a Web client, process the information, and construct a reply on-the-fly. CGI governs how a Web server program interfaces to an external program: via the command, standard input, environment variables, and standard output. The `Html` class is useful in sending a reply.

Input for a CGI usually comes from a user submitting a form resulting in a `POST` (or the older `GET`) query. A CGI program reads, decodes, and checks the URL-encoded form data, and sends a reply. The `FormData` is a general class for treating form data.

EXERCISES

1. Do you have access to a computer connected to a network? If so, find the domain name and IP address for your workstation.

2. Is there anything obviously wrong with the IP address `131.123.5.366`?

3. What is the difference between the partial URLs `/xyz.html` and `xyz.html`?

4. How do you include comments and anchors in an HTML document?

5. To identify a particular server program on the Internet, why do you need both the IP address and the port number?

6. What is the *form* facility in HTML? How does it involve two-way interactions between the browser and the server? In what way does a CGI program also get involved?

7. What is CGI? What are the four aspects of CGI?

8. Take the "Time to Welcome" program, compile it, put the executable in a cgi-bin directory under a Web server, and test it. You may have to contact the system managers of your department to see which cgi-bin to use.

9. Place the user feedback program in a cgi-bin and test it by submitting the form.

10. The Web server passes environment values to a CGI program. A C++ program can find these variables and their values by examining the global `extern char **environ;`. Write a CGI program in C++ that, when invoked, constructs a reply that displays all the CGI environmental values.

11. The value of the environment variable `REMOTE_USER`, if not empty, is the name of the Web user. Modify the "Time to Welcome" program so it greets the user by name when possible.

12. Improve the error handling in the user feedback CGI program. When sending an error reply for missing form entries, specify exactly which missing form entries the user must complete before resubmitting the form.

13. Use a HTML form to allow a user to submit a *Reverse Polish* arithmetic expression. Process this form and return the value of the expression, or an error message, to the Web user. (*Hint*: See Exercise RP-1, Chapter 3.)

14. Improve the user feedback program further by sending back a dynamically constructed form with the completed information plus missing entries marked in red so that all the user has to do is fill in the red entries and resubmit.

15. Make the C++ program you wrote for Exercise 14 into a class library that is useful for reporting errors for any form.

CHAPTER THIRTEEN

Object-Oriented Design

Just because C++ provides good support for OOP does not mean that simply using C++ constructs leads to well-organized object-oriented programs. On the contrary, without a good design created with an object-oriented view, the resulting program will most likely be a procedure-oriented program written in C++. Worse yet, it could be such a program bent out of shape to give rise to classes!

Object orientation requires its own approach to software design. The well-known life cycle model divides software construction into several phases:

1. Requirements analysis.
2. Design specification.
3. Implementation.
4. System testing.
5. System maintenance.

The first two phases produce a set of design specifications that guide the implementation (actual coding) phase. The life cycle model gives a somewhat rigid sequential view of the software creation process. Producing an OO program usually involves an incremental and iterative process where each of the listed steps are done with object orientation.

One technique shared by all software engineering methodologies is "divide and conquer," whereby the problem at hand is decomposed into smaller and more manageable pieces. The individual pieces are made and then put together to achieve the overall goal. Starting with large pieces and breaking them down into smaller ones is considered a *top-down* approach. Collecting small chunks and combining them into larger chunks of the solution follows the *bottom-up* style. How a problem is broken apart is limited only by the experience, creativity, and ingenuity of the designers.

In object-oriented design (OOD), the given problem is broken into interacting objects that correspond to actual or logical entities in the problem domain. A detailed study of OOD would take us beyond the scope of this book. This chapter, however, gives some basic principles, suggests concrete steps to follow to identify objects, introduces the design pattern concept, shows Unified

Modeling Language (UML) diagrams, describes the CRC design method, and provides examples.

13.1 DECOMPOSITION APPROACHES

Before the design process begins, there must be a clear understanding of the requirements and purposes of the software to be constructed. The first step of the design effort usually involves breaking down the whole problem into manageable chunks and defining the interrelationships among them. Decomposition forms a basis for design specifications that, in turn, govern implementation. The three major decomposition methods are:

1. Procedural decomposition.
2. Data decomposition.
3. Object-oriented decomposition.

Procedural Decomposition

One way to solve a given problem is to look at the steps required for its solution. This method of decomposition produces interrelated procedures that combine to form the desired solution.

Taken from the top down, a problem is divided into several major procedures. Each procedure is then decomposed in the same manner. Common procedures are identified, and eventually the procedures are implemented as functions. The bottom-up approach to procedural decomposition considers basic steps necessary in the solution and how they combine to form larger procedures.

With any methodology, after a problem is decomposed sufficiently, we always arrive at a point where procedures are necessary to carry out the computation. The design of efficient procedures (*algorithms*) to solve given problems is a major topic in computer science.

Data Decomposition

Another way to break up a problem is to look at the usage of data. This method of decomposition considers what parts of the solution system deal with which data, how data flow through the system, and which pieces of data are shared by what parts. The data considered include input to the system, information generated for internal use, and results for output. This analysis identifies self-contained pieces and defines their interrelationships.

A need-to-know view should be applied to data decomposition. A system component possesses knowledge of required data only and nothing else. This design principle helps isolate data to restricted parts of the system and therefore reduces the overall complexity.

Object-Oriented Decomposition

The OO view is to decompose a system into autonomous computing agents that correspond to the interacting mechanisms in the given problem. These agents are then modeled by software objects. In a banking system, for example, the objects are customers, accounts, loans, CDs, passbooks, statements, and so on. At a finer level, objects could be addresses, charges, credits, overdrafts, payments, and interest rates.

Each object represents some tangible entity and behaves in a well-defined way. The internal organization of the object can be anything that supports its external behavior. The major advantage of OO decomposition is its flexibility and close relation to the problem domain. Clearly, once objects are identified and put into place, they can support, for example, one particular banking system just as easily as another.

Procedural decomposition and OO decomposition take orthogonal views: One highlights the sequencing of logical solution steps; the other focuses on the interacting entities. Both views are important for the overall design process, but it is perhaps best to first apply the OO view to identify the objects and define their behaviors. Then, the sequencing-of-events view can be applied to the interactions of these objects.

The data decomposition view can also help identify the objects, define their relations, and set limits on knowledge and access of data. The need-to-know principle of data decomposition is enforced very well with OO decomposition. Protected and hidden from unnecessary outside view are not only data structures but also internal procedures. To the rest of a program, an object is completely characterized by its behavior, which is important to good design.

Thus, in one sense, the OO organization is like setting up a company that contains a number of autonomous divisions, departments, factories, centers, and so on. Some of these entities contain other entities, and all have well-defined external behaviors and internal organizations. A company can adapt to many different tasks and react to a changing marketplace because these entities can adapt to different patterns of interaction without major reorganization.

13.2 OBJECT-ORIENTED DESIGN PRINCIPLES

Ideally, an *object-oriented analysis* (OOA) phase produces a set of requirement specifications. The requirement specification becomes input to the design stage. The design stage, in turn, produces a software architecture to achieve the

Figure 13.1 OBJECT-ORIENTED SOFTWARE CONSTRUCTION

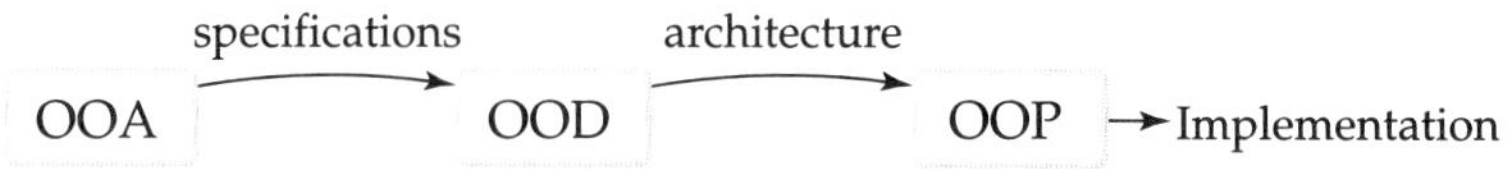

```
              specifications      architecture
    OOA    ─────────────▶  OOD  ─────────────▶  OOP  ──▶ Implementation
```

goals and conditions set forth in the specification. Once an OO architecture is achieved, then OOP, the actual implementation using an OO language, follows (Figure 13.1).

OOD, like other creative activities, does not follow any fixed recipe. There is no magical formula to create a software design. The recommended approach involves an iterative process called the *round-trip gestalt design*, a style that views the system as a whole and emphasizes incremental development and stepwise refinement. A preliminary design is based on what is known and doable; improvements, modifications, and redesigns take place thereafter.

But this does not mean that OO design is completely unstructured. Although the design follows an evolutionary path, the design effort usually involves a sequence of tasks:

1. Identify classes and objects in the entire system.
2. Characterize external behavior of each object.
3. Specify the data and operations within each object.
4. Identify requests answered by each object.
5. Identify services required of other objects by each object.
6. Establish the visibility of each object in relation to other objects.
7. Group similar objects together and develop inheritance relations and class hierarchies.
8. Produce system architecture.

Often, the most crucial step is the first one—in this case, to identify classes and objects.

Identifying Classes and Objects

The software designers examine and reexamine the requirement specifications at hand; become familiar with the terminologies, conventions, assumptions, and solution methods in the problem domain; and through discussions and consultations, form a high-level computation model of the architecture. Interacting problem-domain entities (real and logical) become candidates for objects, and the nouns used in the problem description, such as account, loan, and mortgage, are considered as potential class names.

At this point, the problem decomposition is in the early stages, and the boundaries are not yet fixed. Often, the closer the computation model is to reality, the better the decomposition. The design process not only formulates a high-level abstract view of the software to be constructed but also sharpens the specifications and the attributes of the final software product. Discussing the classes and objects in the design among the designers provides checks, balances, and different perspectives.

External Behavior of Objects

Once classes and objects are identified and listed, each object on the list must be characterized by its external behavior. In other words, each object is considered a "black box," and its actions and reactions to the outside world are prescribed. To do this, the designer acts like a detached customer, demanding functionalities from these black boxes with little concern over how the functions are achieved.

To help the design, a script can be written for each object that describes its role in the overall scenario, including creation, typical actions, and demise. It is also important to look at different scenarios and how the objects interact through their external interfaces in each scenario. These activities may suggest modifications or refinements of the OO decomposition produced earlier.

Finally, a list of objects with external behavior descriptions is produced.

Designing Objects

With the external behavior defined, an object's public interface functions, data structures, and internal workings are then considered. When an object represents a high-level abstraction, it can often be further decomposed using the same OO design methods. Additional objects are then introduced into the evolving design. For each different object, a class is specified to support data hiding and encapsulation. Arguments for public function members should reflect the information necessary to achieve the functionality at hand. Requiring too little information obviously does not work. However, requiring too much information leads to unreasonable designs.

The design produced at this stage serves as a blueprint for the eventual implementation of classes.

Relationships Among Objects and Classes

The goal now is to obtain a comprehensive picture of how the objects in the system interact to perform the desired overall functionalities. By examining requests answered by each object, services required of others by each object, and the direct/indirect relationships among objects, groups of closely related objects can be formed. The behavior patterns and characteristics of objects and classes are then compared to detect any additional is-a, has-a, uses-a, and can-be-implemented-as-a relationships. Objects that can be made plug-compatible are identified. The visibility and invisibility of objects help package classes into files and modules.

In the process of discovering such relationships, certain adjustments of the characterization of the objects may suggest themselves. Thus, the design process is evolutionary.

Implementation

The design process produces a software system architecture including classes, objects, relationships among them, and interaction scenarios. Each class is characterized by its external behaviors and internal organization. Then, we enter the implementation phase.

Implementation is the coding phase. The designed classes, modules, and objects are set down in C++ or some other OO language. But this process is not a simple transcription of the design specifications into codes. Often, implementation exposes unforeseen problems and opportunities that make rethinking parts of the design necessary or desirable. Thus, the design process is iterative.

13.3 DESIGN PATTERNS

Among the multitude of OOD literature, one of the most useful is *design patterns* cataloging a variety of OOD solutions for frequently encountered problems in practice. Design patterns describe and solve recurring problems in programming. Each design pattern is characterized by

- Pattern name, motivation, purpose, and intended application.
- Classes, their relationships, structure, and collaborations.
- Consequences of the pattern.
- Implementational issues.
- Other related patterns.

13.3 DESIGN PATTERNS

There are three large categories of patterns:

- *Creational patterns*: Solutions for creating and building objects with flexibility. An *object factory* allows polymorphic programs to instantiate objects without knowledge of how they are created.
- *Structural patterns*: Innovative ways to organize classes and hierarchies, mix-in interfaces, and apply inheritance. A *composite* pattern, for instance, addresses the need to treat components and the whole as objects of the same type. The fact that a document can be a single word, a diagram, a sentence, a paragraph, a section, a chapter, and so on, illustrates the composite idea.
- *Behavioral patterns*: Setting up objects and collaborators to achieve well-defined overall behaviors for certain goals. An example is iterators and how they glue containers and algorithms.

For example, the iterator concept can be captured as a behavioral pattern depicting how iterators become established and operate in relation to container classes that implement iterators. Figure 13.2 is a typical design pattern diagram. Different containers such as List and Table may implement the abstract Iterable interface and define the functions first() and last() that return iterator instances (think of begin() and end() in C++). A concrete iterator, such as ListIterator and TableIterator, conforms to the Iterator interface and supplies the increment(), getItem(), and equal() operations (think of the C++ iterators ++, *, and ==). A client class can treat Iterable and Iterator objects in a polymorphic way. Such pattern diagrams, when combined with descriptions, examples, applicability, implementation techniques, and critical evaluations,

Figure 13.2 THE ITERATOR PATTERN

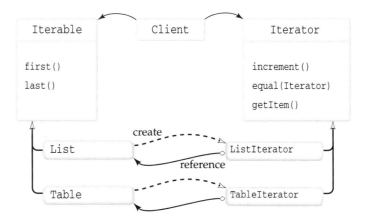

can be a valuable tool for object-oriented design and programming. A good book in this area is *Design Patterns: Elements of Reusable Object-Oriented Software* by Gamma et al. (Reading, MA: Addison-Wesley, 1995).

Class Relation Diagrams

For larger OOD projects, many classes will be involved. There are standard ways to diagram these relations so that the overall architecture can be captured, presented, and discussed clearly. The widely accepted Unified Modeling Language (UML[1]) contains a standard to specify and diagram class relationships. Software tools are available to create the classes, their attributes, and the relationship diagrams. The encoded design can be transferred directly to other implementation software.

Typically, boxes represent classes with a name and key components and attributes. A box is connected to other boxes by lines to denote relations: instantiates, uses-a, has-a (aggregation), has reference/pointer to, inherits, and so on. Text labels on these lines can indicate if the relation is one-way or mutual and how many objects may be involved. Figures 5.1, 9.6, and 13.2 are samples of such notations we have used. See

http://www.rational.com/uml/resources/

for a *UML Notation Guide* and other UML resources.

Class relation diagrams and the CRC can complement each other in specifying your OO design.

13.4 THE CRC METHOD

A particularly effective technique for identifying objects and defining their relationships is the CRC (class, responsibility, collaboration) method. It is especially good for helping beginning programmers learn OO design.

For CRC, a set of regular index cards is used. On each card, the name of a class, its responsibilities, and collaborators (other classes/objects) are recorded (Figure 13.3). Completing these cards is an iterative and evolutionary process; many cards will be revised or rewritten before a design emerges:

- *Class names*: It is important to find the right names for the classes to be created. Names should be natural, conventional (using accepted terms from problem domain), and easy to understand and remember. They

---

[1] See *Communications of the ACM*, Oct. 1999, for more information on UML.

Figure 13.3 A SAMPLE CRC INDEX CARD

CLASS: `ComputeEngine`	
Responsibilities	**Collaborators**
¥ Stores operands, opcode, result.	☐ Calculator
¥ Performs arithmetic operations.	
¥ Carries out control operations.	☐ Derived engines
¥ Produces quantity stores.	
¥ Reports error.	

should not be misleading. Using nouns for class names is recommended.

- *Responsibilities*: These are actions assigned to an object. Responsibilities should be described with short verb phrases. Again, it is important to use the right words.
- *Collaborators*: For each class, names of related objects should be recorded. All objects required to fulfill the responsibilities are obvious collaborators. Classes that require/supply services or data from/to the class under consideration should also be recorded.

With a set of index cards so marked, the designers then proceed to play out execution scenarios and spot omissions or corrections for the descriptions. They also ask "what if" questions to anticipate all conditions that might arise. They can break up complicated classes into more components if necessary. A clear understanding of the problem domain is very helpful because domain knowledge should be used to check and verify the OO design.

13.5 INTERFACING TO EXISTING SYSTEMS

When a complete system is built from the ground up, the OO design techniques that have been discussed work well. Often, however, a software project must use existing systems that are large, old, and not easily changed. Such *legacy* systems affect how the overall system is designed and how object orientation is applied.

The recommended approach is to encapsulate any existing legacy system with specially designed classes that capture and formalize the outside behavior of that system. In this way, the rest of the system can still be thoroughly object-oriented. The interface to the legacy system is made through objects of the interfacing class, thus isolating the legacy system from the rest of the software and reducing potential complications significantly.

Let's examine this approach by considering the class encapsulation of **curses**, a package of two-dimensional terminal screen I/O routines, and then using the legacy system to provide screen I/O for the pocket calculator discussed in Section 5.5.

Using a curses Interface Class

The curses Package

The **curses** package, a screen-updating library of C functions, is available on UNIX workstations and on PCs. It supplies many efficient terminal output operations such as updating the screen, cursor-motion optimization, and so on. The package uses *windows*, which are logical data structures capable of representing the entire terminal screen or a portion of it. If a window is as large as the entire terminal screen, it is referred to as a *screen*. After initialization, **curses** establishes two built-in *screens*:

1. curscr: The *current screen* is for the current state of the terminal screen.
2. stdscr: The *standard screen* is for the next state of the terminal screen.

A program controls terminal display by making modifications to the stdscr and then calling a **curses** function to refresh the terminal screen. All the necessary computations to update the terminal and the curscr are performed automatically. The user is not limited to these screens. In fact, any number of named screens and windows can be established to help manipulate and update the terminal screen. This makes it relatively easy to maintain multiple windows on a terminal screen.

To use **curses** in a program, follow these four basic steps:

1. *Initializing*: Call **initscr()** to properly initialize **curses** (obtain terminal-specific characteristics, establish the screens curscr and stdscr, and record the current terminal I/O control modes for later use). Among other things, the global variables LINES and COLS are set to the number of lines and columns of the terminal. After calling **initscr()**, change the terminal input modes to suit the application. Often, automatic echoing of user input is suppressed and input-line buffering is disabled, allowing a window-oriented program to have each character typed on the keyboard immediately and arrange its own appropriate reactions to the input character.

13.5 INTERFACING TO EXISTING SYSTEMS

2. *Establishing windows*: After initialization, establish additional windows if needed. The library function call **newwin**(line, col, y, x) establishes a new window, whose upper left corner is at position (y, x), with the given number of lines and columns and returns a window identification (wid) for future operations to reference the window. Note that **curses** uses (y, x) for the position line y column x in a window.

3. *Performing input/output:* The basic functions that modify stdscr are **move**(y, x) to move the current position to location (y, x) and **addch**(c) to add the character c at the current position. The two operations can be combined to **mvaddch**(y, x, c). A call to **refresh**() updates the terminal screen according to stdscr. The function **getch**() reads a character from the stdscr. For other windows, **waddch**(wid, c) adds a character and **wgetch**(wid) gets a character.

4. *Finishing*: Before the program terminates, the routine **endwin**() should be called to restore normal terminal I/O modes and perform other cleanup chores.

The CursesWindow Class

To encapsulate the legacy **curses** package, a class named CursesWindow is designed. It initializes properly with constructors, cleans up at the end with a destructor, and supplies member functions that call the set of **curses** library functions.

A **curses** window or screen now becomes an object, an instance of CursesWindow. Data related to a particular window are kept in the object, and all manipulation routines are accessed as members. The header file begins with constructors:

```
///////   CursesWindow.h      ///////
#include  <curses.h>      // C++ header for curses library

class CursesWindow
{ public:
    CursesWindow(WINDOW* &window);    // useful only for stdscr   (1)

    CursesWindow(int lines,           // number of lines          (2)
                 int cols,            // number of columns
                 int begin_y,         // line origin
                 int begin_x);        // col origin

    CursesWindow(CursesWindow* par,   // parent window            (3)
                 int lines,           // number of lines
                 int cols,            // number of columns
                 int by,              // absolute or relative
```

```
                              int bx,              //   origins:
                              char absrel = 'a');  // if `a`, by & bx are
                                                   // absolute screen pos,
                                                   // else if `r', they are
                                                   // relative to par origin

      ~CursesWindow();                             // destructor
```

The header `<curses.h>` supplies declarations that make C-defined functions and identifiers accessible from C++. It may not be standard for all C++ implementations. Some systems offer the `<ncurses.h>` header file that can be used instead. See Appendix K for easy ways to construct such headers yourself.

The three constructors establish the standard `stdscr` (line 1) as an object, obtain a window of given size and location (line 2), and make a subwindow within a parent window (line 3). The destructor takes care of cleanup actions such as releasing subwindows and restoring normal terminal I/O modes, as required.

The class definition continues with many public member functions that provide access to the full complement of **curses** functions. Only a few function members are listed here to give you an indication of what is involved:

```
////////   CursesWindow public functions

// window status
  int Height();                        // number of lines in host window
  int Width();                         // number of cols in host window
  int Begy(){ return w->_begy;};       // smallest y coord in host window
  int Begx(){ return w->_begx; };      // smallest x coord in host window

// reading
  int Getch();                         // read character in host window
  int Getstr(char *str);               // read string in host window
  /* . . . */

// writing
  int Addch(const char ch);            // write character to host window
  int Addstr(char * str);              // write string to host window
  /* . . . */

// screen control
  void       Refresh();                // display host window
  int        Standout();               // highlighting begin
  int        Standend();               // highlighting end
  /* . . . */

// many other function members not shown
```

All nonpublic members are protected and accessible in derived classes. A count of all **curses** windows established is also kept:

```
////////   CursesWindow data members
protected:
   static int     count;            // count of all active windows
   WINDOW *       w;                // the curses WINDOW
   int            alloced;          // 1 if allocated by constructor
   CursesWindow*  par;              // parent, if subwindow
   CursesWindow*  subwins;          // head of subwindows list
   CursesWindow*  sib;              // next subwindow of parent
   void     kill_subwindows();      // release all subwindows
};
extern CursesWindow std_win;    // global object encapsulates stdscr
/* more inline function definitions */

///////    End of CursesWindow.h    ///////
```

Every public member function simply encodes a call to the appropriate **curses** library function. The inline feature can make the interface more efficient. For example,

```
inline int CursesWindow::Height()    // host window height
      {    return w->_maxy;       }

inline int CursesWindow::Getch()     // read one char from keyboard
      {    return ::wgetch(w);    }
```

Positioning a string in the host window, for example, is performed by Mvaddstr:

```
inline int CursesWindow::Mvaddstr(int y, int x, char * str)
      {    ::wmove(w, y, x);
           return ::waddstr(w, str);
      }
```

The full CursesWindow class is contained in the example package. The class can be used to improve the pocket calculator example of Chapter 5 by providing a simulated liquid crystal display window, as we see in the next section.

13.6 POCKET CALCULATOR SIMULATION

For our design example, let's revisit the pocket calculator simulation. Since Chapter 5, we have considered many aspects of this problem in a sequence of exercises. Now we are interested in designing and implementing a more realistic pocket calculator with a simulated liquid crystal display (LCD) window (Figure 13.4) as well as error states. By applying the design principles

Figure 13.4 **POCKET CALCULATOR SIMULATED LCD WINDOW**

explained in this chapter and following the CRC method, we can formulate a design.

CRC Design

The CRC descriptions for the calculator simulation contain five classes:

1. `CalcEng` (*Compute Engine*)

    - *Responsibilities*: Stores operands, operation codes, and results; performs arithmetic operations; carries out control functions such as clear, all clear, and sign change; produces quantity stored in the compute engine upon request; keeps an internal state for error reporting to the outside.
    - *Collaborators*: `Calculator`, derived plug-compatible compute engines with additional features.

2. `CalcFace` (*User Interface*)

    - *Responsibilities*: Receives input keystrokes; recognizes operations and numeric operands; produces next operation and operand from user input; displays operation code; displays operand; displays result; displays error; restricts input under error.
    - *Collaborators*: `Calculator`, derived plug-compatible user interface classes.

3. `CalcWindow` (*Display Window*) derived from `CursesWindow`

    - *Responsibilities*: Establishes simulated LCD window of proper size; shows given character string in LCD window; shows given single-character opcode; clears LCD window; restores normal I/O to user.
    - *Collaborators*: `LcdFace`, `CursesWindow`.

Figure 13.5 **CALCULATOR DESIGN**

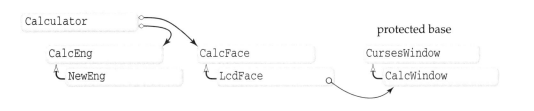

4. LcdFace (*LCD User Interface*) derived from CalcFace

   • *Responsibilities*: Uses *Display Window* for I/O; echoes each input keystroke as typed (otherwise, has same responsibilities as base class).

   • *Collaborators*: Base CalcFace, Calculator, CalcWindow.

5. Calculator (*Calculator Control*)

   • *Responsibilities*: Runs any plug-compatible compute engine and user interface; performs calculator top-level loop; turns calculator on and off; detects internal error; requests display of results and errors.

   • *Collaborators*: CalcEng, CalcFace, and their plug-compatible derivations.

Note that the display object can be a customized CursesWindow object to better simulate a real calculator display. This is simply done by deriving from CursesWindow. Figure 13.5 shows the class relationships.

Implementation

The C++ implementation of the pocket calculator program involves five classes: CalcEng, CalcFace, CalcWindow, LcdFace, and Calculator. The CalcWindow class uses the CursesWindow class that encapsulates the legacy **curses** library. The CalcEng class implements the compute engine and, other than some additional error handling, is not different from that presented in Section 5.5. The user interface is modified through inheritance to use a CalcWindow for realistic simulation.

The CalcFace Class   The base CalcFace class now supports these basic operations: input of numbers and operations, display of number, display of opcode, display of error, and handling of input under error.

Chapter 13 OBJECT-ORIENTED DESIGN

The member input() normally returns the next operation and the operand in the reference parameters op and number, respectively. The return value indicates OK if both operator and operand have been obtained, OPONLY if only the operator is entered, and OFF if the calculator is being turned off.

```
///////    CalcFace.h    ///////
#include <iostream>
#include <string>
using std::string; using std::cin;
using std::endl;

class CalcFace
{   public:
        CalcFace( const int digs,    // calculator precision
                  const char* k );   // operation keys recognized
        virtual int input(char& c, double& number, int err);
        virtual void showNumber(double number) const;
        virtual void showError() const
        {   cerr << "Error" << endl;   }
        virtual void showOp(char op) const { }
        virtual int errInput(char& op);
        enum {OK=0, OPONLY=1, OFF=-2, PREC=6};
        ~CalcFace() { delete nbuf;  }
    protected:
        virtual int inchar() const { return cin.get(); }
        virtual void extractNumber(double&) const;
        virtual void buildNumber(char c, int& i);
        static int nump(char c);
        char*          nbuf;    // buffer[prec+2] for input number
        const string   keys;    // keys
        const int      prec;    // precision, digits displayed
};
```

CalcFace serves as a base for the window-oriented user interface class LcdFace, which adds mechanisms to use a **curses** window object for better simulation of a pocket calculator:

```
///////    LcdFace.h    ///////
#include    "CalcFace.h"
#include    "CalcWindow.h"

class LcdFace : public CalcFace
{   public:
        LcdFace( const int digs,     // calculator precision
                 const char* k );    // operation keys recognized
        void showNumber(double number) const;  // virtual
        void showError()  const                // virtual
```

13.6 POCKET CALCULATOR SIMULATION

```
        {   cw->showOp('E');   }
        void showStr(char* str) const       // virtual
        {   cw->showStr(str);  }
        void showOp(char op) const          // virtual
        {   cw->showOp(op);    }
        ~LcdFace();
    protected:
        CalcWindow*   cw;                   // ptr to window object
        void buildNumber(char c, int& i);   // virtual
        int inchar() const
        {   return cw->Getch();  }          // direct char input
};
```

The constructor dynamically allocates a calculator window of the right size to accommodate the maximum number of digits allowed. An in-memory register nbuf is used to store characters (including . and '\0') for numeric input:

```
///////    LcdFace.C    ///////
#include <iostream>
#include <strstream>
#include "LcdFace.h"

LcdFace::LcdFace(const int d, const char* k)
:   CalcFace(d, k)                          // base constructor
{   cw = new CalcWindow(d);  }              // LCD for calculator

LcdFace::~LcdFace() {   delete cw;  }
```

Dynamically allocated spaces are freed by the destructor.

The showNumber() function is now defined to display a number in the LCD window. This is done by turning the double number into a string and asking the display window to display the string:

```
void LcdFace::showNumber(double n) const
{       static int width = prec+2;
        cw->clearLcd();                     // clears window
        if ( n == 0.0 ) showStr("0.");
        else
        {   ostrstream os(nbuf, width, ios::out);
            os.precision(prec);
            os.width(width);
            os << n << "";          // put n as string in buf
            showStr(nbuf);          // show in LCD window
        }
}
```

Now the input number must be displayed as it is being entered just as in a real calculator. This is done by supplying a new definition for the virtual buildNumber() to display the number as it is being built:

```
void LcdFace::buildNumber(char c, int& i)
{   static int leading_0 = 0;
    static int before_point = 1;
    if (i == 0)                              // reset
    {   leading_0 = 0; before_point = 1;
        cw->clearLcd();
    }
    if (leading_0 && c == '0') return;   // ignore extra leading zero
    if (i == 0 && c == '0') leading_0 = 1;   // first leading zero
    else leading_0 = 0;
    if ( before_point )
    {   if ( c == '.' )
        {   before_point = 0;
            if ( i == 0 ) nbuf[i++] = '0';
            nbuf[i++] = c;
        }
        else if ( i == 1 && nbuf[0] == '0' )
            nbuf[0] = c;
        else
        {   nbuf[i++] = c;
            nbuf[i] = '.';
        }
    }
    else  // after point
    {   if ( c == '.' ) return;
        nbuf[i++] = c;
    }
    if ( before_point ) nbuf[i+1] = '\0';
    else nbuf[i]= '\0';
    showStr(nbuf);
}
```

The buildNumber() function receives characters one at a time and builds a valid decimal number in nbuf. The argument c is the next input character, and reference argument i is the total number of characters accumulated so far for the number. The function contains logic to ignore extra leading zeros and to allow numbers with at most one decimal point. Only valid characters become part of the number being built; other characters are ignored. The accumulating buffer nbuf always contains a proper string.

13.6 POCKET CALCULATOR SIMULATION

The CalcWindow Class The LCD window is represented by an object of CalcWindow, a class derived from CursesWindow. The object shows a string and indicates an opcode, as well as clears the LCD window:

```
///////   CalcWindow.h    ///////
#include "CursesWindow.h"

class CalcWindow : protected CursesWindow
{ public:
      CalcWindow(int digits, CursesWindow* parent = &std_win);
      ~CalcWindow();
      void showOp(char c);      // shows given opcode
      void showStr(char* str);  // shows given string
      void clearLcd();          // clears LCD window
      using CursesWindow::Getch; // reads input char: char Getch()
  private:
      int x0, x1;               // internal positions
      void lcd(int i, char* str); // actual output
      void init();
      void cleanUp();
};
```

The constructor establishes a base **curses** window at a fixed position of just the right size (line 1). It also draws a box around the LCD and enters the direct window I/O mode:

```
///////   CalcWindow.C    ///////
#include "CalcWindow.h"

CalcWindow::CalcWindow(int d, CursesWindow* parent)
: CursesWindow(parent, 5,d+14, 5, 16, 'r') //  (1)
{    int width = d+4;
     x0 = 5; x1 = x0+width-1;              // begin and end of LCD
     Box('#','#');                          // draw box around LCD
     init();                                // init direct window I/O
}

void CalcWindow::init()
{    fflush(stdin);
     fflush(stdout);
     noecho();          // do not echo input characters
     cbreak();          // set to direct input mode
}

CalcWindow::~CalcWindow() {  cleanUp(); }
```

```
void CalcWindow::cleanUp()
{   Clear();
    Refresh();
    fflush(stdin);
    fflush(stdout);
}
```

The destructor does proper cleanup and restores the terminal screen. The basic output routines are

```
void CalcWindow::lcd(int x, char* str)    // output to lcd window
{   Standout();                           // standout mode begin
    Mvaddstr(2, x, str);
    Standend();                           // standout mode end
    Refresh();
}

void CalcWindow::clearLcd()
{   Standout();
    for (int i=x0; i <= x1; i++)
        Mvaddch(2, i, ' ');
    Standend();
    Refresh();
}

void CalcWindow::showOp(char op)          // display opcode
{   Mvaddch(3, x1 + 2, op);
    Refresh();
}

void CalcWindow::showStr(char* b)         // show str in lcd window
{   lcd(x1-strlen(b)+1, b);   }
```

The given string `str` is displayed in standout mode. The complete calculator simulation program is available in the code package (ex13/calc).

The Calculator Class

The `Calculator` class is defined to take plug-compatible compute engine and user interface objects. The calculator object is initialized with pointers to given compute engine and user interface objects:

```
///////    Calculator.h    ///////
// a polymorphic calculator
#include    "CalcEng.h"
#include    "CalcFace.h"

class Calculator
```

```
{ public:
    Calculator
    ( CalcEng*  e,            // plug-compatible engine
      CalcFace* f             // plug-compatible interface
    )
    : eng(e), cf(f) { }
    virtual void on();
  protected:
    virtual void perform(int ind, char op, double number);
    virtual void treatError();
  private:
    CalcEng*   eng;  // plug-compatible engine
    CalcFace*  cf;   // plug-compatible interface
};
```

The calculator top-level loop executes a body that is a separate function (perform()). This design allows the virtual perform() and the virtual treatError() to be modified later with added preprocessing and postprocessing through class derivation:

```
///////    Calculator.C    ///////
#include   "Calculator.h"

void Calculator::on()
{      char op;
       double number;
       cf->showNumber(eng->output());
       int ind;
       // top-level cycle
       while ( (ind = cf->input(op, number, ! *eng))
                  != CalcFace::OFF )
       { perform(ind, op, number);  }
}

void Calculator::perform(int ind, char op, double number)
{      if ( ind == CalcFace::OK )
            eng->operand( number );
       eng->operate( op );
       number = ( op == 'c' || op == 'C' )
                ? 0 : eng->output();
       if ( ! *eng )  treatError();               // (A)
       else
       {    op = eng->opcode();
            if ( op == '=' ) cf->showOp(' ');
            else  cf->showOp(op);
            cf->showNumber(number);
```

```
        }
}

void Calculator::treatError()
{   cf->showError();   }
```

Testing error reported by the compute engine (line A) is done by engine-defined void* conversion.

13.7 SUMMARY

Good OO programs require a combination of thoughtful design and skillful implementation. The two processes form a feedback loop and help programs evolve. The central issue in OO design is the identification of objects and classes in a given system. Decomposition methods break up the entire problem into easier-to-handle pieces. OO design class diagrams, following UML notations, can capture a global view of the design and make discussions easier. The CRC method is particularly helpful during the OO design process. Effective use of the CRC method has been demonstrated with the pocket calculator simulation program design. Design patterns offer descriptions and solutions for common programming problems.

For practical projects, incorporating legacy systems and handling run-time errors are important design and implementation considerations. A class can be used to encapsulate an entire legacy system. The CursesWindow example illustrates this approach by encapsulating the legacy **curses** package.

The complete pocket calculator simulation program offers a small but complete example of OOD and OOP.

EXERCISES

1. Consider the CRC design of the pocket calculator simulation program. Add the CRC description for a derived compute engine class.

2. Experiment with the **curses** package on your system. Test the CursesWindow class on it.

3. Write a class Menu whose objects are initialized with several strings for a menu title and several menu items. The object uses the **curses** library, through the CursesWindow encapsulation, to display the menu and to allow user selection. The member function show() displays the menu, and select() returns the

user's final selection as an index. The interactive user selection should provide normal feedback to the user as different items are visited before the selection is finalized.

4. Exercise Cal-1: Complete the pocket calculator implementation with sophisticated derived compute engines, proper error handling, a simulated LCD window, and a Calculator control that can establish any combination of compute engine and user interface.

5. Take the Menu class (Exercise Menu-1, Chapter 5) and give it a display window with the ability to select menu items by the ARROW keys on the keyboard. (*Hint*: Use CursesWindow.)

6. Apply the CRC method and the OO design approaches suggested in this chapter to design a program for playing Othello. Identify the objects in this game and write the CRC cards for them. Think about the game pieces, game board, moves, board positions, players, move generator, user interface, board display, and so on. Make the design general so that it works for most board games.

7. Take the Othello program design and consider its implementation. Apply inheritance planning and polymorphism. Take into account future extensions and modifications to create other games. Do you find points overlooked in the design phase? Fix the design and start over.

CHAPTER FOURTEEN

Compiling and Preprocessing

To program effectively in C++, a good understanding of how a program is treated by the compiler is fundamental. However, many aspects of the compiler are implementation dependent and somewhat different on different operating systems. Since the official standardization of C++ (late 1998), standard compliant compilers have been increasing in number and quality. Examples are GNU g++ (Free Software Foundation), HP aC++ (Hewlett-Packard), Sun Visual Workshop C++ (Sun Microsystems), and Green Hill C++ (Green Hill). GNU g++, part of the GNU Compiler Collection (GCC), is available for UNIX and PC platforms[1] and free to individuals and educational institutions. Commercial C++ compilers tend to come under an interactive development environment with editor, compiler, debugger, GUI tools, and other facilities.

It is not possible to cover all these systems here. Our discussion is based on general compilation principles for C++. Help for compiling and running programs under **g++** and Microsoft Visual C++ can be found in Section 14.9.

The use of preprocessing is an integral part of C++ programming and is standardized across all systems. Important preprocessing features include header files, symbolic constants, macros, and conditional text inclusion. The practical uses of these features are explained in this chapter.

14.1 COMPILING AND RUNNING C++ PROGRAMS

The compiler takes *source code* files in C++ and produces *object code* files in machine language. This process may produce intermediate files in C or assembly code. Object files can then be combined into an executable file, which is a program that can run on your computer. The compiler treats each source code file separately, and each source code file is known as a *compilation unit*. Distinct compilation units are treated independently by the compiler.

---

[1]Download from `http://www.gnu.ai.mit.edu/software/gcc` for UNIX and `http://www.delorie.com/djgpp/` for PC.

Table 14.1 **FILENAME SUFFIXES**

File Type	Suffix	Example
C++ source file	.C, .CPP	`Account.C, Account.CPP`
Standard C++ header	no suffix	`<iostream>`
ANSI C header	.h, .H	`<string.h>`
User-defined header	.h, .H	`"Account.h", "Account.H"`
Assembly code file	.s	`Account.s`
Object code (compiled) file	.o	`Account.o`

To the compiler, a compilation unit consists of tokens separated by white space. *Tokens* are the smallest unbreakable units used to build a program, and they include keywords (e.g., `class` and `int`), operators (e.g., `+` and `new`), variables, separators/terminators (e.g., `;` and `{}`), constants, and so on. *White space* includes SPACEs, TABs, RETURNs, and NEWLINEs.

Files for different purposes are usually named with conventional suffixes. These suffixes may be different depending on the computer system used. Examples in this book consistently follow the suffix conventions in Table 14.1.

The Compilation Process

A compiler not only translates programs into machine code to run on a particular computer, but also takes care of arranging suitable *run-time support* for the program by providing I/O, file access, and other interfaces to the operating system. Therefore, a compiler is not only computer-specific but also operating-system-specific.

The C++ compilation process consists of five phases (Figure 14.1):

1. *Preprocessing*: Preprocessing removes comments and handles constant definition, macro expansion, file inclusion, and conditional code inclusion.
2. *Compilation*: Taking the output of the previous phase as input, the compiling phase performs syntax checking, parsing, and assembly code generation.
3. *Optimization*: This optional phase improves the efficiency of the generated code for speed and compactness.
4. *Assembly*: The assembly phase creates an object file containing binary code and relocation information to be used by the linker/loader.

Figure 14.1 COMPILATION PHASES

Preprocessing
↓
Compilation
↓
Optimization (optional)
↓
Assembly
↓
Linking and loading

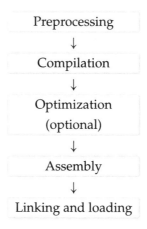

5. *Linking/loading*: The link/load phase combines all object files and links in necessary library subroutines to produce an executable program.

The descriptions here give only a rough idea of the process. At this point, it is sufficient to know that the C++ compiler performs all five phases automatically.

14.2 PREPROCESSING

Preprocessing is the first phase of the C++ compilation process. Your program goes through preprocessing before the main translation phases of compilation. Preprocessing supplies certain well-defined text transformations on the compilation unit (Figure 14.2).

Generally, preprocessing performs two types of text transformations: *automatic* and *requested*. There are four automatic transformations: (1) Every trigraph is replaced (a *trigraph* is a special three-character sequence—see Exercise 2), (2) every comment is replaced by a single space, (3) every BACKSLASH–NEWLINE pair is deleted, and (4) every predefined macro is expanded.

Figure 14.2 C++ PREPROCESSING

Source code file ⟶ Preprocessing ⟶ Transformed source file

Other than the automatic ones, preprocessing makes no other transformations unless specifically requested. You use preprocessing *directives* to request transformations. A directive is given with a # as the first nonblank character on a line followed by a keyword. File inclusion with #include and symbolic-constant definition with #define are the two most widely used directives. A directive for preprocessing is deleted after being processed.

14.3 HEADER FILES

The preprocessing directive #include is used to include another file in a source code file. The line

```
#include <iostream>
```

that includes the Standard C++ I/O stream header has appeared in many programs already. In general, the directive

```
#include <filename>
```

is used to include system header files. The given *filename* should be located in one of a list of standard system directories kept by the C++ compiler.

C++ Standard Library header files have no .h suffix and put the libraries in the std namespace. Examples are <iostream>, <string>, <map>, <vector>, and <set>.

Header files from ANSI C such as <string.h>, <stdlib.h>, and <math.h> are all available. C header files carry the .h suffix and put the libraries in the global namespace. To avoid polluting the global namespace, Standard C++ also offers *wrapper headers* such as <cstring>, <cstdlib>, and <cmath> that place the corresponding C headers in the std namespace. Thus, include <cstring> instead of <string.h> to put strcmp and so on in std. If you do that, you need to refer to strcmp as std::strcmp.

The following header files

<fstream.h>   <iomanip.h>   <iostream.h>   <new.h>   <stl.h>

are provided in Standard C++ for backward compatibility with prestandardization C++ programs and supply names in the global namespace. They are not for use by Standard compliant C++ codes.

When a #include line is encountered in a file (current file), preprocessing does the following:

1. Locates the requested file (target file) to be included.

2. Reads and processes the target file, which may contain other preprocessing directives itself. In particular, it may #include other files.

3. Inserts the resulting target file into the current file in place of the #include line and continues to read the current file.

Therefore, the effect of a #include directive is almost as if the target file were physically inserted in place of the #include line.

To make a call to the operating system (a system call) or a library function in a program, certain specific system header files usually must be included. Required header files will be part of the documentation of a library or system call. Not including the necessary header files will cause errors and compilation failure.

In addition to standard header files, it is also possible to include header files of your own. The preprocessor directive

```
#include "filename"
```

is used to include the file specified. The double quotes are part of the directive. This feature is used to include nonstandard header files. For instance, the wordcount program (Section 3.12) includes the Cirbuf.h header:

```
#include "Cirbuf.h"
```

If *filename* is not found in the same directory as the input file, the standard system directories are searched.

14.4 SYMBOLIC CONSTANTS AND MACROS

The preprocessing directive #define is used to define *symbolic constants* and *macros*.[2] For example, after the definition

```
#define TABLE_SIZE 1024
```

the symbolic constant TABLE_SIZE can be used in all subsequent source code instead of the integer 1024. This makes the program much more readable and easier to modify when the table size must be changed. The general form is

```
#define identifier token...
```

Preprocessing will replace the identifier with the given tokens everywhere in subsequent source code, except in string and character constants. Although

---

[2] Use const variables and inline functions instead of preprocessor constants and macros whenever possible.

14.4 SYMBOLIC CONSTANTS AND MACROS

using any identifier is allowable, using all capitals for symbolic constants and reserving all lowercase identifiers for variables, function names, and so on is advisable. It is then easy to distinguish symbolic constants from other identifiers in a piece of C++ code. Table 14.2 gives some examples of symbolic constants that also show the various forms of numeric constants. In Table 14.2, note how a character (FORMFEED) can be specified with its octal ASCII code, a bit pattern (LOW_BIT) by an octal number, and a special zero pointer (NULL) by ((void*)0).

Whereas a *symbolic constant* provides a fixed substitution, a *macro* is a variable text-substitution mechanism. A macro is defined with parameters in the form

#define *name*(*arg1*, *arg2*, ...) *definition*

For example, the macro SQUARE

#define SQUARE(x)   ((x)*(x))

has one parameter and can be used in such forms as

```
area = SQUARE(side);    // becomes area = ((side)*(side));
r = c/SQUARE(a+b);      // becomes r = c/((a+b)*(a+b));
```

Macros are *expanded* by preprocessing using the definition and the supplied parameters.

Another macro MIN

#define MIN(x, y)   ((x)>(y) ? (y) : (x))

takes two arguments x and y and is defined by a conditional expression. The macro call

MIN(a + b, c - d)

Table 14.2 EXAMPLES OF SYMBOLIC CONSTANTS

```
#define PI 3.14159          #define NEWLINE '\n'
#define DELTA 0.1e-8        #define TAB '\t'
#define MAXSIZE 200         #define NULLCHAR '\0'
#define EOF -1              #define BACKSLASH '\\'
#define TWELVE 014          #define TWELVE 0xc
#define TRUE 1              #define FORMFEED '\014'
#define FALSE 0             #define NULLSTRING ""
#define NULL ((void*)0)     #define LOW_BIT 01
```

is expanded into

```
((a + b)>(c - d) ? (c - d) : (a + b))
```

Although a macro call looks like a function call, it is just an abbreviation to be replaced by its full definition through preprocessing. Note the use of the extra parentheses around x and y in the definition of MIN. This is necessary because x and y can be arbitrary expressions in a macro call. If the definition were given without the extra parentheses, would the example just given still be expanded correctly?

Another commonly used macro is absolute value:

```
#define ABS(a)     ((a)>=0 ? (a) : -(a))
```

Technically, a symbolic constant is just a macro with no arguments. Also, the right-hand side of a macro may involve other macros that may or may not be defined yet. When a macro expansion is performed, the result will be scanned again for any macros to be expanded until no more expansion is encountered.

Redefining Macros

Once a macro is defined, it normally should not be defined again. While redefining with the same definition may be allowed, using a different definition produces a warning message. Often, redefining a macro with the same definition is caused by multiple inclusions of the same header file. (Avoiding duplicate inclusion is the subject of Section 14.7.)

Sometimes, it is also useful to undefine a macro, removing its definition entirely with the #undef directive:

```
#undef ABS
```

Once undefined, a macro can then be defined again with no problems. A macro definition persists from the point of definition to the end of the compilation unit.

14.5 INLINE FUNCTIONS VERSUS MACROS

Preprocessing macros are convenient but error-prone—there is no syntax checking until after substitution, and there is no argument-type checking either. Besides, run-time errors caused by macros are very hard to find. Furthermore, expressions with side effects are dangerous in macros. For example,

```
MIN(i, j++)    (side-effect-in-macro-call trap)
```

looks innocent enough but in fact expands to

```
((i)>(j++) ? (j++) : (i))
```

which is certainly incorrect.

In C++, `const` variables and `inline` functions should be used instead of `#define` constants and macros wherever possible. Thus, the following codes are preferred:

```
const int TABLE_SIZE = 1024;

inline int MIN(int x, int y) { return(x > y ? y : x); }
```

They can be used without loss of efficiency or the side-effect trap. In addition, the compiler performs all the normal checking for an inline function as for a normal function.

Remember that an inline function definition must be seen before a call to it can be compiled. Also, member functions actually defined within a class declaration are automatically inline.

14.6 CONDITIONAL TEXT INCLUSION

Preprocessing also provides a mechanism to include/exclude certain parts of a program. This facility is useful in many ways. For beginning programmers, the primary use is in debugging and testing programs.

If `#define` is given just one token,

```
#define name
```

then *name* becomes *defined* (as opposed to *undefined*). You can include or exclude sections of code in your program, depending on whether certain special names are defined or undefined.

Conditional inclusion can be specified in the form

```
any-if-condition
    source code lines A
#else
    source code lines B
#endif
```

where *any-if-condition* can be `#if`, `#ifdef`, or `#ifndef`. The `#else` clause is optional. If the condition is satisfied, then part A will be included; otherwise, part B (if given) will be included. Table 14.3 lists the possible conditions.

Table 14.3 PREPROCESSING CONDITIONALS

`if` Condition	Meaning
`#if` *constant-expression*	True if *expression* is nonzero
`#if defined(`*identifier*`)`	True if *identifier* is `#defined`
`#ifdef` *identifier*	True if *identifier* is `#defined`
`#ifndef` *identifier*	True if *identifier* is not `#defined`

Conditional inclusion can be used to include debugging code. For example, the `factorial` function (Section 1.5) can be revised as follows:

```
int factorial(int i)
{    int ans = 1;
#ifdef DEBUG
     cerr << "entered factorial with i = " << i << "\n";
#endif // end DEBUG
     /* the rest of factorial */
}
```

The point is to perform the diagnostic output only when the program is being debugged. Therefore, such lines do not have to be deleted for regular execution. Note that a comment is supplied after the `#endif` to mark the end and make it easier to see where the conditionally included code starts and ends. Although not required, this is a highly recommended practice.

To activate such conditional debug statements, either add a line

```
#define DEBUG
```

at the beginning of the source code file or tell the compiler to define the symbol when it is invoked. For instance, the **g++** command supplies a -D option for this very purpose.

Another frequent use of conditional inclusion is to handle system- or hardware-dependent code. For example,

```
#ifdef SUNOS
/* for SUN Operating System */
#define TABLE_SIZE    256
#endif  // end SUNOS

#ifdef HP700
/* for Hewlett-Packard 700 series */
#define TABLE_SIZE    128
#endif  // end HP700
```

14.6 CONDITIONAL TEXT INCLUSION

Here the symbolic constant TABLE_SIZE is defined differently, depending on whether the symbol SUNOS or HP700 is defined (with #define).

You can also position extra code for program testing right in the source file itself. For example, the lines

```
#ifdef TEST
int main()
{   Fraction x(1,30), u(-1,60), v(-1,60);
    Fraction y;
    y = x + u + v;
    y.display();
    return 0;
}
#endif  // end TEST
```

could be put in the file Fraction.C (Section 3.5), which can then be tested by compiling it with the symbol TEST defined.

The expression for the #if directive may involve integer and character constants, macros, arithmetic operators, bitwise operations, shifts, and relational operators, as well as the two logical operators && and ||. If the expression involves an undefined token, the token is treated as zero.

Also, the directives #else and #elif can be used between a pair of #if and #endif in the obvious way:

```
#if FLAG == 1
   . . .
#elif FLAG == 2
   . . .
#else   // default case
   . . .
#endif  // end else
```

You can also use conditional inclusion to exclude code without deleting it, as in

```
#if 0
// This code no longer needed -- John Doe, Date
  .
  .
  .
#endif // end 0
```

This technique gives you an easy way to reinstate the code later or to see what has been removed by whom and when.

14.7 ONCE-ONLY HEADER FILES

In programs, it is common practice to have many source code and header files. The header files often have `#include` lines to include other headers. The inclusion relations among header files can be complicated and may cause certain header files to be included more than once during the preprocessing phase. This is not only wasteful but also introduces preprocessing and other errors. For example, a duplicated class declaration results in a compilation error. An inline function declared more than once is also incorrect. The situation is especially true when using the C++ template mechanism (Chapter 10).

To avoid possible multiple inclusion, a header file can be written as a big conditional inclusion construct:

```
// A once-only header file Cirbuf.h

#ifndef Cirbuf_SEEN__
#define Cirbuf_SEEN__
    .
    .
    .
/* the entire header file*/
    .
    .
    .
#endif // Cirbuf_SEEN__
```

The symbol `Cirbuf_SEEN__` becomes defined once the file `Cirbuf.h` is read. This fact prevents it from being read again because of the `#ifndef` mechanism. This symbol uses the underscore suffix to minimize the chance of conflict with other macros or constant names. It is recommended that all header files be coded in the once-only form suggested here. To keep our examples uncluttered, the once-only feature in header files may not always be shown.

14.8 STANDARD MACROS

C++ preprocessing also maintains a number of built-in macros to make programming easier. The built-in macros are implementation dependent, but the standard macros in Table 14.4 should be available. Since these are preprocessing-defined quantities, the word *current* in Table 14.4 refers to when the predefined macro is being interpreted. The base file is the compilation unit given to the compiler when invoked. The current input file can be any file being read because of file inclusion.

14.8 STANDARD MACROS

Table 14.4 STANDARD MACROS

Macro	Meaning	Type	Example
__FILE__	Current input file	String	"string.h"
__BASE_FILE__	Main input file	String	"Fraction.C"
__LINE__	Line number in current file	Integer	109
__DATE__	Current date	String	"Jan 31 2000"
__TIME__	Current time	String	"21:45:03"
__cplusplus	C++ flag	Integer	#ifdef __cplusplus

Values of some standard macros will change as preprocessing proceeds. They are handy in diagnostic messages such as

```
cerr << "Reached line " << __LINE__ << " in file "
     << __FILE__ << "\n";
```

or in greetings such as

```
cout << "Welcome to WonderProgram Created " << __DATE__
     << __TIME__ << "\n";
```

To further aid program diagnostics, the macro assert defined in the header <assert.h> is available. It is useful for testing various *assertions* (conditions that should hold) at different places in a program. This is done by calling assert with any C++ expression that produces a logical value. If the value is zero (false) at run time, an error message is produced, and execution is aborted. Here is a small test program to show you how to use assert:

```
#include <iostream>
#include <assert.h>
using std::cout; using std::endl;

int main()
{   int x=9, y=8;
    assert(x == (y+1));
    cout << "first" << endl;
    assert(x > y);
    cout << "second" << endl;
    assert(x < y);
    cout << "third" << endl;
    return 0;
}
```

Note that the assert macro is only active when the symbolic constant NDEBUG (no debug) is not defined. This gives you a convenient way to disable the diagnostics for the production version of the program.

The assert macro invokes the Standard Library function **abort**() to terminate the program abnormally without certain cleanup actions usually performed when a program ends (Section 8.10).

14.9 COMPILATION AND EXECUTION

Under UNIX

For UNIX systems, you may have a vendor-supplied C++ compiler, or you can install the Free Software Foundation GNU **g++**, part of the GNU Compiler Collection (GCC). We introduce **g++** usage here. Other C++ compilers under UNIX should work in similar ways.

Compilation with g++ The compiler is invoked at the UNIX shell level with the **g++** command:

g++ *option-or-filename*...

The command takes one or more arguments, each in the form of a UNIX *filename* or a compiler *option*. The filenames specify which files to compile, and the options control compiler actions.

A filename ending in .C (on some systems, .cc) is taken as a C++ source file, and a corresponding object file (.o) is produced. A filename ending in .o is taken as an object file and is loaded into the final executable module. When compiling a single .C file into an executable module, the .o file produced is automatically deleted.

The executable program produced is named a.out unless a name is specified using the -o option. The name of the executable module is used as a UNIX command at the shell level to run the compiled program. Arguments supplied on the command line are accessible by the main program through argv (Section 2.3).

If your program reads standard input (cin), then input data comes from the keyboard. You can type multiple lines of input and, when the input is done, enter ^D (control-D) as the first character on the last line of input. Output from cout is displayed on the screen.

UNIX also allows *I/O redirection* with the notations

mysort < *infile*
mysort > *outfile*
mysort < *infile* > *outfile*

14.9 COMPILATION AND EXECUTION

In this case, cin reads the given *infile* instead of the keyboard, and/or cout outputs to the given *outfile* instead of the screen.

When dealing with a program consisting of multiple source code files, it is usual practice to compile .C files separately into corresponding .o files. The object code files can later be combined with others (with **g++**) to form the executable program. The command

g++ -c *filename*.C

produces *filename*.o.

Linking object codes from the C++ Standard Library is automatic. Other libraries, such as those containing mathematical functions (<math.h>) or curses (<curses.h>), are indicated by the -l option. For example,

g++ -o calc CalcEng.o CalcFace.o Calculator.o calctest.C -lcurses -lm

asks for the mathematical functions library libcurses.a and libm.a.

Consult your computer manual to see all the available options for your C++ compiler. Online manual pages can be easily displayed, for example, with

man g++

A few often-used options for **g++** are listed here:

-c: Suppresses the loading phase and produces .o files only. No executable module is produced.

-o *name*: Names the executable module with the specified *name* instead of the default a.out.

-E: Performs preprocessing only.

-O: Invokes the optional code optimizer phase. Used to produce faster running code, it is generally used only when producing final production versions of a program.

-l*name*: Specifies the library file lib*name*.a to load additional library functions.

-D*name*=*str*: Initializes the preprocessing macro *name* to the given string *str*. If =*str* is omitted, *name* is initialized to 1 (same as #define *name*).

-d: Treats inline functions as regular functions to help debugging.

-i: Leaves intermediate C code files (..c) in the appropriate directory.

The -g option of **g++** is important to know because it asks **g++** to compile a program for debugging with an interactive debugger such as **dbx** (Appendix E).

Compiling Templates
If your C++/**g++** compiler supports the export keyword, then you should use it. Otherwise, you may try the *explicit template instantiation* method. In each template implementation file, add explicit template instantiation declarations at the end of the file to instantiate template

functions and classes. Compiling these .C files produces .o files that include the specified instantiations. Make sure you declare all instantiations required for your application program.

Explicit template instantiation can make compilation much faster by eliminating potential multiple instantiations of templates. For GNU **g++**, follow these steps:

1. Include explicit template instantiations in all template implementation files.
2. Add the #pragma interface line at the beginning of each template header file.
3. Add #pragma implementation at the beginning of each template implementation (.C) file.
4. Use the external template option for **g++**. For example,

    g++ -fexternal-templates VectorND.C testVectorND.C

Compiler Error Messages   A C++ compiler lists errors encountered when processing a file. Errors involve grammar problems, function-call mismatches, redeclaration of variables, missing punctuation, and so on. Each error is indicated with a filename and a line number. The actual mistake that leads to this error is either on this line or just before it. Don't be intimidated by the volume of errors or the strange syntax. There are two reasons why the compiler errors look strange:

- Because of function overloading, each unrecognized function call results in listing all function candidates for the call.
- Because of templates and the STL (even string is based on the basic_string template), some type names look very long and complicated.

On PCs

GNU **g++** is also freely available for the PC (http://www.delorie.com/djgpp/). And it works by commands at the MS/DOS level in ways similar to UNIX.

Another common environment is Microsoft Visual C++, whose usage is briefly introduced here. MS/Visual C++ offers a combined C and C++ *Integrated Development Environment* (IDE) providing a window-mouse-menu-oriented interface to text editing, compiling, linking/loading, debugging, and other facilities.

On PCs, a filename is not case sensitive — uppercase and lowercase characters are the same. Some standard filename extensions are listed in Table 14.5.

14.9 COMPILATION AND EXECUTION

Table 14.5 SOME STANDARD FILENAME EXTENSIONS

Extension	For
.CPP	C++ source file
.C	C source file
.H or .HPP	Header file
.OBJ	Object code (compiled) file
.EXE	Executable file
.DLL	Dynamic Loadable Library file
.LIB	Library file
.MAK	Project file (makefile)

There are two modes in which to use the MS/Visual C++ compiler: within the IDE and outside.

From DOS Level Working outside the Visual C++ IDE, give DOS commands to compile and run your C++ program. For example, the command

cl /c *FILENAME*.CPP

produces the compiled object file *FILENAME*.OBJ. The /c is an option (or switch) that tells the compiler **cl** to produce .OBJ files only and not to make them executable. If you have a complete program in a single source code file, using the **cl** command without the /c option produces the executable file *FILENAME*.EXE.

And the command

cl NEWCALC.CPP CALCENG.OBJ CALCFACE.OBJ CALCULATOR.OBJ MATH.LIB

produces the executable file NEWCALC.EXE (the name of the executable is based on the name of the first argument file given to **cl**). Then, you can run the program by giving the name of the executable file (NEWCALC) on the command line and supplying any appropriate command-line arguments. Clearly, the command **cl** takes source, object, and library files as arguments. Give the command

cl /HELP

to display a list of options that control **cl**. Use the online help facility or consult the run-time library manual for names of header files to include and library files, if any, to specify.

Compiling and Running Under IDE For single source file programs, simply select the **B**uild command from the **P**roject menu. This generates an .EXE file.

Within the MS/C++ IDE, create a project file (.MAK) to manage compilation and execution of a multiple-file program. The project file contains source, header, and library filenames, as well as other information.

To access the project-management functions, use the **P**roject option from the main menu. Select the **N**ew **P**roject option from the **P**roject menu to create a new project file. Use the **O**pen command to select an existing project file.

After creating a new project file, you can add files to the project and set build options. Then, you can save the project file. To compile a program controlled by a project file, simply **O**pen the project file from the **P**roject menu and then choose **B**uild or **R**ebuild to generate the .EXE file. The **E**xecute command from the **R**un menu runs the .EXE file. Any arguments your program needs can be supplied with the **P**rogram Arguments command on the **R**un menu. While your program is running, a user screen is active for interactions with the running program. The user screen disappears after the program terminates.

To separately compile any source code file, use the **C**ompile **F**ile command on the **P**roject menu. There are also facilities to help correct syntax problems detected by the compiler and to perform interactive debugging.

To run an executable program, click **E**xecute on the **B**uild menu. Or to run the program under the debugger, click **S**tart **D**ebug from the **B**uild menu and select options.

If your program reads standard input (`cin`), then input data comes from the keyboard. You can type multiple lines of input and, when the input is done, enter ^Z (control-Z) to end the input.

14.10 SUMMARY

The C++ compiler is available on a multitude of computers and operating environments. Some compilers may not be fully standard C++ compliant. Five distinct phases can be identified for the C++ compilation process: preprocessing, compilation, optimization, assembly, and linking/loading.

Header files are either native C++ or inherited from ANSI C. Standard C++ Library entities are in the `std` namespace. Include the required headers and `using` declarations for correct compilation.

Preprocessing, the first phase of compilation, performs some important program transformations before the output is sent to the compiling phase. Automatic transformations are trigraphs, comment deletion, BACKSLASH–NEWLINE deletion, and expansion of built-in macros (Table 14.4). Other operations can be requested using preprocessing directives.

Each directive takes one line and begins with a # followed by the directive keyword. Line continuation is allowed. The #include directive includes system- and user-supplied header files that may themselves contain #include directives.

The directives #if, #ifdef, #ifndef, #endif, #elif, and #else supply the flexibility to include/exclude portions of a source code file, depending on certain conditions. Multiple inclusion of the same header can be avoided through the once-only technique. It is recommended that all C++ headers be once-only.

There is also a macro mechanism to define symbolic constants and to use abbreviations for code sequences. The #define and #undef directives define and undefine macros. Constant variables (const) and inline functions (inline) should be used whenever possible instead of macros. The built-in macro assert(*expr*) is convenient for checking conditions that must hold at key points in a program.

EXERCISES

1. Consult and learn how to use the documentation for your C++ compiler. Compare it with the general description given in this chapter and note any differences.

2. For systems using a reduced character set, preprocessing allows the use of the following nine trigraph sequences for the corresponding single character:

   ```
   ??(  [      ??)  ]      ??=  #
   ??<  {      ??>  }      ??/  \
   ??'  ^      ??!  |      ??-  ~
   ```

   The preprocessing escape sequence ?? takes effect everywhere (including inside single and double quotes) and is processed before any other preprocessing transformation. Try a test program with ?? inside a string and see what happens. Trigraphs are normally not a concern for anyone using a full character set such as ASCII.

3. Will preprocessing handle circular file inclusion where file1.h includes file2.h, which in turn also includes file1.h? What happens in this situation on your system?

Chapter 14 COMPILING AND PREPROCESSING

4. Will preprocessing handle recursive macro definitions where the definition of a macro xyz directly or indirectly involves xyz itself?

5. Most C++ compilers allow you to process a compilation unit with preprocessing only, leaving the results in a file for inspection. Find out how this is done with your compiler.

6. Consider the following code fragment:

```
#define BUFFER_SIZE 1024
#define TABLE_SIZE BUFFER_SIZE/4
#undef BUFFER_SIZE
#define BUFFER_SIZE 512

cout << TABLE_SIZE;
```

What TABLE_SIZE will be displayed?

7. Consider multiple files, each containing a test main program used for testing the particular file. The test main program is conditionally included with #ifdef. Devise a convenient scheme that allows you to exclude all but a specific main program for any particular test run.

8. Consider the inline declaration. If a function is declared inline, should you put its definition in a .h file or in a .C file? Why?

9. Find out how well your C++ compiler supports templates. Does the export mechanism work? If not, does explicit instantiation work? Or do you have to resort to the inclusion model?

10. Explain clearly the differences and relations among Standard C++ header files, ANSI C header files, and ANSI C headers turned into C++ headers.

APPENDIX A

Summary of C++ Constructs

Class Declaration

```
class Name
{
            friend declarations
    public:
            public members
    protected:
            protected members
    private:
            private members
};
```

A class member is an instance member unless declared `static`, which makes it a class-wide member. The `struct` and `union` constructs have the same form as the `class`. A *nested class* is a class enclosed as a member in another class.

Derived Class Declaration

```
class Name : base-class list
{
            class body
};
```

where *base-class list* is a list of one or more base-class designations separated by commas. Each base-class designation takes the form

```
                    public
    [ virtual ]     protected     base-class name
                    private
```

(The default designation is `private`.)

Function Definition

```
valuetype fn_name ( type arg1, type arg2, ... )   // header
    throw( exceptions )                            // optional
{                                                  // body begin
    declarations and statements
}                                                  // body end

// valuetype can be void, argument list can be empty
// zero or more declarations, statements
```

Member Function Definition

```
valuetype ClassX::fn_name ( type arg1, type arg2, ... )   // header
    throw( exceptions )                                    // optional
{
    declarations and statements
}
```

The `if` Statement

```
if ( expr1 )
    statement-1
else if ( expr2 )    // optional
    statement-2
. . .
    . . .
else                 // optional
    statement-i
```

Iteration Statements

```
while ( continuation condition ) body

for ( init-stat cont-cond ; incr-expr ) body   // all parts optional

do body while ( continuation condition );
```

A `break` statement breaks out of the loop. A `continue` statement jumps to the beginning of the next cycle of the loop.

The `switch` Statement

```
switch ( expression )
{     case constant-expr1 :
        statements          // zero or more
```

Appendix A   SUMMARY OF C++ CONSTRUCTS   511

```
        case constant-expr2 :
            statements
        . . .
        default:                // optional
            statements
}
```

A break statement breaks out of the switch.

The typedef Declaration

```
typedef declaration of Newtype as if it is a variable ;
```

The goto Statement

```
label: statement
...
goto label;
```

Array Declarations

```
type array_name[10];              // linear array
type array_name[10][20];          // two-dimensional array
type array_name[10][20][30];      // three-dimensional array
```

The enum Declaration

```
enum name {  symbol₁[ = val₁],
             symbol₂[ = val₂],
             ...
          };
```

Exceptions

Catching Exceptions:

```
try {    statements
    }
    catch(e-type₁ e)
    {    statements    }
    catch(e-type₂ e)
    {    statements    }
     . . . // any more catch clauses
    catch (...)  // optional catchall clause
    {    statements    }
```

Throwing Exceptions:

```
throw( exception_object )
```

The Function Prototype

```
value_type fn_name(type1, type2, . . . );
void fn_name(type1, type2, . . . );        // returns no value
value_type fn_name();                       // takes no arguments
```

The Function Pointer

```
value_type (* fn_ptr) (type1, type2, . . .);
```

Namespace

```
namespace xyz{ ... }    // puts all enclosed constructs in namespace xyz
using xyz;              // imports all names from namespace xyz
using xyz::ident;       // imports ident from namespace xyz
```

Overloading ++, --, and [ ]

```
type ClassX::operator ++();              // prefix ++ as class member
type operator ++(type arg);              // prefix ++ as nonmember
type ClassX::operator ++(int);           // postfix ++ as class member
type operator ++(type arg, int);         // postfix ++ as nonmember
type& ClassX::operator [](int);                  // read or write
const type&ClassX::operator [](int) const; // read only
```

The overloaded operator -- has the same forms as ++, and * has the same forms as [].

Class-Defined Conversion

```
ClassX::operator type();   // converts host to type
ClassX::ClassX(type);      // converts type to ClassX
```

Offset Pointer to Member

```
type ClassX::* opmd;           // declares opmd data opm
type (ClassX::* opmf)(...);    // declares opmf function opm
& ClassX::xyz                  // gets offset value of member
obj.*opmd                      // dereferences opmd in obj
objptr->*opmd                  // dereferences opmd? in *objptr
(obj.*opmf)(...)               // calls function in obj via opmf
(objptr->*opmf)(...)           // calls function in *objptr a opmf
```

Templates

Function Template:

```
template < type T, ... >       // one or more template parameters
function prototype or definition
```

Class Template:

```
template < type T, ... >       // one or more template parameters
class declaration or definition
ClassX< types >var( args );    // template class object declaration
```

Formal template parameters can be either typename or normal-type parameters.

Template Specialization:

```
template < >                   // zero template parameters
function definition

A normal function template     // for a proper subset of types
```

Template Explicit Instantiation:

```
template
class or function declaration  // with explicit template arguments
```

Union as Class Member

```
union
{   type    id1;
    type    id2;
};
```

Bit-Packing Class Members

```
typedef unsigned int Bit;

Bit dept : 16;    // department code, lower 16 bits
Bit div  : 8;     // division id, next 8 bits
```

```
Bit  rgn : 6;   // region designation, next 6 bits
Bit    q : 2;   // 1st, 2nd, 3rd, or 4th quarter, next 2 bits
```

C++ Keywords

```
and         and_eq   asm           auto        bitand    bitor
bool        break    case          catch       char      class
compl       const    const_cast    continue    default   delete
do          double   dynamic_cast  else        enum      explicit
export      extern   false         float       for       friend
goto        if       inline        int         long      mutable
namespace   new      not           not_eq      operator  or
or_eq       private  protected     public      register  reinterpret_cast
return      short    signed        sizeof      static    static_cast
struct      switch   template      this        throw     true
try         typedef  typeid        typename    union     unsigned
using       virtual  void          volatile    wchat_t   while
xor         xor_eq
```

Among the keywords, the following are keyword versions of their operator counterparts:

```
and     &&    and_eq  &=    bitand  &
bitor   |     compl   ~     not     !
or      ||    or_eq   |=    xor     ^
xor_eq  ^=    not_eq  !=
```

APPENDIX B

Summary of Special Member Functions

Table B.1

Special Member	Inherited	May Be `virtual`	Return Type	May Be `static`	Generated by Default
Constructor	No	No	No	No	Yes
Copy constructor	No	No	No	No	Yes
Destructor	No	Yes	No	No	Yes
operator=	No	Yes	Yes	No	Yes
operator()	Yes	Yes	Yes	No	No
operator[]	Yes	Yes	Yes	No	No
operator->	Yes	Yes	Yes	No	No
operator new	Yes	No	void*	Must be	No
operator delete	Yes	No	void	Must be	No
Type conversion	Yes	Yes	No	No	No

```
explicit ClassX::ClassX( args )                   // constructor
  : base and member object init-list
{ other initial actions }

ClassX::~ClassX( );                               // destructor
ClassX::ClassX( const ClassX& );                  // copy constructor
ClassX::ClassX( ClassX& );
ClassX& ClassX::operator=( const ClassX& );       // assignment
ClassX::operator type ();                         // conversion to type
```

A constructor taking one argument is declared `explicit` to avoid also becoming a type conversion specification.

APPENDIX C
C-Style Strings

Include <string.h> to use these functions common to Standard C++ and ANSI C. Tables C.1 and C.2 employ the notation

- s   (a character string terminated by '\0' to be modified by the library function)
- cs   (a const character string not to be modified)
- n   (an integer of type size_t)
- c   (a single char)

The type size_t usually means an unsigned integer of a certain size, depending on the computer, and is defined in the standard header file <stddef.h>. For most purposes, size_t is the same as unsigned int.

To use any of the string library functions, the header file <string.h> must be included. The functions in Table C.1 actually alter their first arguments. For copying or concatenating, make sure there is enough room in s to accommodate the incoming characters. The **strcmp** functions compare strings lexicographically (in dictionary order), returning a negative, zero, or positive value in case the first argument is less than, equal to, or greater than the second. For **strncpy**, if cs has more than n characters, no '\0' terminator is copied.

Table C.1 DESTRUCTIVE STRING OPERATIONS

Function	Description
char *strcat(s,cs)	Concatenates a copy of cs to end of s; returns s.
char *strncat(s,cs,n)	Concatenates a copy of at most n characters of cs to end of s; returns s.
char *strcpy(s,cs)	Copies cs to s including '\0'; returns s.
char *strncpy(s,cs,n)	Copies at most n characters of cs to s; returns s, pads with '\0' if cs has less than n characters.
char *strtok(s,cs)	Finds tokens in s delimited by characters in cs.

Table C.2 NONDESTRUCTIVE STRING OPERATIONS

Function	Description
size_t **strlen**(cs)	Returns length of cs (excluding '\0').
char ***strcmp**(cs1,cs2)	Compares cs1 and cs2; returns negative, zero, or positive for cs1 <, ==, or > cs2, respectively.
char ***strncmp**(cs1,cs2,n)	Compares at most first n characters of cs1 and cs2.
char ***strchr**(cs,c)	Returns pointer to first occurrence of c in cs.
char ***strrchr**(cs,c)	Returns pointer to last occurrence of c in cs.
char ***strpbrk**(cs1,cs2)	Returns pointer to first character in cs1 and in cs2.
char ***strstr**(cs1,cs2)	Returns pointer to first occurrence of cs2 in cs1. *All four functions return* NULL *if the search fails.*
size_t **strspn**(cs1,cs2)	Returns length of prefix of cs1 consisting of characters from cs2.
size_t **strcspn**(cs1,cs2)	Returns length of prefix of cs1 consisting of characters *not* in cs2.

The **strtok** function is a little more involved than the other functions. The purpose of **strtok** is to scan its first argument and break it up into tokens. A *token* is a sequence of characters forming a word such as a variable name or an arithmetic operator. Tokens in a character string are separated from one another by one or more *delimiter* characters. The delimiters are indicated by the second argument cs. To extract tokens from a string, a series of calls are made to **strtok**, with each call returning a pointer to the next token as a '\0'-terminated string. The first invocation of **strtok** supplies a nonempty string s and receives the first token. All subsequent calls pass NULL as the first argument and receive successive tokens.

The tokens are returned in place by overwriting the first delimiter character after each token with a '\0'. Table C.3 illustrates how **strtok** breaks "ls   /user/fac/pwang" into tokens. In Table C.3, ⊔ stands for a space, ⊗ for a '\0'. Naturally, each token returned contains no delimiter characters. A NULL is returned when **strtok** finds no more tokens. Also, the delimiters contained in cs may be different on each call.

Table C.3 USING strtok

Call Sequence		Token Found Is Underlined
1	strtok(str, del)	<u>ls</u>⊗␣␣/user/fac/pwang⊗
2	strtok(NULL, del)	ls⊗␣␣/<u>user</u>⊗fac/pwang⊗
3	strtok(NULL, del)	ls⊗␣␣/user⊗<u>fac</u>⊗pwang⊗
4	strtok(NULL, del)	ls⊗␣␣/user⊗fac⊗<u>pwang</u>⊗

str = "ls␣␣/user/fac/pwang" and del = "␣/"

Let's examine an actual implementation of **strtok**:

```
#include <string.h>

char * strtok(char * s, const char * del)
{   char * token;
    int i = 0;
    static char *spt = NULL;              // starting position
    if ( s ) spt = s;                     // new string
    if ( !spt || spt[0] == '\0' )
        return NULL;
    while ( spt[i] != '\0'                // find beginning of token
        && strchr(del, spt[i]) ) i++;
    token = &spt[i];
    while ( spt[i] != '\0'                // find end of token
        && !strchr(del, spt[i]) ) i++;
    spt[i] = '\0';                        // terminator in place
    spt = &spt[i+1];                      // record position
    return token;                         // token produced
}
```

A static pointer spt remembers, across calls to **strtok**, the beginning of the string yet to be processed. The library function **strchr** is used to determine whether a character is a delimiter (contained in the string del) or not.

APPENDIX D

Unions and Bit Fields

Basic Concepts

An int variable holds integer values, and a double variable holds double data. Is it possible or desirable for a variable to hold one type of value at certain times and other types of values at other times? Yes, and a union variable has exactly this property. A union is declared with the same syntax as a class. Once a *union tag* is established, it can be used to define objects of that type. The declaration

```
union IntDouble
{       int     ival;     // public members
        double dval;
}
```

creates the union tag IntDouble, which can be used in

```
IntDouble x;
```

to declare a union variable x, which can hold *either* int *or* double values:

```
x.ival = 9;        // x as int variable
x.dval = 4.321;    // x as double var, overwrites int value
```

In effect, a union object is a struct object that stores all its data members at the same location (offset zero relative to the beginning of the object). A union object is given enough space to hold the largest of its data members. Thus, a union object holds only one type of value at a time. The member notations x.dval and x.ival are used not to get different offsets but to get different interpretations of data stored at the same location. Hence, the compiler treats x.ival as an int variable and x.dval as a double even though both occupy the same memory address. It is your responsibility to access a union object correctly to retrieve the most recently assigned value.

Consider dividing one integer by another. To make things interesting, let's define a function that returns either an integer or a double, depending on whether the division is even:

```
IntDouble divide(int a, int b, int& evenflag)
{   IntDouble ans;                        // union object
    if ( (evenflag = !(a % b)) )          // even division
        ans.ival = a/b;                   // ans is int
    else                                  // otherwise
        ans.dval = a/static_cast
                        < double >(b);    // ans is double
    return ans;
}
```

The reference parameter `evenflag` is set correctly so that a calling function of `divide` can examine its value to determine whether an `int` or a `double` has been returned. Thus, we can write a test function as follows:

```
void test(int a, int b)
{   int flag;
    IntDouble x = divide(a,b,flag);
    std::cout << a << '/' << b << " = ";
    if ( flag )
        std::cout << x.ival << std::endl;
    else
        std::cout << x.dval << std::endl;
}
```

Then, when we run the program, the calls

```
test(8, 4);
test(2, 3);
```

should produce the following output:

```
8/4 = 2
2/3 = 0.666667
```

Union objects can occur in arrays and other objects just as class objects can. The notations for a `union` are the same as for a `struct`. In fact, a `union` could be redefined as a `struct` and used without change. The only difference would be the space needed; a union uses less storage because all members are stored at the same location.

A class with a constructor, destructor, user-defined copy, or assignment operator cannot be the type of a union member because the compiler would not know which member to destroy.

Appendix D UNIONS AND BIT FIELDS   521

The artificial example here illustrates the basic concepts of unions. Let's now examine a few actual applications.

Heterogeneous Data Structures

The primary purpose of a union is to create *heterogeneous* structures—that is, data whose elements are not of the same type. This ability allows you to use, for example, either an array of numbers and strings or a list of various types of items. An example uses the union mechanism to build nested lists. Consider lists of the form

```
(A B C D E)
((A B) C (D E))
((A (B C)) (D E))
```

These are nested lists of characters. A *nested list* of characters is one containing zero or more characters and/or nested lists. Therefore, items in a nested list are objects of type NItem:

```
class NList;

class NItem
{ friend class NList;
  private:
    enum CL {CHAR, LIST};
    union       // anonymous union
    {   char    ch;
        NList&  lis;
    };
    CL l_c;   // CHAR or LIST indicator
    NItem* next;
    NItem(char c = '\0', NItem* ptr = NULL)
      : l_c(CHAR), ch(c), next(ptr) { }    // constructor
    NItem(NList& nl, NItem* ptr = NULL)
      : l_c(LIST), lis(nl), next(ptr) { }  // constructor
};
```

As you can see, NItem is a modification of the ListCell class. The value cell in NItem now becomes a union storing either a single character or a NList reference. Correct interpretation of the union is ensured through proper use of the indicator l_c.

If a union is given neither a tag nor a variable to declare, then it is an *anonymous union*. Member names in an anonymous union surface to its enclosing scope and can be used directly there. Thus, for the NItem example, the code fragment

```
NItem a('F');
if ( a.l_c == NItem::CHAR ) std::cout << a.ch;
```

shows direct access of the union member ch. Anonymous unions cannot have nonpublic members or member functions.

Actual nested lists are objects of the friend class NList whose definition is outlined here:

```
class NList
{ public:
    NList() : head(NULL) { }          // empty list constructor
    NList(char c)                      // list with first cell
     : head (new NItem(c,NULL)) { }
    bool putOn(char c);                // put on a char          (1)
    bool putOn(NList& c);              // put on a list          (2)
    bool insert(char c, NItem* e);     // insert a char
    bool insert(NList& nl, NItem* e);  // insert a list
    NItem* last();                     // last item
    bool append(char c);               // insert char at end
    bool append(NList& nl);            // insert list at end
    void display(NItem* p);            // display from p to end (3)
    void display() { display(head); }  // display whole list
    /*   ...  */
  private:
    NItem* head;                       // first cell of list
    void free();                       // free all cells
};
```

The second version of the member function putOn (line 2) helps construct nested lists:

```
bool NList::putOn(NList& nl)
{   NItem* tmp = new NItem(nl, head);
    if ( tmp )
    {  head = tmp;
       return true;
    }
    else return false; // failed
}
```

It puts the given nested list nl at the beginning of the host object. Other member functions may provide insertion at other places in a list. And the function append inserts a new item at the end of the list.

```
bool NList::append(char c)
{   return insert(c, last());  }

bool NList::append(NList& nl)
{   return insert(nl, last());  }
```

The display function is recursive in order to process nested sublists. It can also be given a second argument to control the display of a final NEWLINE:

```
void NList::display(NItem* p)
{   std::cout << "(";
    while ( p )
    {   if ( p->l_c == NItem::CHAR )
            std::cout << p->ch;
        else
            p->lis.display();
        if ( p = p->next ) std::cout << " ";
    }
    std::cout << ")";
}
```

The union saves space by storing different data members at the same location. In addition to the union, C++ offers another way to save space in a program, as explained next.

Bit Fields

A class member can be declared to occupy a few bits in a single word. This ability allows you to pack information more tightly for certain applications. Such members are known as *bit fields* and are either signed or unsigned integer types with the number of bits specified after a colon (:).

For example, consider a departmental quarterly report class. It can have, among others, four bit fields:

```
typedef unsigned int Bit;

Bit dept : 16; // department code, lower 16 bits
Bit div  :  8; // division id, next 8 bits
Bit rgn  :  6; // region designation, next 6 bits
Bit   q  :  2; // 1st, 2nd, 3rd, or 4th quarter, next 2 bits
```

Figure D.1 BIT FIELD MEMBERS

31	30	29		24	23		16	15		0
←	q	→	←	rgn	→	←	div	→	← dept →	

When given consecutively, these four members fit into a 32-bit word (Figure D.1). Bit field members, except for storage, are no different from other data members of a class.

APPENDIX E
Interactive Debugging with dbx

Debugging with dbx

While the C++ compiler identifies problems at the syntax level, you still need a good tool for debugging at run time. On PCs, the C++ program development environment normally supports a convenient interactive debugger. See your PC manual for more details.

A convenient UNIX utility for source-level debugging and controlled execution of programs is **dbx**. It can be used to debug programs written in any source language such as C++, C, f77, or Pascal, provided that the object files have been compiled to contain the appropriate symbol information for use by **dbx**. On some UNIX workstations, you may find **dbx** available inside a window-menu-oriented debugging package that supplies multiple windows and other useful features for easier debugging. The **dbxtool** on Sun computers is an example.

You should use **dbx** as a routine tool for debugging programs. It is much more efficient than inserting `cerr` lines in the source code.

Because **dbx** provides an interactive debugging environment and correlates run-time activities to statements in the program source codes, it is called a *source-level* debugger. Debugging is performed by running the target program under the control of the **dbx** utility. The main features of **dbx** are:

1. *Source-level tracing*: When a part of a program is *traced*, useful information will be displayed whenever that part is executed. If you trace a function, the name of the calling function, the value of the arguments passed, and the return value will be displayed each time the traced function is called. You can also trace specific lines of code and individual variables. In the latter case, you are notified every time the variable value changes.
2. *Placing source-level break points*: A break point in a program causes execution to suspend when that point is reached. At the break point,

you can interact with **dbx** and use its full set of commands to investigate the situation before resuming execution.

3. *Single source-line stepping*: When you are examining a section of code closely, you can have execution proceed one source line at a time. (Note that one line may consist of several machine instructions.)
4. *Displaying source code*: You can ask **dbx** to display any part of the program source from any file.
5. *Examining values*: Values, declarations, and other attributes of identifiers can also be displayed.
6. *Editing source files*: If you want to correct an error, you can edit source code files (for later recompilation) from within **dbx**.
7. *Object-level debugging*: Machine instruction-level execution control and displaying of memory contents or register values are also provided.

To debug a C++ program using **dbx**, make sure each object file has been compiled with a native-mode compiler (e.g., the GNU **g++**) and the -g has been specified. One simple way to achieve this is to compile all source code (.C) files at once using the following command:

g++ -g *source_files*

This results in an executable a.out file suitable to run under the control of **dbx**. Then, to invoke **dbx**, simply type

dbx a.out

to debug the executable a.out file. When you see the prompt (dbx), the debugger is ready for an interactive session. When you are finished, simply type the **dbx** command

quit

to exit from **dbx**.

A typical debugging session should follow these steps:

1. Invoke **dbx** on an executable file compiled with the -g option.
2. Put in trace and/or break points.
3. Run the program under **dbx**.
4. Examine trace output and display program values at break points.
5. Install new trace and/or break points to focus on bugs, deleting old trace and/or break points as appropriate.
6. Resume or restart execution.
7. Repeat steps 4–7 until satisfied.

Summary of **dbx** Commands

Table E.1

Command	Meaning
run	Begins execution of the program.
cont	Continues execution.
step	Single steps one line.
next	Steps to next line (skips over calls).
trace *line#*	Traces execution of the line.
trace *function*	Traces calls to the function.
trace *var*	Traces changes to the variable.
trace *expr* **at** *line#*	Displays *expr* when *line* is reached.
stop at *line*	Suspends execution at the line.
stop in *function*	Suspends execution when *function* is called.
status	Displays trace/stops in effect.
delete *number*	Removes trace or stop of given number.
call *function*	Calls the function.
dump *function*	Displays values related to the function.
where	Displays currently active functions.
set *var* = *expr*	Sets variable to the value of the expression.
print *expr*	Displays the value of the expression.
whatis *name*	Displays the declaration of the name.
list *line, line*	Lists source lines.
edit *function*	Edits file containing *function*.
quit	Exits **dbx**.

APPENDIX F

Functions with a Variable Number of Arguments

C++ supports functions taking an indefinite number of arguments. The concept is natural for functions such as sum, product, max, and min.

The notation

```
int sum(int argcnt, ...)            // variable args notation
```

is used to declare sum as a function of one or more arguments. The first parameter is argcnt, and it is of type int. The ellipsis (...) indicates that the number and type of the remaining (undeclared) arguments may vary. An indefinite parameter declaration must begin with at least one named parameter, such as argcnt in this example. A function declared in this way may each time be passed a different number of arguments of arbitrary types.

At run time, when a function with an indefinite number of parameters is actually invoked, the number and type of the arguments being passed in the particular call must somehow be made known to the called function. There are several ways to do this. If the types of the undeclared arguments are fixed, this information can be hard-coded in the called function. Alternatively, the count and types of the unnamed arguments may be supplied in the leading named arguments. Instead of the argument count, a terminator marking the end of the unnamed arguments may be appropriate in certain applications. Again, the terminator used may be fixed or supplied in a leading named argument.

The principal problem for a function taking a variable number of arguments lies in *referencing the unnamed arguments*. Macros defined in the standard header <stdarg.h> provide the solution. These macros are as follows:

va_list   (argument pointer type—declares argument pointer)
va_start   (variable argument start—initializes access to unnamed arguments)

Appendix F FUNCTIONS WITH A VARIABLE NUMBER OF ARGUMENTS

va_arg (next variable argument—accesses individual unnamed arguments)

va_end (variable argument end—cleans up before returning from function)

These concepts can be made clearer with an example. Let's define the function sum:

```
#include   <stdarg.h>      // header for variable argument list

int sum(int argcnt, ...)   // argcnt gives number of other args
{     va_list ap;          // argument pointer
      int ans = 0;
      va_start(ap, argcnt); // initialize ap
      while ( argcnt-- > 0 )// process all args
          ans += va_arg(ap, int);
      va_end(ap);          // clean up before function returns
      return(ans);
}
```

The type **va_list** is a macro to declare a variable ap (argument pointer), which is used to refer to each unnamed argument in turn. The macro **va_start** initializes ap to point to the first unnamed argument (Figure F.1). To locate the first unnamed argument, **va_start** also needs the last named argument, argcnt in this example. Once ap is properly initialized, the macro **va_arg** is used to return the next unnamed argument on the argument list. The **va_arg** macro also advances ap to point to the next argument. To do this, **va_arg** needs the type, and thereby the size, of the unnamed argument. In sum, the type int has been given. After all such arguments have been retrieved, the pointer ap is then given to the macro **va_end** to perform the required cleanup actions. Notice that the second argument of **va_arg** is a type name and not a variable. Therefore, if a function wishes to obtain unnamed arguments of mixed types, several different **va_arg** statements, controlled perhaps by a switch or an if, should be used. For example, in an arrangement where the type of an unnamed

Figure F.1 VARIABLE-LENGTH ARGUMENTS

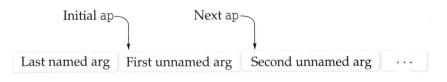

argument is given by a string contained in the previous unnamed argument, you can use a code such as this:

```
double x;   int i; char* t;
/* ... */
t = va_arg(ap, char*);
if ( strcmp(t,"double") == 0 )
    x = va_arg(ap, double);
else if ( strcmp(t, "int") == 0 )
    i = va_arg(ap, int);
/* ... */
```

Because the number and type of arguments are unknown at compile time, the space to receive incoming arguments must be allocated at run time, a principal job of **va_start**. The duty of **va_end** is to return dynamic storage used.

APPENDIX G
Operator Precedence

All C++ operators are listed here according to their relative precedence. An operator on an earlier line takes precedence over any that come after. Operators on the same line have the same precedence. An expression involving operators of the same precedence is evaluated according to the *associativity rule* of the operators. Unary operators and assignment operators are right-associative; other operators are left-associative. Note that the unary operators +, -, and * (value-of) take precedence over the binary forms.

Table G.1   OPERATOR PRECEDENCE

```
::
()  []  ->  .   typeid  4-kind_cast  postfix ++ --
!  ~  +  -  *  &  type()  sizeof  new  delete  prefix ++ --
.*   ->*
*    /    %
+    -
<<   >>
<    <=   >    >=
==   !=
&
^
|
&&
||
?:
=  +=  -=  *=  /=  %=  ^=  |=  &=  <<=  >>=
throw
,
```

APPENDIX H

Implicit Type Conversions

Inheritance-Related Conversions

A derived object, reference, or pointer is implicitly converted to a corresponding *accessible* base type. An opm (offset pointer to member) is implicitly converted from an accessible base type to a derived type. User-defined conversions are also applied by the compiler. Such conversions are applied in passing arguments, initializing, branching and iteration control, and returning value from a function.

Any pointer can also be converted to void* implicitly. Any zero-valued constant expression can be converted to any pointer or opm.

Standard Arithmetic Conversions

When the two arguments of an operator have different types, automatic type conversion is performed before the operation is carried out. The conversion rules summarized here are applied in the order given:

Table H.1

Rule	If one operand is	Convert the other operand to
1.	long double	long double
2.	double	double
3.	float	float
4.	long int	long int

After these rules are carried out, *integral promotions* are applied on both operands. Integral promotions upgrade a char, a short int, an int bit field (or their signed or unsigned varieties), or an enumeration object to type `int`. Then, the following rules are used in the order given:

5. If one operand has type `unsigned long int`, convert the other operand to the same.
6. If one operand has type `long int` and the other `unsigned int`, convert the latter to `long int` if this type can accommodate all values of type `unsigned int`; if this is not the case, convert both operands to `unsigned long int`.
7. If one operand has type `long int`, convert the other to `long int`.
8. If one operand has type `unsigned int`, convert the other to `unsigned int`.
9. Both operands must now have type `int`.

Also a `bool` or an `enum` is implicitly converted to an `int`. Any arithmetic or pointer value is implicitly converted to bool—nonzero to `true` and zero to `false`. Floating to integer conversion is by truncation. Floating to floating conversion is to nearest value.

APPENDIX I
C++ Library Functions Common with C

Character and String Functions

Character-set-independent functions (or macros) are supplied to deal with characters. The header <ctype.h> should be used.

Table I.1

Function	Test For
int **isupper**(int c)	Uppercase letter
int **islower**(int c)	Lowercase letter
int **isalpha**(int c)	Uppercase or lowercase letter
int **isdigit**(int c)	Decimal digit
int **isalnum**(int c)	**isalpha**(c) || **isdigit**(c)
int **iscntrl**(int c)	Control character
int **isxdigit**(int c)	Hexadecimal digit
int **isprint**(int c)	Printing character including SPACE
int **isgraph**(int c)	Printing character except SPACE
int **isspace**(int c)	SPACE, \f, \n, \r, \t, v
int **ispunct**(int c)	Printing character not SPACE, digit, or letter

Function	Meaning
int **toupper**(int c)	Converts to uppercase.
int **tolower**(int c)	Converts to lowercase.

C-style string functions are given in Appendix C.

Appendix I   C++ LIBRARY FUNCTIONS COMMON WITH C

Arbitrary Types as Character Arrays

It is sometimes convenient to process data of other types as a sequence of characters in consecutive memory locations. A set of library functions exists for this purpose. The header <memory.h> should be used.

void ***memcpy**(void *target, const void *source, size_t n)

copies n characters from source to target, which is returned.

void ***memmove**(void *target, const void *source, size_t n)

is the same as **memcpy** but works even if s and ct overlap.

int **memcmp**(const void *cs, const void *ct, size_t n)

compares the first n characters of cs with ct and returns a positive, negative, or zero value (as **strcmp**).

void ***memchr**(const void *cs, const char c, size_t n)

returns a pointer to the first character c in cs or NULL if c is not among the first n characters.

void ***memset**(void *s, const char c, size_t n)

sets each of the first n characters of s to c and returns s.

Floating-Point Calculations

To use the functions listed here, include the header file <math.h>. To check possible domain and range errors, you also need the header <errno.h>, which defines EDOM, ERANGE, and HUGE_VAL. In the following, the variables xx and yy are of type double, and i is an int. All functions return double.

sin(xx)   Sine of xx
cos(xx)   Cosine of xx
tan(xx)   Tangent of xx
sinh(xx)   Hyperbolic sine of xx
cosh(xx)   Hyperbolic cosine of xx
tanh(xx)   Hyperbolic tangent of xx
exp(xx) e^{xx}
log(xx)   Natural logarithm $\ln(xx)$, $xx > 0$
log10(xx)   Base 10 logarithm $\log_{10}(xx)$, $xx > 0$
asin(xx) $\sin^{-1}(xx)$ in range $[-\pi/2, \pi/2]$, $xx \in [-1, 1]$
acos(xx) $\cos^{-1}(xx)$ in range $[0, \pi]$, $xx \in [-1, 1]$

atan(xx) $\tan^{-1}(xx)$ in range $[-\pi/2, \pi]$

atan2(xx, yy) $\tan^{-1}(xx/yy)$ in range $[-\pi, \pi]$

sqrt(xx)   Square root of xx, $xx \geq 0$

ceil(xx)   Ceiling of xx as double

floor(xx)   Floor of xx as double

fabs(xx)   Absolute value of xx

ldexp(xx, n) $xx \cdot 2^n$

pow(xx, yy) xx^{yy}; if $xx = 0$ and $yy \leq 0$ or if $xx < 0$ and yy is not equal to an integer, a domain error results

In addition to the functions just listed, there are also the following functions for fractional parts and floating remainder.

frexp(xx, int *exp)

computes the fractional and exponent parts of xx. The fractional part (fr) is normalized ($0.5 \leq fr < 1$) and returned. The power-of-2 exponent is stored in exp so that $xx = fr \cdot 2^{(*exp)}$. If xx is zero, both parts of the result are zero.

modf(xx, double *ip)

computes the fractional and exponent parts of xx. The fractional part fr has the same sign as xx and is not normalized. The integer part is stored in ip so that $xx = *ip + fr$.

fmod(xx, yy)

computes a remainder of xx by subtracting yy from xx an integral number of times. The result is less than xx in magnitude and has the same sign.

Error-Handling Functions

```
#include <stdlib.h>
void exit(int status)
```

causes normal termination of the program. The value status is passed to the environment.

```
void abort(void)
```

causes abnormal termination of the program as if by raise(SIGABRT).

```
int atexit(void (* fn)(void))   [nonzero]
```

registers the function fn to be invoked when the program terminates normally. Multiple calls to **atexit** set up a sequence of such functions executed at exit time in the reverse order as registered.

Appendix I   C++ LIBRARY FUNCTIONS COMMON WITH C

String-to-Number Conversions (`<stdlib.h>`)

`double` **`atof`**`(CSTR str)`

converts string `str` to a `double`, which is returned.

`int` **`atoi`**`(CSTR str)`

converts string `str` to an `int`, which is returned.

`long` **`atol`**`(CSTR str)`

converts string `str` to a `long`, which is returned.

`double` **`strtod`**`(CSTR str, char **rest)`

converts the prefix of the string `str` to a `double`, ignoring any leading white space. It also stores in `*rest` a pointer to the rest of the string after the consumed prefix, unless `rest` is `NULL`. Overflow and underflow are detected, and `ERANGE` is set.

`long` **`strtol`**`(CSTR str, char **rest, int base)`

treats the prefix of `str` as a number of the given `base` and converts it to `long`. It is otherwise similar to **`strtod`**. If base is zero, the integer constant notations are recognized.

`unsigned long` **`strtoul`**`(CSTR str, char **rest, int base)`

is the same as **`strtol`**, except the result is `unsigned long`.

Date and Time

The header `<time.h>` defines structures, macros, and functions for manipulating date and time. The date is kept according to the Gregorian calendar (in common use). Date and time can be represented in calendar time, local time, or daylight-saving time.

The *broken-down* time structure `struct tm` includes the following members:

`int tm_sec;` Seconds after the minute (0–59)

`tm_min;` Minutes after the hour (0–59)

`tm_hour;` Hours since midnight (0–23)

`tm_mday;` Day of the month (1–31)

`tm_mon;` Months since January (0–11)

`int tm_year;` Years since 1900

`int tm_wday;` Days since Sunday (0–6)

`int tm_yday;` Days since January 1 (0–365)

`int tm_isdst;` Daylight-saving time flag

The value of tm_isdst is positive if daylight-saving time is in effect, zero if not, and negative if unknown. There are also clock_t and time_t, which are arithmetic types capable of representing time.

clock_t **clock**(void)

returns the processor time used by the program since the beginning of its execution or −1 if unavailable. Use clock()/CLOCKS_PER_SEC to convert to seconds. To measure the time spent in a program, the clock function should be called at the start of the program and its return value subtracted from subsequent calls.

time_t **time**(time_t *tptr)

returns the current calendar time in an implementation-defined encoding of type time_t or −1 if not available. The value is also assigned to *tptr if tptr is not NULL.

struct tm ***localtime**(const time_t *tptr)

converts the given calendar time *tptr and creates a broken-down time structure representing the corresponding local time. A pointer to the structure is returned.

double **difftime**(time_t t1, time_t t2)

returns t1 − t2 in seconds.

time_t **mktime**(struct tm *tptr)

takes the (partial) local-time information contained in the given structure *tptr and determines the values of all members in calendar-time form (*tptr is modified). It also returns the calendar time as encoded by time (or −1). This is useful to obtain the broken-down calendar time for a future or past date.

char ***asctime**(const struct tm *tptr)

converts the broken-down time in *tptr into a string in the form

Sun Dec 23 15:35:22 1990\n\0

char ***ctime**(const time_t *tptr)

is the same as **asctime**(**localtime**(tptr)).

struct tm* **gmtime**(const time_t *tptr)   [NULL]

converts the calendar time *tptr into coordinated universal time (UTC) and returns the broken-down structure.

size_t **strftime**(char *s, size_t slen, CSTR fmt, const struct tm *tptr)

Appendix I   C++ LIBRARY FUNCTIONS COMMON WITH C   539

formats data and time given by *tptr into the string s (maximum length is slen) according to the format specified by fmt. The format is analogous to that for **printf**.

%a, %A: Abbreviated or full weekday name
%b, %B: Abbreviated or full month name
%c: Local date and time representation
%d: Day of month (01–31)
%H, %I: Hour (00–23) or (01–12)
%j: Day of the year (001–366)
%m: Month (01–12)
%M, %S: Minute, second (00–59)
%p: Local equivalent of A.M. or P.M.
%U, %W: Number of weeks/year (Sunday/Monday as first day of week)
%w: Day of week (0–6; Sunday is 0)
%x, %X: Local date, time representation
%Y, %y: Year with, without century
%Z: Time-zone name, if any
%%: %% % %

Utility Functions

Functions listed here all use the header <stdlib.h>.

int **abs**(int n)
long **labs**(long n)

returns the absolute value of n.

div_t **div**(int num, int denom)

computes the quotient and remainder of num divided by denom and stores the results in quot and rem, int members of the structure div_t.

ldiv_t **ldiv**(long num, long denom)

computes the quotient and remainder of num divided by denom and stores the results in quot and rem, long members of the structure ldiv_t.

void **rand**(void)

returns the next random integer in a pseudorandom sequence based on a seed given by a prior call to srand. The default seed value is 1. The random integers are in the range 0–RAND_MAX.

void **srand**(unsigned int seed)

sets the seed value for a new random sequence to be used by subsequent calls to **rand**. The same seed value gives rise to the same random sequence.

```
void *bsearch(const void *key, const void *base,
              size_t n, size_t size
              int (*cmp) (const void *key, const void *datum))
```

searches an array located at base with n elements, each of size size, for an element matching the given key. The supplied comparison function cmp takes a key and an array element and produces a negative, zero, or positive int value as **strcmp**. The array must already be in increasing order as defined by the same comparison function.

```
void qsort(void *base, size_t n, size_t size,
           int (*cmp)(const void*, const void *))
```

sorts an array located at base with n elements, each of size size, with the supplied comparison function cmp, which takes two array entries and returns a negative, zero, or positive int as **strcmp**.

int **system**(CSTR cmd)

passes the string cmd to the operating system for execution. If cmd is NULL, then **system** returns zero if there is no command processor. Otherwise, the return value is implementation dependent.

char ***getenv**(CSTR name)

returns the environment string associated with the given name or NULL if no such string exists.

Implementation-Defined Data Limits

The header <limits.h> contains symbolic constants for implementation-defined size limits for integer quantities. The limits must not be more restrictive than the following values:

CHAR_BIT[Bits per character]   8

MB_LEN_MAX[Byte per character]   1

SCHAR_MIN[signed char minimum]   -127

SCHAR_MAX[signed char maximum]   127

UCHAR_MAX[unsigned char maximum]   255U

CHAR_MIN[0 or SCHAR_MIN]

Appendix I C++ LIBRARY FUNCTIONS COMMON WITH C

CHAR_MAX[SCHAR_MAX or SCHAR_MAX]
SHRT_MIN[short int minimum] -32767
SHRT_MAX[short int maximum] 32767
USHRT_MAX[unsigned short int maximum] 65535U
INT_MIN[int minimum] -32767
INT_MAX[int maximum] 32767
UINT_MAX[unsigned int maximum] 65535
LONG_MIN[long int minimum] -2147483647
LONG_MAX[long int maximum] 2147483647
ULONG_MAX[unsigned long int maximum] 4294967295U

Constants and limits related to floating-point computations are contained in <float.h>. The minimum values are listed here (actual values are defined by each implementation):

FLT_RADIX [Radix of exponent representation] 2
FLT_ROUNT [Rounding mode for addition]
FLT_DIG [Number of decimal digits for float] 6
FLT_MANT_DIG [Number of base FLT_RADIX digits in mantissa for float]
FLT_EPSILON [Smallest float ϵ that $1.0 + \epsilon \neq 1.0$] 1E-5
FLT_MAX [Maximum float] 1E+37
FLT_MIN [Minimum normalized float] 1E-37
FLT_MAX_EXP [Maximum n such that $FLT\_RADIX^n - 1$ is representable]
FLT_MIN_EXP [Minimum n such that $FLT\_RADIX^n - 1$ is a normalized float]
DBL_DIG [Number of decimal digits for float] 10
DBL_MAX [Maximum double] 1E+37
DBL_MIN [Minimum normalized double] 1E-37
DBL_MANT_DIG [Number of base FLT_RADIX digits in mantissa for double]
DBL_EPSILON [Smallest double ϵ that $1.0 + \epsilon \neq 1.0$] 1E-9

There are other similar constants. The values for FLT_ROUNDS control how rounding is done for floating-point addition:

 0 Round toward zero
 1 Round to nearest
 2 Round toward $+\infty$
 3 Round toward $-\infty$
-1 Indeterminable

APPENDIX J

C-Style Input/Output

The C++ I/O stream facility (<iostream>) should be sufficient for most purposes. Functions listed here are in a separate I/O library shared with C (<stdio.h>). The stdio supports buffered I/O streams (FILE *) defined in the header. The symbolic constants stdin, stdout, stderr, EOF, NULL, and others are defined in the header. The error value returned by each library function is indicated in square brackets []. Normally, the C++ I/O stream objects should be used to perform I/O. The functions listed here may be needed in special situations. The #define CSTR const char * is used.

Operations on Files

FILE ***fopen**(CSTR filename, CSTR mode)   [NULL]

opens filename for read, write, or update as indicated by the given mode:

Table J.1

Mode	Meaning
"r", "rb"	Open text/binary file for reading.
"w", "wb"	Open text/binary file for writing; discard existing contents.
"a", "ab"	Open text/binary file for appending at end.
"r+", "rb+"	Open text/binary file for *update* (reading and writing).
"w+", "wb+"	Open text/binary file for update; discard existing contents.
"a+", "ab+"	Open text/binary file for update, writing at end.

FILE ***freopen**(CSTR filename, CSTR mode, FILE *stream)   [NULL]

opens filename for read, write, or update as **fopen** but reuses an existing stream, which is returned. This function can be used to redirect stdin, stdout, and stderr.

int **fclose**(FILE *stream)   [EOF]

Appendix J   C-STYLE INPUT/OUTPUT   543

closes the given stream after flushing any unfinished output, discarding unread input, and freeing allocated buffer space.

int **fflush**(FILE *stream)

forces all unfinished output of the given stream to be sent out.

int **remove**(CSTR filename)   [nonzero]

deletes the given file.

int **rename**(CSTR oldname, CSTR newname)   [nonzero]

changes the name of oldname to newname.

int **setvbuf**(FILE *stream, char *buf, int flag, size_t size)   [nonzero]

sets the buffering mode for stream using the supplied buffer buf. If buf is NULL, the buffer will be allocated when necessary. The flag specifies the buffering mode: _IOLBF (line buffering), _IONBF (no buffering), or _IOFBF (full buffering).

void **setbuf**(FILE *stream, char *buf)

turns off buffering on stream if buf is NULL. Otherwise, full buffering on stream is done with the supplied buffer (size at least BUFSIZ).

FILE ***tmpfile**(void)   [NULL]

creates a temporary file with mode "wb+" that will be automatically deleted when closed.

char ***tmpname**(char name[L_tmpnam])   [NULL]

tmpname(null) returns a unique heretofore unused name string as a pointer to an internal static array. The name is also copied into name if supplied.

Formatted Input

int **scanf**(FILE *stream, CSTR format, ...)   [EOF]

reads input according to the given format. Conversion modes for scanf are listed in Table J.2.

Formatted Output

int **fprintf**(FILE *stream, CSTR format, ...)   [negative]

outputs to stream according to the given format and returns the number of characters sent out. Conversion modes in the format are listed in Table J.3. For **printf**, the possible conversion flags are listed in Table J.4.

Table J.2 CONVERSION MODES FOR scanf

Conversion Character	Pointer Type	Input Data
d	int *	Base 10 number
i	int *	Integer; may be octal or hexadecimal
u	unsigned int *	Unsigned base 10 number
o, x	int *	Octal or hexadecimal with or without prefix
e, f, g	float *	Float with optional sign, decimal point, and exponent
s	char *	Characters with an added terminator '\0'
c	char *	Characters including white space (default width 1)
p	void *	Pointer value as displayed by **printf**("%p")
n	int *	Number of characters read so far
u	unsigned *	Unsigned decimal integer
[...]	char *	Longest nonempty input string consisting only of characters given in [ ]
[^...]	char *	Longest nonempty input string consisting only of characters *not* given in [ ]
%		No input assignment; matches a literal %

Table J.3 CONVERSION MODES IN format

Conversion Character	Argument Type	Formatted As
d, i	int	Base 10 number
u	unsigned	Base 10 number
f	double	$[-]m.dddddd$; number of ds given by the precision
s	char *	Characters in a string until '\0'
c	char	Single character
o	int	Unsigned octal number (no leading 0)
e, E	double	$[-]m.ddd\text{e}\pm xx$ or $[-]m.ddd\text{E}\pm xx$
g, G	double	Use %f unless exponent is < -4 or $\geq$ precision
x, X	int	Unsigned hexadecimal (no leading 0x) with a-f or A-F
p	void *	A pointer value (implementation dependent)
n	int *	No output; number of characters output so far is *stored* into the argument
%		Displays a %; no argument needed

Table J.4 CONVERSION FLAGS FOR `printf`

Flag	Description
-	Left-adjusted in field
+	Display number always with a sign
space	Use a space if first character is not a sign
0:	Pad numbers with leading zeros
#	Alternative format: Produce leading 0, 0x, 0X for o, x, X; preserve the decimal point for e, E, f, g, G; trailing zeros not removed for g, G

Character Input/Output

int **getchar**()   Same as **getc**(stdin).

int **putchar**(int c)   Same as **putc**(c, stdout).

int **getc**(FILE *stream)   Same as **fgetc**; if implemented as a macro, it may evaluate stream more than once.

int **putc**(FILE *stream)   Same as **fputc**; if implemented as a macro, it may evaluate stream more than once.

int **fgetc**(FILE *stream)   Returns next character of stream as an unsigned char converted to int [EOF].

int **fputc**(int c, FILE *stream) Writes c out to stream as char and returns c [EOF].

int **ungetc**(int c, FILE *stream) Pushes c back onto stream for next **read**; only one character can be pushed back per stream; returns c [EOF].

String Input/Output

char ***gets**(char *s)   Reads next line of stdin into s, *replacing terminating* '\n' *with* '\0'; returns s [NULL].

int **puts**(const char *s)   Writes string s to stdout, *replacing terminating* '\0' *with* '\n'; returns nonnegative [EOF].

char ***fgets**(char *s, int n, FILE *stream)   Reads at most the next $n - 1$ characters into array s, stopping if a '\n' is encountered; the '\n' is included in the array, which is terminated by a '\0'; returns s [NULL].

int **fputs**(const char *s, FILE *stream)   Writes string s to stream; returns a nonnegative [EOF].

Binary Input/Output and Error Status

size_t **fread**(void *ptr, size_t s size_t n, FILE *stream)

reads at most n objects of size s into space pointed to by ptr. The number of objects read is returned, which may be less than s. Use **feof** and **ferror** to determine status.

size_t **fwrite**(const void *ptr, size_t s size_t n, FILE *stream)

outputs n objects of size s from array pointed to by ptr. The number of objects written is returned, which is less than s only if there is an error.

int **feof**(FILE *stream)

returns nonzero if the end-of-file indicator of stream is set.

int **ferror**(FILE *stream)

returns nonzero if the error indicator of stream is set.

int **clearerr**(FILE *stream)

clears the end-of-file and error indicators of stream.

Moving File Read/Write Position

int **fseek**(FILE *stream, long offset, int org)   [nonzero]

sets the file position for stream as given by offset from the origin org. For a binary file, the position is moved to offset bytes from org, which can be SEEK_SET (beginning of file), SEEK_CUR (current position), or SEEK_END (end of file). For a text file, offset must be zero or a value obtained by **ftell** (relative to SEEK_SET).

void **rewind**(FILE *stream)

is the same as **fseek**(stream, 0L, SEEK_SET); clearerr(stream).

long **ftell**(FILE *stream)   [EOF]

returns the current file position as an offset from SEEK_SET.

int **fgetpos**(FILE *stream, fpos_t *ptr)   [nonzero]

marks the current file position in ptr for later use by **fsetpos**.

int **fsetpos**(FILE *stream, fpos_t *ptr)   [nonzero]

moves the file position to that marked by ptr.

APPENDIX K

Interfacing C++ and C Programs

It is possible to call existing library or user-defined functions written in C from C++. The techniques described here allow you to access any existing C library function as well as use other existing C codes from C++ programs, and vice versa.

Calling C Functions from C++ Programs

Just because C++ admits most, if not all, of the ANSI C constructs from a syntax point of view does not mean that C programs can be freely intermixed with C++ programs. On the contrary, the same exact construct can have different semantics in C and C++. For example, in C++, the function prototype

```
int fn();
```

is the same as

```
int fn(void);
```

and means that the function fn takes no arguments and returns an int. In C, however, the first declaration says nothing about the number of arguments fn takes.

However, it is sometimes desirable (or convenient) for a C++ program to call external functions written in C contained in separate files. The C-defined functions could be user-supplied routines, library functions, system calls, or existing programs in C. Such calls are possible but must be done with great care. Use this appendix as a guide.

Function Name Encoding in C++

For various reasons, function names are encoded by the compiler. The encoded names are the actual names used internally by the compiled program. In some cases, the encoding is simply a matter of adding underscores as prefixes and/or suffixes to a function name. In other cases, it can be much more complicated. This is especially true because of function overloading. Due to encoding differences, a function name abc in a C++ file will not correspond to the same name abc in a C file. The encoding makes it hard to call a C-defined function from a C++ program, and vice versa.

Fortunately, C++ provides *linkage directives*, which can be used to access functions written in other languages, notably C. For example, the linkage directive

```
extern "C" void abc(int);
```

declares the function abc to have C linkage and will be identified with a C-defined function abc. The linkage directive consists of the keyword extern followed by the string constant "C" and then by a usual C++ function prototype. The linkage directive tells the C++ compiler that abc is a function name encoded by the C compiler and is exempt from the usual C++ function name encoding. Also supplied is necessary type information for argument and return type so that the function can still be subjected to full C++ argument-number/type checking.

It is also possible to give a list of function prototypes in a single linkage directive:

```
extern "C"
{      char * xyz( unsigned int );
       int uvw( ... );
}
```

Note the use of the notation "..." to indicate an unknown number of arguments.

Here is a C++ program that uses a C function testfn:

```
///////    interface.C    ///////
// accessing C function from C++
#include <iostream>

// the following enables C++ argument-type checking
// before calling the C-coded function testfn

extern "C" int testfn(int, int);

int main(int argc, char *argv[])
{    cout << testfn(3,4) << endl;
}
```

The C file for this experiment is

```
/******    test.c    ******/
/*  a C source code file */
```

```
int testfn(a, b)
int a, b;
{   return a+b; }
```

Compile `test.c` into `test.o` with a C compiler. Compile `interface.C` into `interface.o` with a C++ compiler. The two .o files can now be linked together and run.

Accessing library functions written in C from C++ can be useful. Instead of using the `<string.h>` of C++, consider accessing the C-defined `strcmp` library function from your C++ program. Here is a sample C++ program that does exactly that:

```
// accessing C library functions
#include <iostream>

// the following enables C++ argument-type checking

extern "C" int strcmp(const char *, const char *);

main(int argc, char *argv[])
{   cout << "strcmp(" << argv[1] << ", " << argv[2]
         << ") gives " << strcmp(argv[1], argv[2]) << '\n';
}
```

C++ and C Header Files

The C++ language has its own complement of Standard Library functions together with associated C++ header files. The most frequently used is the `iostream` header file for I/O.

In addition to native headers, C++ also supplies header files to access Standard C Library functions and system calls. For example, header files such as `<stdio.h>`, `<string.h>`, `<malloc.h>`, and `<signal.h>` exist. Although the same names are used, these header files are *not* the same as the corresponding C header files. They are written in C++ syntax with extensive use of linkage directives to give C++ programs access to the desired C library functions or system calls.

Here is a sample C++ program that uses some C I/O functions:

```
#include <stdio.h>      // gets the C++ header file stdio.h

// For this example
// there are two active lines in the above header file
// extern "C" FILE *fopen(const char *, const char *);
// extern "C" int fprintf(FILE *, const char * ...);
```

```
main(int argc, char *argv[])
{       FILE * out = fopen(argv[1], "w");
        fprintf(out, "this is a %d test\n", 15);
}
```

There are also two catchall C++ header files:

```
#include <stdlib.h>
```

gives you access to most C Standard Library functions, and

```
#include <sysent.h>
```

declares most system calls. However, the naming and the contents of these header files are not standardized. For instance, the GNU C++ system (**g++**) uses <std.h> as the header for system calls. Thus, you must check what your C++ system has to offer before using such header files. There is a possibility that your #include line may pick up a C header file because there is no such C++ header. Compile-time errors usually result from such mistakes. A regular C header file will not work at all in a C++ program.

So what can you do if you want to use a C header in your C++ program to access certain C-defined functions? If your C header is written in ANSI Standard C syntax, it is possible that the declaration

```
extern "C"
{
#include "header.h"
}
```

given at the beginning of your C++ file will make things work. If the header file is in traditional C (instead of ANSI C), then the best thing to do is rewrite each and every function prototype in the header into C++ style and enclose the entire header file inside a "C" linkage directive. In fact, this is exactly how <string.h> and other C header files are transformed to C++ headers.

Calling C++ Functions from C Programs

Although unusual, it may sometimes be useful to call a C++-defined function from C. Because of the special function name encoding used by C++, this is usually difficult.

But if you write a function in C++ with the intention that it be (also) called from C, you should give the appropriate linkage directive (extern "C") to make its name encoding match that used by the C compiler. In case this C++ function is an overloaded function, only one instance of it can be declared with a linkage directive.

APPENDIX L

Header Files

Here is a list of top-level headers available for Standard C++.

Headers in Namespace `std`

Native C++ Headers:

```
<algorithm> <bitset>     <complex>   <deque>     <exception>
<fstream>   <functional> <hash_map>  <hash_set>  <iomanip>
<ios>       <iosfwd>     <iostream>  <istream>   <iterator>
<limits>    <list>       <locale>    <map>       <memory>
<new>       <numeric>    <ostream>   <queue>     <set>
<sstream>   <stack>      <stdexcept> <streambuf> <string>
<strstream> <typeinfo>   <utility>   <valarray>  <vector>
```

Importing ANSI C Headers:

```
<cassert> <cctype>  <cerrno>  <cfloat>  <ciso646>
<climits> <clocale> <cmath>   <csetjmp> <csignal>
<cstdarg> <cstddef> <cstdio>  <cstdlib> <cstring>
<ctime>   <cwchar>  <cwctype>
```

Headers in Global Namespace

ANSI C Headers:

```
<assert.h> <ctype.h>  <errno.h>  <float.h>  <iso646.h>
<limits.h> <locale.h> <math.h>   <setjmp.h> <signal.h>
<stdarg.h> <stddef.h> <stdio.h>  <stdlib.h> <string.h>
<time.h>   <wchar.h>  <wctype.h>
```

Backward Compatibility Headers:

```
<fstream.h> <iomanip.h> <iostream.h> <new.h> <stl.h>
```

Index

+ addition operator, 20, 140, 268, 288
& address-of operator, 40, 126–127, 439
\\ BACKSLASH escape sequence, 26
= class-defined operator, 269–271, 277
, comma operator, 45
?: conditional operator, 32
-- decrement operator, 22–23, 30, 124, 294, 512
/ division operator, 20, 30
*/ documentation close marker, 14
/* documentation open marker, 14
\" DOUBLE QUOTE escape sequence, 26
== equal-to relational operator, 17
() function-call operator, 296
> greater-than relational operator, 17
++ increment operator, 22–23, 30, 124, 294, 512
[] indexing operator, 145, 296
% integer remainder operator, 20, 25, 31
< less-than relational operator, 17
&& logical-and operator, 31
! logical-not operator, 31, 32
|| logical-or operator, 31–32
. member-of operator, 19, 56, 295
-> member selection operator, 295–296
* multiplication operator, 40, 126–127, 268, 439
!= not-equal-to relational operator, 17, 19
~ not operator, 33, 34, 194
\0 null character, 26, 38, 130, 132, 232
\? QUESTION MARK escape sequence, 26
:: scope resolution operator, 57, 84
<< shift left/output operator, 11, 33–34, 232–233, 240–242
>> shift right/input operator, 15, 33–34, 222, 232–233, 240–242
\' SINGLE QUOTE escape sequence, 26
; statement terminator, 11, 13, 20, 53
- subtraction operator, 20, 95–96, 104, 182, 268, 288

\a escape sequence (BELL), 26
abort(), 71
ABS macro, 496

Abstract base class, 322, 344–346
Abstract data type, 55
Abstraction, 3, 51–57
Access
   to class members, 55–56, 173–174
   to inherited members, 260–261
Access control, under class derivation, 259–261
Account, *See* Bank account examples
Actual arguments, *See also* Argument(s), 58
Addition operator (+), 20, 140, 268, 288
Addition of pointers, 128–130, 132
Address arithmetic, 128–132
Address-of operator (&), 40, 126–127, 439
Aggregate, 184
Algorithms, 2, 468
Allocation
   deallocation with delete, 108
   with new, 107–108, 111
   pointers and, 165–169
   of two-dimensional arrays, 165–166
American Standard Code for Information Interchange (ASCII), 26
Ampersand (and) operators
   &, 40, 126–127, 439
   &&, 31
and_test function, 161
Anonymous enumerations, 36
Anonymous union, 521
Appendant members, 252, 253
arblen function, 160–161
ArbList class, 212–216, 262–264, 276–277
   display function, 213
   find function, 214
   remove function, 214
ArbStack class, 262–264
argc argument, 61–62, 71
Argument(s), 8, 58, 97–99, 528–530
   actual, 58
   array name as, 124
   command-line, 61–62

functional, 156–158
   optional, 97–99
   variable-length, 528–530
   See also Parameters
Argument passing, 58–59
   by reference, 59
   by value, 59
argv argument, 61–62, 71, 106, 151, 155, 502
Arithmetic, pointer, 128–132
Arithmetic computations, *See* Computations
Arithmetic expressions, 11, 30–31
Arithmetic operations
   fractions in, 96
   implicit type conversions in, 114–116
Arithmetic operators, 20, 25, 30
Array(s), 37–39, 123
   character, 37–39, 535
   dynamic arrays of pointers, 166–169
   initializing, 124
   names of, 124–125
   one-dimensional, 124–125
   references and, 154
   two-dimensional, 133–135, 165–166
arrayAdd function, 107
Array assignments, 40–41
Array cells, 37
Array declarations, 511
Array entry (element), 124
Array-style initialization, 176
ASCII (American Standard Code for Information Interchange), 26
Assembly, 491
assert macro, 137, 501–502
Assertions, 501
Assignment(s)
   array, 40–41
   derived-object, 274–276
   object, 95–96, 267–271, 276–277
   of pointers, 132
Assignment expressions, 32–33
Assignment operator, 17
Associativity, of operators, 30
Asterisk
   markers (*/ and /*), 14
   operator (*), 40, 126–127, 268, 439
Automatic transformations, 492
Automatic type conversions, 114–116
Automatic variables, 82, 106
average function, 157

average.C file, 12

\b escape sequence (BACKSPACE), 26
BACKSLASH escape sequence (\\), 26
BACKSPACE escape sequence (\b), 26
Bank account examples, 52–57
   of destruction of plug-compatible objects, 353
   of multiple inheritance, 278–281
   of ordered accounts, 352
   of polymorphism, 323–325
   of public derivation, 255–258
   of virtual functions, 326–329
Base, 234
   private, 259, 260
   protected, 259, 260
   public, 259, 260, 265
   shared, 279–282
   virtual, 279–282
Base class, 4
   abstract, 322, 344–346
   inheritance and, 248, 249
base-class list, 250–251
Base object, 4, 251, 253
BELL escape sequence (\a), 26
Binary C-style input and output, 546
Binary input and output, 239–240
Binary operators, 29
Binary search, table-lookup via, 209–210
Bit fields, 216, 523–524
Bit-packing members, 513
Bitwise operators, *See also* Output operators, *See also* Input operators, 33–34
Black box, 4, 52, 322
Block, 13
Bool, type bool, 17
Boolean values, 17, 162
Bottom-up design, 467
Braces {}, 10, 13, 25, 124, 176
Brackets [] operator, 145, 296
Branching, conditional, 16–17
break statement, 44, 46
bsearch function, 210
bsearch template, 377–379
Buffer
   circular, 109–114
   first-in/first-out (FIFO), 109
   last-in/first-out (LIFO), 261
Bugs, *See also* Error(s), *See also* Error handling, 525–527

`buildNumber` function, 189
Built-in object assignment, 267–268
Built-in object copying, 272
Built-in operations for objects, 192–193

C++
 calling C functions from, 547
 evolution of, 5
 features of, 5
 object-oriented programming and, 5–7
 programming tips for, 74–77
C programs, interfacing with, 547–550
C-style string
 composition, 221–222
 extraction, 221–222
 I/O, 220–222
 in-memory I/O, 221–222
`CalcEng` class, 184–187
`CalcFace` class, 187–191, 235, 481–484
`Calculator` class, 191–192, 362–363, 486–488
Calculator simulation program, 183–192
 designing, 184
 for object-oriented design, 479–488
 testing, 187, 190–191
`CalcWindow` class, 484–486
Calendar, monthly, 166–169, 236
Call, *See* Function call(s)
Call resolution, 101, 382–383
 best match, 101
 exact match, 101
 inheritance related, 267
 viable functions, 101
Canonical representation, 94
Cast, dynamic, 331
`catch` keyword, 308–316
Catch or specify, 312
`cerr` object, 15, 18, 70, 71, 230
CGI, 442–464
 example in C++, 461–464
 programming, 458
 receiving form data, 459
 steps, 458
CGI specification, 450
Channels, I/O, 17
`char` data type, 19, 26–27
Character arrays, 37–39, 535
Character C-style input/output functions, 545
Character constant, 26
Character escape sequences, 26

Character functions, 228–229, 534
Character-set-independent program, 26
Character string constant, 11
Checking account, *See* Bank account examples
Choices, 46–47
`cin` object, 15, 17, 19, 70, 230, 233, 265
`Cirbuf` class examples, 109–114
 class-defined `operator=` in, 269–271
 destructors in, 194
 iterators in, 296–297
 once-only header files in, 500
 pointers in, 126
Circular buffer, 109–114
Class, 4, 52–53, 172
 abstract base, 322
 `ArbList`, 212–216, 262–264, 276–277
 `ArbStack`, 262–264
 base, 4, 248, 249, 322, 343–346
 `CalcFace`, 235, 481–484
 `Calculator`, 362–363, 486–488
 `CalcWindow`, 484–486
 container, 211
 `CursesWindow`, 477–479
 data-only, 175–176
 defined, 8–9, 172–174
 derived, 4, 248, 252–254, 348–352
 diagrams, 474
 `EmpStack`, 264
 family, 322, 363–371
 `FormData`, 459
 `Fraction`, 80, 195–196, 239
 friends of, 195–197
 `fstream`, 72, 230, 283
 generic, 263–264
 `Html`, 452
 identifying, 470
 `ifstream`, 230, 283
 instance, 53
 I/O `stream`, 11, 282
 `ios`, 210, 230, 282
 `iostream`, 230, 240, 283
 `istream`, 152, 230, 233, 238, 282
 `istringstream`, 228
 `istrstream`, 230
 local, 299
 nested, 299–302
 `Number`, 364–371
 object-family, 322, 363–371
 objects and, 472

ofstream, 230, 283
ostream, 221, 230, 238, 282
ostringstream, 228
ostrstream, 230
Poly, 138–140, 272–274
Refstr, 291–293
robust, 302
Stack, 262–263, 397–399
stream, 6, 282
string, 63–65, 222–228
stringstream, 228
strstream, 230
style for defining, 76
template, 384, 387–388
Tokenizer, 225
vector, 141–143
See also specific class names
Class body, 53
Class declaration, 174–175, 509
Class declaration styles, 174–175
Class-defined object assignment, 268–271
Class-defined object copying, 272–274
Class-defined operator=, 269–271
Class derivation, 248–251, 259–261
  types, 251, 258, 259
Class member(s)
  access to, 55–56, 173–174
  capitalization of, 53
  See also Member(s)
Class member functions, 57
Class names, 76, 172
Class objects, pointers to, 56
Class scope, 81, 84, 173
Class scope nesting, defined, 252
Class tag, 52, 173
Class template(s), 383–388, 513
  definition of, 383–388
  instantiation of, 383–388, 513
  specialization, 397
Class-wide member(s), 204–211
Client, 55, 118–119
clog, 231
CLOS (Common Lisp Object System), 1
Closing files, 231–233, 542–543
Code
  generic, 35
  hash, 400
  object, 490
  source, 490

Coefficient, leading, 138
Collision, of records, 400
Colon (:), 178, 250
  ?: conditional operator, 32
  :: scope resolution operator, 57, 84
Comma operator (,), 45
Command-line arguments, 61–62
Common Lisp Object System (CLOS), 1
compare function, 25
Comparison
  of keys, 144, 147–151
  of pointers, 132
Compatible types, *See also* Plug-compatible
  objects, 323–325
Compilation, 12, 490–492
  from DOS, 505
  under IDE, 506
  on PCs, 504–506
  under UNIX, 502–504
Compilation unit, 87, 490
Compiler, error messages of, 504
Compiling, templates, 388–390, 503
Complex number objects, 230
Composition, 4
  of derived objects, 253
  of virtual functions, 362–363
Compound statement, 13
Computations
  functions for, 229, 535–536
  handling errors in, 306–307
Compute engine, 184–187
Condition, 14
  continuation, 15, 43
Conditional branching, 16–17
Conditional operator (?:), 32
Conditional statements, 16–17, 32
Conditional text inclusion, 497–499
const identifier
  initialization of, 179
  meaning of, 103
  with read-only variables and parameters,
    103–105, 152–154
  use of, 42, 76
Constant(s)
  character, 26
  character string, 11
  floating-point, 28, 67, 115, 229
  integer, 28, 29
  logical, 17

Constant(s) (*continued*)
   symbolic, 76, 494–496
Constant pointer, 40
Constructor(s), 53–54, 177–181
   copy, 194, 272–274
   default, 54, 66–67, 77, 178, 181
   defined, 177
   `explicit`, 110, 305
   no-args, 54
   one argument, 110, 304
Consumer, 109
Container
   associative, 418–419
   efficiency, 416
   `set`, 429–431
   `stack`, 417
   standard, 413–434
Container class, 211
Continuation condition, 15, 43
`continue` statement, 44–45
Control character, 19, 27
Control variables, 15, 43
Conversion, *See* Type conversions
Conversion ambiguity, 305
Copy constructor, 194, 272–274
Copying, object, 271–274, 276–277
core dump, 71
`cout` object, 11, 15, 19, 70, 230, 265
CRC design, 474–475, 480–481
Creating objects, 53–54
`curses` interface class, 476–479
`curses` library, 476–479
   `addch()`, 477
   `endwin()`, 477
   `getch()`, 477
   `initscr()`, 476
   `move()`, 477
   `mvaddch()`, 477
   `newwin()`, 477
   `refresh()`, 477
   `waddch()`, 477
   `wgetch()`, 477
`CursesWindow` class, 477–479

^D, 19, 27
Dangling else problem, 25
Dangling pointer, 153
Data abstraction, 3, 51–57
Data cell, 128

Data decomposition, 468–469
Data limits, implementation-defined, 540–541
Data members, types of, 5
Member(s), 5
Data-only classes, 175–176
Data structures, heterogeneous, 521–523
Data types, 26–28
   abstract, 55
   `char`, 19, 26–27
   `double`, 28, 115, 229, 304
   enumeration, 35, 36
   `float`, 28, 67, 115
   `int`, 14, 22, 27, 115
Date(s), ordered, 348–352
Date functions, 537–539
dbx utility, 525–527
Debugging, 525–527
Declaration(s), 80, 86–88
   array, 511
   class, 174–175, 509
   defined, 10
   definitions and, 86
   derived-class, 509
   file scope, 86–87
   function pointer, 158
   in functions, 10–11
   internal and external linkage and, 87–88
   local and global identifiers and, 88
   rules for, 88
Declaration order, 179
Declaration statement, 15
Decomposition
   data, 468–469
   object-based, 74
   object-oriented, 469
   procedural, 73, 468
Decrement operator (--), 22–23, 30, 124, 294, 512
Default constructors, 54, 66–67, 77, 178, 181
Default initialization, 180
Default value, 98
`#define` directive
   anonymous enumerations vs., 36
   with preprocessing conditionals, 497, 498
   with symbolic constants, 76, 493, 495, 499
Definition, and declarations, 86
Degree, 138
Deinitialization, 108
`delete` operator, 108, 195, 316–319
Delimiters, 517–518

Dense representation, 183
Derivation, 248
   access control under, 259–261
   class, 248–251, 259–261
   object assignment and copying via, 276–277
   principles of, 258–259
   private, 258, 261–263, 361
   `protected`, 258–260, 361
   public, 255–258
Derived class, 4, 248, 252–254, 348–352
Derived-class declaration, 509
Derived-class template, 397–399
Derived objects, 4
   assignment and copying, 274–276
   composition, 253
   construction and destruction, 254
   inheritance and, 248, 252–254
Design
   bottom-up, 467
   of calculator simulation program, 184
   implementation phase of, 472
   of linked list, 199–200
   model-control-view, 184
   object-oriented, *See* Object-oriented design
   of objects, 471
   round-trip gestalt, 470
   top-down, 467
Design patterns, 472–474
Destruction
   of derived objects, 254
   of plug-compatible objects, 352–353
Destructive string operations, 516
Destructors, 108, 193–195
`display` function, 199, 203
Distinguishable signatures, 99–101
Divisor, greatest common, 89
DNS, domain name system, 445
`do-while` statement, 23
Documentation, markers for, 14
Domain error, 306–307
Domain name, 444
DOS, compiling and running from, 505
Dot (.)
   member-of operator, 19, 56
   selection operator, 295
`double` data type, 28, 115, 229, 304
Double indirection, 127–128, 155
Double power, 99–101

Double-precision floating-point constant, 28, 115, 229
DOUBLE QUOTE escape sequence (\"), 26
Double underscore (_), 29
`double` variable, 519–520
Dynamic arrays of pointers, 166–167
`dynamic_cast`, 331
Dynamic storage, 107–108
   allocation with `new`, 107–108, 111
   deallocation with `delete`, 108
   pointers and, 165–167

Echo command, 61–62
EDOM symbolic constant, 307
`#elif` directive, 499
Ellipsis (...), 99, 528
Else, dangling, 25
`#else` directive, 497, 499
`EmpStack` class, 264
Empty list, 10
Encapsulation, 2, 51–57
`#endif` directive, 498, 499
`endl`, 11
`enum` declaration, 35–36, 210, 511
   in class scope, 210
Enumeration, 35–36
Enumeration type, 35, 36
Enumeration variables, 36
Enumerators, 35
Envelope, 364–368
Environment variable, 62–63
EOF constant, 118, 188, 233
ERANGE constant, 307
`errno` global variable, 307
Error(s)
   domain, 306–307
   range, 307
   standard, 18
Error handling, 70–73, 306–316
   of arithmetic and mathematical computation errors, 306–307
   debugging with `dbx`, 525–527
   functions for, 536
Error messages
   compiler, 504
   displaying, 71–72
Error output channel, 18
Error states, 307–308
Error status, 546

Error treatment and recovery, 308
Error values, 307
Escape sequences, 26, 229
even_or_odd function, 25
evenflag reference parameter, 520
Exception(s)
    bad_alloc, 107, 318
    bad_cast, 331
    bad_typeid, 332
    for class Matrix, 314
    defining your own, 313
    out_of_range, 349
    standard library, 312–316
    unexpected, 312
exception class function, **what**(), 312
Exception handling, 308–316
Exception specification, 311–312
    empty, 312
Exchange rate table, 206–211
Exclusive or operator (~), 33, 34, 194
Exempting, 261
Exit status, 62, 308
Explicit address arithmetic, 129
explicit constructor, 110, 305
Explicit type conversions, 36, 116–117, 266
export, 388
Expression, 11
extern modifier, 83, 87–88
External interface, 119
External linkage, 87
extractNumber function, 189
Extraction, of common operations, 346–348

\f escape sequence (FORMFEED), 26, 229
factorial function, 13–15
Failure of new, 318
Fall through, 47
False (logical constant), 17
Family class, 322, 363–371
Fibonacci hashing, 404
FIFO (first-in/first-out) character buffer, 109
File(s)
    client, 55, 118–119
    header, *See* Header files
    object code, 490
    opening and closing, 231–233, 542–543
    source code, 490
    updating, 237–239, 542
File-position indicator, 237

File scope, 81, 82
File scope declarations, 86–87
Fill characters, 234
find_if, generic algorithm, 426
find, generic algorithm, 426
First-in/first-out (FIFO) character buffer, 109
flags function, 236
Floating-point calculations, library functions for, 535–536
Floating-point constants, 28, 67, 115, 229
for_each, generic algorithm, 427
for statement, 20–22, 43
Foreign exchange rate table, 206–211
Formal parameters, 10, 58
    functional, 159
    template, 375, 380–381
Format flags, 236
Format functions, 234–235
Formatting
    C-style output, 543–545
    functions, 76
    input, 543
    output, 234–237
FORMFEED escape sequence (\f), 26, 229
Forwarding mechanism, 364
Fraction(s), 93–97, 100
Fraction class, 80, 195–196, 239
Fraction subtype, 368–369
Free checking account examples
    of destruction of plug-compatible objects, 353
    of multiple inheritance, 278–281
    of polymorphism, 323–325
    of public derivation, 255–258
    of virtual functions, 326–329
Free pool, 107
Free storage
    managing, 316–319
    object with pointer to, 194
Free store exhaustion, 318
Friends, of class, 195–197
fstream class, 72, 230, 283
Function(s), 9–12, 34–35
    as computation unit, 9
    defined, 8, 510
    factorial, 13–15
    formatting, 76, 234
    general form of, 9
    generic, 161–162
    getline(), 65

INDEX

hash, 400
inline, 60–61, 95, 496–497
instance, 57, 204
member, *See* Member functions
names of, 76, 547–549
with optional arguments, 98–99
overloaded, *See* Overloaded functions
overloading, 99–101
recursive, 80, 89–92
returning pointers, 153–154
static member, 205
style of, 75–76
with variable-length arguments, 528–530
virtual, 322, 325–329, 359–363
See also specific functions
Function body, 9, 76
Function call(s), 8, 58–61
   array name in, 124
   to C programs, 547
   pointers and, 151–154
Function call operator (), 296
Function call overhead, 60
Function call resolution, 101
Function definition, 9
Function header, 9
Function members, 9
Function pointers, 157–158, 512
Function prototype, 19, 66, 512
Function template(s), 377–383, 513
   argument deduction, 380
   definition of, 377–379
   instantiation of, 380–383
   overloading, 382
Function template specialization, 381–382
Functional arguments, 156
Functional variables, 156–158
Functor, 427, 431–434
   advantages, 431
   binders, 433
   defined, 431
   instance function as, 439
   standard, 433

g++ command, 502–503
gcd (greatest common divisor), 89
Generic algorithms, 426–429
Generic classes, specialization of, 263–264
Generic code, 35
Generic functions, 161–162

Generic lists, 211–216
Generic programming, different approaches, 407
Generic programs, 156–165
Genericness, 160
Global identifiers, 82, 88
Global variables, 88
goto statement, 45–46, 511
Greatest common divisor (gcd), 89

Handler, for new failure, 318
Hash code, 400
Hash function, 400
Hash table, 400–406
Hash table implementation, 402–404
Hash table operations, 404–405
Hash table template, 400–402, 405–406
Hashing
   defined, 400
   Fibonacci, 404
   keys in, 400, 402
head index, 109–110
Header
   function, 9
   template, 376
   wrapper, 493
Header file(s), 12, 117–119, 364–367
   <algorithm>, 426
   C++ and C, 549–550
   <complex>, 230
   <deque>, 414–416
   different types of, 219
   <functional>, 427
   imported from C, 220
   <iterator>, 425
   <list>, 414–416
   listing of, 551
   <map>, 414–416
   native C, 219
   native C++, 219
   once-only, 367, 384, 500
   in preprocessing, 493–494, 500
   <queue>, 414–416
   <set>, 414–416
   <stack>, 414–416
   for standard containers, 414
   <stdexcept>, 312
   <vector>, 414–416
Header file and namespace, 493
Heterogeneous data structures, 521–523

Hexadecimal byte escape sequence (\xhh), 26
Hierarchies, inheritance, 248–249, 282
Host object, 55, 181–182
   pointer, 97
   read-only, 182
Host pointer, this, 97
HTML, 447–449
   forms, 455
HTTP, 447
   post query, 457
   query format, 456
   response format, 456

i loop control variable, 22
I/O exceptions, 312
I/O manipulator(s), 242–244
   endl, 244
   from <iomanip>, 243
   setw, 243
I/O stream
   error, 240
   templates, 399
IDE, compiling and running under MS/Visual C++, 506
Identifier(s)
   declarations and, 88
   defined, 29
   global, 88
   local, 88
Identifier scoping, 81–84
#if directive, 497–499
if statement, 510
   multiway, 24–25
   nested, 25
#ifdef directive, 497, 498
if ... else statement, 16, 18
#ifndef directive, 378, 497, 498
ifstream class, 230, 283
Implementation-defined data limits, 540–541
Implementation phase of design, 472
Implicit copying, preventing, 274
Implicit type conversions
   in arithmetic operations, 114–116
   inheritance-induced, 265–266, 532
inString function, 43
In-memory I/O, 228
   C-style string, 221–222
#include directive, 237, 493–494
Increment operator (++), 22–23, 30, 124, 294, 512

Index notation, 124, 125, 133
Indirection, 133
   double, 127–128, 155
   multiple, 154–156
Infinite loop, 21
Information hiding, 52, 55–56
Inheritance, 4, 248–284
   access control under class derivation, 259–261
   advantages of, 248
   class derivation, 248–251
   derivation principles, 258–259
   derived classes and objects, 248, 252–254
   derived-object assignment and copying, 274–276
   I/O stream class hierarchy, 282
   multiple, 4, 249, 278–282
   object assignment, 267–271, 276–277
   object copying, 271–274, 276–277
   overloading and, 266
   private derivation, 258, 261–263
   public derivation, 255–258
   single, 4, 249
   specialization of generic classes, 263–264
   type relations under, 265–267
Inheritance hierarchies, 248–249, 282
Inheritance-induced conversions
   explicit, 266
   implicit, 265–266, 532
Inheritance planning, 361–363
Inherited members
   access to, 260–261
   defined, 252
Init-list, 178, 179
Initial values, 4
Initialization
   array-style, 176
   of arrays, 124
   of const, 179
   of curses, 476
   default, 180
   member, 178
   of objects, 175–181
   of reference members, 179
   of static members, 208
   of virtual-base object, 282
Initializer, 11, 53, 124
Inline functions, 60–61, 95, 496–497
inner member function, 67
Input

binary, 239–240
C-style, 542–546
C-style binary, 546
C-style string, 220–222, 545
formatting, 543
library functions for, 6, 230–240
standard input channel, 17
Input operators, 15, 33–34, 232–233, 240–242
Instance(s), 52, 175, 377
of a class, 53
Instance function, 57, 97, 204
Instance member(s), 97, 204–211
Instantiation, 4, 175
of class templates, 387–388
of function templates, 380–383
of templates, 375–377
int data type
long int and short int, 27
signed and unsigned, 27, 116
int_end function, 160
Integer, signed and unsigned, 27, 116
Integer constants, 28, 29
Integer subtype, 370–371
Integral promotion, 115
Interface, 357–359
definition, 358
external, 119
IOable, 358
mix in, 359
planning, 322, 343–352
public, 3–4, 55, 74, 322, 343–352
user, 184, 187–192
Interfacing
with C programs, 547–550
to existing systems, 475–479
Internal-external decoupling, 182–192
Internal linkage, 87–88
Internal workings, vs. public interface, 3–4, 55, 74
Inward conversions, 304
I/O channels, 17
I/O redirection, 502
I/O stream class, 11, 70, 282
I/O stream class hierarchy, 282
I/O stream conversions, 305–306
I/O stream library, 6, 230–240
binary input and output, 239–240
file updating, 237–239
I/O operators, 232–233
opening and closing files, 231–232

output formatting, 234–237
reading and writing, 233
ios class, 210, 230, 282
iostream class, 12, 118, 230, 240, 283
IP address, 444
isEmpty member, 262
isEmpty (isFull) test, 110
istream class, 152, 230, 233, 238, 282
istringstream class, 228
istrstream class, 230
istrstream object, 221–222
Iteration
control of, 42–46
defined, 42
early termination of, 43
Iteration statements, 510
Iterator(s), 296–299
bidirectional, 424
for Cirbuf, 300
const_iterator implementation, 301
creation, 298
iteration loop, 298
<iterator>, 425
random-access, 424
standard container, 421–425
STL conventions for, 297
typedefs, 298

Joint account examples
of class derivation, 249–251
of multiple inheritance, 278–281
of virtual functions, 326–329
Justification, 234
Juxtaposition, string, 221

Keys
comparing, 144, 147–151
in hashing, 400, 402
Keywords, 175, 491, 514
Knuth, D.E., 404

Labels, 46, 81
Last-in/first-out (LIFO) buffer, 261
Leading coefficient, 138
Library function(s), 18, 25, 71, 219–240, 534–546
abort(), 308, 502
atexit(), 308, 536
atoi(), 150
bad(), 240

Library function(s) (*continued*)
    for character operations, 228–229, 534
    cin.get(), 18, 60
    close(), 70, 231
    common with C, 534
    cos(), 229, 535
    cout.flush(), 19
    for date and time, 537–539
    dstrcpy(), 130
    exit(), 71, 308
    fail(), 72, 240
    for floating-point calculations, 535–536
    flush(), 232
    fmod(), 536
    frexp(), 536
    gcount(), 234
    get(), 19, 232–234
    getenv, 63
    getline(), 232, 234
    good(), 240
    ignore(), 233
    implementation-defined data limits, 540–541
    for C-style input/output, 542–546
    for input/output, 6, 230–240
    isalnum(), 229, 534
    isalpha(), 229, 534
    iscntrl(), 229, 534
    isdigit(), 229, 534
    isgraph(), 229, 534
    islower(), 229, 534
    isprint(), 229, 534
    ispunct(), 229, 534
    isspace(), 229, 534
    isupper(), 18, 229, 534
    isxdigit(), 229, 534
    log(), 229, 535
    memchr(), 535
    memcmp(), 535
    memcpy(), 535
    memmove(), 535
    memset(), 535
    modf(), 536
    for numeric computations, 229, 535–536
    peek(), 233
    precision(), 235
    put(), 233, 234
    putback(), 233
    read(), 234
    scanf(), 543
    seekg(), 238
    seekp(), 237
    sin(), 229, 535
    sqrt(), 229, 536
    strcat(), 516
    strchr(), 517
    strcmp(), 25, 129–130, 517, 549
    strcpy(), 130, 516
    strcspn(), 517
    string, 222–225, 516–518
    for string operations, 222–225, 516–518
    for string-to-number conversions, 537
    strlen(), 130, 131, 517
    strncat(), 516
    strncmp(), 517
    strncpy(), 516
    strpbrk(), 517
    strrchr(), 517
    strspn(), 517
    strstr(), 517
    strtok(), 517–518
    sync(), 232
    tellg(), 239
    tellp(), 239
    tmpname(), 543
    tolower(), 18, 229, 534
    toupper(), 229, 534
    utilities, 539–540
    width(), 235
    write(), 234
Library operations
    nondestructive, 517
Library, C and C++, 85
LIFO (last-in/first-out) buffer, 261
lineCompare function, 149
Linkage
    external, 87
    internal, 87–88
Linkage directives, 548
Linked list, 197–204
Linking/loading, 492
List(s)
    base-class, 250–251
    generic, 211–216
    linked, 197–204
    nested, 521–523
List cell, 198–199
List template, 390–397
Local class, 299

Local identifiers, 88
Local scope, 81–82
Local variables, 82, 88
Logical condition
  non-Boolean, 17
Logical operators, 31–32
`long double`, 28, 29, 115
`long int` types, 27
Loop(s)
  control of, 42–46
  `do-while`, 23
  `for`, 20–22, 43
  infinite, 21
  nested, 25, 45
  `while`, 13–16
Loop body, 43
Loop-control variable, 15, 43
`lower` function, 18, 19
lowercase command, 237
lvalues, 102

Macros
  defining, 494–496
  inline functions vs., 496–497
  in preprocessing, 494–497, 500–502
  redefining, 496
  in referencing unnamed arguments, 528
  standard, 500–502
`main` function, 9, 13, 61–62, 161
map, 418–419
  in URL decoding, 419
`match` function, 72, 265
Mathematical computations, *See* Computations
Mathematical functions, 229
`matmul` function, 153
Matrix Class, 135–138
Matrix multiplication, 135–138
`max` function, 528
Member(s)
  access to, 55–56, 173–174, 260–261
  appendant, 252, 253
  bit-packing, 513
  capitalization of, 53
  class, 55–56, 172–174
  class-wide, 204–211
  data, types of, 5
  function, 9
  inherited, 252, 260–261
  instance, 204–211

private, 55, 173–174
public, 55, 173–175
static, 204–210
Member access notations, 56
Member functions, 19, 57
  defined, 510
  special, 515
  static, 205–210
Member initialization, 178
Member-of operator, 19, 56
Member template, 387
Memberwise copy operation, 176
Memory, *See* Free storage
Memory cells, 123
`min` function, 528
MIN macro, 495, 496
`monotonic` function, 44
Monthly calendar, 166–169, 236
`move` function, 438
Multiple indirection, 154–156
Multiple inheritance, 4, 249, 278–282
  mix-in, 281
  scope nesting, 278–279
  virtual vs. nonvirtual, 279–280
Multiway `if` statement, 24–25
`mutable`, keyword, 105
mysort command, 143–151

\n escape sequence (NEWLINE), 26, 62, 220, 229, 491
Name(s)
  of arrays, 124–125
  class, 76, 172
  of functions, 76, 547–549
  type, 11
  of variables, 76
Namespace, 80, 84–85
  alias, 85
  and header file, 85
  declaration, 85
  directive, 85
Negation, unary, 95
Nested class, 299–302
Nested `if` statement, 25
Nested list, 521–523
Nested loop, 25, 45
Nesting, class scope, 252
Networking, 442
  client and se
Networ

new operator, 107, 111, 195, 316–319
NEWLINE escape sequence (\n), 26, 62, 220, 229, 491
No-args constructor, 54
No-op, 21
Nontype parameter, 376
Not operator (!), 31, 32
Null character (\0), 26, 38, 130, 132, 232
NULL constant, 118, 131, 517, 518
NULL pointer, 131, 132, 167, 195, 404
Null statement, 21
Number class, 364–371
Number envelope, 364–368
Numeric computations, *See* Computations

Object(s), 1–2, 52, 172
   base, 4, 251, 253
   built-in operations for, 192–193
   classes and, 472
   creating and initializing, 175–181
   derived, 4, 252–254, 274–276
   designing, 471
   destruction of, 108, 193–195
   external behavior of, 471
   function, 431–434
   host, 55, 181–182
   identifying, 470
   life cycle of, 177
   member of, 56
   ordered-sequence, 344–345
   organizing into hierarchies, 248
   with pointer storage, 194
   pointers to
   problem 65–69
   size

explicit, 274
implicit, 271
Object-based decomposition, 74
Object-based (OO) design
   decomposition approaches to, 74
Object-based thinking, 73–74
Object-family classes, 322, 363–371
object.member notation, 57
Object-oriented decomposition, 469
Object-oriented (OO) design
   calculator simulation for, 479–488
   CRC, 474–475, 480–481
   decomposition approaches to, 468–469
   interfacing to existing systems, 475–479
   principles of, 469–472
OOD, 467–468
Object-oriented programming (OOP), 1–5
   advantages of, 2, 9
   C++ and, 5–7
   concepts in, 2–5
   problem solving with, 65–69
   program structure in, 8–9
Object-oriented programming (OOP) techniques, 322–371
   destruction of plug-compatible objects, 352–353
   inheritance planning, 361–363
   multiple inheritance, 278–282
   object-family classes, 322, 363–371
   ordering text lines, 354–357
   with plug-compatible objects, 322–329
   polymorphism, 4, 322–325
   uniform public interface planning, 322, 343–352
   virtual functions, 322, 325–329, 359–363
Octal byte escape sequence (*ooo*), 26
Offset pointer to member (opm), 413, 434–438, 513
ofile object, 265
ofstream class, 230, 283
Once-only header files, 367, 384, 500
One definition rule, 86
One-dimensional arrays, 124–125
ooo (octal byte escape sequence), 26
OOP, *See* Object-oriented programming
Opening files, 231–233, 542–543
Operator(s), 34–35
   addition (+), 20, 140, 268, 288
   address-of (&), 40, 126–127, 439
   arithmetic, 20, 25, 30
      ssignment, 17
      ociativity of, 30

binary, 29
bitwise, *See also* Output operators, *See also* Input operators, 33–34
comma, 45
decrement (--), 22–23, 30, 124, 294, 512
as friends, 196–197
function call (()), 296
increment (++), 22–23, 30, 124, 294, 512
indexing ([]), 145, 296, 512
input, 15, 33–34, 232–233, 240–242
logical, 31–32
member-of, 19, 56
output, 11, 33–34, 232–233, 240–242
overloadable, 288
overloaded, *See* Overloaded operators
precedence among, 30, 33, 531
relational, 17, 19, 31–32
scope resolution, 57, 84
subtraction, 20, 95–96, 104, 182, 268, 288
ternary, 32
typeid, 331–334
unary, 22–23, 29, 32, 126–127, 268, 439
Operator functions, defining, 288
Operator delete
redefine/overload, 317
Operator new
redefine/overload, 317
operator=, class-defined, 269–271
operator[], 293, 296, 512
for rvalue or lvalue, 294
opm (offset pointer to member), 413, 434–438, 513
Optimization, 491
Optional arguments, 97–99
Or operator (||), 31–32
Ordered bank accounts, 352
Ordered dates, 348–352
Ordered sequences, 344–348
Ordered text lines, *See* Sorting
OrderedSeq base class, 344–352, 354–357
OrderedSeq class
append function, 348
cmp function, 347
partition function, 347
swap function, 347
ostream class, 221, 230, 238, 282
ostringstream class, 228
ostrstream class, 221, 230
ostrstream object, 221
Output

binary, 239–240
C-style, 542–546
C-style binary, 546
C-style formatting, 543–545
C-style string, 220–222, 545
error output channel, 18
formatting, 234–237
library functions for, 6, 230–240
standard output channel, 17
See also I/O stream library
Output operators, 11, 33–34, 232–233, 240–242
Outward conversions, 303–304
Overloadable operators, 288
Overloaded functions, 4, 35, 80, 99–101
defined, 34, 58, 99
display, 199, 203
distinguishable signatures of, 99–101
example of, 99–100
function call resolution and, 101
inheritance and, 266
Overloaded operators, 4, 34–35, 287–290
[] operator, 293
- operator, 95, 288
-- operator, 294, 512
+ operator, 288
++ operator, 294, 512
Overriding, 261

Padding, 211
pair class template, 386
Parameters
read-only, 103–105, 152–154
reference, 59–60, 102, 154
return, 130, 154
type vs. nontype, 376
See also Formal parameters
Parentheses (), 296
partition function, 91–92, 149–150, 163–165
Pass, *See* Argument passing
pe element, 92
perpendicular test, 65–69
Personal computers (PCs), compilation on, 504–506
Planning
inheritance, 361–362
public interfaces, 322, 343–352
Plug-compatible objects
destruction of, 352–353
planning public interface for, 322, 343–352

Plug-compatible objects (*continued*)
   polymorphism and, 324
   programming with, 322–329
Pocket calculator, *See* Calculator simulation program
Pointer(s), 40–41, 123, 125–133
   addition of, 128–130, 132
   as arguments, 151–152
   assignment of, 132
   to class objects, 56
   comparison of, 132
   constant, 40
   dangling, 153
   double indirection and, 127–128, 155
   dynamic arrays of, 166–169
   dynamically allocated storage and, 165–169
   function calls and, 151–154
   to functions, 157–158, 512
   functions returning, 153–154
   host-object, 97
   multiple indirection and, 154–156
   offset pointer to member, 413, 434–438, 513
   ordinary, 434–435, 438
   references and, 154
   smart, 295–296
   to static members, 438
   subtraction of, 130–132
   valid operations, 132–133
Pointer arithmetic, 128–132
Pointer variables, 40, 124–126
`Poly` class, 138–140, 272–274
Polymorphic, defined, 328
Polymorphism, 4, 322–325
   `template` vs., 408
   `void*` vs., 408
Polynomials, 138–141
Pop operation, 262–264
Postprocessing, and virtual-function composition, 362, 363
`power` function, 20–23, 99–100
Precedence, among operators, 30, 33, 531
Precision, 28, 235–237
Preprocessing, 491–502
   conditional text inclusion in, 497–499
   header files in, 493–494, 500
   macros in, 494–497, 500–502
   symbolic constants in, 494–496
   text transformations in, 492
   virtual-function composition and, 362, 363

Primitive-type constructor, 387
Private base, 259, 260
Private derivation, 258, 261–263, 361
Private members, 55, 173–174
Problem solving, with objects, 65–69
Procedural decomposition, 73, 468
Procedure-oriented programming, *See* Object-oriented programming
Producer, 109
`product` function, 528
Program
   for calculator simulation, 183–192
   character-set-independent, 26
   defined, 8
   designing, 184
   generic, 156–165
   readability vs. terseness of, 23
   testing, 187, 190–191
Program structure, object-oriented, 8–9
Program templates, 375
Programming tips, 74–77
Protected base, 259, 260
`protected` derivation, 258–260, 361
Prototype, function, 19, 66, 512
`ptra` variable, 125–126, 155–156
Public base, 259, 260, 265
Public derivation, 255–258
Public interfaces
   internal workings vs., 3–4, 55, 74
   planning, 322, 343–352
   for plug-compatible objects, 322, 343–352
Public members, 55, 173–175
Push operation, 264

`qsort`, 165
Question mark colon (?:) conditional operator, 32
QUESTION MARK escape sequence (\?), 26
`quicksort` function, 91–92, 149–151, 162–165
Quotation mark escape sequences
   DOUBLE (\"), 26
   SINGLE (\'), 26

\r escape sequence (RETURN), 26, 220, 229, 491
Range error, 307
Read-only host, 182
Read-only parameters, 103–105, 152
Read-only variables, 103–105
`readLine` function, 41–42
Records, collision of, 400

Recursion, 80, 89–92
    formula , 90
    of greatest common divisor (gcd), 89
    quicksort algorithm, 91–92
Recursive structures, 197–204
Reference(s), 102–103
    argument passing by, 59
    arrays and pointers and, 154
Reference counting, 290–293
Reference members, initialization of, 179
Reference parameters, 59–60, 102, 154
Refstr class, 291–293
register modifier, 86
Relational expressions, 17, 31–32
Relational operators, 17, 19, 31–32
remove, generic algorithm, 429
Representation
    canonical, 94
    dense, 183
    sparse, 183
Requested transformations, 492
Resolution
    template function call, 382–383
Resolution, function call, 101
RETURN escape sequence (\r), 26, 220, 229, 491
Return parameter, 130, 153
return statement, 43
Return value, 9, 14
Robust classes, 302
Round-trip gestalt design, 470
RTTI, 330–334
Run-time support, 491
Run-Time Type Identification, 330–334

Scope(s)
    class, 81, 84, 173, 252
    file, 81, 82, 86–87
    local, 81–82
    nesting, 83, 252
Scope operator (::), 57, 84
scoping rules, 81
seekp function, 238
Self-pointer, this, 97
Semicolon terminator (;), 11, 13, 20, 53
Sequences
    escape, 26, 229
    ordered, 344–348
setw manipulator, 220
Shared bases, 279–282

shfree function, 317, 318
shmalloc function, 317, 318
short int types, 27
Sign bit, 27
Signatures, distinguishable, 99–101
signed integers, 27
Simple conditional statements, 16–17, 32
Simple statement, 13
Single inheritance, 4, 249
SINGLE QUOTE escape sequence (\'), 26
sizeof unary operator, 208, 210
Slash (/) operator, 20, 30
SMALLTALK, 1
Smart pointers, 295–296
Sorting, 143–151, 354–357
    building class of text lines for, 144–147
    comparing keys and, 144, 147–151
    generic program for, 162–165
    quicksort function for, 91–92, 149–151, 162–165
SortKey object, 144, 147–150
Source-client relation, 118–119
Source code files, 490
Source-level debugger, 525
SPACE, 62, 220, 229, 491
Sparse representation, 183
Specialization, template, 381–382
SQUARE macro, 495
Stack, 261
    pop operation, 262
    push operation, 262
    top operation, 262
Stack class, 262–263, 397–399
Standard container
    iterators, 424–425
    typedefs in, 422–424
Standard error, 18
Standard input channel, 17
Standard macros, 500–502
Standard output channel, 17
Standard Template Library, 413
Statement(s), 12–17
    compound, 13
    declaration, 15
    defined, 10
    do-while, 23
    for, 20–22, 43
    in functions, 9, 10
    iteration, 510
    multiway if, 24–25

Statement(s) (*continued*)
    null, 21
    simple, 13
    simple conditional, 16–17, 32
    successor, 43
    while, 13–16
Statement terminator (;), 11, 13, 20, 53
Static member(s), 204–210
    initialization of, 208, 209
    pointers to, 438
Static member functions, 205–210
Static-storage variables, 106
std::, 11
STL, 413–414
    associative container, 418–419
    container adaptor stack, 417
    container efficiency, 416
    functors, 432
    major parts, 413
STL class, vector, 141–143
Storage, *See* Free storage
str_end function, 160, 161
str index notation, 124
stream classes, *See also* I/O stream library, 11, 282
stream I/O, for objects, 240–242
strEqual function, 38–39, 125
String, 37–39
string class, 63–65, 222–228
    +, 224–225
    append(), 224–225
    c_str(), 224–225
    compare(), 224
    empty(), 224
    find_first_not_of(), 224
    find_first_of(), 224
    find_last_not_of(), 224
    find_last_of(), 224
    find(), 189, 224
    I/O, 223
    I/O Objects, 228
    length(), 224
    object, 222–228
    object creation, 223
    operations, 224–225
String class, reference-count, 290–293
String functions, 222–225, 516–518
    C-style input and output, 545
String juxtaposition, 221
stringMatch function, 44–45

String operations
    destructive, 516
    functions for, 222–225, 516–518
String tokenizer, 225–228
stringSearch command, 72–73
stringstream class, 228
strstream class, 230
struct keyword, 175
Subtraction operator (-), 20, 95–96, 104, 182, 268, 288
Subtraction of pointers, 130–132
Successor statements, 43
sum function, 528, 529
swap function, 59, 163–165
switch statement, 46–47, 510–511
Symbolic constants, 76, 494–496

\t escape sequence (TAB), 26, 220, 229, 491
Table-lookup, via binary search, 209–210
Tag, 52, 173
tail index, 109–110
Template(s), 6, 156, 375–409
    class, 383–388, 513
    compilation model, 388–390
    defined, 375
    degree of specialization, 382
    derived-class, 397–399
    explicit instantiation, 389–390
    function, 377–383, 513
    hash table, 400–402, 405–406
    instantiation of, 375–377, 380–383, 387–388
    list, 390–397
    program, 375
    specialization, 381–382
    void* vs., 407
Template class, 384, 387–388
    notation, 384
Template formal parameters, 375, 380–381
Template function
    call resolution, 382–383
    explicit call, 381
Template header, 376
Ternary operator, 32
Testing, of calculator simulation program, 187, 190–191
Text, sorting, 143–151, 354–357
Text inclusion, conditional, 497–499
Text transformations, 492
TextLines object, 144–147, 354–357

this (host pointer), 97, 181
throw keyword, 308–316
Tilde (~), 33, 34, 194
Time functions, 537–539
Time objects, 98–99
tmp pointer variable, 130
Tokenizer, string, 225–228
Tokens, 225–228, 491, 517
Top-down design, 467
Tree
    generic, 335–343
    internal node, 336
    iterator, 339
    leaf node, 335
    traversal, 338
Trigraph, 492
True (logical constant), 17
try keyword, 308–316
Two-dimensional arrays, 133–135
    allocating, 165–166
Type, compatible, 323–325
Type conversions, 114–117, 512
    ambiguous, 305
    explicit, 36, 116–117, 266
    implicit, 114–116, 265–266, 532
    inheritance-induced, 265–267, 532
    inward, 304
    I/O stream, 305–306
    outward, 303–304
    rules for, 532–533
    string-to-number, 537
    user-defined, 303–306
Type name, 11
Type parameter, 6, 376
Type relations, under inheritance, 265–267
Type-cast
    const_cast, 117, 300, 359, 393–394
    dynamic_cast, 117, 330–334, 340
    explicit, 36, 116–117, 266
    reinterpret_cast, 117, 161, 215, 350, 355
    static_cast, 116, 167, 266, 421
Type-cast notations, 116
typedef declaration, 105–106, 511
    in class scope, 84, 210
    dynamic arrays of pointers and, 166
    functional variable declaration and, 158
    multiple indirection and, 156
    pointers to member functions and, 437
    in template, 387

typeid, 331–334, 423
typename, 376
typename declaration, 423

UML, 474
Unary negation, 95
Unary operators, 22–23, 29, 32
    address-of operator (&), 40, 126–127, 439
    value-of operator (*), 40, 126–127, 268, 439
#undef directive, 496
Underscore (_), 29, 76
Unicode character, 26
Unions, 216, 513, 519–524
    anonymous, 521
    bit-packing members and, 513, 523–524
    as class members, 513
    heterogeneous data structures and, 521–523
UNIX
    compilation under, 502–504
    dbx utility of, 525–527
unsigned integers, 27, 116
Updating files, 237–239, 542
URL, 447
URL encoding, 419
User, 55
User-defined type conversions, 303–306
User interface, 184, 187–192
Using, identifiers in namespaces, 85
using, keyword, 85
Utility functions, 539–540

\v escape sequence (VERTICAL TAB), 26
va_arg macro, 529–530
va_end macro, 529, 530
va_list macro, 528, 529
va_start macro, 528–530
Value(s)
    argument passing by, 59
    Boolean, 17, 162
    default, 98
    error, 307
    initial, 4
    lvalues, 102
    return, 9, 14
Value-of unary operator (*), 40, 126–127, 268, 439
valuetype, 10, 14
Variable(s), 29
    automatic, 82, 106
    enumeration, 36

Variable(s) (*continued*)
    functional, 156–158
    global, 88
    local, 82, 88
    loop-control, 15, 43
    names of, 76
    pointer, 40, 124–126
    read-only, 103–105
    reference, 102–103
    static-storage, 106
Variable-length arguments, 528–530
vector class, 123
    begin(), 143
    constructor, 142
    deleting element, 143
    initial capacity, 143
    insert(), 142
    of objects, 142
    push_back(), 142
Vector2D constructor, 65–69, 84, 271
VERTICAL TAB escape sequence (\v), 26
Virtual base, 279–282
Virtual base object initialization, 282
Virtual function(s), 322, 325–329, 359–361
    composing, 362–363
    declaration and use of, 325–329
    implementation, 330
    pure, 345
    selection of, 325, 326
    table (vtbl), 330
Virtual multiple inheritance, 280
Virtualized object, 330
    type-cast, 266
void, 10, 14
void pointer, 159–162
void*, vs. template, 407

wc command, 114
Web
    browser, 447
    page generation, 450–452
    server, 447
while statement, 13–16
White space, 220, 232, 491
Wide character, 26
width function, 235
Window, 476
Window object, 2–4
World-Wide Web, 446–448
\x*hh* (hexadecimal byte escape sequence), 26

^Z (control-Z), 19